Praise for
False Self: The Life of M

"In this portrait, clinical psychologist Hopkins draws on thousands of letters and scores of interviews to bring to life a charismatic, cultured, brilliant, immature, and ultimately demented individual. . . . [This] thoroughly researched and well-written life is essential for psychotherapists and historians of the rise and decline of post-World War II psychoanalysis. Hopkins deftly handles a large treasure of material, including interviews with Khan's colleagues, friends, patients, and wives."
— *Library Journal*

"Hopkins offers an unnerving and sympathetic portrait of the enfant terrible of postwar British psychoanalysis and convincingly suggests that Khan suffered from undiagnosed bipolar disorder."
— *Publishers Weekly*

"[Hopkins's] biography goes far beyond relating Masud's life. Her balance breathes fresh life into this Lear-like man who lost his kingdom, his wives, and his way while still staking out a claim to have shown analysis a new and much more intimate, much more loving, way to present itself. . . . An absorbing read."
— *Republic of Letters*

"This scholarly, lucid book offers a balanced view of Khan's rich and extremely problematic life and work. Linda Hopkins has done a masterful job of investigating the complexities of history and psychology."
— Joyce Slochower, Ph.D., A.B.P.P.,
author of *Holding and Psychoanalysis*
and *Psychoanalytic Collisions*

"I didn't want this book to end. A hush fell with the last page, the hush of a shadow of life. I can't thank Linda Hopkins enough for the truth of this book, the detailed care, the love of life that it reveals."
— Michael Eigen, Ph.D.,
author of *The Sensitive Self*,
The Electrified Tightrope, and *Lust*

"Linda Hopkins demonstrates how seamlessly threads of inspired genius and impaired living are woven together in the life of Masud Khan. While admirably empathic toward Khan's vulnerability, she does not whitewash his accountability. There is so much to be learned from Hopkins's labor of love, and we all owe her a debt of gratitude."

— Dodi Goldman, Ph.D., William Alanson White Foundation; author, *In Search of the Real: The Origins and Originality of D.W. Winnicott*

"Sensible, intelligent, scrupulously researched, and clear as a bell. This is an important biography, for its reference points are the relevance and standing of psychoanalysis in today's world, the crossroads between Western and Muslim culture, and ultimately the contemporary conflict between dramatic image and authentic life. Linda Hopkins has made an extraordinary and successful attempt to get Khan's larger-than-life character into ordinary human proportions, where he becomes a flawed man living a flawed life."

— Bob Hinshelwood, Ph.D., professor, Centre for Psychoanalytic Studies at the University of Essex

"Linda Hopkins paints a remarkable portrait not only of a pivotal individual, but of a cadre of professionals who had a major hand in shaping the psychoanalysis of then and now."

— Margaret Crastnopol, Ph.D., cofounder and faculty, Northwest Center for Psychoanalysis, Seattle

"*False Self* is a biographical gem, compelling, brilliant, and evocative. Dr. Hopkins provides us with a compassionate exploration of the depths of human suffering and frailties in the context of Masud Khan's life, resonating deeply with our own souls and psyche."

— Purnima Mehta, M.D.

FALSE SELF

The Life of Masud Khan

Linda Hopkins

KARNAC

First published in 2006 by Other Books, New York
This edition published by Karnac Books in 2008
Photo of Svetlana Berisova in Swan Lake © Zoë Dominic
Photo of Masud Khan and Svetlana Berisova © Henri Cartier-Bresson
Photo of Number 3 Hans Crescent appears courtesy of Rebecca Smith and Tara Stitchberry
Photo of Masud Khan and Svetlana Berisova in Monte Carlo © Zoë Dominic
Khan Bibliography © 2006 Harry Karnac

British Library Cataloguing in Publication Data

A C.I.P. for this book is available from the British Library

ISBN-13: 978-1-85575-628-1

Typeset by Vikatan Publishing Solutions, Chennai, India

Printed in Great Britain

www.karnacbooks.com

For J., B., and P.

TABLE OF CONTENTS

ACKNOWLEDGMENTS

I did not know when I started this project thirteen years ago how much it would enhance my professional and personal life. Of the many people who helped me, three in particular stand out. These are Wladimir ("Wova") Granoff, the recently deceased French analyst (d. 2000); Robert ("Bob") Rodman, the recently deceased California psychoanalyst (d. 2004); and Harry Karnac, the founder and original owner of Karnac Books. Granoff had been Khan's crucial friend in the early 1960s prior to a major estrangement, but he had the grace and honesty to talk to me about the extreme pleasure he took from the friendship in the days when it was going well. We met in Paris several times and, in an era when e-mail was not yet popular, we exchanged many faxes. Right from the beginning, he trusted me and gave me access to his extensive correspondence with Khan. Bob Rodman was still working on his biography of Donald Winnicott (*Winnicott: Life and Work*, 2003), when we met, and we shared substantial material concerning our separate and overlapping research subjects. Bob had unfailing energy and a sensitivity to the nuances of life that kept me going through many difficult times. Harry Karnac originally had doubts about the importance of the work, but after I won him over, he spoke with great generosity of his personal experience with Khan and Khan's world. Then, wearing a very different hat, he guided me through the long process of dealing with various crises involving publication that were, I was to learn, just part of the process. Harry and his wife, Ruth, have been unflinching in their hospitality and their support. Karnac also put together the Bibliography, an impressive project for which I am deeply grateful.

Prior to becoming a psychologist and an analyst, I studied Arabic as an undergraduate at Brown University and then as a graduate student at the Johns Hopkins School of Advanced International Studies (SAIS) in Washington, D.C. This educational experience got me interested in Islam and, after I changed careers, led me to investigate Khan's writings once I learned that he was Muslim. In Philadelphia, I got a Ph.D. in clinical psychology at Temple University and became a certified

analyst and then a training and supervising analyst at the Philadelphia
School of Psychoanalysis. I studied Khan on my own in my student
years—his work was never assigned and I heard his name spoken out
loud only once, in a talk by Salman Akhtar, a Muslim analyst who practices locally. My private study was greatly facilitated when I became a student at a school dedicated to the study of British psychoanalysis, under
the leadership of Jill and David Scharff. This school is currently known
as the International Psychotherapy Institute (IPI) and located in Bethesda,
Maryland, but when I studied there it was part of the Washington School
of Psychoanalysis in Washington, D.C. This was the first time that I
had the chance to learn from others about the British object relations
analysts. The Scharffs are masterful teachers who have fostered a lively
and supportive community; they also provide the opportunity to meet
leading British analysts who come to the school as guest teachers. All
the IPI faculty and students are deserving of my acknowledgment and
I am particularly grateful to six members of the community, in addition to the Scharffs: Anna Innes, Michael Kaufman, Kent Ravenscroft,
Michael Stadter, Charles Ashbach, and Frank Schwoeri.

Nothing had been written about Khan's life when I started my work
in 1993, but Judy Cooper's short biography *Speak of Me As I Am* (1993)
came out a few months after I started. Her description of the basic facts
of Khan's life was an invaluable resource. Whenever I started to doubt
the value of another Khan biography, my good friend Jane Widseth, a
Haverford College psychologist who has studied at Tavistock, was un-
failingly enthusiastic and encouraging. The American editors Michael
Moskowitz and John Kerr also believed in the importance of another Khan
biography. Over the years, I have been supported in the work by Joseph
Aguayo, James Anderson, Leon Balter, Philip Bennett, Sandy Hershberg,
Asher Keren-Zvi, George Moraitis, Paul Roazen, and Catherine Stuart,
who invited me to speak about Khan to their organizations.

Two people stand out for their capacity to always have an answer or
find an answer, no matter what question I asked. Douglas Kirsner of Australia, a scholar of psychoanalysis and author of *Unfree Associations* (2000),
has studied overlapping material and he has helped me on many occasions at the same time as he has become a comrade. David Cast, an art
historian from Bryn Mawr and an Englishman, is an old friend, and I
have turned to him with a wide variety of questions ranging from the

history of the Mongols to contemporary British politics. Both of these men have amazing minds.

My agent, Georges Borchardt, helped to educate me about publishing and he was always available for consultation. Furthermore, I had four editors, all quite different. Sally Arteseros was my editor at a time when the book was twice as long as it is now, and she was a sensitive critic and a patient tutor. My sister Marsha Havens, a professional editor from Arizona, read the next full draft, and with her suggestions, I learned things about language and sentence structure that I had never imagined I did not know. Finally, my Other Press editors, Rosemary Ahern and Stacy Hague, put all the finishing touches onto the book. Rosemary read just a portion of the manuscript, but her feedback was right-on. Stacy read every word with care, and her comments had a major effect on the structure and content of the final manuscript. My assistant Elizabeth Larkin went far beyond the call of duty in the many tasks I asked her to complete and her devotion and talent are greatly appreciated. In Paris, Jacque and Jacqueline Lang generously offered their bilingual skills as translators.

In the course of my work, several sections of the biography have been published as journal articles, and for these I received editorial assistance from Jay Greenberg at *Contemporary Psychoanalysis*, James Anderson at the Chicago Institute for Psychoanalysis, and Peter Rudnytsky at *American Imago*. The articles were also critiqued by my colleagues David Mark, Noëlle Burton, Madeleine Page (d. 2003), and Rick Webb.

In addition to Harry and Ruth Karnac, there were a number of people who read the entire manuscript in various stages of completion. Paul Roazen (d. 2005) actually chose to do his reading before I started my major cutting, and his enthusiasm was surprising and welcome. Two fellow psychologists, Joseph Delvey and Stewart Hockenberry, read a later version and made many helpful comments. My thinking about India was checked by a peer, Sanjay Nath, and by Robert Nichols, a South Asian scholar from the University of Pennsylvania. Another South Asian scholar, Thomas Thornton of the University of Maryland, provided helpful consultation, as did Salman Akhtar, who shared his thinking about the influence of Islam on Khan's professional life. John Charlton (d. 1998) of Hogarth Press and Mark Paterson of Sigmund Freud Copyrights, together with Paterson's assistant Tom Roberts, helped me to

understand the extent of Khan's editorial contributions to psychoanalysis. The Boston analyst David Mann guided me through the current literature on addiction and helped me to grasp the tragedy of Khan's
alcoholism, as did John Benson, a Philadelphia analyst. Leslie Johnson,
a scholar of Russian literature as well as object relations theory, was a
thoughtful and informed resource as I wrote about Khan's delusions
concerning Fyodor Dostoevsky's *The Idiot*—a book that I had read and
loved when I studied Russian as an undergraduate, one that Leslie also
knows well.

My access to Khan's unpublished Work Books came about through
a collaboration that became a friendship with Sybil Stoller, the widow
of Khan's crucial friend Robert Stoller. Through Sybil I became recon-
nected to a man who had had an enormous influence on me many years
earlier: my Temple University dissertation adviser, J. Herbert Hamsher.
Herb lives in Aspen and Los Angeles now, and he is the longtime partner of Jonathan Stoller, one of Sybil's sons. He has an almost magical
quality of transmitting courage and energy, and I am thrilled to know
him again. Herb and Jonathan both read and critiqued major pieces of
the manuscript.

One of Khan's London relatives (anonymous) told me about two relatives in Texas who might be willing to speak with me, and thus it was
that I discovered Khalida Riaz Khan and her sister Fatima Ahmed. These
women were the daughters of Khan's much older half-sister and, as
children born at about the time of Masud and his brother Tahir, they
had a great deal to tell about the facts of Khan's childhood. Khalida keeps
in close touch with the extended Khan family and she generously researched several items that seemed important to me. Khalida and her
cousin Zubair Sadiqi read the chapters on India to check for accuracy.
Her husband Riaz Khan (d. 2003) supplied me with details of Khan's
university life in Lahore.

It was surprising to me that I was able to meet or communicate in other
ways with almost all the analysts and therapists whom I contacted to ask
for an interview. People who talked to me about their personal knowledge of Khan include the following. In England: Bernard Barnett, Michael
Brearley, Ron Britton, Patrick Casement (by e-mail), Judy Cooper, John
Davis (by e-mail), Sadie Gillespie, Rosemary Gordon, R. H. Gosling (by
letter), Kenneth Granville-Grossman (d. 2000), Jeremy Hazell (a short

talk), Robert Hinshelwood (a short talk), James Hood, Judith Issroff (who helped me in many ways), Marcus Johns (by e-mail), Brett Kahr, Pearl King, Gregorio Kohon (by e-mail), Lionel Kreeger, Peter Lomas (by letter), Marion Milner (d. 1998), Susie Orbach, John Padel (d. 1999), Gerald Phillips (by e-mail), Malcolm Pines, Eric Rayner, Charles Rycroft (d. 1998), Anne-Marie Sandler, Joseph Sandler (d. 1998), Hanna Segal, Harold Stewart (d. 2005), Ken Wright (by e-mail), and about ten others who have chosen to remain anonymous. In France: Georges Allyn, Marie-Claude Fusco, André Green (who shared his correspondence with Khan), Joyce McDougall, J.-B. Pontalis, and Daniel Widlöcher. In the United States: Luise Eichenbaum, Eleanor Galenson (by letter), John Gedo (by telephone), Nasir Ilahi (by telephone), Harriette Kaley, Charles Kaufman (by telephone), Peter Kramer, Melvin Mandel (by e-mail), Werner Muensterberger (d. 2003), Leo Rangell, Johanna Krout Tabin, Robert Wallerstein, Milton Wexler, Earl Wittenberg, and Elizabeth Young-Bruehl. In other countries, with communication by e-mail, telephone, or letter: Gisela Ammon from Germany; Augusto Colmenares from Spain; Olaf Dahlia from Sweden; Andreas Giannakoulas from Italy; Max Hernandez, Saul Peña, and Elizabeth Kreimer from Peru; and Jeffrey Masson from New Zealand. The Canadians Dean Eyre and Peter Elder (who has since moved to Wales) both met with me and corresponded at some length.

Khan had many friends outside of the analytic world, and these people were also surprisingly cooperative. One of the most important sources of material was Barrie Cooper, the analytically trained internist who was Khan's private physician for many years. Barrie shared his deep understanding of Khan through comments and questions over the years of my work. Zoë Dominic was a close friend to both Khan and Svetlana and, in the course of many meetings, she shared her memories and her beautiful photographs, now owned by Dominic Photography. She also helped me to get an interview with Khan's second wife, Svetlana Beriosova (d. 1998), who was a recluse before she died, and that opened up the chance to get Svetlana's permission to read her correspondence with Khan. Zoë also gave me access to her private correspondence with Khan and, after Svetlana died, to Svetlana's correspondence with her father, written in Russian, which I happen to be able to read. The noted scenic designer Tony Walton, who had been Khan's close friend in the early 1960s, had wonderful stories to tell and his positive energy was a constant inspiration. Tony was influential in helping me to arrange a long phone interview with his first wife, the actress Julie Andrews, who had been Svetlana's intimate friend in the 1960s. Henri Cartier-Bresson (d. 2004), who had been a close friend of Khan as well as Svetlana, chose not to meet, but he allowed me to purchase at a very low price several of his photographs of Khan and Svetlana.

Other nontherapists who had been part of Khan's life and were willing to talk were the following: In England: Jonathan Benson, Jill Duncan (archivist at the Institute of Psychoanalysis), Mary Drage Eyre, John Forrester (by e-mail), Maureen Harris, Anne Jameson Hutchinson, Anita Kermode, Frank Kermode, Anne Money-Coutts, Jane Shore Nicholas, Hilda Padel, Frances Partridge (by telephone), Melanie Stanway Purnell, the actors Corin Redgrave and Lynn Redgrave (by letter), Ruth Rosen (who shared with me the unpublished autobiography of her deceased analyst husband Ismond), Lydia Smith (daughter of Martin James—by e-mail), Ted Lucie-Smith, and Joy Stewart. In France: Soula Aghion (by letter), Lucie Arnold, Paul Moor (by e-mail), Babette Smirnoff Soria. In the United States: Jeanne Axler, Harold Bloom, Keith Botsford, Sybil Christopher, Hildi Greenson (by letter), Leslie Kayne, Gen LeRoy, Roger Stoller, and Earl Wittenberg; and in other places: Nazir Ahmed of Pakistan (by letter), Björn Benkow of Sweden (by letter and telephone), Augusto Colmenares of Spain (by letter), Rina Eyre of Canada, Phyllis Grosskurth of Canada, Eugene Lerner of Italy, Hal Shaper of South Africa (by letter), and Sahabzada Yaqub Khan of Pakistan.

Many people who had not known Khan helped me to understand the story. These include Morton Axelrod, Paul Benson, Robert Boynton (author of a long interview with Khan's analysand Wynne Godley), Margaret Crastnopol, Michael Eigen, Lawrence Epstein, Michael Fisher, Gladys Foxe, Christopher Gelber (who provided invaluable help with the Robert Stoller archives at UCLA), Raeland Gold, Dodi Goldman (a Winnicott scholar), Gladys Guarton, Cooper Hopkins, Joel Kanter (author of a recent book on Clare Winnicott), Richard Karmel, Jerome Kavka, Deborah Komins, Ed Levenson, Howard Levine, Peter Loewenberg, Frank Marotta, James McCarthy, Purnima Mehta, Joan Ormont, Richard Papenhausen (d. 2003), Prajna Parasher, Don Pippin, Irv Rosen,

Marcia Rosen, Janet Sayers, Don Shapiro, Joyce Slochower (a Winnicott scholar), Stanley Spiegel, Charles Strozier, Frank Summers, Judith Vida, Roger Willoughby (himself the author of a recent Khan biography), David Wilson, and Irvin Yalom.

Khan's controversial behavior left a trail of conflicted people and as a result I had to deal with legal issues from the very beginning of my project. Just a few weeks before he died, Joseph Sandler helped me get in touch with Robert Tyson, who advised me about how to work with the International Psychoanalytic Association to clarify the rights to use the Stollers' copy of Khan's Work Books. A grant funded by Marvin Sussman at The Union Institute helped me pay for legal advice on international copyrights relevant to the Work Books. In another matter that straddled the areas of legality and ethics, I was greatly helped by the American analyst Glen Gabbard, a man who is wise in many ways.

Like Masud Khan, I have three crucial friends. In addition to Jane Widseth, Susan Mathes and Karen Saeger have always been present as I did this work.

AUTHOR'S NOTE

There are undoubtedly parts of this biography which some people will question as being exaggerations or untruths. I am an American woman writing about a Muslim Pakistani man who lived in London, and my knowledge of Khan and his world is limited due to our differences. Furthermore, I have the disadvantage of writing about a person who regularly exaggerated and otherwise distorted the events of his own life. I have tried hard to exclude what I consider to be outright lies (usually these are from Khan's final decade), and to report my sources of information. In cases where Khan was the sole informant, the reader is told that he is the only one reporting, and may have an opinion different from mine about the validity of the report. Some areas where I personally remain unsure about what to believe are: the details of Khan's apparent admission to Oxford in 1947 and his subsequent acceptance into analytic training, the exact nature of his analytic contract with Winnicott in the period 1956–1966 (i.e., whether he had formal sessions five or six times a week for those ten years or whether the "coverage" was at times more casual), and the account of the crazed relationship with Yasmine during the Dostoevsky period. It is likely that new information will be revealed in years to come that will help other biographers to tell a more complete story.

No one can deny Masud's talent. But it is also impossible to deny his sickness and his evil nature. When you have met someone like him, you know that the mind is not simple.

André Green

Much of what I have to say about Masud sounds critical and even derogatory. But it's odd, because I feel, and have felt ever since he died, a great sense of loss as if a large part of the gaiety of life was extinguished in his death.

Corin Redgrave

One cannot lie with one's body; only with one's mind.
Masud Khan[1]

Masud Khan (1924–1989) always attracted attention, no matter where he was. In Northern India, as the youngest of nine living sons of a prominent Muslim landowner, he had been the adored "pet" in his extended family, where he was the token scholar. In London in the austere postwar years of the late 1940s, he was noticed in part because he was rich. At a time when the city was just beginning to recover from the trauma of World War II, he lived in an ancestral suite at the Savoy Hotel and had a chauffeur who drove him around the city in a Rolls-Royce. At age twenty-two, he spoke English fluently and was obviously well educated. And he was clearly an intellectual—in his first days in the city, he attended twenty-seven consecutive performances of *King Lear*. The British were not used to such an Indian, especially an unknown with no apparent connections.

His physical presence was in itself impossible to ignore. He was tall—at least 6'2"—and thin, with a ramrod-straight military posture. The combination of dark skin, Oriental features, and thick black hair, which he wore swept to one side, was unusual and, in the West, he was regularly described as "beautiful" by men as well as women. People remember his deep resonant voice, and women in particular remember the attractiveness of his hands and feet.[2] Only a small number of people observed that underneath the sweep of his hair on the right side, he had a severely deformed ear that was overly large and lacking in cartilage. The congenital disfiguration in a man so handsome reminded those who saw it of his complexity and added to their fascination. (A surgical repair in 1951 helped, but the ear was never normal.)

In manner, he had a haughtiness that fooled people unless they understood that it masked a deeper shyness. His intelligence and wit were obvious and pleasing, and he had an intellectual air that most people found charming, with a lit cigarette constantly dangling from his mouth, ashes dropping unnoticed onto his clothes. At first, trying to fit in, he wore Western-style suits—with just a hint of differentness in his navy blue or black beret or a gray lambswool "Jinnah" cap, also called a kara-kuli. In later years, he dressed in Eastern-style robes or black collarless clothing with silver jewelry. Regardless of what he wore, he always looked exotic.[3]

Khan came to London in October 1946, supposedly to study litera-ture at Oxford—and to have a personal psychoanalysis, since he was a deeply disturbed young man. His homeland was in what is now Paki-stan, but in 1946 he was technically an Indian, because Pakistan was born a year later, in 1947, when British Colonial India was split into India and Pakistan. In those first months in the West, while his own country was also headed toward a new identity, the shape of Khan's future evolved in an unexpected way. He would leave Oxford almost immediately, moving to London to start his analysis and to enroll in the training pro-gram of the British Psycho-Analytical Society.

The psychoanalytic movement flourished in the postwar years, and the handsome Indian would become such a leader that in 1976, the American analyst Erik Erikson exclaimed, "The future of analysis be-longs to Khan!" He was by then a prolific writer, speaker, and editor as well as an innovative clinician. His lasting reputation was ensured by his writings—clinical and theoretical contributions in which he wrote openly about what he really did in the consulting room, in stark contrast to the formality and evasiveness of most analysts of his time. When he died in 1989, he left behind four books, three of them highly regarded and the last one scandalous: *The Privacy of the Self* (1974), *Alienation in Perver-sions* (1979), *Hidden Selves* (1983), and *When Spring Comes: Awakenings in Clinical Psychoanalysis* (1988; published as *The Long Wait* in the United States).

In addition to Khan's own significance, it is of great importance that he was the principal disciple of Donald Woods Winnicott (1896–1971), one of the most influential analysts since Freud. Khan referred to Winni-cott as "the man who was destiny for me," and Winnicott experienced Khan as the son he never had. It was a strange and almost unbelievable alliance, because the two men were a study in contrasts. Winnicott was a pixielike man who was raised in the proper world of the British middle class, in a home dominated by women.[4] He complained that he had experienced such security that he had to search to find his "madness." Khan grew up with a patriarch father who sired fifteen children with three of his four wives—and his "madness" was barely in control on the best of days. Winnicott, who had twinkling blue eyes, liked to start his day by sliding down the banister of his staircase giving a cheery imitation of a clucking chicken, while Khan was, as one of his analysands said, "the kind of man who you just know would have a dagger in the next room."[5] The Winnicott–Khan connection is central to the story of Khan's life in the West.

Khan's private life would match his professional living in its star quality. In London, his second marriage was to Svetlana Beriosova, a tall Russian beauty who was at the time of their marriage the number two ballerina with the Royal Ballet, about to become number one, after Margot Fonteyn's planned retirement. Together, Beriosova and Khan created a salon where they entertained the major stars of the art world, including Michael Redgrave, Julie Andrews, and Rudolf Nureyev. The Khans invited these artists to their home along with the less well known but equally talented "greats" of the analytic world, creating a mix that was as lively as it was strange.

What only his intimates knew was that Khan suffered all his life with depression and serious psychological problems. In mid-life, he began a long and unremitting fall from grace, struggling to survive the pain of divorce, the terror of a supposedly terminal cancer, and the ravages of alcoholism. He ended his life in disgrace, having been ejected from membership in his psychoanalytic group, the British Psycho-Analytical Society, as a consequence of inappropriate socializing with analysands as well as published writings that included a vicious anti-Semitic tirade. He died in 1989, just a few months after the society rejected him. Almost to the end of his life, however, he continued to write, and even the last book contains material that will live on.[6]

Many people read Shakespeare and see their own lives mirrored, but not many people live life on a scale grand enough to match the fictional characters of the great tragedies. Khan did live such a life, a life that has a striking similarity to the fictional lives of his favorite characters: Shakespeare's King Lear and Dostoevsky's Prince Myshkin, from *The Idiot*. Whether it was Destiny (arranged in part by himself) or Fate (something totally outside of his control), he had a rise and fall as major as those of King Lear and Prince Myshkin, and he left behind, as they did, both inspiration and destruction.

As I proceed to track Khan's life in more or less chronological order, it will become clear that no matter how much information is revealed, he remains something of a paradox. The British analyst Eric Rayner told me: "Masud's soul came from the Devil and his writing came from the gods." This biography is an attempt to show these sides of Khan, and other sides too, in the spirit of Khan's clinical thinking, where he was firmly convinced that people have multiple incompatible selves that are all real. The way to understand a person, he said, was to "explicate the paradox," not to try to resolve it, and indeed this idea is one of the major contributions made to psychoanalysis by Khan and by Winnicott.

AUTHOR'S NOTE

It was surprisingly easy to find a great deal of unpublished material about Khan's life, probably because he wanted to be written about posthumously. As he wrote in his diary, "In a strange way I am leaving behind materials which I hope someone will put together and that will constitute the verity of Masud Khan."[7]

Of all my sources, the most significant material came from Sybil Stoller, whose husband Robert (1924–1991) was a Los Angeles analyst and one of Khan's best friends. When I first talked to Sybil on the telephone, she told me: "I'd be glad to tell you about my husband's relationship to Masud." I was ambivalent about making the trip to California because her words suggested that she did not have much to say, but some instinct told me to go. I knew that on the same trip I could look at the Khan–Robert Stoller correspondence, which is held in Stoller's archives at UCLA.

Sybil picked me up at the airport and drove me to her home in the Pacific Palisades. When I walked into her living room she waved at a pile of letters and manuscripts that was three-and-a-half-feet high and said, "This is my relationship with Masud." It turned out that Sybil had had her own friendship with Khan, which included a correspondence with letters fifteen to twenty pages in length written to her over a period of twenty-plus years.

And there was more to discover. Sybil did not tell me at first that she also had a complete copy of Khan's unpublished Work Books, a 3,045-page personal and professional diary covering the years 1967 to 1980 (with patient information mostly excluded), which Khan had given to her and Robert over the years for safekeeping and possible publishing. Since the original Work Books are in an archive held by the International Psychoanalytical Association and frozen until the year 2039, I had not thought I would be able to read and use them. Then, on my third or fourth research trip to California, I was interviewing Roger Stoller, a son of Sybil and Robert, and I discovered that Roger's twin, Jonathan, was involved in a long-term relationship with a psychologist named J. Herbert Hamsher. By strange coincidence, Herb happens to have been my beloved dissertation adviser at the graduate program in clinical psychology at Temple University. He and I had been out of touch for more than two decades, as he had left the Philadelphia area to start a new life with Jonathan in Aspen and in Los Angeles. The synchronicity of this connection surprised all of us, and it influenced Sybil to trust me with the Work Books. To a biographer, this "find" has been like a buried treasure.

In addition to the Stoller correspondences, I had access to fourteen other relevant correspondences, all unpublished, nine of them from private collections. Since Khan's preferred mode of intimacy was correspondence, these were invaluable. They cover the span of his entire Western life.

I sought out the major people from Khan's life and most of them agreed to talk with me, so another important resource was in-person interviews that I conducted in the years 1993 to 2004 in Europe, South America, Canada, and various cities in the United States. (At least twelve of the people I interviewed are now deceased.) Very often, people first told me that they would have little to say about Khan—and then went on to speak at great length, surprising themselves with the extent and the intensity of their memories. To my astonishment, about half the men whom I interviewed *cried* at some point. And it became a common experience that seventy- and eighty-year-old women spoke with great pleasure, a sparkle in their eyes, about times when they were young and sexual and daring. This would have pleased Khan, who liked to provoke people to "come alive."

Quite a few of the interviewees have asked me to quote them anonymously, and all of the women who had personal and sexual relationships with Khan asked for a pseudonym. I will make note of a disguised identity the first time a person is mentioned, but after that, the name will appear as if it were the actual name, without quotes. The pseudonyms I use were chosen by the subjects, whenever they had a preference. In a few cases, identifying information has been altered, and those cases are noted in the text.

In three cases, I had numerous lengthy interviews with people who, upon reflection, did not give me permission to use any information from the interview. Two of these people felt that they and their families had been harmed by Khan and that the retelling of their stories might do more harm; and the other had a different personal reason for opting out. The missing information is interesting and it would add to themes discussed by others, but it is not crucial to the story.

The book is organized chronologically into nine parts, and five of these parts include separate chapters with transcripts of interviews with analysands and supervisees who describe Khan's clinical work. I am grateful to these people for sharing their information, as it illustrates Khan's clinical genius, as well as his gradual deterioration. The interviews are highly personal and, even though I am a practicing psychoanalyst, I will not make anything other than a superficial comment on the content. I do not want to second-guess my interviewees by assuming that I know more than they do about their own selves—so their words stand alone.

PART I

COLONIAL INDIA

(1924–1945)

CHAPTER I

EARLY YEARS IN MONTGOMERY

No matter how much I have translated it all into metaphor and
myth, my childhood is still alive and real to me, and my feudal
upbringing gives me any virtues I possess.
Masud Khan[1]

Masud Khan's childhood home was in Montgomery (now Sahiwal), an area in the northwest part of the United Provinces of India known as the Punjab. The land had been conquered by the British in the latter half of the nineteenth century after a savage conflict in which Khan's father and uncles were allied with the British.[2] After the conquest, his family continued to maintain close military ties: of his eight half-brothers, seven would have celebrated careers in the Indian and then the Pakistani army. In the West, Khan claimed, probably accurately, that his was the first generation in which there had not been a murder. He told a friend: "In my country, life is very cheap. I could have men disposed of for a mere five hundred rupees—that is how we might deal with difficult situations. My people do not feel Judeo-Christian guilt: my people feel vengeance."[3]

As an adult, Khan was always aware of the powerful influence of his "savage" Eastern roots.[4] In the West, he wrote:

[I]n all honesty I have to confess that in some deep dark recesses of my soul I am still hankering after an ideal of heroism which is essentially miltaristic, impersonal and political. The taint of my ancestry. The victory of my imaginative-intellectual sentiments is not yet complete over this dark inheritance. [I have an] inner craving for heroic social battle

and a dark fascination with war and soldiery. . . . That is perhaps why I
live away from my country. Because in it I will eventually get seduced
into action.[5]

Khan's father, Fazaldad, was a Shiite Muslim[6] who was born a peasant. Because of their alliance with the British, he and his two brothers
were richly rewarded, acquiring significant power and wealth. An old
photograph shows a tall (6'5"), light-skinned, and handsome Fazaldad,
proudly wearing military dress that includes two medals around his neck.[7]
Family legend has it that he received one of these for his bravery in carrying a wounded British general to safety in a battle in Mesopotamia.

After the British conquest, Fazaldad's name changed to Khan Bahadur
Fazaldad Khan. "Khan" and "Bahadur" are terms of respect for people
with power, not family names, and indeed Punjabis did not use family
names until after the British came. Fazaldad's descendants use Khan as
their last name and it is a name that has become common in Pakistan.
This group of Khans, however, is no ordinary family. The wealth accumulated by Fazaldad has been passed on to members of a large extended
family, and his landholdings in several different locations in Pakistan,
including Chakwal and Faisalabad (formerly Lyallpur), are still held by
family members.

As the Punjab settled into peacetime, Fazaldad switched from being
a warrior to being a farmer. He specialized in breeding and selling horses
that the British used in their army and for polo, and he became a self-
taught horse veterinarian. He made his home in the remote countryside of Montgomery and he also owned land in other parts of Northern
India. The social system was feudal, and the peasants who lived on his
land were required to work for him.[8]

Fazaldad, by the custom of his religion, was free to marry four times,
and he did so.[9] His initial marriage was to a first cousin, as was common. When she was unable to bear children, there was a divorce.

His second wife, Badsha (d. 1955), was a Muslim from the Pathan
tribe, a fair-skinned group that includes Hindus as well as Muslims.[10]
The couple had eight children together, four sons and four daughters.
As a Pathan, Badsha did not share the Rajput tradition of contempt
for females, and she made sure that her daughters were educated, albeit secretly. These daughters then encouraged their own daughters

to be educated. Masud was especially close to Badsha's granddaughters Khalida Khan and Fatima Ahmed, who were his age. "Uncle" Masud and his "nieces" played together as children and attended university together. These two women, both professionals living in the United States, are major sources of information about Khan's early life.[11]

Amir Jan, Fazaldad's third wife, was a courtesan who came to the marriage having already borne an illegitimate daughter.[12] Fazaldad had started the relationship with her while Badsha, who was pregnant, was making an extended visit to her family. Badsha accepted Fazaldad's new wife, even as the two women had children in overlapping years, and Amir Jan's illegitimate daughter was allowed to stay with the family in a kind of nursemaid role. Amir Jan had four children, all sons, with Fazaldad. She died in the 1920s at a young age and Badsha then raised the sons.

Fazaldad's fourth marriage took place in 1923, when he was seventy-six years old—an age the family considered to be inappropriate for infatuation and sexuality. The new bride, Khursheed, was a dark-skinned beauty, and, like Amir Jan, she was a courtesan with an illegitimate child. She claimed to be seventeen, an age considered to be the peak of beauty and sensuality for Punjabi girls, although she was probably a few years older.

After the marriage, Fazaldad insisted that Khursheed's illegitimate son Salahuddin ("Salah," 1914–1979) be sent away. Salah went to live with Khursheed's brother in Jhelum, a town about 100 miles north of her new home. Khursheed had grown up in Jhelum, and her extended family still lived there. She would visit Salah every year, always traveling alone.

This marriage upset the family balance. Fazaldad's oldest son, Akbar, took Badsha to live with him in Lahore, eighty-five miles away, an act that broke with the tradition of multiple wives and their children living together on the patriarch's land.

Khursheed and Fazaldad had three children in quick succession: Tahir (1923–1983), Masud (1924–1989), and Mahmooda (1926–1942). Masud was born in Jhelum, at his mother's family home, on July 21, 1924. He was born with a defect known as an "elephant ear" or "cauliflower ear." It was a deformed and oversized right ear, and it would remain a stigma all his life.[13]

Khan wrote about his childhood: "[L]ife was gloriously feudally phobic. Everything was really simple. No one travelled far or left. Relationships were direct and simple, even though often very violent. No one ever used boats, and planes were science-fiction to us. One's farthest reaches were limited by the abilities and capacities of a horse."[14] As a toddler, he was adored by the servants: "I lived in a benignly autistic stance, closely and warmly environed by the servants. I was perpetually in their care & respected with deep affection in their holding presence."[15] But he was not a peaceful child. Chaudri Nazir Ahmed, whose father Mustaq Ahmed had been estate manager when Khan was young, reports that "from the very beginning" Khan was overly talkative.[16] In a contrasting account, an anonymous friend remembers Khan saying that, as a boy, "he was autistic, enclosed in himself—he felt he existed in the midst of nothingness and he never fit in."

It appears that Khursheed devoted herself to her new husband. She regularly stayed in her bedroom until around 4 p.m., at which time she would emerge exquisitely made up and dressed with bracelets and jewels. Late in my research, I learned that there was a family secret: Khursheed may have been addicted to opium.[17] This would explain her late rising and her remoteness. Fazaldad apparently had a secret bank account that was used to buy the illegal opium, and upon his death the bank account (and the responsibility) was transferred to Masud.

As adults, Masud and Tahir joked about hearing their parents make love on hot nights, when the whole family would sleep outside on the terrace; they remembered their parents as having had a romantic sexual relationship.[18] But the marriage was, from the perspective of others, tainted by Khursheed's history. One of Khan's Indian/Pakistani friends told me: "I think that when Masud was young, he was probably taunted for being the son of a courtesan. I mean, it was better that his parents were married, but it was still very bad. So that experience went into his soul and he carried not only a chip on his shoulder—he carried a rock."[19]

Despite his mother's relative absence, Khan was close to her: "It was in my mother's ambience and sentient presence in my early childhood that I evolved my sensibility."[20] According to Khalida Khan, Khursheed had a gentle disposition and rarely showed negative emotions. Masud was acutely sensitive to his mother's feelings and two early traumatic experiences had a huge effect on him. The first occurred when he was four years old:

> Living has never been natural to me, since I saw my mother in an epileptic seizure, at the age of four, convulsed, with a pathetic local doctor convinced she was going to die. She had just been delivered of a stillborn foetus. I stood crying and praying by her. Maids wanted to take me away, but I refused, and my father, normally a cruel and authoritative feudalist lord, ordered I be allowed to stay.
>
> My mother recovered. I do not remember the rest. But the gossip by the maids and sisters was that for three years I did not speak.[21]

One wonders why Fazaldad would have allowed his son to witness such a scene. The fact that Masud developed the symptom of mutism afterward shows that it was overwhelming to him.[22]

The second traumatic experience occurred when he was seven, when Khursheed went to visit her parents and Salah:

> This time, my mother betrayed a promise to me. She was going to . . . Jhelum and she promised to return in thirty days. My father didn't believe that she would return when she said she would, but she made me her accomplice in believing her, and I convinced my father. On the twenty-ninth day, a telegram arrived, and she was delayed for fifteen more days. My mammoth and majestic father raved in panic like a child. For fifteen days he made the whole estate a living hell of barbarous cruelty, maudlin self-pity, and abusive threats of vengeance against my mother and her family. "I shall kill, kill, kill," he kept shouting and whimpering.
>
> Mother did arrive on the fifteenth day. [But] I refused to drive to the railway station to receive her. When she reached the mansion, she sent for me. I went, but refused to greet her: very insolent indeed. She said, "You have not greeted me." In the most lucid Urdu, I replied: "You have dishonoured my father and let me down." She slapped my face—she, who had never slapped me, ever! I quietly said, "I will never speak to you again, unless you ask for me and order me." I never did, to her dying day.[23]

He was almost certainly exaggerating when he said that he never spoke to his mother again, but he did grow distant from his mother as he grew up. He experienced her as a simple woman prone to "anxious chatter" who could not keep up with him: "My mind as it evolved estranged me from my mother."[24]

Tahir seems to have been always in the shadow of his younger brother,[25] while Masud had a closer relationship with his younger sister, Mahmooda. She was dark-skinned and beautiful like their mother, and she was much adored. Because she was brought up separately from the brothers for her first years, Masud only got to know her when she was four years old and began to come to the family meals. This was also a time when her father first began to see her regularly, and he made sure that she always had multiple gold bracelets to wear, bracelets being a status symbol in that world. Khalida Khan recalled Masud's devotion to his sister:

> One Easter when we were visiting, Mahmooda had a pet bird that died, and she wanted to bury him using Islamic rites. Girls weren't supposed to dig graves, so she asked Masud to do it. He agreed because he would do anything for her. We had a ceremony and we all cried.

Masud had to fight hard and be very clever in order to earn his father's recognition, as this story shows:

> My father hardly knew me when I was young. But a few days before my fourth birthday, my mother and the governess were talking with me about what to ask for as a birthday gift. I said, "Four million rupees." They cajoled me to ask for less. So when my father came to ask me what I wanted, I said, "A penny." He roared with laughter and produced it immediately. The women were disheartened that I had asked for so little. But later, when I was thirteen, my father handed his estate over to me and he said, "All this goes to you because you were content with a penny." This is how I learned the importance of gestures.[26]

Fazaldad marked the significance of his "discovery" of his four-year-old son by changing his name. Masud had been named Ibrahim at birth, but his father renamed him Mohammed Masud. Mohammed was the first name of all four sons born to Badsha, so this gesture may have been an attempt to integrate Masud into the larger family.[27] Names were important, as in a story Khan told a Western friend:

When I was nine, I went for a short time to a school in Montgomery. A teacher called the roll; when my turn came, he asked me to tell my name. I did not answer. The question had never been asked of me before. He sent me home. I asked my esteemed father, "How do I answer someone who wants to know my name?" and he replied with asperity: "He who does not know your name will learn little from your telling it to him."[28]

Fazaldad's favorite child at the time when Masud was born was Mohammed Baqar, a son born to Badsha. Baqar was an intellectual, different from his brothers, who all had military careers. He was a student at Oxford when he was killed in a motorcycle accident at age nineteen, in a family tragedy that still evokes sadness in his family. The accident occurred in 1923, a year before Masud was born. Over time, Fazaldad encouraged Masud to take Baqar's place as the family intellectual.

Mohammed Masud would become his father's new favorite son. From the age of four, he accompanied Fazaldad as he conducted the business of the estate. When Fazaldad presided over the local court,[29] Masud wore a velvet suit as he sat silently and listened. He was being groomed to take his father's place.

Masud remembered Fazaldad as "a gaunt, bleak, monumental presence, either utterly still or raging in wild temper."[30] The sons competed for his affection. Every day, they were required to line up and proceed in front of him and bow, with Masud always last, since he was the youngest.[31] Masud was the only son never punished with a beating. Instead, Fazaldad controlled him verbally and with "sulks & restrictive & punitive gestures."[32] Even as a favored child, however, Masud suffered under his father's high standards:

> I recall the long hard years of learning to ride and jump, under father's vigilance, and not being praised for taking all the high fearful jumps on a seventeen hand horse—a very tall horse!—and my father at the end of some seventeen jumps in the ring not recognizing and endorsing the fact that a tiny tot of a boy (I was eleven then) had achieved the critical deed; instead he berated me for not being able to hold the horse still while he was talking to me. Of course, I had at the time burst into tears.[33]

Some of Khan's childhood stories include accounts of violence and sadism. Even if untrue, they carry an emotional truth that is worthy of consideration. The following stories were told to me anonymously by two of Khan's female friends:

> Masud used to suffer at school because the other boys would taunt him about his large ear. One day he confided to his father that he was being bullied. Soon after that, a group of his father's servants showed up at the school, and they buggered [i.e., sexually assaulted] the other children as Masud watched.

> Masud told me a story about a man who had raped a woman on the family estate. His father had the man hung upside down and he was beaten until he had a brain rupture or stroke. He was never okay after that. Masud told me this proudly, as an example of how his father cleared the estate of crime.

Khan never criticized his father's harsh style. He wrote, "[I was] nurtured by love and care, but apprenticed in cruelty and service,"[34] and "I was brought up a much indulged child under an iron discipline, and the chief ideal presented to one was that one should spare oneself nothing. Both in terms of the good things in life and in terms of effort and application."[35] In considering writing a biography of Fazaldad, he said, "I know what I shall write: an epical, lyrical, metaphorical, simple biography of my father. I shall sing this man. It is not often that one meets a person whose whims have to be met and pampered because there is real dignity, virtue and affection in them."[36] An anonymous Western friend remembers that Khan idealized his father and talked about him "as if he were God."

But Robert Stoller, who knew more about Khan's early history than any other Westerner, believed that Fazaldad's extreme personality had been harmful: "[Fazaldad's] love was so dangerous, conditional, and distant that Masud could use it only to sketch in stability—not ever to feel it as foundation. The father fed [Masud] a diet of love and humiliation, and that is a fiery mix."[37] Stoller thought that the young Khan had been traumatized by unprotected exposure to violent experiences. Khan himself hints at this, without providing details: "Yes, childhood is destiny. [Mine has] provided me with both the ferment and the sensibility that I am harvesting now [in adult life]. And also all the phobias and terrors that I shall never rid myself of."[38]

CHAPTER 2

A FEUDAL UPBRINGING

[The American analyst Karl Menninger] asked me to describe
my background. My simple answer: "Feudal, Sir!" "What does
that mean, son?" "A loving, tyrannical father; vast space; peasants
and horses!" This had us both at ease with each other.
Masud Khan[1]

In 1937, when Khan was twelve, Fazaldad moved his family to a country estate that he had built to serve as a horse-breeding facility as well as
a homestead. Another reason for the move may have been that Fazaldad
wanted his favorite son to have a separate estate, where sons from his
earlier marriages would not interfere.[2]

The estate, which was named Kot Fazaldad Khan ("Kot" means
"home of"), was in the outskirts of Lyallpur (now Faisalabad), a town
named after the English commissioner Mr. Lyle. It was a few hours' drive
from the larger city of Lahore, where Khalida and Fatima lived. Fazaldad
and his brothers had been given land grants in the area and, over time,
they became instigators of development in the entire region and owned
most of the businesses in town.

Kot Fazaldad Khan was built on a grand scale. The central mansion
was surrounded by a huge walled courtyard. Outside the wall, there was
space for horses and for cultivation, as well as a mud hut village where
the peasants lived.[3]

Khan hated the move. He felt it marked the end of his childhood.

I recall vividly our father driving Tahir and me to the village in Lyallpur,
which was just being built (it was April, 1937). I was hushed and quiet

during the long car-trek across dirt roads. I knew my father was nervous about leaving me alone with my year-older brother Tahir, and my
favourite servants from Montgomery. He stayed for four days to settle
me in. We were temporarily living in the guest house; the mansion proper
was still being built and the rest of the family were due to move in sometime in June or July.

On the morning of the last day, just as my father was ready to leave
for Montgomery, I complained of acute hernia pains in the right groin,
and poor father had to take me back with him, via Lahore, where I was
examined by a surgeon, who found nothing and advised rest. I could sense
the dejection in my father all the way back, but he said not a word of
complaint. Most unusual for a man of his intolerance of weakness of any
sort in his children.

It was my mother who was startled into enraged dismay and panic at
seeing me back. She bluntly accused me of faking. I remember her contained but wild despair in remarking, "Now you will not inherit Lyallpur
for sure!" I was crushed by her refusal and hurt disappointment in me. So
much so that I convinced my father in two days that I was fit and wanted
to join my brother, who must feel very alone and lonely. In spite of his
misgivings, my father drove me back the same day . . .

I don't think I have ever felt at home in any space since then: certainly not in Lyallpur.[4]

One of the biggest changes was that Kot Fazaldad Khan was close
to a city, in contrast to the wild countryside of the Montgomery home,
and as a result there was a strong British presence. Fazaldad and his family
were accepted into British social life because of his horse breeding and
veterinary skills. Khan wrote: "I recall vividly how, every Sunday, we
would be sent by father to ride in the morning with our British neigh-
bours; and then, in the evening, we would go with father to other friends'
estates to play croquet with the 'ladies' and their brood."[5] He was deeply
impressed by the colonizers: "I [grew up] among the Imperial English
of the Administration: civilians & militarists who were steeped in the
lore of the Victorian self-image of 'great men.'"[6]

The British influence had also been present in Montgomery, although it was not part of everyday life. Field Marshall Lord Birdwood
was, by Khan's account, his godfather. In 1931, Birdwood was retiring
and he came for a final visit to the Khan estate. Aware of his godchild's

verbal precocity, he suggested that Fazaldad hire English-speaking teachers for Masud to prepare him for higher education in England rather
than an army career. From that time one, Fazaldad hired British tutors
to provide both Masud and Tahir with a private education. Prior to that,
they had not been taught to read or write in any language.[7]

One tutor, a man named P. I. Painter, had a huge impact:

> Early in my adolescence, Painter [was the] most crucial and pivotal for-
> mative influence in my life. As I grow older and become more myself, I
> realize with a sense of profound indebtedness how much I owe to him.
> He had studied at Oxford, where he was a favourite and devout student
> of the philosopher R. G. Collingwood. Then he was a high ranking
> Imperial Civil Service official who resigned on issues of philosophical
> and political differences over the Imperial policy of jurisprudence in India.
> He was loafing around idle when my father employed him to tutor me
> privately.[8]

Guided by Painter, Khan abandoned an interest in Persian and Urdu
poetry in order to immerse himself in the tragedies of Shakespeare, along
with other great works of Western literature. Later he wrote: "If anyone wants to know the true matrix of my sensibility, he shall have to look
to . . . the climate of these books that created that tension in me in the
years 1940–1946 which actualised itself in my becoming an analyst and
living the life I do in London."[9]

Through reading Shakespeare, Khan began to be psychologically
reflective—that is, he learned to think about his thinking.[10] In his world,
this type of psychological development was almost nonexistent: "I grew
up in a climate of relationships where affectivity was not spelt out into
emotions of any complexity. It all stayed larval, intense, and reticently,
as well as explosively, mute."[11] Shakespeare taught him how to put feelings into words, something he would not have learned elsewhere: "The
question of how to interpret Shakespearean tragedy constituted one of
the archetypal preoccupations of my adolescence."[12] Writing from Pakistan in a later year, Khan described the immensity of the contrast of
East and West on this matter: "The persons around me here move in a
sentient transparent physicality, and they are poetic as well as subtle of
sensibility—but they are not, in the European sense, psychological. Our
culture could no more produce a Kafka than it could a Freud!"[13]

Eastern and Western culture now existed in parallel in Khan's mind, without blending or merging. He was fluent from childhood in five languages—Hindi, Urdu, Punjabi, Pashto, and English—but even before he moved to the West, his psychological and intellectual life developed almost exclusively in the English tradition. When he moved to London, the culture was already so familiar, so central to his very self, that he claimed he did not have culture shock. The huge influence of Painter and Western civilization is acknowledged in this quote from his Work Books, where he refers to the impact of his education in India: "Adolescence is destiny—the personal destiny as against the given destiny of infancy and childhood."[14]

In 1940, Khan lived at home as he attended Gout College in Lyallpur. There he met a Hindu girl with whom he had an adolescent love relationship that led to an enormous upheaval. The Punjab had a tradition of Hindu–Muslim cooperativeness, but that did not mean that Hindu and Muslim youth could freely date. Local politics was dominated by the Muslim League, which promoted a strong Muslim identity as part of the movement toward an independent Muslim state, so Khan's relationship with the Hindu girl was provocative and potentially dangerous. His parents joined with his teachers in pressuring him to break up with the girl and, reluctantly, he did so.

Within a few months, at age seventeen, he was severely depressed and suffering from anorexia, a rare symptom for a male. His father must have been quite alarmed, because he took the unusual step of having his son seen by a local psychotherapist. Khan's symptoms got better, but the therapy did not touch deeper problems that had caused the symptoms. He later claimed that this early love experience left him unwilling to experience longing. He said that when he lost his girlfriend, he developed a "basic unappetite" that he masked for the rest of his life by overproductivity.[15]

Psychologists generally believe that identity crisis and rebellion against parental norms are growth-promoting experiences in adolescence. Khan, however, did not feel that his brief revolt was helpful: "It was adolescence that hurtled me into militant and cussed autonomy, and the success of the venture alienated me from myself."[16] Later he would write that adolescence presents an opportunity to correct childhood psychopathology[17]—but this did not happen for him.

He stifled his rebellion and convinced himself that his father in particular had handled the situation well: "My adolescence . . . made inordinate demands on my father's generosity of spirit to meet its antics. Little wonder no-one has ever replaced my father in my inner life."[18] His already shaky relationship with his mother was never restored: "My mother and I got estranged during my adolescence: quietly and without conflict. We never found our way back to each other."[19]

In order to get away from the scandal that resulted from his relationship with the Hindu girl, Khan enrolled at University of the Punjab, in the nearby city of Lahore, where Tahir was already a student. There he received a B.A. (honors) and then an M.A. in English literature.[20] Stimulated by the intellectual and social life of the university, he began to recover. Then two major tragedies occurred that would have enormous repercussions.

The first tragedy was the unexpected death of his beloved sister. Mahmooda died on December 26, 1942, at age sixteen. Different stories are told about the cause of her death—an overdose of the new drug penicillin, typhoid fever, or a urinary tract infection that was untreated because the doctors were unwilling to catheterize a high-class Muslim girl.[21] It was a huge loss for Khan, because he had adored his sister and she had adored him: "[Mahmooda] was my first and model love; we were utterly mutual and in trust."[22] "I taught her to dress fashionably, speak English and do mathematics. In short, I was her all-in-all."[23]

Then in 1943, just a few months later, Fazaldad died. One biographer[24] suggests that Fazaldad died of a broken heart over the loss of his beloved daughter, but we have to remember that he was already ninety-six years old, a man who had been bedridden for several years due to circulatory problems secondary to diabetes.

Khan was devastated. As an adult, he said that his father's death was a turning point in his life because he lost the person who was his secure base: "With the death of my father in my teens, I was left with no expectancy of a traditioned discipline; I was instead impaled on the intensity of my own will and temperament."[25] He described Khalida Khan's memory of him from this period:

[Khalida] said that the family all thought I had no other existence but to live for my father. To them, it seemed I had dedicated myself to one man, and when he died, I had so arrogantly isolated myself that I was like a person possessed with some dark mission in life. They were all frightened because I started living like a lunatic after my father's death, with no real friends, only my servants, horses, eccentric snob dress habits, books, and haughty superior isolation. My subjective memories of the years 1943–1946 are of a youth confused, terrified and bewildered, inconsolable and bleak, who drew a sort of magical circle round himself and survived by isolation.[26]

At the advice of Painter, Khan went into psychoanalytic therapy in Lahore with a psychiatrist named Dr. Latif. Latif had trained in London under Anna Freud, in a special shortened course of study that was set up for students coming from a great distance.[27] He was known for being a helpful therapist, despite the fact that he was something of a "ladies' man."[28] Khan felt helped by Latif and it was this experience that led him to conclude that he should seek a personal analysis in London.

One consequence of Fazaldad's death was that Masud and Tahir got to know their half-brother Salah, Khursheed's illegitimate son. Fazaldad had forbidden his presence on the estate, but now Khursheed brought him to live at Kot Fazaldad Khan. Salah, who was a town boy, not an aristocrat, regularly visited Masud and Tahir in Lahore, where he introduced his half-brothers to clubs and other social life. Khan later said that Salah saved him from being completely rustic.

Throughout the ages, in all parts of the world, family secrets are publicly revealed when death leads to a redistribution of wealth. The victories and wounds at such a point are of enormous consequence to the living, since they are frozen in time and unchangeable—the deceased person being unavailable for further negotiation. Khan's status of "favorite son" was confirmed for posterity in 1943, when Fazaldad died.

Muslims living in India at that time were mostly of the Sunni branch. Their tradition, at that time and in that location, was to distribute wealth according to Islamic laws where a larger portion is divided equally among the sons and a smaller portion is divided equally among the daughters. Fazaldad, however, was a Shiite Muslim, not a Sunni, and in his tradition, sons received everything, with the eldest son getting half of the estate and the rest divided among the other sons.[29]

Oddly, given his heritage, Fazaldad gave his youngest son a disproportionately large inheritance. Masud alone inherited his physical property—Kot Fazaldad Khan, as well as two other estates. Apparently the decision about inheritance had been made in 1937, when Fazaldad was influenced by a close friend, Nawab Sir Mehr Shah, to transfer the land and villages to Masud in a way that would supersede Islamic law.[30]

The will was an extreme insult to Tahir because, as the older son, he should have either shared in the inheritance of land or received all of it. Fazaldad's will did give Tahir a significant sum of money, but Masud got more. The only way in which Fazaldad followed tradition was by giving his wife and daughters nothing. Khursheed was now dependent on Masud for money and for the right to continue living at Kot Fazaldad Khan. Khan appreciated the inheritance, even though it created problems:

> As my father was dying, he reached out his feeble and trembling hand and said to me: "Sudi, I have given you the title, the estates, and money you will gawp at!" He died a few minutes later. What had he left me: the hatred of my half-brothers and sisters, and the deadly envy of my mother . . .[31]

By 1946, Khan was experiencing major psychological problems for which he could not get effective help in India. Furthermore, he was living in a country that was on the verge of a dangerous struggle for independence. With feudal India about to disappear and his father gone, there was little reason to stay and at least some hope that he could make a life for himself in the world he was so familiar with from his reading. He decided to follow the advice of Lord Birdwood and go to Balliol College at Oxford to study "Modern Greats."

World War II had just ended, and it was difficult to get permission to leave. But Field Marshal Sir Archibald Wavell, an old friend of Fazaldad, intervened, according to Khan.[32] He arranged for Khan to be one of the first Indians allowed to fly to England in the post-war years.

PART 2

EARLY YEARS IN LONDON

(1946–1959)

CHAPTER 3

A MISUNDERSTANDING

Yes, Destiny is the summation of all those circumstances we
pre-arrange unknowingly.
Masud Khan[1]

In October 1946, Khan arrived at Oxford. At age twenty-two, he was alone
in a totally new environment: "I [had brought] 37 suitcases of luggage,
and was told that only one suitcase was allowed. So I put all the rest in the
hotel opposite, which was fortunately available. I was shown my room. I
had grown up in vast mansions, and here was this small attic room, with
one small bed, a mirror, table, and no heating. I slept every night fully
dressed in my clothes and overcoat; even so, I nearly froze to death."[2]

Prior to leaving India, he had written Dr. John Bowlby, training
secretary of the British Psycho-Analytical Society (BPAS), to discuss
arrangements for a personal analysis. Bowlby wrote back asking him to
telephone upon his arrival. Thus it was that, immediately after settling
in to his quarters at Oxford, Khan went to London. He checked into
the Savoy, a luxury hotel, called Bowlby's office, and was given an appointment for the next day at 11 a.m.[3]

His life was about to be dramatically affected by a surprising mistake. Even though Khan had no background in medicine or psychology, Bowlby assumed that he was applying to become a candidate at the
Institute of Psycho-Analysis, the part of the BPAS that handles the training and administrative activities. Thus Bowlby viewed their meeting as
an admissions interview for the training program.[4]

The situation was complicated by internal politics in the BPAS of
which Khan had no knowledge. His tutor, P. I. Painter, had consulted

the London analyst Margaret Lowenfeld, who was a friend, and Lowenfeld had recommended Dr. Edward Glover as Khan's analyst. Khan had addressed his letter to the training secretary of the BPAS, because that was an address he saw on an old copy of the *International Journal of Psycho-Analysis* (IJPA), and he asked that his letter be forwarded to Glover—but Bowlby kept it. Bowlby and Glover were on opposite sides of a feud that had led to Glover's resignation from the BPAS in 1944.[5] Had Bowlby sent the letter on, Khan presumably would have had a personal analysis with Glover while doing graduate work at Oxford. It is possible that Bowlby deliberately confused things, perhaps wanting to deprive Glover of a good referral or perhaps out of a desire to recruit an intelligent Indian for training at the BPAS.[6]

Here is Khan's description of the fateful meeting:

> I arrived at Bowlby's office, immaculately dressed. Was surprised to see how shabbily everyone was dressed. I had no idea what the war years had done to the English. I had read about the war, and my brothers had fought in it, but I had no image of what it had done to people.
>
> I was told to go up a poky little staircase and sat in a dingy room. I was punctual, Bowlby was late. Some 20 minutes later a middle aged, red-faced, pug-nosed man wearing a crumpled tweed suit . . . [emerged and] introduced himself as Dr. Bowlby. He rather embarrassedly told me he was busy and could I wait till 12 o'clock and then he would see me. I asked for some book to read meantime as there was nothing but newspapers in the room. He showed surprise at this request but acquiesced.
>
> He arrived around 12:30 and I was peeved by now. He invited me to lunch . . . "We will make a dash for the restaurant, it is only round the corner," Bowlby explained. It was drizzling so I said, "Why not use my car?" "You have a car, already?" "No Sir, I have hired one." "You have a license?" "No Sir, I never drive myself." He refused my chauffeur-driven Rolls and we walked our distance. I had by this time a distinct feeling that Dr. Bowlby thought he had a lunatic on his hands.
>
> We got into the restaurant and it was crowded. We squeezed in and sat in a corner at a table for two. A typed menu was presented where the choice was between mushroom omelette and roast duck. Bowlby asked me what I would have and I replied: "You choose, Sir. I am your guest."
>
> The food that arrived was simply awful. I ate a few mouthfuls politely. Alongside Bowlby made the most inane sort of conversation. Quite

irrelevant and meaningless, punctuated by huge and heavy silences. When coffee was served, he asked me whether I had any references because I had sent one and it was customary to have two references. I didn't quite understand and Bowlby explained ponderously that he needed the names of two persons whom he could write to and ask about me. I thought for a while and said the two people who would perhaps serve his purposes best were Field Marshal Lord Wavell, Governor General of India and Sir Bertrand Glancy, Governor of Punjab. Bowlby shuffled awkwardly and asked: "Do they know you personally?" "Yes Sir, very well indeed, and they also know the family well." There was a most uncanny atmosphere following this little conversation.

We gulped our coffees in silence. The day had cleared outside and Bowlby asked me if I would care to walk round Regent's Park with him. I said: "I have no objections Sir." When we got out he asked me: "Do you always address people as Sir?" and I replied: "No Sir, not the people. Only a gentleman if he is 20 years or more older than me, which I reckon you are, Sir!" In Regent's Park he explained to me a great deal of the architecture and pointed out which flower was what. Utterly useless chatter. Then he became conscious I was getting bored so he asked: "Do you like flowers?" "Not as a rule, Sir! but I think all this is very pleasant."

By this time, it was nearly 3:30 and he said he must get back to the Clinic. On our way back he met a lady and started talking to her, completely ignoring my existence. Then turned to me and said: "Dr. [Sylvia] Payne, this is Mr. Khan from India. When can you see him?" Dr. Payne shook hands with me and smiled in a kindly generous way which made me feel at ease for the first time. She said she could see me at 5:50 p.m. the next day. And we parted. Bowlby explained to me that Dr. Payne was the President of the British Society. When we reached my car, he said he would walk and I didn't fuss. Just as he was about to leave he asked me: "Have you anyone particular in mind for your analyst?" "Yes Sir, Dr. Glover." He replied rather too sharply: "That is not possible as he is no longer a member of the British Society—but you can discuss that in your interview with Dr. Payne tomorrow."

The whole episode left me confused, peeved and utterly disoriented. I had no clue as to what this man had been after. I went to my hotel. Changed. Had tea and slept. In the evening went and saw Sir Laurence Olivier in "King Lear" at the New Theatre and forgot all about my lunch with Dr. Bowlby for the time being.[7]

In Khan's account,the issue regarding his request for analysis was clarified and then resolved when Dr. Payne made a decision:

When I arrived at Dr. Payne's consultation room the next day I was a bundle of nerves: taut, stiff, awkward and pouring with sweat. My mouth was dry and my eyes staring with a mixture of terror and panic. Dr. Payne received me in a very gentle and courteous manner and asked me to sit down. She told me Dr. Bowlby had rung her about me. Then with a mirthful smile she asked: "Are you a good sportsman?" This immediately put me at ease and for the next hour I chattered away about my horses and riding and polo. She listened with keen interest and told me her husband had been a Cambridge Blue and so was her son. I knew she was a wise kind person and apologised: "I am sorry I have talked so much but I am very nervous." To which she replied: "You can at least talk when you are nervous. Most people cannot utter a word." This pleased me. She had a sense of humour. Now she started to ask me questions. At some point she asked me: "Whom have you loved most in your life?" I burst into tears; she came over, patted me on the head, offered me a glass of water. She then talked for another ten minutes and said it would be better if we met again the next day at the same time. I left feeling I had met a real person who had understood me. Just as I was leaving I said: "I didn't answer your question, Dr. Payne. It was my father I loved most. He died in 1943." "Oh! I am sorry!" she said. "No, my father was ripe for it, Dr. Payne. He was 96. Only I never thought he would ever die." And I rushed away in nervous pain.

Next day when I arrived at Dr. Payne's I felt both confident and relaxed. She asked me about my education and I told her I had a B.A. (Hons.) degree in Political Science and an M.A. in English Literature. She then enquired about my plans and my answer was: my family wants me to go to Oxford and do Modern Greats and after that study for Barrister-at-Law and return home and be a politician. I told her that I had no intention of going back home to become a politician as we, the Feudalists, had had our day and what was to follow was corruption, demagogy and chaos. I was looking for a profession which would enable me to earn my living anywhere in the world. I would like to go to Oxford, as I was registered there, and do Law, perhaps International Law. But first of all I would like to have a good analysis. She asked me what I meant by "a good analysis." I said I didn't quite know. She then asked me what sort of an analyst I had in mind. I told her he or she must be English, well-bred, sensitive, kind, very patient and firm and well-read in literature. She was amused.

She had, she said, given my situation a lot of thought and her suggestion was I should go to Miss Ella Sharpe for analysis. That Miss Sharpe was one of their best, most sensitive and experienced training analysts. She had talked to Miss Sharpe personally last night and Miss Sharpe was willing to take me on.

She then produced a form and said, "I think you should apply to the Institute for training. I cannot promise they will accept you. You are very young. Anyhow, I shall strongly recommend you." . . . There was a happy, kind, benevolent, protective look on her face when we shook hands to part and I had not felt so safe and cared-for since my father's death.

When I reached my room I wanted to celebrate but I knew no one. Then I felt very dismal suddenly. Got up, washed, changed and went and saw "King Lear" again. I was to see it for 27 . . . evenings that month.

Ten days later Dr. Bowlby rang me and said I had been accepted and should contact Miss Sharpe. I started my analysis with Miss Sharpe on the 17th of October, 1946, as a candidate. It was also the third anniversary of my father's death that day.[8]

It is intriguing that Khan reports seeing twenty-seven performances of "King Lear" that first fall in London. Shakespeare's tragedies were already a significant part of his life, so the play may have felt comfortably familiar. Furthermore, his current life situation resonated with major themes of the play, including the role of fate and destiny in a person's life[9] and the problematics of favoritism and betrayal in a family. He would reread *King Lear* throughout his life in the West.

With his passion for literature and his superb analytic and writing skills, Khan would undoubtedly have made significant contributions to the field of literature had he pursued his original plan. However, an anonymous analyst commented that fate had been kind in directing him to a career in psychoanalysis: "Literature was Masud's real milieu. He was totally enmeshed in it. But psychoanalysis was a necessary mistake for him, because it allowed him not to go even further inward to dissolve into psychosis. He needed the relationship to reality that psychoanalysis offers, and a literary career would not have had that." Khan thought similarly: "The questions and curiosities that literature had engendered in me during my adolescent years of study could have been pursued sentiently only through clinical psychoanalysis. I needed Freud's clinical space and method to actualize all the intellectual torment I had gathered inside myself: both subjectively and heuristically."[10]

An alternate view is that of the Kleinian analyst Hanna Segal. She comments on the difference between a therapeutic analysis, which is given to ordinary analysands who have psychological problems, and a training analysis provided for candidates who in theory are already fairly healthy. The therapeutic analysis goes deeper and is less intellectual. In the current structure of training, people sometimes have a therapeutic analysis first and then a training analysis, but in the 1940s, in England, a person was given one or the other—and Khan had a training analysis. Segal argues that he needed a therapeutic analysis, because he was so ill, and that it was a tragedy that he was accepted into analytic training: "Masud was a gifted man and very intuitive, in the way very sick people often are. I personally would have accepted him into analysis, even though I'm not sure that he was analyzable—but I would never have accepted him as a student."

Khan was not headed for a peaceful experience in the BPAS. He arrived just after the Extraordinary Meetings and the Controversial Discussions, a series of heated theoretical debates held in 1943–1944. The complexity of the situation is described in several sources[11] and goes beyond the scope of this book. However, a summary is necessary to give context to the analytic world that Khan had entered.

Prior to World War II, there had been three large and thriving psychoanalytic societies, one located in Berlin, one in Vienna, and one in London. Each society had different theories and techniques, but they were cooperative rather than antagonistic.[12]

Things began to change when Melanie Klein emigrated to London in 1926. Klein was welcomed by the British analysts, who were interested in her writing about early childhood and the role of hate and aggression in development. She became a member of the BPAS in 1927 and a training analyst in 1929. But an acrimonious relationship developed between the followers of Klein and the followers of Anna Freud in Vienna. Klein and Anna Freud both specialized in children and they disagreed on many theoretical and practical points. Furthermore, there was a personal rivalry as each struggled for recognition as the "true heir" to the ailing Sigmund Freud.

The Anna Freud–Melanie Klein tension intensified on the London scene in 1933, when there was an influx of German analysts loyal to Anna Freud. The tension became even worse after the eminent British analyst Ernest Jones helped Sigmund Freud and his family, along with other Viennese analysts, move to London. All the refugees were given immediate membership in the BPAS, where the close contact of the Kleinians and the Anna Freudians ignited their rivalry.

Eventually, there were three major groups in the BPAS. Those who adhered to Melanie Klein's ideas became known as the A group. The followers of Anna Freud became the B group. And the original English analysts who refused to be designated as A or B became part of what was called the Middle Group (later known as the Independents). Most analytic societies faced with similar tensions split into separate groups, but the BPAS stayed united.[13]

The rivalry of the three groups would be a constant backdrop to Khan's analytic life. Initially, he had the advantage of not having been present during the Controversial Discussions, so that he had not needed to choose sides. His first contacts in London were with people who had been major players in all the subgroups.[14]

CHAPTER 4

FIRST YEARS OF TRAINING AND
PERSONAL LIFE IN THE WEST

I first met Masud in 1946. He was an immensely handsome
young man with a charming wit. What he wanted most
of all was to be accepted by the English.
Sadie Gillespie, London analyst

Since Khan was the kind of young man who comforted himself in a
strange country by going to see *King Lear* at twenty-seven consecutive
performances, Ella Sharpe, a scholar of Shakespeare, was a natural choice
to be his analyst. In a letter to a colleague, she referred to the new Indian referral with pleasure, commenting on her "constant need . . . to
shift out of ruts and see the world through other eyes than Western
ones."[1]

Sharpe accepted the fundamentals of classical psychoanalysis but
she focused on the creativity of her patients rather than their psychopathology. She believed that the analytic relationship was essentially
a "serious dramatic play" and that the main goal of treatment was to
help the patient get access to his or her "ordinary creativity."[2] Khan
remembered: "Ella Sharpe used to say all analysts must be able to read
AND ENJOY Alice in Wonderland!"[3] Sharpe stretched her role to
help him feel comfortable in a new country. She gave him a letter of
introduction to the analysts Adrian and Karen Stephen (Adrian was
Virginia Woolf's brother) and by Khan's report, he was invited to their
at-home Sunday tea gatherings. Looking back at this early exposure
to the world of Bloomsbury, he commented, "I was so young and naïve,
my God!"[4]

Charles Rycroft (1914–1998), a London analyst who would become one of the major creative thinkers of the 1960s, was one of Khan's early friends and colleagues. He had also seen Sharpe for analysis, and he was critical of her work: "My analysis with Ella Sharpe never got anywhere actually. [She] treated me as though I was a rare bird. I got the feeling that she'd never encountered anyone like me before."[5]

If Ella Sharpe thought Rycroft was "a rare bird," she must have had similar thoughts about Khan. But, unlike Rycroft, Khan liked being watched over. Hanna Segal believes that, overall, Sharpe was helpful to him: "Ella Sharpe couldn't have coped with Masud's psychosis in those days, because it was only in later years that we understood how to work with that kind of pathology. But she didn't collude with him the way the others did." The analysis lasted only seven months because in 1947 Sharpe died suddenly of heart failure.

While the Western world, including England, tried to return to normalcy after World War II, India was preparing for independence. Its Muslim and Hindu populations were at a boiling point of ethnic mistrust and hatred and, despite extreme efforts, Mahatma Gandhi and others did not succeed in forming a new government that would be accepted by both groups. Just after midnight on August 14, 1947, India split into a Muslim Pakistan and a secular but primarily Hindu India. Overnight, the India that Khan had left became Pakistan. Muslims fled north to Pakistan, and Hindus and Sikhs fled south to the new India, in the largest mass migrations in recorded history. Freedom was costly— the violence claimed well over a million lives. Khan's immediate family was relatively safe because they lived in the country and because seven of Fazaldad's sons were part of the new Pakistani Army. Two of these brothers were generals. As things turned out, Kot Fazaldad Khan was untouched.[6]

Lacking Indian friends in London and trying to fit in, Khan did not talk to anyone about the death and confusing rebirth of his homeland. He would never have much of an interest in politics—he cared about individuals, not about large movements.[7] His concern for what happened in India would be for the human suffering: "In my early years, I saw such body-misery, poverty and destitution of existence in the Hindu–Muslim culture of India, that I will never believe that a civilization is worth a

bean if it does not look after the ordinary welfare of its citizens, no matter
how excellent it is with the metaphysics of the soul."[8]

After Ella Sharpe's death, Khan chose John Rickman to be his analyst.
He had been impressed by a series of seminars Rickman gave at the
Tavistock Clinic, and he may have been further influenced by Pearl King,
a classmate who was seeing Rickman for her training analysis. Rickman,
who was a Quaker, had been one of the founders of the BPAS in 1919.
He had also played a major role in helping Ernest Jones set up the IPA.

    Like Khan's later mentor, Donald Winnicott, Rickman had sided
with the Kleinians during the Controversial Discussions before becoming part of the Middle Group. In 1947, when Khan was beginning his
analysis, Rickman was already shifting his allegiance. The Kleinians had
been critical of Rickman's thinking, claiming that his openness to considering the influence of the environment led to a watering down of
analytic essentials. In 1948, Rickman made a formal break with the
Kleinians after a "big row" with Melanie Klein.[9] Pearl King told me that
Michael Balint, who was chairman of the Education Committee, passed
the information to both her and Khan that "your analyst is no longer a
Kleinian." That same year, Rickman was elected president of the BPAS,
following Sylvia Payne's presidency.

    Khan did his first clinical work at the Tavistock Clinic, which was then
located in a dingy house on Beaumont Street. The clinic had been founded
in 1920, and it became a popular training site after the war years, through
the influence of Rickman, Wilfred Bion, and others. Candidates who saw
patients at "The Tavi" were usually paid for their work, but Khan had to
pay to work there, apparently because he had no prior clinical experience.
He was allowed to join a group led by Bion and to attend Rickman's seminar, and after some time he was referred several patients as training cases.

    He moved through the training requirements at a rapid pace, in part
because he was financially secure and did not have to have an outside
job. His first case, which began in October 1948, was supervised by Dr.
John Kellnar.[10] This case was terminated in June 1949 for unknown
reasons, at the suggestion of the Training Committee, and he started a
new first case, supervised this time by Melanie Klein. Then in October
1949, he started a second case, supervised by Anna Freud. (One implication of Rickman's break from the Kleinians was that his analysands

were now free to choose their supervisors from any of the three groups of training analysts.) By December 1950, Khan had been elected to associate membership, which meant that he could call himself an analyst. Starting in 1950, he added training to become a child analyst, and his supervisors for child work were Donald Winnicott, Marion Milner, and Clifford Scott.

Khan admired Rickman: "The really great teacher I have known was an analyst called John Rickman. He was a Quaker by upbringing and his talks were like sermons; he dug deep into one's sensibility."[11] Rickman's Quaker traditions of hospitality, generosity, and respect for others reminded Khan of feudal traditions, and Khan contrasted Rickman's style to what he experienced as the tactless crudity of many other analysts. Decades later, Khan repeated with admiration advice Rickman had given to his students: "You should never tell a patient something that you wouldn't tell a guest in your sitting room."[12] The Quaker influence also facilitated Rickman's ability to use silence effectively in his clinical work and Khan valued that.

In many ways, Rickman was an ideal analyst for Khan. He was a strong male figure not only because he was important but also because he was physically large, like the men in Khan's family. And he was a blunt-spoken man with good common sense who did not hide behind analytic jargon.[13] Once, early in his training, Khan read an analytic paper that was critical of Mohammed, referring to his writings as "toilet paper." He was so angry that he wanted to stop training, but Rickman persuaded him to stay.[14] When Khan gave his first paper at the BPAS and almost fainted from anxiety, Rickman was kind and accepting.[15]

As a firm believer in the importance of hard work, Rickman taught Khan to take his career seriously. The analyst Sadie Gillespie remembers Rickman telling her privately that he worried about his ability to do effective work with Khan because "How can you analyze a man who goes to Paris every weekend and has a servant to put his boots on in the morning and pull them off every night?" Rickman told Khan that if he lived on inherited income, he would never develop the skill and insight required to be an effective clinician. Khan promised that after he qualified as an analyst and could charge regular fees, he would stop drawing on his inheritance for living expenses, and from 1950 on, until he became seriously ill, he used his inherited money only for luxuries. He later wrote about that decision: "I grew up like royalty, but now I didn't have money. [Rickman's advice] almost killed me."[16]

Rickman went even further than Ella Sharpe in granting favors to Khan. Hanna Segal told me that Rickman used to have coffee with Khan after their analytic session at a restaurant where the next patient often saw them together: "It was torture for that patient." Rickman invited his analysand to professional dinners at his house and took him as a guest to the first postwar International Psychoanalytic Congress (IPAC), held in Zurich in 1949. Khan was, by his report, the only student at the Congress. Rickman also invited him to help edit the *British Journal of Medical Psychology* and the *International Journal of Psycho-Analysis* (IJPA) and showed him drafts of papers he was writing, asking for feedback. Khan later reported: "I did all my editorial apprenticeship with [Rickman]."[17]

Khan never forgot or took for granted the mentors who helped him. But the special treatment by Sharpe and Rickman prevented him from having a full analysis. Analysis requires a bounded relationship where an analysand can freely make projections onto the analyst. "Outside" favors ruined the analytic space, and Khan knew this: "Each of [my analysts] helped and sustained me, without my being able to talk to any of them significantly about myself ever. . . . Ella Sharpe and Rickman never even suspected that what I said about myself was not me ever. It narrated events that had happened to me—no more!"[18]

Rickman also influenced Khan negatively through the example of his writing practices. He had collaborated with the anthropologist Geoffrey Gorer in a book entitled *The People of Great Russia*, published in 1949. According to the psychoanalytic historian Paul Roazen: "Rickman 'dramatized' things [in the book]. . . . His examples were drawn from several individual instances, but they were only 'dramatically true.'"[19] The compounding of data to create a supposedly accurate figure, with no reference to the process, is a kind of "lie" for which Khan would be harshly criticized many years later.

In 1951, Rickman died of a heart attack while sleeping under a mulberry tree in Regent's Park. He was sixty-one years old. Khan had now lost two analysts to heart attacks. Harold Stewart, a British analyst who trained a few years after Khan, suggested to me that despite Rickman's weaknesses as an analyst, this was a major loss: "It's a great pity that John Rickman died. He would never have put up with Khan's nonsense."

While in analysis with Rickman, Khan fell in love with Clara (pseudonym), an English woman who was a student in an evening program in child analysis at Anna Freud's Hampstead Clinic. They started dating in 1947, and from 1949 to 1951 they were engaged.[20] A classmate remembers that they were a striking couple: "Masud looked like Omar Sharif, with his dark skin and eyes so filled with expression. He had a tempestuous quality—he reminded me of Heathcliff. [Clara] was, in contrast, gentle, even ethereal, with delicate features, beautiful blue-green eyes and a luminous complexion."[21] But Clara's family as well as the analysts of both Masud and Clara discouraged the marriage on the basis of their racial differences, and the engagement was called off.

The story of Masud Khan is a story not just of one man, but of an entire community. In his new life in London, there were leaders and followers, friends and enemies. Everyone knew everyone else, there were regular meetings and people were excited about their work. In the post–World War II years, an extremely gifted generation of analysts was active. Wilfred Bion wrote to his wife, Francesca, describing his London colleagues in 1951: "There is one thing about the psycho-analytic world [in London]—we may all be freaks, but there are very few I meet who do not seem to me to be intelligent and interesting people."[22] As a much adored student and then a peer, Khan provoked, entertained, stimulated, and enraged his new family members. He had as large an impact on the British analysts as they had on him.

But he was at the same time an outsider. Nobody I interviewed admitted to looking down on him for his ethnicity, but racial discrimination is often unconscious, and many people commented that "others" probably had trouble accepting him.[23] As one colleague put it, "To the English, he was [always] from Pakistan."[24] A subtle but pervasive example of Western racism involved Khan's very name. The "Kh" of "Khan" is a guttural "Xh" sound—but Westerners rarely pronounced it correctly and analysts as well as close friends regularly misspelled it as the usually Jewish K-A-H-N, something that never failed to upset Khan.[25]

CHAPTER 5

SETTLING IN AND STARTING ANALYSIS WITH WINNICOTT

*I was a complete stranger in London, strange in my way of life, wayward
and insufferably arrogant in my style of living. . . . I was isolated and
I flaunted my aloneness as a superior and elected way of being. A great
deal of it was bluff and both exhausting and painful for me. It was
hellishly annoying for everyone, but—this being England—individuals
are never extinguished; they are merely bullied through a persistent
and cussed politeness and negation.*
Masud Khan[1]

[Winnicott is] the analyst whose genius has been destiny for me.
Masud Khan[2]

John Rickman's death opened up a new opportunity for Khan as he chose
Donald Woods Winnicott ("DWW") (1896–1971), the supervisor of his
first child case, to be his next analyst. Winnicott is now an enormous
figure in contemporary psychoanalysis, and there are many published
texts describing his theoretical and clinical contributions. Khan himself
would become an important source of information on Winnicott's work.[3]

He had been impressed by Winnicott in 1948 when he heard him
give a lecture in his position as chairman of the Medical Section of the
British Psychological Society: "This gnome of a being spoke with a clarity
and conviction that allowed both for doubt and debate. From then on I
was determined to find out more about him and his way of working."[4]
Later, Winnicott allowed him to attend one of his child psychiatry consultation clinics at the Paddington Green Hospital where he used the

children's drawings to explain their problems to both the parents and the children.

In 1951, the year Khan entered into analysis with him, Winnicott was just beginning to develop his theory that the analysand's interpersonal experience with the analyst could be as important as verbal understanding and interpretation. With this contribution, Winnicott would directly oppose his Kleinian peers as well as supporters of ego psychology, the dominant force in international psychoanalysis.[5] Winnicott's clinical work was consistent with his new thinking and Khan wrote about his significant skill:

> As I look back over some 20 years of working with Winnicott, what stands out vividly is his relaxed physicality and a lambent [i.e., radiant] concentration in his person. Winnicott listened with the whole of his body, and had keen unintrusive eyes that gazed at one with a mixture of unbelief and utter acceptance. A childlike spontaneity imbued his movements. Yet he could be so still, so very inheld and still. I have not met another analyst who was more inevitably himself. It was this quality of his inviolable me-ness that enabled him to be so many different persons to such diverse people. Each of us who has encountered him has his OWN Winnicott, and he never transgressed the other's invention of him by any assertion of his own style of being. And yet he always stayed so inexorably Winnicott.[6]

Prior to starting the analysis, Winnicott insisted that Khan have surgery on his deformed ear.[7] It is remarkable that no one else had influenced him to do this, as the ear was extremely disfiguring. Winnicott's intervention illustrates his belief that the "real" environment is as important as the transference relationship, and also his willingness to intervene outside of ordinary analytic boundaries. After the surgery, Khan's ear was greatly reduced in size and, by wearing his hair long, he could easily hide it.

Winnicott accepted and encouraged his analysands without excessive interpretation,[8] and he focused on their strengths, as described by Khan: "DWW . . . knew and allowed for the margin of weakness and error in every human individual and he worked with the three percent that was creative and vital."[9] He did not try to analyze inconsistent parts of a person down to a single understanding, because he believed, as Khan would also, that people had multiple separate selves; a goal of personal development, in his thinking, was to know and accept irreconcilable differences within oneself. The thinking about multiple selves matched Khan's personal experience well: "My existence in Pakistan, as in London, is riddled with paradoxes. I coexist parallelly in multiple realities, external as well as internal."[10] Khan experienced their relationship, which lasted for twenty years in various forms, as a secure base in the West: "One of the most valuable contributions of DWW's long protective care and coverage . . . has been that he has changed a catastrophic threat of loss of object into separation anxiety."[11]

Khan's pathology included a tendency to be offensive and arrogant, attitudes that masked his insecurity. The bookstore owner Harry Karnac remembers meeting Masud and Tahir in 1951. They came into Karnac Books looking for first editions and made no attempt to hide their opinion that a first-rate bookseller should not be selling new books.[12]

His closest friends in the early 1950s were people whom he met in his training—Charles Rycroft, Pearl King, James ("Jim") Armstrong Harris (d. 1973), Barbara Woodhead, and Rosemary Gordon (a Jungian). King, Gordon, and Rycroft all told me that in those early years they were not bothered by Khan's arrogance—in fact, they enjoyed it.

Jim Harris was Khan's very best friend. Harris was a physician who had been in general practice before training as an analyst. "He looked like a farmer," according to his widow Maureen Harris, and his Harley Street practice owed some of its success to a down-to-earth style.[13] Harris and Khan often met at Khan's flat on Eaton Square to drink brandy and talk, and they traveled together on at least one vacation to Paris. Harris never could master theory, and Khan gave him special help with the theory section of his membership paper for the Society. Khan would later write that the relationship with Harris was one of only three in the West where he received back more than he gave.[14] We do not know what Harris did for Khan to merit such high praise.

Khan had a close intellectual collaboration as well as a friendship with Charles Rycroft, who was ten years older but only a few years ahead of him in training. Rycroft was a physician who held numerous offices at the BPAS during the 1950s and he is remembered for his innovative thinking about creativity and for being the analyst of the radical psychiatrist R. D. Laing, who became well known in the 1960s for his willingness to do analytic work with schizophrenics. Judy Cooper, Khan's first biographer, remembers Khan telling her: "What was valuable to me about Rycroft in the 1950s was that we used to have lunch every day together and never say a word." But Khan valued Rycroft's insights as well as his silence: "Charles has been the only person in my generation whose mind I respected and who has deeply influenced me and my thinking."[15] And Rycroft returned Khan's admiration, telling me: "At one time I thought Masud was one of the few people worth talking to, very bright indeed."

Khan and his colleagues established the 1952 Club, a private group that promoted the presentation of informal psychoanalytic papers in a relaxed home setting. The Club was started by Khan, Harris, Woodhead, King, and Rycroft, and membership was by invitation only. The 1952 Club still exists.

Charles Rycroft and Rosemary Gordon both told me about socializing in the early 1950s with Khan and his new girlfriend Jane Shore, who later became his wife.[16] Shore was a ballet dancer at Sadler's Wells Theater Ballet (which in 1957 became the Royal Ballet), and she came from a traditional English family. Her father was Bernard Shore, a famed viola player. "Jane was beautiful," Rycroft told me, "and she had a sense of humor that Masud totally lacked."

Jane Shore, now in her seventies, is a short and strikingly pretty woman, with straight gray hair and lively eyes. In an interview, she was eager to tell me her experience of marriage to Khan and a subsequent breakdown. Her account provides a glimpse into their everyday life.

The two first met in 1949 through the dancer/choreographer Hans Zullig (1914–1992),[17] who brought Khan backstage at the ballet to make the introduction. Shore invited Khan to her twenty-first birthday party, shocking her conservative parents, and soon she was in love: "I fell under Masud's spell very quickly. I thought he was wonderful and handsome. He seemed to know everything. As a dancer, I had met a lot of men, but so many of the men in the ballet world are homosexual and none of them ever made me feel in love. Masud did that for the first time. He sexually seduced me and I wanted nothing more than to marry him."

At the time of their marriage, Shore had already left the ballet world. By her own admission, she had not been a brilliant ballet dancer, and

she contrasted her role as rat in *Sleeping Beauty* to the princess role in
the same ballet danced by Svetlana Beriosova, Khan's second wife. Shore
had real talent, however, and she was now the principal dancer at the
revue *London Laughs*, which was playing at the Strand Theatre.

Khan and Shore got married at the Kensington Registry office on a
Saturday in 1952. The bride and groom made a striking impression, as
is seen in a photograph where they sit in a car with Tahir and his Indian
girlfriend Uma Vasudev. Shore is wearing a two-piece leopard print dress
and Khan is in a suit from a designer named Felix; they are each wearing a gray wool karakuli cap, the Indian hat that was part of Khan's everyday wardrobe. After lunch at the Ritz with Shore's parents, there was a
reception at her parents' flat, a studio with skylights on Kensington High
Street. There were one hundred guests, all Westerners except for Tahir
and Uma. Shore's parents tried hard to accept Khan, but there was noticeable tension about an interracial marriage.[18]

The show had to go on at the Strand Theatre. On the night of the
wedding, Shore performed twice in *London Laughs*, with Khan sitting in
the front row. The director announced the marriage to the audience and
put a spotlight on him. The next day, the couple left for a week-long
honeymoon in Geneva, where they spent much of the time with Hans
Zullig, who lived there.

The newlyweds lived in a small basement flat in South Kensington
that Khan had been renting for some time.[19] He saw patients in the front
room. Shore remembers that the space was dark, with no kitchen—only
a kettle and a hot plate. They lived a modest life: "There was a restaurant nearby to which Masud and I went regularly and he would eat the
same meal every day: veal schnitzel. At home he would cook a favorite
pudding for himself, because he had a strong sweet tooth: he would boil
a tin of condensed milk until it turned brown, and then he would eat it
with a spoon."

The Khans' next apartment was at 8 Harley Street, an impressive
upper-class location just south of Regents Park, known for being the
home of fashionable physicians. The flat had little prestige other than
location, however; it was a small maisonette on the fourth and fifth floor
with shabby furniture. There was no elevator and visitors had to climb
up eighty-nine stairs, according to an analysand who walked up the stairs
many times.[20]

On Sundays the couple had a ritual of joining Khan's analyst friends for tea at the elegant Grosvenor House on Park Lane. Shore never fit in and she experienced the conversation as vulgar: "The group was always talking about sex and masturbation and they would analyze to shreds everyone who wasn't there."

When *London Laughs* closed, Shore became unemployed. The only opening she could find was as understudy to Rosalind in *As You Like It* at Regents Park Theatre, but Khan would not allow her to take the position, which he considered to be too lowly. Neither would he allow her to collect "the dole," compensation for her unemployment. She finally got a minor role in *A Midsummer Night's Dream*.[21] Against her wishes, she had to leave her new husband to tour with the play for four months in the United States. The change in her career status was especially disappointing because she had believed that Khan would be able to help her to become more of a star. It is probably accurate that Khan wanted to mentor her and that he too was disappointed with her career.

From the beginning, Khan resisted Shore's attempts to influence him. For example, he refused to bathe in the English manner. Instead, Shore told me, "he soaked himself in scent." Khan called his bride "Bunnies" and was affectionate, but their sex life was disastrous. Shore remembers: "He either couldn't or wouldn't do foreplay: he said it was 'against my principles.' I had the impression that sex was just something that he felt you had to do. He often came to bed three hours or more after I had fallen asleep."

To Shore's consternation, her husband approached food in a manner that was similar to the way he dealt with sex. He had a large appetite and he "gobbled" food, with no appreciation for the pleasures of a slow and drawn-out meal. He would eventually learn about eating and about sex from people who were connoisseurs in both areas: the French. But at this early time in the West, he had just begun to frequent Paris and he had no idea about how to charm a Western wife.

The newlyweds were deeply unhappy from the beginning, and their relationship quickly deteriorated into bickering and negativity. After a few frustrated years, Khan started a secret affair with Beriosova, who was by then a major star. Shore was distraught when she discovered her husband's infidelity: "I discovered that Masud was in love with Svetlana one terrible day in 1956. I remember leaning out of the window and seeing them kiss on the street below. I wanted to hurl a vase at them! It soon became obvious that Masud didn't want me around any more." Shore stole Khan's green diary and read all about the affair—in her belief, he had left it out for her to find. Things got worse: "I became suicidal, but I didn't have the courage to kill myself. I was pathetic, like a flat piece of jelly, a total wreck. I felt that I had no individual personality, only unhappiness, that I was nobody unless I was his spouse. I felt that I couldn't live without him."

After Khan and Beriosova got together, there was no chance to restore the marriage.[22] Khan pressured Shore to move in with her parents, but she refused. When she seemed on the verge of a nervous breakdown, he insisted that she get help from Winnicott. Winnicott had no openings at the time but, at Khan's urging, he agreed to see Shore in the hours that had been Khan's, while Khan temporarily stopped his analysis and instead worked for Winnicott as an editorial assistant. Winnicott knew that he and Khan could work together in this manner because they had already collaborated on a book review published in 1953.[23] After about a year, Winnicott apparently found the time to resume Khan's analysis. The combined analytic and editing relationship continued until 1966, when the analysis ended, although it is likely that some, or even most, of these years involved what Winnicott called "research analysis," where therapeutic "coverage" took the place of formal analytic hours[24] (see Chapter 20).

Eventually Shore was hospitalized in what she called "a looney bin"— Shenley Hospital in Hertfordshire. She was still able to see Winnicott for analysis, and she drove herself to the daily sessions. She would never return to 8 Harley Street.

Shore's analysis lasted for five years and she comments: "That referral was one good thing Masud gave me."[25] Her divorce was final in June 1958, and eventually she found another husband with whom she has "a long, happy, and fulfilling relationship." She has had a successful career in dance administration for which she was awarded the O.B.E. (Officer of the Order of the British Empire) for "Services to Dance."[26] She is thankful that Khan ended the marriage: "I do believe that if I had stayed with him, I would have committed suicide. He used to write me letters after we separated, saying 'You'll be grateful one day!' He was right."

Khan's analysis with Winnicott went much deeper than his earlier analyses, although Jane Shore never got the benefit of his growth. In the decade of the 1950s, he was able to think about his personality problems, which suggests that he was open to change,[27] and he was working hard in his sessions and in everyday living to understand and control his behavior.

We get a sense of Khan's struggle to manage his aggressiveness in two letters from 1957, written to Svetlana Beriosova prior to their marriage. He reflects on his misbehavior in a professional meeting where he had been overly critical:

> In the late evening I have done one of the typical aggressively over-sincerely critical Khan-acts, which, though I do not sense them as such, are devastating in fact. I am feeling guilty, lonely and sad. My criticisms were just and true and yet I erred in the way and manner in which I voiced them. Jim Harris presented a case to our group and he hadn't prepared it. It was a badly treated case and presented without any method or thinking. That really gets my goat. He is an able clinician, so all the more deplorable that he should present us such a mess at such length.
>
> And did I go for him. Coldly, acidly, point after point. I must have been really lethal because it pulled everyone up and the discussion was sober and thoughtful, and Harris was left obviously bewildered. Only in retrospect, when Harris had left early and it was pointed out to me that I had been very severe and harsh, did I realise the hurt I must have caused him. . . .
>
> And something clicked in me: I can see now that I suffer and have suffered from a curious delusion of sincerity. I never attack those I don't care for. And so when I am critical I do not lose my affection, but that is not how the other party experiences it. I really molest savagely. I am going to watch my tongue in future.[28]

> I am gradually reaching a point of self awareness where the only conclusion I can draw is that for me to speak, say or write what I wish to express of my feelings and thoughts only hurts others and gets me nowhere. It is both sad and ironic that for over two decades I have tried desperately and over-anxiously to say what I feel and make sense of it, and haven't got anywhere. Until now, I had always thought it was because others were dense, unintelligent, insensitive and unsympathetic, but I do not believe that any longer. The absoluteness, maturity and ripeness of your love,

sympathy and compassion for me have convinced me beyond doubt that
the fault and the failing are in me. . . .

Somehow, though all this should be depressing and dismal, to me
it is not so. So long as I know how things have become what they are,
I can bear them and start anew. That is where I am right now, my
beloved, but I am neither hopeless nor daunted, only sad at the waste
of it.[29]

Khan believed that his peers contributed to his problem when they
backed off from confrontations that he thought would help him: "[I] feel
that I only seek a dialogue. I do not think what I say is absolute. If it is
challenged and corrected I am all too willing to see it. The pity is that
everyone withdraws behind a quiet cold rejection and I am left holding
an angry dissociated monologue."[30] It was a problem that plagued him
throughout his life in the West. More than a decade later, in a letter to
a colleague, he wrote: "Why are my friends so tenderly careful with me?
I am not really all that fragile and I promise not to collapse if criticised!
Please don't spare me your incisive judgment. I need it."[31]

The overpoliteness of his peers might have been less of a problem
for Khan if Winnicott had been willing to deal directly with Khan's
aggressiveness. But Winnicott regularly avoided confrontation and, over
the years, he tolerated outrageous conduct by Khan, making no attempt
to control it. Malcolm Pines, a younger peer, told me about meetings of
the BPAS during the time when Winnicott was serving his first term as
president, from 1956 to 1959: "Masud would sit halfway back in the
room; sometimes he sat with Rycroft. Masud was very prominent; he
would nearly always say something or ask something and he was always
witty and brilliant. When Winnicott was chairing the meetings, Masud
used to be quite rude to him, arrogant and challenging. Winnicott was
always laid back, sometimes he would even go to sleep at those meetings. As students observing this, we [worried] that an analysand was attacking his analyst." Khan hated Winnicott's tendency to back off from
confrontation: "DWW traumatised me by his public Christian masoch-
istic humility: so phoney and yet so him."[32]

Another characteristic of the analysis was that, from the very beginning, Winnicott gave Khan special treatment, as had so many others.
Charles Rycroft told me: "I remember thinking about Masud, 'This is a
man who needs to be treated as a human being, not as someone special.'"[33]

Winnicott placated Khan when he should have just continued the analysis. Winnicott's highly unusual agreement to allow Shore to take Khan's analytic hours was "a terrible mistake" according to Marion Milner (1900–1998).[34] Khan had been deprived of treatment at a time of great stress, and, with the editing, he was given a status that compromised his experience as an analysand.[35]

Khan qualified as a child analyst in 1952. Initial success had come easily. Rycroft told me that he and Khan were stars who enjoyed what Rycroft referred to as "meteoric careers" in the BPAS of the 1950s.[36] Harold Stewart, who started training in 1956, told me that Khan was a "golden boy" in these years, and he added: "A 'golden boy' doesn't have to work his way up. And once you do that to somebody, they are ruined."

But the easy success was mixed with some obstacles. Candidates for full membership had to present a paper to the entire Society at a scientific meeting, with voting conducted at a later business meeting. Khan read his paper twice before it was accepted in December 1954.[37] The vote in 1954 was thirty-two in favor, and fifteen against. Anne-Marie Sandler, a contemporary British analyst, writes that he was turned down the first time for not disguising his case sufficiently.[38] But Pearl King remembers things differently. She told me that the analytic community at that time was so small that it was almost impossible to read a paper without someone recognizing the patient and that Khan was turned down because he was "overly eager," an attitude that the Kleinians did not like. King was so angry about the way Khan's membership application had been treated that when she became secretary of the society in 1956, she successfully fought to change the system so that candidates read their papers to a group of twelve people on a membership panel, not to the whole society.

Khan's application to become a training analyst, the highest level of analytic recognition, was also delayed. He tried unsuccessfully three times (twice in 1955 and once in 1957) before he was finally approved in November 1959. The final application may have been successful only because Khan had an analysand who had been accepted for training, and the institute had the incentive of wanting to cooperate with that student's request to keep seeing Khan for analysis. (It is standard analytic procedure that a candidate must be seen by an official training analyst.)

Another setback was that several submissions to the IJPA were turned down. Years later, when he had access to the journal files, Khan discovered that the editor, Willi Hoffer, had not even read these submissions. The analyst/editor Joseph Sandler confirmed to me that Hoffer despised homosexuality, the topic of Khan's papers, and would not have wanted the topic discussed in the IJPA. (Sandler added that Hoffer disliked Khan and used to mock him in private, referring to him as "Elephant-Ear.")[39]

But Khan had the obvious sponsorship of Winnicott and his overall career was extremely successful. In 1959, through recommendations from Sylvia Payne and Winnicott, he began doing editorial work for the IJPA under the guidance of the editor, John Sutherland. This position would be an important stepping stone in his career.

Khan had several very intense friendships in the 1950s, in addition to the friendship with Jim Harris. Khan and Charles Rycroft became personally close after Jane Shore was hospitalized, because Rycroft then became Khan's flatmate. (Rycroft lived in the flat but saw his patients elsewhere.) According to Khan, "[Rycroft] used to pay me 5 pounds a week for a room, linen, food, maid's services, laundry, telephone, light, drinks, meals out, theatres, heating, cinemas, etc. and he always felt he was doing me an economic service."[40]

Rycroft told me that Khan was a difficult flatmate who suffered from significant anxiety and instability. He had terrible sleeping habits and he could not tell the difference between being anxious and being hungry. Rycroft experienced Khan as being so vulnerable that he had to control any expression of aggression lest he cause Khan to crumble. And he was extremely competitive. When Rycroft bought a new car, Khan immediately went out to buy his own new car. Once, during a discussion, Khan was amazed to find out that Rycroft took dreams seriously—Khan said he had *never* had a dream. The very next day, he started dreaming.[41] Another irritation was that Khan sometimes stole small things, such as fountain pens.

In the late 1950s, Khan's best friend was Ismond Rosen (1924–1996), a Jewish analyst from South Africa who trained with Anna Freud at the Hampstead Clinic. Rosen spent half his time working as a sculptor of large stone works, for which he attained considerable renown. He was a highly regarded intellectual despite the fact that he was known to be a "mystic" who believed he had the capacity for extrasensory perception. He was firmly convinced that all coincidences in life had meaning; for example, if a person were driving and came to a red light, that meant that he should not continue going straight after the light turned green. In Rosen's thinking, he and Khan were predestined to be friends, the proof being that he had been teased as a child in South Africa about his name, Ismond, with his friends calling him "Ishmael Mohamed"—this meant that he was a "Mohammedan" like Khan.[42] Rosen's mystical thinking was never acceptable to Khan, but he greatly valued his friend's intelligence, humor, and interest in the arts, and he was impressed by his eidetic imagery—Rosen had automatic and complete recall of verbal and visual events going back to his childhood.[43]

Through Rosen, Khan became friendly with the Cassou family in Paris. Jean Cassou (1897–1986) was a poet and art critic who was chief conservator at the Musée d'Art Moderne (1945–1965). He tutored Khan in modern art and introduced him to the work of the Fauvist/Cubist painter Georges Braque, who became Khan's favorite artist. With Cassou's guidance, Khan purchased Braque lithographs that eventually became valuable. Cassou introduced him to other major artists such as Léger, Clavé, Richier, Calder, Bonnard, and Soulages—and to Aimé Maeght, owner and founder of the world-famous Galerie Maeght. The Galerie Maeght was an important center for the exhibition and selling of contemporary art and, in the years to come, Khan would be a regular visitor.

Jane Shore remembers that the Cassous adored Khan and related to him as a favored son. Isabelle, their daughter, was especially fond of him—Shore remembers Isabelle saying: "It is so marvelous to be kissed by Masud Khan on New Year's Eve." Khan's friendship with the Cassou family floundered in the late 1950s when the newly single Khan failed to have a romantic interest in Isabelle. The Cassous had no idea that he was already in a serious relationship with Beriosova.

Another close friend in the 1950s was Harvey Kayne (d. 1974), a wealthy American builder from Baltimore who had an apartment in Paris. They met in Paris in the early 1950s, at La Bella, a bar near Place de Furstenburg that was owned by two American folksingers. An anonymous close friend told me: "Masud used to say, 'If I ever had a love relationship with a man, it would be with Harvey Kayne.'" Leslie Kayne, who became Harvey's wife in the 1960s, told me that she is almost certain that the two men never had a sexual relationship, but the friendship was obviously important to both. She remembered Khan's intensity, which was a match for her husband's: "Masud had remarkable insights—he could see through anything or anybody. And I always thought he was preparing himself for posterity. It was as if he was producing his life so that when he was dead there would be a play written or a movie made about him."

Through John Rickman, Khan became a friend of the cultural anthropologist Geoffrey Gorer (1905–1985).[44] Gorer, a lifelong bachelor, socialized in the highest levels of London society and intellectual life. He was friendly with George Orwell, W. H. Auden, Edith Sitwell, Ernst Kris, Vladimir Nabokov, Margaret Mead, and Lucian Freud. He liked to entertain on weekends at his country estate, a very special property located in Sussex that had been built in 1692. Gorer grew prize flowers on the grounds, and inside he had a large collection of modern paintings. Since Khan loved to mingle with the rich and famous, he was pleased to be part of Gorer's social life.

Khan returned to Pakistan only once in the decade of the 1950s, although he maintained contact with family and friends from Pakistan who were living in London or visiting. His closest connection was to Tahir, who had come to London in 1947 with Uma Vasudev, his Hindu girlfriend. Tahir never had professional success, although he trained as a barrister and then became a portrait photographer. After Vasudev returned to India,[45] Tahir married a Jewish woman, with whom he had a daughter,[46] and his relationship with Masud became strained. Khan also kept close ties to two boyhood friends, Jamil Nishtar, an international banker, and Ijaz Batalwi, a businessman. They lived in Pakistan and Khan saw them whenever they came to London on business. Khan's single visit to Pakistan had occurred when he went by himself around the time of his marriage to Jane Shore. It is clear that he was trying hard to keep his Eastern and Western lives separate.[47]

CHAPTER 6

EARLY CLINICAL WORK
(INTERVIEWS)

In the very early years, Anna Freud said to Masud:
"Mr. Khan, you have been authorized to start supervised treatment.
Do you think you can take care of two people?" Masud replied:
"Miss Freud, if I can take care of 25,000 peasants,
I believe I can look after two people."[1]
Anonymous French analyst

Khan had no trouble establishing an active practice after qualifying as an analyst in 1950. Psychoanalysis was popular in London and there was a shortage of analysts, so the better-known analysts readily referred their overflow to colleagues.

Since he had also trained as a child analyst, some of Khan's referrals were children and adolescents. In the mid-1950s, Winnicott referred him a twelve-year-old boy, and this treatment, supervised by Winnicott, shows Khan's early talent for working with a patient who would normally be considered too disturbed for analysis. Winnicott had told him that the boy was "eminently suitable for analysis," but Khan's description shows how generous (and radical) Winnicott was in that evaluation:

I found that though [the boy] came punctually and left in a very docile manner, during the sessions one could only describe his behavior as a manic, berserk mess, and all attempts at interpretation merely aggravated his condition. Also, he always came eating an apple, and he would spit a lot all over the place. His behavior was extremely chaotic and unmanageable, and often I had to use force to restrain him from throwing the furniture around in the consultation room. All attempts to interpret this

to him in terms of internal anxiety situations were also utterly useless.
[He] gave absolutely no account of his life outside, and if I talked to him
he would block his ears with his fingers.[2]

It is characteristic of Khan and also of Winnicott that they saw this
case through to a satisfactory ending. The technique was a kind of exorcism that was primarily nonverbal, and Khan came to understand
the child's behavior as a communication concerning his bizarre family
situation. This kind of clinical understanding about nonverbal aspects
of analyst–analysand relating was new and did not become popular until
decades later.

Two adult analysands who saw Khan early in his career have been
willing to talk about their analyses, and their reports are presented here.
In contrast to Khan's work with the boy, these accounts show Khan
working in a relatively conservative style. His conservatism may be in
part due to the fact that he would have been in supervision at least until
1959, when he qualified as a training analyst.

INTERVIEW WITH ANALYSAND
H.K. (1957–1967)

H.K.[3] is a well-known bookstore owner. He started analysis when he
was thirty-five years old. I initially spoke with him in 1996.[4]

> I was referred to Masud Khan in 1957 by Barbara Woodhead, an analyst
> and a customer in my store. I went not because I needed it, but because
> I wanted to learn more about the subject—or so I fooled myself. I went
> for eleven years, five times a week for six years, then three times a week,
> then twice weekly.
>
> I thought then that he was brilliant—I guess I think that still. He
> was like Bobby Fischer the chess player, a brilliant mind with the emo-
> tional maturity of a twelve-year-old, and with all the aggression of a
> genius child.
>
> When I started analysis, Masud's office was on Harley Street. I
> thought that he was living there with Jane Shore, but he wasn't, only
> Charles Rycroft was living there. Later I read in the newspaper that
> Masud Khan the "psychiatrist" was being divorced on the grounds of

adultery. This shocked me terribly. I remember he apologized to me, saying that I had found out in the wrong way.

I didn't have any symptoms. What was wrong with me was that I didn't know what I was all about. He asked me once to describe myself and I told him that I had built an invisible glass cube around myself so that nobody could hurt me. He said: "The trouble with those bloody glass walls is that they keep pleasure out as well as pain." I found that very useful.

Another time I remember I related a ghastly dream to him. First he said, "Hmm . . . ," which often meant that the session was over. But then he went on and asked me to tell the dream again in Yiddish—that's my native tongue, I was born here in an East London ghetto. So I told the dream in Yiddish, and I hadn't said a single sentence before I suddenly understood the meaning of my dream. There was something about a newborn foal, and when I translated that word, it was what my mother used to call her younger sister, a word that also meant horseflesh. How he knew to do that, I have no idea. He certainly didn't speak Yiddish himself.

After five or six years of analysis, I sometimes would have coffee with Masud and Svetlana when they came into my shop. He also invited me once or twice to supper while I was still a patient. My wife disapproved of this greatly because she was in a Kleinian analysis and her analyst stayed so separate he wouldn't even come to my shop to buy books.

I had just finished the analysis when I had a very bad time—my son was killed in a road accident. Masud was about to go on vacation and he actually postponed the trip. He canceled his flight and took a taxi to my house. I remember he put his arms around my shoulders and said: "We have both suffered great losses." He took my wife to the hospital, at her request, to say good-bye to our son; I couldn't go because I had already identified the body and I was too broken up to go back. Later I would go to see him in his office and just talk, cry. He was the rock on whom I leaned the most after my boy was killed. It's a debt I wish I didn't still owe. I put up with a lot from him in the years to come because of what he had done for me.

Would you call it a successful analysis? Look at it this way. If he hadn't helped me to destroy that bloody glass wall, I wouldn't have been so hurt by him later. The answer has to be "yes."

One and a half years later, in 1998, I interviewed H.K. again and he had had a dramatic change in the way he thought about Khan, particularly with regard to Khan's helping him out after the death of his son. He said that his change was due to having read my article (Hopkins 1998), which included information about Khan's behavior in later years. In this second interview, H.K. told me more about socializing with Khan and seeing his misbehavior firsthand.[5]

> Your article made me realize that something actually did go wrong with my analysis. I don't feel grateful to Masud anymore—I realize now that his helping me about my son had nothing to do with me, it was for him. I didn't realize that until things started coming back in my memory, little pieces.
>
> I thought more about that afternoon when he canceled his trip and came to my house. For example when he put his arms around my shoulders and said: "We have both suffered great losses"—what did he mean by that? What was his loss that he was supposedly sharing with me? You can't compare the loss of a child with any other loss, and he hadn't had that. And I remember that somebody had asked him if he wanted tea, and he said yes, he was starving, and could he also have bread and jam. He turned to my daughter, who was fourteen years old at the time, and he said: "You go and get it for me!" She wasn't a spoiled girl, not at all, but she had never been spoken to like that. Later, she asked my wife: "Is he always so horrid?" and my wife replied: "He doesn't understand children because he doesn't have any of his own." What she wanted to say, but didn't, was "He's used to servants."
>
> What I think now is that Masud didn't help me in the analysis. By convincing me he was so good and so clever, he got me to tell him things I would never tell anyone. So I helped myself—it was not his interpretation that helped.

It is ironic that the part of the treatment valued most by H.K.—Khan's support after the death of his son—led to negative consequences. H.K. felt indebted to Khan and, for this reason, he allowed a postanalytic social relationship to develop, even though it was extremely unpleasant. If H.K. had not known Khan in "outside life," he would have been able to hold on to his private therapeutic image of Khan.

H.K.'s report that he got beyond the feeling that he was constantly surrounded by a glass wall suggests that the analysis was helpful. Even if H.K. did the work himself, Khan provided the space for that work, and this is not easy to do. The feeling of "separateness" is something that is not always helped by analysis.

INTERVIEW WITH ANALYSAND
L.U. (1954-1964)

L.U. (pseudonym chosen by the subject) is a biological psychiatrist, now deceased, who lived and worked in London until he retired in 1985. He saw Khan as part of analytic training at the British Psycho-Analytic Society (BPAS). When he started analysis, he was twenty-five years old. He ended his training and his analysis in 1964 because his wife was expecting their first child and he needed to devote more time to his family. He has had almost no contact with the analytic community in London since that time. Our meetings occurred in 1996.

I was analyzed by Khan for ten years, beginning in December 1954, first a personal and then a training analysis.[6] I had qualified as an M.D. in 1952 and I was very keen on psychiatry, so I applied to the Institute of Psychiatry, and then I also wanted to do psychoanalytic training. I went and was interviewed by Winnicott and also by Clifford Scott. Winnicott suggested that I see Khan for analysis, so that's what happened.

I learned to smoke during the analysis. He smoked all the time, all through the session, some kind of cigarette called State Express 555, with no filters. And that was the cigarette that I started to smoke.[7] There would be an ashtray on the floor and I smoked as I talked. I'm not blaming him for getting me started, but that's how it happened. I only gave it up a few years ago.

About two years into the analysis, Khan told me something that shocked me. He said that he and his wife were getting divorced. My parents were separated, and I had been saying how terrible divorce is, and he thought that I was talking about him and his wife. Really, I didn't know that. I thought that healthy analyzed people didn't get divorced, so I was just shocked.

He was good with dreams. I'm Jewish, and I remember once I had a dream in which there was the Hebrew word *merkazie*, which means "central"; I told him the dream and he gave a brilliant, absolutely true interpretation. It involved his name, his full name, which is Mohammed Masud Raza Khan. He showed me in the dream interpretation how *merkazie* actually referred to him.

He pretty much kept to the frame. Or, more accurately, the frame was broken, but in a way which at the time I thought unimportant. Indeed, I believed it fostered what would now be called "bonding." For example, towards the end, I would get there at my time which was 7:50 or maybe 7:30, and I was his first patient, and he would turn up in pajamas, like he was just out of bed. He would make us both a cup of coffee, Maxwell House coffee, and we would sit and talk for awhile. I thought that he shouldn't do that, but I didn't say anything about it. I then started drinking Maxwell House coffee myself, and that was the only kind of coffee I would want to drink.

He gave me occasional presents—books, etc.—in the same way a teacher might to a pupil. But perhaps the most serious breach, in retrospect, was my doing little favors for him. I remember once I told him I was going to Paris and he asked me to bring back a copy of William Burroughs's *Naked Lunch*. This must have been in 1960 or thereabouts, when the book wasn't available in London—I believe it was banned as obscene. So I smuggled it through customs and I felt we had become co-conspirators. I really don't think these breaches did any harm.

And, by the way, he did come to my wedding. He came alone. It was 1963 and I was near the end of my analysis. All my guests thought he was so good-looking and so interesting. He gave us a wedding gift that was a print of a still life of pumpkins with a plate and a knife signed by Braque. It had been on his consulting room wall, and he took it off of the wall and handed it to me as a gift.

Another thing he did for me is that he introduced me to existentialism, for example Rollo May's work, and that has been helpful to me. I have stayed very identified with him in his interest in books—I now have bookcases everywhere!

Although this interview tells us very little about the psychological impact of L.U.'s analysis, the details are interesting, as they demonstrate that Khan was a fairly traditional analyst in this period, despite the gifts, favors, and his attendance at L.U.'s wedding. I had a second interview with L.U. a few days after this one and, like H.K., he told me about a disturbing experience with Khan long after his analysis had ended. Details of this experience and its impact on L.U. are told in Chapter 36.

PART 3

THE DIVINE YEARS: KHAN AT HIS PEAK

(1960–1964)

CHAPTER 7

MASUD AND SVETLANA

One either surrenders to the dynamism of life—inside and outside
oneself—or one stays petrified in a manipulative spectorial attitude
towards it. I want to live, and be lived through by, life.
Masud Khan[1]

How very drab and colourless most humans are.
And how infinitely lucky I am to have you, my love.
(Letter, Khan to S. Beriosova)[2]

Masud Khan's deepest and most lasting love, without question, was
Svetlana Beriosova (1932–1998). A year into their affair, while he was
still married to Jane Shore, he told Beriosova that their relationship was
something completely new for him: "I actually had never experienced
the reality and necessity of a woman until I met you. I had 'wet-nursed'
them all. Only in you, through you and with you did I realise my needs,
emotions and demands as a man from a woman."[3] Thomas Main, a fellow analyst, commented, "Svetlana was the jewel in Masud's crown."[4]
Khan would write that the best relationships are ones in which people
change each other, and certainly he and Svetlana met this criterion.

Whether or not it is true that people can have only one true love,
that was their experience. After the relationship ended, Khan wrote,
"No one can replace Beriosova in my life. We met at a critical moment of growth in our lives and we shared a dreaming that was taskful
and utterly demanding. . . . One does not love twice in a lifetime."[5]
On their deathbeds, both Khan and Beriosova would be thinking of
the other.

Beriosova told me about her first meeting with Khan. It was in 1956, at a time when she was a twenty-four-year-old dancer at the Royal Ballet, second in her position only to the world famous Margot Fonteyn (1920–1991): "Masud had liked watching me dance and he asked Hans Zullig[6] to bring him backstage to meet me. I remember a charismatic person wearing an astrakhan hat. I fell instantly in love. He came alone the next evening and asked me out after the performance. He told me that his wife was away dancing in the U.S. and that his marriage to her was ending."

A few weeks later, Beriosova was invited to a party at the Khans' home.[7] She plotted to get Khan to drive her home in the early morning hours: "In the car, I turned to Masud and kissed him. I didn't feel guilty—I was in love! I didn't care that Masud was married to Jane. After that night, he fell in love with me too."

Khan and Beriosova were ruthless in pursuing the relationship, despite the pain it caused Jane Shore. The two lovers met regularly at 8 Harley Street, after Shore left, and sometimes Khan took short European trips to watch Beriosova dance. They traveled together several times to Stuttgart, where Beriosova's father, Nicholas ("Poppa") Beriosov, was ballet master at the Opera House. It was not long before Khan moved into Beriosova's flat at 3 Herbert Mansions, 35 Sloane St.

Beriosova's best friend and roommate on tour was Mary Drage.[8] Drage and Beriosova had a glamorous social life when they were on the road. A mutual friend told me: "We all would get drunk and go out dancing. Svetlana was ravishing. She loved to disco and she had plenty of fun."[9] It is an odd coincidence that Drage had also been Jane Shore's best friend and her tour-roommate in the early 1950s.

Traveling with Beriosova in the United States in 1957, Drage started receiving nightly phone calls from Shore, in which Shore agonized over her separation from Khan, whom Drage had always disliked. At that very time, Beriosova had obviously fallen in love with a man from whom she was receiving daily letters, whose identity she kept secret. When Drage learned the identity of Beriosova's correspondent, she was horrified that a man she so despised was Beriosova's secret lover. However, she was also pleased for Beriosova, who was obviously happy:

I had already seen tragedy come to Jane, and now I was afraid that I would see it happen again, with the same man. I was afraid that Svetlana was going to be "arm candy" for Masud, that he just wanted to have a greater star. But then I came to believe that Masud and Svetlana did have something. I don't think Svetlana was deceived in love. I began to think, "Here is a man who has loved two of my best friends, he can't be all bad news." And in those days, Masud was more eager to please than he was later; his arrogance was less evident, and he was very charming. He had a talent for totally absorbing the attention of whoever he was with.

When Beriosova was touring, Khan made sure that she received a letter from him every day. This meant that he was often writing and posting a letter from London a week or more before Beriosova left. Here is a sampling from letters written prior to their marriage.

Hello Gee,[10] my love!
9 a.m. As I lean steep out of the window I can see the mail-van discarding its contents up the street. I do not think it will arrive here before my patient, who is due any minute.
10:10 am. No letter in the post, my love. Vagaries of our mail system. Or perhaps you returned too late and exhausted from your club party on Thursday night in Houston, so shan't get time to write till Friday night.
2:30 p.m. No letter in the afternoon too! How greedy and childish I am. It is certainly linked with my not being able to place you anywhere specific in my imagination. Feels as if I am totally out of touch with you today. You are in a train and so I am all adrift. . . . No! Gee, Svetlana, your Sud is not happy today. And it has crept upon me rather of a sudden. Feel sad and disembodied and very zestless. This is a heavy week and today is a heavy day. [I will go to the]1952 Club tonight and shall linger on to 11 pm or so.
11:30 p.m. Today has been a no-letter day and this week is bound to be staggered and deprived for me.
With all my love, Your Sud[11]

Hello Gee, Svetlana my Beloved!
Welcome to Sydney and I hope you are not too exhausted. And please remember, long air journeys have a very depressive effect that lasts a day or two; so if you feel too blue just let it be.
In London it is already a truly autumnal day today. The air nipping eager and the cool of the day rather sharp. Autumn has begun to mean

inevitable separations from you: year after year. And yet the logic of it makes sense since it all evolves round your growth and expansion as an artist. Creative lives cannot be always cosy.

Of course I am an inveterate cheater. Already I am thinking of the hour when you are warmly nestled in my arms, with all the warmth of success and exhaustion of the travails and we can really settle down to finding a home for ourselves and establishing its materialities. I am beginning to feel the excitement of it now: keenly, avidly. For a long time I carry a dream in my head and heart: surrounded by utter stillness; letting it ripen into fullness. Then one day it begins to stir in the whole of my being and compels action. I cannot hurry it, my love. Now our house is stirring to action in me and I know we will find, create and make one. Yes Gee my Svetlana! together we start a real home on your return. The time is ripe now.

Abientot my Svetlana! Love, Sud[12]

On Saturday, January 23, 1959, shortly after his divorce, Khan married Beriosova at the Chelsea Registry. Poppa, Poppa's sister, and a few friends were the sole witnesses. Beriosova had designed her own dress and the Covent Garden wardrobe mistress had sewed it for her—a lace-topped evening gown of champagne satin, covered by a choirboy jacket. She told me that she never took off her wedding ring—when she played a maiden role on stage, she covered it with elasto-plast.

Two receptions were held at Beriosova's flat.[13] She told me that she remembered "chaos, lots of champagne, a poached salmon, and a wedding cake from Harrod's—and then a three-day honeymoon at the Madison Hotel in Paris." The marriage was widely reported in London newspapers, with Beriosova referred to as "Covent Gardens' No. 2 Ballerina" and "The Real Cinderella," while Khan was inaccurately described as "the brother of Pakistan Premier, Malik Firoz Khan Noon."[14] (At the time of the wedding, General Ayud Khan, who was not a relative, was prime minister of Pakistan; he became the first elected president in 1960.)

Khan wrote about the day:

I was 34 years old and Svetlana was 25. [She was actually twenty-six.] We were both young and at the threshold of success and living: in life and in our careers. . . . We were a startlingly handsome couple and matched each other in every sense.

I recall the day so vividly. It was a brisk, chilly, sunlit winter morning. I had driven with Tahir Bhai Jan,[15] Poppa Beriosov and Svetlana to the Russian Church in Addison Road at 8:30 a.m. for a "Russian blessing" ceremony. I was startled to see Svetlana in her beige wedding dress. I have never seen any person of such beauty, clarity and purity again. As the priest blessed us in Russian, the sun streamed onto the Madonna ikon in the background. We felt and were blessed.

We had returned to 35 Sloane Street and then at 11 a.m. we were legally married at the Chelsea Town Hall. I recall that an uncanny sudden dread shivered through me when Svetlana burst into a nervous mocking giggle (which she smothered quickly) as a silly civil servant was pompously reading us our "duties" and declared us wedded husband and wife. Something in me sensed disaster.

Our wedding was a joyous international happening. Yes, I and Svetlana were happy. We had launched our life together.[16]

Soon after their marriage, Khan and Beriosova made a bold statement announcing their presence on the London scene by leasing an extraordinary flat in Knightsbridge. They took Flat 9 on the fourth floor of Number Three Hans Crescent, a handsome brick building in the ornate style called Pont Street Dutch.[17] The actor Michael Redgrave lived on the third floor with his wife Rachel Kempson and teenage children Vanessa, Lynn, and Corin, and the Venezuelan consulate was on the first floor. The building faced the back entrance to Harrod's Department Store,[18] where the Khans now became regular patrons,[19] often sending their staff to the food court to buy take-out dinners as well as caviar and other delicacies.

Flat 9 was a large space that took up the entire floor. Khan's consulting room was in the back, with the dining room doubling as a waiting room for patients. There were bookcases everywhere, because Khan's collection was constantly expanding. In addition to analytic books, he had a fairly complete collection of world literature, and a valuable sampling of oversized books containing limited edition prints by contemporary artists. Modern art was present throughout the flat—framed pictures as well as sculptures, purchased by Khan, often with Beriosova's money. The most valuable pieces were a pair of large Braque lithographs of swans flying in opposite directions, given to Beriosova by Geoffrey Gorer, and a signed Picasso Cubist original. Khan loved living in this building. And Beriosova had a similar attachment—she said of Hans Crescent that it was her first real home. It would be the place where they spent the happiest years of their lives.

Joining them in the flat was Beriosova's poodle, Kalu, whom she adored and treated like a child. Khan also loved Kalu, and he was obsessive in his concern for the dog's well-being.[20] In 1961, while away from home, Khan could not stop thinking about Kalu, who was staying with Zoë Dominic, a close friend. He wrote to Dominic: "Kalu is a very dear & beloved person [sic] in my life and I do miss him terribly much. We know each other so well & have a profound respect for each other's quirks of temperament."[21] His anxiety about separations included separation from the dog.[22]

The flat included ample space for the people whom Khan referred to as staff,[23] and there was private living space for a full-time houseboy. The Khans would have a series of houseboys on whom they were dependent for all kinds of chores, from welcoming patients, to walking the dog, to cooking the evening meal.[24]

Zoë Dominic was an essential part of the Khans' daily life.[25] The threesome, along with Kalu, formed a clan that functioned as a family, and they had dinner together whenever possible, often five nights a week. Dominic was a single woman who had a business specializing in the photographing of artists, and she and Beriosova had met on a photo shoot. Khan approved of her because she met his essential criteria for women: she was intelligent, attractive, and physically fit. As a woman with enormous common sense, Dominic became something of a parent figure to both Khans. She was especially devoted to Beriosova, which Khan appreciated: "I am grateful to you for your quiet affection, devotion and friendship for Svetlana. She is such an isolated & alone person that it is a great relief for me that she has found such a dear & trusting friend in you. Thank you, dearest Zoia!"[26]

The actress Julie Andrews was a close friend to Svetlana and to Zoë Dominic, and she and her then-husband Tony Walton were included as members of the clan.[27] Svetlana was godmother to Emma, the daughter of Andrews and Walton, and was present at the hospital when Emma was born in 1962. The extended clan spent many evenings together, talking and playing games. Andrews told me:

Once we were playing a game about what our biographies should be called and Masud said to me, "I know yours, Julie: 'Tiptoe Through the Cut Glass.'" That seemed then and still seems utterly right for me. I am a very careful person. Masud could do that, say exactly the right thing about you.

It was the era of the Cold War, and once we played a game about what we would do if we had a six-minute warning that we were going to be bombed, so we would definitely die. I said: "I'd climb into bed and cuddle." But Masud said: "I would climb to the top of a mountain and scream at God: 'How could you do this? This is outrageous!'"

The clan also got together in smaller groupings outside of London. Charles Kaufman, an American analyst, once invited Khan to a dinner party at his Long Island home. When Khan asked if he could bring a guest, Kaufman readily agreed. He was amazed when the guest turned out to be Julie Andrews, whose friendliness charmed everyone. Later, when Kaufman was staying with Khan in London, Andrews came over one night and Kaufman recalls: "A focus of the conversation was Julie saying that she had had the strangest offer: of all things, she had been asked to play Mary Poppins! She had doubts about whether she would accept, because she was afraid it would make her into a certain 'type.'"

For ten years, from 1956 to 1966, Khan and Beriosova were mutually infatuated and deeply enmeshed in their relationship. Khan wrote: "I recall Winnicott ruefully remarking: 'You never had a real analysis and transference with me because you were so much in love with Beriosova all those years when you came to analysis.'"[28] At first, Beriosova was the star, with Khan watching in adoration.[29] She helped him to calm down as he struggled, with some success, to control his mercurial temperament: "I wish you were here, Gee, because then I will feel strong and quiet and contained."[30] Khan particularly admired his wife's ability to focus on her work: "This is what I envy Svetlana most: her aesthetic austerity, economy, and containedness of concentration: nothing but the essential is let through, and nothing but the assimilated quintessence is expressed."[31]

Beriosova may have had the greater fame, but she was equally adoring of Khan and equally dependent on him. The symbiotic quality of the relationship worked well when times were good, as was the case in the early 1960s. Corin Redgrave told me his adolescent impressions of the couple: "It is hard to describe that flat and their relationship without having recourse to the sort of soft porn which in those censored days used to be published by Maurice Girodias at the Olympia Press in Paris. Soft porn masquerading as literature. *L'Histoire D'O, Belle du Jour*, etc. Svetlana seemed like the heroine in one of those fantasies. Often she seemed to be Masud's patient, but even more of the time she seemed his prisoner, though always a willing prisoner."[32]

The Khans lived an intense life. Their crowd was a certain type of 1960s group, where alcohol rather than drugs or politics fueled the dynamism.[33] Corin Redgrave told me: "Masud hunted personalities. Being himself an immense personality, and having, it seemed, always more than enough money, he had no difficulty collecting what in earlier times would have been called a 'salon' where many of the most gifted people would congregate." Andrews and Walton introduced the Khans to people from the arts, who became friends. Khan loved to mix different types of people at his parties, and the conservative analysts of his professional world now got to know Mike Nichols, Chita Rivera, Richard Burton and his then-wife Sybil Christopher, Peter O'Toole, and other actors, as well as the writers T. H. White and J. P. Donleavy. Tony Walton remembers that one of Khan's mischievous pleasures at these parties was to introduce people with a remark that was "just the thing you'd prefer not to have a brand-new acquaintance know about you. So you then spent most of the evening, or much of the new relationship, trying to untangle whatever it was that Sud had cheekily inferred."

On his thirty-seventh birthday, Khan was alone, and he wrote:

> When I take stock, I cannot but feel very grateful to the Lord for his endless kindnesses to me. I live in a state of grace. I have such wonderful friends [and] a really invaluable companion in my wife, whose love and care are always with me, around me and sustaining me. I have a healthy body, an alert mind, a successful and creative profession, a lovely spacious home, the cuddly love of Kalu and our adorable Antonio [the houseboy]. To be 37 and have all this is really a great blessing.
>
> Antonio cooked me a very special dinner and as I sat alone in the candle-quiet of the dining room, I was profoundly aware of the gift of being alive. At such moments, I always wish my father could be alive, so

that he could see and share it. That would give him greater peace and happiness than 10 paradises put together. It was his devout wish that I should become established in a creative and comfortable life. Thanks to his prayers and all his love, industry, and devotion, I have achieved it. And what he started, Svetlana has brought to fruition.[34]

Having lived in the dance world all her life,[35] Beriosova was now at the peak of her career.[36] She received worldwide publicity in 1961, when the renowned photographer Henri Cartier-Bresson photographed an article on her for *The Queen* entitled "Ballerina of Fire and Snow."[37] In a series of exquisite photos, Cartier-Bresson revealed Beriosova's exotic beauty, adding in his commentary: "She has the intelligence, sure and simple, born of an instinctive knowledge of what is essential in life." Soon after this publication, Beriosova became the number one dancer at the Royal, as Margot Fonteyn retired and began to perform only as a guest artist.[38]

In her private life, Beriosova's family was limited to Khan and Poppa. Her mother was long-deceased, and her extended family lived in Lithuania and Russia. She loved Poppa, but he was an unreliable womanizer who was constantly traveling.[39] She showed me a poem she had written about him that she considered to be an accurate description of her feelings:

My father, my brother, my life, my joy—sometimes a cruel, macho boy—
     You broke many beauties and that includes me . . .
     I will always search for your unreachable star.

Khan and Poppa hated each other from the time of their first meeting.[40] Khan resented Poppa's often-successful attempts to control his daughter, while Poppa felt he had every right to continue to do this, especially with regard to her career. Beriosova told me she had felt trapped between these two men with their strong personalities.

Even as her career was skyrocketing, Beriosova continued to be modest and undemanding. She sewed the ribbons on her own ballet and toe shoes, she washed her own tights, and, whether at home or on the road, she always lit a candle at night to watch over her ballet items. The analyst Sadie Gillespie remembers going to a dinner party at the Khans' after a performance and being amazed to see that Beriosova, on arriving home, took off her makeup and then made supper. When Gillespie complimented her on some window curtains, Beriosova told her she had sewed them herself. Khan was irritated at his wife for saying this—he did not value domesticity.

Whenever he could, Khan attended Beriosova's performances. He traveled regularly to Europe and to the United States, especially New York City. He was a calming presence in the hotel room as Beriosova silently paced in the daytime hours prior to a performance. He ordered flowers for her backstage dressing room, and often he bought her gifts, such as jewelry from Tiffany's. She loved the way he spoiled her, because she never spoiled herself.[41]

Often the demands of Khan's career kept him from being with his wife on tour. He rationalized that the separations were helpful: "Our separations put a distance across which we can meet again: explore & experience the separate identity of each other. It is always a small miracle to me to meet [Svetlana] again after a break."[42] But Tony Walton remembers that Khan did not do well when he and Svetlana had to be apart. He would become aggressive and so rattled that it was almost impossible to calm him down. Khan wrote of such experiences, "When Svetlana leaves, the whole atmosphere changes. The houseboy drags, the poodle won't eat, and Masud [referring to himself] frets with peevish stillness."[43]

In 1962, Fate would play a major role in the trajectory of Beriosova's career. This was the year when the great dancer Rudolf ("Rudi") Nureyev (1938–1993) came to England. It was a few months after his dramatic defection from the Soviet Union in Paris, an event that commanded the attention of the entire world.[44]

Ninette De Valois, the director of the Royal Ballet, hired Nureyev almost immediately. Everyone knew that the ballerina who became his partner would achieve worldwide fame overnight. Beriosova would have been the natural choice, except for the insoluble problem of her height. At 5'8", she would have been several inches taller than the also 5'8" Nureyev when dancing en pointe—and, in the highest circles of international ballet, dance partners had to be a perfect match. Fonteyn, however, was a petite woman who was only 5'4". And so it was that, even

though the world had already said good-bye to her, Fonteyn now returned to the stage to be Nureyev's partner.

Nureyev and Fonteyn made their debut at Covent Garden on February 21, 1962, to a full house that included the Queen Mother. Seventy thousand ticket requests had been turned down, and tickets sold
on the black market for four times their face value. Fonteyn gave the
performance of her lifetime as "Nureyev's carnal ardor was the perfect
foil to [her] eloquent purity."[45] On that night, Beriosova lost her number one status.

The significance of Fonteyn's return was not immediately obvious.
Beriosova was still an international star, dancing mostly with her new
partner, Donald MacLeary, but also at times with Nureyev. It was expected that Fonteyn would dance only for a year or two, and Beriosova
still had a huge following of fans.[46]

August was vacation time and the Khans almost always went to Monte
Carlo. Many of the dancers from the Royal Ballet were also vacationers in
the area, and Beriosova, along with her collegues, took classes in the morning with the esteemed Marika Besobrasova, who had a school nearby. In
the afternoons, she would sun-bathe or swim. Khan, who hated the sun
and had a lifelong phobia of water, would sit all day under an umbrella
and read.[47] After a late nap, the Khans would have a long dinner with friends
at one of many restaurants in the area. Dinner was regularly followed by
an intense poker game that continued into the early morning hours.

With one exception, the summers were almost exactly the same. That
exception was the summer of 1964, when the Khans went for a long visit
with Mike Nichols. First they went to New York City to see the play
The Knack, which Nichols had directed, and also *Hamlet*, where they were
guests of Richard Burton, who was playing the lead. Then they went to
Nichols' home on Martha's Vineyard. Khan was phobic of anything
having to do with the ocean, and instead he went horseback riding, returning to a childhood passion. He rode with a group of teenagers, all
girls, between fifteen and twenty years of age, and at the end of the visit,
he threw a "drinks party" for the girls at the Nichols' house.[48] Harvey
and Leslie Kayne, also friends of the Nichols', had driven up from Baltimore, and the six friends socialized daily with a heady intellectual
crowd.[49] Then the Khans drove south with the Kaynes to spend a few

days at their "glass house" on the Maryland shore. Returning to London, both Khan and Beriosova felt this had been an overly active vacation.

In December 1964, Khan received word that his mother was ill and might be dying. He had not been in Pakistan for ten years and he had never taken a Western acquaintance there. Now he decided to say good-bye to his mother and to take Beriosova with him.

Despite their distant relationship, Khan knew that Khursheed would welcome him: "I have neglected my mother these past 20 years in order to find and establish my own identity. Now that I have achieved my basic shape and conviction, I will try to take my leave of her and receive her blessings as well. She will not understand, but she will forgive and accept."[50]

He guessed correctly that Beriosova would help to ease the tensions of the visit. As things turned out, the visit was a great success—and Khursheed did not die: "The really beautiful and profound experience has been the way Svetlana grew into the very pulse and rhythm of the way of life in my village. It came to her so naturally, as if she were to the manor born. Without effort or artifice. And it made my mother alive with a new hope and vigour. It has given me a revitalized anchorage in my past."[51]

Beriosova told me: "When we went to Pakistan, I wore long robes, and I had to walk behind my husband. I brought a little Christmas tree, and they loved it. There was no electricity. I remember little colored birds on the orange trees—and beds that were on sort of stilts. The mother was a lovely, wrinkled woman. She would put her hand on my stomach and say 'bocce,' which I was told means 'children,' and I wondered if I would ever fulfill her wish for that."

Mary Drage told me that she thought, based on this visit, that Beriosova and Khan might have been able to live successfully in Pakistan: "Masud aspired to European things like a monogamous marriage. But he wasn't temperamentally suited to be with just one wife—he demanded too much of people. I remember Svetlana talking about how much it meant to her to go to Pakistan with Masud. She felt well accepted. Oddly enough, she was probably the type who could have made a life with him there, and it might have been healthier for him if he had stayed close to his roots. She used to even joke about it, how she wouldn't mind if he took on a 'junior wife,' as long as she could be the primary one."

Even in the Divine Years, there was a hint of darker times to come. During a fight that occurred in June 1962, Khan hit Antonio, his house-boy, in the head with sufficient force to break Antonio's eardrum.[52] Antonio pressed charges and Khan was taken to the Chelsea Police Station by two plain-clothes policemen who came to Hans Crescent with a warrant for his arrest. After being fingerprinted, Khan was discharged on bail, paid by Dominic. The next day, the judge at Marlborough Judge's Court let him off with a fine rather than a jail term, since this was a first offense. Antonio was fired.

On vacation in Monte Carlo two months later, Khan was still fuming about the incident and he did not feel regret: "The very mention of the name 'Antonio' upset me last night. Foolish and unrealistic, but there it is. His name fills me with shaming rage, violent disgust and disdain, and most of it with myself. The impotence of my humiliated fury only adds insult to injury. Never have I been so betrayed by a useless, feeble & vicious human being. The real pain of it is that we nurtured him with such tender care & affection. How adamantly another human being can disregard the nature & quality of one's devotion is one of the deepest sources of my shame."[53] His shame was not of the type in which a person regrets his actions: he was ashamed because an employee had been able to harm him. This was a situation far removed from anything his father would have tolerated—Fazaldad might well have had Antonio killed. Dominic remembers that when she chastised Khan, saying "Of course, you must never physically punish your staff," he had looked at her with incomprehension.

In a letter to Dominic the next day, Khan showed another side of himself as he was thoughtful and felt regret: "I have had a moment of epiphany. The trouble with me is that rage always precedes insight. Nature has endowed me with a mind and a capacity to understand which are vastly beyond my emotional capacities and the limits of my temperament. Hence I am always being pulled apart between the insights of my mind & the feudal prejudices of my temperament."[54]

Even as early as this, Khan recognized that he had two completely different selves: one that had the capacity for relatedness, insight, and change, and another that was rigid and overly comfortable with violent and socially inappropriate behavior. The frightened, symptomatic, playful Masud was accepted and loved in the West, even when he bragged or exaggerated—while the arrogant and violent Masud was neither understood nor respected. Khan's eventual success or failure would depend on his ability to develop the first self and control the second.

CHAPTER 8

WORKING IN A TIME OF REVOLUTION

*Up to our epoch, madness was a private state, nurtured in
adamant secrecy. Now, sanity is a state of which everyone is ashamed!
Sanity has become misidentified with mediocrity and
the ultimate sin is to be mediocre.*
Masud Khan[1]

*Masud dwelled in a world where passionate engagement was valued. He
held in common with Winnicott and I expect with many of their
analysands a desire for intensity of experience and for quality of being, a
kind of existential aspiration which is I think no longer fashionable.*
Anita Kermode, friend[2]

In the late 1950s and throughout the 1960s, major innovation occurred
in psychoanalysis, and there was a new freedom to deconstruct rigid
Freudian dogma. Winnicott, Khan, Michael Balint, Marion Milner,
Nina Coltart, Charles Rycroft, and R. D. Laing[3] worked with supposedly
untreatable patients in England; in France, Jacques Lacan was recom-
mending destabilization of the ego as a way to get closer to the unconscious; analysts in Argentina were treating schizophrenics[4]; and, in the
United States, Arthur Janov, Harold Searles, Frieda Fromm-Reichmann,
John Rosen, Milton Wexler, and Ralph Greenson were exploring, each
in his or her own way, the treatment of deeply disturbed patients using
modified psychoanalysis.[5]

The climate of the 1960s was ideal for psychoanalysis. People willingly made enormous sacrifices of time and money in order to be

analyzed, and analysand and analyst alike expected treatment to be an all-consuming experience.[6] An anonymous analyst said to me: "Things have changed so much in psychoanalysis since the 60s. Today's students have no idea about how it used to be. I think of the climate of those analyses, people who regressed to where they were ready to die—such a passion that they lived! What a comparison to today. Today, psychoanalysis has become a rivulet of tepid water. It used to be incandescent, it was fantastic."

In the world of international psychoanalysis, London was one of the most important places for innovative work. Peter Kramer, the American psychiatrist and author, was analyzed in London at this time, and he told me, "Compared to the U.S., the U.K. felt like the center of the analytic world." British analysts, especially those of the Middle Group (re-named the Independent group in 1964),[7] treated seemingly hopeless patients using modifications of technique; they talked about their own "mad" countertransference experiences and insisted on finding out for themselves what really worked.

Khan was able to be innovative and still stay part of mainstream psychoanalysis. As a full member of the British Psycho-Analytical Society (BPAS), he regularly taught the introduction to psychoanalysis course and he was an active member of the Education Committee, in addition to functioning as honorary librarian and doing editorial work for the *International Journal of Psycho-Analysis* (IJPA). The inner politics of the society continued to be tense as the Kleinians battled with the non-Kleinians,[8] but Khan's various positions kept him in close contact with all the groups.

His colleagues, both Kleinian and non-Kleinian, were often critical but they also admired him:

I first met up with [Khan] fully in the mid-1960s when I joined a discussion group in which he was a leading member. He was a tall man but with nothing of the bully about him either physically or mentally; there was no threat or punitiveness in his tone. However, his urge to fill the room, or haughtily be centre-stage, never failed him. What he had to say obviously had stature; it was always fascinating and to the point. . . . I remember his generosity and encouragement when many analysts can forget about such things. (Eric Rayner[9])

Khan was certainly an impressive, even flamboyant, figure and usually seemed to join a meeting a bit late so making a noticeable entrance. Compared with most of us dullards he was quite theatrical. He was clearly very intelligent and very well-read. I thought his writings were extremely interesting—outstandingly so. But I never for a moment thought of referring a patient to him. Why? I never felt, rightly or wrongly, that he was sufficiently in control of himself or reflective enough of the counter-transference. (R. Gosling[10])

As a teacher, Khan was known for being brilliant, eccentric, and intimidating. He was also known for choosing a favorite and a scapegoat in his classes, which naturally made the students uncomfortable.[11] An analytic trainee from this period, told me about a controversial incident in the early 1960s:

Masud was leading a small seminar which I was in and there was a visiting guest, an anthropologist from Australia. Masud came in late and nobody introduced the anthropologist who happened to be wearing a cardigan sweater [with buttons down the front]. The following dialogue occurred:

 M.K.: You're wearing a cardigan!
 A.A. [Australian anthropologist]: Yes I am. Do you mind?
 M.K.: Yes I do.
 A.A.: Would you like me to leave?
 M.K.: Yes I would!

Upon which the anthropologist left! And the seminar proceeded without discussion of the incident.[12]

For most people in the analytic world, Khan's presence was welcome. His knowledge and his commitment to psychoanalysis were reportedly inspiring, and he kept things interesting. His mischievous behavior was experienced as playful.[13]

It was during this decade that Khan acquired an international reputation. He gave his first lecture in the United States in spring 1962, when he spoke at the Downstate Medical Center of New York, at the invitation of his friend Charles Kaufman. Then in April of 1963, he went on a more ambitious tour, speaking in New York, Chicago, Topeka (at the Menninger Clinic), and Maryland (at Chestnut Lodge). He reported to

Zoë Dominic that he was "unwell, paranoid-irritable, and scared stiff" but still able to function well.[14]

For Khan's third professional visit to America, in the spring of 1964, his friend Wladimir Granoff asked him to write in detail about the tour, and we can see from these letters that Khan was accepted at the highest levels of his profession. The description of his analytic activities is combined with accounts of an active social life that he obviously enjoyed.

Karl Menninger and his daughter Rosemary provided what Khan remembered as the highlight of the trip: horseback riding on the pastoral grounds of the clinic.[15] From Kansas, Khan went to California, where he gave several papers and met the Stollers for the first time (see Chapter 11).

In 1965, Khan went on another major trip to the United States. The big names of American psychoanalysis were in New York City for a meeting of the American Psychoanalytic Association, where Khan presented a paper, "On Symbiotic Omnipotence," at a panel on trauma headed by Leo Rangell. When the American analysts Erik Erikson, Heinz Hartmann, Rudolf Lowenstein, and Max Schur came to the panel and sat in the front row, he knew that he had been accepted by the Americans. This pleased him enormously: "I must say the [American] analysts are really kind and positive to me. They meet me with such fervour and respectfulness. I have now started to accept that I am important, significant and a creative mind among analysts."[16] This positive reception from the Americans suggests that Khan was adjusting well to the West.[17]

CHAPTER 9

CLINICAL WORK [INTERVIEWS]

Masud had a certain style of work that he presented very well in his case histories. It goes like this: "Comes this young man in a dirty sweater. I send him home to get decently dressed before I will begin the analysis. The young man comes back and starts smoking, and he keeps letting the ashes build up on the cigarette butt. So I say to him, 'It takes great effort to keep those ashes from falling. Instead of showing your ability by holding this cigarette and not dropping the ashes, better that you use all that energy on another level.'" That's Masud.
Wladimir Granoff[1]

In the 1960s, Khan had his pick of patients and was seeing up to eleven a day, many of them artists, musicians, or people from the literary world. Barrie Cooper, who was the personal physician to many famous people, felt comfortable referring patients who demanded special attention because, as he told me, Khan knew how to keep them in treatment.[2] When Khan successfully treated a well-known rock musician, he got several other referrals from that world.[3] He had a following both within the institute and in London's artistic community.[4]

Now that he was officially a training analyst, Khan could dare to work more in his private version of Winnicott's style, because he did not have to report to an outside supervisor. As the following cases show, Khan the analyst was primarily motivated by an attempt to help his analysands to become aware of their various selves and to establish a dialogue with those selves—not, as in more conservative analysis, to resolve conflict and to strengthen the ego. Khan's thinking at this time came straight from Winnicott: "As I see it, the characteristic feature of DWW's

[Winnicott's] theorising is that, whereas Freud saw conflict as the central issue of human experience, DWW considers paradox [as in co-existing contradictory selves] as the essential human reality. For Freud, resolution of conflict constituted the aim of therapeutic effort, and for DWW it is the realization of paradox without its resolution that constitutes psychic health and creativity."[5]

INTERVIEW WITH ANALYSAND JAMES HOOD (1959–1965)

James ("Jimmy") Hood is a psychiatrist/psychoanalyst who had his training analysis with Khan in the 1960s. He worked with Winnicott at Paddington Green for many years and is now in full-time private practice in London. I interviewed Hood in 1996.

> I was a child psychiatrist in Glasgow, and I came here to London for analytic training in 1959. Khan was my training analyst from 1959 to 1965. I certainly experienced him in his best years.
>
> When I first arrived, I was working with Winnicott at Paddington Green, and Winnicott steered me toward Khan. He took me to a scientific meeting, even though as a student I wasn't allowed there—and he showed me who some of the analysts were. He pointed out Khan and I decided to see him for a consultation.
>
> Have you seen any pictures of him? He is [sic] a very tall and handsome man. He was always courteous and gentle in style.
>
> At the first interview, Masud only said one thing, and that was at the very end: "You are anxious." I was comfortable with him and I decided I would see him.
>
> I felt lucky. With me, he did very good work, and he was always consistent. He respected privacy. For example, one time, about eighteen months after I started, it was winter, and I had a serious pneumonia. I was quite ill, and my mind was wandering. I missed about eight sessions, and he didn't contact me at all. When I went back, he never asked where I'd been, although of course I told him. Privacy is very important to me. I see a lot of analysts' kids, and I never talk about them. I think I got that from Masud.
>
> He was an analyst who incited extraordinary transferences. What was striking was the level of his attention and his sensitivity. You thought that he lived for you! And he had a great sense of humor.

He was such an exciting person to know. Like Yeats. People say of Yeats, "His manner was such that you felt he had a sword upstairs." Khan was like that. Or they said of Yeats, "After you saw him, you would feel like you had $200,000."

I also believe he was, as they say, "a man of action." He was a hunter of deer, I think—and I am a hunter of hares. He told me that he used to hunt in Pakistan and, instead of using dogs, they used trained cheetahs. They really did that—he was an honest man, and, in those days, he wouldn't have said it if it wasn't true.

There was a window in his office that looked out onto the street. My sessions were at 8 a.m., and one morning there was a terrific racket of bin-men—you know, collecting the garbage. He went to the window and shouted at them: "Stop! You are interfering with my work!" And they did stop. Nobody else would have done that, I am sure. It shows how protective he was of the environment.

His greatest strengths, as an analyst, were his interest in the self, and the fact that he wasn't tied to classical theory. Also, his interest in the patient's experience.

You know, I worked with Winnicott and used his child consultation techniques all the time. It took me decades to get Winnicott out of me and find my own self. Not so with Khan. He always encouraged me to be my own self.

It is clear that Hood felt greatly helped by Khan. In this case, Khan kept to a strict frame even as a strong transference relationship developed.

INTERVIEW WITH ANALYSAND PETER ELDER (1960-1966)

I first heard about Peter Elder via L.U., another Khan analysand (see Chapter 6) who remembered Elder from their training days in London. In 1997, the year of the interview, Elder was actively engaged in a successful career in Canada. He had been chief psychiatrist at a children's hospital in Ottawa, and then moved to Toronto, where he was in private practice, with fifty percent of his time devoted to work with children. About a year after the interview, he retired from practice and moved to Wales.

I'm originally from Edinburgh, and I came to London to go to medical school. As a medical student, I became an analysand of Adam Limentani. He was good for me, but too conservative—he didn't know about personality disorder, and that's what I had. When I decided to do analytic training, I asked Limentani who I should see and he gave me three names —Eva Rosenfeld, Khan, and someone else. I would never have seen a Kleinian [Rosenfeld's orientation]. Khan was the only one I saw. And you know, to me it's as if it were yesterday. My analysis feels timeless. It is still a part of me.

At the first interview, I had expected to meet a diminutive Indian sage, so I was surprised by his looks. Masud was a tall man, in semiformal dress, as always. You sensed immediately that you were in the presence of someone serious, learned, and important. He was not what you would call "amiable," but he was very human. I was quite at ease. He told me right then that he would accept me for analysis, and I was pleased since I had known someone who had been rejected by him for analysis.

I saw him five days a week for fifty minute sessions. Sometimes on a Sunday, just for emergencies, he would see me for an hour and a half. He always called me "Dr. Elder," and I called him "Masud." Maybe once, after the analysis, he called me "Peter."

I would say about the atmosphere of the sessions, you always knew you were talking to a sensitive, well-disposed person. I wouldn't say he was lovable, but he was admirable. He was eclectic and broad minded— a very wise man. And he never let me down. He was always very much the analyst in his demeanor.

He got fed up in the end, because I never had a major regression. He told me it had been the same for him, that he had never had a regression with Winnicott. Winnicott had written about regression to dependence, and so it had become godlike, as if you had to have it in order to have a complete analysis. Winnicott really did a disservice with that idea.

I did know enough of a regression, though, to get a taste of being "held" by him. It was about letting go, and I was able to do that. But I was always able to keep working.

In technique, he was hard and persistent. He wouldn't let me off the hook. His interpretation of the negative was constant. At times I thought that he was driving me mad! When I would hear from others about empathy in their analysis, or read about it, I couldn't imagine what it would be like. But I think the emphasis on the negative was very helpful to me. I needed that.

He had a taboo on any mention of his wife, Svetlana Beriosova, the ballerina. I would see her sometimes in the corridor, sometimes with their dog, and sometimes she was obviously angry at him. When I came for an emergency visit on a Sunday, she would be visibly annoyed that I was there.

Masud always respected my marriage. When I was first seeing him, I had a son, and my wife was pregnant with our daughter. And after my daughter was born, Masud made it clear that if we had another baby, he wouldn't go on with the analysis. He felt that the drag of domesticity would be a prolonged hold-up, that it would prevent me from doing the internal work. I think he was right. He was no fool with these things.

I don't know if my ex-wife would say that she felt he contributed to the breakup of our marriage. But he did aid and abet that. It was at the end, after many years of analysis, and not until she had been in analysis herself for over two years. The threads of hope had all run out for us, it seemed, and Masud encouraged us to separate. He was like Winnicott—he sometimes gave advice, in a professional manner.

One day, I remember, I was very ill, I think from something dental. And instead of a session, he took me to a bedroom, and let me sleep.

Also, I was impecunious, so he charged me very low fees. I appreciated that very much. In connection with that, I remember that once I had been to a bookstore and I saw a book of Chagall reproductions that I felt I HAD to have. It cost 5 guineas, which was a lot. I was embarrassed to tell him about spending the money since I was paying him so little, but I did tell him, and his response was to stop the session. He took me into his grand living room and showed me his large collection of books, paintings, and sculpture. There was one enormous sculpture—a tall, long abstract figure, seven feet tall. It may have been a Giacometti, since he said once that he had been a model for Giacometti, but I don't know for sure about that. I do know that there was more than one Braque on the wall. I don't remember him saying anything. I think this incident illustrates a sensitive balance in Masud's awareness and timing. My neediness was already painfully experienced. What I longed for was acceptance of my interest and passion for art, and that was beautifully acknowledged. His intervention worked. By that I mean that I wouldn't have to steal from his world. He would share it with me.

And he looked after my training needs. For example, he talked about what seminars and supervisors I might choose. I knew Rycroft and Martin James through him. He was a great buddy of John Sutherland, who is also from Edinburgh, and he was very friendly with Anna Freud. He got me into Anna Freud's seminars. She was extremely boring, but as a commentator on papers, she was a gem.

I can't remember a single one of his interpretations. But he was a real person. That's the most important thing, the thing about Khan that I would emphasize above everything else: he was always real with me, none of this oedipal stuff or the Kleinian stuff about primary envy, which was a devastating and witchlike theory. He was down to earth and also serious. And he respected me, all the time. His attention to what was going on was very powerful, and I needed that because my own father had been distant. Khan could do both, provide the attention and the negative interpretations.

Limentani had been different. He tried to interpret my complexes, and he was kind, but he was never a real person like Khan. He didn't have that quality of attentiveness to every detail.

Khan and Winnicott were a good pair. Khan was more extraverted in a superficial way: Winnicott couldn't swagger! Or wear a cloak when seeing patients! But I found Winnicott's humility very frightening, because it was misleading—there was such a powerhouse inside. I was always frightened of him. Of course I admired Winnicott, but I felt "penetrated" by him—he had this quality as if he could see through everything. He was not a gentle mother.

One thing I feel sorry about is that Masud wouldn't let me acknowledge him as real. For example, once I dreamed about Svetlana, that she had been very kind to me. It was actually my gratitude to him. But he swept it aside, he wouldn't discuss it. I think that was unfortunate.[6]

Overall, I think I disappointed Masud because I wasn't successful enough. I mean, I wasn't going to be a doyen of psychoanalysis, just a clinician. I wasn't going to write important papers. Once I wrote a paper about my treatment of an adolescent girl—I was working then in the children's unit at Tavistock—and I gave him the only copy of the paper, and he lost it. I always felt that he had lost it because he was ashamed of my level of functioning. He would have liked me to have been an intellectually superior candidate. I didn't write anything psychoanalytic for a long time after that. And he didn't apologize—he wouldn't have done that. He wouldn't have apologized. He was such a meticulous filer of things—he took all these notes on 3 × 5 cards and he was so organized— that I knew there was a reason why he had lost the paper. I'm a good clinician, that I believe, but I couldn't write well.

I'm sixty-eight years old now. I think I was bright enough for him, but I wish I had written more. My work in Canada has been phenomenal—but I can't write about it.

Masud definitely influenced my clinical work. He taught me that you don't have to "cure" people, though you can bring them closer to health. And he showed me how to be real. His theory is something that you can take in and really use. I'm so grateful for that. I don't have to posture and pose with my patients, and I got that from him.

I suppose it's ironic that I got that experience of realness with Khan, when he is so often criticized for being haughty and false. But his arrogance was really rather splendid. You knew that there was a defensive and vulnerable person right underneath. And most of the time I was seeing him, he was very highly regarded in the analytic community. In those days, you were cast in the dye of your analyst, and I felt proud to be with such an outspoken and capable man. I still feel proud.

I am glad to have had an analysis with Masud. The world has become very superficial in comparison to those intense days.

After the interview, Elder had some further thoughts that he sent to me in an e-mail:

Here are some afterthoughts about our interview. Before now, I've not come up with anything I could write. If one were to ask ten theoretical analysts to give their opinion on my analysis, I expect one would get at least four different constructions. My view is Winnicottian.

The long process was essentially a "holding"/working through situation, without any massive regression. Masud's interpretation of the negative was my most prominent experience over time. Solace under those circumstances would have avoided my anti-social tendency.

It must have taken much determination and genuine regard on Masud's part to help me to shoulder and survive rather than escape. He was acutely attuned to the power of acting out and its place in our relationship. Whatever hurt I gave to others in my social life, I experienced as hurtful to him—I could sense that in his countertransference. The analysis was a protracted working through, to a worthwhile degree. His ability to care without stepping one inch on the side of softness and sentimentality was remarkable, and it gave me the privilege of self regard and more life of my own. Eventually, as a result, much that was caring in me took a surer place in myself.[7]

As with Hood, Khan's willingness to be "real" with Elder and his intense focus on the content while keeping to an analytic frame appear to have been deeply curative. The account of the lost paper shows why an analyst has to be careful about all interactions with the analysand, whether in the session or outside of it, because they can have a symbolic meaning that may not be intended.

INTERVIEW WITH ANALYSAND
JOHN MALLINSON (1959–1969)

John Mallinson was between high school and medical school when he started analysis with Khan. He went on to qualify and work for twenty-five years as a doctor. He was known for having had a silent analysis, which Khan described in a published article, with Mallinson referred to as Peter.[8] My interview with him was in 1998.

> I grew up about forty miles outside London. My father and mother were both physicians. I was seventeen when I started seeing Masud, just out of high school. I was in limbo, in a frozen state, unable to move forward. Martin James referred me to him, and the analysis was five days a week for a year. Then I started medical school and we reduced the frequency. I don't know if I can say that I was "in analysis" in the formal sense, really. I remember very little in detail of the sessions. There was a lot of silence but at other times I was able to talk quite freely.
>
> Sometimes I'd lie on the couch, sometimes sit in the chair opposite him. I am the patient Khan wrote about in his article, "Silence as Communication." I was a very silent patient and he was remarkably tolerant in the face of what seemed at times a trial of strength. When he sometimes lost patience, he didn't hesitate to show it. He got me through a "patch," a difficult time. I give him credit for that. And he was incredibly insightful. He was one of the most impressive people I have ever met. He was charismatic, and he had a power of attracting people to himself, which worked for good and for bad. I thought of him as grand and glamorous and of myself as a country lad. I was never sure what Masud was up to. He seemed to be very proud of me, as if he felt I was a great success. Perhaps I was, more than I care to acknowledge. He made much of my passing exams, as if I were the most brilliant young doctor in the

country. This was flattering, but more often I found it patronizing and irritating. I've never been able to stand compliments.

At some time in the first year, Masud found me a job sorting books at Karnac's book store on Gloucester Road. Another of Masud's ideas was to encourage me to go ice-skating, which I did regularly in that year. In retrospect the metaphor seems odd—putting this frozen boy on ice— but I think he was right in seeing physical movement as a key to a mental thaw.

Later Masud introduced me to Winnicott and I lived in his basement flat with another medical friend. Winnicott had severe heart problems and he wanted a medical presence in his house. I lived there for about two years and, though I didn't know Winnicott or his wife Clare well, they were both very friendly. Clare called me when he finally collapsed in the night but sadly there was nothing to be done. I went to Winnicott's funeral with Masud. We never had a formal ending. Our relationship just gradually became more social.

I would say that Khan rescued me. He saved me.

Khan's article about Mallinson describes treatment through silent sessions, with an underlying theoretical rationale based on Balint's (1968) theory of the basic fault. The description of silence as a communication, rather than a resistance, is something that is still a radical notion.

CHAPTER 10

THE CURATIVE FRIENDSHIPS

*I am fickle and arbitrary with people who are non-friends. I jilt them, or
forget them. But not my friends—they are a thing apart, sacred. The
curative friendships and the malignant loves . . . and yet humankind has
always insisted on representing it the other way round.*
Masud Khan[1]

Quite a few people remember Khan as the best friend they ever had.
The Pakistani diplomat Sahabzada Yaqub Khan said to me: "Masud was
a loyal and dependable friend. I've known him to defend his friends like
a tiger." Khan chose his friends carefully and made them feel special:
"Masud bestowed his love on you—it was as if you were 'knighted' by
him."[2] Although he is sometimes criticized for being overly interested
in important people, he was not a simple social climber—he wanted to
be surrounded by people who had a true zest for living. And he gave
back as much as he took. Barrie Cooper, Khan's longtime physician and
friend, told me: "Masud had a particularly rare gift for catalyzing. He
wanted something to happen with you and with him. He wanted these
experiences with others because, as he would say, 'How else can I know
I am alive?'"

The ideas promoted in Khan's various writings did not always
match his lived life—but in the domain of friendship, his actions almost always matched his values. In his theory, friends took the place
of God. He wrote that human beings had "from time immemorial"
needed an "other" to relate to in order to have stability and to learn
about the self and, in prior eras, people used God as the "other" with
whom they could relate.[3] But as religion became less personal, the

relationship to God was replaced by friendship with mortals, and mortals served the purpose as well as God had: "To sense oneself alive in another's preoccupations is to be in a state of grace."[4] Love relations were important, he said, but friendship lasted longer and was more conflict-free than love.[5]

His passion was for male friendship. He felt at ease with certain men in a way that he never could with a woman, even a woman who was his lover, and he speculated that women might actually be dispensable in the essential experiences of men.[6] He resented the intensity of male–female relationships in Western life, an intensity that was a contrast to the greater separation of the sexes in India and Pakistan. Khan was upset, not pleased, when his French friends J.-B. Pontalis and Victor Smirnoff and his American friend Harvey Kayne developed lasting love relationships, possibly because it disrupted an internal fantasy of the friendship. For example, although he was very fond of Harvey Kayne's wife, Leslie, he wrote: "I managed to sustain Harvey as an embodied abstraction private and personal to me, all these thirteen or more years since 1951. When I met Leslie I felt a sense of doom."[7]

Since childhood, Khan had always had close male friends with whom he experienced great pleasure.[8] The friendships were homosexual in the sense that, as the French analyst Daniel Widlocher suggests, one can think of any passionate relationship with a same-sex person as homosexual, whether or not it is acted upon genitally. Widlocher related to me: "I remember being with a bunch of analysts and their wives at Hans Crescent. Masud told us that he was very proud of the boots he had just bought. He called Susu [the houseboy] to bring the boots to show them to the ladies. What he was really doing was using the ladies to show the boots to the men. The ladies were not important to him—he just wanted the men to watch him charming the ladies. It was a kind of homosexual display. This is the quality that you could see in his passionate friendships with my colleagues. Passion in a friendship is an expression of homosexual trends, even if it is not acted out."

There were many rumors about Khan, and one of these was that he was an active homosexual. Charles Rycroft told me that he was certain that Khan had homosexual experiences in Paris in the 1950s, and this belief was based on an accidental meeting they had there, which he did not want to describe further. The art critic and poet Ted Lucie-Smith thought that Khan had homosexual encounters in London: "I do think that Masud was actively homosexual, in a very covert way. I suspect he probably had 'episodes' with at least one houseboy—he probably raped him. [This houseboy] was scared of him, in the manner of an abused child. Masud's manner to [him] was always a curious mixture of the caressing and the sadistic." Lucie-Smith's report is uncorroborated, however, and in all my years of research, with the exception of his mention of the houseboy, I never heard any gossip about specific men who might have been sexually involved with Khan.

Not surprisingly, Khan's friends and peers have a range of thoughts on the question of his sexuality. Joseph Sandler remembered Khan staying late at parties, where, after Svetlana had gone home, he engaged in homosexual banter with men and sometimes danced with them. And a girlfriend told me, "I think Masud wanted to be homosexual, but wasn't."[9] But a longtime friend who knew Khan very well says that she never saw any evidence of homosexuality and she was certain he would have talked to her about that. She added: "Masud always had a woman at his side or in his bed."[10] Barrie Cooper viewed the issue in another way: "I think Masud was ambisexual, not bisexual. By ambisexual, I mean a free-floating capacity to attach. Masud fancied sexualized relationships and gender was not ultimately the primary thing."

Khan's friendships with women were less intense than his friendships with men, but all evidence suggests that they were much more intense than most nonsexual friendships between men and women. His female friends were mostly from outside the field of psychoanalysis, and they were all remarkable people in one way or another.[11] Khan cared about looks in a woman, but, in order for her to be taken on as a friend, she had to have talent and vitality as well. With just a few exceptions, he kept his relationships with female friends completely nonsexual. There were several instances when women friends tried to sexualize the friendship and Khan responded by distancing himself.

In an article written in 1970, "The Catalytic Role of Crucial Friendship in the Epistemology of Self-Experience in Montaigne, Rousseau and Freud," Khan[12] stated that there was a particular kind of friendship that was the deepest and most important of all friendships: the crucial friendship. In crucial friendship, shared confidences catalyze significant development in the other that would not have happened otherwise. Crucial friendships are characterized by very full relating that may include hate as well as love. Accordingly, there is an uncommon degree of forgiveness and generosity.

In letters and in his Work Books, and in the tradition of Aristotle, Khan developed this idea further. He theorized that crucial friends had to be of the same sex, to preclude the influence of sexuality (his examples were all of men relating to men). Furthermore, the friends had to live at some distance from one another and meet only occasionally, because distance allowed for intensity. And crucial friendships always come to a bad ending, he believed, because one friend outgrows the other: "[H]uman beings with rare gifts, where they use the other as a catalyst towards the fruition of their self-experiences, have to face the responsibility of destroying the agent into the bargain."[13]

Khan illustrated his ideas through a discussion of crucial friendships in the lives of the philosophers Montaigne[14] and Rousseau,[15] but his primary example was the Sigmund Freud–Wilhelm Fliess relationship. Students of psychoanalysis know that Freud and Fliess were intimate friends from the late nineteenth century into the early 1900s, at a time when Freud was on the threshold of making his great discoveries. In 1887, when they met, Freud was living in Vienna and Fliess was living in Berlin. Their relationship was carried on mostly by correspondence, with occasional meetings which Freud called "congresses." In Khan's opinion, Freud could not have made his early discoveries were it not for this friendship, in which Fliess was a supportive presence and a catalyst. Even the self-analysis that Freud conducted in these years was possible only because of Fliess: "One needs another to know oneself with."[16] The friendship ended, in Khan's opinion, because of an imbalance of talent: "In spite of Freud's courtesy and adulation, the correspondence leaves one in no doubt that Freud was and considered himself to be the more significant and creative person. They both outlived their friendship. Fliess was, perhaps, more hurt from the lapse of the friendship than Freud."[17]

Khan felt that he understood the Freud–Fliess relationship well because of his own similar experiences: "I know so well the truth of

Freud's statement to Fliess: 'No-one can replace the intercourse with a friend that a particular—perhaps feminine—side of me demands.'"[18]

The concept of crucial friendship is essential to an understanding of Khan. He had three crucial friends: Wladimir Granoff, Robert Stoller, and Victor Smirnoff.[19] Each of these relationships will be examined in detail in subsequent chapters.

CHAPTER 11

WLADIMIR GRANOFF

*Wova [nickname for Wladimir] plays at life with a zeal
and intensity that is both epic & absurd. That, I reckon,
is the secret of a style of living.*
Masud Khan[1]

In the years 1963 to 1965, Masud Khan and Wladimir Granoff (1924–
2000), a French analyst, had a friendship so strong and so transformative that it definitely qualifies as crucial. The story of the friendship comes
from interviews with Granoff as well as from the extensive Khan–Granoff
correspondence, which begins in September 1963, and ends in November 1969, several years after the friendship ended.[2] In addition to having significant effects on both men, the relationship led to two major
developments in psychoanalysis: the exportation of the thought of the
charismatic and iconoclastic French analyst Jacques Lacan to England
and the exportation of Winnicott's ideas to France.

To understand the Khan–Granoff friendship, it is important to have
a rudimentary knowledge of the state of French psychoanalysis in the
late 1950s and early 1960s. The French analysts did most of their
speaking and publishing in their own language and their movement had
developed somewhat separately from British and international psychoanalysis. In comparison to mainstream psychoanalysis, the French tradition had closer ties to poetry and literature and less of a connection to
the medical model of health vs. illness, and they were much more influenced by Lacan's thinking.

Their major analytic group had split in two in 1953, leaving a conservative Paris Society affiliated with the International Psychoanalytic

Association (IPA), while members of the young and perhaps more exciting society, Société Francaise de Psychanalyse (SFP), were denied
membership in the IPA.[3] Lacan and Granoff were both members of the
SFP, with Lacan being the central figure of the group and the analyst
or supervisor of many SFP members.

Like all psychoanalysts, Lacan was interested in helping his patients
get access to the unconscious mind, but in contrast to many of his con-
temporaries, he was willing to do this work through the destabilizing of
defense mechanisms, rather than trying to make the defenses stronger.
A controversial technique developed by Lacan was the variable-length
session, in which analytic sessions lasted anywhere from a few minutes
to several hours. He believed that sessions of uncertain length led to
intense feelings that facilitated the analysis.[4]

When the SFP tried to get membership in the IPA, it was blocked by
conservative British and American analysts who disapproved of Lacan's
variable length sessions. The IPA holds a combined business and professional meeting called a congress every other year, in odd-numbered
years. In 1961, at the Stockholm Congress and then again at the 1963
Edinburgh Congress, the Executive Committee granted the SFP study
group status only. But in 1963, the IPA gave Granoff full individual
membership, a clear signal that his group would be accepted if it got rid
of Lacan. Later that year, in a coup organized by Granoff, the SFP became defunct as a new group was formed that did not include Lacan—
the Association Psychanalytique de France (APF). It fell to Granoff to
be, in his words, "Lacan's executioner," because he was the only one of
the leading SFP analysts who had not had a personal analysis with Lacan.[5]
The IPA gave full membership to the APF at the 1965 Amsterdam
Congress. Lacan then founded a new training institute and that group
developed outside of the IPA.

The friendship of Khan and Granoff was at its peak while the APF
was working to get its membership in the IPA. It is saying quite a lot to
say that their friendship was just as charged as the politics of that time.

Granoff was born in Strasbourg, France, in 1924, to parents who were
Jewish intellectuals who had emigrated from St. Petersburg.[6] He first
considered a career as an actor or painter, then pursued medicine and

psychoanalysis. He became an important analyst, teacher, and writer, and he is remembered for his charm and his generosity, as well as his professional achievements. A description by the historian Elisabeth Roudinesco illustrates the intensity of his personality:

> [Wladimir Granoff] with his double-breasted jacket, his habit of kissing hands, and a discreet carnation in his lapel . . . cultivated intrigue in the manner of the Czar's officers: with a baroque sense of truth bordering on the ludicrous. Every deed was for him a question of life or death. If a weapon was loaded, it had to be aimed at either himself or another, whether the best of his friends or the most formidable of his adversaries. No morality for Wladimir, rather an ethic in which the drama of a destiny— with the richness of its pleasures and the bleakness of its despair—was to flourish.[7]

Khan and Granoff met for the first time in 1953, when Granoff brought Lacan to London to meet the English analysts. Khan, along with Pearl King, was introduced as a young and promising colleague. They met again at the 1961 Edinburgh Congress, where Granoff was lobbying to get the SFP accepted for IPA membership. But it was when they met for the third time, at the 1963 Stockholm Congress, that they truly became friends.

Both men were prolific writers. In the first years of their friendship, they exchanged letters every day and they got together in Paris or London several times a year. (There was no language barrier, because Granoff was fluent in English, as well as Russian, German, and French.) Granoff told me: "For the first two and a half years, Masud was absolutely central in my life, as I in his."

Their mutual appeal came from having in common a number of traits, not all of them admirable—verbal eloquence, an attunement to style, a tendency to snobbery, and a passion for dramatic living. Remembering how they would drive around Paris in his 1930 Bugatti convertible, Granoff laughed as he told me: "Masud and I made quite a pair. We were 100% lacking in modesty, impossible megalomaniacs—and it was wonderful! For other people, we were probably unbearable, but we didn't care."

The first letter of their correspondence concerned the theory and treatment of perversion. The next letters involved Khan helping Granoff to get a paper published in the IJPA and referring a patient for consultation. Khan wrote regarding the referral: "I am very intrigued by your way of thinking, and wish to exploit this opportunity to see if we cannot match our respective experiences."[8]

Soon after they started writing, they visited each other in London and Paris. Khan introduced Granoff to Svetlana, and Granoff sent roses to Svetlana when she danced in Paris. Within a few weeks, Khan wrote: "The more I see of you as a person, Granoff, and the more I read of your works, the better I like you. I feel indeed very happy to have launched on the beginnings of a relationship with you."[9]

In fall of 1963, Granoff wrote a letter saying that the extra room in his home was now to be Khan's, with or without notice, whenever he came to Paris—and he would be welcome to bring a friend. He sent Khan a set of keys. In return, Khan gave Granoff an open invitation to a room in his Hans Crescent suite. By January 1964, both men were signing their letters "With much love."

In March 1964, Granoff wrote that they would now enter the second phase of their friendship. The first phase, he said, had been a blind bet, guided by intuition. The second phase would be one in which they taught each other things, and this would make them a magnificent pair. Khan responded immediately: "Your letter is in perfect accord with my own feelings and assessment of the beginning and growth of our relationship as well as my aspirations about it."[10]

Their mutual respect for expensive living was often expressed through gifts. Granoff bought Khan a small clock (that Khan mourned when it finally broke in 1975), and Khan bought Granoff a decanter, a thick book on cars, and an engraved silver Hermès match box (that he showed me when we first met). On one occasion, awaiting Granoff's arrival in London, Khan reported: "[I am] excited like a child because I know Wova is bound to bring me gifts. And I have a surprise for him too: a ceramic model of a 1908 Bugatti."[11]

Khan became obsessed with the work of Jacques Lacan very early on in the friendship. Under the tutelage of Granoff, he became one of the first English-speaking analysts to grasp what Lacan was saying. (Lacan wrote in French and his work was not yet translated into English.) Khan recognized Lacan's genius when almost everyone in the IPA was dismissing him due to his deviations in technique and the scandals of his private life. If Lacan wore lifts in his shoes to make himself taller, if Lacan had a reputation as a womanizer, if Lacan broke rules and was deceptive at times in order to get his way, Khan did not care—the more important point was that he was developing an innovative theory: "You write that I shall have to put up with Lacanism. I do not have to put up with it, my dear Wova, because I enjoy it!"[12]

Lacan believed that the unconscious of all people is structured like a language, but Khan thought that Lacan's ideas were particularly well suited to people who spoke and thought in French. While he admired Lacan's thinking, he was also a critic. He was bothered by what he saw as Lacan's lack of concern for facilitating health in a patient: "I think Lacan is lacking in the human responsibility and responsiveness to the analytic clinical process."[13] And he disagreed with Lacan's privileging of language as the way to study the unconscious: "I do think that Lacanians fail to understand that language, although a creative instrument, cannot become a substitute for affects or relationships."[14] Khan's critique was a contrast to the thinking of most of Granoff's peers.

Upon Granoff's urging, Khan introduced him to Middle Group/ Independent ideas such as nonverbal relating and the True Self—ideas that had not yet crossed the Channel to France. Granoff told me that Khan exposed him to this thinking for the first time.

Throughout his London years, Khan gravitated to Paris. He resonated with French thinking and French life, and he knew that he could learn things from Granoff that he could not learn in England. Living in the West, it was clear that he had to modify the patterns he had learned in childhood, but he was temperamentally at odds with the principles of compromise that guided British life. Granoff showed him a totally different way of getting things: he was a charmer and a master of the use of intrigue, scheming, and behind-the-scenes statesmanship. Khan would not adopt Granoff's style in dealing with psychoanalytic politics, but he did take in important new information about the subtleties of personal relating.

In the spring of 1964, as Khan was preparing for a lecture tour in the United States, Granoff felt compelled to mentor him about how to "conquer" America. He himself had traveled widely in the United States and he thought he had important things to teach his friend. In his letters, Granoff encouraged Khan to retain his exoticism and not to try to fit in, because, he wrote, it would be better if the Americans wondered about who he was and even felt some anxiety.

As things went, Khan had an extremely successful tour of the United States. Now Granoff wanted even more for him: he wanted Khan to succeed in France. In a strongly worded letter, he did his best to convince Khan to try it his way, claiming that what worked in Great Britain and the U.S. would not serve for France. He advised a strategy in which Khan would make more use of references to French authors in his publications and completely avoid references to the work of the American ego psychologists, who were not valued in France.[15] Furthermore, he urgently insisted that Khan immerse himself in studying French, with the goal of becoming a fluent speaker and writer.

Khan wrote back immediately, accepting only parts of Granoff's advice:

Wova! Your letter was magnificent. I shall not quibble with inaccuracy of detail here and there. Instead, let me thank you heartily for a wonderfully insightful, explicit and articulate letter.

When you advise me to really learn French and not toy with it anymore, I respect your insistence. I promise you, my good friend, that I shall learn French in the next year.

I want to learn French not because I want to publish analytic papers in French or practice in Paris—I assure you that I find the resources of the English langauge more than adequate for that purpose—but because I find that I need it as a nutrient and an expressive idiom. My mind and sensibility militantly are searching for that increment of language and metaphor which, to my way of feeling, only the French literature and language can provide. But it is essentially for my creative mind that I need it. And this brings me to my basic disagreement with your letter. Let me start again from a slightly different angle.

So far, we have met and experienced each other essentially as persons and individuals in society. We have not encountered each other as intellectuals. I am essentially an intellectual. By this I mean that the life, activity and rhythm of the creative mind is my basic pursuit in life. It is precisely this that has brought me out of my feudal backwater in the Punjab to London, Europe and America. The life of the mind and its

fullest expression is my only true obsession in life, and towards its realization I expend all my energies: moral, aesthetic, libidinal, social, professional, and familial. Even psychoanalysis is not an end in my life: it is
a means to the articulation and realization of my creative mind. . . .

I am not really interested in the politics that infest the psychoanalytic societies. . . . It is the creative mind, in myself and others, that fascinates and interests me.

If I use a certain jargon in my papers, it is not to solicit the sympathy
of any group or person, but because at present that complex of concepts
I find handy and useful to think with about my clinical material. I shall
never borrow a concept or avoid another to promote myself either politically or culturally. No, I shall never corrupt myself with that sort of
intrigue.

You, my dear friend Wova, are essentially an aesthete who is a man
of action and a political animal. I am not. I act merely to survive. Otherwise, all actions in me are in the service of the creative mind and its life.
I do not mean anything grand or noble by the concept "the creative
mind." To me, it is just a way of life.

Of course I would like to experience and be involved with the mind
of the European analysts: learn and be influenced by them. But not because I want a politico-geographical cultural cum professional habitat for
myself.[16]

If Khan had been a more political man, the two friends would have
been a formidable pair and they might indeed have taken Europe by
storm, something Granoff was hoping for. But they were now coming
up against the limits of their compatibility. Granoff was fascinated by
"psycho-politics" while Khan lacked that interest and preferred to think
about the creative power of the psychological mind. This is perhaps why
Granoff, in contrast to Khan, succeeded in having a huge impact on
psychoanalytic politics, while Khan's influence was more related to clinical matters.

The opportunity to watch Granoff take his time in working toward
a goal would be a more important contribution to Khan's personal growth.
Waiting was foreign to his temperament and to his learning—in Pakistan, his family could get what they wanted just by taking it. He wrote
to Granoff again a few days later, reflecting on their basic differences in
"style of existence":

No, it is no use matching and comparing our respective styles and techniques of living. We wager differently and we play the game called living with extremely divergent rules and expectations. Of course that is what constitutes the real attraction and interest we have in each other. . . .

I have just re-read your letters of the past three weeks. Your way of coping with the events you initiate and launch fascinates me. I am very interested in your capacity to keep so many events in alerted animation. You strive after results but are in no hurry to push happenings to a conclusion. This is so foreign to my temperament. . . . I am neither sly nor capable of complex intrigues. The identificatory pleasure of watching you at work is enormous.[17]

Events that occurred in 1965 would lead to the ending of this crucial friendship. But Khan would later write: "There was a very deep and joyous friendship between Granoff and me at one time, and I have rarely been so happy in a carefree way under anyone's coverage as in Granoff's."[18] And Granoff, talking with me more than thirty years later, recalled Khan with pleasure, nostalgia, and loyalty. "It was a friendship that ended badly," he said, "but it was an honor to have had such a time together."

CHAPTER 12

THE STOLLERS

The good Lord blesses me through my friends. I gloat
and do not feel guilty about my good fortune—it makes
me feel very special and spoilt indeed.
Letter, Masud Khan to Robert Stoller[1]

I am hungry to get to London and to really talk with you—to laugh
and yell and argue, to be astonished and thrilled and to be together
again in the loving friendship we share.
Letter, Masud Khan to Robert Stoller[2]

Khan's crucial friendship with the California analyst Robert ("Bob") Stoller (1924–1991) was even more significant than the one with Wladimir Granoff, and he had a separate close friendship with Sybil Stoller, Robert's wife. Considering the chance circumstances of their meeting and the fact that the relationship had huge ramifications, it does not seem overly dramatic to say that the friendship between Khan and the Stollers was meant to be.

They met in 1964, when Khan came to Los Angeles to give a talk at a meeting of the American Psychoanalytic Association. When the person who had planned to pick up Khan at the airport became suddenly ill, Robert went instead. The two men, who were meeting for the first time, connected with each other during the short drive. Stoller dropped Khan off at the Ambassador Hotel, where he was sharing a suite with the analyst Eleanor Galenson and her then-husband, the analyst Sam Guttman. Khan had requested this arrangement because he was phobic of hotels and wanted company.

Galenson told me what happened there:

Masud looked like royalty, and even had special dress, including a tur-
ban hat that he wore everywhere. Sam and I went to dinner with him
that first night. I wore a mink coat and lots of jewelry, which I had brought
with me from New York, because Sam had a political position in the
group, and we knew we would be doing a lot of socializing.

    The next night, on entering our joint suite, it was obvious that some-
one had been there. I think they were looking for Masud's baggage, because he had bought a lot of silver that he was taking back to the U.K.
But his silver was in a locked suitcase beneath his bed, and the thieves
never found it. Instead, they took my coat and all my jewelry. It was antique jewelry that my father had given me. My loss was great.

Galenson was so distraught about the robbery that she returned to
New York. Guttman no longer wanted a suite, so he canceled the remaining days of the reservation. Khan, now left alone with his hotel
phobia, called Robert to ask if he could stay at his house. Both Stollers
welcomed him, and the Khan–Stoller story began.

The Stollers' world was an American variant of the world of wealth and
culture that Khan had known in India.[3] Their home was a sprawling
structure of stone, wood, and glass, nestled in the serenely beautiful hills
of Rivas Canyon in the Pacific Palisades area just north of Los Angeles.
There was also a beach house in a walled community in Malibu.[4] The
entire Stoller family, which included four young sons, was blessed by
physical attractiveness. One acquaintance, a European man now in his
seventies, told me that Robert was the most handsome man he has ever
seen.[5] And an anonymous family friend recalled the Stoller boys on the
beach at Malibu: "They looked like gods: tan, blonde, and athletic."

    One thing that Khan especially valued was that the Stollers, who were
world travelers, were not intimidated by him. Roger Stoller (b. 1954), a
younger son and twin brother to Jonathan, told me: "I remember Khan's
first visit well. He was like a regal prince, walking around in capes and
tunics, clearly of a different world. He fit into our environment like a
great piece of living sculpture."

    Khan gave his paper at the conference, then chose not to attend the
other talks. Instead, he spent his days with Sybil as she went about her

errands. In the evenings, he joined in family activities and then stayed
up late, talking alone with Robert. He summarized that first experience
"chez Stollers" (Khan's phrase) in a letter to Robert:

> Meeting your family, as a group and as individuals, has been a deeply
> enriching experience for me. From our very first talk . . . I felt at ease
> and confident with you. This is rather rare for me. My social alacrity of
> manner is a mere screen for both shyness and a built-in negativity against
> all strangers. It has taken me a long time to accept that the species has
> more people in it than my father's peasants. This sounds ridiculous, but
> it is true.
>
> When I met Sybil, I was nervous and diffident. So often, my rela-
> tion to a man has been thwarted and crippled by the simple fact that they
> had wives [sic], and I could not bear these good ladies. Sybil found such
> a quietly affluent good-humoured and ironic way of putting me at ease
> that we were friends before I had recovered from my defensive edginess.
> What sponsored this mutuality was partly that safely traumatic experi-
> ence of being driven by her from the Ambassador Hotel to Rivas Can-
> yon at 70 miles an hour. I was convinced she was colour blind because
> she interpreted all amber light signals for green and hurtled on happily.
> When we reached your home, I felt safe in her hands and in trust. This
> was a very wonderful feeling indeed. She has a way of being [that is]
> without strain or anxiety, yet with a quiet of reserve, which is marvelous.
>
> And then your children: the whole sapful bunch of them, with their
> alert, lively and shy quietness of manner. How unlike the American chil-
> dren I have met before.
>
> And so the Stollers grew on me and seeped into my sensibility.[6]

Upon his departure, Khan left a short note for Robert: "Thank you
for sharing your home and your family ambience with me. If there is
anything you can get from me, it is yours for the asking."[7] On the plane
home, he wrote to the Stollers as a couple, with special points addressed
to each of them separately.[8] From London, he wrote two letters, both
to Robert. In the first one, he said that he would like to establish a correspondence with Robert, adding: "I write with pleasure, it is a way of
living for me."[9] In the second, he enclosed several of his published articles with the request that Stoller read them and respond with comments. He also laid out terms for a separate relationship he wanted to
have with Sybil. He gave Robert a decree: "Please tell Sybil I am going

to establish a split technique of correspondence to you two. The letters to you will be typed because they are thinking letters, and I need their copies to be able to refer to. To Sybil, I shall write with the inchoate extravagance of my own handwriting."[10]

Writing his first letter to Sybil a few days later, Khan told her he wanted to correspond with her and he set three requirements. First, he said, the correspondence had to be private—she could share it only with Robert. Second, he wanted acknowledgment of all his letters and a prompt response. And third, he asked that she stamp all the letters adequately, so that there would not be any postage due. Sybil readily agreed to all these terms.

For the next two decades, Khan maintained separate correspondences with both Stollers, with intellectual letters to Robert and more personal ones to Sybil. The Stollers carefully preserved the correspondence, with Robert also preserving drafts of his responses. True to his word, Khan's letters to Robert were almost always typed, while the letters to Sybil were written in his large script, with the flowing black ink of his Mont Blanc pens. Many of the letters to Sybil are over twenty pages long.

At the time when he met Khan, Robert Stoller was known only in his local analytic world. A psychiatrist and psychoanalyst on the faculty of the University of California–Los Angeles (UCLA) Department of Psychiatry, he was a leading expert in the fields of sexuality, gender development, erotica/pornography—and the sexual practices of primitive tribes in New Guinea. He is especially remembered for theories about core gender identity and "primary femininity," work that called into question the Freudian idea that biology is destiny. Although Stoller was in general a conservative man, some of his ideas were controversial; for example, he claimed that perversion should not be a separate diagnostic category, since all people are perverse. By the end of his life[11] he had achieved a lasting international reputation, as the author of eleven books and over 150 articles.

Stoller was aware that there was an apparent discord in the fact that although he seemed to be an exceedingly wholesome person, he was studying the darkest sides of human nature: cruelty, revenge, humiliation, and hatred. He addressed the discrepancy in a letter to Khan: "You know, it is really odd. I write of rage and corruption, and I live in peace and love. There should be some kind of hypocrisy therefore in my papers, but I don't feel it. And yet I certainly don't learn about hatred and destruction from Sybil and the boys."[12] He said that his own life really was rather mundane: "[My] story is, of course, as empty of drama and pain as your life is full."[13]

He was attracted to Khan, who was a very different kind of person, because he knew they could be complementary—as a family member commented, "Masud had much of what Bob wanted." Stoller was lonely at UCLA and did not feel stimulated by most of his colleagues; he almost always brought his lunch in a brown bag and ate alone. His favorite colleague at UCLA was Ralph ("Romi") Greenson (1911–1979),[14] a man who, like Khan, had a flamboyant charisma. (Greenson has acquired international renown as the author of a conservative book on psychoanalysis, but he was better known locally for his outspoken manner and his willingness to treat difficult patients, such as Marilyn Monroe, in a nontraditional manner.)

Stoller responded quickly to Khan's letters. In response to the first letter, he agreed to enter into a correspondence: "What I ask of you is your friendship, to be able to talk with you about analysis and analysts, to argue ideas, to relax as we talk together."[15] In response to the second, he wrote that he had read the articles and admired the "honest, solid, and dependable work" reported in Khan's case descriptions. Over time, the two friends shared their frustration with the dishonesty of analysts, who they believed hid the details of their actual work with patients and used jargon for the purpose of impressing others rather than sharing information.

For the first years of their friendship, Khan was Stoller's mentor. Up to this time, Stoller had been working in relative isolation: "My main excitement comes from discovering my own thoughts on a subject."[16] Even for his important work on core gender identity, he had not read the relevant literature: "I have a feeling that keeps recurring while reading your papers: an awareness of my ignorance of the literature related to mother–infant relationships. As you move so easily and gracefully through this literature, I am for the first time aware of my ignorance."[17] This weakness meant that his writing was not taken seriously in the analytic world. Khan was an expert at distilling the essence from an author's works and putting it into context, and over the years he helped Stoller by introducing him to a wide range of analytic writings.

One of Khan's first mentoring gestures was to send Stoller a copy of Winnicott's *Collected Papers*.[18] Then, acting as review editor of the International Journal of Psycho-Analysis (IJPA), he asked Stoller to write a book review—even though Stoller had never published there and was relatively unknown to most of the readers. The IJPA reached a large and important audience because all members of the International Psycho-analytic Association were required to have a subscription. Stoller did not feel qualified to write the review, but he accepted Khan's offer knowing that it would be a growth experience. Later he regretted the decision, believing that he had compromised a personal commitment to succeed on his own.[19]

Writing came easily to Khan, but not to Stoller, who told Khan: "Getting ideas is so easy; making them intelligible and interesting is very difficult for me."[20] It is obvious from Stoller's letters that he was capable of excellent writing—some of his descriptions of Khan are exquisite, especially in a correspondence he had with the French analyst Victor Smirnoff. Yet he failed to use his verbal gifts in his professional writing. As a proponent of precise empirical reporting, he presented much of his research in the form of verbatim transcription and videotaped interviews that did not include data analysis or theoretical speculation.[21] Khan's feedback to Stoller was that his writing was lucid but not deep enough. He felt that Stoller's easy life limited him from taking risks, a belief that Stoller shared: "I used to want to gobble up the world—to do and be so much. However, it is hard to maintain that attitude when one is physio-logically and psychologically fully gratified."[22] Khan tried to help with tips on writing,[23] but his professional influence on Stoller was mostly in the area of introducing him to the wider psychoanalytic world, thereby facilitating his international fame.

Stoller's contribution as a crucial friend to Khan would be significant. In his own person, and through his wife and children, Stoller provided a Western home where Khan could have stability and sanity, things he desperately needed. Jonathan Stoller told me, "Bob [the Stoller children called their father by his first name] was a role model for Masud about how to sublimate perversity and still have a house and a wife." Khan wrote to Stoller, "I am grateful to you for your solid common sense and sympathy."[24]

One of Stoller's early gifts was that he helped Khan to set priorities. He encouraged him to concentrate on editorial work and writing, and discouraged him from giving too much of himself to the institute. Stoller was a champion of Khan's unique gifts to psychoanalysis, and he wanted him to protect his time and energy: "Be careful not to burrow into the organization (the Institute and Society) so deep that you won't surface. I am sure everyone is grateful to you for doing a beautiful job, but we don't have forever to get around to the creative things. You are spending yourself with administrative and teaching work and they will gladly eat off your flesh and it may even feel good to you while they gnaw away. But you are an artist and there are so few in psychoanalysis."[25]

Khan came to have enormous respect for Stoller, and in his Work Book comments, he is consistently positive about him. He thrived on Stoller's compliments: "Received a letter from Bob about my introduction to DWW's *Collected Papers*. Bob's praise is so knowing and solid and supportive. . . . This harassed and sagging day is suddenly singing with joy."[26] Both men regularly signed their letters, even typed professional letters, with "Love," the same way that Granoff and Khan signed their correspondence.

Sybil Stoller was not a crucial friend to Khan and the two did not effect deep change in the other. What Sybil did do for Khan over time, however, was extremely important: with her expectation of high standards of behavior, she stabilized him and had a healthy impact on his life. Khan described Sybil as an "extraordinarily ordinary" woman,[27] and she does seem to fit that description. Roger Stoller said about his mother,

> Sybil flows easily on a surface level and she doesn't perceive the deeper levels. She's very uncomplicated. Bob used to say that she hadn't ever experienced trauma. In Hawaii two years ago, I sat with her every morning on the beach and I asked her to tell me all her memories. And her most traumatic memory was when her dog died.

Right from the beginning, the two enjoyed, in Sybil's words, "a click of personality." She did not mind Khan's strangeness—in fact, she enjoyed it. She told me that she experienced him variously as "a boy," "a girl-friend," "an exotic bird," and "a charmer." Although she was close in age and very attractive, the complications of sexuality were not present because, as Robert's wife, Sybil was off-limits for Khan. He admired her enormously, however, writing in his Work Book, "The only happy, healthy and wholesome as well as handsome American woman that I have ever met is Sybil Stoller."[28]

Sybil made sure that the Stoller family would not be embarrassed by Khan. He was notoriously contemptuous of fat people, and when he visited, she vigilantly kept him away from anyone who was overweight. One time, at a California party, Khan somehow insulted the analyst-host, and Sybil insisted that Khan write a note of apology. More importantly, she was one of the only people in Khan's life who directly confronted him about his drinking, and as a result, Khan was never intoxicated when he was with the Stollers. Sybil told me,

> Alcohol wasn't a problem for Masud in the beginning of our relation-ship, and later, when I saw that he was drinking too much, I wasn't going to put up with it. I wrote him a letter saying I would not be in the room when he drank. After that letter, he never touched a drop when we saw him in London. When he came to California, I let him have one glass of wine a day— and I hid all the alcohol in the house. Once he tried to bribe our male housekeeper with $20 to buy Scotch and, when I heard about it, I told him, "If you want to drink, I'll take you to the airport."

Due to a phobia of water, Khan never took showers, although he was always clean.[29] Throughout their friendship, whenever they were together, he would ask Sybil to wash his hair, and she reports that she did so with pleasure. She also did other favors for him. Soon after their meeting, he sent her a check and asked her to open an American check-ing account for which either of them could be signatories. After that, he regularly gave her projects, like buying books or subscribing to journals.

Khan sometimes needed help to spend money, and Sybil was a good shopping companion.[30] She had excellent taste. On one visit to Lon-don, she helped him make one of his most extravagant purchases—an eighteenth-century Lord Nelson desk for his study from a London antique shop, costing 2800 pounds. This desk was his most prized piece of furniture.[31]

Over the years, Khan never doubted Robert's support, but he often worried that he might alienate Sybil. Once when he was involved in a relationship with a much younger woman, he wrote: "I wonder what Bob and Sybil will make of us. I have no anxieties about Bob, but Sybil can be fatuously American and puritanical in her judgments of lived life. Madness is foreign to her experience of living!"[32]

Khan related to the Stollers as individuals and also as a couple.[33] His own parents had had an intense sexual connection, and he saw this in the Stollers as well. But Fazaldad and Khursheed were of such different ages and the Muslim society was so sexist that they could not provide a model for Western-style mutuality. Khan needed this, because his lovers were now almost exclusively Western women. Commenting as he was leaving California after one of his visits, Khan wrote: "A quiet soft pain at leaving Bob and Sybil . . . Their style together gives me a model [for how to live as a couple]."[34]

The Stoller sons were another important part of Khan's learning about the West. He was fascinated as he watched them living their California lives in the 1960s and 1970s. Roger Stoller told me:

> I remember Masud in 1973 at the family beach house. He was amazed at me and Jonathan. We both had long curly hair like a lion's mane—blonde, from all our time in the sun—and we would come in from surfing and sit on the deck and meditate. He was interested in our meditation and he didn't know whether to laugh or to take it seriously. I had just taken est— Werner Erhardt was my seminar leader—and he didn't know what to make of that either.

The Stoller family had their share of problems, but Khan failed to see them. With this pattern, he had plenty of company. Roger told me: "As a family, we seemed to be perfect. It was hard for my brothers and me to develop as individuals, because the Stoller myth was so compelling and we were attached to it. Masud never saw these parts of the family —he bought the myth completely."

Over the years, Khan and the Stollers shared their friends with each other,[35] although Khan kept his Eastern friends separate. Through Robert, Khan became part of a subset of the California psychoanalytic world. The principal members of this subset were successful and somewhat flashy analysts. This group tended to affiliate at international

meetings, where they were distinctly noticed by more mainstream analysts. An anonymous Los Angeles analyst who was not part of their group,
commented with a mixture of bitterness and envy: "That whole group,
Wexler [Milton Wexler was Greenson's partner], Greenson, and Khan,
they all pranced across the scene at IPA meetings like little phalluses.
Robert Stoller too, he was pretty, pretty as could be, he fit right in."

Khan's favorite of Stoller's friends was Ralph Greenson. The two
men collaborated on several cases and Khan, like Stoller, experienced
Greenson as a kindred spirit.[36]

As the reader will see, Robert and Sybil Stoller continue to have a major
presence in almost every chapter that follows.

PART 4

CONTRIBUTIONS
TO PSYCHOANALYSIS

INTRODUCTION

*I am convinced I give of myself better to people through my work
and writing than through my living with them.*
Masud Khan[1]

To have a lasting impact, an innovator in psychoanalysis has to publish,
and Winnicott and Khan made enormous contributions through their
written records. Winnicott published in professional books and journals
as well as in the popular press. Khan published primarily in journals and
his major papers are collected in four volumes: *The Privacy of the Self* (1971),
Alienation in Perversions (1979), *Hidden Selves* (1983), and *When Spring
Comes* (1988; published as *The Long Wait* in 1989 in the United States).
The first three volumes of Khan's collected papers contain the writings
that are his most significant contribution to the literature of psychoanalysis.

The Privacy of the Self is a relatively conservative book that contains
papers showing how Winnicott's ideas about infants can be applied to
the treatment of adults. This first book was and is extremely well regarded; reviewer Janet Malcolm summarized it as "a sane and civilized"
book that "with its meditative essays on psychoanalytic history and

clinical theory and humane Winnicottean case studies, remains one of the best introductions to psychoanalysis in the contemporary literature."[2] An article entitled "The Concept of Cumulative Trauma," contained in this book, is the most widely cited of Khan's contributions.[3]

The next two books show Khan elaborating on Winnicott's work with more originality. *Alienation in Perversions* contains Khan's theories about perversions and also about relationship problems in people with False Self pathology. *Hidden Selves* is the most clinical of Khan's books, and it includes details of how Khan actually worked in analyzing patients who had pathology of the self.

The last book, *When Spring Comes*, was published without editorial revision at a time when Khan was a demented and dying man. It inspired, in Adam Limentani's[4] words, "a remarkable degree of hostility and criticism" and "a more than justified sense of revulsion," owing to a lack of respect for the usual analytic standards and the report of a case that included offensive anti-Semitic remarks. Although *When Spring Comes* contains some valuable material, it is not considered to be an essential part of Khan's legacy, and it caused enormous damage to his reputation.

Khan's writings in general provide many examples of the application of Winnicott's thinking to the analysis of adults. The American Harold Searles is perhaps the only analyst who has published a comparable amount of case material. Searles himself was an admirer of Khan's contributions:

> As a psychoanalytic clinician and theoretician, Masud Khan is unique. He possesses a most rare creativity of thought and of analytic technique, coupled with an encyclopedic knowledge of the contributions of his predecessors and contemporaries. In addition, he writes with lucidity and absorbing narrative skill concerning his work with his patients. . . . I have admired and never failed to learn from, Khan's writings for many years. His description of his work conveys far more of the living reality of psychoanalytic therapy (and of psychoanalysis) than do nearly all the descriptions of interviews that one ordinarily encounters.[5]

In the first four chapters in this part, I focus on the innovative theories that underlie Khan's clinical work. In Chapter 17, I describe Khan's editorial contributions to psychoanalysis, which include substantial editing of Winnicott's writing. Discussion of the controversial material from Khan's fourth book is deferred to Chapter 38.

CHAPTER 13

TRUE SELF

The essence of any enquiry into the concept of Self is the acceptance of a
paradox. The Self has to be autonomous to experience its Selfhood and yet
it (the Self) is viable in lived life only through and with the other.
Masud Khan[1]

Winnicott's (1960) theory of true and false self is one of his most important contributions to psychoanalysis. The theory was elaborated upon
throughout the 1960s by both Winnicott and Khan[2] and this chapter
describes their ideas, with an emphasis on the implications for clinical
work. (See Chapter 14 for a discussion of treatment of the False Self
through regression to dependence.) Khan's unique contributions include
ideas about how to work therapeutically to help people develop and
actualize what he referred to as their personal metaphor.[3]

Although Winnicott referred to the True Self in papers on regression in the 1950s, it was not until 1960 that he put forward his major
theory. The True Self, he said, is part of health and creativity. In contrast, the False Self sacrifices development in order to be safe.

Winnicott chose not to attempt a precise definition of self. He said
that the True Self was identifiable through its actions, specifically actions that showed spontaneity or creativity, and through an internal sense
of feeling real. Khan agreed that a definition was impossible and unnecessary: "Though each of us feels sure about what he means when he uses
the concept self, it is hard to communicate the meaning to another."[4]

In a paper that would elicit considerable controversy, Winnicott wrote
that the True Self is an "isolate, permanently non-communicating, permanently unknown, in fact unfound."[5] This idea of self as isolate has

been challenged by many writers. But, as was often the case for him, Winnicott did not totally accept his own idea—he also wrote that the self was intrinsically embedded in the outside world. In fact, he had enraged the Kleinians in the 1950s by emphasizing the importance of the outside world, saying in a famous quote, "There is no such thing as a baby."[6] Winnicott was not troubled by his contradictions, while Khan tended to have a more logical and internally consistent set of ideas, even if they changed over time.

Winnicott and Khan were psychoanalytic radicals working in an area that had little to do with the classic analytic thinking about drives, fantasies, and defenses. Their central concern was to create a space where the analysand could just "be," with the analyst contributing by not-interpreting. Winnicott stated that this kind of work was meant for patients who could not make use of interpretation, but, as Khan wrote, Winnicott worked in his modified manner with almost all his analysands, even those who were able to benefit from interpretation: "DWW was incapable of conducting a 'classical analysis' by his private sensibility and character, though he knew how it could be done. He chose only those patients who were not suitable for 'classical' technique, but who would fit his style of relating and non-relating. One hesitated to tell the truth about what DWW did, because what one told could so easily damage the true comprehension of his work."[7]

In one of many clinical illustrations of his own Winnicott-influenced style of treatment, Khan wrote about a patient who had not improved in a prior classical analysis:

[The patient] did something very simple in [a] session which was unusual for him. He took the blanket from the chair and wrapped himself in it and lay down. After a little while, he complained that I had given no interpretation at all, to which I responded that any interpretation on my part would undo his gain from having experienced respite from his mentation during the pain incurred by him over the weekend from his surgeons. He lay down quietly and gradually his breathing sank to a low rhythm, and he fell asleep. He woke himself up automatically just about five minutes before the end of the session. . . .

The next session [he] cried the whole length of the session; then he gradually collected himself, sat up, thanked me for not having disrupted his experience, and said that so far as he could recall, this was the first time he had experienced himself as a person living through a private emotional state to which he had absolutely no clue. . . . The real gain to this patient from this experience of himself was that he felt he now had available to him in himself a real experience of quietude and affective sentience, which he could contrast to the "chatter" in his head.[8]

Khan wrote that this work led to a dramatic change in the patient's outside life, so that he could now feel a private existence of self instead of being compelled to manic relating. The usual idea that symptom relief occurs through transference interpretation had nothing at all to do with the patient's improvement: "One of the paradoxes relating to Self-experience in the transference is that one can do nothing with it. It just IS."[9] Khan's technique here was a conservative application of Winnicott's theory. He had not yet added his personal signature.

By the middle of the 1960s, Khan was ready to start making his own contributions, as Robert Stoller had encouraged him to do. He told Stoller: "I have devoted two decades in the pursuit of [an apprenticeship to psychoanalysis] and I now have to wean myself from it and find my own style. I shall certainly give it a good try."[10]

In comparison to Winnicott, Khan was the more radical thinker. He began to believe that Winnicott's depiction of the isolate self was an idealized notion, something not seen in real life: "In humans today, an autonomous Pure Self is little other than a morbidity and a sickness."[11] Khan new idea was that psychological health involved interrelated living in both the internal and the external worlds: "Happiness is the capacity to be able to share oneself with oneself and with others."[12] Once he started thinking on his own, he never deviated from a belief in the importance of the outside world to the True Self.

Another difference in the ideas of the two men was that Khan saw potential for enrichment from the environment, while Winnicott thought that the environment could only facilitate or impinge.[13] Thus while Winnicott believed that it was extremely important to protect the True Self from impingement, Khan was more concerned about the problems of isolation: "Yes, the true MIND in each of us speaks only from isolation—and yet how terrible is the abyss of this aloneness & how many it has driven crazy."[14] Applying his thinking to clinical technique, Khan wrote that outside living facilitated growth in ways that went beyond analysis: "Yes, until life-experience augments and corrects the analytic experience, a person does not grow in analysis."[15] "Nothing can substitute for the curative sentience of actual living! But [often, our patients] shirk and evade living."[16]

Khan's privileging of environmental experience meant that he always wanted to know about his patient's life outside of the consulting room, a topic that is of less interest to the classical analyst: "Most analysts believe they can know a patient from his exclusive relating and communicating with them. I think that gives us a very biased view. How often have I been startled about a patient when they have quoted someone else's opinion of them."[17] He actively promoted a patient's activities in the outside world, both cultural and interpersonal.

An example of Khan applying his idea that the True Self is enhanced by interactions with the outside world comes from an analysand who was a musician and composer. The patient was in a panic because, by accident, he had heard music on the radio, and he felt it was adulterating his inner working out of a new song. Khan told him that the True Self did not have to fear adulteration, because it could assimilate and digest not-Self elements and stay intact.[18] It was, he said, inevitable and even preferable for the True Self to maintain a dialogue with the outside world and also with the False Self.

Khan's respect for the role of the environment is an enormous challenge to the main body of psychoanalytic thinking. The integration of a belief in the health of the True Self (which could be a composite of various selves) with a belief in the importance of the outside world is an achievement that is elusive even today. Khan in his heyday achieved this integration as well as anyone else has.

Khan's writing about intersubjectivity, one of the newest topics in contemporary psychoanalysis, is consistent with the most recent thinking.[19] For example: "All therapy is mutual—analysts forget that all too often. What is not mutual as cure is either magic or tyranny or swindle!"[20] "It takes two bodies and two minds for [psychotherapy] to actualise separately an experience which, though mutual, is unshareable."[21] In the preface to *Hidden Selves*, he provides a concise summary of his thinking: "[I am trying to show how] the clinical process gradually involves two persons in a mutuality of relating and, if things fare well, in time enables them to part from each other in a state of grace and awakened unto their hidden selves."

One of Khan's most prescient contributions involved the relationship of the self to the self. "Personal analysis, with the right person, always helps one, not so much to know oneself, as to render oneself Other to oneself, and thus gain the necessary distance for discourse with oneself."[22] This capacity is referred to in modern theory as reflexive self-awareness or mentalization.[23]

Khan made repeated reference to True Selves, implying that there is more than one Self, even in health. This idea is a precursor to contemporary thinking about the self.[24] Khan also proposed, in direct contrast to Winnicott's thinking, that the True Self could have significant pathology. For example, the True Self could be overly idolized, first by the mother and then by its own self.[25] And a person could have too much True Self functioning: "One must learn to protect oneself from oneself. The greed of knowing all of oneself is a perversion & a folly! One should let oneself be surprised from within—Yes!, but not overwhelmed and over-run."[26]

Following Winnicott's lead, and perhaps influenced by Lacan, Khan came to believe that cure was not an appropriate goal in analysis: "The [analytic] task is not so much to eliminate an illness or to render it innocuous, as to put a person in the total possession of his affectivity and sensibility, both in its positive and negative aspects, so that he can live to the maximum of his potential and in terms of full awareness of the handicap and the illness it entails for him."[27] Khan was rejecting the medical model of psychoanalysis, which assumed that analysands are sick people who need to be healed by the analyst. He saw his analysands— indeed, all people—as being like plants that, if healthy, were always growing and never at an end-state. Analysands did not need symptom relief—their symptoms would automatically disappear or become tolerable if the patient achieved "aliveness."

Winnicott had chosen not to emphasize the radical nature of his technique by disguising it as "research analysis." In contrast, Khan presented his work as an acceptable and even preferable alternative to traditional analysis: "My style in private practice has changed. I have shed all symbiotic bonds with dogmatic classicism. I now explicitly no longer take on patients for analytic care. I only take people on for 'Masudic care'—although I have never been more classical in my outlook."[28]

When Winnicott conducted "research analysis" or Khan provided "Masudic care," there was an implication that the analyst had permission to act outside of the usual analytic frame. In the consulting room, Winnicott was willing to hold the hand or touch the forehead of a patient,[29] something Khan did less freely. Both Winnicott and Khan were available at times for extended and even unscheduled sessions. Khan wrote that he saw one analysand "on a hot summer Sunday—that being the only time I could fit her into my schedule. I have learnt from Winnicott that in this type of case, one either sees a patient on demand or it is useless."[30]

Winnicott intervened mostly in the service of protecting his patients, but Khan often acted to provide aid or to enhance the outside environment. For example, he writes about handling a situation where a patient had stolen books by returning them himself, helping a wealthy patient to find and manage appropriate staff, and calling a connection in India to help a young adult patient gain admission into an exclusive ashram.[31] He also provided career guidance to patients. Many analysts make this kind of intervention for certain patients in special circumstances, but for Khan, intervention in the patient's environment bordered upon routine for his noncandidate analysands.

The theory underlying Khan's technique was actually quite simple. He believed that people lost the connection to their True Self when they constructed what he called a self-cure, a term he used to describe the workings of the False Self. The self-cure consisted of symptoms, addictions, or elements of personality style that were developed in order to control anxiety at the expense of being genuine. Khan's theory of treatment is in many ways a return to early Freudian thinking. Patients need to endure anxiety and even terror, as they shed the self-cure and face the deeper illness that has been masked: "The need of the mad . . . is to be and speak!"[32] "Psychic pain pushed to the limit becomes its own cure."[33]

One of Khan's favorite friends, the Pakistani diplomat Sahabzada Yakub Khan, gave me an example of how Khan described his thinking to people who were not analysts:

Sometime around 1980, Masud had invited me and two other non-analyst friends to dine with him at his home, which was also his professional office. As we waited, we heard the doors to the consulting room open and close as Masud escorted his patient out. His final words were, "Now remember—your trouble is that you are not prepared to suffer." We heard that very clearly. Then he came into the dining room and I said to him, "We have nothing to do with your professional life, so we don't need to know the details about your patient. But here she has come to see you, a person who is in agony, she is paying a high fee—so what do you mean by saying this to her? You are her only solace and consolation and you tell her she is not prepared to suffer! Why?"

Masud answered very briefly, making it clear that he would not discuss his patient. He said this: "Suffering is like a minefield that you have to go through and you have to grit your teeth and nobody will be able to help you. But if you will endure, then you will end up suffering immeasurably less than if you try to deny or repress your suffering—because it will return to you in disguised ways, it will fester, it will be redoubled—and you will be perplexed, as you will not know the source of your troubles. But if you face it, then—and only then—you can control it."

In considering Khan's contributions, it is essential to make a distinction between contributions made when he was a relatively healthy man as opposed to those from the period when he was deteriorating. Starting in the mid-1960s, he began to have extraanalytic relationships with patients that were often in the service of his own needs. Usually, his need was for companionship. For example, he went to movies with patients, shared dinners with them and their spouses, played card games, and watched TV with them.[34] In the extreme, his need was for a sexual relationship. This openness to outside relationships with patients was a consequence of his willingness to break the classical frame. Once the analyst starts breaking rules and adding parameters to the treatment, it requires considerable self-discipline and self-analysis to keep an exclusive focus on the patients' needs.[35] Significantly, Khan did not write about his "outside" relating to patients in the articles of his first three books.

REGRESSION TO DEPENDENCE

If you don't give up the False Self, you can't find the True Self.
But as you give up the False Self, it is a dangerous experience,
so you have to be absolutely and reliably "held" by another person.
Harold Stewart, British analyst[1]

The concept of regression to dependence took to an extreme the ideas that emerged from the new thinking described in Chapter 8. In the 1950s, Winnicott and his peer Michael Balint had written about its value for certain analysands,[2] but the idea of providing a space to allow for analytic regression did not become well known until the mid-1960s and later.[3] The Khan analyses reported thus far show that he originally worked in a relatively classical manner, with analysands experiencing limited regressions. In contrast, all the accounts of Khan analysands in the chapters to come illustrate his willingness to work with regression to dependence. This chapter describes the theory of regression as it was developed by Winnicott and modified by Khan.

In the course of my research, I spoke with many people who had been analyzed in England in the 1960s. With the exception of those analyzed by a Kleinian, they all spoke about whether or not they had experienced a regression to dependence in their analysis. That appeared to be the single criterion for determining if they had gone deep enough in their analysis to find their True Self, or if they were doomed to just being adaptive for the rest of their lives. Most of the analysands reported with regret that they had not experienced a full regression to dependence.

When people in England refer to regression to dependence, they are not talking about the kind of regression that many or most people experience in a deep analysis. Regression to dependence (also referred to as therapeutic regression to dependence or regression to psychotic dependence) is something much less common. Analysands enter into a state of neediness where they cannot be responsible for their own survival. This means that, like babies, they require absolute protection from others. People having this experience have to be able to take time out from ordinary life, and sometimes they cannot maintain a job or be responsible for child care until they come out of the regression, which can take weeks or months. As one analysand told me: "Most people didn't have the opportunity to have the experience because, as Khan used to say, 'To have a major regression, you have to have money.'"[4]

Neither Winnicott nor Khan ever said that regression to dependence was a necessary part of a complete analysis. Regression to dependence was meant only for analysands who present primarily with a False Self, where a conservative analysis would not work because the analyst would not be able to communicate with the True Self. Nevertheless, it seems obvious that those who believe in the value of regression will promote the experience in subtle or unsubtle ways. A man who went for a consultation with Winnicott remembers that his first question was: "Do you have any cot [i.e., baby crib] recollections?"[5]

Analysts working with regression to dependence use the same technique as that described in the previous chapter to help people find the self: they provide a safe space and refrain from interpretation. When the patient presents primarily a False Self, a significant regression develops automatically, without the analyst's urging. The patient experiences an "unfreezing" as the False Self is shed and a True Self is experienced.[6] As the patient lives the experience, there is no need for verbal understanding.[7]

An essential component of regression to dependence is what Winnicott refers to as management, in which the analyst assumes responsibility for ensuring the patient's safety, usually with the help of family members. The content of the sessions is not important—as Winnicott wrote: "[E]verything boils down in the end to what I have tried to describe as the survival of the analyst. [W]hen the patient gets towards this very serious state of affairs, then almost anything can happen and it is irrelevant. The only thing is arriving at the point at which the risk is taken and the analyst survives or does not survive . . . without retaliation."[8]

Although it might be imagined that regression to dependence is a kind of passive bliss, it is usually a terrifying and painful experience. Patients lose their sense of having a base as they experience infantile feelings without the added support of adult defenses. Thus Winnicott wrote, "If we are successful we enable the patient to abandon invulnerability and to become a sufferer. If we succeed, life becomes precarious to one who was beginning to know a kind of stability and a freedom from pain, even if this meant non-participation in life."[9]

Regression to dependence is inherently a two-person experience. The analyst simultaneously experiences a personal regression, even as he/she continues to be an observer and regulator.[10] The experience will lose its intensity unless the analyst *allows* a descent to madness, rather than trying to bring the patient to a sanity that would be premature.[11] Winnicott wrote that this kind of work was suitable only for therapists who were able to tolerate extremes of emotion: "The analyst must be temperamentally suited for this kind of deeper work which is not always successful in terms of cure [and] could be described as cruel. When it succeeds, of course, the cruelty and the suffering are forgotten."[12]

At times, a regressed patient may develop a delusional transference that causes the therapist to have a direct experience of the patient's primitive state. Several analysands of Winnicott remember him crying at times during their treatment, and a regressed patient may have been responsible for his first coronary.[13] Winnicott protected himself by taking only one patient at a time into full regression to dependence, but he never wrote about limiting the number of regressed patients, and other Independents who worked using regressive techniques did not impose such a limitation on their practices.

Khan was an excellent student and as he learned about regression to dependence from Winnicott, he incorporated it into his practice and wrote about it. In one of his first published articles, he described a long treatment of a woman who went through a three-month regression to dependence:

> Though the working towards the regressive experience had been gradual and controlled, its ultimate emergence was sudden and absolute. . . . She lay down and quietly said: "Yesterday I was by that old lake again." I knew she meant she had been suicidal.

Then she started to cry, quietly, gently, and with the whole of her body. I could feel its reality and pain in myself. There was nothing of her strength left, she felt; and this also I could feel. It is hard to define this in words, as in my counter-tranference experience I registered it with the whole of my mental and body sensibility. In this phase I had to learn more and more to rely on and use my body as a vehicle of perception in the analytic setting. . . . I told her that I knew how much pain and frustration she was experiencing, but that it was exactly for this that she had sought treatment. Now she was really ill and helpless. I bluntly asked her how much she could manage for herself. "Ten per cent" was her answer. I told her that I would try to help her find the rest of the ninety percent, but she would have to be very patient with me.

[D]ependence on me was near-absolute. I helped her with her reality affairs whenever she asked for help. My role in the situation was basically and dynamically this: to be there, alive, alert, embodied, and vital, but not to impinge with any personal need to translate her affective experiences into their mental correlates. I tried many experiments with modes of being still with her. If I was not all there in my body-attention she would register it straight away. I could never quite find out how she registered it, but I could always sense it had happened by the change in the affective rhythm or a new slant of material emerging next day.[14]

Failure experiences occur when a benign regression becomes malignant,[15] where nothing the analyst does is helpful and the safety of the patient cannot be assured. Management of the situation is then an extreme challenge for the therapist. Khan wrote: "Nowhere does an analyst's personal style show so vividly as in the handling of the regressed patient."[16]

The early experimentation with regression to dependence included examples of patients who ended up doing badly. One of the most disastrous of the failures, especially disastrous because it involved several innocent people, occurred in the practice of Winnicott's analysand, Harry Guntrip. In 1965, one of Guntrip's patients (who had already had ten years of treatment) began to remember for the first time some extremely traumatic memories. When he became increasingly regressed and agitated, Guntrip gave him an emergency session, where the patient reported that he was thinking of killing himself and Guntrip as well. The session was just prior to a weekend, and Guntrip made plans for the patient to enter a hospital that Monday. However, the patient and his wife went on to have what the wife called "the happiest weekend she could remember,"[17] and the husband then refused to enter the hospital. The next week, however, he got worse, and Guntrip was too busy to give him another emergency session. The husband then killed his wife, their two children, and himself.

Guntrip experienced the murder/suicide as the worst tragedy of his entire career. He realized that the regression had gotten out of control and become too real, and that he had failed to understand the significance of the good weekend, which might have been a consequence of his patient's relief at having made a decision to act. But Winnicott reassured Guntrip with an unusual comment: "I think you were as near to a perfect 'cure' in this case as you will ever be."[18] With this, Winnicott seems to have been referring to the patient's statement in the emergency session that he had considered killing Guntrip. If actual murder had not taken place, the verbalization would have been an example of Winnicott's concept of object usage,[19] where the patient psychologically kills the object (analyst) and the object survives, showing the patient that he could feel the most extreme destructive thoughts without actually harming anybody.[20]

Even though Winnicott was an early expert on the acceptability of hate in analysts (and in mothers), having written a groundbreaking article "Hate in the Countertransference" in 1947, he was not known for being especially skilled at protecting himself from destructive forces in his practice. He was better at tolerating his patients' hatred than he was at expressing hatred, and he might not have modeled effective therapeutic responsiveness to hate for Guntrip.[21] Khan was probably a more effective analyst than Winnicott or Guntrip in the face of homicidal and suicidal regression because he was quite willing to hate his patients and to insist that he was the one with greater power. He refused to be tortured by patients and he felt free to interrupt what he described as victimization of the analyst.[22] It is interesting that there are no reports of Khan's analysands committing suicide or even requiring hospitalization, perhaps because of his comfort with negativity. In contrast, Winnicott was known for "dumping" regressed patients in hospitals and for the high number of successful suicides in his practice.[23]

A description of how Khan worked with malignant regression involves a case that was an emergency referral from a female colleague. The patient, an adolescent girl, had just pulled the analyst's hair and physically wrecked the consultation room. Since this was not the first time the girl had been violent and since she had already had a hospitalization, the analyst concluded that she could no longer "hold" her patient. She asked Khan to see the girl right then at 8 p.m. Khan agreed and he describes what happened soon after the patient came into the consultation room, refusing to sit down and "staring around like a caged animal":

> [The girl] threatened: "I am going to wreck this room, too. It has too many books and things." She looked menacing and I felt she meant what she said. So I said to her: "Before you try any of your antics, please come and let us shake hands." She hesitated, did not move, but put out her right hand. I stood up, went over, and took hold of her hand firmly.
>
> "Please try and squeeze my hand," I demanded.
>
> "I won't!"
>
> "In that case, I will squeeze yours!" . . . She taunted me: "You won't!"
>
> I started to squeeze her hand, harder and harder. Within a minute, she was crumpled on the floor, shouting: "Let go! Let go! You are hurting me!"
>
> "I mean to," I responded. There was a knock at the consultation room door. "Come in," I said, and I let go of her hand. Hearing her shouting, the houseboy had come, fearing there was trouble. She stood up. I told him it was all right and he went away. She was pretty shaken. I sat back in my chair and said firmly but gently to her: "You see, you cannot wreck my consultation room; Not only am I physically stronger and more agile than you, but I have staff to provide me with coverage. I don't need hospitals."[24]

I was able to interview this patient and I asked her if Khan had really acted as he described. She told me that the facts were not as stated. She had indeed destroyed her first analyst's office, but in the consultation, Khan had used words and a stern demeanor in order to make his point that she would have to behave differently with him. He had not squeezed her hand and she had not fallen to the floor in pain. Nevertheless, she said, the article provided an accurate description of the essence of what she had experienced.[25]

Much of the work of the Independent analysts of the 1960s has survived—for example, awareness of the importance of nonverbal experience, a willingness to treat more severe pathology, recognition of the importance of infant experiences in the adult—but the kind of treatments reported here have in general not survived. Today's innovative therapists must be willing to face ethical charges, malpractice litigation, and even criminal lawsuits—things that Winnicott and Balint and Khan never had to worry about—and as a result, experimentation is much less common. Patients still regress to dependence, but the regression is usually controlled through medication and it is not curative. As a consequence, there is less risk of malignant regression, but individuals who could benefit from a deeply regressive experience may not be able to find a therapist who will work in this way.[26]

PLAY THERAPY FOR ADULTS[1]

Psychotherapy has to do with two people playing together.
D. W. Winnicott[2]

Playing is the only antidote to all the daily fatalities of existence.
Masud Khan[3]

Winnicott wrote extensively about using play in therapeutic work with children, but in none of his writings did he give examples of how the therapist might play with an adult. It would be Khan who filled this gap by expanding Winnicott's theory to cover the adult population and providing clinical examples.

A rare story of Winnicott's play with adults comes from noted scenic designer Tony Walton, who saw him for a highly successful consultation in the mid-1960s. Walton's account shows Winnicott working in his inimitable style, which looks easy. It is only as one studies the complexity and seriousness of Winnicott's intervention that it becomes clear that his light and playful style emerged from an acute sensitivity to the individual person. The account of the consultation is presented here as a contrast to Khan's play style, which will be discussed later.

As described above (see Chapter 7), Tony Walton and his then-wife, actress Julie Andrews, were close friends of Khan and Svetlana in the early 1960s. Walton often stayed with the Khans when he was working in London and he had become especially close to Khan. In 1965, Walton was depressed about the ending of his marriage to Andrews, who had been his childhood sweetheart, and he went for a single consultation with Winnicott:

I've forgotten a lot of this because it was during my breakup with Julie and I was totally raw. Masud and Mike Nichols were my good friends and they were amazingly patient in making me talk. My nature would have been to conceal my emotions. Mike had referred me to an analyst in New York whom I saw for two or three sessions, which was very helpful. And Masud was always talking about Winnicott. I was about to leave for London, on my way to Spain, where I was designing the film of *A Funny Thing Happened on the Way to the Forum*. I'd been telling my story to Mike's analyst in a stiff-upper-lipped way—but then he asked me something about my baby daughter, and I completely came to pieces. At that point, he wrote out a slip of paper and gave it to me to take on the trip. It said, "I think you'll be okay, but, if not, contact this man: Donald Winnicott." Of course, I remembered that it was the same person who Masud was always talking about.

I hadn't thought that I would call Winnicott, but then, while I was in London, I felt a little flurry, so I made an appointment. Winnicott was by then quite deaf[4] and I had to shout to tell him my story. He asked all kinds of details about the relationship. Having to shout my answers was actually kind of hilarious.

Winnicott ended the consultation saying, "I don't know the girl, I've only seen her in movies. But I think I can tell from what you say that you were quite happy with her. Is that right?" "Yes," I answered. "Well," he said, with some drama, "then count your blessings, cut your losses, and cheer up!"

A week or two later, on location for the film in Spain, I felt that a dark cloud, which until then had owned me, had just lifted. I remembered his words and I thought, "Nobody could have said anything more perfect." I wrote immediately, with great gratitude, to tell him so. I was, and am still, profoundly moved by the consultation.

In this example, Winnicott perfectly matched his intervention to the subject, sensing correctly that Walton would remember his words and (eventually) be able to put them to therapeutic use. Walton is a man with an almost unbelievable amount of positive energy, and, although he was in despair at the time of the consultation, he was well suited temperamentally to make use of an intervention that a more sullen type of person would have dismissed or considered foolish. He was also immersed in the world of entertainment, and he could laugh at Winnicott's words. In fact he liked the words so much he later shared them with the film director Sidney Lumet, who gave them to the character Dorothy in his movie *The Wiz*—a most unexpected forum for the wisdom of Winnicott.

Winnicott developed his ideas about play through his spatula intervention. In thousands of mother–infant observations, he observed the rhythm and style of five- to thirteen-month-old babies in handling a spatula while sitting in their mothers' laps.[5] Babies who had the capacity to play showed three distinct stages: a heightened awareness of the presence of the mother; a period of hesitation; and then play, in which the focus shifts from the mother to the spatula. Infants, children, and adults play in a related manner, and their play occurs in an area of creativity that is variously called potential space, transitional space, or the area of illusion. This is a psychological space that is intermediate between internal and external reality, where illusions are not tested against reality. For example, a child's precious teddy bear is allowed (by the child *and* the mother) to have its reality as perfect-best-friend unquestioned.

Winnicott was interested in the problems that occur in adults who have not developed a transitional space. Not only are these adults unable to play, they also cannot use symbolism, fantasy, or dreaming.[6] Psychoanalysis is a kind of play, where the as-if experience is and is not real, and the adult patient sometimes needs to learn to play before anything therapeutic can happen: "[W]here playing is not possible, then the work done by the therapist is directed towards bringing the patient from a state of not being able to play into a state of being able to play."[7]

In Khan's opinion, a major flaw in analytic technique was that although a wide variety of play was used in child analysis, the adult patient was usually allowed to play only in words: "In adult analysis, we believe that analysands regress to childhood in the transference-neurosis, yet we refuse them playing outside the permutations of . . . language."[8]

Khan was one of the first analysts to understand that adult analytic technique could benefit from studies of the mother–infant relationship. He wrote: "Today, we are in danger of being smugly cocooned in those of our theories that make good sense and not letting our clinical experience question them. . . . The way out of this paralysis, so far as I can see, is to try and integrate the researches into the infant–mother relationship with our daily clinical work."[9] His awareness of the link of therapy to the care of babies is seen in a joking entry in his Work Book:

"The phone rang, I picked it up. A woman's voice enquired: 'Is this Knightsbridge Nannies?' [He was then living in the Knightsbridge section of London.] I replied: 'Almost, Madam, though not quite.' She banged the phone down. I was stating the truth alright!"[10]

Regarding technique, Khan wrote that the most important part of the treatment was to make a connection to the analysand: "I really do believe devoutly that the first obligation of every analyst is to meet the patient as a person, to find the patient as a person, no matter how fragmentarily and transiently, and only then to work on him or her with all the expertise of our skill and theory."[11] Here is one of his clinical examples:

> Saw the patient Barrie Cooper had asked me to see urgently. A calculatedly frozen [man]. I told him: "You have an illness in you alright, but you have not found a language to speak it!" He was sullen and willfully unmutual. I teased him into an as-if smiling tentativeness towards talking together. It worked. Shall see him again.[12]

This style of relating to adults is remarkably similar to the style described by the contemporary infant researcher Beatrice Beebe[13] for mothers who are optimally attuned to their infants. These mothers match the nonverbal patterns of the baby to establish a connection, and then modify the match by exaggerating some part of the connection, leading to heightened affective moments.

An early example of Khan working to develop the transitional space comes in a report of a child consultation he did in Pakistan:

> [Writing from Lyallpur, Pakistan:] Called on one Dr. Ihsan-ul-Haq. He is [a physician] from Edinburgh; a very quiet and thoughtful young man. He asked me to see a girl of seven with him. The child was reported by the mother to suffer from mild "attacks." It was obvious that they were of an epileptic nature. I watched carefully while Dr. Ihsan examined the child, who never left the mother's lap. She could speak only a few words, though she understood a great many. What impressed me was the mother's placid unconcern about her child as ill; she put all the emphasis on the symptoms, as a foreign body that the doctor should eliminate. There was little doubt in my mind that this mother had nurtured an autistic child. When I discussed it with Dr. Ihsan he was rather surprised

at my diagnosis, because the elder child is totally autistic and almost a mental defective at 11 years of age.

The mother, who comes from a very wretchedly poor family, has been jilted by her husband and lives with her parents. Evidently these children are her only source of security and sustenance. When Dr. Ihsan asked me how he should proceed with the case, I advised that slowly he should try to rouse a little concern and anxiety in the mother about her daughter as an ill person. Only then will the mother allow that distance where the child's ego-capacities can begin to function autonomously.[14]

In studying Khan's clinical contributions to adult play therapy, it is important to separate his earlier work from his later work. The early deviations from classical technique are lasting contributions to psycho-analysis. One such case was a twenty-four-year-old woman who was unable to function verbally or symbolically:

When she arrived for her first session, she announced in a maniacal voice: "I am not going to lie down and talk." I replied that [this] did not disturb me very much. I added, however, that it was not my usual style to have a patient trumpeting all over the place, and that whenever I got fed up with it I would ask her to leave, and there need be no ill-will on either side. There is always the next session. She looked up at me in a strange way and could barely hide her smile. Now I knew she had linked up with my playful and teasing use of the word "trumpeting." I was following a guide-line of Winnicott's here, who believes that if a patient has any capacity to engage the play in the clinical relationship, a lot can be done for him.[15]

In this example, we see Khan using words as a medium for play, not for the purpose of communicating meaning. In another article describing the same case, Khan tells how he supported the development of the transitional space by allowing the girl to scream at him, to stand during sessions, and to move around and touch his books: "Only touching per-sonalized the space and time for her and made it bearable for her to be in the analytic situation."[16] He made no attempt to interpret her rage or her incapacity to speak, but over time he introduced the use of words:

It would be wrong to say that the whole encounter was always mute. She spoke a little bit here and there, and I would verbalize the fluctuation of her mood or feelings as I could sense them in her body-presence. Gradually from this we built up a trust in each other, because she could now really believe that I could not only tolerate her incapacity to use language, but work with her at least minimally in spite of it. It was from these little details that an illusional space began to establish itself between us, and a distance was created which related us, and in this illusional space and distance she could begin to explore language as playing.[17]

As time went on, Khan's work in helping patients develop a transitional space included active intervention. Khan claimed that although he was getting "more personalised in my total social relation to the patient," he was at the same time "rigorously abstract in my psychic & affective responses."[18] This may have been Khan's goal, but evidence suggests that he was not staying as abstract as he claimed. It is at this point where readers may begin to diverge in their various judgments of Khan's work as being somewhere between "brilliant" and "destructive."

In a case presented in his third book, Khan writes about using games to help a patient develop his potential space. The patient was a wealthy and successful young man who suffered from paranoia, anxiety, and an inability to establish meaningful relationships. Khan tolerated lateness, bragging, and secrecy, and understood these not as resistance but as attempts to communicate. He took it upon himself as the analyst to help the patient to acquire the trust necessary to make a commitment. The analytic work was proceeding slowly when the patient brought Khan a backgammon set and offered to teach Khan how to play the game:

> While Jonathan was setting up the board to play, myriad ideas and apprehension scampered through my head. Was he intent on asserting his omnipotence and humiliating me? Was he trying to subvert the whole analytic process by this ruse? Then I recalled that only a few weeks earlier, when he was bemoaning his incapacity to converse with people, I had interpreted that he always tried to astonish or dominate with what he spoke, and did not realize that conversation in ordinary social intercourse is playing. Now he had brought me a game. I had the potential to change his gamesmanship into playing. I took the chance. . . .[19]

While playing backgammon with Jonathan, Khan decided that he could use the opportunity to teach his patient to play well, by converting his gamesmanship and his need to slaughter into relating, where he took into account the "person" of the other. As Khan and Jonathan played, they also talked and Khan got an understanding of how his patient had not had the opportunity to develop his self because he was always accommodating others.

In another case, Khan described playing in a more aggressive manner. In this case, words were again used as a medium of play. Mr. L. was a successful artist and furniture maker, despite the fact that one of his hands was severely mangled from a childhood injury. He suffered from an acute depression in which he had stopped working and stopped eating. He told Khan that his problem was that he was evil but he refused to tell why or to relate his history. Khan tolerated the noncooperation.

When Mr. L. finally started to engage Khan, he talked in a manner that Khan experienced as a contest in which dialogue alternated with long silences. At times of separation, such as vacations, Mr. L. withheld crucial pieces of information, which kept Khan tantalized and teased. Instead of interpreting, Khan engaged in playful verbal combat with his analysand. Mr. L. became unfrozen and, like a baby playing with his mother, was able to discover himself (and to revise the story of himself as evil) at the same time as he related to another person. When Khan wrote up the case, he reported that his technique had essentially been play therapy: "I felt sure that enabling Mr. L. to 'play' verbally into conversation what was so rigidly controlled intrapsychically, was more important than intruding with insightful interpretations."[20]

A very controversial example of Khan's play technique is seen in a case that he reported to the Los Angeles analysts Ralph Greenson and Milton Wexler, as part of a project they were conducting on "unexpected failures in analysis."

Mr. [Q.] [disguised initial] had unexpectedly brought his rather unruly and savage dog [a large and aggressive breed] to a session. It had created a climate of terror in my environment, because when the servant had opened the door and encountered the dog with him, he had shown distinct signs of fear and panic. Then our pet small poodle, smelling a dog, had come rushing in, and been so terrorised by the huge dog that it had wetted the carpet and the servant had picked him up. When I came to collect the patient, I met the servant and was told of the presence of [Q.] with his dog. When I collected him from the waiting room, I too had a distinct sense of threat of violence. I tried to behave casually and accepted the situation as such.

In the consultation room, the patient quietly lay round and started to talk in his usual rigid and compulsive way, as if no new element had been introduced by him. Meantime, the large dog walked around restively. I was distinctly frightened. The only interpretations I offered towards the end were that: 1. He had made no reference to the presence of the dog during the session; and 2. He had brought his violent savage Self in the shape of his dog, but it was dissociated from him and no part of his organized self-experience as his own savage murderous potentiality. The session ended. I noticed a smug look on his face. He remarked: "Sorry you have been traumatised by my dear dog and look so afraid. I wish I could experience fear sometimes." The session ended.

In the next session, before it started, I found myself chiefly concerned with the patient's remark: "I wish I could experience fear." Quite spontaneously, I decided to surprise him. I instructed the servant to send the patient straight to the consultation room. I knew he was coming alone because I had told him he cannot again bring the dog with him, and instructed my staff not to let him in if he did. When I heard the patient come, I placed myself quietly behind the door. As he entered, I playfully but with firm aggressive strength grabbed him by the back of his neck. I did not attack and alongside said, "Hello, Mr. [Q.]." . . . The patient was frightened but did not experience this as a traumatic or humiliating event. Quite the contrary, the patient made of it a positive play experience and it released a sort of confidence in him which enabled him to tell me of other destructive actions in his childhood.[21]

Khan considered his technique of jumping out and grabbing his patient to have been effective. In claiming that he did not attack, he is suggesting that the case shows successful object usage, where the analyst does not retaliate in response to aggression. Greenson and Wexler agreed: "Romi was enthusiastic and responsive but had little to say. Wexler was quietly attentive and made the very pertinent point that it seems I understood this patient very deeply at the unconscious level—his and mine—but not at the surface overt level. That is true."[22]

It is worth noting that, even if the intervention was successful, the use of action compromised the provision of a safe space, and, indeed, Khan goes on to report that the treatment ended prematurely.

Another example of Khan intervening aggressively is provided by Harold Bloom, the well-known literary critic and Shakespeare scholar. In the late 1960s, Bloom was referred to Khan by Professor Theodore Lidz of Yale. He describes his encounter with Khan as follows:

In the middle of the journey, at age thirty-five, now thirty years ago, I got very wretched and for almost a year was immersed in acute melan- cholia. Colors faded away, I could not read and scarcely could look up at the sky. Teaching, my most characteristic activity, became impossible to perform. Whatever the immediate cause of my depression had been, that soon faded away in irrelevance, and I came to sense that my crisis was spiritual. An enormous vastation had removed the self, which until then had seemed strong in me. At the suggestion of my Yale psychiatrist, I went abroad, but found myself so depressed in London that I went to see an eminent Pakistani psychoanalyst, at my doctor's recommendation. An instant hatred sprang up between the London analyst and me, so that I refused to see him again after three visits; but my fury was therapeutic and partly dislodged me from the dark night of the soul.[23]

Bloom gave more details in a letter he wrote to me:

Khan loathed me at first sight and let me know it, and I rapidly recipro- cated, though I believe that generally I am amiable enough. All that I truly recall is that he attacked me for being unkempt (I still am), told me innumerable times that he was much more intelligent than I was, and seemed to have read my earlier books. What I remember most vividly is that I walked out half-way through the third session because his abusive- ness became overtly anti-Semitic.[24]

Bloom came out of his depression after the consultation with Khan and went into a very productive period. He had a kind of religious con- version in which he immersed himself in Gnosticism, a nondogmatic way of knowing that emphasizes creativity, imagination, and aliveness.

The clinical problem originated as a clash regarding style. Khan believed in the importance of an immaculate self-presentation, whereas Bloom did not (and still does not, by his own report). Khan's rationale for his attack was that physical presentation is revealing of a person's effort to relate to the world and that sloppiness in a patient implies a sabotage of the treatment.[25] It is a credit to Bloom's ego capacities that he could mobilize reactive rage and emerge intact from the consultation.[26]

Every person has his/her own preferences for play. Winnicott's playful consultation with Tony Walton is characteristic of his gracious, wise, and endearing style, just as Khan's playful work with Mr. Q. and others reflects his relative comfort with aggression, haughtiness, and offensiveness. Khan played more roughly than Winnicott did. Although Winnicott tends to be revered while Khan is often maligned in current times, people who knew both men did not always prefer Winnicott, and, as the preceding chapter showed, Khan's willingness to be aggressive was at times effective and even lifesaving. A problem here is that rough play needs to be differentiated from bad play, which would be an interaction that the other person does not enjoy and in which he/she might even be harmed.

CHAPTER 16

PERVERSIONS AND ISSUES
OF SEXUAL IDENTITY

*I am sure that I myself have learnt more about the structure of character
and perversion from Masud Khan than from any other author.*
Eric Rayner, British analyst[1]

One of Khan's most important analytic contributions is his theory of perversity.[2] The term perversity refers to sexual behavior that is outside of the norm. For Khan, perversity was an aspect of False Self pathology, not a separate diagnosis. The sexual experiences of a False Self, he said, are repetitive, nonmutual, and ultimately unfulfilling, and the person does not feel "real" in the relationship. This was perversion, in his opinion, no matter how ordinary the physical actions or the fantasies were.

Even in his first years of training, Khan was comfortable talking and writing about the extremes of sexuality. The case presented in his membership paper was a homosexual, and he wrote about that case in two (unpublished) articles in the 1950s, a time when homosexuality was a much more controversial topic than it is now.[3] His later writing expanded to more unusual perverse practices and again, he was not reticent about writing on the subject of what his patients were telling him. In *Alienation in Perversions* and also in *Hidden Selves*, he provides such explicit sexual details that the American analyst John Gedo commented to me, "Some of Khan's papers are absolutely unique because they are subtly pornographic. Nobody else has gotten away with that in our 100 year history."[4] Khan's writing goes beyond Winnicott's, because Winnicott has almost no references to the sexual behavior of adults.

Given Khan's new way of looking at perversion, it was logical that the way to treat a pervert was to help him or her gain access to True Self functioning. Thus Khan wrote: "I have never started the treatment of a pervert with any intention to cure him of it or change it into something as-if-normal. The real issue is one of self-realisation."[5]

The development of his thinking over time can be studied by comparing accounts of a man with a foreskin fetish whom he saw for three separate analyses over a span of more than twenty years.[6] This adult man, who was a homosexual, was compelled to find uncircumcised young men on whom he could perform fellatio and then masturbate into their foreskin. He often was successful in his quest, but the relationships were never mutual and he was never satisfied. Over time, Khan came to see that the interpretation of internal dynamics was not helpful—instead, the man simply needed to be "companioned" and understood. As the man became more real in the analytic relationship with Khan, he experimented with mutuality in the outside world and was able to start living in new ways, rather than being compelled to repeat prescribed rote behavior. The American analyst Muriel Dimen, who is a contemporary expert on perversion, finds Khan's theory to have anticipated current thinking and she refers to the articles on foreskin fetish as "remarkable" and "exceptionally moving."[7]

One of Khan's most radical ideas was that a patient's outside engagement in perverse behavior *while in analysis* could be helpful for the treatment. This is an extreme contrast to the idea that the person should not act out the perversity, but instead talk about it in the sessions and allow it to become part of the transference, where it could be understood and interpreted. Khan believed that in actuality, patients do not generally bring their perversity into the transference, so that classic technique left the perversity unanalyzed. His observation was that analysands who were actively engaged in perverse relationships had current material that could be used in the sessions to further understanding. Furthermore, the fact that there was another person involved, a person with a separate subjectivity, meant that the perverse script might be disrupted as the patient started to be more mutual and care about the needs and wishes of his/her partner.[8] Through the outside liaison, the person could get access to the True Self, which, Khan said, always longs to be known: "Acting out through the technique of [sexual] intimacy breaks down the primary sense of isolation and establishes contact with an object, and through an object with the self."[9]

In the area of bisexuality, Khan and Winnicott together made an important contribution. They developed the idea that all people have a dissociated self that possesses qualities of the opposite sex. The idea was not new—it is a central part of Jungian thought—but Winnicott and Khan applied it to their clinical work involving issues of the self.

In one of his most well-known articles, Winnicott wrote about a session with a male patient in which, in the countertransference, he suddenly had the sense that the patient was reporting penis envy— something that a girl might feel, but not a boy. He came to understand that the patient knew he was male and presented himself to the outside world as a male, but that he had a dissociated side that was female. What the "girl self" needed more than anything was recognition. Winnicott's prior work with the patient had not been effective because he had never spoken with the "girl." In outside life, she had stopped the man (i.e., her male self) from having satisfying sex, because she had envied him and did not want him to find release in sex: "[The 'girl'] has always hoped that the analysis would in fact find out that this man, yourself, is and always has been a girl. . . . "[10]

Winnicott reported that although he had long been aware of bisexuality, he had not realized that there could be a complete dissociation of the male and female selves. His new understanding led to dramatic change in the patient: "Now that the new position had been reached, the patient felt a sense of relationship with me, and this was extremely vivid. It had to do with identity. The pure female split-off element found a primary unity with me as analyst, and this gave the man a feeling of having started to live."[11] Winnicott used this experience to develop his thinking about the differences between (female) being and (male) doing, two types of experiences that are present in both men and in women. This was a radical idea, since female being does not involve conflict, whereas conflict is the core of a person's existence in classical analytic thinking.[12]

Winnicott specifically stated that the female element in a man should not be considered homosexual. He said this was something that was difficult to discuss, since analysts were quick to label nonmale elements in a man as homosexual. In his view, homosexuality was a secondary matter that was "less fundamental and rather a nuisance when one is trying to get at a man's woman identification."[13]

Khan followed up on Winnicott's idea in work with an analysand who was a female with a dissociated male identity.[14] His patient was constantly discussing her promiscuous sexual behavior, but Khan, in the countertransference, did not experience her descriptions of sexuality as tantalizing; in fact, she herself did not seem aroused by the promiscuity. After a few months, the patient started talking about a foreign culture where males adopted younger boys as partners, and Khan sensed that she was experiencing herself in the transference as his boy partner. When he suggested to her that she had a male self that had not been expressed, she associated to an important dream where she had dressed up as a count. As they discussed her boy-identity, she began to feel more real and to have more satisfying and more committed sexual relationships. Her boy-self could now watch over her female behavior and protect her from being exploited by men. Khan acknowledges that with this case he was applying Winnicott's theory for the first time and that the interpretation seemed at first to make more sense to the patient than it did to him; he was surprised at how effective it was.

CHAPTER 17

EDITORIAL WORK AND PROMOTION
OF WINNICOTT

What I admired about Masud Khan was his editorial
drive and integrity.
John Charlton, editor at Hogarth Press

Khan's mastery of the English language was remarkable, especially since it was not his native tongue.[1] In the West, he showed sensitivity and significant talent as he edited a whole generation of international analytic writers. A colleague commented on files that he examined after Khan's death: "A cursory examination of [Khan's] personal papers revealed evidence of the care with which he dealt with hundreds of reviews, introductions to books, letters concerning the editing of papers and books written by friends and strangers."[2]

His talent was first used by his peers when they appointed him honorary librarian for the Institute of Psychoanalysis, which was the training and administrative arm of the British Psycho-Analytical Society (BPAS). In the early 1950s, he shared the position with Charles Rycroft and then from 1954 until 1974, he was the sole librarian.[3] From 1962 to 1967, he served as book review editor for the *International Journal of Psycho-Analysis* (IJPA), and from 1965 to 1968 as associate editor, under the editorship of John ("Jock") Sutherland. He was known for being open to publishing high-quality work, even when he disagreed with it.[4] At a time when international psychoanalytic writing tended to be conservative and somewhat boring, Khan and Sutherland kept the IJPA interesting. Khan loved to quote Sutherland's comment: "Our task has been to save psychoanalysis from the psychoanalysts."

As honorary librarian, Khan was automatically a member of the Publications Committee, and that meant that he was intimately involved with the International Psycho-Analytical Library (IPL). The IPL published books by analysts through a cooperative agreement with Hogarth Press, a subsidiary of Chatto & Windus. The Publications Committee of the BPAS chose the books and vouched for their content, with Hogarth's role limited to copyediting. John Charlton, editor at Hogarth/Chatto & Windus, told me that Sutherland and Khan "breathed new life" into the series, with the energy coming mostly from Khan: "Masud did all the real thinking on the Publications Committee for years." When Sutherland retired in 1968, Khan became editor of the IPL, and Sutherland became associate editor. Khan held this position until 1979 and he was the editor of thirty books, many of them psychoanalytic classics.[5]

Sadie Gillespie, a Kleinian analyst, remembers that Khan was supportive of new and inexperienced writers: "Masud was capable of acts of pure kindness. At meetings, he would often come up to me and, with nothing personal to gain, he would say, 'Sadie, write a paper. I'll help you—just ring me, I'll come over.' I was a nobody then."[6] The British analyst Peter Lomas also recalls Khan-as-editor in a positive light: "Many years ago, I was asked to edit a book for the Institute of Psychoanalysis. Khan was series editor and I sent the manuscript to him. He promptly telephoned and harangued me, with evident scorn, for including a contribution which he considered unworthy. It didn't take me long to realise that he was absolutely right. I agreed to change it and he helped me bring this about. I remain in his debt for this."[7]

Khan believed that it was his duty to contribute his editing skills to psychoanalysis, a duty he performed in the tradition of his feudal heritage: "The models of one's parental idiom stick deep to one's soul. I learnt the logic of impersonal devotion to service from my father's example."[8] He contributed thousands of hours to institute work, even though it took him away from his own writing and was not always enjoyable. Referring to a ten-volume publication of Freud's work by Penguin, he wrote to Victor Smirnoff: "I had to do slavish dutiful labour on the Penguin Freud's content list tonight. . . . It is the sort of work I really loathe doing and yet I have great expertise and facility with it."[9] He worked in the style of his father, making decisions mostly on his own:

"Editorial chores—one learns again and again that what one does not do oneself never gets done by others."[10]

But his work came at a price, and much of that price was paid by others. Ann Jameson (née Hutchinson) worked as secretary to the editor at the IJPA for eight years, starting in 1960. The office was in Mansfield House, New Cavendish Street, in those days, home also to the institute and its library. Jameson remembers that Khan was around more frequently than Sutherland and his presence had a huge impact: "Masud's powerful personality flowed onto everything, and we talked about him endlessly." Khan often treated the staff poorly, and she found it strange that Sutherland, who was always a gentleman, gave him total support. The library secretary at that time was a young country girl and Khan would treat her like a servant, ordering her around and criticizing her: "Why did you do it that way?" "Hurry up with the phone call!" etc. Jameson got better treatment, perhaps because she was in analysis with one of Khan's peers. But she still had to deal with Khan's arrogance: "When I first arrived on the job, I left him a note using the name 'Masud,' and he wrote back a huge scrawled note: 'Don't call me Masud.'"

In 1969, Hogarth published Marion Milner's *Hands of the Living God*, with an introduction by Winnicott. This book, a description of Milner's psychoanalysis of a young schizophrenic woman, is still recognized as one of the best clinical accounts of an intense psychoanalysis. It was the first book to appear under Khan's editorship. Here is his account of how he facilitated the publication, from a speech he gave at Milner's seventieth birthday party:

The project of this book started in a desultory and random way. For some time, I heard snatches of Marion's work with a nihilistically omnipresent patient. Then Pearl King started a small group where some of us met to discuss our actual clinical work. I persuaded Marion to offer this case to that group. She smiled and invited me to visit her one Sunday to see the material. I was delighted and arrived expecting a sort of rough, huge, sprawling manuscript. Instead, the experience turned out to be both novel and amazing. She took me downstairs to a room laden with books and some other objects, where normally one expects to find furniture, and then dug out some four or five paper shopping bags that were crammed full of bits and pieces of written stuff, drawings, etc. Each scrap of paper

was an EVENT in itself. Most of them were written over in all directions, upside down and sideways, with a particular bias towards illegibil-
ity. I stood there and gaped. She was perfectly at home in this massive
seething and still world, and knew exactly what was what. It dawned on
me that Marion is an antiquarian of the unintegrated states, and that
suddenly gave me hope about the venture of publishing a book. . . . I
became obsessed with the idea that if only one could bully her relent-
lessly enough, she could make a real, intellectually viable clinical narrative from it.[11]

One thing Khan did not reveal in this talk was that he personally
had gone to great lengths to get outside funding so that the book could
include color prints of the patient's drawings. He did this for the English edition and then again for the French edition.[12]

Khan also served as co-*rédacteur étranger* (foreign editor) for the
French journal *Nouvelle Revue de Psychanalyse* (NRP), holding this position from 1970 until his death in 1989. He was a member of the board
there and one of their most prolific writers, with articles in twenty-eight
issues. Some of these articles have never been published in English.

Khan played a significant role in protecting the integrity of Freud's work
through his interactions with Sigmund Freud Copyrights, where he
eventually became one of the directors. The Copyrights had been established by the Freud family in 1946, with Sigmund's son Ernst as
head.[13] It controls the publishing of Freud material and it has a dual
mandate: to grant licenses for the publication of Sigmund Freud's literary works and letters and to ensure the quality of the publications. Profits
from the publications go to Freud's grandchildren and their heirs. Ernst
died in 1970 and the literary agent Mark Paterson of London became
head of the Copyrights in 1971, a position he still holds.[14] In 1971, Paterson and Anna Freud invited Khan to be a director. They had already
worked with him in various ways and they knew that he would apply his
talents to the second part of the mandate, ensuring the quality of Freud
publications.

Paterson's files show that one of Khan's most significant projects was
completing the publication of the *Collected Works of Sigmund Freud,* translated by James Strachey.[15] In 1971, the publication of the *Collected Works*
was way past its deadline. James Strachey had died in 1967, leaving vol-

ume 24, the final volume, to be completed by his widow Alix, working with an assistant, Angela Harris.[16] Alix was elderly, so most of the work was left to Harris. Harris, however, was overburdened by other commitments including the mothering of young children and she did not make the *Collected Works* a priority.

Khan was determined to get volume 24 published. He pressured Harris to work harder and he got Winnicott, the current chair of the Publications Committee, to add his pressure. Khan and Harris did not get along easily. Khan wrote that their collaboration consisted of "ghastly meetings and paranoid bickering."[17] When volume 24 was finally published in 1973, Khan wrote, referring to Harris: "Human beings take more delight in thwarting each other than in working together."[18]

His private passion at the Copyrights was the publication of Freud correspondences. This was the outgrowth of a longtime reverence for correspondence, his own and that of others: "The reason why I am so intrigued by correspondences is that [they provide] a truer picture of a writer's style of relating to others than any other mode of expression."[19] The Khan–Mark Paterson correspondence, held at the Copyrights, reveals details of Khan's efforts, both before and after he became a director, to facilitate the publication of Freud correspondences such as those with Jung, Weiss, Groddeck, Pfister, Silberstein, Andreas-Salomé, Schur, and Ferenczi. Several of these have since been published with little recognition of Khan's early contributions to their success.

Whenever there was a controversy involving Sigmund Freud, Khan was always on the side of Freud. Two of the controversies involved books written by Paul Roazen, a prolific American historian of psychoanalysis. The first was *Brother Animal* (1969), an account of the suicide of the charismatic Victor Tausk, who, in Roazen's opinion, was treated badly by Sigmund Freud. The second book, *Freud and His Followers* (1975), revealed that Freud had engaged in behavior that is unacceptable in psychoanalysis: unwilling to trust any of his colleagues, Freud himself had been the analyst for his daughter Anna. Roazen had discovered this more than a decade earlier, when he had gotten permission from Khan, in his role of institute librarian, to go through various papers at the institute. Roazen discovered a cache of Ernest Jones's papers in shopping bags in a basement cupboard and the information was in these papers. When Roazen revealed the secret, Anna Freud responded with repeated attacks on Roazen's motivation, and Khan took her side.[20] His correspondence is filled with venomous references to Roazen—for example, "Roazen is the most cunning type of American scandal-searcher."[21] Khan's attempt to discredit Roazen did not succeed, however, because Roazen was publishing important information, not just gossip.

A Freud scandal from the 1980s revealed the maverick side of Anna Freud, who had a weakness for attractive, charismatic men. She fell hard for Jeffrey Masson, a young scholar of Sanskrit who was an analytic candidate in Toronto and a protégé of the American Kurt Eissler, the founder and head of the Sigmund Freud Archives, a group that works to collect and preserve Sigmund's writings.[22] Masson had contacted her with a request to do a full translation of the Sigmund Freud/Wilhelm Fliess correspondence. (Fliess had been Sigmund Freud's crucial friend in the years 1887–1902, at the time of his self-analysis; see Chapter 10.)

Anna Freud had already worked on a publication of a limited selection of the letters and she knew that there was controversial material there. She and Eissler thought Masson could handle this provocative material, even though nobody else thought he was the right person,[23] and they arranged for Masson to be given the rights to translate the entire correspondence. In 1981, Eissler gave Masson the title of research director of the Freud Archives, which meant he had private access to frozen material in the Sigmund Freud archives at the Library of Congress. In the same year, Mark Paterson appointed him a director of the Freud Copyrights, where, along with Khan, he would have power to make decisions about Freud publications.

In those days, Khan was suffering from major health problems, but his mind was still clear. He openly stated to Anna Freud that Masson was not to be trusted. When she objected strongly, he backed off, out of respect for her. He redirected his complaint to Mark Paterson, claiming that Paterson should not have agreed to the translation without getting Khan's approval. In private, he criticized Anna Freud, Masson, and Paterson: "I am enraged that Paterson has ignored me as Director and taken things into his own hands, in connivance with Miss Freud. . . . It is really stupid of Miss Freud to behave in this anachronistic, almost senile and willful way to entrust the translation, the editing and the annotating to a youth like J. Masson, who doesn't really know German."[24]

The Masson translation was eventually published by Harvard University Press and it was warmly received for its scholarship. Ultimately, even Khan had to admit that Masson had done a "splendid" job.[25] But scandal arose when Masson publicized his private interpretation of the material. Sigmund Freud's theory while corresponding with Fleiss had been that the supposed seductions of his female patients were mostly fantasies, but Masson got the idea that Freud had changed his theory in order to cover up actual seductions. He revealed his thinking in a talk at the Western New England Institute for Psychoanalysis, where Anna Freud had friends whom she had met when giving lectures there a few years earlier. He then elaborated on his idea in an interview for an August 1981 article in the *New York Times* and in a 1984 book entitled *The Assault on Truth: Freud's Suppression of the Seduction Theory.*[26] Eissler was enraged, and Anna Freud was dismayed, finally realizing that she had made a big mistake: "For my part, I could only say one thing: that I am deeply sorry that I ever agreed to the publication of the unabridged Fliess letters."[27] Khan was disgusted to the point that he actually made a favorable comment about Paul Roazen—he said to Paterson that "at least Roazen's gossip was based on facts."

In November 1981, Masson was removed from his post at the Archives. He promptly sued for breach of contract and, to avoid further publicity, there was an out-of-court settlement. But he stayed on at the Copyrights, where he had just been appointed (in September) for a three-year term. Khan and Anna Freud wanted him dismissed, but Mark Paterson made the situation workable by keeping Masson largely absent from all decisions.

There was an ongoing conflict at the Copyrights regarding generation of money for the Freuds vs. preservation of the quality of publications. An incident in 1980 shows the intensity of the underlying emotions. At the annual general meeting of the Freud Copyrights, held in Khan's flat, Khan became enraged at a Mr. Kirby, who was the agent for Lucian Freud, the artist son of Ernst Freud. Mr. Kirby was pressuring the directors to do more publishing, leading Khan to the conclusion that Kirby cared more about profit than about quality. After a heated argument, Khan threw Kirby out and, from then on, Khan refused to have the meetings at his flat, because he did not want Kirby there: "Anybody that says he doesn't give a damn about what happens to Freud's works if the money starts to decrease is not worthy of my company."[28] This was his consistent attitude: "We cannot treat the Freud correspondences as if they were mere merchandise to be sold irrespective of the consequences."[29]

One of Khan's greatest editorial contributions to psychoanalysis might have been a publication of the complete Freud correspondences. But he waited to do this because Anna Freud wanted much of the material kept private while she was alive, and he wrongly assumed that he would have years of productivity after her death to work on the project.[30] After Anna Freud died in 1982, Khan wrote to Paterson: "I think that now Anna Freud is no longer there to oversee matters, all the Directors must pool their resources to ensure that the Freud correspondences are impeccably edited in text and well translated."[31] Had he enjoyed better health, there is no question that much of this material would have been published, and published well. According to Paterson, there is a huge amount of Freud correspondence that remains untranslated and unpublished.

Khan's service at the Freud Copyrights continued almost to the end of his life. He worked there longer than he worked anywhere else. In 1987, a change in legal status at the Copyrights meant that there were no more directors, so Khan lost the position.

Khan also worked in a variety of ways to facilitate the publication of Winnicott's ideas. His editorial contributions to Winnicott's works are not widely known, but they were major. Many European analysts believe that Winnicott would not have become an international figure without Khan: "Masud was the midwife to Donald's books. He had the joy of giving birth to Donald in a way that Donald had never before come alive."[32] "What one should never forget—and what hardly anyone knows —is that Masud made Winnicott. He edited, indexed, and published him. Winnicott is the product of Masud's industry and he is a colossal figure now due to Masud."[33] "Let's face it—Winnicott wasn't a good writer. Without Masud, DWW wouldn't have gotten lasting credit for his innovations."[34]

Winnicott, who was an ambitious man, wanted his ideas to survive his death, and Khan was an ideal person to provide assistance. The problem, of course, was that Khan was Winnicott's analysand and an outside relationship was not recommended. But, as discussed in Chapter 5, Khan started helping Winnicott as early as 1952,[35] and the collaboration would continue until Winnicott's death, intensifying after the analysis ended in 1966. Winnicott's early papers are hard to read because the writing is unorganized, colloquial, and lacking in references to the relevant literature.[36] An examination of changes in his publications over time shows Khan's influence: the later writings have a main point, which makes them easier to read, and there are many more references.[37]

Khan's assistance went beyond editorial help. Charles Rycroft told me he was "100% convinced" that Khan literally wrote many of Winnicott's major papers. Ann Jameson told me: "I often typed up Winnicott's papers, and almost always they had been extensively modified by Masud Khan. I knew it was Khan because I knew his handwriting and he always used the black Mont Blanc pens when he wrote. Khan would slash and re-write entire sections of Winnicott's manuscripts, and Winnicott always accepted the totality of the revisions." Khan's personal correspondences suggest that he willingly helped Winnicott with no request for acknowledgment, as in this letter from 1962 concerning Winnicott's upcoming lecture tour to the United States:

> Around 4:45 p.m., DWW rang to say he was completely stuck with his papers and cannot even think of subjects to write on. Could I help! I rushed [the houseboy] to get an extra steak and invited him to dinner. And we have been at it since 7 p.m. I am worried for him. He is having such nightmares (real ones!) about his trip to America. He has a conviction that they will find him out and declare him a phoney. It is so strange and moving to see a man of his genius, experience and reputation get paralyzed by terror and nerves. . . . He has four papers to write between now and the second of October. God help us![38]

The unpublished correspondence between Winnicott and Khan at the Archives of Psychiatry of the Cornell Medical Center gives clear evidence of a writing collaboration that went beyond editing.[39]

Playing and Reality would be Winnicott's last book and it is a psychoanalytic gem to which Khan made a major contribution.[40] The two men had at one time even discussed being coauthors.[41] The book was published in 1971, shortly after Winnicott's death, with Winnicott stating in the acknowledgments: "I am much indebted to Masud Khan for his constructive criticisms of my writings and for his always being (as it seems to me) available when a practical suggestion is needed."[42]

It was part of the collusion between these two men that Winnicott
got most of the credit, even when Khan provided major help. Khan wrote
to Victor Smirnoff in 1971: "The years 1969 & 1970 have been, in a
certain dimension, exclusively devoted by me to facilitating DWW to
get what he had to say, said—and I have succeeded there. Now I realise
how much of my life energy was absorbed by that and I consider it a
blessing in my life."[43] It is noteworthy that all four of Khan's books were
published after Winnicott's death.

Khan's contribution to Winnicott's reputation went beyond the writing. He actively sponsored the spread of Winnicott's ideas and his pro-
motional activity was successful, especially in France.

In the 1950s and 1960s, psychoanalysts made international connections mostly through conferences and through the IJPA, and there were
major gaps in the sharing of information. Winnicott was well known in
England in the 1960s, but even in the United States, where he had lectured, many analysts did not know his work. And there was an even
greater ignorance of his work in France, since most of his writings had
not been translated into French. Winnicott was as unknown and as
poorly understood in France as Lacan was in England.

In today's France, Winnicott's works are readily available in translation. He became popular there in the 1960s and his popularity has
continued. What is not well known is that it was through Khan that the
French discovered Winnicott. Wladimir Granoff said to me: "Winnicott
became an international figure because Masud 'made' him. Masud should
stay forever in our [French] history for having brought and created
Winnicott."

Khan's first approach to getting Winnicott known was by badger-
ing his French friends to read Winnicott carefully. Then, at Khan's
urging, Granoff got some articles by Winnicott translated and published
in the NRP.[44] Later, Khan influenced Winnicott to write introductions
to the English translation of books by Smirnoff and Pontalis, and he
edited these introductions.[45]

Khan knew that the best way to get the French to grasp Winnicott's
genius would be through a live clinical demonstration. If people observed
him working with a child, his work would come alive even if the observers
did not understand English. In June 1966, he arranged through Granoff

to have Winnicott do a two-day workshop at a clinic in Nanterre.[46] The plan was to have small group discussions, a lecture and several live child consultations. Khan was the master planner, although, for unknown reasons, he did not attend.

The workshop was a success, attracting important French figures such as Jean Claude Lavie, Victor Smirnoff, and J.-B. Pontalis. One colleague was in tears at the close of a case presentation, and it was clear to all that an important connection had been established.

PART 5

STARTING TO FALL

(1965)

CHAPTER 18

THE FALSE SELF

Only the True Self can be creative and only the True Self can feel real.
D. W. Winnicott[1]

I have had to invent a "Masud" for myself and live by him.
Masud Khan[2]

Khan had entered the decade of the 1960s with a career, a wife, and a network of friends that left him feeling blessed. He seemed to have made a transition to Western living, and there was every reason to predict a future that would build on the very satisfying present. But by 1965, he was going downhill on a slow and relentless slide. The divine years ended, never to return. The success had been real, but he still had major psychological problems that nobody, not even Winnicott, understood. His damaged foundation was not getting repaired.

When an analysis fails, it can always be said that an analysand failed to make use of the analytic opportunity. It is equally credible to suggest that the analyst failed to provide the kind of space that the analysand could use. Both perspectives can be considered simultaneously. This chapter focuses on Khan's False Self pathology, and it will be shown how, with Winnicott's cooperation, he avoided the experience of regression to dependence, which was the treatment of choice for that condition.[3]

Khan's personal correspondence from the first half of the 1960s shows that he continued to suffer from the problems for which he had come to England seeking help. He describes insomnia, empty depression, feelings of terror, and a variety of stress-related somatic symptoms (fevers, rashes, and back pain). Shortly after his return from a successful lecture tour to the United States, he wrote to Svetlana, who was on an extended tour:

> I really can't account for the past three weeks. Apart from the clinical and professional work, I have vegetated in a sub-human way. This is so hard to describe. I can in retrospect detail it only as a silent invisible inner psychic implosion and a resultant emotional collapse. Occasionally I have lived through acute, fleeting moments of panic and pain. While I am in the dazed ferment, there is no acute conflict. There is no sense of tragedy. Only a bleak aloneness and bare non-existence. While all this is happening the best one can do is suffer it fully and without distraction. . . .
>
> It hurts and aches and pains to be separated from you. Everything has something lacking and dull about it. [But] absence and longing do not create the sort of "dying" and "collapse" I have have just lived through. This is my personal and private predicament.[4]

When he withdrew, he suffered privately in a manner that suggests anaclitic depression: "Sorry I was so opaque and dull last night. There are days where everyone has the feeling of a THING for me."[5]

Khan has been given different diagnoses by various people, but his private writings reveal that he believed his major problem was pathology of the self. "Why is it I have always over-trusted the 'unknown-to-me' person and mistrusted, as well as withdrawn from, the known person?"[6] He writes about this over and over, across the years, in his Work Books and in his correspondence. His symptoms fit those of False Self as described by Winnicott: he lacked a sense of a psychosomatic body and had feelings of being unreal; he did not have the experience of being able to engage his True Self in intimate relationships; there was a disconnect between his inner self and his outer self; and he could fool people (including Winnicott) into thinking he was doing well.[7]

It is very rare, perhaps unprecedented, that an analytically informed person with False Self pathology describes his predicament in detail. But Khan, through his written record, gives us an insider's perspective. Khan also had a well-developed and active True Self that was aware of the False Self. Many people knew him accurately as a True Self. The False Self would come and go, and when it was gone, the accompanying symptomatology was also gone. This suggests that the True Self was always there, but it could not always be accessed—a situation that Winnicott did not describe.[8] Another unexpected finding is that Khan had a complex transitional space even when he was functioning as a False Self— he had symbolic abilities and he could play and participate in culture —while Winnicott had suggested that a False Self would have significant impairment in this area.

A person with a False Self lives in the outside world in a way that feels unreal and Khan describes this:

> All my life I have lived in a silence which I have surrounded with adaptive chattersomeness towards an audience. I have never succeeded in saying what I really felt, because somehow language itself always displaces and dislocates me. . . . [I had] a long analysis with four people, and yet I never managed to have a single session where what I said and what I needed to say were the same.[9]

> I am aware of my profound debt to my colleagues who have put up with all the antic and bizarre provocativeness of my temperament and character. I can now see that all these wild antics which antagonised most of my colleagues were almost a magical way of keeping myself reminded that I was not where I was. . . . It is impossible for anybody outside to relate to a person who is hiding himself.[10]

Social relating alienated him from what he called his "private interiority": "The fact is that all humans distract and dislocate me from my nature and sensibility."[11] Yet he was not comfortable being alone. The paradox of needing to be alone and needing to be with others troubled him and he was constantly trying to arrange an optimal balance of aloneness and socialization. He often wrote that one of the things he loved about Paris was that a person could sit alone for hours at a café with the noise of other people all around—that way he could be alone and companioned at the same time. The Parisian café ambience reminded him of the constant buzz of people at the Khan estate in Pakistan.

Khan's report shows that False Self pathology can block a person from a connection to the True Self. He felt that his True Self was regularly a part of his artwork and his professional work, but when he succeeded in expressing himself, he did not always feel that the work had come from him. For example, he wrote about looking at an album of doodle images that he had drawn for Svetlana in 1961: "It surprised me how alive and pertinent they are as images. But what is even more surprising is the fact that *I* have made them. I really cannot experience in myself any sense of their authorship."[12] Similarly, he commented on a paper he had written: "I have so little control over what comes out of my mind."[13]

Unfortunately for Khan, he had a False Self that could be quite entertaining to others. Many people took delight in his outrageousness and his hostile wit. Some of his closest friends and colleagues, including Winnicott and Robert Stoller, were among those who failed to understand that the person who entertained them was often a False Self.

It is somewhat shocking to find that Winnicott wrote six years before the analysis (or analytic "coverage") ended about a kind of pathology that exactly describes Khan. He discusses the problems that develop when the False Self is located primarily in the intellect, and the mind and the body are dissociated from each other: "The world may observe academic success of a high degree, and may find it hard to believe in the very real distress of the individual concerned, who feels 'phoney' the more he or she is successful. When such individuals destroy themselves in one way or another, instead of fulfilling promise, this invariably produces a sense of shock in those who have developed high hopes of the individual."[14] It is quite possible that the "man patient" Winnicott describes is Masud.

Since Winnicott was an expert on False Self pathology, having invented the concept, we have to wonder why it was that he did not succeed in helping Khan to find adult health. They both knew that a patient with False Self pathology requires a regression to dependence in the analytic situation, where the False Self can be shed and the True Self starts to reveal itself and to develop through interaction (see Chapter 14). When this does not happen, the False Self pathology remains, no matter how much insight there is or how long the analysis continues. But Khan never experienced a regression to dependence: "I have never been 'taken over' by the strength of anyone, only by their weakness and neediness."[15] "It is strange that one can go through some fifteen years of analysis and avoid having a breakdown—in fact, use analysis as a way of not having a breakdown."[16]

The nonregression is unfortunate because, by his own report, Khan had been helped by the few regressive experiences that did occur:

> [I]n some 15 years of analytic relationship with DWW, I did succeed at three points or occasions to sink into my Self, be silent, present in my person and related to him. All these three occasions were physical or rather psychosomatic. He was in his chair seated and I had got off the couch and buried my head into the side of his coat. I can still hear his heart and watch beating. All else was still and sentiently neutral and I was at peace. And DWW never interpreted those three occasions. He had enabled me to reach to that point, allowed it to actualise, and let it pass—without comment. And these three occasions were my only experience of the Self in me in analysis.[17]

Khan had several rationalizations about why he did not have the experience of regression to dependence. For example, he stated that reticence was inherent to his very nature: "There are some of us who cannot share our woes with others. This is neither conceit nor arrogance, but a very personal and private stance of stammer. . . . This is why I made such meager use of analysis: Some of us can find our own comfort only from within our own disciplined silences."[18] He also claimed that male patients in general could not regress to dependence with a male analyst because of fear of the homosexual transference, or with a female analyst because of the threat of a devouring mother figure: "Once one has come through puberty/adolescence, at least in men, A RIGIDITY sets in which can be mellowed and broken down only from within, on one's own. Alas!"[19] But these arguments do not hold—male analysands can and do experience regression to dependence in analysis. Harry Guntrip, for example, described a regression to dependence with Winnicott that was a deep and curative experience.

One of the greatest problems in Khan's analysis involved the analytic frame—the agreed-upon rules of the treatment, such as payment of a fee, ending sessions after a certain period of time, nonsocialization, etc.[20] Thoughts and feelings are understood to be as-if experiences when they occur within the frame, in a transitional space where they are both real and not-real. A real-life relationship with the analyst can be fatal to the as-if quality if it destroys the illusion. It is not safe to "be" a baby, for example, if the caregiver's "real" flaws are seen or if the caregiver requires the baby's assistance in reality.

Winnicott's deviations from the frame were multiple and serious, and they started in the very first years. They did not present a problem in the first part of the analysis, when Khan's primary need was to be psychologically "held"; the socializing and editing may even have facilitated that experience. In the 1960s, however, Khan had enough security to risk working on the issues of his False Self.

Khan's knowledge of the real Winnicott altered and weakened the possibility of experiencing his analyst as powerful: "DWW is so fond and proud of me and yet so ill at ease with me. I have only now realized that DWW is rather afraid of me (God alone knows why!) and covers it up with an awkward bantering."[21] The male figures of his early life had been strong men, and Winnicott could not match them: "I told [DWW] bluntly one reason why I had failed to use him creatively . . . was because I was always larger as a person than him and he could not stand that. He agreed!"[22] Adam Limentani, who knew Khan well, wrote: "Amongst other things, [Khan] was not fully satisfied with his personal analysis [with Winnicott], to the point of being rather disillusioned. Perhaps he was hoping to find again the lost father figure which he had worshipped and feared in his early life, and his analyst did not meet that need."[23]

If Winnicott could not be a warrior or a feudal landlord type of person, Khan's next choice would be that he act like the dignified and serious Imperial English who had been his models in India. But Winnicott liked to be a "ham," as when he would whirl around on his piano stool after performing, once falling off in front of a crowd. Khan hated Winnicott's tendency to self-deprecation. Commenting to Victor Smirnoff about a scientific meeting at the institute where the French analyst Mme. Maud Mannoni had spoken, he wrote: "Winnicott said a few charming things in response and regretted he could not say more because [as he reported] he had fallen asleep for a while at a rather critical point in Mme. Mannoni's narrative of events, as he is old & had had a very hard day. Everyone laughed. Pity he has to clown in this way."[24] For Khan, who valued ceremony in public living, such behavior was intolerable: "In my life, ceremony and metaphor play a predominant role. When I lapse from them, I get dislocated and when others lapse vis-à-vis me in this dimension, I lose them almost automatically."[25]

Instead of having an as-if transference, Khan was experiencing too directly his analyst's limitations. English peers of the two men summarize what went wrong:

> DWW ruined Masud. He kept no boundaries and he seduced Masud emotionally and intellectually. He wanted a "marvelous son" for himself and that's what he got.[26]

> Masud never went to the only analyst who could have helped him—and he knew it. That was Melanie Klein. He only went to analysts who could be seduced by him.[27]

> Masud was never analyzed. He had a long, amusing conversation, using the language of analysis.[28]

In the absence of an experience of regression to dependence, Khan's False Self pathology remained untouched. This was Winnicott's failure, Khan's failure, and their mutual failure. It meant that Khan would never have a lasting sense of being a whole person and that his False Self would become dominant in situations of stress.

CHAPTER 19

DISGRACE IN AMSTERDAM

I have concocted a real nightmare here professionally
& am now fighting hard to survive it.
Masud Khan, writing from the Hilton Hotel
in Amsterdam on July 27, 1965[1]

Amsterdam was a turning point in my destiny and that of Masud.
From then on, nothing was ever again the same in our lives.
Wladimir Granoff[2]

Granoff was filled with dread as he anticipated the International Psychoanalytic Association Congress (IPAC), to be held in Amsterdam in July 1965. This was the meeting that he hoped his work of the past six years would reach a climax as the IPA voted on whether to give the Association Psychanalytique de France (APF) full membership. Several events had occurred that Granoff viewed as bad omens. In December 1964, Robert Knight, an American analyst who was head of the Program Committee, was diagnosed with inoperable lung cancer, leading to significant disarray. Then on February 3, 1965, the Chicago analyst Max Gitelson, president of the IPA, died unexpectedly. Gitelson had promoted Granoff's personal membership in the IPA in 1963 and he had been the main sponsor of membership for the APF, so Granoff was afraid that his group had now lost its chance for acceptance. The IPA itself was in chaos because its constitution did not include a clause about unplanned succession, so it now had no president. Later, in the spring, the entire IPAC program was jeopardized when the patient whose treatment was to be a center of discussion objected to having his case discussed publicly. (This man, who suffered from an obsessive disorder, had apparently not given prior consent.)

Khan wrote to Granoff, trying to reassure him: "Amsterdam is certainly getting to be an ill-fated Congress. We well might have a few more casualties before we arrive there. . . . But don't worry—we will get together and have a good time. Please do not poison yourself with unnecessary forebodings."[3]

As things turned out, it was Khan who should have been worrying. The Amsterdam IPAC was a turning point in *his* life, a marker for the ending of the divine years. The details of the problem at Amsterdam were not widely known at the time when I began my research. The events had been referred to as a "crisis," with no further information, in the official obituary of Khan.[4] For a long time, I could not find anybody who knew what had happened, because most of the people who had been there were long dead or too ill to talk. Granoff turned out to be an invaluable resource for this information.

I learned that Khan's crisis had developed out of letters exchanged between Khan and Granoff in response to Gitelson's death. The first one was written by Granoff. He wrote to tell Khan about his deep mourning, believing that Khan, who had also known Gitelson, would understand how great a loss this was. Wanting to comfort his grieving friend, Khan wrote back immediately, sending Granoff his sympathy and saying that he shared Granoff's high opinion of Gitelson. He said that he had gotten to know Gitelson well after meetings on several different occasions, which he described in detail. Part of their relationship supposedly included Khan having been a mediator in a situation in Chicago, where Gitelson was involved in a bitter feud with the analysts Roy Grinker and Franz Alexander.[5]

Khan's letter had the intended effect of pleasing Granoff. In the context of their very close friendship, he felt that they were experiencing a similar loss. Granoff was so moved that he mailed a copy of the letter to Gitelson's wife, Frances, hoping to comfort her by showing her how much Khan admired her husband.

Although Khan and Granoff were both admirers of Max Gitelson, their relationships to his wife were quite different. Frances, who was also an analyst, was a somewhat formidable woman who was morbidly obese. Granoff had become close to her after meeting with her and Max in

Chicago on several occasions, especially since they shared a passion for cooking. Khan and Frances were also acquainted, but they were not friends. Khan tended to have contempt for overweight people and, moreover, he rejected Frances because of Los Angeles loyalties—Frances had a close relationship with Leo Rangell who was an informal enemy of Khan's friend Ralph Greenson.

Granoff was unaware of the animosity between his two friends, and his sharing of Khan's letter was an innocent gesture. But there were major unexpected consequences. The problem was that Khan had claimed a closer friendship with Gitelson than was actually the case. Additionally, he had exaggerated or even fabricated some of the details of his intervention in Chicago. Lacking Granoff's political sensitivity, he had not respected the intensity of feeling involved in the Chicago rivalry. When Frances read the letter, she was furious.

The wrath of Chicago politics now ignited an international fire. Frances demanded that action be taken by the IPA against Khan for making false claims in the letter. Since there was no ethics committee at that time, nothing could be done until the summer congress. It was in this context that Khan headed to Amsterdam.

The Central Executive Committee of the IPA was the group chosen to deal with the Khan letter. This committee was chaired by William Gillespie, former president of the IPA, acting in the place of the deceased Gitelson. Gillespie, a conservative and proper man who was Khan's associate in London, knew Khan well and did not like him. Other members of the committee were the American Phyllis Greenacre, who was a temporary joint president of the IPA along with Gillespie, and Pearl King, who had an automatic membership on the committee due to the fact that she was serving a four-year term as the first associate secretary of the IPA.

Khan was especially lucky that King was on the committee. She had known and liked him for almost two decades and, over the years, she always defended him.[6] King told me that it was obvious to her that the underlying intentions were positive—Khan had written the letter to impress Granoff and Granoff was truly wanting to comfort Frances.

The committee met at the end of July, just prior to the formal beginning of the Congress. They read Khan's letter and heard Frances' grievance. Then Gillespie met privately with Khan, and Khan admitted to him that some of his supposed memories were of events that had never happened. Gillespie relayed this information back to the committee, whereupon they engaged in a serious discussion of what sanctions should be imposed. But, as King told me: "Suddenly, as we were talking, I saw the funny side of it all. I said something, I don't remember what, and we all burst out laughing. I pricked the bubble. We started to wonder: Why was this so important? Who cared, apart from those who objected to Masud's fantasies or lies?!!"

The committee decided to impose a minimal sanction: Khan was asked, through Gillespie, to apologize to Frances Gitelson. But Gillespie also gave Khan a somber and firm reprimand and he warned him that there could be further consequences at the BPAS when the professional year started in September. Gillespie may have been the first Westerner to officially reprimand Khan for misbehavior.

It is not known whether Khan apologized to Frances Gitelson. He returned to London without saying good-bye to anybody, so he was not present at the celebration party when the APF got its acceptance. He left a note for Granoff:

> I am leaving now. Sorry it has not been possible to say goodbye in person. I wish you and your group every success. . . .
>
> About my "situation." Everyone has been very kind and considerate given the circumstances. Dr. Gillespie talked to me at length and it was a very painful, humbling and fruitful experience. I am at fault and can heal it [*sic*] and myself only slowly over a long time.
>
> I have been and am living through a private nightmare, and for the time being must retreat into a long silent think to re-find my identity and discipline. Please keep in touch. Your affection and friendship are very valuable to me.
>
> I have always needed to be a private person and never managed to be one. These events will perhaps help me to find my privacy.
>
> With much love, Affectionately, Sud[7]

The next day, having had time to reflect, he wrote Granoff again. He said that he had spoken with Svetlana about what happened and they both understood why Granoff had forwarded the letter to Frances. But he said that he no longer felt at fault, since there had been nothing in the letter that was denigrating of Gitelson: "My misconstructions of the basic truth may seem deplorably like outrageous lies when removed from their context and made public—but, in the privacy of a correspondence with a dear friend, they are not so deplorable."[8] This letter was signed with no mention of "Love," a term that now disappeared from their correspondence.

Khan and Beriosova saw no reason to change plans for their yearly vacation.[9] On August 3, Khan wrote to Granoff from Monte Carlo, continuing his commentary. By now, he was even more unrepentant: "My colleagues and especially the Americans have misread the style of the 'flourish': that exaggeration and distortion which, in departing from the facts, invokes the truth.[10] It was childish of me to play with their cramped righteousness."

His next letter to Granoff said that he was *glad* that the crisis had happened, because he could use it as a motivation to stop doing so much work for the BPAS: "Thank God for 'Amsterdam.' It has disengaged me from a rat-race of professionalism that I could not find a way out of by personal volition. Now I can do my own reading and living, my own way. I have paid my dues to my colleagues and owe no more."[11] By the end of the vacation, he had convinced himself that he had unconsciously arranged for the events to unfold as they did: "I had been engineering an anti-climax for myself. The rat-race of avid professionalism was wasting my time, mind & energy too extravagantly."[12] And he decided that Granoff was the guilty party. Granoff told me: "He said that my unconscious should have known that he was fantasying and that I should have known not to share the letter with Frances Gitelson."

With typical drama, Khan thought of the experience at Amsterdam as a kind of murder.[13] He described the events in a letter to Robert Stoller, who had not been present. Stoller agreed with Khan that murder had been in the air and supported his friend, but he also warned him to be more careful:

I'm still quite disturbed by your unpleasant experience in Amsterdam. I cannot believe anyone will be able to "get" you as a result of a private letter, but you've certainly seen the intensity with which some of our colleagues operate. You sometimes act lightly and whimsically, but what for you is defined within yourself as only a trial action, or a game, or an encounter, others may take much more seriously.

I know you are very ambivalent with regard to common sense, and that you would be irritated if you ever had to take my brand of it seriously. Still, I think your creativity is too valuable to waste on the excitements, thrills and disasters of the politics and connivances of psychoanalysis. There is a lot of fun and games in it for all of us, but there's too much murder in it too.[14]

That fall, there was a major war between India and Pakistan over Kashmir. Khan did not even mention the war in his correspondences. Perhaps he was distracted by the continued repercussions from Amsterdam that faced him in London, as Gillespie had predicted. In September, Khan voluntarily resigned from the society's Curriculum Committee, because he did not want to participate in meetings with Gillespie, who was a new member.[15] A more important matter was that there was now a question about whether Khan should be allowed to assume two important positions that had been unofficially promised to him upon John Sutherland's retirement in two years—the editorships of the IJPA and the International Psycho-Analytical Library (IPL). Khan was eminently qualified to hold these posts, having done high-quality work for both for many years. But although the IJPA was officially controlled by the British analysts,[16] it was the unofficial journal for the international community, and since the IPA had just censured Khan, his assumption of the position was problematic. There was less of a problem with the IPL, because the international connection was not as strong.

Both decisions were in the hands of the council of the BPAS, where Winnicott, as the current president of the society, was the most important member. He met with Sutherland and, according to Khan, the outcome was that both men expressed full confidence in him. Sutherland advised Khan to try to be more aware of the envy and insecurity he aroused in people, but, according to Khan, Winnicott actually sided with him: "DWW said [that] I alone can decide: 'This is me and you can take it or leave it!' And he is right, of course. I shall never change one jot to fit in with others: certainly not for expediency's sake."[17]

For more than two years, the council delayed its decision about who would edit the IJPA and the IPL, with various members worrying that

Khan was "arrogant, provocative and impulsive."[18] Khan continued to assist Sutherland at the IJPA and the IPL, but he anticipated that he would be dismissed as soon as Sutherland retired: "There is a lot afoot behind the scenes to discredit me and thus displace me from both the *Journal* and the International Library, and I have little doubt my colleagues will succeed only too easily in that, because I have given away too much ammunition to be shot down with. There is a bizarre mystique in my life of engineering to be reduced to zero point, to start again."[19]

He was underestimating the tolerance of his British peers and their belief in the importance of his contributions. In 1968, the council gave him a ten-year term as editor of the IPL, while Joseph Sandler was named as editor of the IJPA. Khan was asked by Sandler to continue as associate editor of the IJPA. Pearl King told me: "We [i.e., Khan's British peers] just saved his bacon. Masud could have had a public dressing down, but we didn't do that. It was a very English way of dealing with something. We saw two sides of the problem."

The decision was a humane one and it would be beneficial to the world of psychoanalysis but, on a personal level, only Gillespie had made an attempt to provide Khan with the dialogue he longed for.

PART 6

BLESSINGS AND HUMILIATIONS

(1966–1970)

As I traveled in the minicab to the airport in the grey soft drizzle
I stumbled on the right title for my autobiography:
BLESSINGS AND HUMILIATIONS.
Masud Khan[1]

LOSING HIS ANCHORS

*[1966] was a year of sustained terror, violence, confusion and
humiliation and fervid chaos in my life. I lost and willfully
chose to lose all the habitual anchorages that had sustained
me for twenty years in England.*
Masud Khan[1]

Ten great years [Svetlana and I] had together, 1956–1966.
Masud Khan[2]

Amsterdam, 1965, is a marker for the ending of Khan's divine years
because the overall lack of understanding of his letter changed him. In
his private world, it was perfectly acceptable to make a point using stories that were not exact truths and there was nothing wrong with the
letter that had so incensed Frances Gitelson. Khan's preferred communication was through exaggeration, distortion, and even lying, with the
goal of expressing the essence of a truth. In contrast to Robert Stoller,
Khan did not value a straightforward account of events. In fact, he did
not even care about external truth; he told Stoller, speaking seriously,
"My realities are psychic realities."[3] In the West, he often quoted Oscar
Wilde, who shared this way of thinking: "Nothing that actually occurs
is of the smallest importance."[4] People who were willing to "play" with
him did not object to this manner of communication and indeed they
were regularly inspired by it.

When William Gillespie demanded that Khan apologize to Frances
Gitelson, he was asking Khan to go against something that was part of

his core self. Khan did not want to be a person who communicated in ordinary truthful ways. He knew that he had to accept Gillespie's criticism but he felt completely misunderstood by him and by the rest of the analysts who supported Gillespie. He did not feel guilty or even sorry about having written a letter where he had communicated truthfully in "Masudic" style. Writing to Granoff about the apology that he had been told to make, he said: "I shall never surrender my own dignity and independence [and] I shall not let myself be castrated and tailored to fit a very opaque morality of half-truths and social compliance."[5] Granoff understood Khan's reasoning. He told me that Khan had been unfairly treated at Amsterdam: "Masud told Gillespie and the Committee that it was his privilege to fantasy with friends—and I agree with that. On the level of what's exact, he lied. But on the level of what is true, I wouldn't say that he lied at all."

After Amsterdam, Khan saw correctly that the English and most of the West were not going to understand or accept the "flourish" of his style. The cultural milieu is a kind of play space where we live out an illusion of who we are at the same time as we exist in reality—and Khan now gave up on his Western play space. Rather than sacrifice his essence, he retreated to a world where he felt contempt toward those who had criticized him. His Western colleagues would know him more and more as a False Self.

To understand why Amsterdam was so significant, we can look to Khan's article "The Concept of Cumulative Trauma,"[6] where he points out that a person can be severely traumatized by an accumulation of small disruptions that add up. Amsterdam was just one of several aspects of Khan's life that were threatening his Western play space, but it happened to be the one that pushed him over the edge. A major shift had occurred: "To me, only my inner life and its fruition are significant [now]. I aspire to change myself, not others. I am struggling to define a private destiny."[7]

It was a shift that disappointed and demoralized him, because he had wanted to live well, in his own way, in the West. After Amsterdam, he sank into a depressed withdrawal. It was a state that was similar to the experience he had been through after his father died, and he thought it would help him to find his True Self:

I have changed a lot, physically, psychically and socially, since Amsterdam. I feel myself more "en rapport" with the youth I was when my father died, than I have ever felt in the past 23 years. This rapprochement
with myself has cost me enormous mental pain but it has been every bit
worth it. I have never been really a social person, and yet I have lived
through an extravagant sociability. Now I am establishing myself in a
climate of aloneness which is not rejective of others, but not misguid-
edly inclusive of them, either. . . .

[I have been living] through a technique of naïve and childish barter with
other people. They spoilt me, and I served them. Now I am finding the
discipline to do without being spoilt and to serve myself.[8]

Returning to London after his Monte Carlo vacation, Khan stopped
all socializing. His rationale was that he was trying to master a tendency
to over-give to others at his own expense:

[I] am straining to sit still on a detonated time bomb. I have no intention
of fighting. In me, since childhood, there has been an innate voice towards a sort of secular, monastic isolation of being. Somewhere I need
an experience of voluntary, sustained, and progressive loss to find and
establish my private discipline of retreat, reserve, and silence.[9]

I am an impossibly inextricable person who in fact has only a way of
being and no way of relating. All the nightmares of my life derive from
the simple error that I have a facility for relationships which is against
my Beingness. It is this contradiction that has impelled me to cause so
much havoc and pain in the life of others.[10]

As he withdrew, he lost most of his Western friends. He stopped
talking and corresponding with both Stollers and he became permanently
alienated from Ismond Rosen.[11] He had minimal contact with Julie
Andrews and Tony Walton, who were now divorced and remarried to
partners he barely knew. Yet another loss was Harvey Kayne, his longtime friend in Baltimore, already gravely ill with the disease that would
lead to his death in 1974.[12]

The crucial friendship with Wladimir Granoff also ended. They
would continue superficial relating, but the intensity of their connection

was gone. Granoff told me: "At first Masud acted as if Amsterdam had no meaning for us. He said: 'We mustn't make too much of Amsterdam' and 'We've been living in the consequences of Amsterdam, we should retrieve ourselves.' But I had moved on, and it felt like Masud was intruding on my life."[13]

Khan still saw patients and did editorial work, and he continued to read and to study French. But he was uncreative—none of his important papers come from this period. At times he realized he was not doing well: "There is an absolute vigour of psychic pain one should be wary about. Persons like me . . . have only to sink a little deeper inwards, and they become utterly invisible."[14] He thought he might have to retreat to Pakistan in order to survive: "I am about to lose all the objects that I love, but with me it is not so catastrophic, because somewhere my life has been sighted towards a monastic aloneness from the start. I have also got the reassurance of my estate in Pakistan where I can always be in exile until I recover my confidence in life."[15]

Late in 1966, Khan ended his fifteen-year therapeutic relationship with Winnicott. [As mentioned in Chapter 5, the exact number of years of formal analysis is unknown, but Winnicott provided some combination of analysis and "therapeutic coverage" for Khan throughout the period 1951 to 1966.] I was never able to find out exactly when or why the therapeutic relationship ended. Khan has left behind only veiled clues: "DWW . . . faltered in 1965. Not his fault, my lapse!"[16] "My analysis . . . ended in 1966 when DWW and I agreed spontaneously to opt out of our analytic contract with each other."[17] The ending was so bitter that the two stopped talking.[18] Then, after a short period of enmity, Khan resumed his work as Winnicott's assistant for writing and publishing, although Winnicott's analytic "coverage" ended as Khan stopped confiding in him.[19] Khan wrote of their Sunday morning meetings at Winnicott's home: "It was a pleasure for me to help DWW. He would present me with some typed scripts or clinical materials and we would work these into a manageable form and shape for publication."[20]

One reason for the ending of the analytic relationship may have been that Khan was protecting Winnicott from himself—and that Winnicott wanted such protection.[21] Winnicott, whose cardiac problems got worse under stress, literally might not have been able to withstand the intensity of further confrontation with Khan, while Khan was more and more in need of confrontation. At about the time of the ending of the analysis, or shortly afterward, Khan wrote: "Strength is a terrible burden, and very few humans can tolerate the bleak isolation of strength. One must arrange it in such a way that the very few others who are essential to one, are never pushed into a situation where their strength will be tested . . . I have learnt this humility very bitterly in the past year and it is worth learning."[22] Winnicott seems to have accepted the ending, even though he knew that Khan was doing badly. In 1968, in a professional talk, Winnicott made one of his characteristically obscure comments: "It is not a very terrible thing to fail in an analysis. The awful thing is to go on with an analysis after it has failed. Failure in some cases is the beginning of everything. It is the essential thing."[23]

It is ironic that, right at the time when the analysis ended, Winnicott was developing a theory that illustrated a very different way of handling aggression in psychoanalysis. This theory involved what Winnicott called object usage, an experience through which a person acquires a sense of the subjective reality of other people, leading to a dampening of the person's infantile feelings of omnipotence and destructiveness.[24] As we saw in Chapter 14, object usage occurs in analysis when the patient is free to attack ("kill") the analyst, with the analyst then "surviving." Aggression that goes both ways is a central part of the experience. If the object/analyst "fails to survive," the capacity for object usage does not develop, and the patient retains a false and omnipotent belief that the (normal) extremes of feeling are in themselves destructive. Nonsurvival of the analyst can take many forms, including retaliation, withdrawal, defensiveness, or an altering of the analytic setting. Winnicott "failed to survive" when he backed off from confrontation with Khan and allowed the analytic relationship to end.

In 1972, Khan said in a talk about the criteria for termination of analysis that two indicators of health should be present: (1) the analysand should have a self-sufficient ability to grow "as one could," and (2) the analysand should have developed the capacity to be influenced by others.[25] But although Khan *did* have those indicators of health in the 1950s

and early 1960s when his analysis was going well, he *did not* have either
of them in 1966. Later, when he spoke of his analysis, he said that Winnicott had "held" him well in the beginning, but that the analysis was a
failure after the early holding stage. At times, he blamed himself for this,
saying that he would not allow deeper work: "It would be idle to blame
my analysts or their technique. They did the best with what I was capable of at the time. No analyst can transcend & do more than the
analysand's capacities at the time."[26] But some of his comments about
Winnicott were harsh. He said that Winnicott was one more in the series of people who backed off from having a dialogue with him because
they felt overwhelmed: "Why do all my teachers accommodate to me?
I am yearning for teachers who would have the quiet authority that compels me to accommodate to them. Everyone bartered with me, including
Winnicott."[27] "How I eluded DWW, and how it must have aggravated
& hurt him to be wasted thus. He knew it & accepted it with an almost
evil complicity."[28] Eventually, he came to see Winnicott as having been
a savior *and* a destroyer: "Winnicott, from envy and his need of me, was
my most generous yet abominable exploiting accomplice."[29]

The year 1966 was a terrible time to end the therapeutic connection with
Winnicott because, in addition to the losses detailed above, Khan was also
losing his wife. As he isolated himself from his Western connections, he
also grew distant from Svetlana, even though she badly needed him.
    This was a time when Margot Fonteyn was dancing regularly with
Rudolf Nureyev, and it was gradually becoming clear that Beriosova
would not achieve the premier status that had once seemed so obviously
to be her destiny. The person who was most upset by Beriosova's loss of
status was Khan; his feelings about her situation added to his disillusionment with Western life. As Fonteyn kept dancing, Khan stopped adoring
Beriosova and she experienced that accurately as emotional abandonment. A friend commented, "Masud valued people most when they
were shining. Svetlana shone for a long time, but when things started
to go badly at the Royal, that was intolerable to Masud. They had been
equals and he couldn't stand it that she was no longer his equal."[30]
Beriosova needed to dance more than she needed adulation, and she
could have tolerated Fonteyn's return, but she could not tolerate the
loss of her husband, her major stabilizing force.[31] When her down-

ward spiral began, her fall was precipitous, in contrast to Khan's much slower deterioration.

Khan had always experienced his wife in a split manner. His letters and his Work Books show that when he related to her in the role of ballerina, he called her "Beriosova," and when he related to her as a person with human needs, she was "Svetlana." When he was in love, the split was not problematic. Now, as he was losing "Beriosova," "Svetlana" alone was not enough. Years later, he wrote about this time: "With Beriosova, it was her art and not her I understood so profoundly. When it came to knowing Svetlana, I collapsed and let her down abominably."[32]

Spring of 1967 would be the last time when there was vitality in the marriage. Beriosova was on tour in the United States and she had numerous opportunities to dance with Nureyev, giving hope that she could regain her superstar status. In April, Khan came to New York and was in the audience when her Cinderella coach tipped over and she was knocked unconscious (see Chapter 7, footnote 38). He was impressed by the courage she showed in going back onstage, and thrilled by the publicity.

Upon his return to London, he telephoned Svetlana every day. But the relationship was tense and the phone calls were at times upsetting. In May, he wrote to Zoë Dominic: "Svetlana and I had a telephone conversation which I spoilt for her. We are both so ghastly oversensitive and inflammably paranoid, and, given the least provocation, we cocoon ourselves in dismay. Love is really the ideal finishing school for learning bad manners."[33] This phone call led to several days of noncommunication, a most unusual experience for these two.

Part of the problem was that Svetlana's father, Poppa, was traveling with her and, in Khan's opinion, engaging in "a real paranoid splurge against me."[34] Khan claimed that Svetlana was too passive to confront her father, with the result that she displaced her negativity and "refusal" onto others, and he may have been right. When Poppa left for Europe, Khan and Svetlana made a better connection.

By August, the Khans were getting along well enough to make plans to go together to Monte Carlo. Khan's departure was delayed due to the death of his analysand H.K.'s son in a traffic accident (see Chapter 6). Svetlana went ahead with Zoë, so Khan traveled alone to Monte Carlo. Arriving at the Hotel Hermitage, he immersed himself in reading Camus.

(It was on this vacation that he made his first entry into the Work Books.) Although Khan and Svetlana were not especially close, they managed to have a decent vacation.

That fall, the marital problems deepened. For years, his French friends had set a model for extramarital affairs, something that was much less acceptable in London. It was the French who Khan admired, and now, in an act that may have been at least in part imitation or competition, he started his own affair. When Svetlana left on a long tour with the Royal Ballet, he got involved with a young Frenchwoman.

Marcelle (pseudonym) was tall and sensual, with dark skin and hair. By her own description she was sensitive, prone to hypochondria, and moody; in Khan's words she was "authentic, unplaced, apart, and depressed."[35] The daughter of a diplomat, she had lived in many countries and she spoke seven languages. As an adult, she had worked as an interpreter, then as a rebirthing therapist.[36] At age twenty-five, she was divorced from a man whom she had married at twenty.

I met Marcelle in 1998 when she was fifty-six years old. She was retired and living mostly in the country, with a lover who was more than a decade younger. She still kept an elegant flat in Paris, with large windows overlooking a public garden. She told me she was depressed these days, "beaten down by all my sicknesses, tired of traveling, just wanting a simple life." She was eager to talk about happier times thirty years earlier.

> I met Masud in Paris in 1967, when [a mutual friend] introduced us at a restaurant. I was single then, having gotten divorced the year before, and I was young and lost. I was fascinated by Masud—I had never met someone who was so "present," so "there." He had true interest in me. It wasn't just seduction—I was used to men seducing me and I knew the difference.
>
> He was very attractive—imposing, with an exotic masculine beauty. He had a noble hawk-nose and he looked like a warrior. And yet he had something—could have something—feminine in his approach. His anima was strongly developed and he could be very gentle. He knew he was beautiful, so he dressed in outlandish garb, often robes, almost always in black with silver jewelry.
>
> We related in the way people did in those days. I saw him when he came to Paris or when I was in London and Svetlana was away or just asleep—she was often exhausted in those days.

I was on the move then, always in motion, but we kept in touch. I had a boyfriend, but nevertheless Masud and I had a sexual relationship. The sex never meant that much to me—it was the friendship that I cared about.

In Paris, we would dress up like Arabs—I had jellabas [robes] for us to wear. We were both insomniacs and often we would go out at 4 a.m. for onion soup. When Masud got hungry, he never could wait, he *had* to eat. He ate a lot of meat, especially steak. At times he was phobic—he wouldn't go to a restaurant or to a party where he didn't know the people. And he liked to be the center of attention. He was Masud, not anyone else, and you could take it or leave it.

In the beginning years I learned a lot from him—about art, French literature, and psychoanalysis. Sometimes he gave me books—one, the *I Ching*, is inscribed by him to me: "For my tall friend, the book of books." He adored Winnicott, and anything Winnicott said was even more important than the Koran.

[Crying] He was a good friend. When I think of him, I think of the words loyalty, friendship, and respect: that sums him up more than anything. I don't even miss him that much, because he's a part of me. [Crying even more] He brought up a lot of love in people.

Marcelle stands out among Khan's women because she never needed more from him than he was able to give, so he did not feel drained by her. She was a liberated woman who had had many affairs with European men prior to Khan and concurrent with their relationship. She was not in love with him, and her needs were simple: advice, time together, and an easy sexual alliance.

The affair was short-lived and Svetlana never found out about it. Khan was still very much married—he would never master the French skill of having a secret lover. As a man used to having whatever he wanted (with a father who would have dealt with marital problems by taking on a new wife), he was surprised when he felt conflict: "I find that my personality is poorly equipped to deal with conflictual situations."[37] Within a few months, he ended the affair.

Khan continued to watch out for Marcelle all his life. He cared for her almost like a parent. He referred her for analysis to one of his French peers and introduced her to another friend with whom she fell in love and had a long relationship.

After Khan gave up the affair, his marriage continued to deteriorate. The salon at Hans Crescent lost its lively ambience, and hostility often took the place of aliveness. A friend told me about an occasion when Khan was fighting with her and her then-husband at the dinner table. When they decided to leave, Khan refused to let them go. Her husband was furious and decided to use the only exit available: he took her hand and proceeded to walk out across the top of the table.[38] The Khans' fairy-tale living was over.

CHAPTER 2 I

LYING FALLOW

Thus the basis of the capacity to be alone is a paradox; it is the experience
of being alone while someone else is present.
D. W. Winnicott[1]

Two years after the Amsterdam events, Khan began to come out of his
hostile isolation. He did not return to the extensive travel/lecture circuit of the first half of the decade—that period of his life was over. But
he reached out to selected friends and peers in the West and his isolation changed into a kind of creative aloneness.

He built on personal experience as he developed a theory about the
restorative potential of withdrawal. His idea was that a person could "lie
fallow"—retire from activity in the outside world—in order to restore a
connection to the True Self. Lying fallow was characterized by "non-
conflict" and "alerted quietude" and it prepared a person for later creativity: "It is a nutrient of the ego and a preparatory state. [It] allows for
that larval inner experience which distinguishes true psychic creativity
from obsessional productiveness."[2]

Success in the fallow state, Khan said, requires the observing presence of at least one other person. Without a witness, the withdrawal leads
to stagnation: "Although this fallow mood is essentially and inherently
private and personal, it needs an ambience of companionship in order to
be held and sustained. Someone—a friend, a wife, a neighbour—sitting
around unobtrusively, guarantees that the psychic process does not get
out of hand, that is, become morbid, introspective or sullenly doleful."[3]

In earlier years, Svetlana had been a consistent comfort to Khan in
difficult times, but she was now unavailable for him. Khan had to find

other witnesses in his fallow period, and one of these would be Sybil
Stoller. He wrote to inform her that he was a changed person: "My
crisis of the past two years is now ending, and I have dropped many
friends, but not you. I was in NYC for the ballet and I was tempted to
ring, but I decided it would be fatuous and silly to chatter: 'This is
Masud of London, only a different Masud.' You would ask, 'How are
you different?' and what could I answer? I am 30 pounds lighter, now
only French literature obsesses me, and I find my own self the best company. I have changed and feel different to myself and others."[4] Their
correspondence, which had been almost nonexistent for two years, was
quickly restored.

     Khan's most dedicated witness was Winnicott. Working together
on Sunday mornings, the two men had developed a new kind of closeness that pleased Khan enormously. Khan wrote with regard to these
Sundays: "It was from such encounters I learned the most from DWW."[5]
His statement is a mixed compliment, because it implies that the analysis with Winnicott had been of lesser value.

An important development from this period is that on August 14, 1967,
Khan began writing his Work Books. These still-unpublished writings
are a day-by-day reflective commentary, "abstractions towards a general-
ised knowing of myself and others."[6] The project pleased him: "Of all
my efforts at the notation of my self-experience, these Work Books sat-
isfy me the most."[7]

     The first Work Book volumes were written in twenty-three blank
copybooks bound by Tisne of Paris, a previously unused gift from
Wladimir Granoff. Khan's handwritten copy was typed into manuscript
form by a secretary. At first three carbon copies were made, but this
number was soon changed to two because the final copy was too dim.
The first carbon always went to Robert and Sybil Stoller, who carefully
preserved and bound the pages. The location of the second carbon is
unknown, while the (incomplete) third carbon is held by Judy Cooper,
Khan's analysand/biographer, who received it as a gift from Khan.

     Over the years, the Stollers read the Work Books with great enthu-
siasm. Robert wrote, "You can imagine how thrilled we were to receive
the Work Books. They are the most exciting writings being produced
by any psychoanalyst, and whatever can be published some day will be

mined for years after. . . . Every time I pick them up, I grab at them greedily, unwilling to stop reading. They are really marvelous."[8]

The first entry in volume 1 is a quote from *King Lear*: "Is there any cause in Nature that makes these hard hearts?" *King Lear* had been on his mind from his first days in London.

Now that Khan was lying fallow, he was thriving. In addition to reading and letter writing, he started painting and returned to making paper collages. He had taken painting classes with Marion Milner in the late 1940s, then abandoned that interest except for colorful doodles that he had never stopped drawing. Now he again became serious about art, often painting in the early morning hours when he was insomniac: "I paint as I can, but utterly true to my physicality of Being. Painting is the only activity that absorbs the whole of me in a non-reactive and truly expressive way."[9] The return to painting helped him to ground himself: "Yes, clinical work, painting, reading and writing are the four sanities of my psyche."[10]

During this time, he bought a horse, an indulgence and a gift to himself that he had longed for since leaving Kot Fazaldad Khan.[11] Appropriately enough, he named the horse Solo.[12] He rode Solo in early morning, before starting work: "Apart from work, my real joy these days is Solo & in spite of fearfully wet weather here, I have enjoyed some splendid long rides. We are getting to know each other."[13] After awhile, he and Solo started taking polo lessons from a Mr. Walsh, which brought more pleasure: "Solo loves playing polo & for no other reason shall I persist now but for his pleasure in this romp. Every time I missed the ball, and it was often, he spontaneously stopped and turned round urging me graciously to try again. The dignity of a horse's loyal knowing and friendship. If only we humans could sponsor those that fumble like this."[14]

In starting to ride again, Khan was allowing a return of the Eastern self that he had put to the side since coming to England. He was visiting Pakistan more often now, going there twice a year, in January and August. He successfully used the estate in Faisalabad [the new name for Lyallpur] as a place to lie fallow. There he experienced a peace he never had in London. Writing from Pakistan, he commented, "One cannot go too far away from the logic of one's nurture."[15] He sat in his study at

Kot Fazaldad Khan, surrounded by bookshelves filled with English literature, and thought about how fine it was to live in two worlds, with
London a place for intellectual life and Pakistan a place for relaxation:

> From the moment I arrive here, I fuse with my environment. I lose that
> mental distance from which alone one describes things. The physical
> ambience is truly idyllic this time of the year: cold crisp wintry days in a
> vastly generous warm sun. I ride each day. . . . I don't know quite what I
> am thinking inwardly: here even my intellectuality sinks into a sensuous
> haze of muteness and passivity.
>
> Outside the day is dawning. The cacophony of bird-noises has set
> up its coaxing chirp to awaken everyone. I can hear the cocks crow and
> distant faint noises of bells round the bullocks as they trudge their feet
> ploughing the fields. This is a restful ambience and so different.[16]

Life in Faisalabad was not always idyllic, however. Salah, the illegitimate first child of Khan's mother, had been managing the estate for
years, but Khan now came to believe that Salah was squandering money.
Starting in 1966, Khan began to manage the estate himself. This meant
that he always had business matters to handle when he was in Pakistan.

Major societal change was occurring in Pakistan. The entire country was being Westernized and modernized, even as it remained Muslim. In 1966 and 1967, Khan was forced by land reforms to sell a major
part of his property. He used some of the money to purchase the Rex
Cinema on Satiana Road. He also allowed a Bollywood movie to be
filmed on the estate, in return for a substantial fee. But Khan participated in the changes as little as possible—he was attached to feudal India,
never to modern Pakistan. He did not even apply to become a Pakistani
citizen, so from 1947 on, he was a man without a country.

In the two years post-Amsterdam, Khan had written almost nothing and
he had stopped giving public talks. Now, as he returned to living, he
wrote a proposal for a book on perversions, to be based on a collection
of his earlier papers. Sutherland accepted the proposal for the IPL, and
this book was eventually published as *Alienation in Perversions*.[17] In the
fall of 1968, he agreed to give a talk to the society on the work of
Michael Balint, and in preparation, he immersed himself in reading:
"I am phobically obsessed and preoccupied with Balint's writings, all

of which I have read now—some five volumes."[18] For weeks, he struggled with writing and then just two days before the talk, he suddenly knew what he wanted to say. He wrote to Smirnoff that he worked on the paper on November 4–5 from 11 p.m. to 5 a.m. and then stayed up all night on the 5th to finish it: "How easily & pleasurably the act of writing flows out of my hands once I have crashed through the refusal of the mind!"[19] "I am very satisfied with the paper. It is neither clever nor argumentative."[20] In a more combative state of mind, he might have criticized Balint, because he believed that Balint idealized infancy and denied the importance of hatred in human relationships. But he felt like being cooperative, and focused instead on what he felt were the strong parts of Balint's theories.

When he finished writing the paper, he was unable to sleep, despite having had only three hours of consecutive sleep in four days. He called his doctor, John Cardwell, who gave him an injection of pethidine (a synthetic analgesic) that provided respite. That night, he gave his talk to the society, and it was well received: "The paper was a great & genuine success—both with Dr. Balint & the audience. And I delivered it well: with the right modesty of arrogance! The discussion was positive & healthy, which is rare in our Society."[21]

At the time when Khan began to write again, Winnicott was in the United States on a lecture tour. On November 12, he presented his new idea about object usage in a talk "On the Use of the Object" to the New York Psychoanalytic Society. Khan had predicted that the talk would not be understood: "It is going to be very hard for the New York analysts to swallow because it has revolutionary implications for analysis."[22] He was right: the New York analysts responded with a critique so harsh that Winnicott later commented: "I now see why the Americans are in Vietnam."[23] Returning to his hotel that night, he had a serious coronary. The situation at first was very grim, as Khan noted in his Work Book entry: "DWW is seriously ill in New York with heart failure. I pray he can return home and die peacefully in his own home. Amen!!"[24] Winnicott ended up hospitalized in New York City for weeks, at great financial cost. His wife Clare was with him, but she herself became seriously ill with the Hong Kong flu. Since the topic of the talk was the survival of the analyst in the face of attack from the patient, it is an irony of analytic history that Winnicott barely survived his presentation.

In the weeks following Winnicott's coronary, Khan wrote two more papers.[25] He said that he wrote to distract himself from thinking too much about something he could not control: "Strange how nutrient anguish can be. I wonder if I would have gotten my papers written without this extra strain within. It was as if I had to DO something to lance the helplessness I felt vis-à-vis Winnicott's illness."[26] A letter to Smirnoff shows that he was extremely upset: "This has been a wretchedly anxious week for me. Inwardly, I have been preoccupied with Winnicott's severe illness in New York. At one point it looked like he was not going to make it."[27]

John Sutherland was retiring at this time, and Winnicott had been scheduled to give the major toast at his retirement dinner at the Savoy Hotel. Balint asked Khan to take Winnicott's place and he agreed reluctantly, thinking that his colleagues would not welcome him: "I can HEAR their malice so tangibly, their unspoken words are palpable in my ears. . . . A feudal Muslim toasting a Scotsman to an assembly of displaced Jews and what is left of the English. . . . God help us!!"[28] He was again underestimating his peers: the toast was well received.

Oddly, he had not tried to contact Winnicott during the time when his mentor's survival was in question. He wrote only in response to a letter Winnicott sent him, almost three weeks after the coronary:

> My dear DWW,
>
> What a joy to receive your letter in your own writing: I have been patiently waiting for it. Haven't written to you myself because even concern can be intrusive and a strain in such circumstances. Thank God you are getting better and gaining strength each day. Please take time and do not start rushing the full recovery now. I know how tiresome it must be for you to be stranded in a hospital in New York, and of course the strain of it on Mrs. Winnicott. But please try and be patient.
>
> The news of your illness shocked and distressed all of us. . . .
>
> How is Mrs. Winnicott? Svetlana & I think of you both often & pray for you to get home safe and soon.
>
> With love & best wishes for a solid recovery, Affectionately, Masud[29]

Just before Christmas, Winnicott returned to London, traveling with a nurse. Khan made a brief note in his Work Book: "DWW has returned home safely from New York—triumph of the will to live."[30]

Almost immediately, the two were back doing their Sunday work. Khan wrote with admiration about their first post-illness meeting: "Winnicott looked much better than I had expected, and was battlesomely vigorous from his very meagre physical resources, restless searching in the creative ferment of his mind. How enviable to keep alive and creative right to the last dregs of physicality in one."[31] The next day, however, he was more critical: "Winnicott was physically so frail and spent today, and yet he was as willful and unyielding as ever. It is excruciatingly frustrating and depriving—one could almost say castrating—to have to tolerate his refusal and adapt to it."[32]

Despite his frustrations with Winnicott, Khan was relieved to have him back, and he felt secure enough to take more risks in his own writing. In February 1969, he published "Reparation to the Self as an Idealised Internal Object" in the German journal *Dynamische Psychiatrie*—a paper that he liked: "[It is] the first paper in my new Masud style. I am afraid Anna Freud is not going to like it: she will think I am drifting from classicism. Am I? I sometimes wonder."[33] Later in 1969, he wrote "On Symbiotic Omnipotence" for the APF *Bulletin*, and he finished writing his paper on crucial friendship.[34]

He was alienated from most of his peers: "I so starve for human contact in this damnable, Puritan, anti-human culture."[35] But despite a persistent belief that his colleagues were out to get him, he noticed that his enemies were softening. At the Rome IPAC in August 1969, the first congress he attended after Amsterdam, even William Gillespie came over to say hello: "This is most decent of [Gillespie] and by this gesture he gives me his vote of confidence which he had so explicitly suspended in Amsterdam."[36] In 1970 his proposal for a paper for the 1971 IPAC in Vienna was accepted, even though he had been certain it would be turned down. Yet another sign of his acceptance was his appointment as a director of the Sigmund Freud Copyrights in 1971 (see Chapter 17).

Heading into the new decade, it is clear that Khan's professional world was, and would continue to be, in flux. While in Pakistan over the Christmas holidays of 1970, he received word from Victor Smirnoff that Michael Balint had died, an expected but sad piece of news. Khan

182   F A L S E   S E L F

felt a special connection to the older analysts and tended to feel traumatized when any of them died.[37] Later that year, he felt he was also
losing a peer, Charles Rycroft. Rycroft had had what Khan refers to as
a breakdown, and now he was bitterly breaking off contact with the society.[38] Khan wrote: "The devil of it is those of my colleagues who are
not dying of age like DWW are decomposing from within. All this gath-
ers toward a very huge aloneness."[39]

Despite a growing separation from the West, he still delighted in Paris.
He wrote in his Work Book, "The morbid compulsion of my life has been
to love, whereas my true talent is for Paris."[40] It was a city where he could
reliably connect to his True Self, both privately and in social situations.[41]
And thanks to diligent work, he had become fluent in understanding and
reading French. (His spoken French would never be fluent.) He wrote to
Robert Stoller about how important this was to him: "I have been working very hard at acquiring a knowledge of the French language over the
last three years, and suddenly, almost magically, it seems to click, and I
can now function in that environment nimbly and affluently. In fact, at
the present moment, I have put all my concentration of sensibility and
intellectual effort, plus social relationships, with friends and colleagues in
Paris, and I live in London merely to do my professional work."[42] Moving to Paris would be a lifelong, if unrealized, dream.

Granoff was now on the periphery of Khan's Parisian world, but
Victor Smirnoff was there as a new crucial friend (see Chapter 24).
Through Smirnoff, he was accepted into an informal group of intellectuals that included the analysts André Green, Didier Anzieu, Marie
Moscovici, Jean-Claude Lavie, O. Mannoni, and Guy Rosolato; the
analyst/editor Jean-Bertrand ("J.-B.") Pontalis; the anthropologist Jean
Pouillon; and the literary writer Jean Starobinski.[43] These people did
not have "hard hearts" like the English, in his experience. He felt that
his French colleagues valued him as much as he valued them. They appreciated his eccentricity and his vital energy and he felt alive in their
world.[44]

In 1970, Pontalis started the analytic journal *Nouvelle revue de psychanalyse* (NRP) and he invited Khan to be on the editorial board. Khan
agreed, but asked to have the title of "foreign co-editor." Pontalis told
me he agreed because he understood Khan's need to be "a little apart

and different."[45] Khan was pleased, because he had enormous respect for Pontalis' editorial ability. He described his new friend's aesthetic taste as "impeccable."[46]

Pontalis soon became one of Khan's favorite friends. He had a country home where he often invited Khan and other analysts to weekend dinners, and Khan appreciated these evenings because the conversation was "casually and rigorously significant and intellectual, [with] no silly small talk."[47] Khan loved to listen and he also loved to speak. His friend Sahabzada Yaqub Khan told me: "Masud was an amazing conversationalist. I remember once when I was Ambassador to Paris, Khan and Pontalis and I were out to dinner. Masud made some brilliant remark, and then moved on. I said to Pontalis: 'That was such a penetrating remark! It's like a lighthouse in the dark. Suddenly a beam of light comes on, and then it is gone.' Pontalis replied simply: 'That is Masud.'"

A new door opened professionally in October 1970 when Khan went to the Deutschen Akademie fur Psychoanalyse in Berlin, where Dr. Günther Ammon had invited him to give a lecture.[48] He and Ammon had made a good connection in 1964 when they met at the Menninger Clinic in the United States.

This was Khan's first visit to Berlin since his travels in the years 1946 to 1951. He was impressed by the Akademie and its clinic, which were both housed in a suite of rooms on the upper floor of an old building on Wielanderstrasse. Günther's analyst wife, Gisela, ran a psychoanalytic kindergarten on the first floor, where she and her colleagues applied ideas learned from reading Winnicott. She and Günther made their home on another floor of the same building.

On the first night in Berlin, Khan called the Ammons from his hotel, complaining about the noise and demanding to come immediately to their home. They came to get him, and he and Günther then sat together into the early morning hours, drinking whisky and talking about the history of psychoanalysis. Gisela told me: "Masud told us that in all his life, he had never stayed at a hotel and he would have to stay at our home whenever he visited the school. From that time on, he always stayed with us."[49]

Khan's paper was delivered to the students in German, translated by a faculty member. After the talk, he celebrated by buying himself two Mont Blanc pens, a hat, and a knife. That night there was a party for one hundred people at the Ammons'. Khan stayed up late, enjoying the camaraderie: "By midnight I had Masudically established myself round a table in a corner & collected their most promising trainees around me."[50]

On the final night, Khan and his new friends went out to a transvestite club. One of the singers—"a very deliciously handsome Spanish youth"—joined them for drinks, and he and Khan immediately connected. The extent of their connection is unclear, as Khan wrote about the evening: "The difference between a beautiful boy one desires and a beautiful girl one covets is that the boy facilitates one's effort and the girl has to be worked for! This I found out tonight. What taboos about pleasure Christian cum analytic dogma has engendered in me. Still, it is not too late to re-find what nature had lavishly endowed one with."[51]

The last two months of 1970 were a continuation of professional success. In November, after the Berlin visit, he finished the index to Winnicott's *Therapeutic Consultations*; participated (along with Clifford Yorke and Joseph Sandler) in a society panel, giving a paper entitled "Beyond Conflictual Dynamics: A Tribute to Heinz Hartmann"; and published in the IJPA his "Shorter Reviews," a summary of forty books. Then in December, he wrote an article entitled "L'Oeil Entend" for NRP.[52]

This period of Khan's life lacked the glamour of the divine years, but he seemed to be recovering from Amsterdam and getting his professional life back on track, even though his private life was not going well.

THE DYING OF A MARRIAGE

The real horror of a love relationship going sour is not that
the partners start destroying each other, but rather that
they destroy their dreams about each other.
Masud Khan[1]

Sud adored Svetlana, it was obvious. He adored her and he
destroyed her. But she also truly embarked on her own
self torture. It's terrible to think about this.
Zoë Dominic

Khan's fallow period, with all its regenerative aspects, was something
he experienced on his own, without Svetlana. They became increasingly
estranged as Svetlana went rapidly downhill.

In August 1968, the Khans went again to the south of France. This
year, they rented a bungalow at Ramateulle, rather than going to the
Old Beach Hotel. Smirnoff, Jeanne Axler, and Axler's mother stayed a
short distance away in a larger guest house. Khan wrote to Zoë Dominic
that they filled their time "lazing around—privately, separately, or together as the mood dictates."[2]

Axler remembers that Svetlana seemed unhappy and even scared that
summer. She told me: "Svetlana relied on Masud's strength, and when
they weren't getting along, she would be devastated." The others pretended not to notice as Svetlana drank wine all through lunch and then
slept through the afternoon, only to start drinking again when she awoke.
At dinner, she and Khan almost always had a screaming fight, which upset

Smirnoff, because he hated arguments. Axler was amazed at what she was observing: "I thought, who are these aliens?"

When the vacation ended, Khan and Svetlana drove to Paris and stayed for a few days.[3] There he had a recurrence of an old symptom: inner terror that had no apparent cause. It was unprecedented for him to feel the terror while on vacation. He wrote in his Work Book that he was having a problem with accepting and tolerating his feelings—particularly envy, hate, and wishes for revenge—and that he thought that his terror came from trying too hard to control those feelings.[4] When news arrived that Russia had invaded Czechoslovakia, he ruminated about how the whole world was filled with envy, hate, and violence, just as he was.

Returning to London, both Khans were productive professionally. Beriosova was dancing a new role in *Enigma Variations*, which was well received by the press and by audiences. But she was well on the way to becoming a serious alcoholic. A letter from Khan to Geoffrey Gorer reveals that she had collapsed at a weekend party at Gorer's estate. This incident must have been embarrassing for Khan, since he had enormous esteem for Gorer and also for another guest, Diomede Catroux, a well-known philosopher who was a friend of Pontalis as well as Gorer.

> Dear Geoffrey,
>   I hope you will forgive us for our lapses. Svetlana is easily jolted into regressing dissolution of Self at present and this week Anthony Tudor [the choreographer] has been persistently unkind to her—largely from envy of her success in "Enigma."
>   Still, this is no reason why she should collapse on you in your home. You know enough about these states for me to tell you that even that is a way of trusting and being affectionate—I only feel sad the Catrouxes were involved in it because it must have perplexed them greatly. It indeed distresses me beyond the means of my nurture and sensibility.
>   You are very dear to both of us and Svetlana has a deep affection for you. I hope all the fluctuations of her mood did not embarrass you over much and did not cause you too much pain. I know you too care for her deeply.
>   With my love and gratitude, Yours affectionately, Sud[5]

Another part of the 1968 story is an affair Khan started with his analysand Eva (pseudonym). This was no small relationship: Eva was the first woman he loved after Svetlana. (The story of the affair is told from Eva's perspective in Chapter 23.) As with Marcelle, he was risking his marriage, but with Eva the stakes were higher, because he was risking his career by violating the very clear rule that an analyst should not have a sexual relationship with a patient.

He had already been breaking other rules with Eva. They had a significant correspondence beginning in 1963, the year her analysis began[6]; they cowrote a (never-published) paper on Camus; and, beginning in 1967, Eva often came to dinner at Hans Crescent and stayed on to play cards. Zoë Dominic remembers a specific dinner when she suddenly sensed a sexual connection between Khan and Eva, and she knew for certain that they were having an affair. As a friend of both Khans, she decided to mind her own business, so she said nothing. It would be months before Svetlana found out, and when she did, she was devastated.

In a rare gesture of assertiveness, Svetlana issued an ultimatum to her husband: he had to choose either her or Eva. This happened at the same time as Winnicott was hospitalized in New York, and the stress of the situation may explain why Khan was slow to write Winnicott. In early December, just after he learned that Winnicott would survive his heart attack, Khan decided to end the affair and stay with Svetlana. Many years later, he recalled: "I abandoned [Eva] brutally, with the excuse that I must save Svetlana, at all cost to my happiness."[7] Khan regretted losing Eva, but he did not feel guilt about having had an affair with an analysand. He wrote that although he had loyalty to his mentors—especially Rickman, Winnicott, and Sutherland—he did not feel obliged to obey analytic rules: "I do not regret any of the events in [my life] because I sense in them a deeper truer logic than I could have planned and programmed for myself."[8]

At Christmas, Khan wrote to Victor Smirnoff about how difficult the year had been, adding that he also had optimism for the future: "1968 has been an awesome year—so much pain and conflict and chaos. And yet, my dear friend, in me there is a curious unquenchable optimism and verve which keeps itself sustained in spite of all the gloom of my mind."[9] Perhaps, he said, the current emptiness of his life was a signal that there would be a "new beginning," in Balint's terminology. He would put his pain to the side and keep going:

> The hardest thing to learn is that one has to give up by and from choice,
> in order for other new experiences and relationships to have scope and

growth. One would so wish to keep on indulging and that just is not possible. The character of change is defined more by what one decides to give up, than what one chooses to add afresh. I have willfully given up a relationship that had nourished me deeply and meant so much to me both as a person and an intellectual. And there has been no time or scope even to allow myself to experience the sadness of its absence now and forever in my life. I haven't been able to speak of this loss to anyone.[10]

Khan's greatest worry as the new year started was that Solo was sick: "Now even my horse is ill and lame, and this makes me almost more despondent than I can bear."[11]

By January, Khan was back together with both Winnicott and Svetlana and even the horse had recovered. But private living was a nightmare because Svetlana was drinking on a daily basis. In 1969, she was sober when she danced but she regularly got drunk after her performances. Her alcoholism progressed to the point where she began having blackouts. Years later, Khan commented on this period: "I have never really known suffering, except when Svetlana as Beriosova was disintegrating."[12]

Drunkenness was a theme in Svetlana's family history, while Khan had grown up in a Muslim world where there was no alcohol. His scripting included violence, however, that was disastrous when combined with alcohol. When courting Svetlana in the 1950s, Khan had warned her that he was, in his words, a "savage," heir to a kind of behavior that was totally foreign to their London world. For his first twenty years in the West, his violence had been limited to verbal savagery, with the single exception of the fight with his houseboy Antonio. From the mid-1960s on—and only after his analysis had ended—he began episodic heavy drinking and his savage nature was at times expressed physically with Svetlana. These two glamorous people now began to have a very ordinary experience of marital devastation fueled by alcohol.[13]

In May 1969, Khan accompanied Svetlana to New York, where she performed at Lincoln Center in *Swan Lake* and *Giselle*. On an afternoon prior to the performance of *Giselle*, Svetlana went into an angry withdrawal when the hotel phone did not work. Khan described her as "depersonalised, with a violent latency of rage."[14] She became even more angry and upset when Khan left to meet with some editors, because she wanted him to devote the whole day to her as she prepared for her evening performance.

That night, Beriosova put her personal problems to the side and danced flawlessly. It was Mother's Day and Khan was unable to get the usual flowers sent to her dressing room, so he bought flowers and delivered them himself backstage, along with a Chagall picture book. The Stollers were in the audience, having come to New York specifically to see Svetlana's *Giselle*. After the performance, the two couples went to the apartment of Tony Walton and his wife Gen LeRoy for a seafood dinner. It was a companionable evening, free of strife.

Then, returning to the Hotel Salisbury, Khan and Svetlana had a drunken argument that got violent. Khan made an emergency call to Walton, who arrived around midnight and helped them to stop fighting. Nobody slept. In the early morning, Khan left for the airport to book a flight for an early return to London.

On the plane, Khan wrote to Smirnoff. He said he had the feeling that his marriage was over: "[I am feeling] a chilled pain that does not yield even to being experienced as loss or dismay. Something in me has awakened into a quiet hardness of acceptance of the impossibility of a future with Svetlana. We hurt & molest each other too much now. Alas ! ! And yet what a couple we still make."[15] Arriving home, he wrote a second letter, saying that something "definite and mutative" had happened in New York. Svetlana, he said, was attacking not just the marriage but also her career and her whole life, and if he stayed with her, he would be acting as an accomplice to the destruction. He predicted that Svetlana would have no memory of what happened and that they would be unable to talk about the fight: "She has no cognitive recall of the berserk violence of speech and behavior in these 'happenings' and to enumerate it is merely humiliating and enfuriating for her. So I [can] say nothing to console and assuage her. It is this acute incapacity to help that is the real terror of it all for me."[16]

Many years earlier, Winnicott had gone to great lengths to help Khan's first wife, Jane Shore, when she was having a nervous breakdown. This time, however, he was not available. Zoë Dominic told me: "I was desperately concerned about Svetlana's problem with alcoholism. I called Winnicott on the telephone and asked him to help but he backed off, saying 'I can't be bothered by this responsibility, I'm ill.'" It is possible that Winnicott would have tried, had Svetlana been more of a verbal person and desirous of analytic help. But Svetlana put her feelings into physical rather than verbal expression and she did not want talk therapy. As Khan wrote, "One can feel the verity and absoluteness of [Svetlana's] affective logic, but one has no way of sharing it or relating to it."[17]

After Winnicott refused to treat Svetlana, Khan tried to refer her to Michael Balint, knowing that Balint was often willing to treat nonverbal patients. He told Smirnoff about his disappointment when Balint turned down the referral: "Svetlana was not able to start with Balint because he rigidly insisted on a five-times-a-week analysis and a dedication to treatment, while Svetlana can devote [herself] only to her art." Khan added that Balint had referred Svetlana to Dr. John Gould, "a good commonsense psychiatrist," and that Winnicott had agreed to monitor her care, "albeit at long range."[18] In years to come, Svetlana would be treated for alcoholism by many doctors, but she would never try psychoanalysis or even psychotherapy.[19]

In the summer of 1969, the Khans went as usual to Monte Carlo, despite their estrangement. The Smirnoffs were visitors, as was Poppa. Khan felt that Svetlana was happy only with Poppa: "The rest of the time has been as feared & dreaded. Only there seems to be no limit to the variety of the faces of terror & dismay."[20] He left to attend the Rome International Psychoanalytic Association Conference (IPAC), where he met the Stollers, who returned with him to Monte Carlo. The Khans got along better for the rest of their vacation, in part because of the Stollers' calming influence: "We have spent some quiet and genuinely happy days with Bob and Sybil. They are the most normal, genuine and true human beings that we know. I have spent many an hour with them, and it is always so casual, generous and affectionate, without intensity or drama."[21]

After the vacation, upon returning to London, Svetlana decided that she wanted to have a child. It was an old longing that had intensified. A friend told me: "Svetlana felt sorry that she had given up children for her career, when her career ended up not being as successful as she wanted it to be. She said, 'It would have been worth it if I could have really been the best.' She used to become maudlin and talk about children, especially when she drank."[22]

Khan, who might have been willing to have a child in happier times, refused to cooperate: "I am absolutely pitted against the practice of therapeutic childbearing. It seems to me little short of evil that two adults, when they find themselves at odds with each other, should then introduce an infant to sustain their relationship and/or each of them."[23] At times, however, he was ambivalent. Writing from Pakistan, where he had been forced to sell a huge section of his familial land, he told Svetlana:

> One thing I realise now is that unless one has a child, one's life is claustrophobically self centered, with no vista onto the future. An individual's unextended life-space has a very small, though perhaps intense, scope. The horrors that you and I have suffered from life and each other during the past five years are all the result of my incapacity and unreadiness to sponsor and nurture a family of our own. I feel with selling the lands and translating it into liquid money, I have taken a step towards rearing a family. This is all I can say. But somewhere I need a lot more courage and faith to really start a family. Perhaps with God's help I shall find it soon.[24]

Years later he wrote: "It ruined Svetlana and me not to have a child."[25]

It is impossible, of course, to know what would have happened if the Khans had had a child. If children had been involved in a divorce situation, there would almost certainly have been major custody problems. Khan's loyalty was to Islamic tradition and the major statement of Islamic law, the Shari'a, states that men have the right to keep their children after a divorce. One of Khan's (anonymous) mistresses from a later period remembers him saying: "I would never trust a child to a woman."

By late fall of 1969, things were worse than ever and Khan could no longer distract himself with outside activity. He wrote to Smirnoff, "Up till now, all the problems in my life had been created by me from my own temperament and sensibility. The issue now is how to find the discipline and the style for an objective and external nightmare which remains totally outside one's influence or mastery. . . . My dear Pnin, where does one find that extra libido these days which makes one venture into life?"[26] He said that sometimes he felt such terror about survival that he was afraid he would not be able to keep breathing.

In December, Svetlana was admitted to Royal Waterloo Hospital in her first psychiatric hospitalization. Her new physician, Dr. William Sargant, was a biological psychiatrist, and his intervention was limited to detoxification. She was treated with a technique that was then very much in vogue: a chemically induced sleep/coma, in which the patient is allowed to be awake only for a short while each day, to eat and care for various physical needs. Khan wrote to Smirnoff, "[T]hough having Svetlana in a hospital in an ambience of physical psychiatry is frightening for me because I know so little about it, I feel relieved, because she is at last in care and not responsible for willfully battling with her internal nightmare. Up till now, everybody was merely blundering about and then shirking and putting the blame on everybody else. . . . Unfortunately, no amount of reading of Winnicott is going to heal her."[27]

Khan spent Christmas alone. On Boxing Day (December 26), Tony Walton and Gen LeRoy stopped by, together with Emma, Tony's daughter with Julie Andrews. After some difficulty finding an open restaurant, they were able to get a table at the Rib Room. Khan found Emma to be "wondrous, sophisticated, heroic and mellow." When she said, "You know, Sudie, Daddy works all night," Khan told her that he did the same: "Persons like Daddy & me work best at night and we enjoy it, because it is so quiet."[28] Emma learned that Svetlana was in the hospital and insisted on making her a card. As she worked on the card, Walton suddenly burst into tears, and he continued to cry fitfully throughout the dinner.

Thinking back on that evening, Walton believes he was crying as he thought about Svetlana's supportive presence in the hospital on the evening Emma was born. She had been an integral part of one of the most important days of his life, and the contrast to her present state was extreme. He added: "It's likely that I was also crying for the obviously confused solitude of Sud."

On New Year's Eve, Svetlana came home as scheduled and the couple had a short period of peaceful living. But the peace lasted only for a few weeks. In March, Khan wrote to Smirnoff, "I have not been able to write because I am going through another sustained bout of terrible distress and illness in Svetlana. . . . You must forgive me if I am bleak and abrupt, but I am struggling to live through another awesome day where no help can be found anywhere."[29]

He had postponed a Christmas trip to Pakistan and he now arranged it for the end of March, when Poppa could come to watch over Svetlana. He badly needed this trip: "Have never known myself so resourceless, tired and exhausted. Merely existing to survive each day does not fit my temperament."[30]

The trip was at first extremely successful and even blissful. Khan immersed himself in Oscar Wilde's writings and in rereading *King Lear*: "'Lear' is perhaps the most unique example and expression [in all literature] of human hope, rage and helplessness. I find it much more moving than 'Oedipus.'"[31] He was lying fallow—alone, but connected to his Western life, particularly to Winnicott, with whom he corresponded. But he had a premonition of something being wrong. On April 3, he wrote in his Work Book: "There is no way of preparing to receive ill news." Shortly after that, news from London did destroy his peace. The news came in a telephone call from his secretary, Miss Stanway,[32] who told him that Poppa, with Svetlana's cooperation, had dictated to her a letter that had been sent to him in Pakistan. The content was that both Poppa and Svetlana thought that there should be a divorce and they never wanted to see him again. Stanway told me that she called because her primary loyalty was to Khan: "I wanted him to be prepared for the letter and I wanted him to know that I wasn't supportive of its contents."

The letter, dated April 5, 1970, arrived on April 9. Even before it arrived, Khan got telegrams from Zoë Dominic and Winnicott telling him that Svetlana had been hospitalized again. She had voluntarily entered Priory Nursing Home, under the care of a psychiatrist named Dr. Flood, with Winnicott as consultant. Once again, she was getting the drug-induced sleep therapy. Upon hearing the news, Khan left immediately for London.

By the time he got home, Svetlana had already been released and she seemed to be better. Khan wrote to Smirnoff, "I can't tell you of my joy in finding Svetlana truly in her person and presence. It seems she has taken a real hard steady look at herself and accepted that her problems are rooted in drink; and she has decided for abstinence, life, health and work."[33] Then, a few days later, Svetlana drank herself into a near coma and had to be taken by ambulance back to the Priory. She was kept heavily sedated, and whenever the sedation was reduced, she was angry and bitter. This time Khan was more realistic: "I am . . . defeated vis-à-vis Svetlana's ailment. I had been so enthused by her clarity of presence on my return. But it lasted precisely four days. How short the periods of respite have become—and I can no longer hope for a miracle from any direction."[34]

He told Smirnoff that he was feeling a "macabre void and nullity of self experience."[35]

On June 5, Svetlana was released. Khan found it difficult to be with her: "Svetlana is managing to sustain her health, but it is now so precarious that one tires oneself watching."[36] Both Smirnoff and Winnicott were urging him to protect himself by moving out, but Khan did not agree with their advice. He wrote Smirnoff that he thought that he should stay with Svetlana and do a self-analysis in which he faced the torturous feelings of his inner life. He said that, as a result of the current suffering, he was beginning to recall his past "not as metaphorical events, but as it was. Somehow I never managed this in my three analyses with Sharpe, Rickman and DWW."[37] Although he would have to withdraw from the world again to find himself, he was confident that after a little while he would "resurface in myself and unto myself."[38] He thought that Smirnoff and Winnicott could be his witnesses, and that they would be able to understand him without his having to put anything into words.

On July 15, Khan wrote to Smirnoff: "I really have never known myself so tired in my soul." It was a bleak time that was about to get worse.

CLINICAL WORK [INTERVIEWS]

There was something paradoxical about a man [Khan] who was
on the one hand an absentee landlord who regarded his tenants
as little better than serfs—who was dealing, and not always
tenderly, with the neuroses of the London intelligentsia.
John Davis, pediatrician and peer[1]

It is characteristic of Khan that he kept a full practice, even when facing major problems. This chapter gives an account of his work during the years of professional disappointment, personal stress, and marital discord that have been described in the preceding chapters.

As the decade of the 1960s ended, Khan was still working conservatively with analytic candidates, but he at times had "real" relationships with analysands who were not candidates. People who received his "Masudic care" had mixed experiences, ranging from harmful to life-saving. Khan thought he did better work with his noncandidates,[2] but patient accounts do not always support this idea.

There are four cases included in this chapter, as well as some shorter vignettes. Two analysands report successful treatment, one analysand feels that Khan was incompetent and destructive, and one has a mixed memory of a successful analysis that turned into a sexual relationship. The reader has a rare opportunity to hear about analytic work where the True Self is discovered through regressive experiences.

Khan's personal problems interfered with the quality of some of his work in this period, especially the latter part of the analyses of Godley and Eva. Surprisingly, the analyses of Lerner and Eyre appear to have been unaffected.

ANALYSIS OF WYNNE GODLEY (1959-1966)

> *Khan told me . . . how the infant eats the breast,*
> *but that the breast also eats the infant.*
> Wynne Godley[3]

Wynne Godley (b. 1926) was one of Khan's favorite analysands. Zoë Dominic told me this, the very first time we met. She said that although Khan never talked about his patients or revealed their identity, there was one exception in the 1960s: a man named Wynne Godley. Khan had talked about having a special relationship with this man and helping him to have a successful career. The only thing she knew about Godley was that the famous sculptor Jacob Epstein, who was some kind of relative, had used his head as a model for his sculpture *St. Michael and the Dragon* at Coventry Cathedral.

While I was working on this book, I learned a great deal more about Godley. He published an account of his analysis with Khan in the *London Review of Books*[4] and the *London Times*,[5] and he was interviewed by Robert Boynton for the *Boston Review*.[6] I learned that Godley, who is now in his late seventies, is married to the former Kitty Garman, a daughter of Jacob Epstein. Kitty's first husband was the notorious and widely renowned artist Lucian Freud—Sigmund Freud's grandson—and they had two daughters, who were now Godley's stepdaughters.[7] Godley's family has aristocratic Protesant origins in southern Ireland and his forebears include a grandfather who was head of the India Office for thirty-five years, ruling from London without visiting India. After a short career as a professional oboist, Godley had switched to the field of economic policy and forecasting. He became well known in the mid-1960s when, while working for the British Treasury Department in public policy (and still in analysis with Khan), he made some important macroeconomic calculations involving British tax policy as it related to a possible devaluation of the pound.

In 1959, at the age of thirty, Godley had been referred to Winnicott by Frances Partridge, a friend who was part of the Bloomsbury group and who knew about psychoanalysis through James Strachey (Winnicott's first analyst and the brother of Lytton Strachey). He was in a state of "terrible distress," suffering from False Self pathology, which he refers to as an "artificial self."[8] Winnicott was either unwilling or unable to take him on, and he made the referral after asking if Godley had any objection to seeing a Pakistani.

Ten days after the analysis began, Khan left on a planned break. He was getting married to Svetlana Beriosova right at that time and, as he told his new analysand, he would be away on his honeymoon, with Winnicott providing coverage in his absence. Godley then experienced a regression to dependence: "[M]y artificial self came, in stages, completely to pieces, although my adult mind continued to function in a completely normal way; for instance, I continued to work in the Treasury without a break. The meltdown, which took the form of a series of quasi-hallucinations accompanied by storms of emotion, all took place at home. . . . I 'saw' a blanket inside my skull which was very tightly wrapped around my brain. And it began to loosen! First intermittently, then decisively, the blanket came right away like a huge scab . . ."[9] The regression felt like an emotional breakthrough: "I experienced a feelingfulness which had been blockaded for as long as I could remember."[10]

When Khan returned, the regression ended and the treatment became, in Godley's words, a "non-analysis." Even though Khan had "a formidable and quick-acting intelligence, astonishing powers of observation and an unrivalled ability straightaway to see deeply below the surface,"[11] he made no use of the material from the regression—a grave error, in Godley's opinion.[12] Instead, according to Godley, the relationship became, over some years, a kind of battle which included mutual competition and mockery: "[Khan] believed in paying back aggression from his patients in kind."[13] Godley reports that he gave up hope that he would be helped as he retreated into a chronic state of rage that felt "like a kettle that had been left on the flame long after the water had boiled away."[14] (Note: Godley's writings show that he is currently very angry about his analysis with Khan. It is possible, however, that he felt differently at the time when he was in treatment, especially early on. His published account reveals that his symptoms receded and his life situation improved greatly in the years when he was seeing Khan.)

In the final years of the analysis, Khan and Godley began to socialize outside of the sessions. Godley remembers staying up late playing poker with Khan and the analysand whom I call Eva, whose story is told later in this chapter. (Godley gives Eva the pseudonym Marian in his own writing.) Afterward, Khan told him that the poker evening had been the happiest night of his life.[15] Khan pressured Godley, a married man, to meet Eva to see if they might be attracted to each other, and Godley took her to lunch. Khan also played squash with Godley, who was the better player.[16] Once Godley accidentally hit Khan in the face with his racquet, breaking Khan's nose. Khan was such a competitive man that, before having his nose treated, he insisted on playing a game of Ping-Pong, knowing he could beat Godley at that game.[17] On another occasion, Godley was at the Khan flat when Khan and Svetlana Beriosova were having a vicious argument. He was alone in a room when he heard a moan and, going into the hallway, he found Khan lying on the floor in pain. Khan whispered: "My wife has kicked me in the balls." Godley helped his analyst to the bedroom and then discovered Svetlana lying passed out in the hallway.

Godley eventually ended the analysis after an incident in which Khan acted in a hostile and destructive manner to a waiter at a restaurant where the Khans and Godleys were having dinner together. Mrs. Godley had objected to Khan's behavior and Khan called her the next day, attacking her for the objections. She was pregnant at the time, after a history of miscarriages, and after Khan's call, she began to feel contractions and feared she would lose the baby. Godley was distraught, believing that Khan was trying to murder his unborn child. He called Winnicott:

> I rang up Winnicott and said "Khan is mad," to which he said emphatically, "Yes," adding "All this social stuff . . ." He didn't finish the sentence, but he came round to our house immediately, saying that he had told Khan not to communicate with me. As he said this, the telephone rang and it was Khan, wanting not only to speak to me but to see me, which I refused to do. And that was the end of my "analysis."[18]

Ten years later, Khan contacted Godley and asked him to come for a visit. The bond remained so strong that Godley did go to see him.

Godley went on to have another analysis, which, by his report, was extremely helpful, and he states that he is a believer in psychoanalysis. Of Khan's treatment, however, he concludes, "[A]fter untold expense and travail, no therapy whatever had taken place. What a trap! He had reproduced and re-enacted every major traumatic component of my childhood and adolescence. [The damage was] deep, irreparable and wanton."[19]

Thirty years later, while writing his articles, Godley learned for the first time about the close relationship between Winnicott and Khan. He felt betrayed: not only had Winnicott referred him to Khan but he had also failed to warn him over time about the dangers of socialization with Khan. Winnicott would have known about the socialization even if Khan had not told him about it, because Winnicott was seeing one of Kitty Godley's daughters for analysis, and there were several upsetting incidents involving Khan's coming to the Godley home.[20]

Godley wrote his story in a way that made both Khan and Winnicott look incompetent. On the day the *Times* article appeared, an anonymous British analyst wrote me an e-mail: "As you can imagine, London is burning." Making reference to the fact that Winnicott was in his first term as resident of the British Psycho-Analytical Society (BPAS) when he made the original referral to Khan, and again president from 1965 to 1968, when the analysis was going badly, Godley had written, "[W]hat recommendation could I now make to someone in need of help? One answer might be: 'Ask the President of the British Psychoanalytic Society.' But this, it turns out, is precisely what I did, without realising it."[21] He blamed the BPAS for allowing Khan to train and for not "disbarring" him for misconduct.

Godley's articles were noticed in analytic circles all over the world. Perhaps the most important response was a special meeting called by the BPAS in June 2001 to discuss the role they themselves had played in colluding with Khan (see Chapter 39). It is hard to imagine a stronger response to a patient's complaint about a deceased analyst. An indirect follow-up occurred in July 2002, when Dodi Goldman, an American analyst who is an expert on Winnicott, gave a lecture at the Squiggle Foundation (a British group organized to honor Winnicott) on the topic of the Winnicott–Khan collusion in Godley's treatment.[22]

Some of the responses seem like an overreaction. For example, Godley was given a journalism prize from the American Psychoanalytic Association in January 2003, and when Anne-Marie Sandler wrote about the ethical problems in the Khan/Godley/Winnicott situation for the *International Journal of Psychoanalysis* (IJPA),[23] Godley was allowed to publish a response. Sandler's article included mention of Khan's strengths, while Godley's response was completely negative regarding Khan. It is unusual and perhaps unprecedented to give a writing prize to an analysand from outside the field or to allow an analysand to describe his treatment in a professional journal. Due to ethical issues regarding the protection of analysands, a critical response is impossible—there is no "space" for a public discussion by professionals of things that are questionable in the account of a living patient. Several analysts commented to me anonymously that the positive reception accorded to Godley seemed to be an appeasement designed to avoid the underlying issues; that is, those who supported Godley's condemnation of Khan and Winnicott may have been implying that the problem of patient abuse is confined to the work of Independents or "others."

ANALYSIS OF EUGENE LERNER (1964–1966)

Eugene Lerner is an American film agent living in Rome who was first treated by the analyst Ralph Greenson in Los Angeles. When Khan was in Los Angeles in 1964, Greenson asked him to see Lerner for a consultation because he felt unable to handle such an intense case, as he was still upset about the suicide of his patient Marilyn Monroe in 1962. Lerner later moved to London to be treated by Khan in a two-year analysis.

Lerner declined to be interviewed in person but, through our correspondence in 2001, he provided a glimpse of his experience. He believed that the analysis with Khan had saved his life and he said that Khan had always maintained proper boundaries with him. When Wynne Godley's article appeared in the *London Review of Books*, Lerner was surprised because Godley had been analyzed in the same time period, yet the two men had very different experiences. Here is Lerner's commentary from a letter to me written just after he had read the Godley article:

> What to say in response to Wynne Godley's article? My response is anything but easy. It is almost like a Dr. Jekyll and Mr. Hyde theme in a psychoanalytic setting. Whereas, to a point, I can recognize the Khan figure, the Godley portrait of him is unrecognizable.
>
> Godley's version of his experience with Sud begins some years be-

fore mine did. My years with Khan were from 1964 through 1966, and the aftermath of what became an extraordinary relationship built from 1967 to his death.

In my treatment years, there was never any socializing of any kind. Our meetings were entirely limited to the formalities of the analyst–patient syndrome. For example, when at a performance of Svetlana at Covent Garden, we ran across one another during an intermission, there was nothing more than a passing handshake.

When I began my sessions with him, I was in deep depression, contemplating suicide. He kept commenting on and criticizing how I walked, how I dressed, how I made use of the English language. I finally said to him, "Mr. Khan, I've come to you a broken man, lacking confidence in myself, lost, hopeless, and here you are tearing me apart, destroying what little faith I still might have in myself." His voice softened and took on an unforgettable tone, and he replied, "I know I am doing that, but I'm convinced that we will strike granite, and that with the help of God, you will be rescued and renewed. Life and you will be rejoined." From then on, there was no sarcasm, no derogation.

Of course, there were times in the treatment when we had differences, sometimes somewhat harsh, other times touched with humor. There were sometimes sessions in virtual total silence, but never any sign of disrespect. Having spent most of my years in cinema and theatre environments, I recognized that theatricality was part of his nature, and perhaps even one of his gifts. I also recognized his pride in his individuality in a professional world which was, in the main, far distant from his culture. It was he who christened our relationship as "Combat and Camaraderie." And to the end, he never called me "Gene." It was always "Mr. Lerner."

Khan was not for everyone. He recognized and respected simplicity but, I strongly believe, required a considerable degree of mental capacity, culture, appropriate social behavior and innate sensibility from his patients in order to establish a rapport which would function and would bring positive results.

Somehow, I feel that Wynne Godley was not for Masud Khan, that the horrendous experience he recounts, the ghastly failure, stemmed from a dreadful mistake in casting. I cannot help but feel that Winnicott has a heavy responsibility [for what happened], as does Godley himself. And I cannot help but feel that it is unjust, even cruel, to make Sud the sole villain in a tragedy which was born in inevitability which preceded his becoming involved.[24]

Part of Lerner's untold story involves a postanalytic friendship with Khan—something that is informally a taboo in the world of analysis. In this friendship, Khan always functioned therapeutically for his former patient, with no role reversal, so the taboo was broken without leading to problems.

INTERVIEW WITH ANALYSAND EVA
(1962–1969)

Eva is the analysand whom Khan supposedly tried to pair with Wynne Godley. In 1968, Khan himself became involved with her in a sexual liaison, despite the fact that she was his analysand and he was still married to Svetlana Beriosova (see Chapter 22).

Our interview was in 1998. In contrast to Godley, Eva has positive things to say about her analysis in the years before the relationship became social. Her account reveals Khan's talent as an analyst—and also the damage done when the transference became "real." Eva is now a successful artist as well as a wife and mother.

> I met Masud at a time in my life when I was quite lost, trying to recover from a painful relationship. It was 1962 and I was in my mid-twenties. My GP proposed that I go to Masud Khan for analysis, which I did. After the first consultation, we agreed that I would start analysis after the summer break.
>
> He was just about to leave for the South of France when we met. It so happened that I was also going there and he said I could contact him if I became distressed. This I did, as I was so wretched. It was a most peculiar meeting. He was glamorous and dismissive and told me to "lie in the sun and get a tan." I tried but failed—my skin would not tan.
>
> Soon after this rather unhelpful meeting my boyfriend and I were reconciled. Now, I thought, everything would change. We would marry and I would be happy. At last I got a tan. However, the problem was much deeper, and I became increasingly miserable.
>
> Back in London, I arrived at my first session with this relationship a *fait accompli* and Masud was furious. He refused to meet my boyfriend. Their mutual hostility, sight unseen, I came to see as an example of male pathology which I hadn't the independence of mind to be angry about at

the time. Masud warned that if I got pregnant he would stop the analysis, though when later I did, he relented. In fact he helped me to reconcile myself to having a baby on my own as eventually the affair with the father ended, sadly, in hopeless misunderstanding.

Crucially, he mobilized my relationship with my mother, more or less forcing me to relate to her on the grounds that I wouldn't otherwise be able to make progress. It was deeply painful for both of us, but at the same time a huge relief. His intervention was 100% crucial to a new way of being and I couldn't have done without it.

When I started in analysis I had this chewed-up-by-rats feeling all the time. It was a physical anguish, an inner burning, that I'd had all day and every day for much of my adult life. I had associated it with unhappy love but came to accept that it went back to my first three weeks of life, when I couldn't feed and nearly starved. Three weeks into analysis, this feeling went away, never to return.[25] Gradually I began to go into a deeper regression. I was still unhappy but in a new sort of way, and both hopeful and directed. I enrolled in college and began training for the work I was to take up later professionally. I began to believe in myself. Masud was always fantastically encouraging about any creative effort I made.

He always said that he was the only person who could get me through and, true or not, I believed him. He was attentive and patient when I was silent, but when he spoke I felt flooded with a new kind of truth. I felt he knew me to the soul. At times in the sessions he would just put his hand on my head and my heart would relax. The affection in this gesture was natural and unforced. There was a solid and unthreatening warmth about him.

For a long time the analysis was mostly about getting behind the facade which had become habitual. It was an impediment to a genuine experience of the world. Sessions would frequently go overtime and if I was too upset to go home I would rest in the spare room. Susu, his man-servant, would bring coffee. Sometimes I stayed in that room for two hours or more and recovered myself or slept.

I remember one dramatic session in which I had the experience of finding my own voice at last. I was sitting on the couch, talking about the disruptive influence of a friend of my mother. I said: "I'm talking with my own voice from deep inside. It feels like courage." Masud was overwhelmed (so was I) and embraced me impulsively.

When he was on form he was just amazing. Marion Milner once told me: "There is only one other person who can do the magic Masud can in one or two consultations, and that is Ronnie Laing." He could perform this magic in life also, not just in analysis. I watched him do it once at a meeting in 1967. He gave a paper on Camus and afterwards a sweet young man (not a patient) asked a question that Masud, with uncanny intuition, answered with another: "Why did you attempt suicide today?" It seems that the young man had indeed tried to jump out of a window that afternoon. They continued to talk as though they were alone until, one felt, the young man had somehow come through. Truly astonishing.

He had an existential power that you do not often meet. He had twice the weight and presence of anyone I've ever met in my life. His ability to size up a person or situation in a pithy observation could be devastating or transforming. Svetlana hated the way he would "cut up the world," but I was addicted to it. There was a constant flow of ideas between us. Above all it was a relationship without pretense. I could be my own limited self, and that was okay. He was tender, funny and profoundly thoughtful and supportive, in sharp contrast to his sometimes bombastic public persona. If I had been less ill, and he more sound, it might have been wonderful.

I wrote him letters when I had not been able to say what I meant in a session, or when I had thought of something new. They were often desperate letters, and Masud always replied. On paper we were in the closest rapport. His letters were wonderful, often illustrated with abstract collages made of tissue paper, suffused with kindness, grace and, eventually, love.

I remember a session, well into my analysis, when I was very, very upset. I could never have gone straight home—my daughter was a young child then and I was in no state to be with her. The realization that a state of primary dependence was no longer sustainable and that I must take at least partial responsibility for myself precipitated a terrifying crisis, an experience of absolute annihilation. We had spoken of the fear: this was the thing itself, and I could not be comforted. Masud said I could stay in the guest room, where I lay on the floor and desperately wanted to dissolve into the carpet, to go into the fires of the earth, as low and as deep as it was possible to go. I'd never been through or expected anything at all like it. I lost color vision—everything was grey. "I" wasn't there. I had lost my very self. It was like a scream that continues to infinity, except that it didn't feel like me doing the screaming. I didn't think I would ever find myself again. Masud gave me a paper to read—I think by Winnicott—saw another patient, and saw me again for a second session. Again the guest room and another patient. Then he saw me for a third time. He saw me through the crisis that afternoon, and finally I was able to go home.

This unique episode inaugurated an era of dismay, a weaker version of the experience I have described, which I could uncomfortably live with and, eventually, through. Though we did talk about the dismay, Masud was curiously reluctant to go into the meaning of the crisis as deeply as I wanted. In fact he was almost dismissive and admitted that it was not something that he had experienced himself. Later it seemed to me that he was both fearful and envious of my ordeal.

These intense experiences were isolated events which never quite faded into the rest of my psyche. Each time, I had to summon up my resources, carry on and recover, because I had to care for my daughter. I believed then that to some extent it was a decision: you can invite psychosis in and endorse it, almost as an indulgence, as a way to eventually feel better.

Masud had put certain strictures on my way of thinking. I felt at one time that if my ideas deviated at all from his, or if I allowed myself to perceive him as flawed in any way, I would be condemned to be schizoid and sick forever. I was tormented with guilt for my own [separate] insight and truly terrified. Eventually I found the courage to trust my own judgement, but it took a long time, and even longer to speak it. It was the most painful, negative cure.

He objected to my talking about myself, or my analysis, to old friends who tried to understand, on the grounds that I was wasting material on those who could no nothing with it. To some extent I saw the justice in this, but the result was that I became increasingly isolated and lonely. But he introduced me to other patients, some of whom became very important to me. The social atmosphere in their company was one of real companionship. I really don't think this was harmful—I needed support outside of sessions, given the pervasiveness of my regression.

It was sometime in the mid 1960s when our relationship became a sexual one. One day he simply said that there would be no more fees. Whatever happened—nothing much had yet—we would be within the rules. It was not a seduction so much as a development.

I was uncomfortable about Svetlana, whom I revered. He said their marriage was over, and it was alright with her if he was with me. Looking back, how could I have believed it? But he convinced me. He told me that they hadn't had sex for two years, though they had begun with a great romance. He said that Svetlana needed him for protection and se-

curity but that they were remote from each other now. I convinced myself that since Svetlana didn't want Masud, she wouldn't mind that we
were having an affair.

At first he thought that he could continue my analysis unofficially. But
soon this became problematic, so he referred me to Marion Milner. It was
not an intense analysis, but I loved it and I loved her and I learned the freedom of my own voice. We didn't talk much about my complicated feelings about Masud. I felt awkward about it and possibly she did too.

Meanwhile Masud and I were in trouble, because we were looking
for different kinds of love. He wanted love without anxiety, without having to worry about the Other—where, as he said, "You don't have to be
careful." He used to say: "You need me like oxygen, but I'm looking for
a freedom from concern."[26] He wanted to be free of the remains of the
analytical role to which I still clung. Poor man. Poor me. He wanted me
to love rather than need, but I could not do one without the other, and
there it was. What were we to do?

We would meet at my place and my whole life revolved around our
meetings. I remember more than anything else my state of mind at that
time. I felt unhappy and utterly isolated, as if my whole life had become
a secret. He scarcely seemed to know how I felt, though he still seemed
to adore the girl he thought I was. It was the opposite of how he had been
in the first years of the analysis.

After awhile, Svetlana knew about our affair. She was having a bad
time professionally and she was drinking heavily. She went berserk, really, and started to create terrible scenes with Masud, scenes that I only
heard about. She would say awful things about me, abuse him and weep
all night long; sometimes she would physically attack him. He would
never answer back—he was as passive in face of her tirades as I was with
his. One afternoon she came to see me with no warning. I wasn't there,
but she said she would wait and my au pair let her in. She went up to my
bedroom, where she found—and stole—a rare love letter that Masud had
written to me.

Towards the end the relationship became abusive; it would swing
between verbal assaults and reconciliations. His rages were almost demented: his eyes would glare and sometimes there was spittle in the corner of his mouth. He had always been intemperate in his rage, real or
feigned, even during my analysis—usually about some facet of my past
life, especially about anything sexual—but now it had become a habit. It
was worse if he was drinking—one glass of whisky was enough to make

him unstable and he might go either way—charm or cruelty. Two or more and it would all be over.

The situation was past enduring and without Marion Milner I don't know how I would have held together. I wrote a letter to Masud saying that I could bear it no longer. I expected to talk this through with him— but no, he told me that it was the only letter of mine he had ever destroyed, and that we would not discuss it further. He would not let me go. He had to end it himself. When finally the relationship did end, it was with a civilized agreement by the three of us. He came over with Svetlana to announce that they were going to make a new start. I successfully concealed my relief. True, it was painful. But there are different kinds of anguish and some are more bearable than others.

Later, we met from time to time, though on a different footing. I found it surprisingly tolerable. We went riding occasionally and a genuine friendship did survive. I had settled into analysis with Marion Milner and I got on with my life.

The affair that we had is not negative as an influence on my life. I accept that I will never totally sort it out. The destructive and creative elements of the relationship were inextricable. It was wrong in all the ways we know about, but nevertheless it was something wonderful. He changed my perspective, got me to value my own thinking, and helped me to develop my intellectual life. He was my guide, philosopher and friend.

If I went back in time, I still would go to see him for analysis. I was very demanding—I had the demandingness of illness—and I found somebody who would do what it took to see me through. My problem was with reality: How could he help me if it was not real?

It was not a romance or infatuation. It really wasn't like that. It was too important, and there was no sentimentality. If I had been capable of normal self-deception—of romance—I wouldn't have needed an analysis. But it was love. I will always believe that.

Eva had been an important analytic case for Khan prior to becoming part of his outside life. In the Work Book, he wrote that it was out of the work with her that he developed four of his most important analytic contributions: cumulative trauma, symbiotic omnipotence, self as idealized internal object, and the collated internal object.[27]

Khan thought of Eva as one of the great loves of his life and he did not feel guilty about spoiling her analysis. In 1970, writing in his Work Book about analysts who got into trouble for sexual misconduct, he normalized the experience: "Analysts all too easily accuse those [who work innovatively] of sexual misconduct. Who has not been accused of it: Ferenczi, Tausk, Balint, Winnicott,[28] Laing, etc. And the devil of it is, it is always true but not the way it is made out salaciously. . . . It is a professional hazard to those who have sensibility and are really devoted to patients as persons."[29] Years later, writing about Eva, he commented: "What damage one has done to other lives, groping to find the verity of one's own. And regret is as futile as guilt. Carnage is the law of nature! Humans are not exempt from that law in their lived lives; only in their philosophies."[30]

Eva does not regret the "real" relationship experience with her analyst. It is easy to assume that she must be in denial about harm done to her by Khan, but it is perhaps more honest to grope with the possibility that there may be some validity to her subjective experience.

INTERVIEW WITH ANALYSAND DEAN EYRE (1967-1972)

Eyre was born in New Zealand in 1938 and he spent his young years in a boarding school in Hawaii, due to events connected to World War II. After the war, his family returned to New Zealand, where his father entered politics and served in various ambassadorial posts. Eyre went to private school and university in New Zealand, qualifying as an M.D. at age twenty-three, and he then studied psychiatry and child psychiatry in London. After completing his analytic training, he was clinical director at London's Barnet Child Guidance Clinic and in private practice. Later, he moved to Canada, and he is currently an analyst in Ottawa. The interview was in 1997.

> In 1965, I applied for analytic training at the BPAS. Upon acceptance, I consulted with Adam Limentani about which group to join. I liked Kleinian theory but he told me about the strictness of the group and the need to adhere to certain intellectual ideas and principles. I said I did not want, in the process of analysis, to be freed from the prison of childhood only to join another imprisoning, claustrophobic group with set theoretical ideas. He then suggested that I join the Independent group, which I was very agreeable to.

I was referred to "Mr. Khan" for analysis because he accepted lower fees. I knew nothing about him—I had never even heard of Winnicott. I saw him for analysis in the years 1967–1972, and I qualified as an analyst in 1971.

I remember that in the first interview, he was anxious and his legs were in motion—he was often like that. He was smoking either his pipe or one of those French cigarettes, Celtiques. One of my analyst colleagues asked me a few years ago: "How could you have gone to a Pakistani?" and my honest answer was: "I never noticed."

We always shook hands on beginning and ending a session. I called him "Mr. Khan" and he called me "Dr. Eyre." His fee was about three pounds for a session. I remember that when he handed me the first bill, I told him to send it to the Institute, because they were lending me the money for analysis. He said, "No, you have to pay it yourself." He was right, of course.

I remember there was an incident at the Institute about money. I needed to increase my loan, and I had to talk with a man who didn't believe me. He said: "Your father is a Minister, so you have money. You must be gambling on the stock market." And they were going to turn me down. I told Masud, and he wrote a letter to support me. Then he analyzed how I had made that happen—he wouldn't let me get away with it. This was helpful to me, because I hadn't understood my part in the pattern.

When I saw Masud, there were only two other people who could have helped me: Margaret Little or Winnicott. Now I see that they were actually not as good clinically as Masud. He was able to put me in touch with very early memories. Once I had such a strong experience that he got anxious about whether I should continue with the analysis—he was uneasy about the primitive quality of the material I was producing. His 1972 paper "Dread of Surrender to Resourceless Dependence" was originally written about me.[31] He read it at the Vienna Congress in 1971, and I felt like death warmed up when I heard him discussing *me*. I hadn't known he was going to do that. When it was published, he used a different case.

I did have a regression to dependence, although it was completely contained in the analysis—I could still work. In the sessions, I was having a formless primitive experience. Masud was afraid that I would start to regress outside of the analysis. But he tolerated the regression when other people would have freaked out. Masud never gave up on anyone.

The analysis did do quite a lot for me. He helped me to undo my dissociations and understand what had happened to me. More than anything else, he helped me to not be so nasty. I had a personality style of being attacking and he confronted it. I've been considered to be a difficult person all my life, but I was softened. This came from his understanding of the cumulative trauma I had experienced—the way a person gets shaped around a lot of minor traumas which are so subtle they are almost undefinable. My nastiness would have caused me lots of trouble in my life if it hadn't been analyzed.

Khan used to say: "The purpose of analysis is to enable you to continue your self-analysis." And that happened for me. I've done self-analysis and discovered things about myself that he had no idea of. I pay attention to dreams and slips of the tongue and feeling states that don't seem to make sense. I resolved something a few days ago that I'd been wondering about all my life.

I also learned a lot from Masud about clinical work. He was an exceptional clinician. He was like Winnicott in that he was a different analyst for each analysand. There are a lot of analysts who do very good analysis with ordinary people—but for extraordinary patients with difficult backgrounds, they can't do it. Take a patient who might wake up and say he saw ten green men. One kind of therapist thinks immediately about medication. Another type thinks: "Can I tolerate this kind of disturbance of personality?" Masud could tolerate that type and that's what he taught me to do—tolerate the intolerable. Because of that learning I can treat very difficult patients without medication.

Another thing about Masud is that he could look at what was developing in a person. He used a phrase that was later picked up by Bollas: "larval state of being." That's a state between a caterpillar and a butterfly. You have to tolerate not knowing what will emerge. And the person doesn't always come out a butterfly!

He also opened up some doors for me in my training. I was able to work with Anna Freud because of him. If you weren't in her group, you weren't allowed to go to her seminars, but she made an exception for me because of Khan. And he got me to see Joseph Sandler for supervision. I had thought Winnicott, but he said, "No. That's what happened to R. D. Laing—he had analysis with Rycroft, then saw Milner and Winnicott for supervision, and they weren't strict enough—so he went off the road. Only Sandler will give you analytical discipline." He was right.

He didn't deviate from the frame with me, except for one time. My car had broken down, and I was penniless. He said, "I have an old Jaguar in the garage, and you can have it." I refused.

But I knew a lot about his personality. He was very outspoken. Once in a session at Hans Crescent, there was someone ouside in a car honking their horn over and over. Masud leaned out the window and screamed: "You stupid bitch!" The honking stopped and he said to me, "You can hear that I am human!"

I ended in 1972, believing that the analysis itself had been good. Sometimes I have talked with friends about the question, "Why did you finally stop analysis?" And we all agree: it was because of the things that we would bring up that were *not* being analyzed. That showed us it was time to end.

I remember one very funny dream I had that he couldn't handle. It was this: I walk into an empty room. There is a concrete tank of water in the room, and in the tank is a seal with a mustache. A sleek brown seal. The seal looks at me quizically, and I look back.

The seal, of course, was Khan—he always had a quizzical look. And the dream is in part a reference to a James Thurber cartoon of a couple lying in bed. One of them says, "I'm sure I heard a seal bark!" And there really is a seal in the room.

But he couldn't discuss that dream, he just went on to something else.[32]

After I ended, starting in 1973, we had some difficulties. A few years later, I left for Canada, in part because of him.

The norm was that post-analysis there would be respectful acknowledgment, not socializing, and we had a strictly professional relationship. My private practice was on Wimpole Street, and I saw a lot of wealthy people. I referred him a case of a fifteen year old girl from a prominent family, and that led to trouble. I kept getting odd messages from the parents, who were separated. Finally I was told that Masud had started meeting the girl's father for dinner. I wrote him a letter saying I did not agree with this. When he received the letter, he called me up and said: "You are a stupid Puritan. You don't know anything." And he dismissed it. I felt that was as far as I could go on the matter. Then, a month later, he called and said: "You fucking asshole, you bloody shit! You think you are someone special just because your father is a Minister!" He talked like that for a half hour and finally I hung up.

The final thing that happened leading to my leaving is that I presented my paper for membership in the Society, and I didn't pass. The reason is supposed to be secret, but somebody told me that it was because of Masud. I felt I had to leave England because I would be forever known as Masud Khan's ex-analysand. This was what had happened in New Zealand—I was always in my father's shadow.

Some of the greatest contributors to psychoanalysis have been ill people who went beyond the bounds. Yet their contributions are there for all time. The difficult thing is that we tend to look at the person's failings, as if a charismatic figure can't have failings.

Overall, I'd say that Masud was a brilliant analyst. He had remarkable insights because his own personality had been so fractured. He fits into Winnicott's classification of two kinds of people who make good analysts: 1. Very ill people who need lots of analysis, but who have good insights; and 2. Normals who have to learn to suffer in analysis. Masud fits into the first category.

He was a catalytic agent for me. Catalysts don't take part in the reaction, but they are necessary. I strive to be the way with my patients that Khan was with me: I don't impose my own thoughts.

In January 2003, Eyre sent me the following e-mail:

I was just now able, some thirty-four years later, to analyze for myself that seal dream. I was visiting Santa Cruz and I went to the wharf that I used to walk out on when I was six. I remembered how I would look underneath the wharf on the crosspieces, where there were a lot of seals sunning themselves (they are still there), and think how marvelous it would be to be a seal and to be free to swim and do what one wanted. On reading the interview, I realized the dream had a genetic [i.e., historical] basis: I had felt that Masud was my key to psychic freedom. And, in the perspective of years past, that was absolutely correct.[33]

The damage that Khan caused Eyre relates to his professional life: he left the stimulating environment of the British Independent Group, where he would almost certainly have had a very successful career. This proved to be Canada's gain.

These accounts show that Khan was capable of being a gifted analyst throughout the 1960s, although the quality of his work became inconsistent as he experimented with the analytic frame. Several short vignettes from this period show a similar mixed quality of work.

Judith Issroff told me about her negative experience in treatment with Khan in the late 1960s and early 1970s. (She refuses to call the experience "analysis" because she never trusted Khan and there was often a reversal of roles, with Khan confiding in her.) She had been referred to Khan by Winnicott, who was her supervisor, and she went reluctantly— for reasons related to her training there was no alternative. Regarding Winnicott's endorsement of Khan, Issroff speculates: "I suspect Winnicott could never relate to evil aspects of people—he had an extremely generous and tender heart and always tried to find the positive aspects of people. He probably sent Wynne to Masud, as he did me, because he genuinely appreciated our intellectual abilities and could think of no other suitable analyst at the matching intellectual level for us. But here he over-compensated, because he underestimated Masud's capacities for acting in and acting out and sheer negligent destructiveness."[34]

In contrast, Saul Peña, a Peruvian analyst, had a very positive experience in supervision with Khan in 1968 to 1969. Khan saw him without a fee, knowing that Peña's funds were stretched thin, with a condition that Peña promise to teach him back as much as he learned. Peña told me: "[Khan] taught me the importance of integrating clinical experience with theory and the need to consider bibliographical sources and the experience of others, which one could validate or critically differ from, through one's own experience—as well as the importance of being a worldly person who, through life and through books, deeply amplifies the possibilities of analysis."[35]

And the analyst Sadie Gillespie told me another positive story: "[C.] [disguised initial], who died quite a few years ago, was an analyst trainee who said she owed everything to her analysis with Masud. She was an intelligent but very plain woman. I saw Masud go up to her once at a meeting and I was struck by his warmth and kindness toward her. She was an ordinary woman but he could make her glow. This was his strength: he could make a total non-entity into a fascinating person."[36]

Barrie Cooper, who made many referrals to Khan in the late 1960s, believes that Khan's unorthodox work was often effective: "Treatment of the patient is paramount in psychoanalysis, and a maverick quality is essential in relating to certain patients. Masud had that maverick quality. Clinically, Masud showed his genius when he deviated from classical technique." Cooper does not defend Khan's "bad" work; his point is simply that some work that appears to be bad from an outsider's perspective may actually be therapeutic.

CHAPTER 2 4

VICTOR SMIRNOFF

Victor was important to Masud because he was a brilliant reader,
as was Masud.
Wladimir Granoff

To Smirnoff, language was music.
Barrie Cooper

Our friendship is the happiest and quietest experience of my adult life &
I am most grateful for it.
Masud Khan, letter to Smirnoff[1]

Victor Smirnoff was Khan's third and final crucial friend. Smirnoff was
a psychiatrist and training analyst at the Association Psychanalytique de
France (APF) who published on the subjects of perversion and child
psychoanalysis and who had been analyzed by Lacan. Born in St. Petersburg to parents who were both medical doctors, he grew up in Berlin
and Paris. He trained as a physician in Paris, and it was there that he
met Khan in the mid-1960s, introduced to him by Granoff, who was
their mutual friend.

Smirnoff broke the pattern of Khan's usual friendships in that he
was not physically impressive—indeed he was short and overweight.
Khan nicknamed him "Pnin" after the main character in Vladimir
Nabokov's novel *Pnin*—a man who is absentminded, constantly losing
things, and obsessed with health issues.[2] Smirnoff's strengths were
his personality and his mind—he impressed the people who knew him,
and he was well liked by almost everyone. One of Khan's (anonymous)

girlfriends from the 1970s told me: "Pnin was so wholesome and so caring. I used to feel that it was as if my grandmother was there."

Smirnoff would be a new kind of crucial friend to Khan, especially in comparison to Granoff. Jeanne Axler, Smirnoff's second wife, told me: "Victor and Wova were good friends, and they bonded because they both had Russian mothers. But they were very different. Granoff was flamboyant and into display. Once at a costume party, he came as a colonizer, with a black boy following carrying an umbrella and a fan. Victor was different. As a person he was shy and moderate."

At first, Khan, Granoff, and Smirnoff were friends as a trio, but it was not an easy trio. Axler told me: "Victor and Wova and Masud had such competition with each other—whatever one had, the other had to have double—books, women, whatever. It was a nightmare to be with these men!" After the Amsterdam fiasco, when Khan and Granoff ended their friendship, Khan and Smirnoff got to know each other as individuals. Despite his decision to isolate himself from friends during his period of withdrawal, Khan made an exception with Smirnoff.

Smirnoff was as good a correspondent as Granoff had been. He and Khan wrote each other regularly from 1967 to 1975, after which the correspondence became sporadic due to Khan's illness. Khan told Smirnoff that he valued his letters almost as much as he valued meeting in person, and certainly more than connection by telephone: "I deliberately didn't ring you tonight. Telephone is a cheat. One says a few insipid immediate sentences and loses the dynamism of true dialogue. I want to hear you & me talking to each other [in letters.]"[3]

The two friends shared a passion for owning books. Smirnoff could easily understand Khan's comment: "Other people read books; I chase them."[4] When they were together, they loved to spend hours "romping around" in bookstores. On one visit to Paris in 1969, Khan accumulated ninety books, and he wrote to Smirnoff about the difficulty he had in getting them back to London: "I still live with my feudal stance where space was endless and carriage always available."[5] They regularly mailed books to each other as gifts and sought out books for each other in various parts of the world, each one maintaining a bank account in the other's country to pay for these transactions. They cared not only about content, but also about illustrations and binding, and as a result, they both had significant and valuable collections.

Khan was a match for Smirnoff in his overall knowledge of Western literature.[6] But Smirnoff initiated him into a lifelong study of French
literature in particular, for which Khan was an eager apprentice: "Pnin is
a true and devoted pedagogue—and I am perhaps his most devout pupil.
I read what he guides me to."[7] Smirnoff taught him about Baudelaire,
Merleau-Ponty, Gide, Sade, Nabokov, Proust, Camus, Le Clezio, Rim-
baud, St. John Perse, Deleuze, and Genet. He also introduced Khan to
Norman Mailer, Henry Miller, and Nietzsche.

In May 1967, just as he was emerging from his isolation, Khan had written to Smirnoff with a gesture that established him as a crucial friend. The
gesture was a standing offer of a room at his flat that would be available
whenever Smirnoff wanted it. This was something he and Granoff had
done for each other, and it was also part of his Stoller friendship: "Let me
be explicit about the Khanic lore of offering hospitality. . . . When I invite a person to come & stay with me, I offer them: the privacy of a room
and bed to themselves; the services of my staff; and the leisure & quiet of
the flat. It is clearly understood that I yield to them no claims on my time,
person, or attention; nor do I stake such a claim on theirs. In short, I invite a person to share my ambience without obligations towards me or
rights on me. It is in this spirit that I invite you to please come & stay with
me. It will give me great pleasure if you do. Perhaps we shall have some
hours of mutuality when individually convenient."[8]
    In return, Smirnoff made the same offer of a permanent and private
room for Khan in Paris. Khan regularly stayed "chez Pnin" at 15 rue
Duguay-Trouin, a place where he was very comfortable. In his words,
"It was a cosy, very private and particularly Pninian space: cluttered with
books, odd bits of furniture jumbled together and so homesome."[9] In
1976, Khan wrote: "If I were to put together all the days I have spent [at
Smirnoff's flat] it would add up to more than a year in the past decade.
That space was my therapeutic hide-out."[10]
    Another way that Khan marked the crucial aspect of their friend-
ship, several years after it was established, was by asking Smirnoff to
choose and buy new notebooks for him to use for the Work Books after
Granoff's Tisne books were filled up. He was thrilled with the sample
Smirnoff sent for his approval: "I want to thank you for finding me the
ideal format and quality of paper for my Work Book. Please get me 50

of them." He contrasted the ordinary notebook chosen by Smirnoff to Granoff's choice: "The 23 copy-books [that were] given to me by Wova . . . were snobbish, expensive products. Their expensive presence cramped my freedom & style. [The comfort I feel with your sample notebook] is bizarre: a certain cowardly reverence that I entertain towards the thingness of things. It is not a question of economics."[11]

Smirnoff's first marriage was to an Egyptian woman who bore a striking resemblance to Brigitte Bardot. She was an intellectual who was well read in Russian literature and Khan valued her opinions in that area, especially regarding Dostoevsky. The marriage was not a happy one, and they divorced in the mid-1960s. Smirnoff then started a relationship with Jeanne Axler, another Egyptian woman. Jeanne was a psychologist, linguist, and medical student, who was twenty years younger than Smirnoff.

In 1970, Axler and Smirnoff got married. As usual, Khan worried that a woman was going to steal his male friend: "In human life everything changes, like in nature. . . . I am gradually losing a very dear friend, Pnin—and for no fault in him or me or us! Only he has married a very young wife, who will envy him everything that enlarges him without benefiting her. And she will sabotage his loyalty to me. . . . This is what is so treacherous about women: what they cannot partake of, they spoil."[12] His fear turned out to be quite unjustified.

Jeanne Axler always had her own separate friendship with Khan. He had trouble pronouncing the "J" of her first name, so he nicknamed her "My friend the Young-Young." As a strong, feisty, and confident woman, she was not at all intimidated by him, and she has vivid and mostly positive memories of him, beginning in the mid-1960s:

> Who could ever forget the first time meeting Masud?! It was in Paris, and he was coming to dinner. Victor was working so I answered the bell. There is this huge guy, and he says loudly: "I am Masud Khan!," pronouncing his last name with emphasis on the guttural. He entered with a violent approach, very striking. I remember him as being tall, dark, hairy, and constantly smoking.
>
> In the beginning, I was put off by his behavior, the way he treated people, even his ideas. Later when I knew him better and I understood it was all an act, we became friends. Once, at a restaurant, he was playing "king" and ordering the waiter around, complaining that his knife was

dirty even when it was fine—all because he was drinking too much. I remember saying to him: "If you don't stop that behavior, I won't stay to
witness the destruction of this poor man!" He stopped and, when we left,
made sure that I noticed that he gave a huge tip to the waiter—but no
apology. Another time in St. Tropez, I left a restaurant, taking the car—
he had to take a taxi home. He could be mean in restaurants, talking with
his loud voice. Nobody else would ever say anything to him, but I did—
because I was neutral, I wasn't part of the goddamn war or whatever it
was that was going on there with all the men.

Masud used to say he was blessed, and he WAS blessed, because he
enjoyed everything. He had such a capacity to enjoy things—coffee—
wine—the moon. He would just be happy and talk about how nice things
were. That's what attached me to him. It's such a rare quality—most
people tend to see the worst side of everything. He loved beauty. I remember him watching the sea in St. Tropez, and saying how beautiful it
was. Wova [Granoff] needed mansions and cars, but Masud was happy
sitting at a table drinking coffee, watching people, and talking.

He was a good and decent person—provided you were part of his
world. He was generous and kind to "his people" and very, very protective. He loved to give gifts to his friends, and he was constantly giving
me things, calling the gifts gestures or tokens. He would say: "Keep that,
take it!" if there was anything of his that you happened to admire. But he
was cruel to outsiders—he had a princely way of protecting his kingdom.

After Axler finished medical school, she and Smirnoff got divorced.
She left France to start a new relationship and pursue a medical career
in California.

By 1975, Smirnoff had recovered from the loss. He became president of the APF and he found a new companion, Marie Claude Fusco,
a female analyst who would be with him until he died. This time Khan
was pleased about his friend's girlfriend: "It gave me a strange quiet
pleasure to find Pnin companioned at last by a woman's participant intelligence. I hope and pray their relationship will grow."[13]

What did Smirnoff get back from Khan? He had died by the time I
started my interviews, so I never had a chance to ask him that question. There is, however, correspondence that can be used to gain some
insight. Some of Khan's letters to Smirnoff reveal that he was a mentor
in encouraging Smirnoff to write more boldly and more personally: "You

sounded so disheartened and doubtful about your paper on fetishism: those are healthy symptoms of creativity, my friend Pnin. Those that sit down in ease and manufacture to order produce only a debris of platitudes. . . . Do not let yourself be demoralised into merely reiterating the work of others."[14]

Khan's insight regarding a writing block that Smirnoff was temporarily experiencing is something to which many writers may resonate: "There is a sort of meanness in the mind, and almost a malice towards the audience, which it feels [is] as yet indifferent towards its precious creation. So what it does is it swallows up what it has created and refuses to yield it. I think one has to travel a very long way on the route of charity on the one hand, and sufficiency of narcissistic isolation on the other, to find the generosity in oneself to write what the mind creates without too much concern for the possible audience."[15] In another letter, he encouraged Smirnoff to keep writing and not give too much of his time to analytic politics: "A debris of abandoned drafts is accumulating around you ringed by a neon-lit sign: 'one day.' That day is always today or never!"[16]

It is clear that both men took enormous pleasure in their meetings. Here is Khan's description of planning to meet with Smirnoff the next week at a conference of English-speaking analysts to be held at Oxford: "[4 p.m.] What a child I stay! Am so excited about meeting Pnin that I cannot sleep at present. [7 p.m.] Pnin has rung from Paris. He is just as excited about meeting me as I am about him. He wants me to make sure we have rooms next to each other at the hotel, so that we are in easy reach of each other."[17] After their day together, Khan wrote: "I am so happy and nourished by Pnin's company and affection. It is a rare and cherished good fortune to have his affection. Between us, trust is so natural and belonging so easy."[18] And it was always like that for these two. There was a delight in each other's presence that is rare for adult men.

In 1986, Khan was lying fallow at Kot Fazaldad Khan and, upon receiving a postcard from Smirnoff, he responded with a letter that summarized their friendship: "Your picture post-card has made me nostalgic. You are such a living dynamic vital part of my Paris. From 1965 to 1985, some twenty years, you tutored me, with the same sagacity and economy of effort, in readings of French literature and culture, as my Prof. Painter had done in the years 1940–1946 regarding Greek literature and English culture and literature. . . . You 'housed' me, nursed me, and unobtrusively curtailed me: with never a harsh word of reprimand or masked censure."[19] Smirnoff would continue to be a loyal friend for the rest of Khan's life.

PART 7

"AND WORSE I MAY BE YET"

(1971–1976)

Edgar: Oh gods, who is 't can say "I am at the worst?"
I am worse than e'er I was
And worse I may be yet. The worst is not
So long as we can say "This is the worst."
King Lear, *IV.ii. 27–31*

CHAPTER 2 5

"THE MOST TRAUMATIC YEAR"

This [1971] has been the most arduous and
traumatic year of my entire life.
Masud Khan[1]

The year 1971 got off to a bad start. Khan had gone alone to Pakistan, where he went "from a private nightmare in London straight into an anarchic mess in my estate affairs."[2] Pakistan was in crisis as there was a presidential transition and stress regarding the politics of East Pakistan, which would soon split off to become a separate country. In the midst of this turmoil, Khan was forced to sell over half of the land surrounding his estate. Seven peasants were claiming ownership of a portion of the land he was selling, so he negotiated a 350,000-rupee settlement with them through the inspector general of police. He wrote to Smirnoff on January 1: "Pakistan is seething with anarchic socialist unrest and the whole population is just waiting with impatient zeal to grab hold of all varieties of properties. There are no civic values or intellectual perspectives. It is all an almost hysterical ferment in which anything could happen to anyone."

It was clear that he was no longer a feudal landlord with inherited rights: "I have just shaken hands with all the peasants in the voluntary end to a tradition that my ancestors have nurtured over centuries. They knew and I knew we had opted out of an alliance that was always larger than each and all and was handed over from generation to generation. . . . There is no regret or retrieving possible."[3] The large amount of cash he received for his land was poor compensation for the mandated change: "I have never been able to value money as an object in its own right. To me, it has always been an expendable commodity, a means and not an end."[4]

Returning to London at 10 p.m. on January 24, Khan found in his mail the proofs of *Playing and Reality*. He longed to call Winnicott, but because of the time, he decided to wait until the next day. Then, in the very early hours of January 25, Winnicott died.[5] This was the start of what Khan would call "the terrible year."

Eight months previously, he had arranged for John Mallinson, an analysand who was a physician (see Chapter 9), to live in the basement of Winnicott's home to provide medical support. When Clare discovered her husband's body in the living room at around 4 a.m., she immediately called Mallinson. Knowing at once that Winnicott was dead, Mallinson picked him up and put him into his bed.[6] Khan provides additional details: "[Clare Winnicott] had found DWW seated on the floor with his head comfortably poised on an armchair seat, and stillfully dead. [Later, when we talked,] she kept asking me whether I thought he had suffered much pain, and why hadn't he awakened her. I told her candidly what Dr. John Mallinson had told me: he must have felt unease, gotten up, and then died suddenly from heart failure. She again asked: 'Why didn't he shout for me?' And I gave her the only answer which I know is true of him: he was too private a person to demand or seek a witness to his death."[7]

Khan regretted not calling the night of his return, since he believed that Winnicott had wanted to see him one last time: "I know [Winnicott] was deeply concerned about my visit to Pakistan and safe return because he wrote me some seven letters—most unusual for him. He was keeping me sustained and in his own subtle way reminded me that I owe it to him to return. For the first time I have left five of his letters in my estate papers, so that a bit of him shares my life there."[8] "DWW died after waiting for me to arrive—this Mrs. Winnicott tells me. The last remark he made to her before retiring to bed was: 'I am sure Masud is back at 3 Hans Crescent.'"[9]

These details are indicative of the close relationship Khan had developed with Winnicott after the analysis ended, one where Khan believed he gave back as much as he received. After Winnicott died, Khan wrote to Smirnoff: "I think I am right in saying at the end, it was only me he allowed to carry his fragile & vulnerable states."[10] To Robert

Stoller he wrote: "Yes, my good friend, it is no boast on my part to state that if [DWW] anchored me in my being, I maximalized his last years as him!"[11]

Other letters refer to the complexity of the relationship. Khan wrote: "[M]y greatest debt to [DWW] was in terms of TIME. For two decades he provided coverage by his presence and support for me to grope towards my own style of sensibility. [He] never took a stand against me from values other than those that were authentic to my nurture. Often this caused him great confusion & private pain."[12] And Robert Stoller commented in a condolence letter: "It must have amused [DWW] in the most wry way that it was you, of all people, who persisted in helping him and loving him and finally writing for him what he would not have known how to do himself. A cosmic joke of the greatest importance to psychoanalysis. I wonder how the years of his relationship with you changed his thought—humbled him—re. his confidence in his capacity to judge his own love and hate."[13] Khan wrote back to Stoller that he felt well understood by him, adding: "[Winnicott] was more to me than [an analyst]. We were friends: mutually and variously. And we loved each other at the end, after an arduous combat over more than a decade. . . . He was much larger than me in his genius but I was vaster than him in my heritage and character. In the end we augmented and cherished each other."[14]

A long obituary notice written by Khan appeared in the *London Times* on January 27. On January 29, after the memorial service at Golders Green Crematorium, Khan wrote in his Work Book: "So we have taken our final leave of DWW. The funeral ceremony was reticent and true."

Khan knew that as Winnicott's favorite "son," he would be called upon to perform special duties in the analytic community. On the Sunday after the memorial, he wrote: "So many persons have rung me this week to seek support and to give support. Some of them I don't even know. The elders among my colleagues: Lydia James, [Marion] Milner, Anna Freud, Fanny Wride, and [Paula] Heimann, have all said that now the younger generation is going to look towards me for guidance, and I have to honour that responsibility. Lydia and Heimann have sagaciously pointed out that I must not let my temperament trip me up. That DWW's absence puts a huge and large responsibility on my presence amongst them. Yes, that is true."[15] A day later, he commented: "I enjoyed a protected childhood with Winnicott. Now I must assemble myself and become an adult."[16]

Having anticipated Winnicott's death for some time, he had thought he was ready for it. At first, however, he was overwhelmed with pain: "I have not geared myself to the new year. I am not even fully in the know of [Winnicott's] absence. I only feel it as an opaque negative fact of life."[17] "Strange how enigmatic is the experience of another's death. One had been fearful of the loss, and that turned out to be the least of the problems. What is so ungraspable is the absence of DWW's presence in my life. I so desire his company. . . . I have escaped into the machinations of a busy life & overloaded it with tasks. That obliterates a day, but yields no experience of it. One works, one does, but one just fails to BE."[18]

By March, he had recovered enough to resume work on various papers. He thought that he would be fine as long as he was careful about his behavior: "Suddenly I feel lithe and alive. The issue is how to keep it non-manic and in style."[19] He wrote an obituary for the *Bulletin of the Psychological Society*, the journal of the Institute of Education at University College, where Winnicott had lectured on his squiggle technique. To Smirnoff, he said of this obituary: "How he used to enjoy romping around with [the students.] I wish I could have found a way of simply stating: 'Winnicott loved playing.'"[20]

At the end of the month, he went to Berlin to Gunter Ammon's school. This time he gave several seminars on perversions and a talk, "The Scope and Limits of Playing in the Analytic Situation." Ammon was as volatile a man as Khan and he shared a predilection for heavy drinking. One night, the two men had a violent fight, in which Ammon went into a rage and smashed a chair. They made up the next day and the visit ended in success: "Yes, the visit to Berlin has been a true success; even its mishap was authentic."[21]

Back in London, he felt alone but productive: "Have a sense of total wakefulness in myself. The mourning of DWW seems to have passed its climax. . . . I feel separate and positively distanced from everyone."[22] By the end of June, he completed a draft of *Alienation in Perversions*. In July, he wrote yet another Winnicott obituary for the *British Journal of Medical Psychology*.

Winnicott's death was one of the great losses of Khan's life. In 1975, writing the introduction to his mentor's *Through Paediatrics to Psycho-*

Analysis, he used complex grammar to make a simple statement: "Winnicott was one such the like of whom I shall not meet again." It was a dramatic and accurate statement.

By 1971, Svetlana's alcoholism had started to affect her work. She began to be unreliable, failing to appear for performances. But John Tooley, the general administrator of the Royal Ballet, adored her, and he insisted on keeping her even though the new artistic director, Kenneth MacMillan, gave her fewer and fewer roles. For the past five years, she had always been sober when she danced, but sometimes now she would drink just before going onstage. Nobody knew she was doing this, because she had a private dressing room.

One evening in the spring of 1971, Beriosova was dancing the role of tsarina in *Anastasia* at Covent Garden, and the unthinkable became reality. Zoë Dominic was in the audience, sitting in one of the front rows, and as Beriosova came onstage, Dominic noticed a glazed look in her eyes. Moments later, Beriosova rose *en pointe* and fell down—then rose and fell down again. The curtains dropped and she was carried offstage, drunk. Her career with the Royal Ballet was over. Soon after the fiasco, John Tooley asked Dominic to come with Svetlana to a meeting where he terminated Svetlana's contract.

For years to come, Khan tried to figure out what had gone wrong with his wife's career, which had once been so stellar. He finally gave up, writing in his Work Book: "Who killed Beriosova? I shall never know the answer."[23]

Following upon these terrible events, there was more trouble in Pakistan. Earlier in the year, a longtime employee, Mustaq Ahmed, had warned Khan that Salah was cheating him. Salah had been dismissed from the position of estate manager in 1966, but he still handled the books in Khan's absence. Khan responded by firing his half-brother and appointing Ahmed as estate manager. Khan wrote to Smirnoff, making reference to Salah's illegitimacy: "I don't mind the money Salah has cheated from my income, but that he has ruthlessly swindled the peasants, that I could not forgive. How unequal the environment at birth renders us."[24]

In May, he went to Pakistan, and there he suffered a loss that he said was even greater than the death of Winnicott.[25] Salah came to Kot Fazaldad Khan to gather his belongings and while there he persuaded

Khursheed to move back with him to Jhelum. Khursheed left with Salah, leaving Khan bereft: "It is not only a terrible emotional blow, but an awesome loss of face. I have been literally prostrate since then. This is a vast mansion of a house and the absence of my mother howls in its silences."[26] It was an emotionally charged situation that involved all three of Khursheed's sons—Salah, Tahir, and Masud—although the exact nature of the internecine conflict is unclear.

Returning to London, Khan started to recover. On June 8, he wrote Smirnoff: "My mind is beginning to come alive a little." Then on June 10, he got a telephone call telling him that his mother had died. In Muslim tradition, burials are performed within twenty-four hours, so he left immediately for Pakistan. When he arrived, his mother's coffin had already been lowered into the grave, but it was not nailed shut. His half-brothers removed the top of the lid so that Khan could see her one last time. The memory of his mother's face was with him when he went to her grave site two days later, at 5 a.m., just prior to returning to London: "Have just returned from praying at Mother's grave. So still there. And the memory of my last sight of her face so engraven fresh in me. How final and simplifying is death, and what fuss and complications we humans make of existence when alive."[27]

Arriving home again, he reflected on his losses: "Within six months I have lost two beloved persons who alone anchored me in two cultures: Mother in Pakistan, DWW in London. And now that both are gone, all my tradition is within me, and I can drift anywhere. Freedom and alienation are at root the same. There are many beginnings in a lifetime . . ."[28] And he experienced a strengthened connection to the world of his past: "I am a feudal Punjabi to my roots today, as I was at birth. This is, perhaps, my greatest achievement so far. Even though I have lived in London since 1946, the love and language of my people is my sensibility. There is no doubt it has been vastly enriched by European cultures and . . . psycho-analysis. But these are additives to the root-culture."[29]

His mourning took the form of somatic symptoms as well as psychic pain. Late at night on June 18, he wrote, "Have been totally invalided by a grief and sadness that is utterly a physical state. Cancelled some of my evening patients. My lowest point was at 6:30 p.m. and I suddenly realised this is the exact hour by Pakistan time that I had seen Mother's face the last time and then nailed the coffin myself. Only I had no privacy then: all the family around. Tonight, in my consultation room alone, I was private and could mourn."[30]

Still he managed to keep active professionally. In late June, he went to Paris where he read a paper to Smirnoff's society and talked with Pontalis about the next *Nouvelle Revue de Psychanalyse* (NRP) issue on the topic of cannibalism. Back in London, he finished a paper, "Toucher pour Voir: The Role of Illusion in the Analytic Space and Process."[31]

In July, he developed aches and fevers and retired to his bed for several days. He was feeling exhausted, demoralized, and panicky. One morning at 2:20 a.m. he wrote, "Have given myself a 'sleep-cure' of some thirty solid hours of absence from wakefulness. . . . In the sleep-state, a strange continuous psychic life printed itself in endless imagery, recalling crucial relationships and events of my life since 1937. Some very painful, others harrowing—but all manageable. Have woken up partially now and feel distanced and almost coherent in myself."[32] In mid-July, his Pakistani friend Ijaz Batalwi, in town on business, stayed at Hans Crescent. They talked late into the night in their childhood languages (Urdu, Punjabi, and Persian). For the first time since losing his mother, Khan was overcome by the "howling ache" of grief: "I feel weak from the sheer catharsis of the experience. Ijaz was wondrously receptive, mutual and healing. I had no idea so much anguish had piled up."[33]

Later that summer, Khan's Winnicott died a second time. Winnicott had literally "failed to survive" when he died, and now he "failed to survive" psychologically when a secret betrayal was revealed. Everyone in the analytic world had assumed that Khan would be named Winnicott's literary executor, but when his will was read, it turned out that Winnicott had not named anyone for that position, which meant that by default it was given to his wife.[34] Winnicott's second "death" was worse than the first, because it was unexpected[35] and, for a favored son, humiliating.

Clare's biographer, Joel Kanter, believes that the terms of the will were set by Clare, with Winnicott giving in to her pressure.[36] This idea is supported by Khan's comment, "Mrs. Winnicott has always envied her husband's relations with me,"[37] and his complaint that Clare never opened the door to greet him or invited him to lunch on Sundays.[38] The rivalry went both ways. The analyst Sadie Gillespie told me, "Masud felt Clare was the real intruder in his love affair with Donald, and Clare felt the same about him." And Marion Milner remembered, "Masud said to me, 'I can't bear Clare telling me one more time how she made Winnicott potent!'"[39]

Khan makes no mention of Winnicott's betrayal in the Work Books or in any of his correspondences. It is as if, by not writing about it, he could pretend to himself (and to posterity) that it did not happen. He dealt with the deception indirectly, by turning again to *King Lear*, the plot of which involves deception in inheritance. He went to see Peter Brooks' film of a stage production of *Lear* at Stratford-on-Avon and then, the next weekend, set out to acquire copies of the play in three different editions, visiting seven bookshops before he was able to find them all. He was looking to Shakespeare for inspiration. "'Lear' engrossed me all through adolescence and I shall get back to it now and write about it. It contains the mystery of all of Shakespeare's sensibility and power. The basic conflict is ours today: man's unacceptance of man!"[40] He ended Work Book 13 with a dramatic quote in capital letters, repeating the words of Cordelia, the betrayed daughter who later reconciled with Lear:

> I end this Work Book with Cordelia's words to Lear:
> "WE ARE NOT THE FIRST
> WHO, WITH BEST MEANING
> HAVE INCURR'D THE WORST."[41]

Throughout Khan's life, there would be a history of unexpected and destructive wills. All of these can be seen as examples of a failure of object usage: hostility is expressed after the death of the writer, with no opportunity for interaction. Fazaldad had broken with tradition to make Khan his chief heir, thereby surprising his wife, insulting his other sons, and causing an enormous rift within the family. Winnicott acted in the opposite direction, honoring his wife over his "son." Khan himself would eventually write a will in which he attacked his wife and his Western friends, and Svetlana would die with no will at all.

The next trauma occurred in August. Khan had gone to the Vienna IPAC with the Stollers and then on to Pakistan. When he returned, Svetlana announced that she was leaving Hans Crescent, and on September 10 she moved out. Khan's Work Book entry for that day reads: "Seventeen years can suddenly stop, like a clock."

Svetlana moved into the servants' quarters at Zoë Dominic's home, taking with her only her clothes, her writing desk, and a single mattress (half of the double bed).[42] The precipitant to her leaving is unknown, but probably unimportant. The relationship had been headed toward an almost certain crash for some time.

In years to come, the months of August and September would remind Khan of the final separation, and he would feel intense psychic pain and an overall inertia. He said that his unconscious mind was "addicted to anniversaries." Here is an example from a Work Book entry on September 10, 1975: "Four years ago to this day Svetlana moved out. How vividly I can hear her walking from room to room all night long, desperate and bereft. Why does the mind cling to pain?"

The unfolding of devastating events was relentless. Khan no longer had Solo (for unknown reasons), and in September he wrote, "I shall search for a new horse. Horses make better companions for me than women."[43] On the morning of Sunday, October 10, he was trying out a polo pony named Pug Ugly that he was thinking of buying. After his ride, he had just headed the horse toward the stable when a group of riders cantered up to join them, startling Pug Ugly. The horse bucked and, throwing its head back, hit Khan hard on the nose. Attempting to get control, Khan pulled the reins forcefully, upon which the horse reared and they both fell to the ground.

He was taken to Kingston Hospital where it was discovered that he had a concussion and three fractured ribs. Forced to stay for forty-eight hours in the hospital and then to rest at home without working, he found the experience surprising helpful: "In a strange way, I felt extremely safe and protected. This week has been the first sane, wholesome, private, unharassed and unencumbered week that I have lived for God knows how many years. Being totally stranded in this [space] with nothing holding me but acute physical pain has rinsed me. I feel today that what has been has been and I can start again."[44]

In late October, against the advice of his doctors, he went to Berlin to teach Gunter Ammon's students and to give a lecture, "The Finding and Becoming of Self." Ammon invited him to become a full member of his academy, and Khan accepted. He returned home via Paris, where he enjoyed meeting his best friends: "Conversation with friends in Paris has limbered up my mind. My intellect finds its shape and character through dialogic interaction with the other. Only then can I withdraw and write creatively."[45]

There would not be an easy ending to the terrible year. In December, as a consequence of Pakistan's defeat in war with India, East and West Pakistan split into separate countries, with East Pakistan becoming Bangladesh. Pakistan had never had strength relative to India, but now it was greatly weakened. Watching events from afar, Khan worried about his property: "This weekend has been churned up by the horrific happenings of the Pakistan–India war. There seems to be no end to the disasters in my life this year, and all my estates seem to be direly threatened."[46] The world he was so nostalgic about was now gone forever:

> The holocaust of events in Pakistan has not only perturbed me, but devastated me—much more than I could ever have imagined it would. Having lived for more than a quarter of a century in London, I had engendered a sort of make-believe illusion in myself that the fate of my country and my culture is no longer intrinsic to my experience of life—but the impact of true and real events has proved it otherwise. Some six hundred years of feudal culture in West Pakistan are reaching catastrophic disruptions from which nobody will be able to retrieve that tradition.[47]

At the last minute he decided not to go to Pakistan for Christmas. Smirnoff invited him to Paris, but he declined the invitation, wanting to be alone. He spent Christmas and Boxing Day sleeping: "Twenty one hours of oblivion. Feels as if I have succeeded in putting a blank space between me and all that has happened in 1971."[48] After this retreat, he felt restored: "1971 was disastrous! Now I [will] pull down a curtain on it. And start afresh."[49]

He then went to Paris to be with Pontalis on New Year's Eve. The next day, he met André Green and his wife for dinner and then on the 2nd, joined Jean Pouillon for lunch, spent several hours listening to jazz with Jean-Claude Lavie, and had an at-home dinner with the Smirnoffs. Contact with his French friends left him feeling hopeful about the coming year: "I couldn't have had . . . a more true joyous start to 1972. Yes, in 1972 I shall teach myself to befriend myself and actualise my mind to the maximum."[50]

CHAPTER 26

THE ABSENCE OF WINNICOTT

*How right DWW was to say it takes two for one to be **alone**.*
Masud Khan (Khan's bold type)[1]

At root somewhere, I am self-destructive,
and I actualise it through women.
Masud Khan[2]

Khan had relied on Winnicott to keep him stable and it was now a life-time struggle to function on his own. His friends wanted the best for him and they were easily fooled by the fact that, on the surface, he seemed to be alright once "the terrible year" was over. However, even though he would be professionally productive for some time to come, his public persona was essentially a False Self. The losses in 1971 had been huge, and Khan coped with his feelings by denying them, even to himself: "I cheated [in 1971] and didn't allow myself the necessary period of mourning for all the catastrophic losses that happened to me."[3] "The hardest thing in human experience is to bury one's loved objects in God's earth. [Sometimes] one buries them in oneself and thus becomes a living walking graveyard."[4]

Robert Stoller was one of the friends who believed that Khan was recovering well. Throughout the 1960s, Stoller had encouraged Khan to develop his own theories, separately from Winnicott. Now, he thought, Khan would be free to find his own strength: "What is important and necessary for you, as I keep remarking, is that you move into your own created sphere of action, continuing your life beyond Winnicott. Beyond Winnicott."[5] After Khan's death, Stoller wrote to a friend (anonymous):

"[Masud] hid behind Winnicott. For years I scolded him that it was now time for him . . . [to] let go of Winnicott (the Winnicott he invented) and to discover in himself original ideas that could survive regardless of how wonderfully well he could write. He agreed benignly; oh, how he could play the benign aristocrat. But he had too much rage and not enough courage. Had he put the two together—rage and courage—he could have really broken out."[6]

In contrast to Stoller, people in England wanted Khan to continue working in the service of Winnicott. Their requests for his written and spoken words about his mentor continued for years, and Khan was always cooperative. On the first anniversary of Winnicott's death, for example, he wrote and delivered the eulogy, "Homage to Winnicott," for a memorial meeting. Preparing the talk the night before, he felt "empty and alone."[7]

Clare Winnicott needed Khan's help to handle her husband's unpublished work, but she hated Khan, as Khan hated her, and there was a violent clash whenever they had to work together. Most of the time Clare won, because she had the legal power. The hostile relationship between Clare and Khan is described in many Work Book entries, including these: "A gentle and nudging letter from [the publisher] has alerted me into action about finishing my Introduction to DWW's *Fragment of an Analysis*. Clare Winnicott has been most uncooperative. Today I rang her and said I'll give up the Introduction unless she makes the patient's file available to me, so that I can establish dates and data correctly."[8] "Talking to Mrs. Winnicott on the phone is like being trapped in a scream!"[9] Despite the problems with Clare, Khan worked willingly on various manuscripts: "It is my moral responsibility and my debt of love to DWW to see to it that all his works be published in the way he would have liked them to be."[10] Winnicott's *Therapeutic Consultations in Child Psychiatry*, published in 1971, bears witness to Khan's major editorial contributions, and his often-quoted introduction to *Holding and Interpretation: Fragment of an Analysis* was completed a few years later.[11]

Bypassing Khan, Clare set up a committee to handle the disposition of her husband's papers. This committee eventually established the Winnicott Trust, a conservative group that still handles the rights to Winnicott's papers under the guidance of Mark Paterson, the same man who controls Sigmund Freud Copyrights.

One of the casualties of Khan's war with Clare was that he did not get permission to work on a standard edition of Winnicott's collected works, a project that he longed to take on. (According to Mark Paterson, this project is now in preparation and it will run to at least fifteen volumes.) Another casualty was that Khan was not encouraged to write an authorized Winnicott biography.[12] In June 1973, he wrote to his agent Patricia White saying that his *Winnicott: A Critical Study* would be ready for publication by Payot in November 1974.[13] But, with Clare objecting, the project was canceled. Clare then asked her friend Madeleine Davis to write the biography. That project was canceled by Clare when Davis insisted that the complete story would have to include an accurate account of Winnicott's important relationship with Khan.[14] The biography was eventually written by Adam Phillips, a Khan analysand.[15] Phillips' *Winnicott* is highly regarded, but it is an intellectual history, lacking the personal insights that Khan would have included.

In 1972, Khan did start to do work that went beyond service to Winnicott. In February, he published an article entitled "Pornography and the Politics of Subversion and Rage" in the [London] *Times Literary Supplement.*[16] (He argued that the main problem with pornographic literature was that it was poorly written.) In May, he delivered his paper "To Hear with Eyes" to the medical section of the British Psychological Society, where a large audience responded with a "vital and creative" discussion.[17] In the fall, he finished a paper for the NRP, "Cannibalistic Tenderness in Non-genital Sensuality."[18]

In the years 1972 to 1974, Khan revived his career. He had a successful practice, worked as an editor, taught courses at the institute, and published and spoke regularly. He was controversial but respected. A British analyst who was a trainee in these years told me his memories of Khan as a teacher:

He taught me Winnicott and also went beyond that. He was hated by the Kleinians, and he was courageous in coming back at them, more so than most of the other Independents.

Was his erudition real? Yes and no. He was a showoff, and some of the quoting was for effect. But he *had* read a great deal. I did a first degree in English and I don't remember catching him out on anything.

The students felt he was "larger than life," because he wasn't like an ordinary person. A word I would use about Masud Khan the teacher is "memorable." You would never forget him.[19]

In Khan's personal life, the years 1972 to 1974 were characterized by high drama and suffering. He had women in his life, because he always had women—as he wrote, "Romance has ruled my life, gloriously as well as sordidly."[20] He continued the pattern of serial monogamy but the relationships he got involved in were either superficial or dangerous—and the dangerous ones were the ones he liked most. Excessive drinking was part of all of his relationships with women, especially when they were going badly.

He made a vow to be monastic in January 1972,[21] but he broke that vow almost before he made it. His new partner was Roz (pseudonym),[22] a wealthy divorcée from South Africa. She was a portrait painter and photographer, part of an artistic and politically radical world that Khan had previously known about only through his patients.

They had met in October 1971 through Deirdre Redgrave (wife of Corin), who was a mutual friend.[23] A few days later, Khan had his horse accident. When he returned from the hospital, Roz helped him to recover: "After my fall with the horse, Roz came into my life with singular willfulness on her part. She loved, nursed and healed me enormously. In fact, she alone enabled me to cope with the chasm left by Svetlana's absence. I was all smashed up: physically, psychically and emotionally."[24] After a few months, they began a very intense, albeit short-lived relationship.

One of Roz's intimates, a man who asked to be identified as "The Eyes," told me about the affair. The Eyes, who is now a film producer, was himself in love with Roz in those days. He was thirty-four when Khan and Roz got together, Roz was in her late thirties, and Khan was forty-seven.

Roz had a Sephardic look: dark features, beautiful eyes, and an uneven nose. She also had an absolutely perfect figure—in South Africa, she was a "prize" on the beaches. The openness of her personality operated on both a physical and a social level. She had had a lot of sexual experience. She liked marijuana, and she was inclined to get involved with dangerous men—she had had an affair with Hakim Jamal.[25]

Her mind had a primitive quality and, although she was largely uneducated, she gave me a new intuitive way of looking at things. I doted on her, the way a young man dotes on an older woman who allows this because it suits her to have a young man around to do things with when she is not otherwise occupied. There was nothing I wouldn't do for her.

Roz was in London for nine years, and I pursued her that whole time; it was a long time to pursue someone. She would have sexual experiences with others, and I would be insanely jealous at those times.

Masud was the most charismatic man I have ever met. He was always the central person in a room—you couldn't ignore him. When Roz met him at Corin and Deirdre's, she fell under his spell immediately. I could tell, because when she was infatuated, the tone of her voice went down half an octave. I don't think this was conscious, but it contributed to her seductive power.

I was on the outside once again, as Roz fell in love with Masud and told me all the details. I remember her telling me: "Although Masud is a man of the mind, he has a troubled mind." She said he wanted her to just be with him—she could do whatever she wanted, crochet or whatever, and only then could he get on with his writing. Her presence calmed him. Lots of times they wouldn't speak for hours at a time. Roz was good at being quiet.

Then, a few months later, it started to go wrong. Roz said that he was too dominant. When they broke up, she came and hid in my apartment, saying: "This is going to be the hardest thing I've ever done. But I've got to get away from him."

Masud immediately began searching for her, and since I was her confidant, he rang me. He was like Humbert Humbert in Nabokov's *Lolita*, who became totally out of control when he lost Lolita—there was that same desperation, a sense that something he had to have had been taken from him. He begged me to tell him where she was. Before that, I had been hardly noticeable to him as a person. It was obvious that Roz held some extreme power over him.

That was it. Roz saw him once more for dinner, and then she went back to South Africa.[26]

In writing about the rocky relationship with Roz, Khan describes anguish and, occasionally, unspecified violence. By Khan's account, the decision to separate was his:

The past month has been hellish. We can neither leave each other, nor build together. So the nightmare goes on, with patches of real pleasure and peace. Through [Roz], I have discovered what I really need and want

from a woman. Pity of it is there is no chance of our making it together.
Now I am trying to separate from her in an honourable way [but] she is
viciously vindictive. Can't blame her.

   I have to free myself. . . . Then I'll take a long rest and recover fully.
Strange how a woman can both make and destroy one.[27]

After they broke up in spring 1972, he thought about the danger he
had just barely avoided: "I am gradually healing & recuperating. And
there is mercy in that. How I have survived, managed to keep working
and even write significantly truly astonishes me."[28]

He immersed himself in work and that summer he made several trips
to France, where he had a new friend, the painter Philippe Bonnet. He
bought a large and expensive landscape by Bonnet and wrote that his
purchase of an important canvas meant that he was accepting that he would
be staying in England, not moving back to Pakistan: "Up till now I have
lived some 25 years in London in a 'transitional state.' I have acquired
things I could travel with: pack and get out. This canvas states a right for
space that will be permanent. It announces a decision in my life."[29]

In November, he canceled a scheduled presentation ("The Necessity of Illusion") at the Pastoral Society in Edinburgh. This was the first
time he had failed to honor a professional commitment and it was especially upsetting because arrangements had been made through John
Sutherland, a mentor whom he would not have wanted to disappoint.
Due to being in a severely depressed state, which may have occurred in
conjunction with alcohol dependence, there was no alternative: "I have
to accept that I am at present demolished in myself."[30]

As 1973 began, he was in a deep depression, isolating himself from
everyone except his patients. He wrote to Smirnoff: "If you have been
wondering whether I was dead, you would not have been far wrong. The
unconscious is a cruel time-keeper, and I sank into the deepest clinical
depression I have ever known, over the past two weeks and more, and I
am just emerging from it. All I could manage was my clinical work;
outside of that, I was utterly paralysed and inert. It is really quite extraordinary how depression can cancel out all ego functions. To see it
in one's patients is one thing, to live it in one's person is another."[31]

Despite the depression, he was sporadically able to write and to write
well. In February 1973, he wrote a paper on Camus called "Suicide in

the Condition of Consciousness,"[32] a paper entitled "Ego-Orgasm in Bisexual Love,"[33] and a preface to Laplanche and Pontalis' *The Language of Psychoanalysis.*[34] Commenting on the Camus article, he wrote: "How my mind always surprises me. I never know what it will say."[35] In April, he stayed with the Stollers and gave a paper entitled "Dreams" at the Los Angeles Psychoanalytic Society.[36]

The Stollers regularly brought out the best in Khan, and through their influence he began to recover. He wrote to Smirnoff from California: "It is a beatific and bounteously companioned time for me here. Bob and Sybil . . . cherish me with reticent affection and care, and they share a lot of thought and laughter."[37]

After the visit to California, he did well professionally and personally for some time. In early May, he revised a paper on perversion for publication in the NRP and agreed to write a tribute to his colleague Paula Heimann for a festschrift.[38] Alix Strachey had died on April 28 and he delivered the obituary address to the BPAS on May 16. In June, he gave a talk entitled "The Role of Anti-Social Tendency in Hysteria" to André Green's Paris Society. Green did the translation.

And he was able to get involved with a woman who was not destructive. At a small dinner party at the home of Philippe Bonnet, he met a woman who would be his girlfriend for the next few months, and a friend for the rest of his life. Janet (pseudonym) was a forty-year-old actress. Khan referred to her as a "gay tramp" and gave her the nickname "Dodo," a word from a French lullaby meaning "go to sleep." She was a Frenchwoman whose father had been a well-connected businessman. As a child and later as the young wife of an American, she had lived all over the world. She was now divorced and living in Paris.

Khan called the Bonnets the day after the party to tell them he felt "sympathetique" toward Janet and that he hoped to see her again when he returned to Paris the next month. When Bonnet's wife told this to Janet, she replied: "Oh I don't know if I'll be here. I could be in Jamaica, or in India—or dead."[39] But Khan had already charmed her. She remembers that he seemed to understand her almost immediately. He knew that she needed simple affection, something that she had lacked as a child.

They met again the next month and, according to Janet, they were mutually infatuated: "He had the sensibility of a nine year old child; he was shy and so was I. We were so in love—he said I suited him like a glove." Khan began staying with her when he came to Paris and they roamed around Paris at night, dancing at clubs and returning to her apartment at 4 a.m. to eat cheese-and-onion sandwiches. Khan wrote at this time, with apparent reference to their sexual relationship: "Nothing is more authentic and sincere than the way two persons' bodies experience and share each other mutually, if they accept and relish one another."[40] He took great pleasure in the time spent with her: "Yes, your laughter permeates all your gestures. How did you acquire this generosity towards life, yourself and others?"[41] "He [referring to himself] had spent eight gorgeously quietly mutual days chez [Janet]. He so readily accepted her devotion and hospitality. . . . Yes, humans alone [are] the cure of humans."[42]

From London, he sent Janet postcards addressed to "My Mockingbird."[43] He also sent books, including a huge dictionary, and, over time, a collection of black dresses, which she still keeps in a trunk in her living room. And he celebrated his happiness by buying a new Volkswagen in a color that was lavishly called "Texas yellow." He wrote that this, his first new car in fifteen years, was a symbol of the fading of old patterns and the beginning of a new way of living.[44]

Although Janet remembers that they had a serious love affair, Khan's writings suggest that he was less involved. He wrote to Smirnoff about the "quiet luxuriance" of being an intimate friend of a woman without falling in love.[45]

His preoccupation at this time was his own self. He was trying to stop drinking and he was often anxious, phobic, and withdrawn: "How very little he [referring to himself] participated in the ordinary vulgar human milieu."[46] Robert and Sybil's son, Roger Stoller, stayed with Khan in mid-summer of 1973, and he remembers that Khan was doing badly again: "I spent every evening with Masud then. His regal manner was becoming shabby around the edges and he seemed in decline. It was painful to see what was happening to him."

In August, Janet asked if she could go with Khan to Pakistan. He refused, saying, "You can't go to Lahore—it's too hot and you can't eat fruit.'" He went by himself and, with some success, tried to relax: "He [writing from Pakistan, referring to himself] lived in God's time and rhythm."[47] Life at his estate was quiet and familiar, but the terror that had been haunting him remained: "His mind [referring to himself] had gone inert. He quietly preoccupied himself with exotic irrelevances, like getting jewelry made to his specific designs, without knowing for whom, having clothes tailored from native materials etc. Today he had woken up awakened. He didn't know what he would do. But he would act now! What act? He had not a clue. He was awake, and he felt a lucid fear, verging on terror inside him."[48]

He flew to Paris from Pakistan and went with Janet to Corsica. She remembers that they were both happy there. Khan would read under a tree or go book hunting, while she sat in the sun or went into the sea. They got along so well that Khan invited Janet to live with him in London, and she agreed.

Back in London, Khan's friend Anne Money-Coutts had a King Charles Spaniel that had just had a litter. To complement his new domesticity, Khan asked for one of the puppies. He liked the breed because it is a longtime favorite of the English royalty; by a decree from King Charles II, dogs of this breed must be accepted in any public place, even the Houses of Parliament, and it is the only dog allowed to travel (for free) on buses.

But the comfortable threesome of Janet, Khan, and the puppy lasted only a short time. Janet was not a woman prone to settling down. As an anonymous friend told me: "[Janet] is like water—you can't hold her." In the midst of an argument, she said that she needed to return to Paris "to marry Dr. Theater," referring to her acting career. Khan replied, "Do it!" So she left.

After the breakup, Khan gave the dog to his housekeeper, Mrs. Penning. Later he told Janet that he gave the dog away because it reminded him of her, and that was too painful to bear.

In September, just prior to the breakup with Janet, his old friend Jim Armstrong Harris died. Khan believed in honoring the dead, and he was upset when very few people attended Harris's memorial service: "What impressed [me] most at the cremation ceremony was a tangible noiselessness in the atmosphere. Only a handful of friends and colleagues. This was rather sad. How soon people forget one and lapse away. Jim was a gregarious and convivial person, but his invalidism the past two years had distanced him away from others, hence the paucity of those present."[49]

A few nights later, at 3 a.m., he wrote a very depressed poem:

Deadness lay over him,
like a lover.
Flowers withered in his flesh.
Nothing festered.
All was dry.
Sun's light fed the dark.
No colours rose
to answer
the bird's song.
Sand was true and Plant.[50]

"Sand" and "Plant" in the last line of the poem refer to Khan's paintings of those titles.

With Janet gone from his life and the Stollers' influence fading, his overall psychological health continued to deteriorate. He now regularly referred to himself in the third person, as in these Work Book entries: "He [referring to himself] had a notion of a mystical existence with his isolate self which in fact was utterly arid and inert for him."[51] "Strange how different the evaluations of others were from his [my] self experience. To them, he seemed to be a man with inexhaustible vitality and creativity."[52] Referring to his almost-final draft of *The Privacy of the Self*, completed in November, he said: "In a strange way, I feel so separate from what I have written. My Self is private from even my writings."[53] He declined to write the index for this book: "I who have indexed DWW so excellently could not index my own book. So it has a meagre index by someone unknown; that is a pity indeed."[54] More than ever, he was feeling connected to his Eastern origins: "Father died, exactly thirty years ago, this day! Were he to encounter me today, he would hardly recognise the son he had reared as his future. And yet I am exactly what he nurtured me to be. And in my self I have honoured what I have been given by him."[55]

Khan spent New Year's Eve in Paris. "Chez Pnin" he wrote: "If 1972 taught me the folly of getting involved with a woman, 1973 has taught me that I can no longer share my private space and time with anyone. I have to be separate and alone henceforth. Friends are the exclusive idiom of my relatings now ! ! !"[56] He was still suffering from the unexplained attacks of terror, but he was optimistic that he could deal with whatever was causing the terror: "Seems to me that [life] is a question of choice and courage now. Little of choice and more of courage in fact."[57]

Khan and Svetlana had not stopped caring for each other, even though they both knew that divorce was inevitable. Khan wrote, "It is possible for the relationship between a husband and wife, a man and a woman, to go dead and inert. This does not mean that their capacity to feel concern for each other and to relate affectionately, or even to love each other in themselves, has perished as well. In fact, the reverse can happen . . . "[58] He described the tension they both experienced in the final stage of the divorce:

> The divorce hearing in Court was settled for January 30th [1974]. I scanned through the evening papers nervously to find what scandal the Press will make of it! Nothing!! I was relieved but disturbed as well. Nothing in the morning papers on January 31st either. Then my lawyers rang me around 11 am to say, "Mr. Khan, you would hardly believe it. Mrs. Khan never turned up at the court yesterday. She left her flat at 9 a.m. on the 30th and her lawyers haven't been able to find her since!"
>
> Of course my first reaction was—panic of concern! My lurid imagination traumatised me with a thousand horrible images of all vagaries of derangement: had she got drunk enroute & been taken by the taxi driver to a police station? or done herself in? or . . . ?
>
> But I didn't act. I sat down and asked myself, where would she go . . . ? and I rang [Zoë Dominic's flat]. Svetlana answered and blandly told me: "I decided on the way not to go. So I came here. But I will put it right next time."
>
> These Russians: some characters !![59]

After the aborted hearing, he comforted himself by buying a "thing" at Asprey's: an 18 carat gold Montblanc pen to add to his collection. The cost was 450 pounds. He wrote: "How vicariously one cures oneself."[60]

It was a time of change. For years, the poodle Kalu had been a regular visitor but now Khan stopped having Kalu come for visits. He also ended his relationship with his houseboy Susu, who had a new job. Then his secretary announced that she was leaving. Always vulnerable to feeling abandoned, Khan was distraught. He felt better when he got a new houseboy and a new secretary.[61]

On May 9, his analyst friend Walter ("Wally") Joffe died in his sleep, just a few hours after Khan had talked with him on the phone. It was an unexpected and sudden death of a man who was very much in his prime, and it left Khan dismayed. He wrote: "Yes, one has reached the diminishing years in one's life. One has not the initiative or resources to make new friends, and one's old friends start to disappear one by one. Death does not diminish the dead; only the living."[62]

In 1974, things continued to go well professionally. After finishing the final draft of *The Privacy of the Self*, Khan immersed himself in preparations for what would eventually become his second book, *Alienation in Perversions*. In the spring, he read a paper entitled "The Vicissitudes of Responsibility in Modern Psychotherapeutics" at the Extramural Studies Course at London University, he wrote a discussion of a paper by André Green for the *Scientific Bulletin* and a paper for the NRP called "Secret as Potential Space,"[63] and he gave twelve lectures to candidates at the society. His paper "The Beginnings and Fruition of the Self—An Essay on D. W. Winnicott," coauthored with Madeleine and John Davis,[64] was published at this time, and in March he completed another paper, "Freud and the Crises of Responsibility in Modern Psychotherapeutics."[65]

In April, there was a lecture tour in the United States, with papers at analytic meetings in Philadelphia and Washington, D.C., and at Menninger's in Kansas. In May, he presented "Secret as Potential Space" to a scientific meeting at the BPAS where the response pleased him: "For the first time in the past twenty years a paper of mine given at the Society was listened to with hushed attention by a packed house representing all factions of the Society."[66]

The Privacy of the Self was published in June, with a dedication to Beriosova "whose discipline and genius taught me the true measure of effort, with love and gratitude."[67] The response to his first book was significant and positive. A number of reviews were written, including an unusually long twelve-page review in the IJPA by Paula Heimann.

These accomplishments were from a period when Khan also had a full private practice. But he was not in fact doing well. He felt "real" only with Smirnoff or when he was alone. We see how easy it is for a talented person to hide False Self pathology.

In June 1974, Khan started seeing a new woman, and once again he flirted with self-destruction through a relationship. Megan (pseudonym)[68] was a wealthy British woman who was separated from her husband, a well-known businessman. She was as dangerous as Roz, but different. An anonymous friend told me: "They were an enormous contrast: [Megan] had a blonde, English, 'Grace Kelly' look, in contrast to [Roz], who looked like a dark Jewess. You can see the difference also in the drugs they took: [Roz] liked marijuana, but [Megan] liked cocaine and heroin." (Of Khan's girlfriends, Roz and Megan were the only ones who took drugs regularly, an indulgence that Khan never cared for.)

The details of Khan's initial connection to Megan are unknown, except that it was immediate and intense. He wrote to Robert Stoller: "If you and Sybil had witnessed the momentum with which I launched myself with [Megan], it would have amused and frightened you a little. André Green has described me to [Megan] as a cyclone and wished her a joyous nestling in the eye of the cyclone."[69]

Things went well at first: "[Megan], so far, has managed to contain me. I am happy with her and she with me in an ordinary mutual way, and we need each other. All these experiences are new for me, and for her as well."[70] Megan had young children, and Khan liked being part of a family, as we see in this Work Book entry on his birthday: "I am fifty years old today. The good Lord has travelled me a long zig-zag route and nestled me with a home and family at last—thanks to [Megan]! I shall try to my utmost to live familially and creatively."[71] He moved into her spacious townhouse, where he had his own writing room—an attic space that was "vast, bare, white and elegantly stark."[72]

Soon, however, the relationship was a disaster. Megan may have liked heroin, but she also liked alcohol, and that was the greater problem. Khan wrote,

Love is not a healer. . . . God had blessed me with freedom for my 50th birthday, and I imprisoned myself in another nightmare.

It was a mistake to move into [Megan's] space and spread all over it. Deep down, [Megan] didn't want it, in spite of her overt giving and generosities. And she has used the bottle to have her Say. . . . My years with Svetlana should have taught me how at root alcoholism is a murderous assault on the self and the other.

God has chastised me for my greedy grab of [Megan's] space. I wanted my life to be abundant instantly and I did not wait and work for it. It was joyous fitfully, and I found my capacity to love again—but now I am bereft, harassed and shamed.[73]

That summer he moved out and then back in again. In August, he and Megan traveled together to Los Angeles to visit the Stollers, where they had a good time: "Our stay chez Stollers was idyllic in every sense and measure of that word. They are such generous, reticently & casually abundant hosts. They provided us an ideal human ambience to grow together and know each other: quietly & fervently. . . . We left the Stollers sad and buoyant. So unobtrusively they had nurtured our relationship with each other."[74] From California, the couple traveled to Washington, D.C., to visit Sahabzada Yaqub Khan, and then to Baltimore to see Harvey and Leslie Kayne.

But even the Stollers could not work lasting magic on this pair. Back in London, the relationship continued to be "a sordid mess."[75] They lived apart, but saw each other every day. Stoller wrote to Smirnoff that the two were engaged in "a sad, painful and dangerous interplay."[76] Referring to the contrast between his inner romantic vision and the reality of his relationship with Megan, Khan commented, "My dreams are broken glass."[77]

CHAPTER 2 7

BAD DREAMS

This year, 1975, will make or ruin me; either way,
I shall be the exclusive agent! Of one thing I am sure:
Unless I stay utterly dry I shall flounder horribly.
Masud Khan[1]

The year 1975 was pivotal. It was a time when Khan was balanced between healthy and pathological influences and he could have made a decisive move in either direction.

He started the year determined to abstain from alcohol. A pressing issue was that the lease on the Hans Crescent flat was expiring while his finances for a new flat were stretched, since the transfer of money from Pakistan was temporarily impossible. In February, the foliage of a large plant that he and Svetlana had fondly named "Abundance" suddenly turned "rigid and inert" and the plant had to be thrown out. Khan wrote of the dead plant: "Every event in my life is metaphoric."[2] Despite the bad omen, he easily found a suitable flat. It was at 7 Palace Court, near Kensington Gardens in Bayswater, on the opposite corner of Hyde Park from Harrod's and Hans Crescent. He paid £35,000 for a forty-six-year lease.[3]

Bayswater was a lively neighborhood of ethnic groups and popular restaurants. His new building was an ornate and turreted red brick structure on a block with similar buildings—classy, but a step down from Hans Crescent. The flat itself was long and L-shaped, with more than ten rooms. He hired an architect named Moya to help with the interior design: "I told Moya: 'I want a Masudic white monastic library with some cosy spaces for friends: stark, spacious and daunting!' Moya laughed at the word 'daunting' and said 'I'll do my best.'"[4]

Except for accumulating books, he was trying to live simply. His sole employee was a secretary, Jill Standen; the houseboy from the previous year was gone and the new Filipino houseboy Adel Almontero would not start until June. Khan prepared his own dinners, specializing in steak, rice, and peas, which he could prepare in just fifteen minutes: "Who could have envisaged that Fazaldad's favourite son, me, at 50 plus and professionally successful, would be cooking my own meals, making my bed, and tending my clothes on my own!"[5]

The relationship with Megan had continued into the new year, but it now ended. The final ending came after a late evening fight. Khan, while intoxicated, drove his car into her building, causing significant damage and police involvement. Robert Stoller commented favorably on the breakup: "The dream was lovely; the reality [has been] a nightmare."[6]

In the absence of a turbulent private life, Khan was able to be reflective. He concluded that he had been living reactively, responding to things that happened rather than making them happen: "In a curious way I have never arranged my life or decided about any person."[7] With female lovers, he decided, he had been allowing unsuitable partners to choose him, allowing external chaos to distract him from his internal emptiness. "There was an unassuageable pain in him [referring to himself] that he struggled vainly to mitigate through easing the pain in others; and at times, rather perversely, first causing it in order to remedy it afterwards."[8] He thought he should stay out of committed relationships.

At the end of March, he went to court for the drunk driving incident. He was fined £50 and lost his driver's license for three years. The sentence felt mild: "The Good Lord was merciful. I celebrated the respite by acquiring a gorgeous silver necklace for myself, with the letter 'M' in silver, a leather toilet-case, a suitcase, and two books."[9]

Professionally, he was again at the top of his field. That spring, he was appointed by the Publications Committee to be chief editor of a festschrift for Anna Freud's eightieth birthday and he was invited to give two papers at the upcoming London International Psychoanalytic Association Congress (IPAC). In March, he finished writing a preface for the French translation of Winnicott's *Holding and Interpretation* and his paper "Grudge and the Hysteric" was well received at the Hampstead Child-Therapy Clinic.[10]

When Jacques Lacan came to town to give a talk, Khan held a private dinner for him. They had met once before, in the 1960s, and this second encounter strengthened their friendship.[11] A few days later, Khan went to Geneva to give a talk entitled "The Absent Patient" and then, soon after his return, accompanied André Green, who had been appointed to the Freud Memorial Chair, as Green gave his Inaugural Lecture.[12]

Robert Stoller was encouraged by Khan's positive state of mind, but still worried. Their crucial friendship had changed, with Stoller now functioning as a parent/therapist figure: "You are so full of life again, sparkling and yet solid, enthused and original, like a river that has been turned loose to flow where it will and where it should. Now if only you will continue to have the good sense not to fool yourself into some new damaging act. [Y]ou sometimes too hastily protect yourself from dull contentment by manufacturing risks—and when your judgment of the percentages is off, playing at risks shifts into true danger. Sometimes you barely escape with your skin . . . "[13]

Stoller was right to worry. Khan had started to have severe anxiety that pervaded his waking hours as well as his sleep: "Who will restore to me my sleep at night? Strange I can manage sleep only in daytime at present."[14] "Another utterly WHITE night. Where has my sleep disappeared to?"[15] When he did sleep, he had bad dreams—a completely new experience.

He threw himself into planning the renovations. He wanted Palace Court to be a place where he could indulge his agoraphobia by staying in as much as possible: "I am constructing a home around my aloneness."[16] Through Moya, he commissioned the design firm Holloway White Allom to purchase furnishings, then panicked at their £25,000 quote, which seemed extravagant. When Holloway White Allom raised their estimate to £34,000, Khan fired them. In their place, he hired the more reasonable Dale & Co., who had decorated Hans Crescent fifteen years earlier. In his Work Book, he reported an obsessive trait that he had never mentioned before: "Numbers have to be odd with me. I had acquired two woolen slip-over jackets a month or so ago. So went over to Harrod's and have added a third."[17]

Even with occasional relapses, it was his longest period of sobriety in years. Returning to London from Berlin, where he had given his talk

"Grudge and the Hysteric," he wrote to Smirnoff: "It has been quite a new experience to relate to others from sustained and unadulterated quiet and ordinariness."[18] In early June, he spoke to a group of students at the country residence of a Suffolk psychotherapist, Marie Singer,[19] about applied psychoanalysis. It was "an exhilarating experience."[20]

But even though he was sober, he was not doing well. He was sleeping only two hours some nights and the bad dreams continued: "A ghastly foreboding has darkly gathered up in me the past few days. I have tried to evade it, but my mind in sleep throws it at me."[21] In May, he developed a flu-like illness that he could not shake, despite antibiotics and bed rest. By June it was obvious that something was very wrong: "I lose my jouissance so readily at present and sink into invalided self-care. A terrible waste of life that. Couldn't sleep last night till 6 a.m. Got up at 8:20 a.m. Saw two patients and collapsed into bed again to rest."[22] He wondered whether he was unconsciously engaged in self-sabotage of his new stability.

At the end of June, he made plans to go to Paris for an NRP editorial meeting, then on to Geneva for a meeting of the Center for Advanced Psychoanalytic Studies (CAPS).[23] Before leaving, he consulted with Barrie Cooper about his physical state. Cooper gave a tentative diagnosis of chronic appendicitis, but advised Khan to go ahead with the trip, with possible surgery upon his return.

After one day in Paris, he felt too sick to stay. At Orly airport, waiting for a return flight, he wrote, "Exhausted I am. This feels more like flu to me than appendicitis. I really have not been fit in feeling and in fact since I had flu some four weeks ago. . . . The refusal to rest is perverse."[24] Back home, Cooper ruled out appendicitis and prescribed sleeping pills. With his work week already canceled, Khan immersed himself in long bouts of sleep.

He returned to work feeling better, but soon was worse again: "Attempt to sleep hasn't worked. This faceless unrest in me which I do not experience either as anxiety or stress, but know only through the ego's insomniac vigilance. In itself, my life is so well arranged now, but on its fringes I sense menacing ghosts!!"[25] "Dread, dismay and panic have devitalised me today. Best to retire to bed and recuperate."[26]

It was in 1975 that Khan completed a trio of papers on dreaming, begun in 1962, that are among his most important contributions to psychoanalysis. These seminal papers are "Dream Psychology and the Evolution of the Psychoanalytic Situation,"[27] "The Use and Abuse of Dream in Psychic Experience,"[28] and "Beyond the Dreaming Experience."[29]

In the first paper, he described what he called the "good dream." "Good dreams" contain symbolism and they have a restorative quality because they deliver messages from a person's unknown "Other" to the awake and conscious self: "By a 'good dream,' I mean a dream which incorporates through successful dream-work an unconscious wish and can thus enable sleep to be sustained on the one hand and can be available for psychic experience to the ego when the patient wakes up."[30] The clue to recognizing a "good dream" was the feeling tone of the dreamer—a "good dream" feels like a personalized real experience. Khan wrote that it is important that the analyst recognize when dreams are not "good" because dreams that are compulsive and overabundant can look valuable when they are really a kind of meaningless clutter that screens the absence of good dreaming. These dreams should not be given much attention, because then the patient will continue with superficial dreaming.

In Khan's view, the capacity to have a "good dream" is a developmental achievement that is a sign of psychic health in the adult. It is a marker for the existence of transitional space,[31] something that is necessary for success in psychoanalysis: "It is my clinical experience that patients who cannot have a 'good dream' also cannot creatively use the analytic process."[32] Patients who could not dream well needed to be taught to dream. This is an elaboration of Winnicott's idea that patients who could not play had to be taught to play.

The second paper developed the idea that "good dreams" occur in a dream space, in contrast to nonsymbolic dreams, which do not occur in such a space. If a dream were a play, the dream space would be the stage. A person can use the dream space to actualize an experience, he said, with benefits just as significant as if the experience were lived in outer life; for example, he or she can work through a conflict, or develop a creative idea, or try out a new way of being while asleep. People who had not developed a dream space were doomed to express their conflicts in actual living: "I am suggesting that it is the incapacity in a patient to use the dream-space to actualise the experience of the dream-process that leads to acting out of dreams into social-space."[33] Dream analysis, Khan theorized, is similar to Winnicott's squiggle work—people dream into the dream space just as the child uses paper and a writing instrument to draw doodles.

The final paper in the series distinguished between the dreaming experience and the dream text. Khan wrote that dreams do not have to be remembered in order to be beneficial, because in the dreaming experience, the message is communicated to the self even if it is not remembered[34]: "A person in his dreaming experience can actualize aspects of the self that perhaps never become overtly available to his introspection. And yet [the dream] enriches his life . . ."[35] "Have started writing my paper on Dreams and found the exact statement to launch my argument: 'The remembered dream is a negation of dreaming.' That should make them [his peers] sit up!"[36] Khan's theory implies that dream interpretation, a central part of traditional psychoanalysis, is not always necessary or even helpful.

Khan's dream theories came from personal experience. He needed a dream-filled sleep, but not remembered dreams, in order to feel refreshed upon awakening: "The mysteriousness of the experience of sleep. One can sleep for an hour and sink into it with a relaxed wholeness, such that one can wake up feeling one has slept for a whole night. Per contrast, one can sleep for 11 hours and have little experience of rest. I have been sleeping terribly poorly for over a week, and suddenly this afternoon, I slept for little more than an hour and feel so refreshed and whole from it."[37] "I heal only in the dream-space. Conscious introspective attempts at understanding myself merely torture and dislocate me. I rarely remember my 'healing dreams,' unlike DWW, who always did."[38]

The importance of the dreaming experience to Khan's psychological health is demonstrated by the fact that, as he lost access to his own dream space, his "lived life" went downhill. First, however, he had a brief reprieve, inspired once again by seeing the Stollers.

The IPAC meeting was in London in summer 1975, and Khan was a featured speaker. Robert and Sybil Stoller were staying with him, and their presence calmed him: "I always feel so safe amidst others when the Stollers are here."[39] Socializing with mutual friends, including Cooper, Green, and Pontalis, he was sober and happy: "These have been idyllic days of companionship."[40]

On a panel called "Intimate Voices," Khan discussed the correspondences of Sigmund Freud.[41] Separately, he presented his ideas about dreams in a paper, "Beyond Psychic Reality: The Dreaming Experience." He wrote that his international colleagues were enthusiastic in their response: "Yes, I have established myself as THE intellectual creative thinker of my generation with this Congress."[42] "[In talking to peers] I gathered reactive momentum and was a man lit up with his own being."[43]

Though Khan's remarks may seem manic, he did truly get a great deal of attention and praise at IPAC: "Pontalis called and told me that in the summing up of the Congress, my dreaming paper was singled out by the reporter for its imaginative quality."[44] "[The analyst] Colmenaris tells me that Erik Erikson had remarked to him: 'The next decade in psychoanalysis belongs to Khan.'"[45]

After IPAC, Khan was alone as he faced the ending of summer. He had decided to stay in London to prepare for his move, and he was distressed to be losing the space he had once shared with Svetlana: "A terrible gnawing madness clings to and seeps from every object here [in this flat]. Even that which was once beautiful and exultant now has an anguished bite in it."[46] "How many fugitive and anonymous little deaths one dies. These sudden panics that seize and paralyse me at present [are] a way of clinging to this space."[47]

In September, the flat was filled with tea chests that were used for packing, inspiring one analysand to comment: "It looks like Napoleon's army breaking camp."[48] The move was on September 16. One his last day at Hans Crescent, he wrote a note to Svetlana: "Svetlana Gee! I hope this finds you in good health. I am quitting our home here today. God be with you and bless you with health. Much love, Sud."[49]

In preparing Palace Court, Khan had been personally involved in selecting all the furnishings, from desks and couches down to towels, sponges, and the toothbrush mug.[50] He gave up the attempt to be a proper English gentleman in favor of expressing a self that was an idiosyncratic blend of English and Indian. After the move, he even changed his style of dress, often wearing Eastern-style robes that he bought in the ladies' department at Harrod's: "Loose housegowns suit me ideally."[51] He had a vision that Palace Court could be the Western equivalent of Kot Fazaldad Khan: "I am nurturing Flat 7 into a Masudic village."[52]

Prior to the move, he had started an intellectual and social group with three young people whom he referred to as his "villagers." The "villagers" were analytic candidates who were also his analysands, and they met regularly to discuss analytic material. They were two male medical doctors, whom I will refer to as X and Y, and a female Ph.D., Margarita [pseudonym], united in a "brotherhood" in which they vowed to be totally supportive of each other. X was an English Jew from an academic family, Y was an Orthodox Christian from a Southern European country, and Margarita was a young Jewish scholar who would play a major role in Khan's life in the next few years. (She would not be a formal candidate until that fall, but she was working as a therapist and was already well read in the analytic literature.) Margarita's husband, who was not part of the "Masudic village," was an advanced psychoanalytic candidate in analysis with Joseph Sandler.

In the fall, after several months of sobriety, Khan started to drink again. "[I] am drinking again. That can't be helped. So much confused ungraspable stress."[53] His explanation was that his serenity kept being destroyed by the feelings of meaningless terror, and the terror was relieved only by alcohol. Smirnoff urgently pressured him to control his drinking and Khan wrote to him in a period when he was temporarily sober: "As you rightly say, I underestimate to myself the quantity of alcohol I can gulp across the night. I have searched hard for what started it this time. Among various little irritants, the only major reason is my acute phobic dread that [a female friend] was getting too fond of me and was too much in my life. I cannot tolerate intimacy or indebtedness to any woman now. Or any man even. My private reactions shame me because they are so ungracious."[54]

In mid-November, he went to a CAPS meeting in Geneva. There he sank to a new low when he stole a small clock from one of the local shops. He was caught by the owner, who summoned the police. Brought to the police station and kept there, he called on various people he knew to help him get out. Because of his social status and perhaps also because a local colleague had a brother who was a judge in Geneva, he was not imprisoned beyond the first night. But he was asked to leave the country immediately and informed that he would not be allowed to return to Switzerland for several years. He dealt with the incident by rationalizing that he had wanted it to happen: "I never wanted to attend CAPS in Geneva last month and I had to make it impossible to go again. I did."[55] He seems to have made no attempt to understand his behavior and instead tried to forget it: "How much one has to forgive oneself to regain self-esteem."[56]

Even though Khan had known for several years that he had a problem with alcohol, he pretended that everything was fine. The buoyancy of his December Work Book entries is unconvincing: "I dreamed that I was in a bookshop which had beautiful bound books and I felt happy and whole. From this dream, I know I have emerged from my bout of sickness."[57] "To live and travel to one's destiny, it takes the expanse of a desert! I have created that expanse."[58] His optimism yielded at times to a more realistic despair: "I, who know others so well, know myself so very little."[59] He canceled a Christmas trip to Paris because he knew he would drink too much there. He even considered the drastic step of asking Barrie Cooper to perform a medically unnecessary appendectomy, so he could use the enforced sobriety of a hospital stay to dry out. Home alone, he missed Svetlana: "If only I could forget Svetlana, for even an hour. I live with her absence all the time."[60]

CHAPTER 28

THE ALCOHOLIC SOLUTION

*[I]n the alcoholic there persists underneath a search for total
mutuality of belonging and authenticity. This is what mobilises
concern and care in others. But one cannot break the stranglehold
of the alcoholic solution on the person.*
Masud Khan[1]

Even though Khan's peers were highly skilled analysts, people did not
understand that he was slowly becoming a severe alcoholic in the 1970s.[2]
In my interviews, most of his friends and colleagues gave him a primary
diagnosis of narcissistic personality disorder, and indeed he seems to
have been a haughty and grandiose person throughout his life. He was
also diagnosed as being psychotic, a psychopath and—not an official
diagnosis!—a demon. But by 1971, or possibly earlier, he was alcohol
dependent and by 1975, alcohol was destroying his life.

Since alcoholism has not been widely discussed as a central factor in
understanding Khan, I will start by illustrating the severity of his problem. These two accounts come from the later years of his life, when his
drinking problem was obvious.

The first story is from André Green:

I remember a scene in a restaurant in London in the 1980s. Smirnoff and
Pontalis were with us. The tables were connected, and Masud was at the
end of our table, which connected to another at which two couples were
seated. I am a good observer, and I noticed that Masud was behaving
strangely. He was pushing our bucket of champagne with his elbow.

Eventually the champagne fell to the ground. And Masud made a scandal. "SEND ME THE BOSS!" he yells. And he tells the boss that the man at the next table had pushed the champagne off the table. The boss offers to replace the champagne, but Masud says: "No! I want the gentleman to apologize." The boss doesn't know what to do, so he says: "Sir, the gentleman at the next table wants to talk to you." Masud starts up: "I am Prince Masud Khan!" "Oh yeah? And I'm the Duke of Edinburgh!" "You have thrown my bottle!" "Not on purpose. But if I did so, I regret it." That ended it. All Masud wanted was to humiliate that man in front of the women. We all knew it.

Georges Allyn, a psychoanalytic psychotherapist and Khan supervisee, is the only person I interviewed who suggested that Khan's decline was primarily due to alcoholism. He tells of an experience in 1986, when he was living in Paris:

People were gossiping about Masud that he had become increasingly schizoid and aggressive. Then I saw him myself and I had a very different perception.

I had gotten a phone call from Victor Smirnoff that Khan would be in Paris and he asked, would I make a gesture to see him? I said I would, of course, and Masud then called and asked me for lunch. He was staying at the Hotel Lutetia, in a small room on the top floor. The curtains were all drawn.

When I arrived, Masud was still in pajamas and a bathrobe, and he was so hung over that he was trembling. He was there with a Pakistani woman who said very little and seemed embarrassed. He told me that he was ill and asked what I wanted to drink. I had tea, and he had a small bottle of wine.

Masud took one sip of wine, and with that first sip he started to slur words and he became almost delusional. I remember a slip of the tongue he made. He meant to say the word "circumscribed" and he said "circumcised." He couldn't keep his words straight and he was just babbling. He talked with venom about Winnicott, saying things about his impotence. I didn't like being told that. It was unsettling because it was an attack on someone he loved.

I saw a man who was clearly hung over. I've rarely if ever seen anyone so drunk in Paris. And I was amazed at how little wine it took to get him totally inebriated.

It was very clear to me that this was not psychosis, as the gossipers were saying—it was alcoholism. I wondered how much people who were calling him psychotic didn't pick up on his alcoholism. Some people are so good at disguising alcoholic behavior, they pass themselves off as having a different stigma than the one they have.

Allyn's story suggests that Khan suffered from serious end-stage alcoholism, where even a small quantity of alcohol can cause a toxic response. This would have developed only after many years of alcohol abuse.

Alcohol had not been present in Khan's Muslim childhood and, in his first years in the West, Khan was extremely critical of excessive drinking. This attitude can be seen in letters to Svetlana from the early 1960s:

Sud has been to the movies, Gee! Jack Lemmon and a rather austere-pretty girl in a film "Days of Wine and Roses." Rather drably sordid, though Jack Lemmon gives a very good performance and so does the girl. It was rather grimly factual and in its documentations of how a person can be taken over by alcohol very grimly graphic.

I am very sensitive to the horrors of alcoholism! It is the greatest insult to human dignity and God and I found the whole film rather grossly accurate and disturbing, without any "leverage for redemption." It is no news that alcoholism destroys, degrades, and annihilates the human mind, personality and the soul itself. And we are destroying the very nerve of the human soul if we become over-indulgent towards self-pitying hysterics of drunken, debauched and drugged mental states.[3]

I have done something clinically only half an hour ago which I have never risked doing before: A patient (a new case) turned up and bemusedly, complacently, told me he had got drunk last night and is still pretty drunk. I asked him, had he tried to stop getting drunk? He changed my question into the statement: "I do not know why I got drunk." I told him that I hadn't asked him why he got drunk, but whether he had tried NOT to get drunk. He said "No!," he had not tried. I politely but firmly told him that, in that case, there was no use going on with the session. . . . I had no use for a drunk patient: it merely wastes his time and mine. That he is an adult intelligent person and should be able to control himself and arrive sober. That I was not interested in the equation: "Poor patient, he does not know why he gets drunk. Let us help him find out." He was rather taken aback by this. I gave him another appointment and showed him out.

It became clear to me that this patient has learnt all the tricks of exploiting the status of being "neurotic, ill, helpless," and hides behind these to live exactly as he pleases. If one gives in to the myth of the patient's total helplessness, then one becomes the victim and accomplice of their omnipotence. No adult is ever totally helpless.[4]

The second letter shows insight about the treatment of alcoholism that went beyond the analytic thinking of the time. Khan was aware that traditional analysis would be of no help to somebody who was actively alcoholic. In that era—and sometimes even today—the standard analytic thinking about addiction was that it was a symptom of a separate disorder, and that it would disappear if the disorder was successfully treated through analysis. Khan concluded the letter with a clear statement that he did not believe that analytic insight would help his patient unless he stayed sober:

To some extent, psychoanalysis has sponsored this myth of the helpless neurotic who can be helped in spite of his effort to destroy himself. We believe that if only we succeed in imparting true and full knowledge, people will act nobly and responsibly and creatively. But that is not true. People or a person can have all the necessary self knowledge and yet refuse to make use of it.

Over time, Khan would develop an alcohol problem that was much worse than that of his patient. His problems began when Svetlana started heavy drinking at the time when her career was collapsing. But in contrast to Svetlana, he did not drink every day in the late 1960s, and neither his physical health nor his career were compromised at first. He continued to be judgmental of people who drank too much, including himself: "The alcoholic derangement and mess that I became last night [was] a failure of discipline, privacy and separateness."[5] "Alcoholism is not a helpless habit, but a nihilistic attitude towards life and others."[6] By 1973, however, he knew that he was an addict: "I have lived a very alcohol-poisoned existence these many berserk years."[7]

Several of Khan's friends and peers told me that they felt Khan's alcoholism was "his own fault." However, anyone who has dealt with addiction knows how hard it is to break the pattern. Whether alcoholism is seen as biological and/or psychological in origin, a balanced understanding includes respect for the power of addiction along with a questioning of why the addict does not make use of resources that would help him/her recover.

Current writings on psychological problems that predispose a person to addiction—fear of helplessness, vulnerability to separation and loss, and mistrust of others[8]—describe Khan surprisingly well. After becoming aware that he was an alcoholic, Khan did not ask anyone for help, but instead tried to solve the problem by himself. A colleague who was fond of him suggested that pride may have gotten in his way: "I sound like an old-fashioned mediaeval moralist in saying this—but pride was [Khan's] sin and his downfall."[9]

In the early years of his excessive drinking, confrontation might have been helpful. Sybil Stoller, for example, was always able to keep Khan's drinking in good control when he was in California, and Zoë Dominic had the same success in her London home. Sahabzada Yaqub Khan told me he never saw Masud drunk. In those years, the person who probably could have been most effective was Winnicott. Winnicott could have used the power of the transference to make a major impact, even after the analysis had ended. But Winnicott had trained as a pediatrician and as a psychoanalyst, where the topic of addiction was not a significant part of the training, and it appears that he did not understand the centrality of Khan's problem.[10]

Over time, Khan lost his conviction that behavioral control over the drinking was more important than insight. As his addiction worsened, he adopted the more typical analytic view: "Alcohol is a 'self-cure' of ungraspable terrors we fail to render psychic in our self-experience."[11] He may have deliberately avoided people who might have confronted him about his behavior; for example, he stayed at a distance from William Gillespie, who had demonstrated in Amsterdam that he was not afraid of confrontation. Instead, he seems to have picked intimates who were complicit in the sense that they joined him in not seeing the severity of his problem.[12]

Today there is more awareness in the analytic world of the dangers of alcohol addiction, and it is quite possible that Winnicott would have made more focused interventions if he were working now. In the current climate, when psychoanalysis is used as the treatment for alcoholism, technique is modified and alcohol abuse is confronted even if the patient does not bring up the subject.[13] Referrals are often made to rehabilitation programs and to Alcoholics Anonymous. If the patient is believed to be using alcohol to self-medicate symptoms of depression or anxiety, he/she is given antidepressant medication (which treats anxiety as well as depression). Khan, of course, might not have cooperated with such treatment. The first step in the Alcoholics Anonymous program is to "surrender," which could have been problematic for him. But it is notable that he was a late-onset alcoholic who did not enjoy drinking: "Once unpoisoned by alcohol, how lucid, orderly and insomniac my mind becomes. The devil of it is, I do not even enjoy alcohol."[14]

Thinking psychiatrically, there is another matter to be considered: the possibility that Khan's alcoholism was part of an underlying bipolar illness, an inherited disorder popularly known as manic-depression that is often associated with creative genius.[15] Bipolar illness in adults has a sixty to seventy percent comorbidity with alcoholism. This is a perspective that psychoanalysts have historically neglected, out of the idea that alcoholism is a purely psychological problem. But Khan had a family history that suggests a genetic predisposition: his brother Tahir was given a diagnosis of manic-depression while living in London and their mother was reportedly addicted to opium. Khan's depression is well documented, and much of his writing about himself fits the description of the manic phase of a bipolar illness, for example, "Sometimes I feel I am like these images of the Indian gods: with two heads, six arms, four legs! I am one person with too many functions seething to come alive. If I were less endowed, perhaps I could be more containable and achieved."[16] "I have dragged my feet all day, but come the evening and I can sense the whole of me begin to simmer with wakefulness. Ever since adolescence, there was been a refusal in me towards daytime and daylight. If I could, I would work all night and sleep through the day: like Dostoevsky."[17] Throughout his life, the manic symptoms alternated with periods of depression and withdrawal, in a kind of cycling that is typical of this disorder.[18]

Khan's symptomatology fits the current psychiatric description of bipolar disorder extremely well,[19] including the fact that his problems began in adolescence and worsened in his mid-thirties. Looking at his symptoms, the only question would be whether he suffered from what is called bipolar I disorder or the less serious bipolar II illness. If his symptoms are considered to be severe enough to be called psychotic, his diagnosis would be bipolar I.

In the 1960s, the recommended medication for a bipolar disorder was lithium, which was in fairly wide use.[20] But his physician told me that Khan was never given a sustained trial of lithium—only a brief unsuccessful trial in the 1980s, when he was too ill to tolerate the side effects.[21] One reason for the possible oversight may be that the diagnosis and treatment of bipolar II disorder was not well understood until recently. Bipolar II was given the name "cyclothymia" and the general psychiatric thinking was that it was a personality disorder, which is not helped by medication.

Consideration of the possibility that Khan might have had an illness that went beyond a purely psychological disturbance opens up the possibility of understanding him differently. From this perspective, he can be seen as a man who suffered from the ordinary and expected consequences of untreated bipolar illness exacerbated by alcoholism. Many people deteriorate in their later years, and just about anybody would be deranged when drinking a bottle and a half of Scotch a day, as Khan was by his final decade. One hopes, however, that in cases of uncontrolled illness, there will be family or friends who make sure that a person's deterioration is kept private, something that was not the case for Khan.

Undated photo of Fazaldad Khan, Masud Khan's father (circa 1846–1943), in military dress and wearing medals that were awarded by the British for service in the Indian Army.

Masud Khan as a young boy, dressed in Western clothing for a formal picture, at the family home in The United Provinces of India (now Pakistan).

Masud's sister, Mahmood (1926–1942), standing in the back row, inherited her dark-skinned beauty from her mother Khursheed, who was Fazaldad's fourth wife. Mahmooda is pictured here with a woman and other children from the extended family.

This picture is probably of the first post-war International Psycho-Analytic Congress, held in Zurich in 1949. Masud attended as a guest through the influence of his analyst, John Rickman, and he was the only student at the Congress. Masud is in an upper row toward the right, a tall man looking away from the camera.

Masud with analytic colleagues in the early 1950s. Charles Rycroft is second from the left and Marion Milner is on Masud's right.

Wedding photo of Masud's first marriage in 1952. Jane Shore, the bride, wore an Indian karakuli cap matching that worn by her new husband, and she is joined in the car by Masud's brother Tahir (1923–1983) and his Hindu girlfriend from India, Uma Vasudev.

Masud and Svetlana Beriosova in Monte Carlo, 1957 or 1958. Svetlana and Masud would marry in 1959, but at the time of this photo he was married to Jane Shore, from whom he was estranged. (Photo by Zoë Dominic)

Svetlana Beriosova dancing the lead role in *Swan Lake* for the Royal Ballet in the early 1960s. (Photo by Zoë Dominic)

Number Three Hans Crescent in the fashionable Knightsbridge section of London. As newlyweds, Masud and Svetlana took a long lease on Flat 9 on the fourth floor, with neighbors on the third floor Michael Redgrave, Rachel Kempson and their teenage children Vanessa, Lynn and Corin. (Photo by Rebecca Smith and Tara Stitchberry)

The famed photographer Henri Cartier-Bresson was a personal friend of the Khans and he took several significant photos of them, including this one from the early 1960s, with Masud wearing his karakuli cap.

Masud in the 1960s, with an ever-present cigarette dangling from his mouth. A decade later, he would be diagnosed with lung cancer.

In the late 1960s, Masud returned to his childhood passion for horseback riding when he bought a horse he named Solo and rode daily in Richmond Park, London.

Masud holding Kalu, the much loved household pet. On the mantel are photographs of Svetlana, a Russian ancestor who may be her mother, and Mike Nichols. The print on the wall is one of a pair of bird prints by Braque, given to Svetlana by her wealthy admirer, Geoffrey Gorer.

Mike Nichols, Rudolf Nureyev and a very pregnant Julie Andrews at the Khan flat. The picture is from the early 1960s, in the period Masud called "The Divine Years". He and Svetlana established their flat at Hans Crescent as a place where actors, authors and artists mixed with psychoanalysts in notable post-ballet parties. Note the picture of Kalu on the bookshelf.

Masud and Svetlana out to dinner with Robert and Sybil Stoller in the late 1960s.

Masud and his houseboy, Susu, in 1967.

Masud and a longtime friend at dinner in the late 1970s or early 1980s, a period when Masud regularly dressed in his own variant of Eastern dress, often in black and silver.

Masud in his flat at Palace Court looking thin and distant, from a period near the time of his death in 1989.

CHAPTER 29

CLINICAL WORK [INTERVIEWS]

From Masud I did learn about silence, quiet and integration;
and about being. I do not think I could have gained the
conviction of the power of analysis with many,
if any, other analysts.
Anonymous Khan supervisee from the 1970s

Khan always sought to please his elders, and with just a few exceptions (e.g., socializing with Wynne Godley), he did not allow his personal problems to affect his analytic work while Winnicott was alive. After Winnicott died, Khan's clinical work became, at times, more aggressive and more sexual. Working without supervision, he did not tell anyone the truth about what he was doing.[1] He seems to have believed that he could keep his personal problems separate from his work. In 1972, he wrote, "I am utterly crippled inside at the present moment but, for some strange reason, can manage my clinical work adequately."[2] But Khan did not abandon all discipline in the post-Winnicott years. Much of his work was still good, especially his work with regressed patients, which helps explain why it took so long for his peers to act to control him.

There are four interviews in this chapter. The accounts of one supervisee and one analysand show Khan doing strong, positive work. These are followed by two accounts from analysands who started out having a fairly traditional analysis involving regression, and then became involved in "real" relationships with Khan that destroyed their analysis.

INTERVIEW WITH SUPERVISEE
GEORGES ALLYN (1971-1972)

Georges Allyn is an American who moved to London in the late 1960s
to have analysis. While there, he worked as a therapist and was supervised by Winnicott and then Khan. He now makes his home in Paris,
where he is a practicing Buddhist, a gourmet cook, and a psychoanalytic therapist. We met for the interview in 1997.

> My first supervisions for child observations and pediatric testing were
> with Winnicott, and they ended abruptly in 1968, if I remember correctly,
> when he had a heart attack. Then I started seeing Masud for child therapy
> supervision. I found him to be a sensitive supervisor, very tuned in to my
> case of a difficult child.
>
> Winnicott had taught me that interpretation must be therapeutic,
> rather than an attempt to explain or indoctrinate. So I learned to observe
> and store things, giving them a silent place in my memory so that if needed,
> they can be called back. Masud worked in that style with patients and with
> supervisees. Once I told him about a session that was intensely painful for
> me, and his response was to go get a cup of tea for me. We then sat in
> silence—there was no need to talk or explain. He considered his role as
> supervisor to be to help *me*—he was very different from other supervisors
> who tend to blame the therapist when things aren't going well.
>
> He understood the schizoid piece in patients and the vulnerability
> of nonexistence. He must have experienced that himself. He also knew
> about helping people to find their self. Once he said, "I have to invent
> each person's therapy in such a way that the patient can invent himself."
>
> They say history is written by the winners. It's very easy to take pot-
> shots at someone who can't defend himself, but there are always at least
> two sides to every story. If I could summarize anything about Masud, I
> would think about the way a child develops—you can't just take single
> photographs, you have to have a composite picture over time, because there
> is a continuously evolving story. Masud was very different at different times.

INTERVIEW WITH ANALYSAND ALEXA
(1973-1975)

Alexa (pseudonym) is a Spanish woman[3] who had a short analysis with
Khan that included regression to dependence. At the time, she was in

her late twenties doing graduate work in London. She is now an academic working in the United States. The interview was in 2000.

I was referred to Masud by my cousin, who was already an analytic candidate in London. He told me: "Masud's main quality is that he goes straight to the essence of things." Masud had been my cousin's supervisor and he was the only analyst who centered him, showing him the limits. Masud taught him that he should stop being everyone's darling and commit himself to a real life. I felt that was exactly what I needed.

I remember the moment I met Masud. I was in the waiting room, and he opened the door and peered in. I was impressed by this huge, tall, extremely handsome man, who had such a careful way of opening the door and gently entering the room. He even seemed timid. From the very first moment, he was aware that he was entering the space of another person, entering my space, and he was careful not to burst into the space. He bent over as he came in, almost as if he was asking "May I . . . ?"—as if he was quietly warning me that he was there and showing me respect. That may be the side of him that people know the least about, the way he was so respectful of the privacy of others. People today think of him as the opposite of that.

I became intensely involved in the analysis right from the very beginning. Halfway through the initial interview, I had found myself sitting on a cushion on the floor, leaning against the couch, and I began to cry and cry. I didn't know why I was crying, and it was surprising, because I was not usually a crier—but something had opened up in me. He touched something inside me that nobody else had ever been able to grasp. It was like my cousin had said: Masud went straight to the core. I welcomed the newness of these feelings he aroused in me. I thought: If I choose to be in analysis with this man, my life will change. It's a big risk. Do I dare to take it? And I answered, to myself: Yes.

One of the most helpful sessions came early in the analysis. It was a 5:00 session on a Friday in the wintertime. When I rang the bell, the houseboy, Susu, opened the door with a concerned look on his face. He said, "Mr. Khan apologizes, he was going away this weekend and he had to take an earlier flight than expected, so he isn't here." That was the first and only time that he missed a session. My husband had planned to pick me up after the session. So, rather than have me stand out in the cold, Susu said I could wait in the secretary's room and I did that, even though I worried that I was breaking a boundary.

Then Susu offered me tea, and as I sat there I got more and more anxious. I wondered if Susu knew that patients weren't supposed to sit in their analyst's secretary's office and to have tea. Susu left the room, but I was so nervous I couldn't drink the tea. I was troubled for Susu and for myself—I was afraid he would get into trouble and I didn't want him to feel bad about being so kind.

The issue of the tea was with me all weekend. In the Monday session, Masud accepted my upset about him not being there. But with regard to the tea, he said: "Look, I could interpret your feelings and fantasies about the tea—we could write ten volumes about it. But the only thing I will tell you is this: what a pity it is that there is so much between you and a cup of tea!" It was such a perfect comment—he allowed me to just BE. That ended up being his greatest contribution to me—he freed me from constantly having to analyze myself. It's paradoxical, I know.

As the analysis went on, I began to get more and more regressed. I would curl up like a fetus under the blanket on Masud's couch. (He had a tartan blanket, which I think came from John Sutherland, who was Scottish.) After awhile, I regressed to something close to infancy. For at least a week, my experience of the ground became altered. It was as if I was a young child learning to walk and not sure of my balance or of where the ground was. I wasn't scared by this—everything was just different and new.

He gave me an extra session one weekend. I came into the room and immediately fell asleep on the couch. While sleeping, I had a powerful dream, which seemed absolutely real. I dreamed that I was enveloped all around my body by something that was of a different density than the air—I was totally surrounded, like a larva, by something that wasn't hard but neither was it soft. I felt totally peaceful. And in the dream state, there was a dog in the room, similar to a German shepherd my mother had once, and it was taking care of me, looking out for me. The dream went on and on, with nothing happening. I was just there and the dog was by me.

When I woke up, I came back gently into the present. I told the dream to Masud and he was totally quiet. We both knew that the dog in the dream was him. The word for "dog" in my native language, is "can," which sounds equal to "Khan."

This was a very important session, a session that changed me forever. I used to get depressed a lot; I felt that I had a weight inside me and that it shadowed my life. After the session, I was never again depressed that way. The weight of that depression was gone and something had been restored. Even now, I only get depressed when there is some real reason. Years later, an analyst friend who had been supervised by Khan suggested to me that Masud had enabled me to regress to a state of infancy previous to the point where I had taken in my mother's depression. I think she was right.

I had a year and a half of this kind of restorative analysis. Masud was always appropriate, all the time. I knew absolutely nothing about his private life and he didn't show off. It was a time of enormous growth for me. I was totally involved in the analysis, thinking about it all day long—just like all my peers. That is how we lived then. It was exhilarating.

The analysis ended because I moved to the United States, where I saw a new analyst. The work with Masud prepared me to make the most out of the second analysis.

Thinking about all this takes me far back—my life now is so different from what it was at that time. But as I think about it, I remember him very well. He had an enormous influence on me. He was an extraordinary clinician and a wonderful teacher. He left people with seeds that could grow for the rest of their lives.

INTERVIEW WITH ANALYSAND
FRANCISCO ALMADA (1970-1972)

Francisco Almada is a practicing psychic who lives in Soho, a lively section of New York City. The son of Eurasian parents (both of them a mixture of Portugese and Chinese), he grew up in Hong Kong and then, at age thirteen, attended a Jesuit boarding school in England. Later he studied composition at the Royal College of Music, attended Nottingham University, and went to art school. Our interview was in 1998.

It's important to say right at the beginning that I am fifty years old, born in June, a Cancer-Cancer.

When I was at Nottingham University in 1969, I had a kind of breakdown. I was depressed, perhaps because I didn't know how to "come out" as a gay man. I ended up in a hospital, where I was given semi-narcosis. That was a technique where you are given heavy tranquilizers and you basically sleep, but you are woken up every twelve hours to use the bathroom.[4] It lasted about a week and it did help me.

At the hospital, I saw a Scottish psychiatrist, a man whom I liked. He said to me: "I thought you were a paranoid schizophrenic and that you wouldn't make progress. But you have recovered well and I'd like you to try psychoanalysis." He sent me to a pompous, unpleasant psychoanalyst in London to get a referral for analysis. That man said to me: "Are you racially prejudiced?" I WAS prejudiced, but I replied: "I can't afford to be, because I'm of mixed race myself." That's how I got referred to Khan.

Khan started the analysis by saying at the first meeting: "You know what to do." Really, I didn't know. Now I realize that he was checking me out to see if I was a suitable candidate. But I did talk and at the end, he said he could help me. I was flattered because he seemed to want to see me. Now I wonder if he was being manipulative with that. He is [sic] such a complicated person.

He impressed upon me from the beginning that he was learned and cultured and from the upper echelons. He quoted Auden and T. S. Eliot, and he would make reference to modern French painting. He was imposing and pompous. And the truth is, I did care about those things, because I had been brought up in an English public school.

I thought he wanted me to talk about my childhood, so that's what I did. Five days a week, I lay on the couch. He was sometimes listening intently, but then at other times he didn't seem to be paying attention. He would shuffle papers and write things and I was sure he wasn't writing about me. And he would take phone calls—his secretary would buzz him and tell him who was calling.

Sometimes he would be harshly critical, and I wouldn't know what to do with that. Once I said: "You are right, I am a wimp." Then later he asked me: "What did you think of my onslaught?" as if he wanted me to evaluate what was behind his attack. I answered: "I suppose if things aren't difficult here, I won't make progress." Other times I thought that he shouldn't have attacked me and he was just venting, letting off steam. I was always polite when he attacked me. I never confronted him, never talked back.

At other times, he was sympathetic and he would praise things I did. That meant a lot to me because I felt my parents had never been interested in me.

Once, he was very pushy about me seeing a medical doctor. It was some public holiday and I wasn't that sick—I only had a sore throat—so I wanted to wait until the next day. He insisted: "You must phone the doctor right now." I said: "You are being as aggressive as my parents." My parents had never "heard" me and I felt he wasn't listening either. That is the only time I ever contradicted him. I can imagine now that he was jubilant that he had gotten me to say something a little angry. I ended up seeing the doctor and paying a fortune for the visit, because it was some Harley Street specialist.

Maybe I should tell you about the ways that [Khan] was good for me. It was he who encouraged me to go to art school. I had dropped out of university and he had seen some of my work. He was very pushy about it. I had the thought that actually HE wanted to be an artist, and that I was going for him. But ultimately I was glad that I went and I don't think I would have gone if he hadn't been pushy.

Also, he asked me to illustrate some books he had. One of his books, *Knots*, by R. D. Laing, had blank pages, and he said "Draw directly into this book." I did some very fine ink drawings directly into the book, which involved considerable risk-taking. When I gave it back to him, he asked me to sign it. He also asked me to illustrate his copy of Camus's *L'Etranger*. He was a parental figure who appreciated my work, and I valued that.

I remember once I was very upset telling a story about my mother. He reached over and put his hand on my head for awhile and that was comforting. Because of my hunger for empathy, that meant a lot to me. It was appropriate and it worked.

He did not share my interest in music, so we rarely talked about it. But we did share one musical experience, and this is a strange story. It touches on something important. Every once in a while he wanted to socialize with me, something that I knew was verboten. On this occasion, I had had two teeth extracted under general anesthesia, and he insisted I spend the evening in his apartment. He had ice cream brought in, because my mouth was sore.

I don't know where the music came from. Maybe I brought a record? It was a woman singing Persian poetry to the accompaniment of a harmonium. He claimed to understand the Persian language, and he was deeply moved. He said: "Isn't this beautiful?" And I said to him: "Mr. Khan, there is someone else in this room. We are not alone." I felt a presence—and this is before I knew that I would become a psychic. Later he said: "As I listened to the music I knew my dead sister was with me. She used to sing with a harmonium." This experience created a bond between us.

As our relationship changed, I saw his pettiness and his control issues. He needed to be respected and in some way feared. When I would feel disempowered, I thought that that was what he wanted. He would intimidate his secretaries mercilessly, sending them out of the room quivering and in tears. And then he would send ME to say to them: "Mr Khan will see you now." Sometimes I felt that he was relating to me as if I were a son.

The issue of homosexuality was something he didn't want to discuss. He said "That's not why you are here!" He almost pushed me toward having sex with women. Once he insisted that I go with another of his analysands to Paris for a long weekend. He had wanted me to be an artist, so he helped me with that, but he had no wish for me to be a homosexual.

I was young, insecure, and impressionable. I got caught up in the thing in a way that was exciting and fascinating, and for a time very interesting. And then . . . I don't know the sequence . . . the socialization changed things. We did more and more of it. Once Susu [the houseboy], Masud, and I went to a movie. On another evening, Susu came to dinner with us.

There were more and more intrusions. When DWW died, he said: "Winnicott died today." So I said: "Look, if you don't want to do a session today, I understand, we can skip it." And he said: "No, no, no. This is your time." Then fifteen minutes later he said: "I think I do want to stop." Later that year he told me: "My wife left me today, my marriage is over." I didn't know what to say.

He wanted to be sure that I, the analysand, was not the one calling the shots. That's why he didn't stop the session when I first suggested it on the day that Winnicott died. It was a contrast to his experience in analysis where, he told me, he used to say: "DWW, you aren't in the mood for a session today, so I'm leaving."

I saw him for about eighteen months. In that time, he was always critical of my friends, accusing them of having loose morals. He said of the woman I shared my apartment with: "She's just a slut." He knew that offended me. The next day he asked me: "How did you feel when I said that?" I didn't discuss it because there seemed no point. I felt that he wanted to arrange my social life by handpicking my friends and getting me to socialize with his analysands. Once he said: "You better brush up on your French, because I may move to Paris." I was flattered, but I also thought: "How presumptuous!" How could he assume that I would follow him?

Near the end of the analysis, I was upset because he kept insisting that my father had married my mother because she was good at sex. There was a seventeen-year age difference, and he said: "She must have been a seductress," implying that she used her sexual wiles to seduce my father.

It felt like a violation of something when he insisted on this. It was impolite, irrelevant.

Then there was an incident that finally caused me to end. It involved his rudeness at a dinner party at Hans Crescent. He instigated a fight and then threw out the guests, everyone but me. He said: "No! you stay! I haven't finished talking to you!" He took advantage of my trepidation— I was afraid to object.

I couldn't respect him after that. The next session, I refused to sit down and I told him I would not continue. He told me: "I will leave all your sessions open for the rest of the week. You can come or not."

I didn't go back. As I said, I'm a Cancer-Cancer and, you know, the moon in Scorpio means I'm stubborn and into self-defense. These people can sever relationships with terrifying finality.

A week after the ending, he sent a letter. It said: "I don't claim to be the only analyst in town. But you are an extremely disturbed sick person and it is imperative that you have treatment or it will be a disaster." This was revengeful, inappropriate. He knew it could harm me. I understood that he was angry because I had taken control and made the decision. The next night he told a friend of mine, who was his analysand: "A clinical disaster has occurred." He was referring to me.

I did have a relapse of depression. In 1977, after I broke up with a boyfriend, I became paranoid again. But I wouldn't go even to an M.D., because I was traumatized by the therapy with Khan. I just stayed inside and was agoraphobic for several months.

I'm too much of a coward to ever return to psychoanalysis. I considered it in 1996, after another breakup, but I didn't go. Because by definition, if you see a therapist, you are going there to deal with things you are afraid to see on your own, and I wouldn't trust a therapist to help me. In some ways that is good, because I have a sense of my own internal strength.

Khan's birthdate is July 21, 1924. He's right on the cusp of Leo-Cancer. And he's Cancer. That means we would share the same traits. The crab. Hard on the outside, soft on the inside. Two Cancers would be doomed.

After the interview, Almada showed me some of his drawings and paintings from the time when he was seeing Khan. (He abandoned his art career after ending the analysis.) One was a superb pen sketch of a well-known musician, a Khan analysand who had become Almada's friend. There was also a series of pages of white paper with tiny colorful oil paintings on the four corners. The painting of these corners had obviously taken an enormous amount of time, and they were hauntingly beautiful. I wondered silently why a man of such talent would have abandoned his art career.

INTERVIEW WITH ANALYSAND CAROLINE (1970-1973)

I heard about Caroline (pseudonym) through Francisco Almada, who had been her friend in London in the early 1970s. Almada said that she was a private person who probably would not want to be interviewed, but he agreed to forward a letter from me to her home in Toronto. More than two years passed before Caroline answered the letter in 2000, and when she did, she expressed an urgency to meet as soon as possible. I was planning to be in Toronto a few months later on unrelated business, but she told me that was too long to wait "now that I've started thinking about the whole thing." So I flew to Toronto within the month to talk with her.

Caroline is a married artist, now in her early fifties. She grew up in Canada, the sixth of seven children. As a young woman, she had characteristics that Masud especially favored: she was beautiful, foreign, a talented painter, and wealthy.

Where should I start? Well, let's see. The most important thing is that I'm now a member of Alcoholics Anonymous.

When I first knew Khan, I hardly even drank. But I was skinny then and he said I should have a glass of wine with every meal. After awhile I was drinking way too much. He sent me to his doctor friend, Barrie Cooper—the great Barrie Cooper, physician to Elizabeth Taylor. He told me that my liver was enlarged, and that I should stop drinking alcohol and start drinking bouillon instead. Really! I don't know if Masud ever knew about that.

One way that I was unlucky as a child is that I am dyslexic. No matter what I did, I never achieved at the level of my siblings. My parents sent me to a finishing school in London to try to pass the A levels, but I never wrote the exams.[5] When I started analysis, I was working as a typist in the evaluation department of Sotheby's.

My mother gave me analysis as a twenty-first birthday gift. Her analyst in Canada referred me to Winnicott. I was having a hard time. I was emotionally up and down a lot and totally unable to feel anger. I also felt bad that I couldn't finish my education.

It was the summer of 1969. I saw Winnicott in a bright airy room, very white. He was a tall thin ascetic man, and I felt he was cold. I did not take to him. [Note: Winnicott was, by other accounts, a short man, no taller than 5'6".]

I was just as happy to hear that he was too busy to take me on. He said he had to refer me, as he was too busy, and he asked: "Would you have anything against seeing a Pakistani analyst?" The words were so odd—what a way to "pitch" a person! He made no mention of Khan's talents, just asked if I would mind that he was Pakistani. I had no objection, so that's how I got referred.

I remember that Khan was warm, right from the beginning. The office was dark, and I experienced it as cozy and womb-like, in contrast to the bright open space of Winnicott. There were lots of deep red and brown colors. I got to sit in a chair for the first visit and look at him, rather than lie on the couch. I asked him if he was a Freudian, and he answered with a snort, no words. That snort may have meant that he thought my question was stupid, or maybe he was implying that he had gone far beyond Freud.

Khan had a Spanish houseboy named Susu who would answer the buzzer. He was studying silversmithing—jewelry making—and he gave me this. [She referred to a handcrafted silver cross that she was wearing around her neck.] I think he gave it to me because I used to give him money at Christmas time—that was Masud's suggestion. I'd been brought up to be polite, so I was glad to do it.

I remember once Beriosova answered the buzzer and let me in. It was awkward, because I knew that our lives weren't supposed to overlap. But she was kind and I felt positively toward her. That meeting inspired a dream that I had late in the analysis. I dreamed that Beriosova came to me and said: "Pack your bags and leave this place." It was a comforting dream, a caretaking dream. I should have followed her advice.

But in the beginning, I liked him very much. I went five times a week, for fifty minutes. I think in all the years, he canceled or was late only one or two times. My mother paid him. I don't know what he charged, but I can tell you this—the fee was high.

At first, I would just lie there and a lot of times there would be no words at all, for five or six sessions in a row. We would both be totally silent, and he was usually smoking. I found those sessions to be comforting. The chance to have somebody be silent with me was quite wonderful. The analysis helped me then. It kept me from becoming an alcoholic.

One time, I was on some kind of emotional edge, and I just turned up at his door and rang the bell. He wasn't at all bothered that I had come. He put me in the spare bedroom with a blanket, and I fell asleep instantly. I had a feeling of total safety.

Khan was never boring. He made me feel alive. One of the most wonderful things was that he believed in me. After all those years of being the one who failed in school, he told me that I could pass my A level exams and I knew he believed that. His unquestioning stance on this topic was that I could go to university if I wanted to. So I went to what is called a "crammer's school"[6] and I wrote the exams, but I only passed one of the three. The funny thing is that when I didn't pass, it didn't matter. He then steered me to go to a school of interior design—Mrs. Inchbold's school—where I had a wonderful time and developed my best talents. Coming from a family where I had felt like such a failure, it meant a great deal to me that he assumed I was a competent and intelligent person.

I had very painful menstrual periods at that time, and lots of people, including doctors and therapists, had given me the interpretation that I wasn't accepting my femininity. Khan had a different approach. He said "Put your knees up, with a pillow underneath you and a hot water bottle on your stomach." He looked on it as a physical problem. To me, it felt like acceptance.

Once I was feeling depressed, and he came to where I was living. He didn't call first. It seemed very odd. He came into my bedroom and just sat there with me. And once Francisco Almada was sick, and Khan and I went together to see him. Other than that, we never socialized outside of the sessions.

He was so attractive then. You were always aware of him as a man. He liked to consult with me on my appearance. Once I had just bought a dress and he asked me to model it for him. I changed right there in the office.

The breaking of the trust was a sexual thing. It started in 1971, when I was twenty-three years old. We started to "go all the way," but didn't. It was cunnilingus and fellatio, and it was only for a few sessions. We didn't do it to climax. It was meant as a Pygmalion kind of thing. I was a virgin, and he wanted to be the person who initiated me into the world of sex. It felt like he was doing it for my benefit, not for himself—it was a gift.[7] But I screwed it up because, when he went away to Pakistan, I got drunk and had sex with somebody. After that, he got furious—he took it as a personal betrayal. He said: "You did that to get back at me!" And he stopped making advances, so there was no more sex.

Looking back, I wonder if I wasn't being self-protective when I lost my virginity. Maybe I knew it was a way to stop the sexual thing. Maybe I knew that he wouldn't be interested after that.

Was I in love with him? I have thought about that. The answer is "yes and no." I had my first serious boyfriend at the same time, so it wasn't that he was like a boyfriend. But it would have been pretty hard not to be in love with him then. He was so sexy; it was as if he was a movie star. It was flattering just to be noticed. And at that time, I wasn't able to say no to him about anything.

After the sex ended, we never talked about it. But the analysis changed. We started meeting in the living room, which we had never done before. Lots of times he sat in a chair and I sat on the floor at his feet, and we listened to music—jazz or blues. Sometimes we played backgammon. We didn't talk much. He often wore his caftan—a robe with long sleeves—rather than formal clothing. I thought he seemed depressed. Somehow I knew that Beriosova had moved out—it was something about the furniture and the mood in the flat, it had become like a bachelor's place, lacking the female touch.[8]

All these sessions lasted for the usual fifty minutes, and my mother paid for them. She never knew what was happening, of course.

Khan had this great belief in himself, that if he accepted you, then that was God's stamp, things would be really great for you. And in a way that was true. He was such an alive person in the beginning, electric, joyous. It did rub off. He was one of the few really alive people I have ever met, and he made me feel alive too.

But when the trust was broken, it was different. He didn't sparkle any more, and neither did I.

I ended the analysis in 1973. He had begun to have headaches a lot and it was clear that he mostly wanted company. In the sessions, we usually just played backgammon. He was going down in some way and I had a sense that I could be pulled into something destructive.

There were three things that contributed directly to my stopping, one more important than the others. The first is that he used to cheat at backgammon, and that bothered me. We played for prizes, and I won a big French–English dictionary that he gave me. Then I won the other volume, the English–French dictionary, and he wouldn't give it to me.

The second thing is that my sister told me that Khan was known for sleeping with his female patients, and that made me angry. She heard this from a friend, who was another of Khan's patients [the friend was Eva; see Chapter 23].

The final thing was that once in the living room I asked for a Coke, and Khan made Susu add Scotch to it. He insisted, and I didn't have the courage to refuse. The thing was, the mixture ruined the Scotch and it also ruined the Coke. That was my breaking point. It wasn't about the sex, because that had been over for a long time. It bothered me that he would override my wishes.

After we ended, he contacted me twice. The first time was a few weeks later. He phoned me to tell me that my mother was late in paying the last bill. I was surprised that he was calling me, since I had never had anything to do with her payments. He ended the conversation by saying: "You sound depressed." And that made me angry, because it seemed like a ploy, as if he were saying: "See, you can't make it on your own."

Then another time, years later, I had moved back to Canada and I got a letter from him. He said that [a man we both knew] had gotten into trouble with the law about something, and he asked if I would donate money to help him out. I didn't answer.

I didn't start to get angry until a few years ago when I went back into therapy. I was seeing a woman therapist and she was furious when she heard the story. She helped me to talk about how he had disappointed me. I got so angry, I wanted to just scream at him—even though I'm not a screamer.

Eventually I got past the anger, and now I can forgive him. He was damaging himself at that time, spiraling downward and really in trouble. I forgive him because he was a fellow alcoholic. I know about that—I've been there, too. Now that I know about his alcoholism,[9] I understand him better.

I wish I would have seen him to tell him that I forgive him. I wish I had told him about how I stopped drinking through Alcoholics Anonymous and I'd like to have encouraged him to do that for himself. I remember that he himself had been very good to somebody who called on the phone during a session, somebody who was upset because they had just "slipped" about the alcohol; he didn't say this, but I think it was a friend of Beriosova.[10] He was calm and encouraging. I would like to have done for him what he did for her.

When I think of Khan now, I remember the acceptance that he showed me, the way he saw no barriers to my going to the university. That has stayed with me, and it's a precious gift. He didn't do enough damage to rob me of that gift. He was a wonderful person to know in the beginning. I'm sure that I wouldn't be the person who I am today, if not for all the experiences I had with him.

But I would never, never go back to a male therapist.

Caroline reported that she was not traumatized by the sexual relationship with Khan. Many readers may believe that she, like Eva, is in denial, still protecting her abuser. But she seemed to speak sincerely as she related her story.

CHAPTER 30

MOVING ON

I have lived for some 45 years serving, accommodating
to what was asked, and spasmodically erupting into anti-social
acts of "hidden self-actualisations." At 52, that style no longer
suits me. I want a total break with my past . . . How to
assemble a beginning is the real task now for me.
Masud Khan[1]

In 1976, Khan again started a new year determined to control his drinking. Newly sober, he was able to sleep, but still feeling unwell: "How easily I sleep ten hours and more each night. Yet it is a strange sleep—dreams seem to be living my day life for me at present. In wakeful private time, I am utterly inert. I sense no depression, only a passive ease. Lack of reading and writing and my total lack of interest in any person puzzles and bothers me a little."[2]

When the Stollers visited in February, he collapsed into sickness, knowing that his friends would "hold" him while he regressed: "Bob and Sybil somehow did enable me to let go of my last bit of self-holding. . . . I stayed in bed the whole weekend and lived through my past in the dream-space."[3] He easily accepted Robert Stoller's advice to cancel plans for a paper, "The Clinical Toleration of Unrelating by the Borderline Patient," planned for a conference at Menninger's later in the year.

Throughout the spring, he stayed phobic and exhausted. Barrie Cooper diagnosed him with postviral depression, but Khan felt his essence of his problem was his False Self living: "[Throughout my life] my circumstances compelled me to fabricate a phenomenon called 'Khan' who has very little to do with the private, true me, 'Masud.'"[4] Another problem was alcohol. By now he had liver damage for which temporary sobriety was not a cure.

A letter from Victor Smirnoff to Robert Stoller reveals that it was finally becoming obvious to others that Khan was doing badly: "[Masud] made somewhat of a scandal at [a BPAS meeting]. . . . He was in a paranoid state, polishing his jack-knives, talking about how he could defend himself against aggressive patients, how he was still physically strong, although the time would come where he would be weak and helpless. He seemed shattered by his Geneva experience although he was telling almost everybody about it."[5]

In the same letter, Smirnoff described behavior that is an eerie foreshadowing of something that would make more sense later that year. Smirnoff had come to London to have a routine medical exam, which revealed that his health was fine. Khan, however, telephoned their mutual friend J.-B. Pontalis and told him that Smirnoff was suffering from a fatal illness. Pontalis believed the story and it was only later that Smirnoff, with some effort, was able to convince him that he was totally healthy. Later Khan did the same thing again, lying to French friends that a colleague, Annette Lavers, had cancer, and to English friends that Hanna Segal had cancer.[6]

André Green had been Khan's friend since 1969. As two of the most talented writers and thinkers of their generation, they had engaged in open admiration and competition. Now their relationship was strained as Khan became offensive in professional meetings, especially after Green began to make theoretical contributions that expanded on Winnicott's thinking about transitional objects.[7]

Green was program chair for the 1977 Jerusalem International Psychoanalytic Association Congress (IPAC), and the planning was well underway in 1976. Khan was hoping to be invited to be a main speaker, especially since the planning committee included his friends Pearl King and Adam Limentani. However, as Green told me, the invitation never came, for a good reason: "If the congress had occurred at any location other than Jerusalem, Masud could have been the main speaker. I told him why he wasn't being invited. I said I had been in Jerusalem two weeks earlier and the Israeli soldiers were doing physical searches of everyone entering the country. I asked Masud 'Would you stand for that?' His answer: 'If anyone touches me, I will call my cousin Hassan, and Israel will be invaded!' But he still didn't understand."

In late spring, things took a dramatic turn for the positive. Khan seemed to be succeeding in the struggle to establish himself in his new space: "I feel I have shed a sickness; but I really don't know what that sickness was."[8] Not surprisingly, this improvement coincided with his continued abstinence from alcohol.

In May, the French translation of *The Privacy of the Self* came out, with a title coined by Pontalis: *Le Soi Cache* ("The Hidden Self").[9] There was an introduction by Green[10] and a blurb by Pontalis on the back cover. Khan attended the festivities in Paris and was pleased. He wrote to Robert Stoller: "The launching of *Le Soi Cache* was a real event for me, and it has restored my morale. . . . I can feel the sap in my hands reaching out towards my mind. Yes Bob, I am healthy and quietly in my own person."[11]

That summer, he was again considered for the editorship of the *International Journal of Psycho-Analysis* (IJPA), the position that he had lost as a consequence of Amsterdam. According to Khan, the Selection Committee (William Gillespie, Hanna Segal, Adam Limentani, Pearl King, and Geoffrey Thompson) had unanimously agreed to recommend him, with further support from the retiring editor Joseph Sandler.[12] Perhaps they believed he could control his provocative behavior in an editorial position, since his editing work and his writing had remained uncompromised, even as he went downhill in other areas.

Khan wanted the position. He knew he would have to stay dry in order to do good work and he was determined to do so. Barrie Cooper was in strong support of the idea. After a checkup, Cooper told him that blood test results were "better than you deserve"—the liver damage was mild enough that over time it might be reversible.

However, an incident from this time suggests that things were not going as well as they appeared to be. He had taken a female friend to dinner at Deux Magots, and as they sat outside, a woman came up with a "lit and flaming gadget" that frightened Khan: "She was very near to us and I felt that the gadget could blow up in our faces. I got up and told her to go away because I feared fire. She said: 'Don't push me.' I stood still and she tried to blow the flame at me. I put up my hands and stood still. Police intervened and took her. I came back to my seat. Suddenly some 30 youths surrounded me in a most menacing way. I told them I was an outsider and feared fire and bombs. They kept shouting at me while I paid the bill. [My friend] was white with terror. I kept my cool and walked away to a taxi with her. She nearly fainted when we got into the taxi."[13] Later he wrote that he was almost stabbed by one of the youths.[14]

The story does not quite make sense, perhaps because Khan is leaving out details of his own provocativeness. In response to a letter from Smirnoff concerning the incident, Robert Stoller wrote: "I suspect Masud may be a bit volatile these days and I only hope that neither he nor anyone else lights a match."[15]

The match that Stoller and Smirnoff were worrying about was already lit. It involved the brotherhood of analysand/trainees who were meeting at Khan's "Village Flat 7." The fallout from one meeting led to events that would ultimately have major consequences. André Green had been a special guest, along with an editor friend of Khan who was currently in psychoanalysis with a Kleinian. The evening was so stimulating that the editor complained to her analyst that her own treatment was never as exciting. That complaint triggered an inquiry into Khan's socializing with students.

The Education Committee conducted the inquiry in the summer of 1976, under the leadership of Hanna Segal. (The institute still lacked an ethics committee.) X, Y, and Margarita were all asked to come for an interview. Margarita remembers: "Hanna Segal asked me what was going on with the socializing. That word, 'socializing,' had become a crime."

Khan knew about the investigation, and he told Stoller and Smirnoff about it. He said that although he was not worried, it meant that he had once again lost his chance to be editor of the IJPA.

In August, Khan went to Pakistan, where he had not been for several years. The estate was tranquil and unchanged, although the city development was getting closer and closer. The first thing he did was to visit his father's grave: "Sat by the grave and prayed, with the oldest peasant Kakuana beside me also praying. Of the old generation, he is the only one left. The rest are all gone, like the land itself."[16] He spent his evenings in his father's study, immersed in rereading *King Lear* and various works by James Joyce and Samuel Johnson. He read into the early morning hours, noting: "Here all time is my time."[17]

When he felt the staff was too noisy, he issued an order: "Everyone here talks in a shrill loud voice and without any pauses. I shall now instruct everyone to speak in a low voice. I have the feudal authority both to demand and command this."[18] Things got quieter after that and he wrote that he was relaxing in a state of "phobic monastic aloneness."[19] The estate, he said, was "so mine, tall and silent."[20] Mustaq Ahmed, the elderly estate manager, and his son Nazir indulged his every whim.

Salah had by now reconciled with Khan, and he lived on the estate, together with his wife and three daughters. On this visit, Khan developed a connection to the youngest daughter, Shehnaz, whom he nicknamed "Giggles." Shehnaz, who was now twenty-one, told Uncle Masud that she had been missing him during his absence and that she had been in love with him since childhood. Khan wrote in his Work Book, "[Shehnaz] said that my absence from her life the past five years has dried up the very sap of life in her."[21] He appreciated her feisty courage.

Toward the end of the visit, Khan attended the wedding of the granddaughter of one of his half-brothers, to the son of an Indian prince, the Nawab of Bahawalpur. The private ceremony was attended by eighty people and the reception at the Governor's House was for three thousand.[22] Khan's wedding gift was the twenty-four-volume *Collected Works* of Freud, a gift he was fond of giving, even when the recipient had no connection to the world of psychoanalysis.[23]

Returning to Kot Fazaldad Khan, he received a phone call from Margarita. She told him that she had decided to separate from her husband, who was threatening to create a scandal about her overly close relationship with Khan. Khan wrote in his Work Book: "Of course, [Margarita's husband] will scandalise me. But I can tolerate damage. That is of little importance compared to a young woman finding the freedom, time and space to achieve her own person."[24]

As he packed to return, he discovered the keys to his mother's almara —a wooden chest—so he opened it. The contents reinforced his memory of his father's "mammoth presence" in years past: "Discovered all my father's medals there and some extraordinary photographs of him with peasants and generals."[25] On his last day, he went to the mosque to say prayers, visited his father's grave again, signed over a power of attorney to Mustaq Ahmed, and got his gun license endorsed. He then went by car to Lahore, where he had dinner with his cherished friends Jamil Nishtar and Ijaz Batalwi.

At the airport the next morning, Khan wrote: "This has been my happiest, quietest, and most constructive visit to my own country since I left in 1946."[26] After a trip that took twenty-three hours, due to various complications, he arrived in London, where he unpacked his father's prayer carpet, retrieved from the almara, and laid it out in the living room.

The new work year began, with a busy life and a heavy load of patients (eleven a day). He had a dinner party for Nawab Sir Mehr Shah, an elderly friend of his father. A few days later, he gave a paper on masochism to a packed audience at the Congress of English-Speaking Analysts of the European Societies.

Tahir visited in late September. He was unemployed and getting divorced from his wife, after a seven-year separation. Even though he had lived in London for almost as long as Masud, Tahir had no accomplishments. Suffering from bipolar illness and alcoholism, he lived alone in a Hampstead flat, unemployed and bitter. Khan worried about his brother but also wanted to keep a distance, because Tahir's hate and envy toward him were "so palpable, I could touch them like one touches steel."[27] Tahir had spent a lifetime in his brother's shadow and now he was particularly resentful that he was being kept out of management decisions at Kot Fazaldad Khan.

But the main event of the early fall involved his relationship with Margarita, who had just started her formal analytic training. It was her second year in analysis and, like many analysands, she felt that she was in love with her analyst. Khan also felt that he was in love, as often happens to analysts—but in this case, rather than maintaining the frame and analyzing the transference and countertransference, he became a real-life lover.

Here is Margarita's description of the how the analysis began to shift to a "real" relationship, a shift that had started months earlier. She is referring to events in the period before Khan left for Pakistan, when they were not yet physically intimate and she was still living with her husband.

My first year of analysis with Masud had been a deep and transformative experience. But some months later, he began to fail in the analytic stance. The first time this happened in a session, it was a very intense experience. I have no idea what I was talking about, but he made a physical movement of some kind and I just froze. It scared me. Somehow his gesture made me realize that he was being a real person, not an analyst. And something stopped being what it had been. It's like if you were a child, and you were talking about monsters and Superman, and then you saw your dad climbing onto the window sill getting ready to jump off. Things are supposed to be imaginary in analysis, but they were becoming "real."

Margarita told me that her decision to leave her husband in the summer of 1976 was not consciously a decision to be with Khan—it came from unhappiness in the marriage. Her parents opposed the separation and her husband was, apparently, enraged. Soon after his return from Pakistan, Khan, acting in the role of Margarita's analyst, held an extraordinary meeting with Margarita, her parents, and her husband in order to try to ease the tensions. Barrie Cooper, X, and Y were also present. Khan reported that he was brutally candid in his support of Margarita's decision. "At the end [of the meeting]," he wrote, "I was nearly violent, but avoided it."[28] One of those present (anonymous) recalls that Khan, having become enraged at something the husband said, picked up a sword and waved it threateningly.

A few days later, Khan surprised Margarita by telling her that he was in love with her. Not knowing what to do next, he invited Adam Limentani, president of the BPAS, to dinner, where he explained the situation and asked for advice. Surprisingly, Limentani did not recommend that Khan analyze the situation and stay out of a "real" relationship; instead, he recommended that Margarita change analysts, thereby giving tacit support to an affair. After the consultation, Khan invited Margarita to move into Palace Court, and she did so. She immediately began a new analysis, choosing a well-respected woman with whom she thought she could speak freely.

Neither Margarita nor Khan tried to keep their relationship secret, so Margarita's fellow students soon found out what was happening. They knew that a "real" relationship between patient and analyst threatened the very essence of the discipline in which they were training, and that led to enormous tension at the institute. An anonymous person who was a fellow student told me: "I was in the class right behind the husband of the woman Khan was having an affair with. Everyone knew about it. It was very painful for different individuals."[29] Oddly, the students knew about the situation long before Khan's peers.

Khan was aware on some level that he was making a mistake. He wrote in his Work Book: "How I jeopardize myself so willfully every time I am plenitudinous with living."[30] His decisions, however, were so influenced by impulse at that time that sanity had only a minor impact. He was out of control and nobody was stopping him.[31]

CHAPTER 3 1

FORTUNE, GOOD NIGHT

Kent: Fortune, good night. Smile once more, turn thy wheel.
King Lear, *II.iii.189–190*

The stable world I had built has suddenly come apart, and I feel lost.
Masud Khan[1]

For three weeks in the early fall of 1976, Khan and Margarita luxuri-ated in the pleasures of their relationship. It was one of those rare peri-ods in life when one is newly in love and nothing else matters. Then at the end of September and again in early October, Khan felt feverish and so tired that he canceled his clinical hours and stayed in bed. He wrote: "These have been strange weeks. I really have not gathered into my person since my return [from Pakistan]."[2] Then he developed a new symptom—dipsomania, the excessive drinking of fluids. Throughout the day, he drank huge amounts of orange juice and his thirst was insatiable.

Neither of them was worried. Khan had a cough, but he was a heavy smoker, so that was not unusual. Margarita remembers that he became convinced that *she* was ill: "Masud said: 'I'm concerned—you have a strange cough and you aren't aware of it.' He insisted that I see a chest doctor, Dr. Hickman. He was unrelenting, so I went to see Dr. Hickman. I told him that I was sure I had nothing, but Masud wanted me checked out. He sent me to East London Hospital for a chest x-ray, and a few days later I got a letter with the report 'There is no sinister background to your cough.'"

On the night of October 14, Khan was at home reading, while Margarita was out with friends. He sucked on his pipe and his throat went into a violent spasm in which he coughed up cup after cup of clotted blood. This continued throughout the night. Margarita was horrified when she returned and saw a huge amount of blood in the sink.

At 8 a.m. the next day, Khan called X, who immediately came over. X called Barrie Cooper, who arrived at 9:30 a.m. and made arrangements for x-rays and throat swabs, as well as an afternoon referral to Mr. Holden, an ENT doctor (British surgeons go by the title "Mr." rather than "Dr."). Mr. Holden found that the bleeding was coming from an area just below the tongue, but he would not give even a tentative diagnosis until he saw the x-ray results.

At 10 p.m., Barrie Cooper came in person to Palace Court to deliver dismaying news. The x-rays had revealed a mass on an upper lobe of the left lung. A bronchoscopy was required for further diagnosis, and Cooper had already spoken with a world-famous heart and thoracic surgeon, Mr. Ross. Ross was in Chicago but he would do the procedure upon his return the next day, a Saturday.

Khan was stunned and terrified. He was admitted to the Harley Street Clinic on the morning of October 16, and the "villagers" (X, Y, and Margarita) were there all day, providing support. Svetlana heard the news and made several panicked phone calls that Khan asked Margarita to handle. He thought about calling the Stollers, then decided not to worry them.

That evening, after first performing heart surgery on another patient, Mr. Ross did the bronchoscopy, accompanied by Barrie Cooper. The results were encouraging: Khan's lungs appeared to be clear. The villagers left and Khan took sleeping pills. When the pills did not work, he called the nurse for a pethidine injection that helped just a little: "The nurse laughingly said, 'This will keep you asleep till mid-day!' Well, I was wide awake at 6 a.m. Feel so healthy and wholesome. Henceforth I shall take more vigilant care of my body-self. I have only nurtured and cultivated my mind these past 30 years."[3]

Khan was relieved by the bronchoscopy results, but the surgeon was not. The mass on the lung still had to be diagnosed. Mr. Ross scheduled a three-dimensional x-ray called a thermogram and warned that exploratory surgery might be necessary. Hearing the news, Khan worried about his relationship with Margarita: "I feel sad because now, at 52, with these ailments (still anonymous) how can one take from the sap

288   FALSE SELF

of a young woman's youth, when one has so little to offer in return, not even the certainty of shared living?"[4]

When the thermogram yielded suspicious findings, he had to face the likelihood that he had cancer:

> So cancer it is in all probability. Mr. Ross and Barrie came in about half an hour ago. Mr. Ross very candidly told me he had now seen the latest x-rays and thermograms. There is a lump and it must be surgically removed. Only then can it be found whether it is benign or malignant. . . . When I asked him if it was a serious and major operation, Mr. Ross replied: "For me it is recreation, but for you it is a serious and major operation."
>
> So my life and future are really in a balance. I have told Almontero [the houseboy] to postpone his vacation in the Philippines. He readily agreed.[5]

The dipsomania now made sense—it is a symptom that occurs in certain cases of lung cancer, when hormones are released that affect the body's water-electrolyte regulation.[6]

Surgery was scheduled for October 20. At 9 a.m. on October 19, Khan dictated a new will to his secretary, who took the draft to his lawyer, Paul Kimber. Kimber brought the formalized will to the hospital for a signature at 7:30 p.m. Khan bequeathed Palace Court and all his money to Svetlana, the art books and lithographs to the Victoria and Albert Museum, and various specific items to his favorite people: "I have left [the Stollers] complete copyright in all my writings, published and unpublished, with the royalties to be divided between Margarita, X, and A [pseudonym for a candidate/analysand who was not a villager]. To Pnin [Smirnoff], I have left the Hermès cigarette case, Cartier silver lighter and the silver Mont Blanc pen. To Pontalis, I have left the golden Mont Blanc pen. To Bob and Sybil, I have left my ancient ceramics and the hand of Buddha, the Chandler's desk, and all my reading library, hoping they can place it in some university in its entirety."[7] Khan telephoned Harry Karnac to ask if he would be executor of the new will, as he had been for an earlier will, and Karnac agreed.

That night, he received phone calls from King, Limentani, Smirnoff, and Pontalis, and another visit from Barrie Cooper. He was touched by their affection: "All this is very moving and makes life worth fighting for tomorrow."[8] Late in the evening, Mr. Ross stopped by with his students to ask if he should contact relatives after the surgery. Khan responded: "I told him 'Only if I die, because they will be interested only in the inheritance.' [Mr. Ross] said: 'Then we will keep them clear of it.' I asked him to kindly talk with Margarita, whom I am going to marry, and he said he would."[9]

Khan had a fitful sleep, with violent dreams: "I was all night vividly aware of the raw youth who were hurtled against machine guns and mortar fire at the Normandy invasion. Who cared where they would be hit and wounded? And here I am, so cared for and arranged for. Same culture creates these contradictory situations: that is the true absurdity of human cultures."[10] (Years later, I told Margarita about this dream, and she commented: "I think the 'raw youth' stood for his students.")

The nine-hour surgery began at 3 p.m. At Khan's request, Barrie Cooper was present in the operating room to assist with surgical decisions. The doctors found the expected tumor near the larynx. This meant that removal involved cutting phrenic nerves that would affect Khan's voice. Cooper told me: "We had to make a decision about how much voice to preserve at the cost of how much tumor to leave. It was an awesome experience, very difficult." Their decision was to remove most of Khan's left lung, despite the sacrifice of the vocal cords. Margarita was alone in the waiting room when Cooper came out. She remembers: "Barrie looked bad when he came out—his face was gray."

Khan awoke in the intensive care unit with multiple tubes coming out of his body and a sixteen-inch wound across his back and chest. He received heroin and morphine for pain. Two days later, he was moved to a private room.

He had been Winnicott's "nonregressing" patient because he was terrified of giving up control. Now, in the private room, he regressed with a panic so severe that it bordered on psychosis:

After having faced and lived through the bronchoscopy and the lung removal, I panicked somewhere inside. The regression to absolute dependence on care by others went deeper than I had let myself realise. The panic started when Mr. Ross told me the nurse would pull out [a

drainage tube in the lung] without local anaesthetic. He said: "You will
feel merely a tiny pull." She did the job painlessly with tender caring. All
the same, I felt unsafe.

But the real dynamic factor was the shift from being [in the care of]
Mr. Ross in the Intensive Care Unit, to moving towards real life, transfer-
ring to this room, with one lung. Even the journey sitting in a chair exhausted me. I was frightened by my frailty and physical resourcelessness."[11]

There was no trusted elder to "hold" him as he regressed. He had
dropped his False Self functioning in an atmosphere that was not secure. This is a terrifying experience for anybody and it is the reason why
Khan and Winnicott had always taken extra care to protect their regressed patients. Margarita was there, of course, but she was a lover and
recent analysand, not a therapist/parent figure. The Stollers or Smirnoff
might have been helpful, but the situation had arisen too quickly for them
to come to be with Khan. Khan would later say that he was never the
same after experiencing this terror.

Margarita canceled all her commitments in order to be with Khan.[12]
She remembers that he was in terrible pain and unable to speak. His
terror was obvious, as he experienced waves of anxiety in which he would
perspire heavily. After the panic came pain, which was easier for him to
tolerate.

The biopsy results were complete a week later and they were bad.
Khan had oat cell carcinoma of the lung, an extremely aggressive form
of cancer. His prognosis was three to six months of life. The chance of
a one-year survival was five to seven percent; the chance of a two-year
survival was well below five percent.[13] After hearing the news, Khan
wrote: "In this aseptic room, life is so unreal. I am dazed by what has
happened so suddenly."[14]

When Khan was in the ICU, Margarita had slept on the floor. After
he moved to the private room, she bought a folding bed to sleep on and
never left the room. Khan did not want nurses to touch him,[15] so she
bathed him, helped him use the bathroom, and was constantly on call.
(He had a bell so he could alert her when he needed help.) The abrupt
transition from the pleasure of the early fall felt like a nightmare to her:
"I had thought of Masud as this godlike person, and we were in the very
beginning of an intense love affair. This person who had been taking

care of *me* was now dying in the ICU, and I was caring for *him*—he was just clinging to life. I can vividly remember Masud with a grey face, lying on that bed, with Y on one side and me on the other. Life was suddenly so frail."

At Khan's request, Margarita wore traditional Eastern clothing, such as tunics and jewelry—he said that soothed him. One day, Mr. Hickman, the doctor who had seen her in September for the supposed cough, came by and, seeing her in Eastern clothing, did not recognize her. She reminded him of the consultation and said: "Now we understand the sinister background to my cough."

When Khan's voice started to come back, it was first a faint squeak, then a whisper. He would have another surgery in a few months that restored his voice a little, but he would never get back his deep, resonant voice. He wrote that he felt "hacked around like a carcass."[16]

As so often happens when illness is severe, many people expressed concern. Soon after the surgery, Smirnoff came for a four-day visit, spending days at the hospital and nights in the "Pnin room" at Palace Court. Pontalis and his wife also visited quickly. The Stollers heard the news from Barrie Cooper and Robert Stoller wrote to Khan immediately:

> We still cannot digest your illness or come to terms with your suffering.
> It has been shocking for us, the only relief being that Barrie has kept us
> up-to-date and informed us that you are recovering from the surgery well,
> beginning to be comfortable, and embarked on your convalescence. I
> suppose it will be many weeks before you are fully back at work and able
> once again to be fully with yourself, in a peaceful and creative way. Just
> be sure not to leave yourself any choices but to heal physically and psy-
> chologically so that you can recapture all your strengths and value.
>   And whenever it is time for us to help, I know you will instantly let
> us know what you need and how best to get it done.
>   You have constantly with you our concern and love. Heal gently and
> quickly and be back with us.[17]

Jeanne Axler, who was in medical school, remembers that she and her friends were incredulous at the idea that Khan was almost certainly dying: "Masud was the kind of person who was supposed to live forever. If he could die, anyone could die." Khan felt the same way. When Axler visited him in the hospital, he said: "I will not die!" and defiantly proclaimed that he would keep smoking. Axler remembers: "When Masud said he wouldn't die, I believed him. He is [*sic*] not someone you see dying. There was a force of nature in him, something that made it seem he just couldn't die—God wouldn't let him, because he hadn't finished doing what he had to do. I believed this even though every book I had said that there was a 100 percent mortality within six months." She told me that Khan seemed to take it personally that God had allowed him to develop cancer.[18]

He recovered quickly from the surgery. The Stollers made plans to visit, and Khan asked that they meet in Paris. Sybil handled all the details and Khan wrote that he was deeply moved and determined to fight the cancer:

> Now I am in the care of fate and physicians. [But] as long as I have friends like Bob and Sybil, who can fly from LA to surround me, the love of [Margarita], etc. I need only to use myself and reactivate my mind and being. And that is precisely what I am going to do. So help me God. When death comes, it will be an end not of my concoction and instigation. I mean to live what I have in me cleanly, vigorously, and creatively. It will take mammoth effort![19]

In Paris, he had more energy and stamina than anyone had expected. "I was alive! Am alive! How long, does not matter a damn. I knew Bob and Sybil would awaken me."[20] On Christmas Eve, he invited his favorite French friends to a gathering, telling them he wanted to be with the people he loved. At the end of the evening, they all went to a midnight mass at Notre Dame.

Paris and the Stollers lifted Khan's mood. He wrote that he was "more in the world, [not just] wrapped up in a private opacity of existing."[21]

From California, Robert Stoller wrote an appreciative letter, recalling their various adventures:

> I cannot tell you how happy we were to have been with you and [Margarita], to see how well you are cared for, and how beautifully you have responded physically and emotionally. When people ask how you seemed to us, I relive the experience and now, after these several days, I am still astonished and enthused.

I cannot find the proper words to describe the style of your response. It was not courage but beyond that, a quiet, firm, natural, joyous total presence in the world, acceptance, honorableness, intelligence, wit and fortitude. But of course, all of these qualities (which at times you like to pretend are not important) are woven into our dear and familiar friend. Masud has not disappeared, instead another facet, another capability, another depth is visible.

Sybil and I [were surprised that] you were quite unencumbered by illness. I shall never forget . . . your plunging through traffic after La Coupole to get a cab, or midnight mass, or still more soup at 2:30 am, or the strength to dominate the dinner with friends in the restaurant in Paris. And kindness, and generosity, and laughter, and happiness. Not bad.[22]

On December 31, back in London, Khan tried to distract himself from the void that he experienced after parting from his friends. He and Margarita spent the afternoon buying gifts: whisky for Mr. Ross; a basket of cheeses and sweets for Mr. Hickman and his family; and clocks from Asprey's for X and Y. Returning to the flat in the late afternoon, the atmosphere felt oppressive, so he went out again by himself. Just before the shops closed, he bought a black cashmere skirt and poncho for Margarita and a diary for Almontero. That night, Barrie Cooper and his daughter Vicky dropped by to exchange gifts.

When the Coopers left, Khan made a final Work Book entry for the year, referring to himself as "he"[23]:

So much had happened since his return from Pakistan in September, and he was in a quietly frightened and dazed frame of mind still. Of course his tape-recorder mind had registered every detail of the happenings, but as yet his psyche, sensibility, and his being could print little of it. Hence the acute and persistent passivity in him: he could neither read nor write; or even see anyone but his closest friends.

As he sat and looked around the salon, a strange sadness suffused his whole being. His living and existence had strangely lost perspective into the future.

He paused and relaxed. He was amused. How like his father he was. He had built this flat, which he called his "village," as if time existed palpably and with perpetuity. One's death did not destroy the permanence of things. He recalled how, standing in Notre Dame for the midnight Xmas mass with Margarita, he had felt this quality of the concreteness of time captured into things. Now, all had changed. There was no permanence to time left.

[Margarita] is up. He could hear her so gently moving around. He had nothing to say any more tonight. 1976 was ending. He was alive and healthy. His friends loved him and he loved them. The rest was all a blank now.

PART 8

NINE LIVES OF A CAT

(1977–1980)

I noticed how everyone was surprised I was still alive. Martin James
with his typical vulgarity and veracity remarked kindly:
"You have the nine lives of a cat."
Masud Khan, after a meeting of the 1952 Club,
which Khan attended for the first time in seven years[1]

SURVIVAL

He [speaking of himself] felt sure that slowly, given a patient
tolerance of non-being . . . , he would come alive [again].
Masud Khan[1]

The Education Committee continued its investigation into Khan's
socialization with students even after the committee members learned
of his cancer. Then Joseph Sandler, the analyst of Margarita's husband,
reported to Hanna Segal, the chair of the committee, that the husband
had told him that Khan was having an affair with Margarita. Segal's
response was to suggest that the alleged affair was probably a fantasy of
the husband. Sandler told me: "Segal said the affair was fiction and that
I should analyze [this candidate] more."

Kleinians are often criticized for giving such privilege to the importance of fantasy that they neglect reality. Segal's incredulity may be an
example of this. She was also following proper procedure—in her
administrative role, she held to the principle that nothing could be acted
on in response to second-hand information. As soon as the husband made
an official complaint, she investigated further and discovered something
that all the students already knew: Khan and Margarita were living together openly.[2]

The Education Committee—Hanna Segal, Ilse Hellman, Eric Rayner,
and Pearl King—now had a very serious situation to deal with. They set
to work in earnest and completed their review in the late fall, a short time
after Khan's surgery. Eric Rayner, who was at the time a junior analyst,
told me that they tried hard to do the right thing: "I remember, with some
pride in my fellows, how decent and fair everyone was towards Masud."

In the bylaws of the British Psycho-Analytic Society (BPAS), it was mandated that the committee investigate a situation and then give recommendations to the council, a totally separate body. The council would then implement the recommendations. The chair of the council was the president of the BPAS, who at this time happened to be Adam Limentani.

The committee reported to the council that Khan had "a past history of instability, mood lability and an incapacity to stop hurting himself" but that all the prior complaints about him had been unofficial.[3] They had three recommendations: that Khan's title of psychoanalyst be taken away, that he be excluded from the BPAS, and that candidates and supervisees currently seeing him be required to change to a new analyst or supervisor.[4] They were well aware that if these recommendations were followed, Khan's career would be over. In contrast to most of his peers, he had not had any training in psychiatry or a related field that would give him separate credentials as a therapist. It was only through the title of psychoanalyst that he was able to see patients.

Barrie Cooper had a strong response to the recommendations. He knew about Khan's psychological problems, but he also knew about Khan's clinical skills and his dedication to his analysands and supervisees. Cooper called and then wrote to Adam Limentani to express his opinion: "[I]t seems to me extraordinarily sad that so much additional stress and distress be imposed upon Masud at a time when he is striving with some success to 'return to life.'"[5] Limentani responded with a phone call, and the two men had a heated exchange. The central issue was where the society's primary loyalty lay: with the analyst or with the analysands? Limentani, thinking Cooper was not concerned enough about Khan's patients, said to Cooper: "And YOU call yourself a physician?!" Cooper, thinking about Khan's personal suffering, responded: "And YOU call yourself a psychiatrist?!!"[6]

Khan was still in the hospital when he got a letter asking him to attend a council meeting on January 14, 1977, where he would be advised of the committee's recommendations. In December, everyone, including Khan, learned that a decision had already been made—the council had decided to allow him to keep his membership in the BPAS, deviating from procedure by not acting on the committee's recommendation. The cancer had saved his career. Hanna Segal recalls: "Being the soft marks that we always are, we decided not to act against a dying man." A recommendation that was enforced, however, was that Khan's candidates had to change analysts if they wanted to remain trainees. At the time, this ruling affected three men: X, Y, and A. They now had to choose between their analyst and their future career. (It is unknown how many people were seeing him for supervision.)

Khan was not grateful for the compassion he had been shown. Believing that he was being harassed at a time when he was in a weakened state, he was unforgiving: "Limentani, Pearl [King], Segal & Co.—they can all go to hell!"[7] He wanted to continue the analyses of his candidates. When Limentani called to pressure him to facilitate their transfer, Khan was indignant: "I told him that I come from some 600 years of taking care, and I cannot just abandon people."[8] But that decision was not open to question. Limentani was especially disturbed by the fact that X and Y had been present at the confrontation in September when Khan met with Margarita, her parents, and her then-husband. "After all," he wrote to Cooper at this point in the negotiations, "would you not agree that those two students who were involved in some very dramatic scenes concerning a third student, have been sufficiently traumatised and that they need a serene state of mind in which to continue their analysis and training?" Limentani's compassion for Khan is evident in his closing sentence: "[D]o remind [Masud] that I am his friend and I only want to contain the disastrous course which he seems to be determined to follow."[9]

Khan's friends finally persuaded him to give up the fight. A few days prior to the January 14 meeting with the council, he called Limentani to tell him he would write a letter to Hanna Segal agreeing to "retire"—not "resign"—from teaching and training. This meant that he would not be able to be a training analyst for candidates, but he could still see noncandidates, because he would still be an analyst. Limentani was relieved and helped him draft the letter. The council meeting was canceled.

A series of compromises followed, all mediated by Limentani. One of these was that A would be allowed to continue his training analysis with Khan, since he was almost finished and he had not been deeply involved in the socializing. A separate matter involved Khan's positions of chairman of the Publications Committee and editor of the International Psycho-Analytical Library (IPL). Joseph Sandler and Peter Hildebrand were demanding that he be removed from both. The council,

through Limentani, refused to act on this demand. And then there was
the question of whether Margarita should be allowed to continue her
training. The majority of the Education Committee wanted her to be
suspended, but Pearl King reminded her peers of the widely accepted
ethos that the analyst is responsible for what happens in an analysis, not
the analysand. So Margarita remained a student.

As things turned out, only A would become an analyst. X saw two
different analysts and then dropped out of training; Y resigned from training and continued his analysis with Khan; and Margarita was forced to
drop out of training a few months later when she changed analysts a second time—something that was not allowed for a trainee, no matter what
the reason was.[10] Many people told me that it was a tragedy that X and Y
did not become analysts, as they were very talented, and some suggested
that a more sensitive handling of the situation might have enabled them
to stay in training. The ending of Margarita's analytic career, however,
was probably inevitable. As Pearl King told me: "[Margarita] didn't have
a chance after the affair with Masud. Her copybook was blotted forever."

Khan was bitter. He had accumulated a large stack of get-well cards
and notes of concern from his colleagues, and he decided to tear them
up without acknowledgment, commenting in the Work Book: "Why did
they have to wait for him [me] to be either dead or crippled, to register
and acknowledge his talent, services and necessity to them?"[11] His
anger and hurt are obvious in a letter he wrote to Nina Coltart, a fellow
Independent:

> My dear Nina,
>   . . . I have behaved totally honourably and still continue to serve the
> Institute in spite of the fact that my solicitor and counsel advise me to
> sue the Institute for their compelling me to resign from teaching and
> training without giving any formal written reasons for it. It is written on
> the graves of all of my ancestors, that he who harms one of us harms all
> of us, and I promised my father when he was dying that I would uphold
> our tradition. I am lapsing from it with the Institute [because] I know
> that a lawsuit would just destroy it. . . .
>   I too know what ethics are, and I know them at a level of responsi-
> bility and care which none of you has been brought up to. If I am not a
> middle-class Christian, or a refugee Jew from Warsaw, that is not my
> fault. I was born a royal feudal duke and I am being picked upon. That I

do not mind. But when my students are picked upon, then I do care, and I act to protect them.

You know perfectly well what deep affection and respect I have for you, and I hope that it will stay the same between us.

Much love, Masud[12]

He came from a world that believed in retaliation. Now he openly declared that he was going to cut Limentani's throat and he made telephone threats against the Sandler family. Joseph Sandler told me: "It was hard on us. Masud would phone, often late at night, ranting and raving. My son was a weekly boarder at Westminster School, and once Masud made a threat on his life, saying something like: 'One can hire a person through the Mafia.'" Khan also made threats against the institute building and for a while an armed guard was hired to stand watch there. After a few months, however, it became clear that his ravings were not to be taken seriously.

There was no official discussion about the scandalous events, so rumors and exaggerations were widespread. For those directly involved, the trauma of dealing with loss and de-idealization was intense. The wounds would take a long time to heal, and for some, they would never heal. For every person who wanted Khan restricted, there were others who believed he was being treated unfairly. Many people thought that an anti-Winnicott bias was being acted out via Khan; by punishing Khan, the Kleinians were sending a message to Khan's and Winnicott's heirs. (The Kleinians had long disapproved of the techniques of Winnicott and his followers, which they considered to be too "action-oriented." A Kleinian in the BPAS commented to me anonymously about the situation today: "We do a lot of things right [at the BPAS] but we still can't deal with Winnicott's progeny.") A supervisee who had been required to stop seeing Khan told me: "Masud's followers were killed off to make sure that he would not leave descendants in the society. It was like in Shakespeare's *Richard III*, where the brothers' children have to be killed so there won't be any heirs."[13] Another candidate from that era suggested to me that the committee and council had acted impulsively out of a need to get relief from their own anxiety. This person had sympathy for Khan, although he had Kleinian training: "It was persecutory anxiety: the need to destroy things that seem dangerous, as if these things will contaminate you. We project our own evil onto other people and Satanize them, and then we feel clean. We can't stand to feel our own part in the evil."

There was no obvious solution. Many training institutes have had to deal with the situation of analysts having affairs with patients and candidates, and the situation has been handled in different ways, always leaving some people hurt and angry. One way that the Khan case is different from most other scandals, however, is that Khan felt no regret. His case is not the same as that of the analyst who acts out only once—his behavior was not going to stop, and that meant there would be more trouble ahead.[14]

Khan cared about what was happening at the institute, but he was preoccupied with his own health. Understandably, he was terrified that his cancer would return. He watched the people around him and thought he saw them planning for a future when he would be gone:

> Almontero [the houseboy] asked me for a favour. The management of the hotel where his wife works as a maid has asked him to work Saturdays and Sundays, 11 a.m. to 4 p.m. [He wants to know] whether he could leave me on the Saturdays. I immediately agreed. Yes, they all smell transience and mortality in me and are re-arranging their lives.
>
> Today, "the little one" [his nickname for Margarita] asked whether she could entertain a girlfriend of hers at [her vacant flat] and sleep there. So even she is preparing for my death and re-building her own space and life.[15]

In February 1977, he decided to go back into analysis. He chose to see Anna Freud, whom he had known since 1948. They had bonded over the years on the basis of their mutual devotion to preserving the reputation of Sigmund Freud. Khan had written: "Thanks to the mystique of ceremony, respect, and reverence, I have felt more at ease with Anna Freud than with anyone else in the British Society. She respects my style and my tradition of nurture. Hence we are equally generous to each other."[16]

At first, he saw Miss Freud once a week, and then, very quickly, he began to see her twice a week.[17] She was now an old lady, not far from death, and she was totally ineffective. Even in her prime, it is an open

question whether she could have helped an adult with problems as serious as Khan's, because she was an extremely traditional analyst.[18] Her
efficacy would also have been weakened by her "real" attraction to him.
Joseph Sandler told me, with reference to earlier times: "Anna Freud
would go all coy when Masud was around. He could 'turn it on' with
her and she was completely gullible."

What Miss Freud could provide was support. She cared about Khan
and he respected her. But they shared a belief that the Kleinians were out
to destroy both of them, and this belief bordered on paranoia. Victor
Smirnoff wrote to Robert Stoller, referring to Miss Freud's Hampstead
Child Therapy Clinic: "I heard from the Hampstead people that Anna
Freud is caught up in a common delusion with Masud that the Kleinians
are after them, and that this is all part of the huge scheme to get rid of
both of them."[19] In his Work Book, Khan wrote:

> At the end of my session, where I had spelt out the way the Education
> Committee is persecuting me through terrorising my candidates,
> Miss Freud remarked, "Now you have some idea of what my father and
> I had to cope with, with the Nazis." I retorted, "Is this not tragic for the
> British Psychoanalytic Society, that after having saved Professor Freud,
> they themselves have become the Nazis and the Gestapo!!"[20]

As he recovered, Khan abandoned his English colleagues and related
almost exclusively to the Stollers and his friends in France. The French
colleagues had not rejected him for his behavior, perhaps because they
had their own acting-out analyst to gossip about: Jacques Lacan, who
was even more defiant of norms than Khan. Commenting on the difference in the reaction of the two cultures, Khan wrote: "Yes, the French
always have style, whereas the English have their virtuousness!"[21]

He had started the year determined to do some serious writing, no
matter what happened to his health. On New Year's Day, he wrote,
referring to himself in the third person: "He knows this could be his
last year. Hence the necessity to get written what was in him."[22] He
immersed himself in writing a paper on a topic he had been thinking
about for years, "On Lying Fallow," for an issue of the French journal
L'Arc dedicated to Winnicott. By March, however, he was withdrawn
and unproductive: "I live affectively in my dream-space only."[23] He could

no longer write, even though his mind was full of thoughts: "My hands are so phobic and refusing. My head is teeming with thoughts, most of them militantly anti-life, but some creative. I cannot write at all."[24]

Part of the problem was that he was drinking again. By the summer of 1977, he was drinking a bottle and a half of scotch each day, plus red wine.[25] He thought it did not matter, because he was dying anyway. Looking back on this period a few months later, he wrote: "I can see now only too clearly that I could not accept, or to put it more accurately, the omnipotence in me could not accept my situation. I wanted to find my own death through alcohol before cancer could get me. Also, I could not accept the physical handicaps that the operation in October [1976] imposed on me. So I abandoned both my body and my consciousness, and I [lived] in a transitional psychic state in which I was stuporous from alcohol and where even dreaming was unfeasible."[26]

Margarita was the one bright spot in his life: "[Margarita], so young, shores me with her presence and being."[27] She was naive about alcohol and had no idea that he was alcoholic, because in this period he would sleep when drunk. When he was sober, she told me, he seemed more troubled: "When Masud was dry, he'd be withdrawn from the world, almost autistic, living in the shadow of sickness. He used to have these mysterious fevers. It was like the character from Dostoevsky's *Crime and Punishment*, Raskolnikov, who would get fevers from his guilt and fear. He seemed terrified, as if there was something dangerous outside—but there was nothing there."

In the late summer, Khan's mental and physical health both improved. The prognosis of three to six months of life had been definite in October, but it was almost a year later and he was not dying. He emerged from his withdrawal and stopped drinking. In July, he learned from Barrie Cooper that his remaining lung was clear and blood tests (sedimentation rate) showed no indication of a recurrence of cancer. He felt blessed by God and immediately called Anna Freud to tell her the results: "She was ebullient with joy. Yes! To her I matter as a person and as a mind."[28]

In August, he stayed in London while Margarita went on vacation to Nice. He was finally saying no to the kind of vacation that he had never enjoyed: "I have at last found the courage to tell Margarita that I detest the sea and the sun, that some 19 years of Cote d'Azur are enough for my lifetime. So she, with her unfailing generosity, agreed to go alone, because she needs the sun and the sea."[29]

The doctors had said that his prognosis would improve in the very unlikely event that he could be cancer-free for a year. By the end of the summer, Khan and his friends were beginning to think, as Jeanne Axler had, that he was just not the type of person to die.

Then, a few weeks before the one-year anniversary, the cancer returned. It was a metastasis of the original cancer, this time in his neck area, in a gland that had to be surgically removed: "So I am, once again, to be carved up, with the medical excuse for keeping one alive."[30] The surgeon found no evidence of local spread, but a precautionary course of radiation was prescribed, to be followed by chemotherapy in early 1978. The recurrence meant that the prognosis was once again very poor.[31]

This time he did not panic, and he resumed work almost immediately after the operation. On October 20, he celebrated the one-year anniversary of his first cancer surgery, writing in his Work Book: "I have survived a year! Lord's mercy in that."[32] The next day, his colleague Harold Stewart called to invite him to give his lecture "Khan on Khan" for a course on British contributions to analysis. The Editorial Committee had banned Khan from all teaching and training activities, and Stewart knew this, but, as usual, Khan's peers were forgiving him and welcoming him back. At Margarita's urging, Khan agreed to give the lecture.

He had stopped going out in public after he essentially lost his voice in the first surgery. Now he began to make a few public appearances, despite the fact that he could only talk in a high-pitched whisper. In November, he went to the Jungian Society where his paper, "On Lying Fallow," was read by a colleague and he gave short responses to audience questions.[33]

He continued to receive multiple speaking invitations from around the world, most of which he turned down. But he did accept an invitation to be keynote speaker for a conference at the William Alanson White Institute in New York City in the late winter/spring of 1978. He agreed to stay for two weeks, doing a combination of lectures, seminars, and supervision. The Americans had no idea that Khan had been ill in any way. In January 1978, however, Earl Wittenberg, the director of White, canceled the conference. He told me that his reason was that Khan was refusing to honor an agreement to present new material in his lecture—he was insisting on using already published material. Seven hundred and twelve people had already signed up for the conference and Wittenberg was "obviously peeved,"[34] not knowing at the time how lucky he was that a potential catastrophe had been averted.

As was now typical, Khan started the new year with a gesture toward sobriety. This time he agreed to a brief hospitalization at Regent Park Nursing Home. By March, however, he was unable to think clearly after just a glass or two of whiskey, and he regularly drank himself into oblivion. He slept for fifteen hours at a time, getting up only to see patients; between sessions, he sat and stared at the wall. He developed a new difficulty with walking that was probably related to nerve damage caused by excessive drinking.[35]

Barrie Cooper knew well the danger Khan was courting. More than once, he wrote up a solemn pact of abstinence that was signed by Khan, witnessed, and dated to enhance its seriousness—only to be violated within a few days. The French analyst Joyce McDougall was Cooper's ally in recognizing the severity of the problem. She told me: "Masud continued to smoke and drink all the time. I asked him why and he replied, 'Who wants to live forever?' I said, 'Masud, that's suicidal, you have to take options for life.'" By now, even Margarita had lost her naïveté: "I told him, 'Masud, you can conquer the cancer, but your drinking is going to kill you.'"

That spring, Khan began to make scurrilous remarks about Winnicott in public. At a professional meeting, he stood up and announced that Winnicott had been impotent throughout his life.[36] His British colleagues were surprised and pained as they witnessed a favorite son attacking the father. His colleagues could no longer deny his illness, and in April the society took away the honorary librarian/archivist position that he had held for more than two decades. He was replaced as editor at the IPL by Clifford Yorke. These sanctions occurred at a time when he had a full analytic practice and was still receiving referrals, mostly from abroad.

In August, he went to Pakistan to lie fallow. He spent his days sleeping, reading, and going to movies at the Rex Cinema.[37] His niece, Shehnaz, asked to talk with him again, as she had in 1976 when she confessed that she had fallen in love with him. Her secret passion had progressed, according to Khan, into an obsession.[38] This time, they met for five hours, and made an intimate connection. Khan wrote, "One thing is certain: nothing has evoked such a deep response in me since Svetlana, and it is totally non-carnal."[39] A few years later, Khan would bring this niece to London to live with him. (At that time, he referred to her mostly as "Bibi," a generic term of affection for a female family member.)

Leaving Pakistan, he was uneasy: "A strange foreboding in me that a tragedy [related to Margarita] awaits me in London."[40]

It was a terrible autumn. Khan was drinking and his mood was, in Cooper's words, "uncaring, nihilistic, and passively destructive."[41] In October, the dipsomania returned, and he began drinking huge amounts of orange juice and tea, along with alcohol.[42]

Cooper reported to Robert Stoller that Khan was not reading or writing and he had developed a phobia about leaving his flat. He asked Stoller to stay in touch as much as possible: "[If] you cannot close the distance physically, the more you can close the distance by letter and telephone the better. You know that Masud respects you and, with a certain loving terror, Sybil, more than any other of his living friends. Your influence is profound. I will hold the situation as best I can, uncertain that my resources will remain adequate; I still have the hat, but I am fresh out of rabbits."[43]

Margarita had stayed loyal through unimaginably difficult times, but she was getting impatient because she wanted to be with people her own age. She remembers: "I was feeling increasingly claustrophobic and trapped in the situation, like I wasn't really alive. I remember how, after work, I would return to the flat, and I would hear the noise of Masud's feet dragging on the floor as he walked around, drunk. I didn't feel I could leave, because he was so unwell." Finally, with the support of her analyst and some good friends, she moved out. Khan wrote on October 8: "[Margarita] has left and taken all her things. So two years have come to a nullity of end. I am sad in a way I have never been before. This is a tragic but necessary loss. . . . A few minutes after our last supper, she packed what remained of her clothes in her car, handed me the house keys, and left, saying, 'I love you.'"[44] With uncharacteristic maturity, Khan accepted that he alone was responsible for the breakup. He knew he had abandoned Margarita when he succumbed to withdrawal and alcoholism: "She had no option left except to save herself by leaving me—and that she did. That my sickness destroyed her love shall always stay a deep sadness within me."[45]

Having rented out her own flat, Margarita had no place of her own to go to. For a few nights, she stayed with Svetlana—they had become friendly while talking on the telephone during Khan's illness. Then she quit her job and went to live alone in a tree house in a forest in the London countryside. This was a quite amazing round structure that her friend Judith Issroff had built on a small private plot in a forest on the outskirts of London. It was a setting where Margarita could contemplate her future in peace. As she rested, it became clear to her that she needed to stay away from Khan. She decided to leave London to start a new life somewhere else—and, after about a year, she did.

Throughout October 1978, after Margarita left, Khan's situation deteriorated even further. Smirnoff came to stay for awhile and he reported to Stoller that Khan had totally stopped drinking, but was in a state of severe depression. He would talk to Smirnoff for no more than fifteen minutes at a time, and then would fall silent, declare that he was tired, and retreat to his dark bedroom: "He does not read at all, never writes a line, doesn't even watch the 'telly,' eats little except for broiled meat, some cheese, a few potatoes and orange juice and iced tea." Khan was no longer interested in other people except to talk about how he was being persecuted—his persecutors being Barrie Cooper, the institute, Jews, the British Empire, and Margarita. One of the worst signs, Smirnoff wrote, was that Khan had no interest in showing off. The flat was a mess and Smirnoff did the shopping, made tea, and even washed the dishes. The situation elicited a humorous remark from Khan: "Now my guests have become my servants." He still saw patients and cared about his clinical work. But even in that area, he was slipping; he had thrown several patients out of his office, telling them that they were not worthy of him.[46]

What Smirnoff did not know was that there was hope right around the corner for his friend. Just before Margarita left, a woman named Yasmine (pseudonym) had become interested in Khan's work, written him a letter, and started to visit. Margarita told me: "I knew immediately that Masud would be taken in by [Yasmine] and that they would have a relationship. It was in part because I knew that another woman was going to be there that I felt I could go." As the next chapters will show, Margarita's intuition was exactly on target.

ANALYSIS WITH ROBERT STOLLER

My life is plenitudinously full of sensuality, fun and affection.
The lady is Arab and handsome. She has a marvelous home
of her own and we live according to what the Bedouins say:
"Let us put our hearts together and keep our tents apart."
Masud Khan[1]

In the fall of 1978, Yasmine[2] became Khan's analysand and, very quickly, his lover. Soon they were spending every evening together in addition to their daily analytic sessions.

Yasmine was a Muslim from a prominent family in Saudi Arabia, the first of Khan's Western lovers to have Eastern origins. Newly divorced from a wealthy film producer, she was slender and stunning, a dark-skinned Arab beauty with a predilection for dramatic dress. As an artist with exquisite taste, she used her wealth to make her surroundings beautiful. She told me that Khan appreciated her talent, and that she was determined to keep him surrounded by beauty. He also valued her upper-class origins, which were a contrast to Margarita's: "Yasmine is a royal aristocrat, highly sophisticated, and I am a damnable snob. This is why [Margarita] could never reach me, in spite of all her love and devotion. She was not one of us."[3]

Although she had already had one analysis in London, Yasmine had resonated to Khan's writings, and she wanted to see him for a second analysis. Harry Karnac remembers that she had come into his bookstore early in the year, picked up *The Privacy of the Self,* and asked him how to get in touch with Khan. Karnac did not want to be responsible for the connection and he told her to contact the publisher. She then got Khan's phone number from Barrie Cooper.

Yasmine told me about her analysis with Khan and the sexual relationship they had even as the analysis continued:

I was thirty-four years old and very lost. I'd always had everything, but now
my marriage of ten years had collapsed. After reading Masud's books, I
was sure that he could help me. Barrie Cooper was my medical doctor and
I knew he was friends with Masud. But he hid Masud—he didn't want us
to meet because he sensed a potential disaster. I told Barrie that I'd find
him through other Pakistanis if he didn't arrange it, so he gave in.

When I went for my first session, I got terrified. I had expected somebody small, almost Jewish, a kind of English country gentleman version
of a Pakistani. But Masud was an enormous giant, wearing black robes
and silver jewelry. I think I must have fallen in love instantly. He later
told me that he also had an instantaneous reaction: He looked at me and
he said to himself: "Disaster!"

I wouldn't take the couch in the beginning. He said, "Can't you see
that there are several chairs? But at one stage you'll have to use the couch."
The problem was that all I wanted was to sit on his lap.

Even though my analysis was short, nobody helped me as much as
Masud did. He had a fantastic mind and he was an extraordinary listener.
He could get to the essence of a problem in a second. He opened up my
fears and he taught me to speak.

One time I called in the middle of the night, in crisis. The tension
was enormous over the phone. I went over for an emergency session.
Somehow I knew that Margarita was there. I ended up in a sexual situation with him, all dressed up. It felt like lightning had struck.

The sexual connection was always very intense. I've never felt so
comfortable with anyone. It was like making love to yourself in a positive way. I never thought anyone could come as close to my soul as he
did. It was a fusion—by far the most intense relationship of my life. I
never thought you could think of another person as a land. But with
Masud, I could go for kilometers and kilometers. And he felt the same
about me. It had something to do with textures of the skin—we had the
same skin.

Masud knew that I was terrified of a commitment, even though I felt
passion for him. And he was like that too. The more you got into a relationship with him, the more he got phobic and restless. He could only
be my companion because I had another life and he was never part of
that. I wanted him privately—I didn't want to be known as his woman.
We never went out in public. I felt strongly about this.[4]

On December 23, not long into the relationship with Yasmine, Khan went to California for a four-week stay with the Stollers. This visit turned into a more important experience than he had anticipated.

One night "chez Stollers," Khan was in a relaxed state, enjoying the affection, care, and concern that he always got from Robert and Sybil. As they talked, Khan suddenly had the idea that he wanted to have a short-term "psychoanalysis" with Robert:

> It all started in a rather quaint way. I was telling Sybil that in 1979 I needed to find myself a new houseboy and a fresh female companion, and I wanted her to find them for me. The woman had to be tall, lissom, university educated and a sharing companion. Preferably half Chinese and half Red Indian. It was part joking and part serious.
>
> Bob had been quietly half-listening while he read *The New Yorker*. Suddenly he said, "I'll give you an interpretation. You want to re-find your bi-sexual self in a woman. You lost it with the lung operation as you handed over all your Female Self to [Margarita], who provided maternal care and love. But you became sterile and uncreative. Now you have to find the discipline to create that dialogue with your True Self, which has produced all your writing and your unique thinking." I was very deeply moved by this interpretation.[5]

Robert agreed immediately to do a "trial analysis" of his friend.[6] He took a risk and broke the analytic taboo on treating friends in just this one case because, as a strong believer in the therapeutic power of analysis, he thought analytic understanding and the power of transference just might work a miracle. It was obvious to him that Khan was killing himself with alcohol, and Robert thought that desperate measures were warranted to try to save a man who still had major contributions to make to analysis.

From that evening on, they had sessions in Robert's study every night, with length ranging from three to four hours. All the rest of the time, Khan was a houseguest who shared their ordinary living as well as professional meetings attended with Robert, and various social occasions, including the Stollers' thirtieth wedding anniversary.[7]

Khan was staying in contact with Yasmine, who was in the Middle East, visiting her family. In the early morning hours, after his analytic session, he and Yasmine fought, suffered, and loved with great intensity, all by telephone. Their talks provided material that Stoller used the next evening to help Khan understand why his relationships kept failing.[8] Khan kept a record of the vacation cum analysis, as seen in these excerpts from his Work Books:

> My conversations with Bob have had a profound effect on me. I can now see that he is right when he says there is a perversity in me that doesn't let me actualise the total me. Instead, I have loved "mad" women for some 20 years. There is a macabre masochism and self-nihilism in my relationship with these women, which is entirely lacking in my relationship with my real friends.[9]

> [After repeated unsuccessful phone calls trying to reach [Yasmine] to wish her a Happy New Year] Yes, the new year has launched itself. And I have to carve a new way of life and living this year. Shed the torpor, the terrors (so hidden), re-active negative living, alcoholism and nostalgia. And find my own life with myself.[10]

> I have to be careful that I do not displace my dependency from [Margarita] onto [Yasmine]. I must re-establish my own ambience of relationships with my friends and my work. . . . Both of us are going through a critical transitional period, and we must retain our spaces and separateness.[11]

> Have been unwell today with sickness of the soul. So have stayed in bed, inert! Last night I had discussed with Bob at length a dream which we interpreted very insightfully. Now I must dress to go to Pasadena to dine with the Stollers and two of their sons and friends.[12]

> (12:45 a.m. the next day) I discussed the dream further with Bob and it became obvious that all my life I have dealt more with death than with living. And this "death" I actualise through the women I love.
>
> (1 a.m.) Why am I persisting with this long-range coverage and holding of [Yasmine] by telephonic relating, when I know perfectly well that she could be more deadly for me in the end than Svetlana, [Megan] or [Margarita]? I somehow escaped total catastrophe with them; I won't with her.
>
> (2 a.m.) [Yasmine] rang back. She has no clue to her incapacity for a sustained relationship. I told her, borrowing from Bob's interpretation of my dream, that each of us is carrying on a combat with death. In my

case, it eventually became cancer. . . . We had our first real conversation on the phone tonight.

(11 p.m.) Torrential rain all day: the one thing no one wants who lives in this canyon. Went with Sybil to buy gum-boots and raincoats to cope with the impending flooding of the canyon. Had lunch—a sandwich with beer at a nearby English bar. Then in the late afternoon, more outburst of rain. Canyon totally flooded, with cars stranded. There is real danger of canyon being unusable if rain continues.[13]

(1:45 a.m. the next day) Rang [Yasmine] and talked for some 45 minutes. I have been misguided in trying to provide coverage and care for her by nightly phone calls. I have mistaken her depressions for neediness and she has exploited me. In fact, she has been having a great time. Tonight she was aloof and rejecting . . . talked of settling down in [her homeland], asked me if I would visit her there. It was all gamesmanship, speaking words that had no relation to reality, private or social. It was painful to sustain a quiet responsiveness vis-a-vis her erratic conversation. The game is injurious to me, both physically and affectively.

(2:30 p.m.) Went with Bob to participate in the casual seminar on homosexuality that he holds. It was quite an experience because both the professors of Criminology and Anthropology were practicing homosexuals and told their data of homosexual clubs in Los Angeles and Mexico from personal experience. It was done with total candour and no exhibitionism. I made my contribution on Pathan sexual habits and homosexuality.[14]

Tonight [I told Bob] something that I have known for years, but in none of my other analyses was I able to speak it. I have never been able to love a woman as woman. I have been able to love only older men, like Rickman, Painter, Braque, Cassou, Winnicott, Sutherland, etc. All my "love" of women has been either aesthetic, as with Svetlana, or from the reparative drive, or purely sensual. Yet I have over-promised love to all my women, with disastrous end which was built into the very beginning. Bob commented: "If you have realised this, then you must love your mind and its products and stop over-promising." True![15]

Out of the material from their evening sessions, Stoller came to believe that Khan hid from his True Self because he was afraid to confront a deeply rooted fear of abandonment. Stoller thought that Khan avoided feeling his terrors by associating with people who distracted him with their talents or a sensational lifestyle. Khan tells how Stoller made use of a transference interpretation to demonstrate this:

> A dream awoke me. In the dream, I was talking with Winston Churchill on the Onassis yacht, and he was saying, "What a pity you didn't join the Army—because you have an innate style of strategy. . . . I thought the dream had to do with disillusionment with old men, because in the dream Churchill looked feeble and rather senile. But Bob interpreted it entirely in terms of transference. He understood it to be saying that I was pulling back from my analytic alliance with him. That it is no longer the rich Stoller house and Dr. Stoller that I talk from and to, but now the richer Onassis yacht and the "hero" Churchill.
>
> And how right Bob is. I know from a certain nervousness in me at present that I am afraid to [return to London] on my own and unprotected. My way of dealing with the upcoming absence from Bob is to preempt the predicament by substituting a grander mythic alliance as against our real mutual dialogue. I am also worried about the absence of Sybil when I get home.[16]

Two days later, Khan continued to reflect on Stoller's interpretation: "One thing Bob has really achieved for me is to show me the necessity of being ME henceforth, without reference to any externals."[17]

Another focus of the analysis was Khan's attachment to a death wish. Stoller believed that the death wish was coming not from a universal human tendency, as in the Freudian model, but rather from forces that were the result of childhood experiences so awful they left Khan with a wish to die. He thought that this explained Khan's drinking, his tumultuous relationships with women, and perhaps even the development of cancer. Stoller wrote to Smirnoff: "It was especially to Masud's destructiveness— of others and of himself—that I continuously went [in the analysis]. He is in a prolonged fuck with Death, and my efforts were aimed primarily at trying to get him to release that mutual embrace."[18]

Khan came to agree with Stoller's interpretations of his death wish. He had always thought about himself in an almost literal identification with the tragic characters of Shakespeare and Dostoevsky, so this was not a big stretch. Stoller had helped him to understand something he had known for a long time: "Since childhood, I have had an emotionality in myself that I knew one day would compel me to kill myself."[19] Khan and Stoller agreed that Khan often used women to externalize his internal drama.

Then, abruptly, the "analysis" came to an end. It was unsettling to stop the treatment, which was incomplete:

> [Writing "chez Stollers" on the last day of the visit] How quickly time has passed and yet at the same time I feel I have been living here for years. What wonderful hosts Bob and Sybil have been. And my "analytic encounter" with Bob is something I shall always treasure and give him credit for.[20]

> [On the plane to London at 6 a.m.] This is London time already, and we should be landing within an hour. So I am now nine hours and thousands of miles away from Bob and Sybil. It has been so idyllic with them. Everything in London threatens me. . . .
> The only and incalculable question now is that of my relating with [Yasmine]. I am not sure that I can dole myself out so extravagantly any more. Specially after all the insights that Bob has so quietly but solidly instilled into me.[21]

Yasmine met Khan at the airport and easily persuaded him to spend the day with her. He telephoned the Stollers from her home and, by luck, was able to get through. He told Robert and Sybil that he was "alert and watching," worrying about the future, and already missing California.[22]

In an ideal world, Khan's mini-analysis would now lead to a miraculous recovery: he would begin to think and feel rather than act, he would not have to numb himself with alcohol, and he would salvage the last years of his life and career. Stoller was hopeful but not overly optimistic. In a letter to Smirnoff, he expressed skepticism: "It is probably the case that [Masud] has too much erotized destruction. We shall wait, with great concern and modest hope, to see whether he will begin to extricate himself. It depends on the alcohol."[23]

Stoller had more hope for the possibility that Khan might be able to start writing again. Before, during, and after the "analysis" he continually emphasized this. As he had told Smirnoff earlier, "[Writing] is all that really should count for Masud now—it was always his beauty. I can only wish that his writing might tickle him unconsciously to rise up, as if from the dead, and restore his creativity. That would be a miracle, but not one beyond his reach."[24] To Khan, he now wrote, "You are an artist and, since art is in such desperately short supply in psychoanalysis, we have need of you in ways that would never be demanded of the rest of us."[25]

Without question, the short treatment had been effective. Stoller had opened up Khan's deepest pathology and "held" Khan in an experience of regression to dependence that addressed his False Self pathology. In hindsight, however, it seems that Stoller erred in the same way as Winnicott had, by failing to insist that Khan continue in treatment, whether with himself or someone else.

In fact, Khan almost returned to California just a week after he left. A fight with Yasmine left him so distraught that he was tempted to resort to alcohol and he did not think he could resist the pull on his own: "I shall fly to Bob and Sybil and be nursed, because I know here I shall drink myself to death. Lord! how generous they are."[26] The Stollers agreed to have him back and he even made a plane reservation. Unfortunately, he canceled the trip under pressure from Yasmine to stay in London.

Back in his London routine, Khan initially resisted temptation and made a major shift toward health. He started to write again, he socialized with friends, and he stayed away from alcohol for months. Ever the optimist, he concluded that the "analysis" had worked: "Bob succeeded in making me accept myself as someone both crazy and exceptional."[27]

It was a productive period. When Khan gave a short talk at a memorial commemorating the 100th anniversary of Ernest Jones's birth, his presentation went so well that he decided to start attending meetings of the Publications Committee again.[28] Clifford Yorke was now the editor of the IPL, and Khan agreed to edit one last book, a collection of articles by Pontalis. He wrote an article for NRP after Smirnoff told him that his work had been greatly missed by the French in the last two issues.[29] In the late spring, he wrote a long book review for the IJPA[30] and he made final revisions on his book *Alienation in Perversions*, which was being published that year by Hogarth, with John Charlton as editor. He had delayed finishing this book out of a fear that the material would upset Miss Freud; now, with Stoller's encouragement, he dared to write what he wanted to say.[31]

Yasmine did not like alcohol and that helped him to succeed in his determination to control his drinking. For the first time since the divine years with Svetlana, Khan felt that he had a satisfying private life, although he constantly dreaded the ending that he was sure would be coming soon: "There will be no ready instant substitute for me once my life with [Yasmine] disappears. [She has] provided the armature of a way of life for me. . . . Who else will ever again give and share such a full and elegant life with me?"[32]

But a closer look at Khan's life in this period reveals that things were not as good as they might seem to be. His Work Books show—and Yasmine confirms this—that immediately upon his return from California, he was seeing her for regular analytic sessions at the same time as they had an intense sexual relationship.[33] He was making a mockery of psychoanalysis and thereby denying the importance of his experience with Stoller.

In the analytic sessions, Khan and Yasmine discussed her relationship problems making reference to Yasmine's lover as "he," as if the man were a person other than Khan himself. Here is one of many Work Book entries where Khan comments from the combined perspective of the analyst and the lover: "Yasmine came for her session. . . . We were both very severe and correct. She talked of how her friend had hurt her again. The 'friend' was me, and I talked of myself in the third person singular. She tried every ruse and she is manipulative indeed, but I was prepared and didn't give her an inch. Eventually she asked to sit in my lap. I let her."[34]

The analytic relationship ended in late spring, although the personal relationship continued. Khan thought that the treatment had been successful: "[Barrie Cooper] says he is quite amazed at my dissociative approach to Yasmine: I am so deeply involved with her on the one hand, and yet I can find the distance to see through all her antics of psychopathology so clearly and lucidly."[35] "I am not sure that I have totally failed with Yasmine; only for the time being. I have sown seeds in her soul that, if luck favors her, will grow to plants and flower as her true being."[36]

Yasmine still thinks that the dual relationship was perfectly acceptable. She told me: "Masud socialized with his patients so that people would feel that analysis was part of their life, and not a separate, isolated thing. That way they could bring the analytic and outside parts of their self together." And she understands Khan's claim that an especially close relationship was justified for certain cases: "Masud was an unorthodox analyst only in cases like mine where he felt that he couldn't help the person without getting involved in their life."[37]

In the years since her relationship with Khan has ended, Yasmine has had a difficult but personally rich life. She remembers him saying something that still feels true for her inner world: "I have kept a vigil around your suffering." And she considers the time when she was with him in the dual relationship to have been the best period of her life: "How many people do you know who can say they were in a totally satisfying emotional relationship, however short-lived?"

There had been additional problems in the first months of 1979. Khan's friendship with André Green had ended after behavior that Green experienced as a betrayal. Green, who was divorced, had visited London with a female friend that spring. Khan invited them to dinner, and everything seemed normal. Afterward, he told mutual friends that Green was having an affair with a patient. It was a total fabrication—Khan was the one who was in a relationship with a patient—and Green was understandably outraged. On another occasion, Khan wrote a seven-page letter that was filled with distortions presented as facts, all meant to ruin Green's reputation, and he sent copies to various colleagues.

When Khan wrote later to ask if they could get together in Paris, Green replied that the only way he would resume the relationship was if Khan apologized to him and to all the people who had received his letter. But Khan wrote back: "I know that I have misbehaved—but I don't even think of saying I'm sorry."[38] That was it for Green. The friendship was over. This was a significant loss because they had had an important friendship. It is a credit to the quality of the original connection that Green still remembers the positive: "Masud provoked a very strong attachment in me. I would never have thought he could betray me as he did. Despite all that has happened I would still say that Masud is one of the people I have liked most in my life."[39]

Another problem was Svetlana. Throughout the spring, she had been in the midst of a severe alcoholic breakdown and nothing was helping her. In May, Khan wrote: "Horror of horrors: Svetlana started ringing me, progressively more drunk, accusative, demanding, threatening and incoherent each time. . . . I feel so unbearably sad and resourceless. I rang [Zoë] Dominic to see if she could help, but she had been harassed the same way."[40] Her situation tortured him: "Have woken up very anguished and aware of Svetlana. Yes, her predicament haunts me and dislocates me from my person. I cannot accept that at best she is now an ambulatory casualty. Once I hear her voice, she seeps into me and for days I am paralysed. This reveals to me how, despite some nearly nine years, I am still utterly incapable of handling Svetlana intrapsychically: time, in that respect, has stood still."[41]

Khan's understanding of Svetlana's problem was not that she was alcoholic—it was that she had never "lived through" her madness.[42] He started reading biographical accounts of Virginia Woolf, hoping to gain insight about other geniuses who had broken down. One of his conclusions was that the creative genius inevitably lives just on the edge of disaster.[43] The unanswered question was how such a person could keep from succumbing to the disaster.

As his connection to Yasmine collapsed, Khan stopped living well and retreated to his inner world. He wrote: "I live at one remove."[44] "How psychic illness dislocates us from authenticity and makes liars of us all."[45] He mocked his past attempts to live in the world and all his gains from the analysis with Winnicott (and also, indirectly, the work he had done with Stoller): "I am false to my back teeth. This works better for me than my True Self à la DWW."[46]

At the same time as he made these comments, he also took comfort in the idea that he was making a contribution to psychoanalysis by describing his False Self living. He thought that his Work Books, which he expected to be published after his death, would provide to the world a clinical description of the pathology he and Winnicott had described:

> [My secretary] has just finished typing the [most recent] Work Book. It is almost entirely a record of my inner fight against relating to [Yasmine]. Superficially read, it sounds silly, weak-minded, lacking in resolve and purpose, eruptively irresponsible in action, incoherent in its affectivity, etc. etc. And yet I feel it is a true record, without literary subterfuge or romantic alibis. It tells exactly how one man fails, in spite of his personality and knowledge, to coordinate and harness affectivity into a relationship that he needs and dreads.[47]

In June 1979, there was still a question about whether Khan would be able to stay on the controlled side of creative psychosis. "Madness is a private state of confusion and lucidity; hence it is not conflictual, but paradoxical. A person can contain it and live with it."[48] Robert Stoller had said that the most important factor was whether or not Khan could stay away from alcohol. Khan was doing well in that area, but still living, as Virginia Woolf and Svetlana had, just on the edge of disaster. The next few months would be crucial.

CHAPTER 34

MURDER, FRENZY, AND MADNESS:
READING DOSTOEVSKY

That vast make-believe which is literature somehow to me feels more
authentic than the living presence of most people.
Masud Khan[1]

Midsummer of 1979 would be the most bizarre period of Khan's life. As he and Yasmine ended their relationship, he immersed himself in a highly personal reading of the writings of the Russian author Fyodor Dostoevsky. Khan became so identified with the character Prince Myshkin from Dostoevsky's *The Idiot*[2] that he lost the distinction between fiction and real life, and made life decisions based on the delusion that he was Myshkin. It was a time when his psychotic living was, in his view, by choice: "I am not only mad, but so willfully perverse about staying mad."[3]

The Idiot was Khan's favorite Dostoevsky novel, and he had read it many times. In a lifetime of reading, *King Lear* and *The Idiot* were the most consistent literary influences on him. At various times in his life, he identified strongly with the major characters and themes of both.

He had read Russian literature as a teenager in India, under his tutor's guidance. Two fictional women, Nastasia Filippovna (who is murdered in *The Idiot*) and Anna Karenina (the heroine of Tolstoy's *Anna Karenina*, who ends up killing herself) had, he said, prepared him to find and experience Svetlana: "In a strange way I actualised them both in my vécu. It was in Tolstoy and Dostoevsky that I first encountered Svetlana: while still raw and in my teens!"[4]

The first mention of Dostoevsky in his writings was in 1965 just after the Amsterdam scandal. Resonating to a theme that is present in *The*

Idiot, which he was rereading, he worried that he might be trying to kill either himself or Svetlana with his problematic behavior.[5] He wanted to discuss the book with a friend, but he felt that Robert and Sybil Stoller, his main correspondents at that time, would not understand such dark themes. So he wrote to Babette Soria, the ex-wife of Victor Smirnoff. Soria shared Khan's interest in literature and he asked her to reread *The Idiot* so they could discuss it together. He was quite insistent: "Have you a copy of Dostoevsky's *The Idiot*? Please acquire a copy and start [reading it again] because I want to discuss it with you. It is not sufficient for you to have a vague memory of it. I shall need the certainty of the knowledge that all the references I make you can refer to and are freshly en rapport with. . . . Of course this is an absurd request. Let me hear your decision. Please! Thank you!"[6] The response to this plea is unknown.

Dostoevsky's intent in *The Idiot* had been to show that a truly good person could not survive in contemporary Western life. It is a modern variant of the story of Jesus. Khan saw himself in the good, innocent, and misunderstood character Myshkin as early as 1968, when he compared himself and Myshkin to Jesus, T. E. Lawrence, and Albert Camus, all "[doomed by] a fatal authenticity of self which is insupportable in lived life; hence their fatedness."[7] In 1973, he wrote about Myshkin in a discussion of "superior men" who hide themselves from others using various masks[8]; obviously he included himself in that group.

In the crazed summer of 1979, Khan no longer felt similar to Myshkin —he believed that he *was* Myshkin. And at the same time as he was Myshkin, he believed he was also another character from *The Idiot*—the murderous Rogozhin. (In Khan's interpretation of the book, Myshkin and Rogozhin were different selves of a single person.) This dual identification meant that a passionate and destructive self coexisted with a passive and loving "idiot" self: "In my sensibility, I am a bizarre conglomerate of both 'the idiot' (Prince Myshkin) and the murderous peasant Rogozhin."[9] Similarly, he came to believe that Yasmine *was* the character Nastasia Filippovna, a woman whom Rogozhin kills.

The precipitant to his insanity was a movie. On June 17, he went with Y to a theater called The Electric in Portobello Road, where they saw Akira Kurosawa's film *The Idiot* (1951), a Japanese adaptation of the novel. Several dramatic scenes show Prince Myshkin having epileptic seizures.

While watching the movie, Khan suddenly had a vivid memory of watching, at age four, while his mother had a seizure and almost died after giving birth to a stillborn infant (see Chapter 1). Khan had repressed the memory and now he was overwhelmed by feelings of helplessness and panic.[10]

He had been sober for six months, ever since the mini-analysis with Robert Stoller. Now, retraumatized by the sudden emergence of the childhood memory, he went home and started to drink again.

In his Work Book, Khan describes a horrible week following the viewing of the movie, a week that culminated in the only overt suicide attempt of his life. Under the influence of alcohol, he wrote a seven-page letter to Yasmine, telling her that he was breaking up with her. He wrote that because he was Myshkin and Yasmine was Nastasia Filippovna, he had to leave in order to save her life. He then read her the letter over the telephone. Not understanding his distress, Yasmine suggested that there was no need to create such drama. Khan felt deeply misunderstood and hung up the phone, then destroyed the letter.[11]

As his thoughts developed further, he decided that he needed to retreat into a personal asylum in order to save Yasmine and himself. He thought that he should isolate himself from everyone, except patients, and let himself have a breakdown: "I have shirked living through my madness these 40 years or so. I cannot dodge it anymore. How I shall contain my onslaughts of panic and madness alone in this asylum I do not know."[12]

The next night, he had a huge fight with Yasmine, undoubtedly fueled by alcohol. For a long time he had been troubled by the fact that Yasmine had more wealth than he had and now he insulted her about something regarding money. Yasmine responded by slapping him, upon which Khan threw her down in the hallway and tried to strangle her. He then took a knife and violently stabbed a cushion of her black leather couch, thereby enacting Rogozhin's stabbing of Nastasia Filippovna: "I [took] a cushion from the black sofa and stabbed it with a long flick-knife, saying, 'This is the Idiot become Rogozhin killing Nastasia Filippovna.' Some of it was enacted, but the core of it was true to my madness."[13] The extent of Khan's insanity at this moment is astonishing.

He tried to reconcile by sending Yasmine thirty-five red roses on the following day. (His reason for sending "thirty-five" flowers is unknown.)

Then, in a phone conversation, Yasmine told him that she could not tolerate his drinking and the relationship was over; she was insulted by the roses, she said, and had sent them to Alcoholics Anonymous.

The thought of losing Yasmine aroused Khan's separation anxieties and he went into a panic: "If I can last till August 4th, when I leave for my estate in Pakistan, I have some chance to survive. Otherwise, I'll ask Barrie [Cooper] to anonymously hospitalise me."[14] In his wild state, the recurrent theme was murder. He believed that he was in danger of being killed by Yasmine—or by his own self: "I have to protect myself from me, MASUD."[15]

He had brought his car out of storage that summer[16] and on the night of Yasmine's rejection of his request to reconcile, he drove drunk to her home. Things did not go well. Yasmine was out, and he drove his car into her parking alcove. When she arrived home in her Porsche, he left. As he parked in the space outside of his own house, he was involved in an accident: "Some idiotic woman rammed into me." His car had broken headlights, but the two agreed that they would not report the accident. His Work Book comment at 1:30 a.m. was: "Yes, this is the end!"[17]

The drama had not reached its climax. The final event was Shakespearean in its violence and its inclusion of multiple characters (including three of his former lovers) in a grand finale:

[He describes the early morning of June 22, sometime after 1:30 a.m.] Last night I went completely mad. I rang [Yasmine] and told her I cannot live without her. She curtly said: "You will have to!" and I replied: "Then I will cut my throat." She put the phone down. I went to the kitchen and tried with various knives to cut my throat, but they were all blunt and merely scratched the throat, and it began to bleed. I panicked. Rang Svetlana and told her I had tried to cut my throat, please come over. She did, at once. She dabbed antiseptic on the scars, tried to find Barrie but couldn't reach him. I made her call [Yasmine] and [Yasmine] came over, a strange hating look on her face. [Megan, Khan's former girlfriend] and Mehnaz [his secretary] arrived also. Svetlana mocked: "Look—all your harem is here!" After awhile they all left.[18]

The evening ended as Yasmine left together with Svetlana—a truly odd pairing—while Khan screamed at Yasmine that *she* was killing *herself*.

Khan's return to alcohol marked the end of his love affair with Yasmine. If she had been colluding in the living out of his life script of murder/suicide, she would collude no more. They continued to talk on the phone for another six months, but Yasmine was moving on.

His peers seem to have been unaware of the fact that he was having another affair with an analysand and that he was having a psychological breakdown. In the summer of 1979, in the midst of his insanity, the same council that had condemned him for his sexual relationship with Margarita decided to honor him: "Adam Limentani called in person to give me a pair of silver cufflinks. The Council of the British Psychoanalytic Society has decided to honour my services to the Society as Hon. Librarian and archivist (for some 30 years) and various editorships for over 18 years."[19] Looking back, it is unsettling to observe Khan's success in hiding his pathology.

Khan was a brilliant interpreter of the self in his patients but when it came to understanding himself, he was inconsistent. Just days after the suicide attempt, he made a Work Book entry describing patients with problems very similar to his own—with no apparent awareness that he shared their pathology. He was writing about people who are unable to utilize symbolic thought, so that they cannot make use of affective experiences to develop the self: "These patients have a knack for concrete experiences, intrapsychic and inter-personal, but all such experiences fail to build an experiential tradition of the private self."[20]

In the same time period, he also had significant self-insight:

I have come through a crisis and realise that only tasks relate me to others; otherwise I am really autistic, and yet can't bear that state. [Yasmine] became emotionally indispensable to me because she provided the first and only experience of familial sharing and living to me. I sabotaged it out of fear that she would/could end it any day. . . . I make the simple act of living so absurdly cruel and torturous for myself; my problems are all inventions of my own sensibility.[21]

Khan "lived" literature, even when he was relatively sane. Literature was so similar to real life for him that the boundary between reality and fantasy was regularly blurred: "Strange how few of my friends are really

326   FALSE SELF

immersed in literature. It is not that they do not read literature—of course they do. But it has not an engrossing, continuous presence in their lives. They do not experience life through language and literature as I do."[22] High drama, the idealization of beauty, and the mixture of passion with murder and suicide were intrinsic parts of Dostoevsky's great novels—and of Khan's experience of himself and others. Writing from Pakistan in 1965, he had told Zoë Dominic: "Have been involved in one long familial wrangle. Only Dostoevsky could do the events justice—in fact he anticipated us in *The Brothers Karamazov*. Read it and know us!"[23]

His Work Books read at times like fiction, as he describes prescient and dramatic feelings, especially regarding women. These accounts are similar to that of the fictional Myshkin, who fell in love with Nastasia the moment he saw her photograph (or even earlier, in a fantasy or a dream). During the marriage ceremony with Svetlana, Khan claimed that he had felt "an uncanny sudden dread that shivered through me. . . . Something in me sensed disaster."[24] He described his initial meeting with Yasmine with similar drama: "A strange dread made me shiver. I knew at once I would fall in love with her, and that if I failed in this relationship I would have a psychotic breakdown."[25]

In 1979, he was interpreting *The Idiot* in a personal manner in an attempt to meet his own needs. This in itself is not pathology—it is something characteristic of an involved reader.[26] Nor was it problematic that he identified strongly with Myshkin/Dostoevsky. The identification makes some sense. In addition to their similar life situations (coming from a foreign country, being accepted at high levels of society, never quite fitting in), the fictional Myshkin and the real-life Khan shared some exceptional qualities, one of these being an ability to help people to see parts of themselves that they had not previously held in conscious awareness.[27] The problem was the *extent* of the identification. In his madness, the "as-if" quality of literature vanished. Khan was having a direct response to Dostoevsky's fictional world, not playing with it in his imagination.[28]

Somehow Khan made it through the summer. In August, he went to Pakistan, where he calmed down. That fall, his identification with Myshkin weakened and his relationship with Dostoevsky became sublimated into an intellectual interest; at last, he began thinking about his feelings and thoughts rather than living them. In October, reflecting on the mad period he had just emerged from, he wrote: "What has the past year been all about? An elaborate attempt at exorcism of the IT in me, an attempt that has failed all the way. One has to befriend one's devils within, and not shed them onto others: that is the only lesson I have learnt from the past year."[29] He started work on an article for NRP about Dostoevsky, something he had thought about writing for years.[30]

For three months, from December 1979 through February 1980, Khan was totally immersed in writing the article, as he filled his study with books and articles by and about Dostoevsky. His usual pattern of reading was to leaf through sections of a book; his memory made it possible for him to write and talk as if he had read the entire work. Now he broke from that style, reading every page of the material with intense concentration. Unable to sleep, his mood was "adrenalized and taut."[31] At times, he felt he was in a state of ecstasy. When he stopped to see patients, he was impatient to get back to his reading. He seemed to be identifying with Dostoevsky: "[Dostoevsky] could live, relate, and create only from a state of frenzy—like all his created characters."[32]

By late January 1980, he was ready to write. The title of the article was "Meurtre, Frènèsie et folie," which translates as "Murder, frenzy and Madness." He was writing about how supposed victims may invite their own destiny, using Dostoevsky's characters to make his point.[33] The idea was not new to him, but he was inspired by his recent experience with Yasmine, which he considered to have been both suicidal and murderous. When, after weeks of reading and thinking, he finally began writing, he noted the occasion in his Work Book: "This weekend is the fateful one. It is now a question of shifting to the mental-work of abstraction. I start the article with the sentence: 'One definition of some murders could be: suicide through the Other.'"[34]

The Dostoevsky period of Khan's life ended in February 1980, when he finished his article.[35] Somewhat amazingly, the completion of the article coincided with his entering into a serious and meaningful relationship with a new woman. As he moved into the next stage of his life, he commented: "Everything becomes so absurdly exaggerated, intensified, and dramatic with me, no matter what care I take. I just cannot be ordinary."[36]

FORTUNE SMILES: LAST LOVE

But it is well known that a man carried away by passion,
especially a man getting on in years, is quite blind, and prone
to find grounds for hope where there are none.
Fyodor Dostoevsky[1]

Khan was like a man come back from the dead as he fell in love one last time and began to live more fully in the outside world. Fleur (pseudonym) was without question one of his most important loves. She belongs in this category along with Svetlana, Eva, and Margarita. With four great loves, he was repeating his father's history—Fazaldad had had four wives. And, like his father, Khan's final love was a very young woman. For Fazaldad and Khursheed, the age difference had been more than fifty years; for Khan and Fleur it was twenty-four years (he was fifty-five years old and she was thirty-one). It may or may not have been sheer chance that the twenty-four year age difference between Khan and Fleur was almost exactly the same as the age difference between Fyodor Dostoevsky and his wife Anna, to whom he was married while writing *The Idiot*. Just as Dostoevsky worried about being too old for Anna, so Khan was haunted by a fear that he was too old for Fleur. But he was also thrilled by the synchronicity.

The relationship had a special provocativeness due to the identity of Fleur's mother, a woman (anonymous) who was an intimate and long-time member of Khan's circle of friends in Paris. Fleur had grown up knowing Khan well and, as seen in Work Book entries from over a decade earlier,[2] he had favored her over other children of friends. Since

Fleur had always related to him in a child's role, there was an incestu-
ous charge to her new status. Furthermore, her mother, who was Khan's
age and single, would be sure to feel slighted. It is likely that Khan delighted in these complications.[3]

In December 1979, Fleur was living and working in Paris. She called
Khan to ask for a referral to an analyst who could help her to get rid of
what she referred to as ghosts from her past. In the course of their conversation, Khan told her about the Dostoevsky article he was writing
for NRP. Fleur asked him to send her a copy of the draft and she then
responded with a critique that impressed him.[4] Her mother happened
to be staying with Khan at the time, but as soon as she left Khan telephoned Fleur and convinced her to come to London for a short visit.
Almost immediately they became mutually infatuated.

The two related to each other in person, on the telephone, and in
letters. Khan was amazed at how healing it was to be involved in this
relationship:

> [Fleur] has arrived [for a four-day visit]: looking so fresh and wholesome.
> The flat is resonant with her quietly ebullient presence. . . . How strange
> and wonderful it is that at age 55 I can still encounter a young, beautiful,
> sensitive, intelligent woman and evoke emotion, passion and mutuality.
> I adore her way of being![5]

> [Fleur] has left for Paris. We had such joyous, quietly mutual and shared
> experiences together: read, ate, cuddled and laughed. She completes me,
> and I am utterly authentic and in a true measure of affectivity with her.
> I can also be creatively alone and work in her presence.[6]

> I have started to really read, think, and write again, after three years of
> inertia and torpor.[7]

On a visit to London in February, Fleur gave Khan a copy of Anna
Dostoevsky's *Reminiscences,* the book she wrote while pregnant and traveling with Fyodor throughout Europe as he wrote *The Idiot.* Anna describes her husband with great tenderness in this memoir, and Khan read
the book with such pleasure that he hated to finish it:

I quietly and with deliberate slowness am "living" Anna Dostoevsky's narrative with her. I have not encountered in life, or read anywhere in literature, such an authentic, moving and candid account of a lived and shared mutuality in life and work, as between Anna and Fyodor.[8]

Alas, tonight my companionship with Anna Dostoevsky would end, as I shall finish the book. But it shall live on in me to the end of my days. I have not in all my life finished a book with such a deep sadness that it has come to an end. [It is] so private that one feels one has been eavesdropping on someone meditating their own life . . . yet so robust and militant in her loving regard for her husband's nobility of soul.[9]

Khan concluded from the book that he shared two characteristics with Dostoevsky: they both needed to be involved with a woman in order to write, and they both were difficult men who required a special kind of devotion from their female partner: "[Dostoevsky] wished to be treated as a titanic genius but indulged as a child."[10] Admiring Anna's tolerance, he thought about how much he wanted a partner who would willingly and lovingly meet his own difficult needs: "I need and demand a being-held-alive within the awareness of the other. I urge and need the other person to be autonomous and independent, yet to not forget me for a moment."[11] He wrote that he had found that with only four people: his sister, his father, Svetlana, and now Fleur. He decided that Fleur was just *like* Anna—he could relate symbolically by now.

He had a nine-day vacation at the end of February, and he made plans to stay with Fleur in Paris, even though she would be working. In recent years, he had always stayed with Smirnoff in Paris, so he knew there would be a problem explaining to his French friends why he was not there. The relationship was still a secret—only Smirnoff and the Stollers knew about it.

As new lovers wanting only to please the other, Khan and Fleur were both anxious about the visit. Fleur worried that her flat was too small, while Khan was afraid of being a burden at night:

Have written to [Fleur] and hinted that her "spoken" worries that her flat is too small are really irrelevant. I can live in an egg-shell, so long as it is clean and I can have endless mugs of tea. My apprehensions are that I may disturb her nights with my restless insomniac habits: reading, making tea, writing, trying to sleep only to get up and grab a banana. Her insomnia is so quiet and still, and I fear I may exhaust her from lack of night-rest, when she is working hard each day.[12]

For years, Khan had complained about his tendency to disperse himself by getting overcommitted and then resenting his commitments. It was part of his character and, as such, very difficult to change. This time, he limited his commitments, making plans to see friends only in the daytime hours when she would be at work—the evenings were to be theirs alone. The one exception was a dinner invitation from Henri Cartier-Bresson and his wife, Martine, friends who had never met Fleur.

He was trying hard to control himself, and determined to learn from the errors of his past relationships:

> I have woken up with that lucid, gentle and pervasively transparent psychic pain, which crystallises from a true knowing of the Self and the Other, accepting the limits of each and the mutuality thereof. [Fleur] is impatient to be a woman. It is both her biologic and psychic urgent need now. And I cannot fructify this womanhood in her. I will only cramp it with the otherness of my demands and my incapacity for that abandonment to sensuality and aggressive sexuality that she would need to actualise her womanhood.... All I am truly capable of is the tender generosities and delights of the oasis of sensuousness with a woman.
>
> I am resolved: 1. Not to cramp [Fleur's] growth into womanhood, which she can find with someone other than me; 2. Not to hurt her by suddenly "disappearing" or "stepping aside," both of which I am very adept at; and 3. To curtail my demands on her person, space and time with my massive letters and documents. She says quite explicitly and naïvely that it takes her so much time reading and re-reading my letters that little energy and time are left to her to write to me."[13]

But he worried that even with the best of intentions, he would not be able to be a good partner: "Poor girl, [Fleur] has no clue to what an impossible person I am to relate to: since mostly I relate by non-relating. I am so scared of hurting and damaging her."[14] He was right to be worrying, because he was not able to control his tendency to create drama. At the very time when he was falling in love with Fleur, he accepted a reconnection with Yasmine.

Yasmine, who had not talked to Khan for months, was in an agitated and panicky state as she sold her house and planned a move. She had contacted Khan asking if she could resume her analysis and he agreed, denying the obvious turmoil that would be a result: "Yasmine is just a woman to me, acutely and even desperately suffering. If I can help therapeutically I will, but [there will be] no socialising of any sort."[15] Yasmine told him that she could not stand the classical style of analysis, and that she needed him to be a warm friend who would be available for two to three hours at at a time, sometimes by phone and sometimes in person. He agreed to this, albeit with limitations:

> I distantly and quietly replied: "Yes, I have thought about it, and I know you need to be accommodated on demand." I told her she had to accept two things: the necessity of the frame and my incapacity, from private reasons, at times to be able to meet her need or demand for long sessions. She snarled: "Is it only that to you now?" I said: "Yes. I have abstracted myself from the rest." She tried to involve me with "our past" and I accepted its reality and my failures in it quite genuinely without becoming an accomplice to her mood of the hour.
>
> Gradually she hinted that she had tried gentler, more sane and solid and balanced persons than me—and it had not worked for her. Only I, in her lived-experience, have come near to any comprehension of her which she could use and relate to.[16]

Not surprisingly, Yasmine became emotionally dependent on Khan. She went into a panic when she heard he would be going to Paris for nine days, and she came unannounced to Palace Court, determined to revive their physical relationship. When Khan refused to let her sit on his lap, she attacked him verbally, saying: "So I am now your boyfriend!" Referring to his commitment to Fleur, Khan responded: "In a way, all my friends, male or female, are my boyfriends now."[17] After that exchange, Yasmine left, but she returned in the evening. They talked for hours, drinking whiskey together, and he let her stay overnight when she fell asleep on the couch.

Khan knew that the intensity of Yasmine's feelings would lead her to try to disrupt his vacation, yet he agreed to give her Fleur's phone number (without telling her Fleur's identity). His rationale was that he had to consider her therapeutic needs, even if they interfered with his own: "Well, can I keep it contained? This is the only way Yasmine can heal, if at all! But what will be its disruptive cost to me as a person, to [Fleur] as a person, and to [Fleur] and me in our relationship?"[18]

As the time drew near for the Paris visit, Khan and Fleur became increasingly tense. They were both sensitive people with a tendency to withdraw, and maintaining a connection while protecting the self was a delicate matter:

> No, a relationship between [Fleur] and me will not evolve. And not for lack of affection, but from an acute dread in each of possible hurt from affection. Rang her at 9 p.m. She is so hyper-sensitive and hyper-perceptive to the slightest nuance in my voice, even at this distance. After I had talked to her for two minutes, she remarked that my voice was sad. This was after I had given her my "formula" that she must not expect a lively and alert Masud, but a phobic and introverted one. She said: "So you are not excited about coming to Paris?" Then her voice faded with sadness. . . . We are both so constantly "on guard," intensely vulnerable and fearful; if I "distance" an inch she hides herself away a mile.
>
> I had said nothing about the joy of seeing her again. How vicious are my silence and evasions. I am best left with myself.[19]

When they acknowledged that things were not going to be easy, the situation eased. Khan's villager, X, visited him, and "his presence awakened me to myself and [Fleur]."[20] He telephoned Fleur, and they were again filled with joyful anticipation. Their good moods lasted: "Woke up at 6:00 am, embodied and personalised. Made myself tea and started to write a letter to [Fleur]. Then suddenly at 7:30 am, wanted to taste her mouth and voice. Rang her. She was so happy."[21] That evening they talked again. After "wondrous, joyous chatter," Khan hung up and found himself singing.

The next day he went to Harrod's to buy gifts and necessities for the visit: two pairs of soft house-shoes so that he wouldn't awaken Fleur at night, a half pound of Earl Grey tea for Smirnoff, teabags for himself, a pair of playing cards, and Moustache eau de cologne so that he would not have to shower. He even went to the optician to get his glasses adjusted. Too excited to fall asleep during his afternoon nap, he lay awake feeling happy.

That spring in Paris, Khan must have been a sight to behold. He was still strikingly handsome and he liked to wear dramatic clothing. On this visit, he wore a long Huntsman overcoat along with his ancestral cap. It pleased him when people on the street stared: "If I draw attention, I am being generous: they have a person who is a handsome man to look at."[22]

He felt perfectly comfortable in Fleur's small flat: "This really is a 'perch': a true nest, tiny and cosy on the tallest branch of the tree."[23] He "nestled" and "homed" himself there and felt blessed by good fortune: "A wondrous night of random converse and touch! I feel so at ease."[24]

The dinner with the Cartier-Bressons went well. Their eight-year-old daughter was present, and Khan had brought her a fancy dress from England, which fit perfectly:

> How my friends enjoy me and relish my presence and conversation—as I do theirs. Both Henri and Martine made [Fleur] feel at ease with herself, by noticing her without fuss or demand.
>
> Henri is youthful and alert of mind indeed, a true genius! He is fearful of atomic war that would destroy humanity and the species. I was facetious about it and jibed [sic] that it was perhaps ripe time for another species to take over and make a better job of living together than the humans have done. A sad dismay crept over his face; of course he was thinking of [his daughter's] future. I quickly changed the subject.[25]

At first, the days were happy and peaceful:

> The view from [Fleur's] high perch is so Parisian: chimneys and slated roofs. It is quiet and still here. Yes, the place fits her needs and her sensibility like a glove! Rich and bashful; gay in colours and self enclosed.
>
> We talk so much and so naturally and mutually. . . . How generously life is affluent once again: friends, living, reading, loving, working. Yes, when the archer's bow and arrow are ripe, the target finds it. One must have charity for all the ghastly abuse of oneself and others en route to the finding of the "it" of livingness in authenticity.[26]

> [9 a.m.] So silent and peaceful here. [Fleur] has hurriedly pulled her clothes on to herself, dunked her bread-butter-marmalade in tea, gulped it and left for work: like a bird flutters out of its nest. Adorable creature!

The sun has lit up the grey tiles and the brown chimney-tops with a gentle candour of freshness. In Paris I can see things; in London, I am blind.[27]

Is it because I am again finding a love that meets and greets my love that I am so awake, quiet and happy? Or has sobriety given me back to myself? Or both?[28]

He persuaded Fleur to take an afternoon off from work so that he could buy her a coat. They went to Galeries Lafayette—one of the few times in his life when Khan agreed to go into a department store other than Harrod's—and chose a long beige coat: "It fits her and is that right simplicity of youthfulness which is so 'her.'"[29] Then they went to Galeries Maeght, where Khan introduced Fleur to Aimé Maeght, his aged friend.

Other days, while Fleur was at work, Khan saw friends for lunch, including Jeanne Axler, who was divorced from Smirnoff and about to move to California. When he happened to run into Fleur's mother one afternoon, the mother was amazed to see that Khan seemed totally different from the invalid she had stayed with in London just a few weeks earlier. Astutely, she asked if he was involved with a woman, and he told her that she had guessed correctly: "You know there is always a woman in my life. But differently now. From being self-indulgent and dependent, I have learnt to love my company and share it with a woman without getting taken over by it. The answer for me has turned out to be very simple: live in one country and love someone in another." When the mother said that she was suspicious of what Khan was up to, that he was untrustworthy and could be dangerous, he gave a joking but honest reply: "I share your sentiments. I feel the same about myself."[30]

The peace of the visit was compromised when Yasmine started to make late-night phone calls. The calls brought strain to evenings that were supposed to have been private, and the situation upset all three of them. Yasmine and Fleur were both filled with what Khan called their grudges: jealousy and resentment.[31]

Another problem was one Khan had anticipated: Fleur started to experience him as being overly controlling and demanding. One night

Therese Lion, a literary friend of Khan, came for drinks, and afterward, Fleur told him about her anger:

> [Fleur] slumped from exhaustion on the bed and murmured in a gentle voice: "Tu me devores! [You devour me.] You say 'Do this! Please [Fleur], make Therese more salami-bread. Give her more gin, please. Yes, I would love another cup of tea. Thank you!! etc. etc.'"
>
> How right and true she is. I have devoured her person, her time and her space. Like the locust, I have spread all over and "tout est mangé" [all is eaten].[32]

The next day, determined to make up, Khan cleaned the flat and washed the dishes while Fleur was at work. He spent the afternoon writing and welcomed her warmly when she returned home. But when he asked her to read the twelve pages he had written, she was too tired to immerse herself in the writing. He felt she had become distant and she felt the same about him, so it was a tense evening. After she went to sleep, he stayed up and wrote in his Work Book:

> I had remarked to [Fleur] that I have stayed two days too long. She protested: "No! I'll be so sad when you leave." Yes, that is true, but she will be unencumbered also. She protests that I speak to her as if she were a parrot and I am speaking to myself, without looking at her, needing only her presence. . . .
>
> I am alone and awake beside [Fleur], who is sound asleep. I have indeed exhausted her. In a way I wish I were in my own bed in Flat 7. It is painful to find her asleep, not from tiredness, but from refusal. I have exhausted, over-taxed, and over-stayed my welcome.[33]

The next day was Khan's last full day in Paris, and Fleur had the day off. Khan had scheduled a luncheon with one of Yasmine's friends, to which Fleur was not invited, and he realized that the plan was a mistake. He canceled the date in order to be with Fleur.

Despite the tensions, the visit had been successful. They both were in love and hopeful about the future, although they knew that they would have to work on the relationship. Khan wrote that he felt "vibrant, self-contained, knowing and alive."[34] His well-being is reflected in the fact that with Fleur in his life, his Work Book entries were no longer written in the third person.

Arriving home, Khan wrote to Smirnoff to tell him how well things had gone: "I had ten delicious, quietly mutual, sometimes chequered (momentarily), and truly happy days with [Fleur]."[35] Feeling lonely, he called Fleur, even though it was already past midnight. He found her "cosily tucked in her quilt and so happy with its enveloping warmth. Darling girl!"[36] Then he called the Stollers, who were pleased to hear that he was both sober and happy. He had just put the phone down when it rang.

It was Yasmine. She was angry and accusative, blaming Khan for having dismissed her by canceling the lunch with her friend. They talked for two hours, into the early morning hours. At the end of the conversation, Yasmine demanded to know: "Who is [Fleur]?" and Khan decided to tell her, making it clear that he and Fleur were in love and planning to build a relationship. They hung up in anger and Khan, exhausted, finally fell asleep.

He called Fleur the next day, but she did not answer. At 4 a.m. on March 5, unable to sleep, he called again. Fleur was herself awake, worrying about their plan to go together to an analytic meeting in April, a plan that would make their relationship public. She said she thought they should not go, but Khan disagreed: "I told Fleur that we become their accomplices if we run to hide. I said: 'One is never ready for anything unless one undertakes it. The Germans were ready for the war and lost it; the English weren't and won it.' That she has to dispel her 'ghosts' and not nurture them."[37] He convinced Fleur to stick to the plan.

On the afternoon of March 6, there was a memorial service for Dorothy Burlingham, Anna Freud's longtime companion. Khan's peers seemed glad to see him: "I stayed awhile: some of my colleagues have genuine affection for me."[38] Later that day he had a private meeting with Miss Freud, and she made note of the change in him: "She congratulated me on my recovery to full health: 'In every sense, Masud Khan, you look & talk as you did before your operations!' I was very touched, knowing that she was as-if blessing me into a future she felt herself departing from [because she was old and near death herself]."[39]

That evening, he wrote long letters to Smirnoff, to Miss Freud, and to Princess Marie Bonaparte (a colleague). He was distracting himself because what he longed to do was write to Fleur. He was trying not to drive her away by overattention, still committed to the rare behavior of trying to control himself: "I really have spread across and usurped too much of

[Fleur's] living-time and life-space. She needs her leisurely privacy of clutter with her own 'ghosts,' to sort them out, exorcise a few, nurture some, and re-arrange others. With me in her head and hair, she has little scope to move. This is why she didn't answer the phone [two days ago] and last night did not ring. I have to learn to companion my own aloneness."[40]

Then, to his relief, Fleur called him. She again said that she wanted to cancel the April plans. This time Khan agreed, trying not to be demanding. "[Fleur] remarked: 'We are a little "mad," both of us. We should keep our feet on the ground.' I told her if we weren't more than a little 'mad,' we wouldn't be together. I said I'll be out on Sunday, and asked will she be home: 'I am not sure,' she said. 'I'll try to call,' I said, and left it at that."[41]

The next day, he received a letter from Fleur's mother. She had found out that Khan's new love was her daughter, and she was writing to tell him that he was an "amoral, dangerous and hurtful liar." Khan was furious about her reaction. He called Fleur, read her the letter, and asked her to fly to London that weekend.

Fleur arrived on March 9, "joyous and bashful as a girl of seventeen."[42] They went shopping at Harrod's for tea bags and then to Karnac's bookstore. Khan bought her a one-volume Shakespeare as a gift and other books by Rousseau, Montaigne, Mallarme, and Freud to have for him when he visited. She left the next morning, her suitcase heavy with books. The quick visit had helped them to reconnect. Khan wrote in his Work Book that he was glad that Fleur's mother had sent her letter: "I feel a strange gratitude [for the] acid letter. It gave the cause (how one needs causes!) to reach out to [Fleur] and ask her to fly over. This short intimate visit has completed [our] stay together *chez elle* in Paris. Now we do not need to hide our relationship from anyone."[43]

The two relaxed into easy relating by phone and letter. At Easter time, Khan went back to Paris for a ten-day visit. Their relationship was now public, and they socialized as a couple with Khan's friends, Fleur's friends, and Fleur's brother. During the day, while Fleur worked, Khan read books and wrote a paper, "L'Armature des Femmes."[44]

In March 1980, Khan decided to stop writing his Work Books. He told the Stollers that he stopped because the work interfered with his freedom. The very last entry (page 3045) of his thirteen-year project was written about Fleur:

> How silly it is that even in the privacy of this Work Book, I go round and round not saying that, for the first time since Svetlana, I am in love. I am in love with [Fleur] and I experience this ego state (to use an analytic banality) as both embarrassing and absurd at my age. I am 56 [he was actually 55], [Fleur] is 31. A quarter of a century separates us in calendar time! I have only a short time left to live, and all experiences with me are as intense as they are fugitive. I cannot build, only consume myself with emotions. Hence I must protect the Other, now [Fleur], from myself.[45]

Khan and Fleur stayed involved with each other for the rest of the year. In May, she came to London to nurse him when he was ill.[46] His illness was related to the fact that he had started drinking heavily once again.[47] Fleur was also there in June when he got in trouble with the police for denting a vehicle while parking his car, then leaving the scene of the accident. At the end of June, she was with him when he gave a lecture on countertransference at a meeting organized by Pearl King— and then returned home and got drunk.

In August, Fleur went with Khan to Pakistan. They met with Jamil Nishtar and Ijaz Batalwi in Lahore, and then went on to Kot Fazaldad Khan. It was, according to Khan, still a thriving estate, with a staff of twenty-five. Writing from Pakistan, Khan commented, "[Fleur] adores it here and she is much loved by everyone; because she is shrewdly observant, says little and is naturally compassionate. She has learnt a few native words and uses them with a droll accent, which endears her to everyone. In local native clothes, no one can tell she is French, the clothes are so natural to her."[48]

By autumn, the seeming return from the dead was over. Smirnoff wrote to Stoller about a meeting with Khan in Paris where he had lost the gay and creative mood of a few months earlier: "He is now on and off the bottle and entirely self-centered, egotistic & immersed in a megalomanic narcissism. Over lunch, we heard nothing but the repetitious account of his estates: 7 Rolls Royces, 37 servants, his gun-men and his bodyguards."[49]

Fleur was still in Khan's life in December, but in an uncertain status, as Smirnoff noted: "[Fleur] is still around: Masud has claimed to have married her in Pakistan without her knowledge or consent."[50] Smirnoff went on to say that although he thought one of Fleur's reasons for getting involved with Khan was because "she had some small feuds to settle with her mother & family," another reason was this: "Let's be fair—Masud can be at times, even now, a pretty fascinating figure." There is no evidence to support the idea that there was a marriage in Pakistan.

And then? The details of the ending of the relationship are unknown, because the Work Books stop and Fleur is unwilling to talk about what happened. They went one more time to Pakistan in the summer of 1981, and then apparently broke up, with Fleur continuing to live in Paris. One thing she did tell me in a very short telephone conversation was that the relationship with Khan remains a precious memory.

CHAPTER 3 6

LATE CLINICAL WORK
(INTERVIEWS)

[T]he clinical process gradually involves two persons in a mutuality of
relating and, if things fare well, in time enables them to part from each
other in a state of grace and awakened unto their hidden selves.
Masud Khan[1]

Even in his most disturbed periods, Khan still saw patients. Sometimes
clinical work was his only connection to the outside world. In later years,
he still had the capacity to see a person's potential and inspire change,
but alcoholism and the abandonment of boundaries led to work that was
at times shoddy and even damaging. The high quality of his clinical
thinking can be seen in selected parts of his last books (MK3 and MK4),
as Khan writes about the therapeutic problem of "holding" and "managing" while still maintaining the highest goal of helping the patient to
achieve a breakthrough to the authentic self. His insistence at times on
the acceptability of the analyst's "action" to assist in reaching the treatment goal is less compelling.

The American psychologist/psychoanalyst Harriette Kaley was living in
London in 1977, and she decided to see a few of the psychoanalytic
"greats" for supervision. One of the people she chose was Khan, who at
that time still had a good reputation. Her account shows Khan's erratic
capacity for clinical discipline at a time when he was recovering from a
second bout with cancer and well on the way to becoming severely
alcoholic. Kaley knew nothing about his private life, but it was obvious
to her that he was not a psychologically healthy man:

In 1977, Masud was extremely, painfully boastful, rambling at times, even tangential. Nevertheless, he was erratically and from time to time clinically astute.

He told a story about a patient from that morning who had arrived early and asked the houseboy for a glass of water, which the houseboy brought. Then, in the session, the patient started to complain about the analysis and was feeling hopeless. Khan asked him to describe what he had been experiencing just prior to the session, and the patient told him about the houseboy and the water. Khan replied, "I will see to it in the future that your thirst is not assuaged. In analysis, you must keep the pain alive, you don't put a boundary on it."

Khan himself described good work in this period with a young man who would have been seen as an impossible patient by most analysts:

[A former patient] called at 5:00 pm. He looks like Prince Myshkin: pale, insufferably soulful. But what a difference! The boy of sixteen, whom his father brought some eighteen months ago—from a drug-cure unit [outside of London]—fratricidal in act (not just fantasy), hallucinated and crazy. Today he was humble, in his person and self-knowing: aware of his acute vulnerability to himself and his absolute demands upon himself. Timorous and brave with all his fragilities. It so reassured me about myself. I saw him some fifty sessions or so in all—if that. And I was in my worst period of starting to drink heavily after the second cancer operation. Yet I seem to have done more for this lad than all the psychiatrists he had seen.[2]

And Barrie Cooper remembers: "Masud was still able to help patients after his cancer. One man was a foreign journalist I knew. He said that Masud was the greatest influence of his life. I once asked him, 'So what helped?' and he said, 'He alone understood me.'" I talked with this patient on the telephone and he said that Cooper spoke accurately and Khan had saved his life.

The accounts below of Khan's analysis of a man and his supervision of two therapists give further evidence of the mixed quality of his work.

INTERVIEW WITH THE EX-WIFE
OF ANALYSAND GUSTAV (1975-1986)

A more detailed account of Khan's work from the postcancer period
comes from the ex-wife of Gustav (pseudonym), a now-deceased
analysand. The account, from an interview in 1999, illustrates Khan's
willingness to work with difficult people and the way in which he shared
a social life with certain patients.

> Gustav was from a lower-middle-class background in the north of England;
> he was an unsophisticated and untraveled lad who became relatively
> smooth. We married in 1960 and had two children, a son and a daughter.
>
> He became a successful patent agent.[3] He was extremely good at his
> job, because he was intelligent, obsessive-compulsive, and manipulative.
> He convinced people that he could not tell even the smallest and whit-
> est of lies. Masud himself told me that because Gustav had such integ-
> rity, he was making him his trustee, along with the solicitor Paul Kimber,
> the bookseller Harry Karnac, and his analyst friend Robert Stoller of
> UCLA—though in fact he didn't do so.
>
> It was only after many years that I discovered that Gustav was de-
> ceiving people most of the time, often just for the pleasure of it. He spoke
> in part-truths and ambiguities, so that it was your fault if you "misunder-
> stood." He used to say, with satisfaction: "Patent agents need a devious
> mind." He was not normally a creative person, except for gardening,
> which he loved and had a great talent for.[4]
>
> Gustav had a nervous breakdown in the summer of 1970. Our local
> National Health Service (NHS) physician prescribed antidepressants,
> which were of no help. Then a friend recommended that he see
> Dr. Barrington Cooper, a highly skilled private physician and psycho-
> therapist. Dr. Cooper referred him to various analysts over the next five
> years and continued to see Gustav himself. Whenever any treatment
> showed signs of working, Gustav would find a way to sabotage it. He
> himself used to say to me when seeing a new doctor or analyst: "One more
> professional to outwit."
>
> On Friday, 22 August 1975, he started seeing Masud. His diagnosis
> from the NHS doctor was "therapeutically resistant personality dis-
> order with depression." Dr. Cooper told me that he had wanted to send
> him to Masud first, but the time had not been right.

I first met Masud on 26 August, 1975, when I was summoned to attend Gustav's session. When I arrived, he was lying as if catatonic on the couch, curled in a fetal position with his back to the room. Masud asked me: "Look at your husband lying rigid over there—how would you feel if he were dead?" Ambushed like this, I was astonished to find that my first thought was that it would be a relief. But then I looked at him there on the couch and felt great pity and caring, and I said: "I don't think I know the answer to that." I knew that Masud had observed all my feelings.

Gustav came out of his state and Masud and I went on talking for a bit. I remember that it was high summer, and I was wearing a gaudy 1970s outfit, while Gustav was in a charcoal gray formal suit. Masud commented on the contrast between us, one dark, rigid and tightly shut, the other bright and open to feelings—he searched for a word to describe how I was, and came up with "shimmering." I'm sure he meant my changing expressions and emotions as much as my bright pink, blue, and white clothes. That was the only time I came to a consultation.

I thought Masud was helping Gustav. He became less volatile. I was impressed that he always seemed slightly scared of Masud, which was unusual for him. When Masud got cancer, G. was angry that he had to stop treatment for a while.

Masud made friends of many patients, and my ex-husband was one. I don't think he was capable of deep friendship, but with Masud, it was just that they enjoyed each other. We started socializing with him as a couple after a few years.[5]

I liked Masud very much. I wasn't at all scared of him, as many people were. I found him challenging and stimulating. You felt alive in his presence. His eyes were piercing and they held yours—there wasn't any point in trying to hide anything. He always spoke with great emphasis and you had the impression of submerged power. Liz, Dr. Cooper's practice nurse, who dealt with Masud as a patient, said to me recently: "What I remember most about Masud is his gentleness." Actually, I don't think of him that way at all. But perhaps that's because I always saw him with Gustav, when Masud was the reverse of a patient.

Gustav complained that Masud had no sense of humor, and he may have been right. I never saw him have a really uncontrolled laugh, and I don't even remember him smiling. But he was not malevolent, not at all. Perhaps he was benevolent, although that may be too strong, because he always had a reserve.

The kids met him two or three times. First, one sunny Saturday, we had tea at his place. Masud played backgammon with our son, who suddenly cried indignantly: "You're cheating!" Masud answered: "I always cheat!" (Gustav used to play backgammon with Masud also, during their sessions.) Another time we all went to dinner at Palace Court. And at Christmas, 1983, we invited Masud to spend December 26 with us, along with his then-secretary, Theresa [disguised name]. I remember all those occasions as happy and enjoyable.

Earlier in 1983, Gustav had started an affair with Theresa. Then she stopped working and Gustav "kept" her. In 1987, they had a baby together. I of course knew nothing of this.

He was planning to retire early to create a landscape garden. Early in 1987 we had bought a house on five acres in beautiful countryside far from London. During the week, we lived near his job in London, and then we went to the country for weekends. That year he was particularly bad-tempered and remote. He said we were short of cash, and he borrowed from my pension fund.

Then one Sunday in 1988, when we were in the country, I happened on a puzzling letter. Gustav had brought a gaping briefcase with financial documents prominent and he left them out for me to "find." He was working in the garden, as usual, when I discovered the papers, some of which related to Theresa and the baby. I saw that Gustav had been lying about our finances, saying we hardly had any money when actually there was a lot there. I suddenly understood that this man had long had an elaborate deception going. I had thought that when he hurt people, he did not know, and could not help it. Now I saw in a flash that he knew, and enjoyed it.

He argued that I had given him permission to have the affair. Once when the three of us were dining with Masud in 1983, while Theresa was out of the room, Masud had warned Gustav: "Your feelings for that girl are sexual." I laughed and said: "If you prefer her, you are welcome." I was being ironic, as he knew. But he said he had taken the remark to be literal.

I think he stopped seeing Masud for therapy in 1986. He and Theresa broke up in 1988, I filed for divorce in 1989, and we were then divorced in 1991. After the divorce, he became increasingly depressed and, at times, violent. His professional success continued, but he had a heart attack in 1989, and then died in 1995.

I can't speak for Gustav, but I myself feel stronger for having known Masud. There was something in him that accepted you and saw you as a

person—which implies that you have a sort of value. I was at my weakest
then, and I wasn't very good at feeling valued. He would ask questions
as if he was interested in your reply. He seemed to believe that you had
a right to say what you thought, even if he didn't agree. I find it stimulating to be with someone who's opinionated—I guess I'm attracted to
totally impossible men!

The patient in Khan's article "Outrage, Compliance and Authenticity" (1985a) is almost certainly a collage of various people including Gustav.
In this late writing, Khan did not bother to do much disguising of the case,
and many details fit. His patient is described as an extremely successful
married man with two children, of humble origins, with a brother six years
younger, and a talent for gardening. Furthermore, the man had had two
prior analyses, was referred by a physician who was also Khan's physician, and was seen during a time that overlapped Khan's cancer. All these
are accurate for Gustav. According to the ex-wife, however, about half of
the other facts reported do not fit him, and some important information
about him is totally absent.

The article is an account of noninterpretive work using play and
"management" in an analysis that included outside social contacts. The
goal was to help the patient to find his True Self, and the work was
greatly helped when Khan insisted, years into the treatment, on
having the entire family to dinner. Khan discovered, to his surprise,
that they were "a handsome and joyous family" (p. 124). He then made
use of his familiarity with the wife and children to give the patient
specific advice about being more interactive, and within the year, by
Khan's report, the patient and his family were thriving. Khan appears
to have claimed a greater success than is warranted, given what happened next.

Gustav's ex-wife is not critical of Khan's extraanalytic socializing,
which she believes was helpful. In the 1985 article, Khan wrote: "When
I think a patient, as a person, needs me to hold him by acting, i.e. managing his private life, I act; not always wisely, but never to my personal
benefit" (p. 118). Unlike some other cases where there was "management," he did live up to the quote in treating Gustav—the socializing
was done for the patient, not for Khan's personal gain, perhaps in part
because Barrie Cooper was always there watching.

INTERVIEW WITH SUPERVISEES SUSIE ORBACH
AND LUISE EICHENBAUM (1979)

What follows is an account from two feminist object-relations–oriented therapists, Susie Orbach and Luise Eichenbaum, who saw Khan for supervision in 1979. Although young, they had already made significant contributions to re-envisioning a psychoanalysis that could include the feminist cause. Together, they had founded the Women's Therapy Centre in London, a clinic that recently celebrated its twenty-fifth anniversary. They had written several papers together on the topic of women's issues and they had been commissioned to write a book, *Understanding Women: A Feminist Psychoanalytic Approach*.[6] Orbach had already published a best seller, *Fat Is a Feminist Issue*,[7] that had given her an international reputation.

Eichenbaum and Orbach met with Khan just as he was coming out of his psychotic Prince Myshkin identification and immersing himself in reading and writing about Dostoevsky. They had not heard that he was psychologically and physically ill; they knew only that he had been close to Winnicott and that he was familiar with the work of Fairbairn, Guntrip, and Winnicott. Khan wrote that he was pleased to see two intelligent, eager, and attractive "girls" who were "militant feminists."[8]

Susie and Luise are still close friends, although Luise practices in New York City whereas Susie is still in London. They were interviewed separately in 1998, and their story is told using excerpts from both interviews.

> L.E.: We saw Khan at his mansion flats at Palace Court in Bayswater. His housekeeper would take us to this massive room, I don't know if it was a consulting room or a living room. His chair there was a "throne"— wooden, with a high back.
>
> I remember the first meeting very well. In walks this incredible looking man. He was strikingly handsome—tall and dark-skinned. He wore all black, with a shirt that was buttoned up to the neck. And he had no voice—he had to whisper.
>
> Each time we went, one of us would present a case. He obviously was formulating things in his mind as he listened, but he didn't ask questions. He viewed himself as the authority and he would respond with a summary statement that seemed classical or even Kleinian. You couldn't

detect the influence of Winnicott. There were lots and lots of references
to penis envy in his statements.

Here's an example. Once I was presenting the case of a woman who
was single, but wanted a baby. She was having artificial insemination. He
fixated on that and said: "Of course you can never give her what she needs,
because you don't have a penis." I did think about that a lot—I still don't
know if I think he was right.

S.O.: I knew ten minutes into the first meeting that I didn't want to go
back. I didn't like the way he treated us and I didn't trust him. I thought
it was ludicrous that he sat on this carved, raised pseudo-throne. I went
back only because Luise wanted to.

The second time we came, he gave each of us a copy of a book by the
Marquis de Sade to read. It was a sexual thing. We were attractive and
cute and, because of the strength of our feminism, we had lots of bra-
vado. I didn't like it that sexual ideas were being dealt with in this way.

L.E.: I think he thought we were lesbians (which we aren't) and he was
having sexual fantasies about us as lovers. Did he say that to us? I don't
remember.

He talked a lot about himself, and it didn't always seem relevant. We
were often impatient with his stories. And he told us one bizarre, chill-
ing story that I will never forget. I usually only tell this at dinner parties
after I've had a few glasses of wine:

He had a patient who came to him with his [large] dog. The dog
would lie by the side of the couch. The man was quite hostile and aggressive. One day he was talking about something and Khan could tell
from what he was saying that the dog was going to attack him. So he stood
up, reached over to his desk, and picked up a letter opener in the shape
of a knife. He slit the throat of the dog from ear to ear—he demonstrated
that for us![9] He said he had to do this to show that man that he would
not be able to destroy his analyst with his aggression.

After we heard that story, we really thought he was mad. We went
back only one more time, to terminate.

Even if there is some value to this supervision, Khan's sexual provo-
cations and the ridiculous dog story show that he was out of control in
his work. The dog story he told is a wild elaboration of an earlier story
that may be accurate, in which Khan reported that he jumped out from

behind a door in order to frighten a patient who had brought his intimidating dog to a session (see Chapter 15). Since the supervisory sessions occurred during Khan's Dostoevsky period, it may be of note that
in *The Idiot*, Rogozhin kills Nastasia Filippovna with a knife that he had
been using as a bookmark.

Another part of the account of Khan's late clinical work is the follow-
up work he did with former patients. He often saw former patients for
short consultations after their treatment had ended, a common practice.
But as he lost control in the 1980s, he traumatized returning patients
who had never before seen him act unprofessionally. L.U., an analysand
whose treatment had ended in 1964 (see Chapter 6), told me:

> I went back to him again in 1981. I went for a small problem, perhaps
> two or three times. As we talked, he was drinking red wine and he was
> really quite crazy. He said to me "You must come for seven sessions,"
> and I agreed, even though I didn't know why he was saying seven. After
> three or four meetings, I realized that I could deal with the problem
> myself, so I said that we didn't need to meet anymore. And a week later
> he sent me a very unpleasant letter, demanding that I pay for the extra
> sessions to make a total of seven. Even though I thought he was raving
> mad, I wrote back. I had to preserve his and my dignity by making a re-
> sponse. I said that I would not pay more and I was confident that this
> disagreement wouldn't disturb our relationship. I never heard from him
> again.
>
> I now see that he was a broken man, broken in every way, physically
> as well as psychologically. And I am of two minds. The two minds are
> these: One, I would like to have comforted him, even though he was
> probably too proud to be comforted. And two, I now look on him as a
> monster, a monster who had been held in check by Winnicott, who was
> no longer there to control him.

Some former analysands were forced to deal with Khan's deterioration over time because they had maintained an active relationship with
him. These social experiences were not helpful. H.K. (whose analysis
ended in 1967; see Chapter 6) and John Mallinson (whose analysis ended
in 1969; see Chapter 9) describe taking care of the man who had once
cared for them:

H.K.: After our son's death, I felt I owed Masud such a debt. In the 1980s
he was having a hard time in life, and he turned to me for support. I let
him call me late at night and I listened to him tell me all his woes. I felt
pity for him. He would come into my bookstore and steal books, and when
he got caught I lied for him, telling my workers that he had already paid
for the books at the other shop. They all knew the truth.

In 1984, when I sold my bookstore, Masud got into a rage that I
hadn't consulted him first. I was 65 years old!

The final break took place about a year or two later. I had called him
about something and when he answered the phone, I said: "Hello Masud,
[H.K.] here, how are you?" His response: "Don't you dare address me
like that, you fucking Yiddisher tradesman, I'm a Prince!" He then went
into a string of vituperative insults.

Although it was not the first time he had subjected me to such insults, it was at that point that I hung up and knew that I was now rid of
the debt it had taken me so many years to expunge.

John Mallinson: I would go with Masud and other analysands or former
analysands for a meal or to late-night cinemas. Usually he had a paternal
or avuncular presence, but when there had been too much whiskey, he
was unpleasant, abusive, and confabulatory. He never abused me (to my
face, anyway) but I regret that I was not capable of confronting him when
he was in this state. I was very slow to appreciate just how devastating
the effects of the drinking were. As the years passed and his problems
worsened it became more and more difficult and painful to visit him. I
had very mixed feelings: outrage at his behavior, sadness at the waste,
and extreme boredom. It is surprising to realize that I must have known
him for about thirty years, but the good memories are all from the early
years in the 1960s. My main feeling now is sadness that he couldn't save
himself.

Eva, the analysand who had had an affair with Khan in the late 1960s
(see Chapter 23), continued to care about him and see him, all the way
to his death. She remembers: "[In the 1980s] Masud had a madness about
him. He had been an extremely powerful influence on me and when he
started messing up that authority, you can imagine how disturbing it
was." The charismatic analyst who had enabled Eva to find her own voice
for the first time had been gone for more than a decade.

When people end a successful analysis, they take with them an internal experience that helps them for the rest of their life. If the analyst interacts with the former analysand in a "real" way posttreatment, the internal experience is compromised, and this is why analysts and analysands are advised not to have social relationships when the treatment ends. Winnicott had gone on to have a "real" relationship with Khan but at least in some ways, the postanalytic relating was healthy and constructive, in contrast to Khan's postanalytic relating where his personal neediness had a primarily destructive impact. His former analysands provided him with the kind of care that should have been provided by an extended family or others from Khan's private life, but Khan had nobody to do that for him.

PART 9

MAJESTY AND INCAPACITY

(1981–1989)

Lear: Who is it that can tell me who I am?
Fool: Lear's shadow.
King Lear, I.iv.236–237

For me, the tragedy of [King] Lear rests in the paradox of a majesty
impaled upon an incapacity. This is what lends his imperious
hauteur its absurd pathos. He demands to be an infant
from desire and he claims to be royal without a kingdom.
Masud Khan[1]

THE SHADOW OF A MAN

You have so much inside of you that has scarcely been tapped. But you
cannot simply wait for it to flow out, as was the case in the past. You now
have to warm your cold soul, and that will take courage and persistence.
Letter, Robert Stoller to Masud Khan[1]

Khan's belief in the importance of play was central to his personality,
and for his first fifteen years in the West, he had played very well with
his friends. He told stories, lied, and cheated as part of his play, but the
Westerners understood this and enjoyed him.[2] Zoë Dominic told me
affectionately: "Sud was such a piece of fiction. He had a habit of telling
anecdotes so that you couldn't tell if it was a fable or the truth." She
called this habit his "fable manner." Several people remembered that
Masud loved to say: "If you want facts, go to the encyclopedia. If you
want to talk with me, I'll tell you a story." Ironically, it was a bad sign
when he was factual. Barrie Cooper told me: "You could tell when Masud
was drunk, because then he didn't lie."

As Khan deteriorated, it was no longer fun to play with him or to
listen to his distortions. (See Chapter 15 for a description of the deterioration of Khan's clinical work using play.) In earlier times, he could
be a good loser when he played games, but increasingly throughout the
1970s, he had to win at any cost and he sulked if he lost. One acquaintance from this period told me, "Masud used games as a way to take
power. And as he played the games, he broke every rule there was to
break. He would do anything to win."[3]

Starting in about 1979, in the Dostoevsky period, Khan began to sign
his letters "Prince/Raja M. Masud R. Khan" and he had the titles printed

on his cards and his stationery. The title Raja was not false—in the world
of his childhood, it was an honorary designation given to people of importance. But claiming to be a prince *was* false,[4] and this pretension did
not go over well in the West, even with those who believed it was accurate. Khan mocked the colleagues who believed his lies: "I stand away
from myself and watch with a wry amusement how I befuddle others
with my confabulations. When I really say something factual, they are
instinctively suspicious and questioning."[5] His lies became offensive and
they were no longer entertaining to others; cf. "When Masud would say:
'I am the product of 700 years of feudalism,' he was telling us that he
had to be treated with special regard owing to his princely condition."[6]

An outright lie that Khan told often was that he had some kind of
close connection to Britain's royal family. Many of his friends believed
him, especially those who were not British. An anonymous member of
his Paris circle told me, in all seriousness, "Masud was on the 'Queen's
List' and he was regularly invited to Buckingham Palace." Friends remember that he told his houseboy to say he was "at the palace" when he
did not want to answer the phone. In response to a letter from Khan
claiming that he had been invited to attend the wedding of Princess
Diana and Prince Charles on July 29, 1981, Robert Stoller wrote: "The
wedding. On this subject I have only one thought: how much we shall
enjoy talking with you about the ceremony."[7]

Yet another lie involved his formal education. He had an M.A. from
the University of the Punjab, but he now claimed that he also had a
doctorate in literature and at times added the initials D. Litt. to the "Raja/
Prince M. Masud Khan" on his stationery.

The deteriorating situation is well summarized by Eva: "[In the
1980s], Masud was changing right in front of my eyes. Storytelling was
becoming suspiciously like confabulation. One could not disbelieve
everything, because his life was truly peppered with drama and the dramatis
personae had been impressive in many areas—social, political, and cultural. But the game got out of hand. Was he dining with the Queen, as I
once heard him claim to a caller? Probably not. Did he bring about the
fall of Bhutto? Goodness only knows. [The reference is to Pakistani Prime
Minister Zulfikar Ali Bhutto, who was ousted from power and hanged in
1979.] Did he really have a beautiful red-haired daughter whose mother
was Russian?[8] I doubted it. The confabulatory tendency accelerated as

time went on. One no longer knew how to respond. Did he believe him-self? Did he believe we believed him?"

Robert Stoller described the same experience using clinical termi-nology: "[Masud] is more grandiose than he should be. His story telling does not return to its softer, lower keyed, joking tale-telling. The line inside of him that used to mark for him the difference between reality and fantasy has become permanently smeared and makes him vulner-able to being flat-out delusional."[9]

Many things were changing in Khan's world as the decade of the 1980s began. In 1981, Jacques Lacan died, as did Ralph Greenson. In March 1982, Anna Freud had a serious stroke, and in October, she too died. Clare Winnicott died in 1984. And two favored students were prepar-ing to leave town: Christopher Bollas for the United States and Andreas Giannakoulas for Rome.[10]

He still had followers, but they were not students from the institute. The admiring crowd at Palace Court was all male at this time. His profes-sional acquaintances viewed the scene with disgust: "Masud had an extra-ordinarily beautiful armchair and it was in the center of his living room. It was like a Bishop's chair or a throne. He would sit there, dominating the whole room, and all the others would sit around him."[11] "Masud liked to 'hold court.' He enjoyed that power and influence. But it didn't seem natu-ral to me, even though it was quite lively. I liked Masud better in smaller groups, where he didn't 'put on the style.'"[12] The same phenomenon oc-curred in Paris: "Masud had a 'court' in Paris. People would say 'Oh, Masud is here,' and everyone would come running. He acted like a prince."[13]

On March 11, 1982, Tahir died. Masud and Tahir had stopped speak-ing in 1977 after Tahir, thinking that Masud was about to die from can-cer, had asked him for power of attorney over his estate. Indignant that Tahir was even thinking about his death, Masud denied the request without discussion. But when Tahir was hospitalized for a heart attack five years later, the brothers reconciled and Masud arranged for Tahir to be transferred to a private clinic. Four days later, Tahir had a second and fatal heart attack.[14]

Khan's older half-siblings were also dying. In 1983 alone, he lost three half-brothers, two half-sisters, and three cousins, leading him to comment: "The clan has almost disintegrated."[15]

As the decade progressed, he lived out the T. S. Eliot phrase that he had often quoted: "In my beginning is my end." His Eastern origins were what mattered to him now: "Nothing roots me in London but my work, my books and my lithographs, and the space they need."[16] He returned to reading Persian and Urdu poetry, untranslated, and he acted out the role of a feudal landlord: Westerners were welcome only if they were willing to be in his service, the subjects of his whims.[17] His former friend André Green wrote to him: "We are different. But the main difference as it appears to me, between us, is that you believe more & more in feudalism and less & less in psycho-analysis; as for me, it is the contrary."[18] Khan replied acidly: "I do not believe 'more and more' in feudalism. I never lapsed from a total belief in it. . . . I have never believed in psychoanalysis, neither as a science nor as a therapeutic technique. [My participation in the psychoanalytic world] was a 'conniving complicity'—for some two decades I exercised a 'willing suspension of disbelief'—but now I disown it totally."[19] It is difficult to know how seriously to take this cynical comment.

In the early 1980s, Khan still had some significant professional accomplishments. He told Robert Stoller in 1981 that there were things he wanted to write about: "The solution, the only one left, is output, since I refuse in-put."[20] And he did keep writing: he had articles published in the *Nouvelle Revue de Psychanalyse* (NRP) in 1979, 1980, 1981, 1982, 1984, 1985, and 1987.[21] After years of relative silence, he returned to a regular correspondence with Robert Stoller, who responded with pleasure: "Now that you are standing again—strong, free, and with proper Masudic arrogance—your letters are once more a joy."[22] But Stoller did not forget the severity of Khan's psychopathology: "Perhaps some day you will tell us about the unseen part of you that finally was generous enough to let free its terrible, murderous grip."[23]

In October 1981, Khan asked the Stollers to be his literary executors in the event of his death, and to handle the American portion of his finances. Robert wrote back that they would be pleased to take this on: "Yes. Both Sybil and I accept the responsibilities outlined and will see that your wishes in all these regards are carried out. You need think no further on this; we shall do the job."[24]

Most of the events of Khan's life in 1982 are unknown. His summer visit to Pakistan was canceled when he fell ill with a problem that may have been kidney cancer. The new estate manager Nazir Ahmed (son of the former estate manager Mustaq Ahmed) flew to London to consult with him about various matters and they planned extensive renovations at Kot Fazaldad Khan.

When Khan went to Pakistan in March 1983, he found that Nazir Ahmed had put the plans into action. The mansion had been renovated and redecorated: "The real surprise was my retreat, especially the study and the bedroom. There was a 17th century Persian carpet for the bedroom, two tables with drawers, one for drawing and one for writing, a table with electric lamp, and a sugar bottle in case I have an insomniac need for tea at 2 a.m."[25] By Khan's report, there were 500 people on the estate, including Muslim peasants of different factions, one Christian, and an Iranian scholar who recited the Koran daily at Fazaldad's grave.

In 1983, Khan's book *Hidden Selves* was published by Hogarth. The most colloquial of his three good books, it includes detailed accounts of his clinical work. The reported technique was unorthodox, but he was still respectful of analytic tradition and still working in the service of his analysands. Robert Stoller wrote: "You create the clinical moment so that it becomes real."[26] *The International Journal of Psycho-Analysis* (IJPA) published a review that was four pages long and positive: "[T]he papers in this book provocatively question traditional metapsychology and technique. . . . There are many novel and unique ideas presented, and the case material makes for fascinating reading, richly and vividly portraying the patients, the analyst, their interactions, and the 'holding space' of the analyst's consultation room."[27]

His international reputation was intact, thanks to the inefficiency of communication in that era.[28] His peers in Britain, however, finally understood that the quality of his professional work did not match his reputation. In 1984 they took away his last official position when the Publications Committee informed him that he could no longer be consultant editor at the IJPA. Khan said he did not care.

Barrie Cooper remembers that, even in his last years, Khan could be a delight and an inspiration. But at times he put severe strains on their friendship, as in this story from the 1980s:

I was giving my daughter an engagement party. About 150 friends were
at my house, and one friend was Masud. It was a very "white-ish" apartment, with lots of white furniture. Masud arrived late and he got increasingly drunk and angry because there were a lot of literary and theatrical
types there, and nobody was paying attention to him. He didn't stand
out in that group—they were just as interesting as he. So he deliberately
cut himself with the cutlery. He bled extensively over a very white sofa.
We bandaged him up and I actually had to leave the party to take him
home, because he was incompetent to drive. My daughter said to me later:
"Daddy, I always told you Masud would go to any length to fuck up anything that didn't involve him."

The next day he called, apologized and sent flowers. "Can I buy you
a new settee?'" he asked, "Can I buy you a new house?"

The Canadian author Phyllis Grosskurth, who became a friend of
Khan in the late 1970s, remembers an upsetting interaction from a time
when she visited in the early 1980s with her son: "My son was talking
about something and Masud suddenly whipped out a knife and held it
at his throat. We didn't know where it came from. We left immediately
in a minicab that Masud called, and my son, who was terrified and shattered, said to me, 'I will not meet any more of your friends!'" A few years
later, in 1984 or 1985, she saw Masud one last time at a meeting of the
1952 Club: "He was brutal to me, telling lies and claiming that I had
said things that I had never said. I was amazed that his peers just tolerated his behavior without interfering."[29]

But Khan could still attract women. In the early 1980s, his partner was
his niece Bibi Shehnaz ("Giggles"), the daughter of his half-brother Salah
(see Chapter 32).[30] Bibi came to London to work as his secretary and by
1983, a year and a half after Fleur and Khan had broken up, Bibi and Khan
were living together and presenting themselves as a couple. Most people
who knew them feel certain that their relationship included a sexual connection, although there is no documentation of that. Although this was
not a great love affair, she helped him to stabilize his life. He ate and slept
on a more regular schedule and he started inviting people to dinner again.

Khan and Bibi went to Pakistan for a long visit in 1984, from July to
November, and he celebrated his sixtieth birthday there. The reason for
the unusually long visit was that he was exhausted. For the first time, he
referred his patients to other analysts for the duration of his absence. In

Pakistan, he stayed in bed all day, except for business meetings and two occasions when he made a brief appearance at family weddings. Bibi lived separately, in the ladies' quarters.

One of his goals on this trip was to do a major reorganization of Kot Fazaldad Khan and the other pieces of Pakistani real estate that he still owned. Working with his banker friend Jamil Nishtar, Khan sold various assets, with the goal of raising cash that he could transfer to London. He also fought for the return of some of the land that the government had confiscated—a battle that he won. The business matters were not easy to complete: "Nothing happened the first month, because in the bureaucracy of Pakistan, there is no today, only yesterday and tomorrow, with that fleeting moment when 'yesterday' slips into 'tomorrow'— and everyone is trying to catch that moment."[31] By the end of the visit, he had sufficient funds to allow him to live comfortably in London, even with a reduced income from clinical practice.

Accompanied by Bibi, he returned to London on November 25. His mind was clear, but he did not feel well, probably due to his chronic liver condition. In August 1985, he developed acute toxic (alcoholic) hepatitis, a condition that was potentially fatal.[32] He was hospitalized for a month in the London Clinic, a private hospital across the street from Barrie Cooper's office. Prior to the hospitalization, he gave his power of attorney and permission to handle all business and personal affairs to Bibi.[33] Upon admission, he went into a coma, and Bibi was called upon to make numerous medical decisions, which she did in consultation with Sahabzada Yaqub Khan and Jamil Nishtar.

When Khan regained consciousness, the medication he had been given had damaged his larynx and possibly his heart and brain. A few months later, he wrote Smirnoff about the early days of recovery: "I had to stay in bed and I wasn't allowed to read or write. I had no memory and couldn't even complete a sentence because I would forget the first words I spoke."[34]

While Khan was in the London Clinic, he and Barrie Cooper had a clash that ended their relationship. Cooper had come into Khan's room one day to find him drinking a glass of burgundy, upon which Khan had asked Cooper to join him in a drink. Cooper remembers: "I asked the nurse how he had obtained wine despite my orders and she said, 'If *you* can't control him, then how can *we* control him?' I went back and I said, 'Masud, you are insulting me on my own territory.' On that, we broke."

With a new physician, Khan slowly began to recover, and after a month or more, he returned to Palace Court. His activity was restricted to seeing one patient a day, reading for no more than three hours, and answering correspondence. This was the sickest he had ever been. After two months of bed rest, he remained fatigued, and he was diagnosed with advanced cirrhosis of the liver.

Bibi returned with him to Pakistan where they stayed until March 1986. During this time, Khan organized the contents of his last book *The Long Wait*.[35] At last, he started to feel better.

In June, back in London, he received the news that Jamil Nishtar had died and he immediately left for Pakistan for the burial. Sahabzada Yaqub Khan remembers: "Masud arrived within forty-eight hours. His voice was hoarse and I told him he was looking slim. He said it was from alcohol." Yaqub Khan was impressed that Khan had gone to such effort when he was not well.

Later that summer, Bibi finally realized that she did not have much of a future with her Uncle Masud. Visiting Pakistan with him in August, she decided to stay there. She bought a house and moved in with her mother and brother. Soon after that, she got married and started a family. Khan was not bitter about the breakup. He told an (anonymous) friend that Bibi was going to be his heir, and, in the strange way that events unfolded around his death, that would turn out to be accurate.

With Bibi gone, Khan was without a woman. He told Sybil Stoller that he was doing fine: "I do my own shopping and find it is fun—more books than vegetables I confess."[36] But he told Victor Smirnoff that he was lonely: "Life is peaceful but empty. If you start shedding women at age 62, with one lung and one kidney, you are not likely to find someone tall and handsome! Then all you can pray for is the faith to go on hoping."[37]

He dealt with his loneliness by getting a dog. It was a King Charles Spaniel puppy named Jugnu Rajah, given to him by Mrs. Penning, his housekeeper.[38] He and Janet had had a King Charles Spaniel that he gave to Mrs. Penning when the relationship ended (see Chapter 26), and the new puppy may have been a descendant. He was devoted to his new pet; Jugnu Rajah sat at his feet throughout the day and shared his bed at night. Along with just a few of Khan's closest friends and associates, the dog would be there for him until his death.

CHAPTER 3 8

DEATH OF A MADMAN

*No one can really get the better of me. Only I have
the curious talent to do it for them, to myself.*
Masud Khan[1]

Masud has now made public that he is a madman.
Robert Stoller, *referring to* When Spring Comes[2]

In June 1987, Khan got bad news. The larynx irritation that had been
plaguing him for months was cancer. He was treated with radiation for
five weeks and there were major side effects—fatigue, insomnia, vomit-
ing, and a swelling of the throat such that food was limited to liquids
and he had no voice at all.

Although the cancer was thought to be inoperable, a laryngectomy
was performed a few months later. From this time on, his already-
compromised voice was a whisper, and speaking was such a strain that
he preferred total silence.[3]

By 1987, his ability to write "like an angel" was also gone. He took
advantage of old connections to publish an article in the *Bulletin of the
British Association of Psychotherapists.*[4] It was not up to the standard of his
previous work and it went unnoticed. Then Khan published a book that
suggested the influence of devils rather than angels. This book caused a
huge stir due to content that was offensive and outrageous.[5] Robert
Stoller commented with disgust that it was "a declaration of war on psychoanalytic institutions."[6]

The book was planned as a collection of clinical essays illustrating
the lasting impact of a person's childhood religion. The cases were

analysands who had transgressed against their early religious beliefs. Khan worked on it, he said, "with a lot of handicaps. The worst was not having anyone to discuss my work with, here in London."[7] John Charlton had accepted it for publication by Chatto & Windus in 1986 and, by the terms of the contract, Khan was allowed to be his own editor.

When Spring Comes: Awakenings in Clinical Psychoanalysis was published in 1988. (In the same year, a paperback edition was published in the United States under the title *The Long Wait.)* The text consists of seven clinical cases and an afterword. The chapters from the early 1980s are well-written descriptions of work with difficult patients, and there is important information about Khan's collaboration with Winnicott. But later chapters are poorly written, disorganized, and boastful, and often contain obscure personal references. For example, in a discussion of the idea that each therapist must find his/her own style of work, Khan wrote: "None should be pontifically instructed in this context [of being a therapist]. To do so is to sin against the Holy Ghost."[8]

The declaration of war was most obvious in a chapter entitled "A Dismaying Homosexual" that described an analysis Khan had done years earlier, when he was still married to Svetlana. The patient was a Jewish man who came to Khan as a last resort before killing himself. At one point, referring to a trip Khan was making to Chicago to be with Svetlana, the patient remarked: "But then a man will follow a dame anywhere. They call it loving." Khan writes that he responded with an anti-Semitic tirade that he claimed was therapeutic:

> One more personal remark about me, my wife, my staff or my things, and I will throw you out, you accursed nobody Jew. . . . Yes, I am anti-Semitic. You know why? Because I am an Aryan and had thought all of you Jews had perished when Jesus, from sheer dismay—and he was one of you—had flown up to Heaven, leaving you in the scorching care of Hitler, Himmler and the crematoriums. Don't fret . . . like the rest of your species, you will survive and continue to harass others and lament, and bewail yourselves.[9]

Khan's words shocked the patient out of his narcissistic self-absorption—and indeed, this is a report of an apparently successful analysis. The technique of mirroring the self-attack of a severely ill patient has a theoretical rationale,[10] but Khan provided no such explanation. It

seems clear that the account, which may not even be truthful, was meant
to shock.

Other chapters in the book also contained offensive material. Khan
refers to Yiddish colleagues, saying that they are some of the best analytic clinicians to be found, but "The yids certainly know how to climb
up. My profession is no exception."[11] He insults homosexuals: "Poofs,
especially the gilded ageing ones, do fill me with instant disgust and
disdain."[12] And explicit sexual details are reported regarding a promiscuous female patient, together with quotes of crude and overly sexual
interpretations he supposedly made.[13] Furthermore, Khan refers to having an "affectionate acquaintance" in private life with this patient,
implying that he was having a sexual relationship with her.

It was a book that could have been saved by editing out the offensive material. Instead of creating a firestorm, it could have been a valuable description of Khan's late ideas about how to help a person to
reclaim the self after a life of transgressions. This had been his intention when he submitted the proposal to Charlton a few years earlier. But
he was now more severely impaired than he had ever been. We get details of his state from an anonymous freelance technical editor who had
been hired by Charlton to get the chapters into publishable form (not
to check content):

I went to Palace Court for the first time in July 1986, and Khan handed
me the manuscript. Here was this man wearing a robe and no shoes, with
a haughty look and manner. I was totally unprepared for the strangeness
of the experience. He started blowing his own trumpet, telling me how
famous and rich he was. He said he had had cancer, but he was now cured.

I read the manuscript in one day and when I returned the next night,
I was very nervous. But he was charming—really, I was awed by him. He
called me by my first name and asked me to call him "Prince." I didn't
want to do that, so I just didn't call him anything.

The editing went on for months. I had thought he would be a col-
laborator, but he did very little—he couldn't sustain any work. I got way
too involved. I did secretarial work, which was not my job, and other
things too. Once I took him out to a bank and then to a shop, and he was
so arrogant, I was embarrassed to be with him. It was a Friday and he
said he was going to France for the weekend "to have lunch with President Mitterand." I disbelieved it.

I couldn't see his brilliance. But it was undeniable that there was in-coming correspondence from very notable people. And I had a friend who had been in treatment with him who had been greatly helped. I just didn't know what to believe. He talked about having a child, a daughter, and I thought it must be a delusion.[14]

After the laryngectomy, you had to communicate with him by notes. He just wanted to sit in the dark, smoking. He seemed to have given up on life—and I thought he was out of his mind.

Robert Stoller was horrified. He wrote to Smirnoff, "I found read-ing [the book] to be a most interesting experience—interesting in the way it is interesting to watch a kamikaze pilot in his final plunge."[15] Smirnoff wrote back that he thought that Khan was out of his mind and not responsible for what he had done.[16] Stoller agreed only that Khan was out of his mind—he was outraged at his friend, despite the sorry state of his mental health: "[Masud's] damnable book, with its gross, gauche, nasty-little-boy-piss-on-you scurrility, is a joke out of control."[17]

Most analysts whom I interviewed agree with Stoller that the book was inexcusable:

People in the British Society said goodbye to Masud when he wrote the book, not when he died. We thought, "We've forgiven Masud a lot, but this we won't forgive." (Pearl King)

He sent me a copy of that last book and I threw it away. I thought, He's spitting on and decrying the people who have cared most about him. He's going against everything he's taken from his spiritual mother and father, like a wild child. (Joyce McDougall)

Masud was mad by the time of his last book and he had the cunningness of the lunatic. (Harold Stewart)

Why did John Charlton allow the book to be published with Khan as sole editor of the content? Charlton was a highly respected figure in the world of psychoanalytic publishing, having worked for many years as the liaison between Hogarth and the International Psycho-Analytical Library (IPL). When Robert Stoller wrote asking why he had allowed the publication, Charlton replied that although he had not expected the book to be inflammatory, he was not sorry he had published it.[18] Ten years later, he told me he felt the same: "Even now, I don't wish we had taken the controversial passages out regarding the case of the homosexual man. If the words had been taken out, the chapter would have lost most of its point. As an editor I feel I owe it to my author to support him, and I still support the book."

There were no professional reviews. But Janet Malcolm, an American writer who is knowledgeable about psychoanalysis, published a review in the *New York Times Book Review*, saying that she was surprised and horrified by certain chapters: "Mr. Khan's transgressions against the minimum decencies of psychotherapeutic conduct are so extreme and so grotesque that midway through the book, one ceases to read it as an account of actual encounters with real people and begins to think of it as a kind of recurrent dream of grandiosity and omnipotence, dreamed by an analyst who has perhaps been in practice too long. . . . When one compares this outrageous and repellent book to the sane and civilized *Privacy of the Self* . . . one can only assume that something bad has happened to Mr. Khan in the intervening 15 years."[19]

Khan had prejudices against many groups in addition to Jews. His targets included Americans, the British, Hindus, feminists, and psychoanalysts in general.[20] Anti-Semitism, however, is so central to his legacy that it warrants separate consideration.

The literary scholar Anthony Julius suggests that in calling a person an anti-Semite, we should address the question of what *kind* of anti-Semite he is. Speaking of T. S. Eliot, he writes: "Anti-Semites are not all the same. Some break Jewish bones, others wound Jewish sensibilities. Eliot falls into the second category. He was civil to Jews he knew, offensive to those who merely knew him through his work."[21] Khan's anti-Semitism was of the wounding variety rather than the bone-breaking variety, similar to Eliot's.[22] A friend who was not an analyst said that Khan's anti-Semitism was "curiously unconvincing,"[23] and another friend commented: "Masud's anti-Semitism was a red herring. He was actually very interested in Jews—they were a fascinating subject that he wanted to understand. He used his apparent anti-Semitism to provoke people into talking about their Jewishness."[24] An analysand remembers that Khan supported the existence of Israel and "often used to maintain that there was nothing more impressive than a cultured Jew."[25] And an anonymous British analyst (who is Jewish) told me: "Anti-Semitism was not a central issue for Khan, he just went on about it sometimes. Had his patient in the final book not been Jewish, he would have been just as abusive about some other topic, in all likelihood."

As a child, Khan had not known Jews, and the racism he saw involved Hindus and Muslims. Several anonymous British analysts suggested to me that his anti-Semitism developed in England as an exaggerated mirroring of bigotry that he observed and experienced within the British Psycho-Analytic Society (BPAS). An anonymous Jewish peer said: "The British analysts used Masud to act out their own prejudices. They needed a Satan, and they chose a wonderful actor for their script." And a Protestant analyst told me that anti-Semitism still thrives in Britain and in the BPAS: "There is a high degree of tolerance for anti-Semitism in Britain and in the Society, whatever people may pretend."[26]

It is very difficult to know to what extent anti-Semitism (and its opposite) truly exists at the BPAS, because it is not a topic of open discussion. My own experience is that, in comparison to other analytic/ psychological groups, the BPAS is characterized by more thoughtfulness and tolerance than is average. Nevertheless, there is a history of Jewish–Protestant tension that can be documented. The tension roughly overlaps the clash between the Kleinians, who were mostly Jewish after the World War II emigrations, and the Middle Group/Independents, who were mostly Protestant.[27]

Certainly the BPAS that Khan entered was quite *aware* of the Jewish or non-Jewish identity of its members. Charles Rycroft, who was Protestant, told me how pervasive the tension could be: "Once I was talking to a colleague and I remarked that Masud was 'taller than the average analyst,' and my colleague accused me of being anti-Jewish." In another interview, Rycroft recalled:

At Society meetings, which were always terribly crowded, I remember Winnicott [who was Protestant] coming up to me, shaking me vigorously by the hand and saying, "Dr. Livingstone, I presume?" An anti-Semitic joke I think—It's what Stanley said when he met Livingstone in the middle of Africa. . . . The Society after the war was predominantly Jewish. It wasn't exactly a problem not to be, but you had to be careful. I think that was what he meant. It was a relief to meet a blond Gentile in the woods.[28]

A quote from Clare Winnicott adds to Rycroft's report: "[DWW] was very, very, very, very, very non-Jewish indeed. Very English, actually."[29] Clare seems to be implying that "English" and "Jewish" are mutually exclusive categories.

So Khan may have spoken in part for colleagues when he expressed anti-Semitism. But even if that is the case, open disrespect for Jews is something that has never been characteristic of any group of British analysts. Khan's lack of thoughtfulness about his bigotry is something that is totally unacceptable in an analyst, as he well knew.

The offensive (vs. playful) quality[30] of Khan's anti-Semitism increased over the years. In 1976, when he was disciplined by his peers, he developed a paranoid belief that the Jews in the group were purposely targeting him. With this belief in mind, he began to voice his prejudices with the single goal of being offensive. André Green told me: "In the early 70s, Masud wasn't openly anti-Semitic. That came only at the end after his cancer and after his loss of training status. Then he became anti-Semitic mostly against Hanna Segal." Barrie Cooper made a similar comment: "You don't find overt anti-Semitism [from Masud] before the Institute rejected him. The anti-Semitism was meant as an attack on his colleagues and the Institute. It was a 'professional' anti-Semitism."[31]

It is hard to know if Khan enjoyed the uproar he had created with his final book, since he was dying when it was published. He sat all day in a dark room, watching television and spending time only with his dog. Sometimes he just stared at the wall, not even bothering to turn on the television. He was so withdrawn and depressed that he had stopped writing letters or talking on the telephone.[32]

His peers knew about his poor health but felt that this time he had to be called to account for his outrageous behavior. Pearl King told me: "We knew Masud was dying, but we couldn't let him die having this book in print without our doing something about it." Five members of the society—Lionel Kreeger, Harold Stewart, Joseph Sandler, Malcolm

Pines, and an unknown fifth—made separate formal complaints about the anti-Semitic content of the book. In response, a special meeting of the council and the board of directors was called. At the meeting, Harold Stewart read aloud three offensive passages from *When Spring Comes* and announced that he personally would resign from the society if Khan was allowed to stay. The matter was referred to the newly established Ethical Committee for immediate study and recommendations for Executive Council action.

Once again, Pearl King was intimately involved in sanctioning the behavior of her "younger brother." She had established the Ethical Committee in 1984–5 and she was the current chair. She told me: "People were up in arms about the book, not just because of its anti-Semitism, but also because Masud was openly talking about breaking boundaries with patients. We knew he had been doing these things—we knew about his affair with his patient back in 1976, for example—but no patient had ever complained about him, so we couldn't act. Now we had written proof of his behavior, coming from Masud himself. We had to do something; it was not possible not to act."

Several members of the committee had dealt with Khan in 1976, and they regretted that they had allowed him to remain a member of the BPAS and to continue seeing nontrainee analysands. This time, they were determined to expel him. In June 1988, the committee issued a formal charge that Khan was "bringing psychoanalysis and the society into disrepute" by publishing accounts of patient treatment that were seen as abusive. (His anti-Semitism was not the focus of the charge, even though it had been the subject of the complaints.) The committee members made a unanimous recommendation that Khan be removed from membership, and the council, headed by the president of the BPAS, Dr. Eric Brenman, accepted their recommendation.[33]

A typed announcement of the planned expulsion was sent to Khan by the British equivalent of registered mail—a man on a motorcycle who delivered the letter with the requirement of a signature. At the suggestion of lawyers, a proviso was attached stating that Khan could appeal the decision at any time prior to 9:00 p.m. on July 30, the date of the council's next meeting.

Khan responded to Brenman that he was too sick to come to the meeting but that he was submitting a letter of resignation. The council members knew that, if he resigned, he would be able to join another analytic society and thus remain an analyst and a member of the International Psychoanalytic Association (IPA), so they refused to accept the resignation. Instead, Khan was told again, by letter, that he was being removed from membership and, if he chose to appeal the decision, he would have to make a formal appeal prior to the stated deadline.

One of the analysts who was present at the July 30 meeting remembers that tension was high as 9 p.m. approached. This (anonymous) person said that the council members thought Khan might put in a last-minute appearance and try to incite some kind of drama: "We all sat around until 9 p.m., together with our lawyer. The letter to Khan telling him that he was expelled was prepared, but not yet signed. When nothing happened, the letter was signed and given to the lawyer. As soon as the lawyer left, we started to talk openly, for the first time, about our own experiences with Masud. There were probably fifteen of us there and about a dozen of us had patients who had had a sexual involvement with him." Soon afterward, the council formally expelled Khan and informed the BPAS members and students by letter that Khan had been formally removed from membership.

Judy Cooper, who was in touch with Khan at the time of the expulsion, believes that he was extremely upset: "Being struck off dealt a mortal blow to his narcissism. . . . Indeed, Khan was so broken by all this that he gave up on life and decided to die." She remembers that Khan whispered to her: "If I had voice, I would fight back. Without voice I can do little."[34] Cooper's recall of Khan's words is undoubtedly accurate, but there is little support to her belief that the expulsion led to his death, because his death was already imminent.

Almost all of Khan's colleagues thought the expulsion was justifiable. Even Pearl King agreed, although she interpreted the book as Winnicott might have, as a cry for help. There were just a very few people who thought the sanction was too strong. One was Khan's friend Rosemary Gordon, a Jungian analyst. She told me: "The expulsion by the society was a lousy thing to do. I know the book was terrible, but it was so near the end. That gave the death knoll to him." Khan's early analysand, James Hood, commented in our interview: "I was upset at the lack of respect for a great man. I think that it was a terrible thing to do to a man who was dying." And Victor Smirnoff was a defender to the end. After

Khan's death, he made these comments in a letter to Robert Stoller, not realizing that Stoller would be unsympathetic:

> Our miserable colleagues got their petty and miserable revenge by evicting Masud when he was already a dying man. I had the feeling that Masud —hurt as he must have been—rather took a megalomaniac pride or satisfaction in this. It must have been the final proof that his despicable colleagues of the British Institute deserved the poor opinion he had shown them for all these years. Of course they had many objective reasons for evicting Masud—and had them for a long time—but this came too late. Maybe they didn't have the guts to do it while he was still able to react and might have stirred up a scandal: So they actually spat on his grave. Mediocrity finally always has the last word![35]

  Robert Stoller had already written to Khan with a sentiment quite different from Smirnoff's: "A colleague just back from London brought the news that the British Society had expelled you, supposedly on the basis of the book. I imagine the last giving you an enraged glee. I wish it had not come to this unhappy conclusion; the losses on both sides are very great." Stoller closed with a reference to the title of the book: "When you can—when spring comes—write again. Love, Bob."[36] Upon mailing the letter, he told Sybil that they would not get a response, because Khan would be offended. But Khan did in fact scrawl a brief note a few weeks later. It was his last communication to the Stollers: "My dear Bob & Sybil, God bless you for your persistent friendship. I have been gravely ill with further cancer growths and have had four operations. I have no voice left now so clinical work is possible with only a very few patients. Love to you both, Masud."[37]

In the anti-Semitic chapter of *When Spring Comes*, Khan describes the rapid death from brain cancer of the lover of Mr. Luis (the target of Khan's anti-Semitic remark). The lover, whom Khan called Dave, was a wealthy and important film director. When Dave knew he was dying, he retreated with Mr. Luis to a seaside house in Spain, and Khan reportedly flew down regularly to give Mr. Luis analytic sessions and to provide therapeutic coverage for Dave. This plan had been arranged at a session in Khan's office with all three present, where Khan made a generous offer: "I said: 'Dave, let us make the end sing for you. You deserve it.'"[38] In Khan's account, the end *did* sing for Dave, as he lived his final weeks surrounded by his favorite people in a place he loved. Although it is possible that these people did not exist in reality—Barrie Cooper says they are composites of various individuals, including people from his own practice—the case report is significant in the sense that it suggests the kind of death Khan would have wanted for himself.[39]

But nobody could make the end sing for Khan, even though there were people who tried hard to be present for him in his last months. At this time, he was severely impaired with symptoms that are typical of end-stage alcoholism: he was barely eating or drinking, neurological problems had caused a difficulty in walking, and his psychological state included poor judgment, hostility, and major withdrawal.

Two of his great loves (Eva and Margarita) and the wife of his nemesis (Sadie Gillespie, wife of William) remember how terrible things were at the end:

Eva: I couldn't desert Masud. But every time I saw him, it was like watching the Titanic go down, because he had had such a strong influence on me. I had never known that pity could be such a strong feeling. It was overwhelming, and dreadfully sad.

He invited me to dinner alone one evening very near the end. The meal was to be cooked by his latest housekeepers, a young Yugoslav couple—students, I imagined. They were charming, but either domestically inexperienced or stoned, or both. We sat for a long time, getting gradually hungrier while the couple talked quietly in the kitchen and chopped and chopped. Masud's throat dressing began to leak and it was clear that he also had a fever. I was struck by his birdlike thinness. It was nightmarish.

He couldn't speak and he communicated using a pad of paper. One of his messages told me that he was considering starting a stud-farm with the Aga Khan on the West Coast of Ireland and moving there. I said weakly that he might find the weather too wet. He replied, with a spark of the old animation, that he preferred wet weather to wet people.

At last at about 10:00 p.m. we got our dinner and I went sadly home.

Margarita: I saw Masud just two months before he died. I was in London on business and I decided to visit Masud to say good-bye.

He was very happy to see me. He wasn't at all out of his mind, like some people say he was at the end. There was a Yugoslavian servant guy living there to care for him, and that man's sister lived there too. I could tell they thought of him as an old invalid, and they had no idea that he had been so brilliant.

He couldn't talk, he could only "utter," but I had no trouble understanding him. We sat in the sitting room surrounded by books. We were going to have tea, but then he decided we should have wine. He indicated that the servant should open this bottle of cheap wine but I said no, I wanted to drink a better bottle! which he agreed to, and we laughed about that. It was a part of our dynamic that was there right at the end.

I stayed for the whole day, and he was very affectionate. We mostly just sat, embracing. All the grandiosity and glamor was gone. Masud was living in the servant's sitting room, and the other rooms were almost empty, the furniture and paintings having disappeared.

At one point Masud needed something and he tried to tell the servant, but the man couldn't understand, no matter how Masud tried. That was so sad to both of us, because it showed how impotent he had become. I could have helped out, but I didn't, because I knew that I was going to be gone very soon and I wasn't going to be able to solve anything for Masud.

He took out a piece of paper and wrote me a note: "What a pity that you live so far away. I am very lonely here. My friends are so far away, in France, in the States. But such is life."

He died just as he had lived—alone, terrified, lonely, and sad.

Sadie Gillespie: The last time I saw Masud, it was in 1989 and he had already been kicked out of the society and disgraced.

I was at home and the phone rang and I heard a croaky voice say, "This is Prince Masud Khan. Can I talk to Dr. Gillespie?" He didn't even say hello to me. He invited William to dinner and asked him to "bring your wife," even though I had known him for years! William told me, "You don't have to go," but I wanted to see him.

So we went. We were met at the door by a young woman. I never knew if she was a servant? a girlfriend? a patient? She could have been all three!

It was 6 p.m. William was an old man by then and he was used to drinks at 6:15 and supper at 7, never even a few minutes late. We came in, sat down in some chairs, and for at least an hour, nothing was served. Finally I asked Masud if we could have some water and then I realized I shouldn't be so timid and I said, "Masud! Why not a drink?" He replied, "I don't know if I have anything." The woman went off and found a bottle of some terrible cheap wine. There was still no food. Finally I just couldn't take it anymore and I was concerned that William hadn't eaten. So I said to the woman, "Can I help you with dinner?" to which she responded, "Please." In the kitchen, she confessed to me that she did not know how to cook. She had gone to Harrod's Food Court earlier in the day and bought a large salmon, which she had pushed down into a pot of boiling water. The pieces were floating all around in the water. That was all there was for dinner, no salad or vegetables. I told her we could salvage the salmon if we served the pieces cold with onions and some mayonnaise, and that was what we did.

Masud was pathetic that night, a broken man. This was a person I had known since his first days in England, a man who had always dazzled me by his tremendous success. "Spectacular" is the right word for him—he was oozing with gifts, not just his looks but also his mind. It felt almost sadistic to be seeing him in such a state.

Thinking about all this, I wonder if only our hearts were breaking for Masud; or was his, also?

More than two decades prior to his death, Khan had written: "When I stop growing I shall not wish to live."[40] Winnicott had felt the same way. He had written in his (unfinished) autobiography: "Prayer: Oh, God, may I be alive when I die." Winnicott had been active in body and mind when he died in 1971, but Masud was dead before he died, and he had been dead for a long time. As Robert Stoller would write: "His death was a blessing to him."[41]

He spent his last days in the London Clinic, where he lay in a dark room with his eyes closed—clean-shaven, still attractive, and very thin. He was attended by two physicians, Drs. Geyselink and Janvier. (Having dismissed Khan as his patient, Barrie Cooper did not get the chance to say good-bye.) Several visitors recall his final days:

I was in France when Masud died, but two to three weeks before his death, I went to see him. He said good-bye to me in a princely way. He sat up straight in bed, with his legs out, and we embraced. (Rosemary Gordon)

I shall never, never forget my last phone call to Masud a short time before he died, when, weeping, he said, "Why do you love me so much?" (Eugene Lerner)[42]

I saw Sud shortly before he died. He formally blessed me, hands on, saying: "I am a very sick man." (Charles Rycroft)

I saw him for the last time on April 10, 1989, in the London Clinic. Lying
in his bed in the hospital, he was still handsome. I spoke to him; he smiled
at me silently, and extended his hand. After some time he asked for
paper and scribbled a few lines in a trembling hand: "What an end to my
life. I was getting too sick so I decided to withdraw. I have no friends in
London. Keep in touch." This was my last letter from Masud Khan.
(Victor Smirnoff)[43]

Svetlana's final memory shows the extent to which these two were
an enduring couple. She still believed that she and Masud had had a great
love, and it appears that he believed the same:

I saw Sud in the hospital four days before he died. I brought him some old
photos to look at—pictures of him with his horse, for example, and pictures of him with Julie and Tony. He liked that. The doctor came in and
Sud wanted to introduce me. He pointed to me and in that hoarse voice
he said, "My one and only love." I welled up at that, but I didn't cry.
    When he died, the hospital called me and I came right over, but I
was five minutes too late. He was still warm, so I sat there and held his
hand. It felt right that we had come back together at the very end.

Khan died on June 7, 1989.[44] He had lived twelve and a half years
beyond the prognosis of three to six months at the time of his lung cancer diagnosis in 1976, and it was alcoholism, not cancer, that killed him.

CHAPTER 39

POSTHUMOUS

Masud remained a Muslim all the time when he was living in the West.
It is difficult to take into account foreign cultural factors that Khan
valued, that made him into a man who did not fit easily into the
Western world and who did not necessarily want to fit in.
Werner Muensterberger[1]

[Masud] considered himself always as an "expatriate": his country
was Pakistan, his culture was Islamic, his true language
remained Punjabi, and in spite of all his exceptional knowledge
of the English literature, he kept quoting Koranic verses
whenever he wanted to make himself understood.
Victor Smirnoff[2]

Upon Khan's death, his solicitor, Paul Kimber, arranged for his body
to be sent immediately to Pakistan for burial in the ancestral graveyard
in Faisalabad, next to his father's grave. (His mother's body is in a section of the same graveyard reserved for females.)

Khalida Khan (who was not present) told me that the funeral ceremony would have been a traditional one. His body would have been
washed and wrapped unclothed in fourteen yards of cotton, with the face
left visible. The box for his body would have been a simple one provided
free of charge by the local mosque.

Khan's mischief-making lasted beyond his death in several ways, and
one involved the burial. In his will, he had decreed that his body should
be buried "on my Father's right side in the family graveyard." In Rajput
tradition, however, the site on a father's right side is given to the oldest

son—so that spot belonged to Tahir or one of the half-brothers, not to Masud. It happened to be empty when Masud died, because his half-brothers were buried elsewhere[3] and Tahir had been temporarily buried in a graveyard in England. It is unknown if people in Pakistan broke with tradition to obey Khan's direction.

His intimates heard about his death in a variety of ways, at different times. The Stollers were informed immediately, in a telegram from Paul Kimber. In contrast, Khalida Khan, living in Texas, read about her cousin's death in an old copy of the *International Herald Tribune*. Two women who were close to Khan had extraordinary, perhaps extrasensory, experiences:

> I heard about his death by reading it in the paper. It was telepathy—I never read the Deaths column, and I just happened to see it. (Melanie Stanway Purnell, Khan's longtime secretary)

> When Masud died—this is very odd—I had gone with a close friend to an exhibition at the Royal Academy and I suddenly started telling her all about our relationship. I had never before told anyone about it. We talked for three hours, over lunch—and the next day he was dead. So he was dying while I was weeping about him, having this intense experience. I think his presence was there that afternoon and that's why I was compelled to talk about him. (Eva)

Khan had alienated his peers to the point that nobody in England even considered gathering in remembrance. Pearl King commented: "There was no memorial service for Masud in London—who would have organized it?"[4] Barrie Cooper added: "I was angry. Angry at everyone. Including Masud. The reason there wasn't much mourning is because Masud had used us all up."

Obituaries of Khan were published in the major newspapers, however. The most notable one was written for *The Guardian* by Christopher Bollas, who told Robert Stoller that nobody else was willing to do it.[5] Bollas wrote of Khan: "He was a man of whom it has to be said that he was larger than life, a sense impressed by his physique—tall, big, handsome—and by his carriage: he acted the prince that he knew himself to be." The obituary is accompanied by a photograph of Khan by

Zoë Dominic (without attribution). Bollas reports as facts things that have come to be seen as quite questionable: "As a young man, [Khan] swept Paris and met Matisse and Braque, charming them out of several of their paintings which were signed to him. Giacometti sculptured him."[6] The credulity of the people who were Bollas' sources of information shows how convincing Khan had been with his exaggerations and lies.

The BPAS did not give public notice of Khan's death for three years. Barrie Cooper remembers having a huge argument with Adam Limentani about whether there should be an obituary in the IJPA. Their difference of opinion was the same as in the 1976 argument, when they debated whether Khan should lose his training analyst status. Limentani stressed Khan's destructiveness and the harm done to patients, while Cooper stressed Khan's mental illness and his contributions. Once again, Limentani capitulated. He himself wrote a thoughtful five-page obituary,[7] which began with a reference to Khan as the *"enfant terrible* of psychoanalysis of the second half of the century," then went on to praise Khan for his careful and dedicated work as an analyst, editor, and writer. The obituary ends with the statement, "This was the life of a man who has been said to be a maverick, an iconoclast, and apostate. He was full of contradictions which affected his external and internal relationships. On that basis, his friends and his enemies will form their own judgment."

The government of Pakistan chose not to make a public announcement of Khan's death. Barrie Cooper had contacted Sahabzada Yaqub Khan, then foreign minister of Pakistan, asking him if Pakistan might want to make some kind of statement and that idea was passed on to Shaharyar Khan, the Pakistani ambassador to London. The ambassador wrote back to Cooper, "It would not be entirely appropriate [to do this] for a personality who had spent almost his entire life outside of Pakistan and who was probably not a Pakistani national."[8] The matter was dropped, perhaps appropriately, as Khan was not a citizen of Pakistan (or of any existing country).[9]

There were, however, a few places where Khan's significance was acknowledged without hesitation. The French honored their "intimate stranger" almost immediately by publishing an issue of NRP in Khan's honor.[10] It included memorials from Christopher Bollas (a reprint of his

Guardian obituary), J.-B. Pontalis, Didier Anzieu, Jean-Yves Tamet, Adam Phillips, and Victor Smirnoff. The British journal *Free Associations* also had a special issue with memorials from many of the same people.[11]

In the absence of group mourning, Khan's intimates were left to grieve in their own manner. Smirnoff and Stoller turned to correspondence, expressing very different emotions:

> Smirnoff: Masud certainly was an unusual man: gifted, beautiful, rich, intelligent. But he was also cunning, boastful, narcissistic, stingy, prejudiced and cruel. He was a strange, talented, sometimes disquieting analyst who had style, taste & flair. And he was a faithful friend. *Requiscat in pace!*[12]

> Stoller: Masud burned down the house, while he was inside it. If only he had been schizophrenically psychotic, then we wouldn't have had this sense of his being willfully destructive. [I had thought that I wasn't really mourning] but I realize now that my mourning is taking the form of a complex anger. One can mourn with the thought: "Fuck you! Why did you do it this way?" I join you in RIP (Rest in Peace) for him, but I don't agree that he was a faithful friend. I think he was, in the end, faithless to himself, to the goddamn tradition he was always hooting about, and to the rest of us.[13]

Stoller wrote more generously to another friend, explaining why he would not be writing an obituary of Khan:

> [Any obituary I would have written] would be unacceptable. I would have stomped up and down in my anger at Masud's lying. . . . But to do that would have been to prevent the reader from accepting what all of us close to him knew: that he really was creative, artistic, marvelously astute when the circumstances fit him, so alive, and—something I cannot yet make sense of but know is true—lovable. Viewing him from the outside—as strangers must—he was more than mischievous: he was a villain. The worst part of his villainy was what he did to himself.[14]

Khan had set out to destroy his Western legacy with his final book and to a certain extent he was successful. Although his work is still widely read in England, France, Italy, and perhaps other countries, it is rarely acknowledged in the United States, where he is regularly dismissed as an anti-Semite. For example, in a *New York Times Sunday Magazine* article on the British psychotherapist Adam Phillips, Daphne Merkin writes : "[Phillips was analyzed by] the mercurial Masud Kahn [*sic*], whose sexual peccadilloes and rabid anti-Semitism eventually led to his being ejected from the British Psycho-Analytical Society."[15] There is no mention of Khan's contributions to psychoanalysis.

Most of Khan's supporters agree that his lasting reputation rests on his first three books. In his obituary, Christopher Bollas wrote, *"When Spring Comes* is a repelling work, but if mental illness can be forgiven, and time's passing often does so, then the literary works of one of the most gifted psychoanalytic writers of this century may yet survive his tragically driven effort to dismantle himself before his death."[16] Robert Stoller had the same attitude: "For Masud, the ultimate word will be the judgment on what he published before the last book. And, should anyone care to keep the record straight, the last book will be forgiven, its contexts revealed and understood."[17] And Jeanne Axler, speaking as a personal friend outside of the field of psychoanalysis, told me: "Masud tried to antagonize everyone after God dropped him [when his cancer returned] and he was no longer believing in God. With his last book, he was able to antagonize lots of people at once. But if that ends up being how he is remembered, it is very unfair. That wasn't Masud, just a part of him."

André Green gives an eloquent summary of his one-time friend in a description that acknowledges his contributions as well as his pathology:

> I think there were at least three Masuds. The first one was the brilliant psychoanalyst. He was an original thinker, sharp, intuitive, with a very quick mind. As such he was admired by many of his colleagues. The second Masud was the private one: an eccentric personality who lived by his own standards, spending his nights reading and painting, interested in meeting distinguished people. The many excesses for which he was responsible in his private life were compensated by his gifts as psycho-analyst. Finally there was a third Masud, the psychopathic one, deeply disturbed, cynical, envious, full of resentment, needing to harm his rivals, to debase them and to use every possible way to fulfill his aim.[18]

A piece of mischief from what Green would call the "third Masud" involved the will Khan left—and the will he did not leave. Both were scandalous. He carried on a legacy of controversial wills that he had inherited not only from his father, but also from Winnicott. Eight years before his death, he was already planning this posthumous trouble: "[My will is] a long devious game I engage in with myself & others, starting now and to go on after I am gone; they shall have to consult how to relate to an 'absence' from some Lacanian in Paris."[19] Whether or not Khan was of sound mind when he drafted the final will, it seems likely that he wanted to provoke people by creating trouble.[20]

The final document, dated March 29, 1989, two months prior to his death, was short and simple.[21] He bequeathed his material possessions, his money, and everything he owned in Pakistan to his estate manager, Nazir Ahmed. The one exception was that he gave his Nelson desk, the desk that Sybil Stoller had helped him to purchase, to his solicitor, Paul Kimber. He did not leave anything at all to Svetlana, who desperately needed money and who had legitimate rights to much of his estate. (The art books, paintings and lithographs had been purchased with her money, and the Braque birds had been a gift to her from Geoffrey Gorer.)

Many people were surprised that they were not mentioned in the will, since Khan had promised them specific bequests. He had even put tape, marked with the beneficiary's name, on the backs of specific works of art and on other items. Rosemary Gordon told me: "I felt he took himself away by leaving nothing to anyone. He rejected all his English friends." Barrie Cooper agreed with Gordon: "There was a slightly mocking 'Masudic' denigration of all those he held dear." And another (anonymous) friend commented: "Masud's will was a complete post mortem enactment of revenge." With the exception of Svetlana, most of the people in Khan's Western world did not need Khan's wealth, but they would have treasured symbolic mementoes. They were left wondering whether the deep connections they had made to Khan had been of little or no value to him.

The final will was different from others Khan had written in the years when he was more sane. Various friends report that, in the 1970s and the 1980s, his written wills always left money to Svetlana and made provisions for his library to be placed somewhere as a complete collection. Khan's handwriting on the final will is uncharacteristic and could even be a forgery, although the signatures of the witnesses appear to be credible.[22] Svetlana told me a story that suggests that fraud may have been involved:

I saw Masud regularly in the weeks and days before he died. His mind started to slip and he couldn't get rid of the idea that he had no money. He was surrounded by valuable treasures, and he had plenty of money in the bank, but he wouldn't be reassured. Then this oily terrible little man from Pakistan suddenly appeared. He was a shyster, and he claimed to be Masud's legal representative. I so objected to this horrid person. He sat on Sud's furniture with no shoes, and I said to him "Put your shoes on!!" He conned Masud, saying, "If you sign everything over to me, I'll make sure that all your debts will be fixed." And he convinced Masud to do that. In the previous will, it all went to me—but Masud didn't consult me now about the change.

I didn't care so much about the will; I'm basically a vagabond, and I don't need worldly goods. The lawyer, Paul Kimber, told me, "You wouldn't win if you contested the will," so I didn't object.

In an unfortunate coincidence, Zoë Dominic, who was Svetlana's trustee, was unable to fight for her because she was recovering from cancer surgery. She told me that if she had been healthy, she would have made sure that the will was contested. Barrie Cooper also questioned the will, and he tried, without success, to persuade Svetlana to challenge its validity. In Cooper's opinion, Khan was not competent at the end of his life.

And so the will went uncontested. On November 28, the Braque bird lithographs were sold along with other works of art and the art books in an auction at Phillips, Son & Neale Gallery on New Bond Street. The cover of the illustrated catalogue announces that the sale includes "A Collection of Reference and Modern Illustrated Books from the Estate of the Prince Masud R. Khan." The pictures of items for sale include at least eight from Khan's flat, including several Braques. An anonymous source told me that most of the artwork was purchased by a single (unknown) person. Khan's huge library, all but the art books, was sold as a single item, and it ended in Athens, Greece, through an arrangement made by Andreas Giannakoulas.

I discovered in my research a likely explanation of why Khan left almost everything to his estate manager—an explanation that conflicts with Svetlana's account of the "shyster" from Pakistan. I learned that Nazir Ahmed was the husband of Bibi Shehnaz, Khan's niece. The laws in Pakistan at the time were conservative Shari'a laws, and it was not possible to leave an estate to a woman, so if Khan wanted to leave his money and possessions to Bibi, the only way he could do it was through Ahmed.[23]

But there would be a complication to the inheritance in Pakistan. Another provision in Shari'a law requires that land can only be willed to a blood relative. Bibi was Khan's blood relative but Ahmed was not, and this led to major consequences. Khan's family appealed the will, and Ahmed was eventually forced to give up Kot Fazaldad Khan, as well as two other Khan estates that he had inherited.[24]

Like Winnicott, Khan failed to name a literary executor in his will. Melanie Stanway Purnell, Khan's longtime and favorite secretary, told me she was astonished by the omission: "It was extraordinary. He always believed that he would be famous and that one day his musings would be read by the world. He would have wanted to be sure that happened."

In the absence of a literary executor, Khan's published and unpublished material was left unprotected, along with collections of his various correspondences and the private records of analysands. These papers now belonged to Nazir Ahmed and, if Ahmed could not make use of them (as by a sale), then persumably they would be disposed of by Paul Kimber.

Kimber happened to be the solicitor for the BPAS, so he knew the world of British psychoanalysis. He consulted with Joseph Sandler, then-president of the IPA, about how to handle Khan's papers. Through Sandler, Kimber found three people who cared enough about Khan's legacy to fight to protect the papers: Christopher Bollas, Barrie Cooper, and Victor Smirnoff. Cooper remembers that the BPAS wanted all the papers to be destroyed, to prevent provocative material from surviving: "Victor and I contested the attempt to destroy Masud's records. We fought with Kimber and the institute about the ownership of the material. We wanted to go to court to protect the papers. The institute just wanted to bury everything." At the end of June, in collaboration with Cooper and Smirnoff, Bollas wrote a circular letter to Khan's colleagues, including international colleagues. He informed them that Adam Limentani, currently the honorary archivist at the IPA, had agreed to hold Khan's papers at Broomhills, the London headquarters of the IPA, but Mr. Kimber, who had control, was not convinced that the papers were worth preserving. It would only be through the efforts of

Khan's peers, acting quickly, that they could be protected. Bollas asked people to write to Kimber immediately, giving reasons why the papers should be preserved.

Robert Stoller was one of the colleagues who responded to Bollas' plea. He wrote to Kimber, "It would be a significant mistake to let that collection disappear. Though there is no way to predict the future of ideas, there is no question that Masud was one of the major contributors to psychoanalysis in the last generation."[25]

By the end of July, Kimber had agreed that the IPA could hold Khan's papers in trust, housing them in un-indexed boxes at Broomhills. The agreement between Kimber and the IPA included a fifty-year ban on usage for investigation or research, which meant they would not be accessible to anyone until the year 2039. Bollas and Limentani went to Palace Court and did a rough sorting, in which they discarded patient records and prepared the rest of the material for storage.[26] Kimber wrote Stoller to tell him about the plan and Stoller responded, "Thank you for your news regarding how Masud's effects are to be distributed. In his inevitable fashion, he has made a mess and in that way accomplished half of what he wanted: to make a mess. The other half would have been to protect his intellectual bequest and his professional properties."[27]

And so it was that the papers and correspondences have been saved for future scholarship. The IPA, however, is an odd choice as storehouse and guardian. Khan was not even a member of that group when he died, having been expelled automatically upon his expulsion from the British Society. Khan might have preferred that J.-B. Pontalis control his papers or that Robert Stoller establish an archive at UCLA. But the effect of the non-will was that Khan's potential wishes were not taken into account, especially since Kimber was adamant that the literary estate remain in Britain.

After the brief flurry of Khan obituaries, followed by Judy Cooper's 1993 biography, almost nothing was written about Khan or about his place in the history of psychoanalysis. Then in 2001, Wynne Godley wrote his articles, eliciting a strong reaction in London that included active discussion in the letters to the editor section of the *London Review of Books*. Don Campbell, then-president of the BPAS, was one letter writer, and his response reflected an urgent wish to defend psychoanalysis from having too close a connection to Khan's ethical problems: "Wynne Godley's account of the treatment practised by Masud Khan revealed a grotesque and damaging parody of psychoanalysis. The patient and self-less analyst that Wynne Godley found to undo the consequences of his disturbing experience with Khan [Godley's second analyst] practised the kind of analysis we teach and practice in the British Psycho-Analytical Society."[28]

Campbell's response was no doubt helpful in reassuring the public that the BPAS did not endorse Khan's reported behavior. But other analysts of the BPAS wanted to look more deeply into what had happened and to consider what roles they themselves had played. The Ethical Commit-tee, headed by Anne-Marie Sandler, undertook a retrospective inves-tigation of the Khan-Winnicott-Godley situation and then, in an act of courage and honesty, the BPAS declared a special meeting to discuss Godley's articles. Anne-Marie Sandler wrote in an IJPA article describ-ing this process, "The [British] Society needed Godley's article to begin a long and painful process of self-reflection."[29]

The special meeting was held on June 19, 2001,[30] and attendance was limited to BPAS members, associate members, students, and staff. The topic was "Masud Khan and Winnicott: What Is to be Learnt in the Light of Wynne Godley's Revelations?" An official announcement stated that the Ethical Committee would summarize the main issues in Godley's article and also relate the events regarding Khan's loss of sta-tus as training analyst in 1977 and loss of membership in the society in 1988. There were two aims: "The first is to think together about how as a society we failed to protect the patients and psychoanalysis. The sec-ond is to focus on the institutional issues and the unconscious collusion that took place, in order to attempt to better safeguard the practice of psycho-analysis in the future." People who could not attend were en-couraged to send written comments that would be read at the meeting.[31]

Two hundred people attended the proceedings, and reports suggest that there was a genuine attempt to understand and learn. The attend-ees acknowledged their own failure to stop Khan from his destructive practices and they considered the possibility that his negative influence was still active through "transgenerational transmission of boundary violations," a reference to the idea that candidates who are in treatment or supervision with therapists who transgress boundaries may go on to violate boundaries in their own clinical work.[32]

The very fact that the meeting was held is significant. The BPAS can be criticized for taking so long to talk about Khan, but it should also be acknowledged that analytic societies almost never have open discussions of the private indiscretions of their members.[33]

In assessing Khan's life as a whole, it seems clear that his self was fractured. The True Self–False Self split has been noted throughout this biography, making use of the theories of Winnicott and Khan. The Eastern–Western split is also obvious, but it is perhaps more difficult to understand. Khan lived in two cultures for most of his life and he had Eastern and Western selves that were coexistent and noninteracting. People appear to have known one or the other side, not both, and most people think that Khan himself arranged for this. For example, Eric Rayner wrote, "[Khan] never told us in the West about the East."[34] And Khan wrote on this topic: "The Eastern sensibility is at once 'public' and also hidden and private. The English linguistic medium cannot transmit experiences both alien and unknowable to it."[35] Several of Khan's peers, most notably Werner Muensterberger, Victor Smirnoff, and André Green, were convinced that Khan's Eastern identity was always stronger than his Western identity.

Certainly Khan never worried when his Eastern values came into conflict with the norms of the West. As Zoë Dominic put it: "Masud had a problem in London: he was never Europeanized. You're either Europeanized or you're not." Thinking like this, we see why he felt free to break analytic rules: he had never agreed to follow them. The only powers that he accepted as legitimate were Islam, his father, and the British Royals. As Khan wrote in *When Spring Comes:* "[T]he faith one is born to, one can rarely shed."[36] If Khan is viewed as a wealthy landowner from feudal Muslim Pakistan, then his life in the West becomes more understandable.

When Khan traveled to Pakistan as an adult, he felt at home and real. After his visit in 1970, he wrote: "What surprises me is how inalienably and naturally a feudal Pakistani I am. . . . I know me in my sensibility and character more truly after this long visit than ever before."[37]

But there is a further complication here: he was "at home" in a world that was nonexistent outside of Kot Fazaldad Khan, because the feudal society in which he imagined himself to be living was long gone. André Green speaks to this issue in commenting, "In the end, Masud . . . didn't realize that he was in England in the 20th century. He thought it was Pakistan and the 17th century." If Green is right, and the True Self Khan experienced in Pakistan was based on a fantasized reality, it is of interest to question whether it is appropriate to call it a True Self.[38]

Setting aside the cultural considerations, it is fair to say that much of Khan's life can be addressed by Western thinking. Almost anyone in the West would agree that he was "mad"—"mad" being a term used in England to imply an open connection to one's psychotic core. The condition of being mad is not inevitably tragic; in fact, there is a long tradition of British Independents valuing madness. In that way of thinking, madness is inside us and all around us, whether we like it or not, and effective living requires that we approach madness even when we do not know how to deal with it or what the consequences may be.[39] Khan's tragedy was not that he was mad, it was that he failed to achieve reliable control over his madness.

Most people have lives that contain tragedy, but not great tragedy. Some people's lives, however, are like literature, and Khan's life is one such. He had learned about Western psychology from Shakespeare and for much of his life, to a greater or lesser extent, he imagined himself as a character in a grand novel.[40] He lived as Oscar Wilde recommended: "When people play a tragedy, they should play it in the grand style."[41] But did Khan know that he had other options? This question, along with many others, remains incompletely answered.

I close my story of Masud Khan with a passage that speaks to the Shakespearean quality of his life. It comes from Augusto Colmenares, a philosopher and former analysand of Khan who now lives in Madrid.

Khan was a subject who left tracks on all whom he touched, and all whom he stepped on. One can say, without fear of error, that whatever candidate or analyst, philosopher or poet, was able to have a place with Masud in the golden valley of the Sun, that on the other side of a high mountain which has the same shape, there is the top of a penumbra [a space of partial illumination] which announces the beginning of rain in the darkness.

And somebody could write a tragicomic account of this. The plot might be that there is a reunion in a Great Assembly, filled with witnesses—people who had been touched by Masud's greatness, and those who had been stepped on. The battle of Ayucacho[42] would be a mere shadow of the engagement that would happen here. The drama could conclude with a description of the assassination of all those assembled.[43]

Not many people from the East or the West are commented on posthumously with such intensity.

MEETING SVETLANA BERIOSOVA

I met Svetlana once, near the end of her life. I was not expecting to like her. Our prior interactions, over the telephone and via post-office mail, had left me enraged. I had tried three times to plan trips to London around her schedule (which was totally empty as far as I could tell) and the plan failed each time, always at the last minute. She would say "yes" when I was buying airline tickets and setting up a tight schedule of interviews, and then "no" after I arrived. Later I understood that she was this way with everyone. As Zoë Dominic told me: "You can't have a direct conversation with Svetlana, with a question and an answer. She won't answer, she'll just say, 'Why are you asking that?' She lives surrounded by clouds."

When we met in November 1997, it was only possible because I did not tell her where I was staying, so she could not call to cancel. In the early morning prior to our meeting I had a dream that left me wide awake at 3 a.m. It was a nightmare in which I felt a rage so intense that it may have been the greatest rage I have ever felt. I usually find my dreams interesting, but this time the physical tension in my body and rapid beating of my heart were terrifying. As I lay in bed recovering, I felt empathy with Khan, reflecting that he too had had to put up with this truly impossible woman. No wonder he left her, I thought.

That morning, I arrived at Svetlana's flat at the set time. Along with her one-eyed cat, she was living in a simple two-bedroom flat at 10 Palliser Court, about a mile from Hans Crescent. It was a fourth-floor walkup that she had bought with her father's money after her divorce. She was sixty-five years old, crippled by arthritis, and confined to a wheelchair.

Svetlana was still able to cast a spell. I immediately felt that I was in the presence of an extraordinary person. She was gorgeous in the wheelchair. She wore no makeup and she was very thin, with long dark hair framing an angular face. Her eyes were huge and she was dressed in a simple black shirt with black slacks. I was surprised that the tone of her voice was now soft and sweet, with a quality of seductiveness, and she was friendly and welcoming, giving me no context in which to deposit my anger—so I had to let go of it.

Having talked to Tony Walton and his wife Gen LeRoy, who had visited Svetlana a few months earlier, I was forewarned that the flat would be a mess. Their report was accurate: ashtrays, old newspapers, clothing, and other debris were scattered about.

In the entranceway, the first thing I had noticed was a painting entitled *My New York Nightmare*. Svetlana told me that it had been given to her by Tony, who had painted it after Julie Andrews left him; he had given it to her, Svetlana said, because he could not stand to look at it. The painting was well done but extremely upsetting to view, and I wondered why she had hung it in such a prominent place.[1]

Entering the living room, I saw that on top of the living room fireplace, there was a small gold picture frame with a photograph of Khan as a young boy in British India, seated in full dress on a chair. Inserted in the corner of the frame was a tiny picture of Khan as an adult, handsome and smiling. Tony and Gen had told me that in a side room there was a shrine to Svetlana's father, her other love. The shrine included photographs and mementoes of Poppa's career as a ballet master, along with burning candles. For some reason, Svetlana kept that door closed during my visit.

It was 10 a.m., and Svetlana took me into the kitchen to make tea. She told me she had just finished eating a breakfast of figs and water. I had brought a box of chocolates as a gift, and she ravenously ate the entire box; I wondered if she had enough money for food, as she seemed to be starving. She did have money for cigarettes. She smoked unceasingly.

In the course of our time together, she went from a hand-operated wheelchair onto the living room couch and back, then onto a kitchen chair and back, and it was only after I left that I realized I had never noticed her making the transition. She had been so in touch with her body and so balanced that she moved in and out of the wheelchair with no awkwardness and (apparently) no major effort.

Perhaps the most striking quality I noticed, aside from her physical grace and beauty, was Svetlana's simplicity. She answered every question I asked her directly and without hesitation. However, she was extremely nonpsychological; it was as if she felt only basic emotions, and these she experienced with great intensity. I shuddered to think how vulnerable she must have been to Khan when he was in a bad mood.

Her simplicity unsettled me because I felt obliged to protect her. I knew that this might be my one and only chance to interview her, and I had planned to ask her some very personal questions, for example about her sex life with Khan and their lack of children. But I could not ask those questions—because I knew she would answer me.

Svetlana seemed to like me. She commented, "I know you are the exact right person to write this biography of Masud," and gave me unrestricted permission to quote from the interview and any of her correspondences. She added, however, that she did not know where the correspondence with Khan was, so she could not give it to me.

Svetlana died unexpectedly on November 10, 1998. She had not known she was ill until four weeks prior to her death, when a doctor found that she had cancer in her liver, kidneys, bone, and brain. Zoë Dominic immediately arranged for her placement in a private hospice where she could die with dignity.

At the hospice, she was visited by her most important friends, including Donald MacLeary and Anne Money-Coutts. Zoë came twice a day and Pauline, a former fan who had been her caregiver, was there almost all the time. Svetlana began to fade rapidly because she refused food and would drink only water. When it became clear that it was very near the end, Julie Andrews flew from New York to be with her for the last four days and Mary Drage Eyre, another old friend, also came. Zoë, Julie, Mary, and Pauline stayed at the hospice in round-the-clock rotations, so that Svetlana was never alone. This was an extremely meaningful and private experience for all of them and perhaps one day we will hear about it in some detail. For now, however, I have only a brief account from Zoë:

> Svetlana's death was peaceful and the four of us felt that it was merciful. She was very moved that Julie had come and she appreciated being surrounded by people who had loved her so much in the early days.
>
> I find myself devastated by her death, more than I had imagined.

Svetlana had taken a small purse to the hospice. After she died, Zoë opened the purse, and inside she found two items: a handkerchief and a silver identification bracelet inscribed with Khan's name and date of birth. It was a bracelet that he had worn constantly up to the time of his own death.

The funeral service was held at All Saints Russian Orthodox Cathedral on November 19, and I had the privilege of being present. It was a gray winter's day, and a light snow was falling. Her death had been widely reported in the world press and there were at least four hundred people present. Cremation would follow the service, attended by Zoë and just a few others.

It was a traditional Russian Orthodox service in an unheated all-wood sanctuary with a prominent smell of incense. The open coffin was surrounded by many, many flower arrangements, all white, and the dark room was lit by hundreds of white candles. Upon entry, most people went directly to Svetlana's casket, dropped down to kiss the floor, and then kissed her body directly on the lips. The service, which was conducted in Russian, lasted an hour and a half, and the mourners, each holding a burning white taper, stood throughout—there were no pews in the church, because Orthodox Russians feel it is appropriate to stand in the presence of God. I happened to be with Harry Karnac, who was eighty years old and walking with a cane. He remained standing the whole time, even though there were chairs available.

The mourners were an unusually mixed group. About half of those attending were from the ballet world, people who were easily recognized by their perfect posture and elegant stature—many of them wearing fur coats. The others were fans, and, at least in my memory, they tended to be short and often slightly chubby, with the women wearing babushka scarves and cloth coats. Almost all of the mourners were people who had not seen or spoken to Svetlana for thirty years, yet they seemed to be consumed with grief, many of them quietly sobbing.

The service was a major tribute to a great dancer. The contrast to Khan's death, for which there had been no service at all, could not be more extreme. I had the thought that Svetlana's mourners could experience untarnished memories of her because, unlike Khan, she had withdrawn from the world as she went downhill, so she had not offended people or left bad memories.

A few months after Svetlana's death, Zoë and Pauline took her ashes to Zurich. A Russian priest conducted a small ceremony at the Ensenbuhl Cemetery, in a plot[2] that adjoined Nicholas Beriosov's grave. The mourners included Svetlana's stepmother Doris Beriosova, some Russian friends of Nicholas Beriosov who knew him from his ballet school in Zurich, and a group of dancers from England who happened to be on tour in Zurich at that time. Svetlana's ashes were put in a casket that was buried next to her father's grave and plans were made to put up a stone with her name to match the stone cross of her father.

Following in the tradition of Fazaldad Khan, Winnicott, and Masud, Svetlana left behind a troubled estate. In Svetlana's case, there was a complete absence of a will. Zoë searched and found nothing, and the situation created enormous complications. The nearest relatives were living in Siberia and Chile, and a lawyer had to be hired to find them. Eventually these relatives inherited the flat and a few items of value. Zoë also succeeded in finding a home for the one-eyed cat.

When Zoë cleared the flat a few months later, she found Svetlana's correspondence with Masud under the bed, in an old suitcase. I wondered whether Svetlana had lied to me about not knowing where it was. And if she did so, why?

Zoë and I met again a year after Svetlana's death. As we talked about her memories, she made a simple comment that left her uncharacteristically tearful: "I loved Sud and Svetlana dearly. We had a charmed life, with enough money to do whatever we wanted. Then that life was totally gone. And to this day, I can't understand why it was that they both had to destroy themselves." It is a sad comment about a sad story.

ENDNOTES

ABBREVIATIONS USED IN ENDNOTES

AFP: Anna Freud Papers, Library of Congress

GGP: Geoffrey Gorer Archives, University of Sussex, Brighton

RSP: Robert Stoller Archives, University of California at Los Angeles, Young
    Research Library

WP: Winnicott Papers, Archives of Psychiatry, Oskar Diethelm Library, Cornell
    Medical Center/New York

CORRESPONDENCES

AF/DW: Letters between Anna Freud and Donald Winnicott (AFP)

BC/RS and RS/BC: Letters between Barrie Cooper and Robert Stoller (RSP)

MK/AG and AG/MK: Letters between Masud Khan (MK) and André Green
    (private)

MK/DW and DW/MK: Letters between MK and Donald Winnicott (WP)

MK/GG and GG/MK: Letters between MK and Geoffrey Gorer (GGP)

MK/MP: Letters between Masud Khan and Mark Paterson (Sigmund Freud
    Copyrights, London)

MK/RS and RS/MK: Letters between MK and Robert Stoller (RSP)

MK/SB: Letters from MK to Svetlana Beriosova (private)

MK/SS: Letters of MK to Sybil Stoller (private)

MK/SYK: Letters of MK to Sahabzada Yaqub Khan (private)

MK/TW: Letters of MK to Tony Walton (private)

MK/VS: Letters of MK to Victor Smirnoff (private)

MK/WG and WG/MK: Letters between MK and Wladimir Granoff (private)

MK/ZD: Letters from MK to Zoë Dominic (private)

NB/SB: Letters from Nicholas Beriosov to Svetlana Beriosova (private)

VS/RS and RS/VS: Letters between Victor Smirnoff and Robert Stoller (RSP)

WB: Masud Khan's Work Book: This is the thirty-nine-volume professional
    diary of Khan covering the years 1968 to 1980. (Various secretaries typed
    his longhand notes, and volumes 1 to 13 are referred to as Work Books, while
    Volumes 14 to 39 are called Workbooks; I have chosen to use the earlier

spelling.) The original Work Books are frozen in the archives of the International Psychoanalytic Association until 2039. The copy used here is one that was given by Khan to Robert and Sybil Stoller, along with permission to make use of any of his unpublished material at their discretion. Robert Stoller is now deceased and the permission given to me to read and quote from the Work Books comes from Sybil Stoller.

Note: Names in the endnotes that are not complete names are always pseudonyms, as noted in the main text.

ENDNOTES TO INTRODUCTION

1. Anticahiers 10, undated. Khan's idea is inspired by Shakespeare's "To hear with eyes belongs to love's fine wit," from the 23rd Sonnet.

2. Almost everyone whom I interviewed for this biography commented on Khan's physical appearance. At least nine people used the same three words: "Masud was beautiful." Most women felt a strong physical attraction: "Of course I wanted a sexual relationship with him. Any woman would have" (anonymous lover). His listening skills were part of his attractiveness: "He seduced me by being extremely 'present' when we talked, by his true wish to know me—it wasn't at all the kind of seduction I was used to" (Marcelle, a French girlfriend). Men had other kinds of comments: "When I met Masud Khan in the late 1950s, he was a strikingly handsome man. He looked like a young Adam Clayton Powell" (Tony Walton, set designer and friend). "Masud was a different person from the majority: tall, dark, and good looking with a touch of pride or superiority that included a certain feature of magnificence" (Saul Peña, Peruvian psychoanalyst). "I was brought up among aristocrats and I met in Masud Khan my own kind and one of the most princely people I have known" (Keith Botsford, American academic and friend). "Have you seen any pictures of Masud? He is [*sic*—Khan had been dead for seven years at the time of this quote] a very tall and handsome man, very courteous and gentle" (James Hood, analyst and analysand).

3. Very rarely, Khan's acquaintances remember his physical impression as suggesting an inner disturbance or even something evil. These quotes are uncharacteristic, but important: "I'm an artist and I was fascinated by Masud's appearance. He could have been a highwayman or a pirate" (Joy Stewart, artist wife of Khan's fellow analyst Harold Stewart). "Masud had a combination of seductive-

ness and poison-ness which was quite incredible. I experienced him from the very beginning as a snake" (Hanna Segal, London analyst from the Kleinian group).

4. Robert Rodman, a Winnicott biographer, told me that Madeleine Davis, a now-deceased English analyst, had insisted that, in Britain, Winnicott's family would be called "lower middle class" because their income came from shopkeeping, even though they were well off and their son went to boarding school. Rodman told me: "Winnicott thought of himself as uncultured. . . . He said that the only culture he had been exposed to before public school was 'evangelical religion.' He was simply not one of the educated kids you'd find at Eton or Harrow or, later, Cambridge" (e-mail to the author, January 19, 2004).

5. The clucking chicken information comes from Judith Issroff and the dagger quote comes from James Hood.

6. Biographers have only recently begun to write about the innovative British analysts of the 1950s and 1960s. There is a short biography of Khan by his analysand Judy Cooper (1993) and a recent longer biography by Willoughby (2005), and there are three biographies of Winnicott (Kahr 1996, Phillips 1988, Rodman 2003) and one of his analyst wife Clare (Kanter 2004). Melanie Klein and Anna Freud have been given close attention by a few writers (Grosskurth 1986, Likierman 2001, Young-Bruehl 1988), and there is one biography each of W. R. D. Fairbairn (Sutherland 1989), John Rickman (King 2003), and Harry Guntrip (Hazell 1996), and an edited book about Charles Rycroft (Pearson 2004). There are no biographies of Sylvia Payne, Michael Balint, Marion Milner, Margaret Little, Charles Rycroft, Ismond Rosen, or other significant Middle Group analysts, nor are there biographies of three important California analysts who belong with this group: Robert Stoller, Ralph Greenson, and Milton Wexler. R. D. Laing, who trained as an analyst and was analyzed by Rycroft, has been written about extensively, but there is little overlap with Khan's world, since Laing purposely kept himself at a distance from the analytic community after completing his training.

7. December 15, 1981, quoted in Limentani, 1992, p. 155. Khan's diaries are distinct from his Work Books and I never saw them, nor do I know where they are or if they have been destroyed.

ENDNOTES TO CHAPTER 1

1. MK/WG, December 13, 1964.
2. Fazaldad and his last wife, Masud's mother, were both Muslim members

of the Rajput tribe, even though most Rajputs are Hindus. Rajputi males have a long tradition of fierce fighting against all odds.

3. MK quoted to the author by Barrie Cooper, 1999.

4. "[I]t is true; I am a savage." MK/SB, November 12, 1958.

5. MK/SB, September 24, 1958.

6. Willoughby (2005) states that Fazaldad was a Sunni, but my information that he was Shiite comes from interviews with two close relatives, Khalida Khan and Fatima Ahmed (see footnote 11, below).

7. Brian Simpkin from the medal company Spink of London explained Fazaldad's medals: "The uppermost is the Order of British India, either 1st or 2nd Class. It was awarded for long and faithful service by native Indian officers of the Indian Army. The lower of the two decorations is an Indian Title Badge. There were two types, for Muslims and Hindus, and each came in three classes. It was awarded to civilians and native Indian officers of the Indian Army for faithful service or acts of public welfare" (letter to the author, July 17, 2001).

8. The British land grants were called jagirs and the person to whom the land was given was a jagirdar. The jagirdars in Northern India formed a new landed aristocracy. Since the British system gave landowners the power to collect taxes, the peasants who lived on the land were essentially serfs under the control of hereditary rulers. This is why Khan accurately described himself as coming from a "feudal" society (interview with Robert Nichols, a scholar specializing in South Asian Studies, 2000). Khan's first home is alternately described as being in Chichivotnee, which may be the same as Montgomery.

9. There is a caveat in the Shari'a, the code of Islamic law, that states that in order to take an additional wife, the man must be able to provide for that wife and all his other wives, and the current wives must give their permission. Fazaldad followed this caveat each time he married.

10. Khan referred jokingly to the Pathan identity of his father's second wife in a clinical article (1971a, pp. 238–239): "Before lying down, [the patient] asked me: 'Are you a Pathan from Northern India?' I replied: 'Almost, but not quite.'"

11. Khalida Riaz Khan (b. 1929) is a retired geophysicist living in Texas, and Fatima Ahmed (born in June 1924, a few weeks before Masud) is an M.D. specializing in histopathology and internal medicine, now living in Pennsylvania. Khalida and Fatima were the daughters of Masud's half-sister, Fatima Jehan Begum. In contrast to the lineage of Fazaldad and Khursheed, which has only one living descendant (Tahir's estranged daughter), this branch is large: Khalida told me that she has fifty-two first cousins. One of Khalida's nieces is Maleeha

Lodhi, who was Pakistan's Ambassador to the United States at the time of the 2001 World Trade Center attacks. Lodhi played a major role as intermediary in the forming of an American alliance with Pakistan in the twenty-four hours following the attacks.

12. Courtesans in British India were entertainers—singers and dancers, not simple prostitutes. Rich landowners often married them, although they were not sufficiently respectable to be allowed as a first wife. Robert Nichols told me: "The courtesan is trained not only to entertain, but also to provoke longing for the beloved—this being the subject of volumes of Persian poetry over the ages. Courtesans invoke desire before they make themselves available for sexual gratification" (e-mail to the author, July 19, 2000).

13. As a young boy, Masud was teased mercilessly about the ear. Tahir nicknamed him "Long Ear" and said that Masud would have to have a special coffin: "When you die, they'll have to keep your ear out of the coffin because it won't fit in." His older half-sisters also used to tease him, saying "Show us your ear," which caused Masud to break into tears (information from Khalida Khan). In school, fellow pupils mocked him for the deformity. Once, playing a tennis match, he was mortified when someone yelled out, referring to the ball: "Hit it back with your ear!" (information from Tony Walton).

14. Undated postcard, MK/ZD, summer, 1962.

15. MK/VS, February 18, 1971. Cooper (1993) reported that Khan "lacked touch" as a child, but Eva (interview, 1998), to whom Khan talked about his childhood, "totally disagrees" with Cooper on this matter. Anne Money-Coutts, an English woman who has traveled extensively in India, believes that Eva had the more accurate information. She told me that Indians in general tend to be tactile, especially with their children, who are generally carried by someone in the household until they can walk (letter to the author, July 27, 2001).

16. Undated letter, Chaudri Nazir Ahmed to Roger Willoughby, circa 1996.

17. The information about the opium was given to me by Margarita, and it had been told to her in confidence by Khan.

18. Interview with Eva, 1999.

19. Interview with Sahabzada Yaqub Khan, 1997.

20. WB, June 21, 1979.

21. WB, June 18, 1971. See also MK/WG, December 18, 1964.

22. Selective mutism in children is correlated with severe social anxiety, and the younger the age at occurrence of the mutism, the more likely it is that social anxiety will be found in adulthood. A modern psychiatrist would not be surprised

to hear that, given his history, the adult Khan suffered enormously from social anxiety, with chronic symptoms of agoraphobia and "blind terror."

23. WB, June 21,1979.

24. WB, June 18, 1971.

25. Charles Rycroft told me that people in London believed that Tahir had been scripted in childhood to be Masud's bodyguard.

26. Khan's telling of this story was related to me by Sybil Stoller.

27. As an adult, Khan liked his name: "A female friend [Sue Holland] remarked to me, 'Everything about you bespeaks you: even your name. "Khan" declaims itself, but "Masud" one has has to whisper.' Yes, there is something in that—my father's sagacity arranged it" (WB, October 1, 1971).

28. MK/RS, August 18, 1986.

29. In Punjabi culture, the village system for resolving disputes and making administrative decisions was the centuries-old panchayat, an independent tribal organization run by a panel of five village elders who presided at court (*panch* means five). Usually the court was located in a town, but Fazaldad's court was located in his home. Fazaldad was known for his fairness and for being a good listener.

30. MK/SS, June 15, 1964.

31. "Masud told me he'd be back there in line wishing the brothers would fall down and make fools of themselves" (phone interview with Charles Kaufman, American analyst and friend, 1998).

32. MK/SS, June 15, 1964.

33. MK/VS, April 29, 1969.

34. MK/RS, February 6, 1979.

35. MK/RS, February 19, 1965.

36. MK/SS, June 15, 1964.

37. RS/VS, March 29, 1978.

38. MK/WG, July 27, 1964.

ENDNOTES TO CHAPTER 2

1. MK/SB, April 26, 1964; Khan is describing a talk he gave at the Menninger Clinic, located at that time in Topeka, Kansas.

2. "[The move] was an engineered artifact of my father's policy for my future." WB, April 15, 1970.

3. The mansion still stands, although much of the surrounding property has been sold.

4. WB, May 28, 1979.

5. MK/RS, January 27, 1986.

6. MK/VS, April 12, 1969.

7. Because he learned to read so late, Khan never read any children's literature: "It is a sad lack in my developmental process that I never read any children's literature in any language. From blankness, I transgressed [*sic*] straight into literature proper" (MK/VS, April 19, 1971).

8. MK/WG, October 8, 1964.

9. WB, March 31, 1970. Khan wrote that, because he had a phobia of public libraries, he purchased all his books: "Even at college, I never once visited the library. I accumulated a vast library of English literature of my own—in spite of the war, ships sinking everywhere, and my ignorance about books at that time, 1940–1946. I have read perhaps six books that I do not possess" (MK/VS, September 28, 1969).

10. Harold Bloom (1998) writes that Shakespeare was responsible for the psychological development of the Western world. Through his writings, Shakespeare actually created human nature, according to Bloom. In the case of Masud Khan, we see how Shakespeare's works influenced an individual to evolve from a nonpsychological person (i.e., one not psychologically aware) into a psychological person. The development of the capacity to think about one's thought, also called "mentalization," is written about at length in a recent publication by P. Fonagy, G. Gergely, E. Jurist, and M. Target. (*Affect Regulation, Mentalization and the Development of the Self*. New York: Other Press, 2002.)

11. MK/VS, February 3, 1969.

12. MK/RS, July 3, 1964.

13. MK/RS, April 10, 1970.

14. WB, February 3, 1980.

15. MK/VS, October 23, 1967. Also note: "I have known since adolescence the stance of shut-inness with myself, or shut-outness by the other. I had the means and the temperament to live in an exotic stance of aloneness" (WB, October 21, 1969).

16. MK/VS, December 12, 1970.

17. Khan1963a.

18. WB, June 6, 1979.

19. MK/WG, December 11, 1964.

20. Khan's master's thesis in 1945 was entitled "From Excitement to Epiphany: A Study of [James] Joyce's Development." All copies of the thesis are apparently lost. Khan claimed there were two typed copies—the original and a carbon—and that he himself lost one while the other was lost by T. S. Eliot, to whom he mailed it in 1946 (WB, May 6, 1971).

21. Margarita said the cause of Mahmooda's death was penicillin, Khalida Khan said it was typhoid fever, and Eva said it was a urinary tract infection.

22. WB, March 29, 1975.

23. WB, February 15, 1980. It was only when Khan met his second wife, Svetlana Beriosova, more than a decade later, that he found a female with whom he had a relationship of similar intensity: "I was so devoted to my sister that it was a tragedy for me when she died. It was to take another sixteen years before I was to find another person—you!—whom I could love and be devoted to with the same obsessive absoluteness" (MK/SB, June 5, 1965).

24. Cooper 1993.

25. MK/VS, January 24, 1970.

26. MK/SB, June 5, 1965

27. See MK/WG, October 8, 1964. Cooper (1993, p. 11) writes that Latif was a psychologist who trained in the United States. My differing information is based on information from Pearl King and Riaz Khan (husband of Khalida Khan) and on letters of recommendation to the Institute of Psychoanalysis written by Anna Freud and Donald Winnicott (AFP).

28. The information is from Riaz Khan, who also told me that Latif was a convert to Christianity from Islam. In addition to his clinical practice, Latif taught at Forman Christian College in Lahore, a school with links to the American Presbyterian church. According to Riaz Khan, Latif was strange looking, with a long mustache that curled at the ends—but he added, "Every psychiatrist I've ever known has been somewhat strange looking!"

29. The Shiite tradition was consistent with Fazaldad's tribal Rajput identity, in which estates are also distributed to sons only.

30. Nawab Sir Mehr Shah was an Indian prince who was given the title of "Sir" by the British. In 1980, Khan was in Lahore and he went to visit Nawab Sir Mehr Shah, reporting: "I went to pay him homage. He is the last of my father's friends alive; the rest are all dead and gone. I was very moved by a certain quality of ceremony and affection in him, so aged but still so intact" (letter, MK to Sahabzada Yaqub Khan, December 18, 1980).

31. WB, June 21, 1979.

32. The information about Wavell is from Khan's obituary of himself, written February 6, 1979 (RSP), and it may not be accurate. (See footnote 2, Chapter 3.)

ENDNOTES TO CHAPTER 3

1. WB, June 9, 1976.

2. MK, unpublished obituary of himself, February 6, 1979 (RSP). Cooper (1993, p. 4) suggests that the account of Khan attending Balliol College may be a complete fabrication, an example of what Khan called his "yarns." However, the son of his father's second wife had gone to Oxford, where he died in an accident, so the family obviously knew how to make such a connection. Khan's obituary of himself was written late in his life, when he was prone to exaggerations and lies, but the story about Oxford is also contained in letters he wrote to Robert Stoller (May 20, 1964) and Riccardo Steiner (December 7, 1984). In the obituary of himself, Khan says he arrived on October 5, 1946, but in the letters he gives the date October 2, 1946. Adam Limentani, a peer who had talked with Khan about his history over many years, believed the Oxford story when he wrote his 1992 obituary of Khan, although he mistakenly says that Khan arrived in London in 1943. The exact truth about Khan's arrival in London is difficult or impossible to know at this point in time.

3. Letter, MK to Riccardo Steiner, December 7, 1984.

4. WB, December 25, 1975.

5. Glover practiced analysis in London under the auspices of the Swiss Psychoanalytic Society, but he was no longer a training analyst for the BPAS. The fact that Lowenfeld referred Khan to Edward Glover shows that she did not think Khan was seeking analytic training—she would have known Glover could not treat a candidate.

6. Khan's close friend Pearl King, a member of his training class, points out that the English analysts were worldly intellectuals who would have wanted to be helpful to an Indian. Guilt about the upcoming abandonment of India by England may have caused Bowlby to be especially interested in an Indian emigree in 1946. Bowlby himself had applied for analytic training at age twenty-two, so he would not have been put off by Khan's youthfulness (van Dijken, 1998, p. 64).

7. MK/RS, May 20, 1964. Khan's description may be an exaggeration of what actually occurred. Willoughby (2005, p. 21) claims that Khan wrote from

India to the Institute of Psycho-Analysis inquiring about training, not about personal analysis. And Bowlby, in a letter to the Chicago analyst James Anderson on December 18, 1989, denied almost all the events described by Khan. But Bowlby's letter, written twenty-five years later, shows an animosity to Khan that could have motivated him to deny what happened. Furthermore, Bowlby expresses doubt that Khan's family had significant wealth, and he is definitely wrong about that.

8. Khan's account of his interview with Bowlby has been previously published and discussed in an article in *American Imago* (Hopkins 2004). Khan wrote another version of these interviews with John Bowlby and Sylvia Payne in a letter to Riccardo Steiner dated December 7, 1984. This letter gives further confirmation of the state of confusion regarding just who Khan was, with Payne for some reason thinking he was a Communist activist: "[In the interview] I could not make out why Dr. Bowlby gave me a very long interview and asked all sorts of questions about my family and parentage—something I had never been exposed to before. He told me Dr. Edward Glover had resigned from the Society and I must see Dr. Payne next. I was quite confused as to what was happening until I went for an interview with Dr. Sylvia Payne. After some fifteen minutes in which she asked me only one question: 'Are you not still the President of the Northern India Communist Party?' and upon my reply 'No! Dr. Payne' she said blandly and firmly that she was a true staunch product of the British Empire, that it was regrettable that I could not go to Dr. Glover for analysis, but that she would arrange it with Miss Ella Sharpe, who was a most cultured person and a real scholar of Shakespeare and English literature. She said there was a meeting of the Training Committee that week and I would be hearing from Dr. Bowlby." Payne's fear about Khan's political identity were unfounded. In his college years, the political tensions of an imminent Independence had been a major concern for many students, but his passions had not been ignited: "In the years that I was growing up at college (1940–1946) in Northern India, the bias was for facile revolutionary stances. I became very suspicious of a revolt that was lacking both in tradition and perspective, hence opted out" (MK/RS, January 30, 1968).

9. Bollas (1989) writes that in circumstances of fate, a person has no control over what happens in his/her life; but with regard to destiny, there is a "destiny drive" where there is at least a feeling of being in control. In living a life where the destiny drive is expressed, a person strives to fulfill what he calls "the idiom of the true self" (p. 49).

10. MK/RS, April 10, 1970. Khan would be the analyst of two contemporary analytic writers, Christopher Bollas and Adam Phillips, who also make significant use of backgrounds in literature in their analytic writings.

11. See Grosskurth 1986, King and Steiner 1991, Kohon 1986a, and Segal 1979.

12. The first analysts to whom Khan related in London all had European connections: Sylvia Payne and Ella Sharpe were both analyzed by Hans Sachs in Berlin; John Rickman was analyzed by Freud in Vienna, by Ferenczi in Berlin, and then by Melanie Klein in London; and Winnicott was analyzed in London by James Strachey and Joan Riviere, both of whom had been analyzed by Freud in Vienna.

13. This coherence is, from the perspective of the British analyst Gregorio Kohon (1986), "[a] characteristic achievement of the British psychoanalysts, accomplished through their remarkable capacity for compromise" (1986, p. 45). But many British analysts view the compromise as a weakness, because it covered up bitter disputes without allowing for open discussion. Nina Coltart, a leading Independent who is now deceased, commented: "It's a great pity the Society didn't split. It was like putting together chalk and cheese. . . . If the Kleinians had gone off and formed their own Society, and if the Independents and the Freudians had been left to get on with their view of things, I think the situation would have been far better. We would have been spared this constant nagging, this semi-underground warfare between people and groups" (Molino 1997, p. 172). Khan agreed with Coltart: "Reserve and caution are the British equivalent of belligerent fisticuffs, only the former are much more lethal in their effect and negativity" (MK/RS, May 20, 1964).

14. Sylvia Payne was the main leader for the compromise movement within the society. Ella Sharpe was a solid member of the Middle Group. John Rickman and Winnicott both supported Klein before becoming rather anti-Kleinian members of the Middle Group. Over time, Khan came to be an enemy of the Kleinians due to his close association with Rickman, Winnicott, and Anna Freud. A reminder of the intensity of the Melanie Klein–Anna Freud feud comes from a memory of Khan told by a peer from the 1940s: "All the students told a story about Masud that may or may not have been true. It was that when Masud met Melanie Klein for the first time, she narrowed her eyes, looking as if she might spit on him, and hissed: 'I know why you are here— you are here to spy for Anna Freud!'" (letter to the author from Johanna Krout Tabin, June 23, 2001).

ENDNOTES TO CHAPTER 4

1. Letter, Ella Sharpe to Donald Winnicott, November 7, 1946; quoted in Rodman (2003, p. 146).

2. Rayner 1991, p. 183.

3. MK/RS, May 19, 1964.

4. Letter, MK to R. Steiner, December 7, 1984.

5. Rycroft 1996, pp. 727–728.

6. Nehru's announcement of the split reflects the intensity of a decision that impacted the entire world: "Long years ago we made a tryst with destiny, and now the time comes when we shall redeem our pledge. . . . At the stroke of the midnight hour, while the world sleeps, India will awake to life and freedom. A moment comes, which comes but rarely in history, when we step out from the old to the new, when an age ends, and when the soul of a nation, long suppressed, finds utterance" (speech to the Indian Consituent Assembly, New Delhi, August 14, 1947). The film *Earth*, produced by Deepa Mehta in 1999, gives a graphic depiction of the horrors of independence in Lahore, which were witnessed first-hand by Khan's nieces, Khalida Khan and Fatima Ahmed.

7. In a very rare reference to the politics of Indian independence, Khan gives a completely psychological analysis, saying that the most basic reason for the savagery was the personal distaste that Jinnah (the Muslim leader) and Gandhi (the Hindu) felt for each other (MK/WG, December 2, 1964). Khan would often say, with some accuracy, that he also avoided political struggle in the British Psycho-Analytical Society and international psychoanalysis. He credited Anna Freud for teaching him in the 1950s to stay out of analytic politics, but this seems to have been his tendency even apart from her influence.

8. Khan 1977b, p. 185.

9. Told by Eva Rosenfeld to Pearl King, then told to the author by Pearl King in an interview in 2000.

10. Letter, MK to R. Steiner, December 7, 1984. In the minutes of the informal joint meeting of the BPAS of June 2004 (P. Daniel, Hon., secretary of Ethical Committee), however, it is reported that the first case was supervised by Anna Freud.

11. MK/WG, July 29, 1964.

12. Anonymous girlfriend.

13. Bion 1985, p. 46. Wilfred Bion, who would go on to make major contributions to psychoanalysis, had been analyzed by Klein as well as Rickman, and he

wrote that the Klein analysis went deeper, even though he was not amenable to Klein's views: "The interpretations that I ignored or did not understand or made no response to later seemed to have been correct" (Bion 1985, p. 68).

14. WB, May 16, 1976.

15. The title of his paper, which he presented in either 1950 or 1951, was "The Dissolution of Object Representation in Modern Art: An Essay on Cubism." The discussant was the literary critic Herbert Read, and Khan recalled: "Read had to open the discussion prematurely because, overambitiously and copying the style of my analyst Rickman, I had given the talk from notes and sat down in a faint and daze during a pause in my narrative" (WB, September 5, 1969).

16. WB, September 5, 1969.

17. WB, September 5, 1969.

18. WB, May 3, 1971.

19. Roazen 2000, p. 179.

20. WB, April 8, 1971.

21. Letter to the author from Johanna Krout Tabin, an American analyst who trained in London. Tabin also told me a story that shows Clara's apparent innocence: "I remember the first time I realized how smart [Clara] was: Anna Freud had given us an assignment to pretend we were writing an analytic advice column in a newspaper, and we had to respond to a question from a mother about how she should relate to her seven year old daughter who was begging her to have a baby. I wrote a long essay on the topic, applying developmental theory— it was the longest essay I ever wrote, except for my thesis. [Clara] was singled out by Anna Freud as having written the perfect answer and it consisted of just one sentence: 'Dear mother, Please give your child a puppy.' This answer shows how practical yet sensitive [Clara] was."

22. Letter dated April 28, 1951, quoted in Bion 1985, p. 92.

23. An example of apparently unconscious racism is that many people told me that when Donald Winnicott made referrals to Khan, he first asked: "Would you mind seeing a Pakistani?"

24. Eric Rayner, quoted in Cooper 1993, pp. xi–xii. Also see Said 2003.

25. This misspelling is something I have seen firsthand, to the extent that it is perhaps as common to see Khan's name misspelled as to see it spelled accurately. The misspelling has occurred in analytic articles, in popular journals, and in almost every first draft of a brochure where I have spoken about Khan. (Examples of the "Kahn" error can be found in the otherwise careful writing of

Boynton 2003, Gerhardt and Sweetman 2001, Hazell 1996, Merkin 2003, and Mitchell 1991.) Furthermore, the "Google" listings of my Khan publications occur under "Kahn." If mistakes have an unconscious meaning, as Sigmund Freud showed us a century ago, Westerners might wonder why we deny Khan his name. We may unwittingly be revealing a resistance to accepting that this man who moved in the innermost circles at the highest levels of our cultural world was a Muslim from Pakistan, an outsider. The problem cannot be dismissed as a lack of familiarity with an unusual sequence of letters: How many times has the reader seen the Mongol warrior Genghis Khan referred to as "Genghis K-A-H-N"?

ENDNOTES TO CHAPTER 5

1. MK/RS, May 20, 1964.

2. MK/WG, November 23, 1964.

3. John Sutherland (quoted in Scharff 1994) refers to Khan as "Winnicott's principal disciple," André Green (1997) says Khan was "the acknowledged authority on Winnicott," and John Davis (personal communication) calls Khan "the person who Winnicott felt best understood his work."

4. Khan 1975d, p. xii. The title of Winnicott's lecture was "Paediatrics and Psychiatry."

5. Ego psychology developed within mainstream psychoanalysis, building on Sigmund Freud's late attention to defense mechanisms in personality. The practical implication was that treatment of patients was done through interpretation of maladaptive defenses and their underlying drives; relationship with the analyst was important only for the purpose of a therapeutic alliance and as the space where the transference occurred. Ego psychologists of Khan's era accepted James Strachey's idea that change occurs in an analysis only when transference distortions are interpreted by the analyst and understood by the analysand.

6. Khan, 1975d, p. xi.

7. Joseph Sandler told me that Khan's ear was operated on by Sir Archibald McIndoe, a famous surgeon who had operated on wounded soldiers during and after the war: "McIndoe was really the top surgeon in London. Masud always had to have the best."

8. Winnicott still believed that interpretations had value, and he must have made many of them to Khan. But in an article written after Winnicott's death,

Khan dismissed the value of his interpretations, writing that they interfered with an analysand's journey to discover his creative potential and personal "madness" (1979a, p. 182).

9. WB, February 4, 1971.

10. MK/RS, April 10, 1970.

11. WB, February 6, 1971.

12. At the BPAS memorial service for Ernest Jones, March 8, 1979, Khan himself told a story about his haughtiness. In the early 1950s, he had been working in the institute library when a man walked in one afternoon. At first the man took no notice of Khan but after some time, he asked, "Who are you?" Khan replied, "My father told me that he who does not know your name is not worth telling [it] to," upon which the man was deeply offended and left the library. These were the words his father told him to say to a teacher who did not know his name at age nine (see Chapter 1). Khan recalled that when he then asked the secretary who the man was and learned that he was Ernest Jones, "I nearly collapsed."

13. A story told about Jim Harris is that in 1968 he engaged in a shouting match with an analysand who was a heart–lung surgeon, and then, immediately after the session, Harris suffered a heart attack. The analysand saved his life by giving him a cardiac massage while waiting for an ambulance (interview with Maureen Harris, 1998).

14. "In my 23 years or so in Europe, there are only three instances where I received more than I gave: Jim Harris, the Cassous, and the Stollers" (WB, September 13, 1969). Khan's relationship with the Cassous will be described later in this chapter, and the Stollers are part of his story starting in 1964.

15. WB, October 7, 1970. For more on Rycroft's career, see Pearson (2004).

16. Jane Shore is the maiden name of Jane Shore Nicholas.

17. Khan wrote of Zullig: "When I first came to London, I enjoyed an exquisitely tender & loyal friendship with a male dancer, Hans Zullig, who was a famous dancer of Kurt Joos Ballet. . . . We had great joy of livingness shared ceremoniously between us, but I was always aware of his private pain vis-à-vis me [because] he was a homosexual & I couldn't meet his desire" (MK/VS, August 26, 1968). Willoughby (2005) suggests that Khan "certainly" was teasing and tantalising to Zullig as he intruded into his personal space (p. 70), but Willoughby does not give a source for the information and I found no evidence of this.

18. Shore remembers that one of her father's friends, a retired international banker, was giving an invited speech at the wedding reception and, to everyone's

horror, he made a racist comment about Japanese Netsuke art, in which there is a contrast of ivory and wood. Shore's father stepped in with a spontaneous speech that softened the impact. After the wedding, her aunt, in a letter to a friend, wrote: "My niece has disgraced the family by marrying a Pakistani."

19. The address was 4 Ashburn Gardens, SW7, off of Cromwell Road. Willoughby (2005, p. 24) reports that Khan had been living there with Tahir prior to the marriage.

20. Information about the steps is from H.K.

21. The play was directed by Michael Benthall and choreographed by Robert Helpmann and Frederick Ashton. Shore had a minor role as understudy to Moira Shearer's Titania and there were also ballet sequences in which she danced.

22. "In my first marriage I was not so much unhappy as uninvested in terms of my imagination and interests. So I packed it up: simply and ruthlessly" (MK/WG, December 19–22, 1964).

23. It was a long book review criticising W. R. D. Fairbairn, a Scottish analyst, for deviating from classical theory (Fairbairn 1952). Apparently the review was not well received: "It earned us everyone's spite" (WB, May 10, 1975). It is the only professional publication that Winnicott coauthored, other than work he published with his wife Clare, and its style suggests that it was primarily written by Khan. It is unclear whether the coauthorship was a gift from Khan to his analyst or a gift in the other direction, with Winnicott lending his name to enhance the status of the publication.

24. Willoughby (2005) believes that Khan never returned to analysis with Winnicott after the temporary sacrifice of his hours for Jane Shore. But Khan writes in his Work Book (May 3, 1971) that the analysis lasted 15 years, ending in 1966, and this is the number reported by Cooper, who consulted with Khan about the facts reported in her biography (1993, p. 20). Marion Milner referred to the hiatus in Khan's analysis as follows: "I believe the [editing instead of analysis] went on for a whole year" (Milner quoted in Willoughby 2005, p. 72). I believe that Milner is saying in this quote that the analysis resumed after a year, but Willoughby believes Milner is suggesting that the editing lasted a year, without reference to the analysis being resumed. In my opinion, which is a contrast to Willoughby's, Khan returned to analysis for some period of time. Jane Shore cannot help in resolving this controversy, because she told both Willoughby and me that she did not know if Khan returned to analysis. We are thus left unsure

about the exact nature of the analysis, except to know that it lasted somewhere between five and fifteen years, with Winnicott providing some form of analysis or analytic "coverage" throughout the period 1951–1966. ("Coverage" is a term used by Khan to describe Winnicott's availability as a therapeutic consultant and as a support. See MK/VS, February 7, 1971.) Rodman (2003, p. 206) suggests that even if the contract for sessions was not continuous, Winnicott considered Khan to be his analysand until 1966.

25. Khan sent Shore only five pounds a month, so Winnicott charged her a low fee of two shillings. Shore told me that for a long time all she could do was cry, and then she tended to be overly quiet: "Winnicott would say 'You are decorating again. I want to know what's underneath!'" Winnicott, however, was patient as he waited for her to be spontaneous: "He used to have discreet floral arrangements in his consulting room. Once there was a vase with three flowers, and when he left the room for some reason, I broke two of them off and stuffed them down into the vase. He said: 'I suppose that's a good sign.'"

26. Shore told me: "I believe Svetlana got the C.B.E. (Commander of the British Empire)—one rank higher than mine."

27. The presence of anxiety and the openness to change suggest that the diagnosis of character disorder, which is regularly used to describe Khan, may have been secondary to other pathology in the 1950s. People with character disorders do not experience anxiety and they are generally unmotivated to do therapeutic work to modify their psychopathology. In later years, in response to environmental stress and alcoholism, Khan's character disorder overshadowed his other pathology and he became resistant to change, although he was still prone to anxiety.

28. MK/SB, November 12, 1957.

29. MK/SB, November 18, 1957.

30. MK/SB, November 18, 1957.

31. MK/VS, May 17, 1969.

32. MK/RS, March 23, 1971.

33. Rycroft added: "Everyone treated him like a celebrity, with the exception of me, my then-wife, and Jim Armstrong Harris."

34. I had the privilege of interviewing Milner at age ninety-six; she remembered Khan fondly.

35. If he had followed ordinary analytic protocol, Winnicott would have referred Shore to another analyst and limited his contact with Khan to the analytic

hours. But Winnicott had a grandiosity that led him to be reluctant to give up control over a case by making a referral. As Hanna Segal told me: "Winnicott thought he was the only one who could do analysis right." In a memorial to Winnicott in 1972, Khan commented: "Yes, he [Winnicott] had a huge pride and his self-esteem could be daunted only by his own errors, not the censure of others" (MK, text copy of memorial address, January 19, 1972; RSP).

36. Rycroft 1996, p. 728. Rycroft did not find a lasting home at the BPAS. Looking back, he felt "used" by the senior people. He was especially resentful of Winnicott, who, he told me, stole some of his ideas, using Khan as intermediary: "In those early days, I found that if I wanted to influence DWW's papers, all I had to do was talk to Masud about something and I would soon see it in writing. For example, Winnicott was never very good in thinking about dreams and some of the things he wrote were things I had talked about with Masud just a bit earlier."

37. The first version of his paper was entitled "A Homosexual Episode as a Defence Against Masturbation" and the final version was entitled "Notes on Homosexual Episodes in a Male Patient."

38. A.-M. Sandler 2004.

39. E-mail to the author from Joseph Sandler, September 25, 1998.

40. WB, July 5, 1969. This was a hard time for Rycroft, because his wife was involved in a public affair with another analyst. Khan claimed that Sylvia Payne, Rycroft's analyst, had pressured him to extend the invitation to share the flat because Rycroft was having a breakdown.

41. Khan's rapidly acquired capacity to remember dreams seems to be an example of compliance/imitation rather than a true development. It is, perhaps, an example of the False Self acting out the role of the True Self "*as it would be if it had had existence*" (Winnicott 1960, p. 147 his italics). This idea is supported by the Khan's later statements that although he knew that he had an active dream life, upon waking he rarely remembered specific dreams.

42. Letter, Ismond Rosen to Ruth Rosen, January 18, 1963.

43. In London, Rosen and Khan were regulars at a popular club called The White Elephant, on Curzon Street. They also enjoyed watching squash matches at the Lansdowne Club on Berkeley Square, especially any match that involved the Pakistani master players Azam Khan and Hashim Khan. Rosen was born in 1924, the same year as Masud Khan, but he did not marry until 1963, four years after Khan's second marriage.

44. Paul Roazen, who met Gorer in the 1960s, summarizes him as "an exceptionally intelligent commentator on British psychoanalysis, and altogether a fascinating figure himself" (Roazen 2000, p. 5). Khan's most frequent socializing with Gorer would be in the 1960s, when he regularly consulted with him about cultural influences in psychoanalysis, and when Gorer became infatuated with Svetlana Beriosova.

45. Uma Vasudev had a significant career in India. She was a founding editor of the popular magazine *India Today* and became a well-known political analyst and novelist. She is also the author of *Two Faces of Indira Gandhi*, written under the pen name of Vasudev Malhotra. An undated clipping of an interview in an unidentified newspaper in the 1970s, saved by Khalida Khan, suggests that she never forgot Tahir: "The first time I suffered pain was when I was about 20. I was with my parents in England, fell in love with a Muslim from Pakistan, and settled in London. Realising how intense were my feelings for him, my parents brought me back to India, with the promise that they'll send me back after six months, if my feelings for him remain unchanged. Though my feelings didn't change and in fact grew more intense, my parents wouldn't send me back. There was so much parental pressure, so much opposition, that for two years I couldn't go back. And during this time, he married a German. I was so miserable, totally devastated. I loved him so much that even today, although so many years have passed, yet I haven't been able to forget him. Not only because he was my first love, but, then, it was a beautiful, ideal relationship, so ideal that in spite of the fact that we couldn't marry, no bitterness crept in, although the pain was immense. The only way I kept myself going was to immerse myself in work."

46. Willoughby (2005) reports many details of Tahir's life based on a report written by the analyst Clifford Scott, with whom Tahir had an analytic consultation. Tahir's daughter allowed me to interview her but she was insistent that her name not be used in this biography.

47. When Dr. Latif, Khan's therapist/analyst from Lahore, emigrated to London in the 1950s, Khan did not try to make a close connection. Latif had applied for membership in the BPAS and, upon his request, Khan solicited some letters of support for him. The application was not successful, however, and Latif soon disappeared completely from Khan's London circles. (See letters from Donald Winnicott, Sylvia Payne, and Anna Freud in support of Latif's membership application, AFP.)

ENDNOTES TO CHAPTER 6

1. Letter to the author from anonymous French analyst, December 9, 1997.

2. Khan 1972c, pp. 284–285.

3. The initials "H.K." are accurate and H.K. is aware that many people will know his full name.

4. The format of this interview, and others to come, has been changed so that my questions and comments are eliminated. The interviews are edited but the quotes are verbatim quotes.

5. For more details about H.K.'s socialization with Khan, see Chapter 36. The socialization was Khan's error, not H.K.'s, because the analyst is responsible for maintaining the analytic frame.

6. L.U. was not accepted as a trainee at the BPAS until he had been in analysis with Khan for several years. He was able to convert his therapeutic analysis into a training analysis, because the rules had changed to allow for this kind of transition.

7. H.K. told me that in his memory the only cigarettes Khan ever smoked were French Celtiques.

ENDNOTES TO CHAPTER 7

1. MK/ZD, July 15, 1961.

2. MK/SB, November 15, 1962.

3. MK/SB, November 7, 1957.

4. Sadie Gillespie quoted Thomas Main in our interview in 2002.

5. WB, May 25, 1975.

6. Zullig had also introduced Khan to Jane Shore.

7. Beriosova and Shore knew each other professionally, although they were never close friends.

8. Mary Drage is the maiden name of Mary Drage Frazier Eyre.

9. Interview with Sybil Christopher (ex-wife of Richard Burton), 1998.

10. Tony Walton told me about the affectionate use of nicknames in the inner circle of Masud's and Svetlana's world: "Within our circle we had a habit of calling each other by pet names—usually making use of diminutives. We would add 'is' or 'gee' to the end of names. T. H. White, for example, was 'Timgee'

and I was 'Tonis.' Masud was 'Sud' or 'Sudie' or 'Sudis' and Zoe Dominic was 'Zoia' or 'Zois.' Svetlana was almost always 'Svetlanagee' or 'Gee.'"

11. MK/SB, Tuesday, November 12, 1957.

12. MK/SB, September 12, 1958.

13. The first reception, in the early afternoon, was for dancers who had Saturday night performances, and the second was an evening reception for everyone else. Unlike Jane Shore, Beriosova did not have to dance on her wedding night.

14. Unidentified newspaper clippings saved by Mary Drage.

15. The reference to "Tahir Bhai Jan" is best understood as "my brother Tahir."

16. WB, January 22, 1976.

17. Letter to the author from Corin Redgrave, December 15, 1996.

18. Harrod's is a large and expensive store, where wealthy shoppers leave their Jaguars and Mercedes Benzes for valet parking. Within its 1.2 million square feet of retail space, there can be found a bank, a fire brigade, a pet store, a huge food court, and a personal tailoring service, as well as Europe's largest hair salon (17,500 square feet). (Fawn Vrazo, "E-mail from London," *Philadelphia Inquirer*, January 9, 1997, C-1.)

19. Many people have Harrod's stories as part of their Khan memories. Here is one from Tony Walton: "One Christmas Eve, Sud and I went to Harrod's late in the afternoon to get gifts for Svetlana. There was a long line and we had to wait at least an hour and a half—and Masud hated waiting in line. Just as we got to the front, the poor harassed clerk was about to wait on us and suddenly a little elderly lady pushed in front of us. Masud rose up and said to her in a loud voice: 'Madame! The Good Lord has made you a woman and against that I cannot go! But if this man serves you before he serves me, I shall personally tweak his nose!' And everyone in the line burst into laughter."

20. Khan's affection for Kalu shows his Western identification, because traditional Muslims do not take dogs as house pets. (The prophet Mohammed proclaimed dogs to be unclean and, as a result, traditional Muslims accept dogs only for their usefulness, as in guarding a house.) Khalida Khan recalls that although her father was a veterinarian who cared for the house pets of the British in Lahore, it would have been unheard of for a dog to come into their home.

21. MK/ZD, August 25, 1962.

22. In the summer of 1964, while the Khans were in the United States, Khan

wrote to Zoë Dominic and asked her to go to visit (!) Kalu, who was being cared
for by Winnicott's secretary, Mrs. Coles (MK/ZD, July 18, 1964). Later in 1964,
as he and Beriosova were packing to go to Pakistan for Christmas, he wrote:
"Poor Kalu has left to stay with Mrs. Coles for the Xmas. Packing up his luggage and food was very saddening. Nearly made me cry" (MK/WG, December
19, 1964). Once he described packing his suitcase to meet Beriosova in Chicago
and finding that Kalu was missing: "We [referring to the secretary, the houseboy,
and himself] ran all round and couldn't find Kalu. Then I figured it out. I checked
again in the bedroom and he lay there asleep in the suitcase, all ready to be taken
to Chicago. He must have figured out in his tiny soul that these curious things
always accompany us & return with us; so he housed himself there. What a treat
it would be for Svetlana if I could have taken him with me!" (MK/ZD, June 17,
1965).

23. Khan called his helpers "staff" rather than "servants," because, in his
opinion, "servant" was a vulgar term (Khan 1988d, p. 110).

24. The Khan houseboys included a Filipino named Almontero, an Italian
named Antonio, and a much-adored Spaniard named Susu. One houseboy, Piero
de Monzi (d. 2000), was a homosexual man with exquisite taste who went on to
establish an exclusive men's clothing store on fashionable Fulham Road.

25. "This is what Svetlana and I love most about you: we are relaxed and
natural in your company. We share the aches & nerves, the exultations, the gossip
and companionship, and it is casual and serious" (MK/ZD, March 25, 1965).

26. MK/ZD, September 9, 1962.

27. Khan would have many female friends in his lifetime, but he reported
that he cared the most about Julie Andrews. In a letter to Zoë Dominic, he wrote:
"I have a deep longing of affection for Julie. She is one of the very few people
who has never hurt or outraged me even inadvertently" (June 17, 1967). Their
friendship did not survive the breakup of Andrews and Walton, and Khan never
became a friend of Julie's second husband, the movie director Blake Edwards,
whom she married in 1969.

28. WB, February 4, 1980.

29. Writing about the early years of their marriage, Khan commented:
"Beriosova had genius and was consumed by her own becoming; I had only talent" (WB, May 25, 1975).

30. MK/SB, April 10, 1963.

31. WB, June 11, 1979. Mary Drage remembers that Beriosova never complained about the rigors of her life and that her devotion was an inspiration to

the younger dancers. She practiced every day, even on holidays, when she had a special agreement with the Covent Garden guards so that she could sneak in. Julie Andrews told me that she learned how to work hard by watching Beriosova in the early 1960s.

32. Redgrave continued, "I was, as you may guess, a little in love with her, though I'm sure I never told her so. I don't think I even told myself. Just as well, because winning her, or even borrowing her, from Masud would have been a hopeless task" (letter to the author from Corin Redgrave, December 15, 1996).

33. Margot Fonteyn moved in different circles. On one occasion after her return to dancing, she was arrested on a marijuana charge in San Francisco, and Beriosova temporarily replaced her, dancing with Nureyev. The radical political movements of the 1960s were significant to Khan only as psychological phenomena. Watching the Redgrave family deal with the political activism of Vanessa, he was unsympathetic: "We have been worried sick about Vanessa, who we are certain has been arrested today and will be in gaol for sure. We ran into her yesterday going downstairs and she was in a frantic manic state from anxiety and exhilaration, which makes one wonder whether these youngsters don't really get carried away by the hysteria and collective emotionality of it all. . . . We live in an age which is so free from natural fears and anxieties that in order to lend significance to our over-cerebral lives, we have to think up causes to fret about" (MK/ZD, September 17, 1961).

34. MK/ZD, July 21, 1961.

35. Born in Lithuania on September 24, 1932, Beriosova was the only child of parents who were both dancers. Her biographer tells the following story: "When Svetlana was about 8 years old and had already been studying for a while . . . her father asked her if she wanted to be a dancer. Now, he said, was the time of decision. The life of a dancer was the hardest life of all. Would she not rather grow up as a normal child, playing with other children, instead of turning towards the barre when others were enjoying games and freedom? But to Svetlana there was no question to answer. To dance was already her life, not something to be learnt as a task, or some little skill with which to show off at parties" (Franks 1958, p. 16). During the turmoil of World War II, the Beriosov family emigrated from Lithuania to France, then to England, and finally to the United States, where Svetlana became what was known as a baby ballerina, dancing with various companies. After her mother died in 1942, she was cared for by a series of women she referred to as stepmothers. In 1947, she joined the corps de ballet of the Grand Ballet de Monte Carlo, headed by the Marquis de Cuevas. A few

months later, Beriosova and her father both accepted invitations to join the Metropolitan Ballet in London, and after some time Beriosova joined Sadler's Wells Ballet, the group that became the Royal Ballet.

36. When Khan later considered writing about his life in the 1960s, he said, "For the section on Beriosova . . . I will choose the title: 'The Arabesque Lives: Caetera Fumus'" ["The Arabesque Lives: All Else Is Smoke"] (WB, August 12, 1979). He found this reference to the words of Mantegua in a writing of T. S. Eliot that quoted S. Spender.

37. The article was in the June 7 issue. *The Queen* was a 100-year-old society magazine that was widely read at that time. "[In the 1960s, *The Queen*] was the most vital publication in the country, a barometer of what was cool and worthy" (Levy, S. *Ready, Steady, Go! The Smashing Rise and Giddy Fall of Swinging London*. New York: Doubleday, 2002, p. 204).

38. On several occasions, Beriosova showed exceptional courage as a dancer, and these incidents were widely reported. In 1961, her role in dancing Frederick Ashton's *Persephone* required her to wear a microphone with a battery pack on her stomach, so that she could recite Andre Gide's poetry in French. She suffered third-degree burns when the microphone had a short circuit, but ignored the pain and kept dancing. In New York in 1967, performing as Cinderella in Ashton's ballet of the same name, she came onstage in a gilded carriage drawn by six mice. The pitch of the stage was unfamiliar to the dancers playing the mice, and the carriage tipped over, throwing her onto the stage and knocking her unconscious, upon which the performance stopped. When she regained consciousness, she went back onstage and finished the ballet. Khan wrote to a friend about this incident: "Fortunately [Svetlana] had not been hurt: only bruised and scratched. She continued the performance in true Beriosova style and had thunderous acclaim. It was a great occasion that nearly stumbled to disaster—then recovered and was exultant. But we have all been rattled by it and since then, TV, newsmen, and journalists haven't left her in peace" (MK/VS, April 21, 1967).

39. After Svetlana's mother's death, Poppa married a wardrobe mistress from his dance company; when they divorced, he married an Italian surgeon; and finally, after another divorce, he married Doris, a half-German woman who ran a ballet school in Zurich. It was only with Doris, who was Svetlana's age, that Poppa finally settled down.

40. "Poppa is such a little man that I am deeply affronted even to have to be antagonistic to him" (MK/ZD, May 19, 1967).

41. Khan wrote, "Svetlana lives austerely and the only indulgence she allows herself is in relation to me" (MK/ZD, June 17, 1965).

42. MK/ZD, October 2, 1962.

43. MK/SS, undated letter of 1962.

44. Nureyev defected in Paris on June 16, 1961—for details, see Solway (1998).

45. Solway 1998, pp. 228–229.

46. Khan described a not-atypical day that captures something about Beriosova's continued celebrity status even after Fonteyn's return. Beriosova had danced at Covent Garden and some of her fans sent onstage a huge stuffed rabbit that was holding a bunch of live flowers. As Beriosova made her bows, hugging the rabbit, "poor Bunny's head fell off." After greeting a group of fans back stage, the Khans had an informal dinner party for ten at their home served by their new Italian houseboy, Piero de Monzi. Then, "At 2:30 we broke up. I took Kalu for a stroll. Just as we were nearing our door, I saw a bubble-car with a huge Bunny in it. . . . The fans had seen the head fall off, insisted on taking bunny home, repaired it, and now were bringing it back. I simply could not but invite them up to a drink: much to Svetlana's peeve." The fans left at 3:45 a.m. (MK/ZD, April 10, 1965).

47. Khan was resentful when his contemplative states got disrupted: "A damnable American kid who has a stuffed toy parrot is sitting behind me making incessant parrot talk & everyone is indulging her on. If she doesn't stop soon, she will forget how to talk [like a person]" (undated letter, MK/ZD, August 1963).

48. MK/ZD, August 9, 1964.

49. Khan described a brief encounter with the playwright Lillian Hellman, who had a summer home nearby: "We had to go to coffee with a very complex and evil person in this town, one Lillian Hellman, a woman in her early 50s. She is one of that curious breed & brand of females who acquire a social niche and wield an uncanny amount of disruptive influence on young men & talent. It is inexplicable to me how they get to this point, because they are essentially unattractive, greedy, harsh, and cruelly petty women. Something to do with the inherent bisexuality of the American male & his awesome fixation on the negative castrating mother figure" (MK/ZD, August 1, 1964).

50. MK/WG, December 13, 1964.

51. Undated letter, MK/ZD, January 1965.

52. An anonymous friend claims that the fight involved something of a homosexual nature originating from one or both men.

53. MK/ZD, August 15, 1962.

54. MK/ZD, August 16, 1962.

ENDNOTES TO CHAPTER 8

1. MK/ZD, May 10, 1967.

2. E-mail to the author from Anita Kermode, March 19, 2004.

3. Khan considered Laing's ideas to be an accurate reflection of the spirit of the times, "a creatively symptomatic dogma of the contemporary craving for being saved through annihilation of the established ego-Self" (MK/VS, August 28, 1968).

4. Personal communication from Gregorio Kohon, December 2001.

5. Prior to this revolutionary era, various people had already laid a base of innovative work. In England, Winnicott (1954) had written about regression to dependence and Paula Heimann (1950) wrote about the use of countertransference to understand severely disturbed patients; in the United States there was John Rosen's book *Direct Analysis* (New York: Grune & Stratton, 1953); and from France, Marguerite Sechehaye's *Autobiography of a Schizophrenic Girl* (New York: Grune & Stratton, 1951). In a separate tradition, the American Harry Stack Sullivan inspired Frieda Fromm-Reichmann to work analytically with schizophrenics at the well-known mental hospital Chestnut Lodge, beginning around 1935 (G. Hornstein, *To Redeem One Person Is to Redeem the World: The Life of Frieda Fromm-Reichmann*. New York: Free Press, 2000).

6. Gregorio Kohon, who is an Independent, remembers, "I had to borrow money as part of my mortgage in order to train" (personal communication, December 2001).

7. Khan wrote to Wladimir Granoff about the transition to a new group to be called the Independents: "Tonight was the first meeting of the so-called Independents at our Institute. The Independents constitute the authentic stock of the British Society minus the Klein and Anna Freud groups. Over the past 18 years, they [the Klein and Anna Freud groups] have been steadily stealing all the teaching and programme initiative from the British Group. Gradually a few of us got rather concerned about it and mobilised our inert members into activity and protest" (November 12, 1964).

8. Khan described an incident that shows how much tension there was between Winnicott and the Kleinians: "In the last meeting of our Society, Meltzer

[Donald Meltzer was a Kleinian analyst] read a patently Kleinian paper where he stated openly that only the Kleinian analyst knows and only the Kleinian patient is cured. In response, Winnicott did one of his equal patently Winnicottian stunts: from the chair, he threw his copy of Meltzer's paper on the table & asked what was the meaning of this esoteric language which no-one in the British Society, outside of Kleinians, can understand. He was roundly snubbed by many Kleinians" (MK/VS, May 12, 1968). Winnicott was never allowed to teach a course on the treatment of children, due to these institutional politics.

9. Rayner, Introduction to Cooper 1993, p. xi.

10. Undated letter to the author from R. Gosling, October 1996.

11. The British analyst Bernard Barnett (interview, November 2003) told me more about Khan's teaching: "Khan was, as a teacher, an incredible showoff. On occasions, he would deliberately get a person's name wrong and when the person would correct him, he would wait until they mispronounced his name, as people always did. He was a teaser, sometimes sadistic, especially to Kleinian students. But he knew the material and was passionate about it—so one word I would use about him as a teacher is 'memorable.'"

12. The information is a personal communication from Peter Elder.

13. Anne-Marie Sandler told me about an encounter with Khan that she said was characteristic: "In the 60s, the first synthetic fur coats had come onto the market and my father bought me a synthetic leopard fur coat. It looked stunning. One winter day, I wore it to the scientific meeting because we had to go somewhere afterward. Masud saw the coat and he followed me. His eyes were lit up and he said: 'Let me help you' and reached to help me remove the coat. At the moment he touched it, he felt the light weight and he made a strange noise and just dropped the coat on the floor."

14. MK/ZD, April 26, 1963.

15. Dr. Karl Menninger (d. 1990) and his brother William founded the Menninger Clinic in Topeka, Kansas, in 1925. Khan wrote from Menninger's: "Attended Dr. Karl's Bible class on Sunday morning at 9:30 am. He had a dozen residents and patients come in and sat around talking to them casually and wisely about biblical themes. The specific chapter was 'Sermon on the Mount.' He has a true Episcopal style of speaking, neither earnest nor moralistic. I find him a monumental person. He is vigorous, elemental, moody, whimsical, collosal and abundant. Everyone here kow-tows to him abjectly, and then surreptitiously finds fault with him" (MK/WG, April 26, 1964). (The Menninger Clinic moved from Topeka to Houston, Texas, in 2002.)

16. MK/WG, April 30, 1965.

17. Khan considered health to consist of "aliveness," and his criterion for aliveness was that a person be growing—learning from others and open to change. Note these aphorisms written in the next decade: "Happiness is the capacity to be able to share oneself with oneself and with Others" (WB, March 24, 1972). "Any kind of stasis is sickness and sin" (WB, March 24, 1972). In the early 1960s, Khan appears to have had both aliveness and happiness.

ENDNOTES TO CHAPTER 9

1. Personal communication to the author.

2. Similarly, Peter Lomas, a British analyst, commented, "Charles Rycroft once told me that Khan, although a dilettante and 'rather mad,' was sometimes able to help people when others had failed. It may be that his spontaneity and impetuousity could stir life into some of those apparently beyond reach" (letter to the author, February 15, 2002).

3. None of Khan's more famous analysands are interviewed in this biography.

4. Peter Kramer, who was not in analysis with Khan, remembers that Khan analysands used to buy oversized porcelain teacups, apparently in imitation of the kind of teacup Khan used, thereby making a kind of public announcement that they admired their analyst and wanted to be like him (personal communication).

5. WB, July 16, 1970.

6. Elder's comment that Khan would not let him give back in the analysis is something that other Khan analysands also told me. Khan understood the importance of accepting reparation from the patient and even wrote about it: "One source of stasis in analysis lies in the fact that, for one reason or another, we do not receive or respond to the patient's reparative gestures towards us (symbolic) and/or do not need them, and they react by refusing our reparativeness towards them" (WB, April 8, 1969). His personal need for control may have limited him from applying this awareness to actual practice.

7. E-mail to the author, February 11, 2001.

8. Khan 1963c.

1. MK/SS, April 15, 1965.

2. Personal communication from Hilde Greenson.

3. Khan 1970a, p. 99.

4. MK/WG, September 20, 1965.

5. Khan's ideas were an elaboration of the theory of the French essayist Michel de Montaigne, formulated in the sixteenth century. According to Thompson (1998), Montaigne built on Aristotle's thinking in classifying three types of friendship: (1) friends who offer a source of pleasure; (2) friends with whom we engage in commerce; and (3) friends whom we love simply for being themselves. The third category is the superior "true" form of friendship, and it is this third category that Khan refers to when he uses the word *friendship*. The intimacy of lovers was not included in Khan's conceptualization of friendship: "Love is selfish and possessive of the other—that is its magic and violent virtue. Friendship is other-directed and gentle" (letter, MK to Joan Hughes, quoted in WB, April 15, 1973).

6. WB, November 9, 1969.

7. MK/WG, December 18, 1964. Leslie was Kayne's fiancée at the time of this comment.

8. Throughout his adult life, Khan stayed closely connected to his childhood friends Jamil Nishtar and Ijaz Batalwi, both of whom had stayed in Pakistan. In the West, his best male friends were (in roughly chronological order) Hans Zullig, Jim Armstrong Harris, Harvey Kayne, Ismond Rosen, Tony Walton, Wladimir Granoff, Robert Stoller, Barrie Cooper, André Green, and Victor Smirnoff.

9. The quote is from Eva.

10. The longtime friend is Sybil Stoller.

11. Women who had significant and primarily nonsexual friendships with Khan throughout the years include Sybil Stoller, Zoë Dominic, Leslie Kayne, Anita Kermode, Anne Money-Coutts, Marie-Claire Nivoix, another French woman who asks to be anonymous, Julie Andrews, Regina Pereira, and a woman in Vienna named Princess Lili Schonberg, whose elderly mother was also a friend.

12. Khan 1970a.

13. Khan 1970a, p. 111. Robert Stoller did not agree that crucial friendships

always end badly and he did not think Khan had provided evidence to prove his case (RS/MK, December 10, 1969).

14. Khan credits Montaigne's friend La Boetie with enabling Montaigne to secularize self-experience, which paved the way to Freud's discoveries about the self some 200 years later.

15. Rousseau's narcissistic friendships were presented as a contrast to "crucial friendship," because they illustrated his pathology of not being able to use others for self growth.

16. Khan 1970a, p. 108.

17. WB, November 2, 1969.

18. WB, November 8, 1969.

19. The existence of three crucial friendships is a testimony to Khan's talent for friendship. Henry Adams, an historian who was the grandson of John Quincy Adams, is reported to have said, "One friend in a lifetime is much, two are many, three are hardly possible."

ENDNOTES TO CHAPTER 11

1. MK/ZD, July 7, 1964.

2. Granoff believed in the historical recording of the major events of his life, so he preserved both sides of the correspondence in neat files with a summary of the contents on the inside cover of each folder. The correspondence is thousands of pages long, and Granoff allowed me to read all of it.

3. Roudinesco 1990, 1997, Turkle 1979.

4. "The point [of the variable-length session] was to turn the transference relationship into a dialectic by halting a session at certain significant words in order to reactivate unconscious desire" (Roudinesco 1997, p. 203).

5. The Khan/Granoff correspondence is filled with details of Granoff's strategizing to get his group accepted by the IPA, and Granoff also described this to me. Granoff told me that there was one time when Khan's influence went beyond supportive listening. Granoff and his peers had already decided to "exclude" Lacan from membership in the APF, but a senior colleague then began to waver in the decision, suggesting that Lacan should be invited to join the new group. Granoff told the colleague, "Look, if I try to stab somebody and the knife accidentally hits a rib instead of the heart, I am not going to apologize about that. Instead I will immediately stab him again, but efficiently

this time—or else I will turn the knife against myself. I'm not going to say, 'Oh, I'm so sorry, the knife slipped.'" The colleague was convinced to stop wavering and stick to the plan. Granoff made his point using words that came straight from his new friend: "I used the words that Masud recommended and they made all the difference." (According to Granoff's widow, Martine, the idea that Granoff used Khan's words contradicts an account of the same events in the film *Quartier Lacan d'Emil Weiss*, 1997, which Wladimir Granoff had reviewed for accuracy.)

6. Granoff told me: "I didn't even begin to think of myself as Jewish until after the war and the Nazi occupation."

7. Roudinesco 1990, pp. 279–280. Granoff considered Roudinesco to be an excellent historian. He told me: "All her facts are correct. She is 100% faithful, true and unflinching."

8. MK/WG, October 31, 1963.

9. MK/WG, November 19, 1963.

10. MK/WG, March 5, 1964.

11. MK/ZD, April 10, 1965. Granoff collected fine cars and, in the years when Khan knew him, he had at least one Bugatti, as well as an Hispano-Suiza, a Bentley, an Aston Martin and an Avis that he was restoring.

12. MK/WG, April 24, 1964.

13. MK/WG, December 8, 1966.

14. MK/WG, April 24, 1964. Khan also criticized Lacan for his belief that he was superior to everyone else in analytic skills, so that it was acceptable for him to take on analysands with whom he had complicated personal and professional connections. (Winnicott was similar to Lacan in this respect.)

15. In strong contrast to the American ego psychologists, Lacan believed that there is no healthy ego. Lacan's view was widely accepted in French analytic thinking.

16. MK/WG, October 7, 1964.

17. MK/WG, October 18, 1964.

18. MK/VS, July 8, 1971.

ENDNOTES TO CHAPTER 12

1. MK/RS, June 1, 1964.

2. MK/RS, June 20, 1973.

3. The Stoller wealth came primarily from Sybil, who had received a significant inheritance when her father died.

4. The beach house was a two-story wooden house painted white with green trim, with a large deck that overlooked the ocean. The singer Linda Ronstadt was a neighbor.

5. Letter to the author from Paul Moor, December 11, 1999.

6. MK/RS, May 20, 1964.

7. MK/RS, May 4, 1964.

8. In a comment addressed to Robert, Khan was unaware that he and Robert were the same age, both born in 1924 (Ismond Rosen and Wladimir Granoff were also born in 1924): "The stewardesses on this plane are quite youthfully pleasant! They are nimble and the sap is raw in them. Once one is forty—you will discover this in a few years' time, Bob—the young female becomes an objet d'art. One looks at it and leaves it alone" (letter, MK to Robert and Sybil Stoller, May 4, 1964).

9. MK/RS, May 4, 1965.

10. MK/RS, May 6, 1964.

11. In 1991, Robert and Sybil Stoller were in their car, turning out onto a road near their home, when they were hit broadside by another car. Sybil was unharmed, but Robert died soon after a helicopter transport to the UCLA hospital where he worked. The driver of the other car was a sixteen-year-old Arab boy who was speeding through the hills in a new BMW.

12. RS/MK, March 4, 1965.

13. RS/MK, February 5, 1975.

14. Ralph Greenson was nicknamed "Romi" because his birth name was "Romeo." Stoller wrote to Khan: "Romi [is] the one person here in Los Angeles whom I admire and would want (in certain regards) to be like. [He] doesn't agree with my way of operating (i.e., listening, understanding, not fighting)" (April 6, 1965).

15. RS/MK, May 11, 1964.

16. RS/ MK, June 19, 1964.

17. RS/MK, June 19, 1964.

18. Winnicott 1958. According to Christopher Gelber, this book is in the library at the Los Angeles Psychoanalytic Society and Institute, with a signed inscription to Robert from Khan (personal communication, January 2001).

19. RS/MK, June 8, 1964. Khan was critical of Stoller's insistence on succeeding without help: "There is no Derby winner without the Derby track. Friendships provide precisely the access to that Derby course: no more and no less" (MK/RS, November 22, 1969).

20. RS/ MK, September 15, 1964.

21. Gelber 1998.

22. RS/ MK, April 6, 1965.

23. Khan commented on one of Stoller's papers: "It is always useful to state one's argument at the beginning of the article and then repeat it at the end. Few readers have the discipline to find this out for themselves" (MK/RS, May 11, 1964).

24. MK/RS, August 15, 1965.

25. RS/MK, September 15, 1964.

26. WB, April 29, 1975.

27. MK/WG, April 27, 1965.

28. WB, August 7, 1979.

29. Other people also told me about Khan's phobia of water and showers: "Sud never took a bath. I thought that was the Pakistani way. But he didn't have an odor about him—he smelled wholesome" (Zoë Dominic). "Masud would never wash, only with eau de cologne" (Wladimir Granoff). The origin of this way of washing, so unusual in the West, was probably Khan's early life in a desert climate. Water was precious in the Punjab, and nobody took showers.

30. Harvey Kayne's wife, Leslie, was another woman who shopped with Khan.

31. The Lord Nelson desk would be the only item named by Khan in his final will to be given to a specific person. It was given to his lawyer, Paul Kimber.

32. WB, March 10, 1980.

33. The American psychoanalyst Jill Scharff (1992) has theorized that our minds internalize not only individual people, but also people-in-relationship, such as a married couple or a set of parents.

34. WB, August 27, 1974.

35. From London, Khan arranged for the Stollers to invite Julie Andrews to their home, and he somehow provided wine for the evening. Robert wrote to him about the dinner, which was also attended by the Greensons: "Julie was as you have always described her: sweet, charming, simple (at least these are the cards she plays—she is so graceful that one scarcely notices when she grows

cautious at a moment). We ate well and too much, talked happily and not enough—and we drank your wine and glowed and warmed and swam and smiled and remembered you. It was a lovely evening" (RS/MK, 1964—partially illegible date on letter).

36. "As you know, I have always relished, as well as respected, your clinical acumen . . ." (letter, MK to R. Greenson, December 24, 1973).

ENDNOTES TO PART IV INTRODUCTION

1. WB, December 10, 1972.
2. Malcolm 1989, p. 25.
3. Khan 1963a.
4. Limentani 1992, p. 159.
5. Searles 1982–83, p. 475.

ENDNOTES TO CHAPTER 13

1. WB, October 27, 1975.
2. Winnicott and Khan developed their ideas about self and self pathology at about the same time as the American psychoanalyst Heinz Kohut, working independently, developed a remarkably similar set of ideas. The similarities in their work reflect Western movement into a new social phase where the individual had great importance.
3. Khan wrote that self actualization is the ability "to live from and extend oneself [by means of] style and character" (WB, July 26, 1970).
4. Khan 1972h, p. 24. Kohut also chose not to define "self."
5. Winnicott 1963a, p. 180. The British psychiatrist Harry Guntrip, who wrote about his analysis with Winnicott, felt personally betrayed by this quote because of its implication that Winnicott did not need other people, such as Guntrip himself (Hazell 1996).
6. "I once risked the remark 'there is no such thing as a baby' meaning that if you set me to describe a baby, you will find you are describing *a baby and someone*. A baby cannot exist alone, but is essentially part of a relationship" (Winnicott 1964, p. 115).
7. WB, January 29, 1980.

8. Khan 1969d, pp. 212–213.

9. MK/VS, February 17, 1968.

10. MK/RS, January 30, 1968.

11. WB, January 19, 1973. The same idea about Winnicott's naïveté is expressed by Richards (1996, p. 6), who writes that Winnicott's view is biased by nineteenth century Romanticism, in which the innermost self is pristine and perfect, possessed of an "immanent divinity."

12. WB, March 24, 1972.

13. Winnicott's theory presented the person as being analogous to a daffodil bulb, which, given a good enough environment, grows into a flowering plant with predetermined daffodil qualities (Winnicott 1952). In contrast, Khan's bulb, if given the right nutrients, grows into a plant with certain predetermined qualities, but with additional qualities that vary widely according to differences in the environmental contribution. Khan's theory fits easily into contemporary literature that questions whether the self has meaning as a one-person experience.

14. MK/VS, August 20, 1968.

15. WB, March 7, 1971.

16. WB, August 29, 1973.

17. WB, May 18, 1975.

18. Personal communication from anonymous analysand, 1999.

19. See Aron 1996, Mitchell 1993, Sugarman, 1995, Summers, 1999.

20. WB, April 8, 1969.

21. WB, March 23, 1975.

22. Letter, MK to Georges Allyn, October 22, 1981.

23. See Aron 2000, Auerbach and Blatt 1996, Fonagy et al. 2002. Writing about Fyodor Dostoevsky's capacity to have a distance vis-à-vis his own subjectivity, Khan said: "I envisage this distance as a triangular space, where the apices are: subjective self, reality, and observing self" (WB, July 31, 1973).

24. See Pizer 2000: "[E]ach person develops the competence to bridge a multiplicity of contradictory and paradoxical experiences of self and self-with-other" (p. 113).

25. Khan 1968a.

26. MK/VS, May 30, 1969.

27. Khan 1970c, p. 134.

28. Undated letter, MK/SS, May, 1967.

29. See Little 1985.

30. Khan 1971a, p. 237.

31. The examples are from Khan 1974a, 1981a, 1988b.

32. Khan 1981a, p. 85.

33. WB, February 20, 1975. Like Winnicott, Khan was skilled at seeing through a person's defenses to their inner self. Winnicott's "penetrating gaze" was mentioned to me by several interviewees. With Khan it was not so much the gaze as it was a concentrated attention. Roger Stoller commented: "Masud focused on me with a laser quality. And when Masud focused on you, you really knew that you were being focused on." In the course of my interviews, several people used the same words concerning Khan: "He knew me better than I knew my own self."

34. The information about movies comes from Eva; the information about dinners from John Mallinson and Wynne Godley; and about card games and TV from Wynne Godley and Eva. Godley's information was published in Godley (2001a).

35. Winnicott's "experimental analyses" also led to situations where the "as-if" quality of analysis came very close to being "real." He told Judith Issroff, who was his supervisee at the time: "In working with highly intelligent 'False Self' patients, for analytic work to be effective you have to have a relationship that is so almost-real that it verges on an almost actual love affair, almost-but-not-quite" (e-mail to the author from Judith Issroff, March 27, 1998). In contrast to Khan, Winnicott was able to work on the edge of a real relationship without going over the edge, and he is not known for involving patients in his private life.

ENDNOTES TO CHAPTER 14

1. Stewart 1991, p. 107.

2. Regression to dependence as practiced during the 1950s by Winnicott and Balint built on earlier experimental work by Sandor Ferenczi.

3. The concept of allowing and managing regression in experimental psychoanalysis was by no means limited to British analysts. As Khan wrote, "It is very interesting how a few of us are struggling with the same issues in analytic societies all over the world" (MK/VS, January 23, 1968). Khan may have been thinking of the work of his friend Ralph Greenson, who, along with his colleague Milton Wexler, is known for using modified techniques to treat especially dis-

turbed patients. For example, Marilyn Monroe was allowed to be a participant in the Greensons' private family living.

4. Personal communication from Peter Elder.

5. Godley 2001a, p. 5.

6. Winnicott 1960. Regression, in the theories of Winnicott and Khan, is not considered to be a defense, as classical theory suggests; it is an achievement that comes from cooperation with the therapeutic process.

7. Several interviewees describing a full regression to dependence reported experiences that suggest they were remembering and/or experiencing themselves as infants. These experiences were vividly remembered thirty and forty years later, which suggests that they were coded in the brain in the biologically distinct manner that we now know to be characteristic of memories of trauma and other intense experiences. However, as Ogden (2001) has pointed out, "Regressions in the analyses of children and adults (whether psychotic, depressed or quite healthy) bear a very uncertain correlation with infantile experience" (p. 309). The analyst is advised to tolerate disbelief and not worry about whether or not the reports are actual memories.

8. Letter, D. Winnicott to R. Rodman, January 10, 1969, in Rodman (1987, p. 181). Winnicott's ideas about management developed largely through the influence of his second wife, Clare, who was a social worker (Kanter 2004).

9. Winnicott 1967. Khan (1969b) noted that he and Winnicott had regressed patients who were a striking contrast to those of Balint. Balint's descriptions of patients in regression were "rather quietist images" where the therapist and patient easily maintained an alliance. The regressed patients of Winnicott and Khan were less cooperative and less controlled, showing, in Khan's words "what one can only describe as a maniacal state of greedy hate [along with] vociferous demands for satisfactions plus a violent envy of the analyst's capacity to offer anything to them by way of help" (p. 247).

10. Margaret Little, who wrote about her psychotic regression to dependence while in analysis with Winnicott in the years 1949–1955 (Little 1985, 1990), kept working throughout the period of her analysis. An anonymous account from one of her analysands suggests that she probably should not have been allowed to see patients in this period because she was *too* welcoming of regression:

> I was analyzed by Margaret Little when she was in analysis with Winnicott. He referred me to her and it nearly wrecked my life. She was crazy with a fearsome

strength. She projected her madness on me and tried to get me to merge with her. She kept saying, "You're mad." I remember I once told her in response, "I think YOU are mad!" Another time I was saying "I don't know what I want," and she took my hand and said, "This is what you want. You can't find your real Self." Lots of bad things happened, and I deeply regret the experience.

11. Winnicott speaking to Harry Guntrip, reported in Hazell (1996, p. 261).

12. Letter, D. Winnicott to R. Rodman, January 10, 1969, in Rodman (1987, p. 182).

13. The information about a patient causing Winnicott's first coronary comes from Hazell (1996). An alternate view is that Winnicott's first coronary, which probably occurred in February 1949, was triggered by the death of his father on December 21, 1948 (Robert Rodman, personal communication, November 2001).

14. Khan 1960a, pp. 155–157. Khan reported that he actively held up the patient's regression for two years in order to help her establish ego strength that would allow her to endure the regression and benefit from it. In the first two years, he worked verbally and helped her build an outside life where she had a job and friends who could support her.

15. The terms *benign* and *malignant transference* come from Balint (1968).

16. Khan 1969b, p. 247.

17. Hazell 1996, pp. 251–252.

18. Hazell 1996, p. 253.

19. Winnicott 1968.

20. It appears that Guntrip had underestimated the patient's murderous communications when he denied him a second emergency session. Guntrip seems to have been too generous and then, perhaps because he was exhausted, too withholding. After the tragedy, Guntrip went into a deep depression and was overwhelmed by a longing to regress himself and stop working (Hazell 1996, p. 257). Winnicott interpreted that Guntrip wanted to stop being a therapist in order to avoid facing an unconscious wish that all his regressed patients would die to relieve him of the burden of worrying about keeping them alive. Guntrip agreed with this interpretation, and ultimately went back to doing regressive work, but with better support systems for his own well-being.

21. Winnicott knew in theory about the value for the patient/child of experiencing the hate of the analyst or mother: "It seems to me doubtful whether a human child, as he develops, is capable of tolerating the full extent of his own

hate in a sentimental environment. He needs hate to hate" (1958, p. 190). This was new thinking. It would be four decades before another analyst, Joseph Lichtenberg (1989), wrote about the child's ordinary developmental need to experience and survive aggression directed at himself/herself.

22. Khan 1971c, p. 255. Winnicott (1947) had written that all limits are experienced as hateful acts, but the limits he reports were primarily protective. Khan's limits often had an aggressive, provocative quality. Some examples of this are refusing to see a patient when she came to a session in her nightclothes (1982a, p. 120) and ending a session with a nonverbal angry patient after just ten minutes because he felt "exhausted" in his countertransference (1971c, p. 255).

23. Rodman 2003.

24. Khan 1982a, pp. 109–110.

25. Khan shared his insights and clinical acumen in story form, and if exaggerations made his story more memorable, that was no problem for him. It is interesting that, although Khan's nonfactual reporting of cases has been widely criticized, a respected contemporary analyst actually recommends such a style: "[I]n the current climate of litigiousness, you're in trouble if you don't make up a case. . . . It is considered legally problematic if you use an actual patient for a case" (interview of Robert Stolorow in C. Strozier 2001, p. 312). However, it is also highly recommended that a writer should acknowledge that there are confabulations or fictional changes in a case report, and Khan never did this.

26. R. D. Laing (d. 1989), who tolerated a great deal of regression in his patients, still has disciples in London and in the United States, but his popularity has diminished. His biographer writes that when Laing died, he left behind "a body of work that had once lit up the sky like a comet, but then vanished, out of sight and out of memory, as if it had never been" (Dolnick 1998, p. 136).

ENDNOTES TO CHAPTER 15

1. Major portions of this chapter were originally published in Hopkins (2000).

2. Winnicott 1971a, p. 38.

3. WB, January 6, 1970.

4. Harry Karnac (personal communication) has a different memory: "I have

absolutely no recall of Winnicott being deaf in his later years when I used to see him socially about once or twice a month."

5. Winnicott 1941. In working with older children, Winnicott substituted "squiggle" drawing for the spatula game. In the squiggle play, analyst and child exchange markings from which the other must complete a drawing and they then talk about the meaning of their drawing.

6. Winnicott 1954.

7. Winnicott 1971a, p. 38.

8. WB, July 14, 1977. Interestingly, recent scientific findings are highly compatible with the writings of Winnicott and Khan. Research has shown that successful therapy with adults involves the same basic mechanism of change as successful therapy with children, especially for adults with pathology that is resistant to purely interpretive techniques (Frankel, 1998).

9. Khan 1972c, p. 293.

10. WB, January 8, 1973.

11. MK/VS, December 20, 1968.

12. WB, August 22, 1975.

13. Beebe 1997.

14. WB, January 16, 1971. Khan, like Winnicott and other professionals of that era, believed that childhood autism originated from a problem with the mother–child relationship. The current thinking is that autism is caused by a biological or genetic problem.

15. Khan 1972b, p. 276.

16. Khan 1971c, p. 259.

17. Khan 1971c, p. 259.

18. MK/VS, September 18, 1967.

19. Khan 1976, p. 93.

20. Khan 1981d, p. 177.

21. WB, July 30, 1969.

22. WB, July 30, 1969.

23. Bloom 1996, pp. 24–25.

24. Letter to the author from H. Bloom, January 5, 1998.

25. WB, July 26, 1970.

26. In a letter to Robert Rodman describing these events, Bloom wrote: "When I returned to Yale, I called upon Dr. Lidz (Bloom's psychiatrist) and asked him why he had sent me to a madman, to which Lidz replied: 'Well, Harold, by your own account, your anger helped cure your depression!'" (May 16, 2003).

1. The quote from Rayner is in Cooper (1993, p. xiv).

2. Khan's three crucial friends—Wladimir Granoff, Robert Stoller, and Victor Smirnoff—all had a particular interest in perversity, even before meeting Khan.

3. Khan wrote two papers on the topic of homosexuality that he submitted to the *International Journal of Psycho-Analysis* in the 1950s, and these are the papers that were put aside and never considered by the then-editor Willi Hoffer. One paper, entitled "The Homosexual Nursing of Self and Object," was printed in Dutch in 1955. (See Khan 1984a, p. 2.)

4. Letter to the author from John Gedo, August 31, 1998.

5. MK/VS, February 11, 1968.

6. Khan 1965a, 1979c.

7. Dimen 2001, p. 845.

8. An exception is the rare situation where two people share the identical perversion, and in that case the outside relationship could strengthen the frozen object relationship pattern.

9. Khan 1964b, p. 29.

10. Winnicott 1966, p. 75.

11. Winnicott 1966, p. 76.

12. There is quite a lot of evidence that the case described by Winnicott is actually Khan. Khan told at least two people (Dean Eyre and Eva) that he had been the case. And the description of the patient by Winnicott fits Khan well: the man was a successful professional who as early as 1959 had had a long analysis with Winnicott after seeing three prior therapists—but still did not feel real and did not get a benefit from interpretation (see C. Winnicott et al. 1989, pp. 51, 76, and 170); the patient did not experience conflict in his life; he had an older brother; he had had prior marriages (Winnicott reports two prior marriages); he had largely sublimated homosexual tendencies; he had a history of extramarital affairs; and in 1963 he had a largely asexual marriage (op. cit., p. 76). Finally, Khan makes an intriguing comment in one of his letters to Victor Smirnoff: "Somewhere in my somatic identity of body-self, I have all the mystique of a pubertal girl's virginal self-protectedness. And I mean this literally, not metaphorically" (October 28, 1969).

If the case was Khan, there is valuable information for a biographer. For example, we would know that Khan's mother had hoped that her second child (i.e., Masud) would be a girl; that she had denied his gender and seen him as a girl baby, diapering him tightly as if he did not have a penis (D.W. Winnicott, 1959, in C. Winnicott et al. 1989, p. 51); that his sexual relationship with Svetlana was minimal and he was having affairs as early as 1963; and that he had homosexual relationships when he was in his mid-twenties but then gave these up, although he continued to be tempted.

It would also be tempting to use this material in thinking about the sublimated homosexuality that appears to have been a part of the relationship between Khan and Winnicott. Winnicott writes "the madness was mine" about his experiencing the patient as a girl with penis envy, and he holds to that idea even as he reports that the patient disagrees. Furthermore, Winnicott wrote that homosexual experiences, had they been allowed, would have "established the maleness" of his patient (1966, p. 79). The oddness of this idea suggests that Winnicott may have been dealing with some of his own issues regarding homosexuality.

13. D.W. Winnicott, letter to "M," April 15, 1966, quoted in R. Rodman (1987, p. 155).

14. Khan 1971a.

ENDNOTES TO CHAPTER 17

1. Mark Paterson commented: "Considering it was not his native language, Masud's knowledge of English was amazing. But at times his writing was faulty, especially with prepositions, and Hogarth had to do a lot of work on his typescripts" (e-mail to the author, March 20, 2004).

2. Limentani 1992, p. 156.

3. Juliet Mitchell told me that in the early 1960s, when she was doing research for her groundbreaking book *Psychoanalysis and Feminism* (New York: Pantheon, 1974), Khan was "generous of spirit," allowing her to use the library even though she did not yet have analytic credentials.

4. Khan particularly deplored the ego psychology writings, considering them to be a reworking of outdated ideas coming from "impotence of thought screened by gamesmanship with concepts which have lost all tangible relation with the clinical realities" (MK/VS, November 27, 1968). But he accepted papers in that tradition and personally arranged for the American Leo Rangell to write a long review of the work of the leading ego psychologist Heinz Hartmann.

5. Clifford Yorke took over as editor in 1979. For a list of the thirty books edited by Khan, see Willoughby (2005, Appendix A, p. 245).

6. When Khan took over the IPL in 1968, he divided it into two parts: a series of books with green covers dedicated to the established authors and writers, and a second series that featured the writings of younger analysts who were just developing their ideas.

7. Lomas 2001, p. 7.

8. WB, June 17, 1969.

9. MK/VS, 3 a.m., November 26, 1968.

10. MK/VS, July 3, 1969.

11. WB, March 21, 1970.

12. At Khan's request, Robert Stoller made a significant financial contribution. In the end, Stoller's funds were not needed.

13. In the years before Ernst died, Khan had worked in his role at the IPL to try to convince Ernst Freud to be less zealous in protecting his father's image by suppressing material. Khan was convinced that he had a better sense than Ernst about what would be appropriate to release. "I hope I can persuade [Ernst] to release a little more of the suppressed material. . . . No one need protect Freud from himself" (MK/VS, February 5, 1969).

14. Paterson's agency was originally known as Mark Paterson & Associates. In a recent merger, it became part of Paterson Marsh Ltd. Paterson is assisted in his work at the Copyrights by Tom Roberts, an historian with training in library sciences.

15. In this case, the profits did not go directly to the Freud grandchildren. The Institute of Psychoanalysis had a one-third interest in the translation royalties, and the other beneficiaries were Sigmund Freud Copyrights and the James Strachey estate.

16. Angela Harris at times used her maiden name, Angela Richards, for professional purposes. When Alix Strachey died on April 28, 1973, she willed to Angela Harris/Richards the copyright as well as her share of the translation royalties. Harris would die of cancer at a young age, in 1982.

17. WB, September 21, 1973.

18. WB, September 21, 1973.

19. WB, September 22, 1969. Even before he was appointed a director, Khan had worked successfully to arrange an English translation of the Freud–Arnold Zweig correspondence, which had been published in German by Fischer Verlag in 1968. As a member of the Publications Committee, he had fought for

the translation despite the fact that various German readers had said that the quality of the letters was "very slight." Khan saw things differently: "Freud was always graciously measured in his tone and textures of narrative. But with A. Zweig, he chats as an elderly Jew of distinction and stature . . . relaxes into a privacy of manner that I have not encountered anywhere else [and] mellows to meet the need of a young second rate writer's deep affection for him. . . . It is a book that deserves to be read with a generous goodwill & then it is most rewarding" (MK/VS, February 3, 1969).

20. The alliance of Khan and Anna Freud began in the late 1940s, when she was his supervisor. She had been a consistent supporter when the institute tried to keep him from attaining full membership and training analyst status in the 1950s. Khan was devoted to her: "Anna Freud has always treated me with affection and deference—and indulgently. She has also always respected my mind and devotion to psychoanalysis since my student days. She bet on me, and today I can say I have not let her down" (MK/VS, November 26, 1968).

21. WB, February 28, 1975.

22. The Sigmund Freud Archives has attempted, at considerable cost, to collect all existing Sigmund Freud material, such as letters, manuscripts, publications, photographs, and taped recollections, in one location—the Library of Congress in Washington, D.C.

23. Anna Freud wrote to her skeptical editor, Lottie Newman: "You are quite right of course about Professor Masson. But he is a nice man and I think we will be able to cope with him" (quoted in Young-Bruehl 1988, p. 436).

24. WB, March 5, 1980. Masson did not read or speak German when he asked to do the translation. But he immersed himself in intensive study and, as a brilliant student of language, he did in fact become a fluent reader.

25. Undated letter, MK/MP, 1986.

26. In 1983, the American writer Janet Malcolm published a book about the fiasco, *In the Freud Archives* (New York: New York Review of Books).

27. Letter, A. Freud to K. Eissler, in Young-Bruehl (1988, p. 437).

28. MK/MP, February 4, 1980.

29. MK/MP, February 19, 1984.

30. "As Director of Freud Copyrights, I could easily disregard [Anna Freud's] sentiments. The Freud heirs . . . are so greedy one could buy them off all too easily. But I feel that Anna Freud has a right to her privacy with her father. And I can wait! So why harass her . . ." (WB, October 20, 1973).

31. MK/MP, February 29, 1984.

32. Personal communication from Sadie Gillespie.

33. Personal communication from Wladimir Granoff.

34. The quote is from an anonymous British analyst. Years earlier, Robert Stoller had praised Khan for his ability to make Winnicott's writings understandable. Referring to Khan's introduction to a new printing of Winnicott's (1958) *Collected Papers: Through Paediatrics to Psychoanalysis*, he wrote: "Your Introduction takes Winnicott's elements and, without seeming to have redone them at all, puts them together again [so clearly]. You . . . make it all seem simple [as if] we could all have gotten the essential Winnicott in our own reading. But that is not true; that is only the artifact you generously created and gave to us" (RS/ MK, April 23, 1975).

35. Khan once wrote: "Every paper by Winnicott from 1950 to 1970 and every book by Winnicott has been edited by me" (foreword to Clancier and Kalmanovitch 1987). The accuracy of this claim is questionable, because Khan was ill by this time, and in the same introduction he tells an outright lie about Winnicott having analyzed Svetlana—but, as a "Masudic" lie, it may reveal something that contains an element of truth.

36. See Aguayo 2001, Sorenson 2000. In 1967, Michael Balint had written Winnicott a letter criticizing his lack of references and Winnicott responded in a joking manner: "I have not had time to read that but I shall ask the Honorary Librarian [Masud Khan] to fill this gap" (Rudnytsky 1991, p. 863). Winnicott was not interested in becoming more scholarly: "[My not providing references] happens to be my temperament . . ." (Winnicott 1967b, p. 573). The American psychoanalyst Thomas Ogden has a different opinion on this matter. He thinks that Winnicott's early papers, with their colloquial style and rambling organization, invite the reader to participate in the reading, in a manner that facilitates understanding of the ideas (Ogden 2001).

37. Aguayo 2001.

38. MK/SB, September 18, 1962.

39. See Kahr 2002.

40. "As the end [the reference is to Winnicott's death] approached, Winnicott laboured with some urgency to put his remaining typescripts in order so that they might soon be prepared for publication. Winnicott's amanuensis [meaning: one who takes dictation] Masud Khan made many trips to Chester Square [Winnicott's home] to help with the editing process; in particular, the

two men devoted a good deal of time to the preparation of Winnicott's 1971 book *Playing and Reality*" (Kahr 1996, p. 121).

41. MK/VS, May 25, 1969.

42. Winnicott 1971a, p. ix.

43. MK/VS, March 28, 1971.

44. Khan actively sought out French translators and did his own research on certain important words—e.g., he had a long discussion with Smirnoff about whether "esprit" might be an appropriate term for Winnicott's "mind," since Winnicott's implications went beyond the purely cognitive definition (MK/VS, January 3, 1967).

45. See MK/VS, January 15, 1969 and WB, July 26, 1970.

46. The Nanterre clinic is currently called Center Wladimir Granoff.

ENDNOTES TO CHAPTER 18

1. Winnicott 1960, p. 148.

2. MK/WG, December 13, 1964.

3. A second major problem in the analysis, involving difficulties with aggression, confrontation, and object usage, discussed in Chapter 20.

4. MK/SB, May 23, 1963.

5. MK/ZD, March 31, 1965. This comment describes anaclitic depression, a feeling of emptiness coming from early deprivation rather than from conflict. In psychoanalytic thinking, it is treated through relationship rather than through interpretation (Blatt 1974).

6. WB, August 27, 1971.

7. Winnicott 1960. The American analyst Thomas Ogden (1986) has written about what he calls psychopathology of the potential space, where people "collapse" into the pole of reality or the pole of fantasy, and the connection between the two poles is damaged. Winnicott's strength with Khan seems to have been his ability to facilitate Khan's inner pole (an inner sense of True Self). Winnicott was not skilled at helping Khan to develop the reality pole (the social expression of the True Self), nor did he help Khan develop the capacity to switch easily between the inner and outer worlds. Khan wrote: "I have always been two persons: one devoted to my own inner life and the other over-concerned about the external object" (WB, October 14, 1969).

8. Consideration of Khan's self is made more complex due to the fact that,

from a very early age, he had two primary identities, an Eastern self and a Western self. These selves were kept separate from each other. So did he have one
True Self or two? Is it conceivable that he had two separate False Selves?

9. MK/WG, March 3, 1966.

10. MK/RS, January 30, 1968.

11. WB, April 3, 1970.

12. WB, February 18, 1970.

13. MK/VS, November 4, 1968. The paper was his summary of the work
of Michael Balint (Khan 1969b).

14. Winnicott 1960, p. 44.

15. WB, February 12, 1980.

16. MK/VS, March 27, 1969.

17. WB, May 3, 1971.

18. WB, June 28, 1970.

19. WB, April 2, 1969.

20. The theory of the frame in psychoanalysis had not been developed in
the 1950s, but that does not excuse Winnicott from having acted unprofessionally
by having extraanalytic dealings with Khan. Nonsocialization and other aspects
of analytic neutrality are central parts of analytic thinking dating to Sigmund
Freud's earliest writings, and Winnicott *did* refrain from socializing with other
patients. He would have known that "reality" contaminates the analytic space.

21. MK/VS, August 30, 1969.

22. WB, March 39, 1969.

23. Limentani 1992, p. 156. John Rickman, in contrast to Winnicott, had
been a father figure for Khan: "Rickman was the only father-figure I have encountered!" (WB, May 16, 1976).

24. MK/VS, October 3, 1968.

25. MK/VS, July 2, 1971.

26. E-mail from Harold Stewart to the author, December 18, 1999.

27. Personal communication from Sadie Gillesie.

28. Personal communication from Barrie Cooper.

ENDNOTES TO CHAPTER 19

1. MK/ZD, July 27, 1965.

2. Interview, 1997.

3. MK/WG, February 3, 1965.

4. Limentani 1992, p. 156.

5. In his letter to Granoff, written on February 9, 1965, Khan said that his first meeting with Gitelson had been in 1959 at the Copenhagen IPAC where Khan was reading a paper. Gitelson sat in the front row, along with Winnicott, Anna Freud, and several other important analysts, and in the discussion period and afterward, he made positive comments that Khan greatly appreciated. Then Gitelson came again to hear Khan's paper at the 1961 Edinburgh IPAC, where Svetlana was also present, and the Khans and Gitelsons went out to dinner together, at Gitelson's invitation. Then, Khan wrote, he had been personally involved in a situation in 1964 that involved the *Bulletin* (a companion journal to the IJPA), where Gitelson had published some critical remarks about another Chicago analyst, Franz Alexander, with whom he was having a feud. Alexander threatened the IJPA with a lawsuit, and in response Sutherland, the editor, allowed a letter of rebuttal from Alexander to be published, causing Gitelson to be enraged at Sutherland. Khan happened to be giving a lecture in Chicago at the time and, at Sutherland's request, he spoke with Gitelson and calmed him down. Khan and Gitelson then became good friends: "In fact, I decided that he was a loveable man who both received affection and gave affection, and I was particularly fond of his wife." Later in 1964, Gitelson was president of the American Psychoanalytic Association, and Khan said he personally persuaded him to refrain from mentioning the Chicago feud in his presidential address. Alexander's good friend Roy Grinker came to the talk planning to have an open row and when Alexander was not mentioned, according to Khan, Grinker was left speechless. Afterward, Gitelson supposedly praised Khan: "Thank you, son. I had not realized that it hurts more to have one's name erased than it does to be attacked openly." Then they went out to tea. For a detailed description of the Grinker–Alexander vs. Gitelson feud, see Kirsner 2000.

6. King told me that Hanna Segal once told her: "If ever I found myself in need of support, I'd come to you, after seeing the way you have supported Masud." It is ironic that King had met Gitelson when they had worked on the drafting and implementation of a new constitution for the IPA in 1963, where one point of discussion was the setting forth of procedures to follow in the event of a sitting president's death. Unfortunately, that section had not been approved.

7. MK/WG, July 29, 1965.

8. MK/WG, July 30, 1965.

9. The Khans were just leaving for the airport when Winnicott stopped in to say good-bye, claiming that he wanted to check on Svetlana's foot, which had been troubling her. The three exchanged a few words of camaraderie and Winnicott left. Khan described the encounter: "The Good Lord sent us a blessing to launch us on the vacation. . . . There he stood: the aged grey man, full of wisdom and always timely. Yes, that is a great part of his genius. Unfailing aptness!" (MK/ZD, August 2, 1965). Although Winnicott did not mention the Amsterdam humiliation, Khan believed the visit was a gesture of support meant for him.

10. Khan's reference to a "flourish" is from Fyodor Dostoevsky's novel *The Idiot*, where "the idiot" Prince Myshkin compares English and French calligraphy, and French calligraphy is shown to be more elaborate and more beautiful. It is noteworthy that Prince Myshkin can imitate the handwriting of others with great skill, but he does not possess his own style of handwriting.

11. MK/WG, August 4, 1965.

12. MK/ZD, August 18, 1965.

13. MK/ZD, August 20, 1965. The equally dramatic Granoff agreed that a psychological murder had been attempted at Amsterdam. From his perspective, however, the murderous wishes related primarily to Lacan: "All megalomania aside, it can be said that Masud and I were truly the focal points of this Congress and we experienced our milieu through its death wish against us. Had Lacan been there, he would have been the target and we would have been deprived of the experience" (interview with W. Granoff, 1997).

14. RS/MK, August ll, 1965.

15. Over time, Khan became less fearful of Gillespie and he rejoined the Curriculum Committee. He took great pleasure a few years later when he observed Gillespie in an embarrassing situation: "You know what reticent hurt and bitter rancour I carry against Dr. Gillespie, since his gratuitous and vile attack on me in Amsterdam in 1965. Well! Last night, he proposed the toast to Paula Heimann (a British analyst), since he is her oldest friend in London, and he did it with his typical smooth and deliberated graciousness and charm, plus cultivated wit. We all enjoyed it. Then at the end, he said: 'AND NOW, LADIES AND GENTLEMEN, I WANT YOU TO LIFT YOUR GLASSES AND DRINK TO ME.' There was a loud hush, and he corrected himself: 'TO PAULA HEIMANN.' In one crucial slip of the tongue, he had epitomized and announced his whole true character self" (MK/VS, February 16, 1969; Khan's capitalizations and underlining).

16. The IJPA had been founded in 1924 by the British Psycho-Analytical

Society and it was in those days (and until recently) totally under the control of the society, despite its international name and reputation.

17. MK/ZD, September 6, 1965.

18. See Khan's letter to Marion Milner of January 13, 1968, quoted in Willoughby (2005, p. 139). Even Winnicott may not have been giving Khan full support in this period. In the letter to Milner, Khan writes that Winnicott "failed to endorse my identity in the British Society."

19. MK/VS, February 1, 1968.

ENDNOTE TO PART VI OPENING PAGE

1. Letter to Zoë Dominic, August 2, 1965, written just after Winnicott dropped by as Khan and Svetlana prepared to leave for Monte Carlo (see footnote 9, Chapter 19).

ENDNOTES TO CHAPTER 20

1. MK/WG, January 26, 1967.

2. WB, May 16, 1976.

3. MK/RS, October 19, 1971.

4. Wilde (1894), quoted in Schmidgall (1994).

5. MK/WG, July 30.

6. Khan 1963a.

7. MK/WG, December 8, 1966.

8. MK/WG, December 15, 1965.

9. MK/WG, February 7, 1966.

10. MK/WG, March 3, 1966.

11. Khan had already offended Rosen by publicly stating that Rosen was being tasteless in exhibiting his sculptures to analytic audiences and talking about their analytic meaning. He said that he believed in Rosen's talent as a sculptor, but thought the worlds of art and psychoanalysis should be kept separate.

12. Kayne died of subacute bacterial endocarditis.

13. Khan would miss Granoff: "Without any wish to embarrass you, I can say with absolute candour and sincerity that no-one has ever offered me among

men the sort of generous and all enveloping provision of affection and goodwill as you did" (April 18, 1969).

14. MK/WG, October 27, 1966.

15. MK/WG, March 11, 1966.

16. WB, February 7, 1971.

17. WB, May 3, 1971.

18. See WG/MK, April 3, 1967.

19. Years later, Khan wrote about a patient whose twenty-year analysis had ended in a failure. He continued to see the man weekly because, he said, the man needed the personal contact: "I have learned from Winnicott that, if we fail our patients, we must not abandon them as persons" (1972d, p. 299).

20. Khan 1986c, p. 26.

21. Marion Milner told me in November 1996, "Winnicott didn't give Masud a successful analysis. He couldn't handle Khan's destructiveness." See Hopkins (1998) for a further discussion of Winnicott's problems with anger.

22. MK/WG, October 27, 1966.

23. Winnicott's talk was given at the 1952 Club and the title was "The Transmission of Technique." It is described by Khan (WB, September 24, 1968). This is a typical kind of comment by Winnicott—he leaves it to the listener to imagine *how* failure could be "the essential thing."

24. Winnicott 1968. Object usage is a complex subject and Winnicott's article, while stimulating, is hard to fully grasp. Khan's definition of object usage is more understandable than most: "Finding the object involves empathy with the other's narcissism, and taking the risk of reality correcting one's fantasy into an improved and new experience" (WB, February 11, 1974).

25. Khan's talk, which was entitled "Styles of Termination of Analysis," was given in Copenhagen; details are in WB, June 13, 1972.

26. WB, July 5, 1970. When Marion Milner complained that Winnicott had not dealt with her deepest pathology in his analysis of her, and that he had not devoted himself to her as he had to Margaret Little, Khan blamed Milner for not accepting her own contributions to the perceived failure: "I am disappointed by Milner's way of recounting her relation with DWW. She had an explicit grudge that he had not helped her . . . and little awareness of her grab of him. I felt she wanted him to provide life for her, and no-one can do that for anyone" (WB, February 4, 1971). See Slochower (1996) for a discussion of holding in psychoanalysis.

27. MK/VS, May 4, 1967.

28. MK/SS, December 11, 1980.

29. WB, June 21, 1979.

30. Personal communication from Zoë Dominic.

31. Beriosova was invited to join George Balanchine's company, but she chose not to. Tony Walton told me: "Svetlana wouldn't leave the Royal because she felt an allegiance—she felt it was her family. She experienced herself as a perennial orphan, and she felt that all her other families had evaporated and died."

32. WB, February 3, 1980.

33. MK/ZD, May 15, 1967.

34. MK/ZD, May 19, 1967.

35. WB, October 14, 1969.

36. A rebirthing therapist uses physical as well as psychological techniques to help a person remember his or her actual birth. The underlying theory is that the trauma of birth has been repressed and, upon memory, it will free the person's energy for more full living.

37. MK/VS, November 14, 1967.

38. Private communication from anonymous English friend. Another example of Khan's poor behavior at this time was his loss of his driver's license in 1968. He was driving his Alfa Romeo while intoxicated and he "froze" at a green light. The police were not impressed by his explanation: "I thought 'green' meant to stop."

ENDNOTES TO CHAPTER 21

1. Winnicott 1958.

2. Khan 1977b, p. 185.

3. Khan, 1977b, p. 185. This idea is similar to the distinction that Winnicott and Khan had made between regression and withdrawal. In regression, the person is "held" by the presence of another person, while in withdrawal the person is alone. It is a further development of Winnicott's (1958) idea that the child who plays by himself, knowing that the mother is nearby, experiences something very different from a child who is truly alone.

4. MK/SS, May 15, 1967.

5. Khan 1986c, p. 26.

6. WB, February 23, 1970.

7. WB, March 13, 1970. See also: "[T]hese Work Books are my truest idiom of daily self actualisation" (WB, May 8, 1975).

8. RS/MK, January 8, 1973.

9. WB, February 25, 1970.

10. WB, August 30, 1972.

11. Horses were an important part of Khan's early memories: "I recall one winter at Xmas time, when it snowed. I was ten or eleven—and as we went out riding one morning, my horse caught the nip in the air and was wild with his vigour. At first I was so terrified, but then I relaxed to discover that his vigour and my muscle were mutual, if allowed to be. The exhilaration of that experience lingers in my body to this day" (from letter, MK to Regina Pereira, quoted in WB, February 2, 1972). "There is a strange bond between a horse and me right from childhood. I feel more in my person and being sitting on a horse than in any other relatedness" (WB, February 16, 1974).

12. WB, May 8, 1968.

13. MK/ZD, May 20, 1968.

14. MK/ZD, June 19, 1968.

15. MK/VS, April 20, 1968.

16. MK/VS, April 2, 1970.

17. MK2.

18. MK/VS, October 18, 1968.

19. MK/VS, November 4, 1968.

20. MK/VS, November 6, 1969, 6:30 a.m.

21. MK/VS, November 7, 1968. Later, he expanded the talk into a paper that was published in the IJPA (Khan 1969b).

22. MK/VS, September 15, 1968. The idea that experience in the analytic relationship could be more curative than interpretation was a radical notion in New York.

23. Rodman 2003.

24. WB, November 15, 1968.

25. The papers were published the next year (Khan 1969a, and 1969d).

26. MK/VS, November 23, 1968.

27. MK/VS, November 23, 1968.

28. MK/VS, November 27, 1998.

29. Letter, MK to D.W. Winnicott, December 2, 1968. I thank Robert Rodman for sharing with me a copy of this letter.

30. WB, December 21, 1968.

31. MK/VS, January 5, 1969.

32. MK/VS, January 6, 1969.

33. MK/VS, February 5, 1969.

34. "The Catalytic Role of Crucial Friendship in the Epistemology of Self-Experience in Montaigne, Rousseau and Freud" was written and translated into German for the journal *Dynamische Psychiatrie* in 1969. It was later published in English as "Montaigne, Rousseau and Freud" (Khan 1970a).

35. MK/VS, November 1, 1968.

36. WB, August 1, 1969.

37. When James Strachey died in 1967, Khan wrote: "It is a strange irony of my life that in spite of my young years I have grown up in the climate of the sensibility of these people—Rickman, Payne, Glover, Ella Sharpe, and Strachey. . . . Therefore with the death of each one of their generation, I experience not only loss, but an isolation" (MK/VS, April 27, 1967).

38. Charles Rycroft (along with Peter Lomas) resigned from the BPAS as a statement of protest after a meeting where the other members gave a critical reception to a speaker who talked about his belief that psychoanalysis is a "moral" science, rather than a "natural" science, as Freud had claimed. Khan regretted Rycroft's act, but agreed with him that the Society was stifling of innovation: "We all have to take responsibility for not being able to help and sustain creative minds like Charles and R. D. Laing" (letter, MK to Tom Hayley, recorded in WB, October 7, 1970).

39. MK/VS, October 8, 1970.

40. WB, April 3, 1975.

41. In Paris, Khan frequented two cafés, La Coupole and Deux Magot, both of which had been favorites of Ernest Hemingway.

42. MK/RS, January 29, 1969.

43. Khan wrote regarding Starobinski: "What attracts me to him is nostalgia. He has actualized a route in life I nurtured during my adolescence as a vocation and then opted out of when I settled for analytic training and abandoned going to Balliol, Oxford" (MK/VS, January 27, 1969).

44. "How I am cherished by my colleagues in Paris" (WB, March 15, 1972).

45. In his obituary of Khan, Pontalis (1989) would refer to him as "notre intime etranger"—French for "our intimate stranger." His words capture the idea of being closely connected to a person who is very different from oneself.

46. MK/VS, November 6, 1968.

47. WB, January 3, 1970.

48. Khan's talk, "The becoming of a psychoanalyst," was on the subject of psychoanalytic pedagogy. The Akademie was not a member of the IPA, in contrast to its main competitor, the Berlin Institute of Psycho-Analysis (now called the Karl Abraham Institute). Due to a clash with a colleague, Ammon had resigned from the accredited institute in order to create his own school.

49. Letter to the author from Gisela Ammon, February 1, 1999.

50. WB, November 8, 1970.

51. WB, November 9, 1970.

52. This paper was later published in English as "To Hear with Eyes" (Khan 1971a).

ENDNOTES TO CHAPTER 22

1. WB, March 28, 1972.

2. MK/ZD, August 13, 1968.

3. Khan entertained himself by watching the "coarse actions" of the American tourists and by buying books (WB, August 19, 1968).

4. Khan wrote that he needed and wanted to learn to feel emotions without acting in a manic fashion, in order to get through to the "private and hallowed silence and aloneness" that constituted his "personal idiom" (WB, August 19, 1968).

5. Letter, MK to Geoffrey Gorer, November 11, 1968.

6. Khan preserved both sides of this correspondence but at present, its whereabouts are unknown. Eva told me that, after Khan died, she wrote the IPA asking if it was in Khan's frozen files, but she was told that the question could not be answered until the files are unfrozen in 2039. She will be 103 years old then, if she is still alive.

7. WB, February 15, 1980.

8. MK/VS, January 3, 1969.

9. MK/VS, December 20, 1968.

10. MK/VS, January 4, 1969.

11. MK/VS, January 4, 1969.

12. WB, March 3, 1980.

13. Khan's family legacy did not include violence toward women and he did not feel like himself in these months. "Have never known myself so

resourceless tired and exhausted. Merely existing to survive each day does not fit my temperament. To fail one's own style is the most wretched betrayal of oneself, and I am living in a way entirely foreign and false to me" (WB, March 18, 1970).

14. MK/VS, May 13, 1969.

15. MK/VS, May 13, 1969.

16. MK/VS, May 15, 1969.

17. MK/VS, April 8, 1969.

18. MK/VS, June 13, 1969.

19. Khan wrote that Svetlana saw Winnicott for analysis in his introduction to Clancier and Kalmanovitch (1987), but this is an example of one of his fabrications. My evidence that she never had analysis or therapy comes from Khan's Work Book accounts, from Zoë Dominic, and from Svetlana herself.

20. MK/ZD, July 18, 1969.

21. MK/ZD, August 15, 1969.

22. Personal communication from Anne-Marie Sandler.

23. MK/VS, November 9, 1969.

24. MK/SB, August 22, 1970.

25. WB, February 2, 1980.

26. MK/VS, November 24, 1969.

27. MK/VS, December 16, 1969.

28. MK/ZD, December 28, 1969.

29. MK/VS, March 12, 1970.

30. WB, March 18, 1970.

31. WB, April 9, 1970.

32. Melanie Stanway is now Melanie Stanway Purnell.

33. MK/VS, April 20, 1970.

34. MK/VS, April 28, 1970.

35. MK/VS, May 2, 1970.

36. MK/VS, June 5, 1970. Khan also told Smirnoff how much he hated the "sun-blazed" weather in London and that he was trying to distract himself by working long hours and staying up late into the night watching the International Football Matches, which were being televised from Mexico.

37. MK/VS, July 5, 1970.

38. MK/VS, June 20, 1970.

1. Letter to the author from John Davis, August 17, 1997.

2. Khan said of his work with analytic candidates: "If any of them had been my private patient only, I would have handled them quite differently" (WB, February 28, 1970).

3. Godley 2001a, p. 6.

4. Godley 2001a.

5. Godley 2001b.

6. Boynton 2002.

7. Lucian Freud deserted Kitty and their two children when he ran off with the society belle Lady Caroline Blackwood (see Schoenberger 2001).

8. Godley 2001a, p. 3.

9. Godley 2001a, p. 5.

10. Godley 2001a, p. 5.

11. Godley 2001a, p. 5.

12. Khan's failure to refer back to the material of the regression is not necessarily an error. In regression to dependence, the experience itself is what is important, not the content (Black 2003).

13. Godley 2001a, p. 6.

14. Godley 2001a, p. 6.

15. Khan may have said it was the happiest night of his life, but he was a man who had many pleasurable experiences, and the comment is unlikely to have been something he held to over time.

16. Khan was getting tutored on his squash serve by the well-known Hashem Khan (not a relative), one of the greatest squash players of all time. Hashem Khan's brother Azam was the current Opens champion and he had started a club called the New Grampians Club. When Azam tore his Achilles tendon, Hashem took over. This is the club where Khan and Godley played squash.

17. Khan's nose was repaired by Sir C. Hogg, a surgeon who was knighted due to his ENT service to the Queen (WB, October 28, 1973).

18. Godley 2001a, p. 7.

19. Godley 2001a, p. 7.

20. Boynton 2002.

21. Godley 2001a, p. 7. The attack on Khan was in some ways old news, but the critique of Winnicott and the BPAS was startling and disruptive.

22. In his talk, Goldman tried to understand why analysis had not helped Khan to get control over his problematic behavior. He suggested that Winnicott and Khan may have had a "mutual vulnerability"—i.e., similar personal issues—which led to complications in the transference and countertransference. Wynne Godley was in the audience, along with at least three other Khan analysands: Judith Issroff, Eva, and H.K. In the discussion session, Godley criticized Goldman for being too positive about both Winnicott and Khan; he later expressed the same criticism in a complaint to the Squiggle Foundation.

Goldman's ideas about "mutual vulnerability" may also be relevant to the Khan–Godley pair. A woman who knew them both told me anonymously: "Wynne is beautiful, funny, and charming, so long as you aren't too much taken in by him. In this respect, he resembles Masud very much. They were, in a sense, twins."

23. A.-M. Sandler 2004.

24. Letter to the author from Eugene Lerner, April 20, 2001.

25. Since the time period of three weeks is the same for the infantile trauma and the period of recovery from the "chewed-up-by-rats" feeling, Eva seems to be implying that she reexperienced the first three weeks of life, this time with a better outcome.

26. Khan's view of love seems like a variant of object usage, where a person does not have to worry about damaging another person through intense feelings.

27. WB, August 31, 1969.

28. It is news to me that Winnicott was ever accused of sexual misconduct.

29. WB, October 7, 1970.

30. WB, August 5, 1975.

31. Another (anonymous) analysand also told me the paper was written about him. Since the case described by Khan changed from presentation to publication, it is possible that both men are correct.

32. Eyre believes that part of Khan's reluctance to discuss the dream was his sensitivity about having brown skin, like the seal.

33. In 2001, when the BPAS had its meeting to discuss the Wynne Godley article, members who could not attend were asked to send written comments, and Eyre wrote a letter that put Khan's behavior in perspective: "There was never any breaching of boundaries [in my analysis with Khan] and I have nothing but admiration for what he did for me, and gratitude. . . . I certainly don't think he was the first who had carried on inappropriately in the British Society and I am

sure he will not be the last. . . . It is not an isolated incident in the personage of Masud, the British Society or just psychoanalysts" (letter, Dean Eyre to Anne-Marie Sandler, June 12, 2001).

34. E-mail to the author from Judith Issroff, August 11, 2002.

35. E-mail to the author from Saul Peña, August 9, 2004.

36. Interview with Sadie Gillespie, November 2002.

ENDNOTES TO CHAPTER 24

1. MK/VS, April 15, 1970.

2. Nabokov, 1953. Harry Karnac told me: "The reason why Victor was known as Pnin was that the cover of the Penguin edition of the Nabokov novel of the same name had a sketch of the bald head of a man that could have easily represented, with a little imagination, Victor. It was Masud who gave him the nickname" (e-mail, April 30, 2002).

3. MK/VS, June 19, 1968.

4. MK/VS, August 20, 1968. Eva, Khan's analysand and lover from the late 1960s, told me: "Once Victor was visiting in London and Masud asked him, 'What did your psychoanalysis actually do for you, Pnin?' He answered, 'It didn't do much for me personally, but it libidinized literature.'"

5. MK/VS, August 17, 1969.

6. Khan's expertise was Shakespeare, Joyce, Virginia Woolf, and Dostoevsky. He was also a scholar of the works of Oscar Wilde, T. S. Eliot, Thomas Hardy, Joyce, Thomas Mann, D. H. Lawrence, Pushkin, Tolstoy, and the American poet Walt Whitman. He was not fond of contemporary novelists.

7. WB, February 23, 1970.

8. MK/VS, May 5, 1967. In Khan's flat at Palace Court, his next home, there was also a room dedicated to Pnin: "Yes, the guest room will be called THE PNIN ROOM and you shall always have the first priority to it. This room shall be yours for 46 years! [Note: This was the term of his lease.] I hope you will be happy in it and like the furniture I have acquired for you" (MK/VS, September 8, 1975).

9. WB, April 29, 1976.

10. WB, April 29, 1976.

11. MK/VS, November 5, 1975.

12. WB, September 22, 1970. The quote continues: "Poor Pnin is such a dear and frightened being and at first he will accommodate to [Jeanne Axler's] demands.

No, much worse! He will insinuate and sponsor them to create a need in her that he can gratify. But one day, he will get tired [and drop her]." This description fits Khan's style of relating to women much better than it fits Smirnoff's.

13. WB, July 19, 1975.

14. MK/VS, May 27, 1969.

15. MK/VS, October 30, 1968.

16. MK/VS, February 1, 1986.

17. WB, April 30, 1975.

18. WB, May 4, 1975.

19. MK/VS, February 1, 1986.

ENDNOTES TO CHAPTER 25

1. WB, July 25, 1971.

2. MK/VS, January 12, 1971.

3. WB, January 21, 1971.

4. WB, January 19, 1971.

5. Rodman (2003, p. 369) writes that DWW died on January 22, but Phillips (1988, p. 154) agrees with Khan that he died on January 25.

6. Khan wrote in his Work Book: "DWW has died at 4:00 am in his home, suddenly, and as he wanted it: alive when he was dying. John Mallinson has just rung to tell me this" (January 25, 1971).

7. WB, February 22, 1971.

8. MK/VS, February 9, 1971.

9. MK/VS, February 9, 1971.

10. MK/VS, February 22, 1971.

11. MK/RS, March 23, 1971.

12. MK/VS, February 7, 1971.

13. RS/MK, March 16, 1971.

14. MK/RS, March 25, 1971.

15. WB, January 31, 1971.

16. MK/SS, February 1, 1971.

17. MK/VS, February 9, 1971.

18. MK/VS, March 20, 1971.

19. WB, March 3, 1971.

20. MK/VS, March 15, 1971.

21. WB, April 15, 1971.

22. WB, April 19, 1971.

23. WB, April 4, 1975.

24. MK/VS, February 9, 1971.

25. MK/VS, May 17, 1971.

26. MK/VS, May 17, 1971.

27. WB, June 13, 1971.

28. WB, June 15, 1971.

29. MK/VS, June 16, 1971.

30. WB, June 18, 1971.

31. Khan 1971c.

32. WB, July 11, 1971.

33. WB, July 14, 1971.

34. Robert Rodman remembers the "distinct satisfaction" Clare showed a few years later in telling him how she had turned down Khan's request to be named executor (Rodman 2003, p. 211).

35. Cooper, 1993, p. 26. André Green told me in this context: "Once I asked Masud the meaning of his name and he told me that it meant 'He to whom everything is given.'"

36. Kanter 2004. Winnicott had written his will in 1965, so there had been plenty of time to discuss the situation with Khan. Clare Winnicott claimed that Khan was not chosen as literary executor because he had failed John Rickman by holding onto his papers and not getting them published. But Pearl King told me that Rickman's papers, which were in need of heavy editing, were given to both her and Khan upon Rickman's death, and they had worked together without success to get them published. As late as 1976, Khan wrote a letter to King confirming that he wanted to finish the project: "[Rickman's papers] have lain around too long now. But in 1977, I shall be available for active editing" (letter, MK to Pearl King, July 4, 1976). Unfortunately, he became ill in fall of 1976 and never returned to the project. King held the papers, along with 644 of Rickman's letters, and she finally completed the project of editing them in 2003 (King 2003).

37. WB, June 18, 1979. It is notable that Khan writes here as if Winnicott were still alive.

38. Khan 1988b, pp. 26 and 33.

39. Interview with Marion Milner, November 1996. Winnicott's first marriage had been unconsummated but he did have a successful sexual relationship

with Clare, first in an affair and then in marriage, according to Robert Rodman (2003).

40. WB, July 24, 1971. The entry continues: "When I find my way to writing about 'King Lear,' the title of it will be: 'The Unaccommodated Man.' Because it is this that constitutes the essence of that play" (WB, July 24, 1971). The reference is to Tom O'Bedlam, the fool (Edgar-in-disguise) who accompanies Lear after he is thrown out of his home into a wild tempest. Edgar is the legitimate son of the Earl of Gloucester and he is betrayed by an illegitimate half-brother.

41. WB, July 25, 1971.

42. WB, August 27, 1975.

43. WB, September 1, 1971.

44. MK/RS, October 19, 1971.

45. WB, November 28, 1971.

46. MK/VS, December 6, 1971.

47. MK/VS, December 27, 1971.

48. WB, December 26, 1971.

49. WB, December 27, 1971.

50. WB, January 2, 1972.

ENDNOTES TO CHAPTER 26

1. WB, April 3, 1973.

2. WB, July 30, 1974.

3. MK/RS, July 12, 1972.

4. WB, December 18, 1972.

5. RS/MK, April 30, 1975.

6. July 7, 1989. André Green saw things differently. He told me that what Khan needed was an analysis with Winnicott that would never end.

7. WB, January 18, 1972. Khan's homage to Winnicott was published later that year in the *International Journal of Child Psychotherapy* (Khan 1972g).

8. WB, February 22, 1975.

9. WB, March 2, 1975.

10. Undated letter, MK to Ishak Ramzy, 1971. The letter is quoted in Rodman (2003, p. 357). Rodman adds the comment: "Khan's correspondence took on an authoritative tone when Winnicott's work was the subject, as if he would now take over for him and do the job he imagined he was best fitted to do."

11. Winnicott's text was first published in Giovacchini (1972) without Khan's introduction. Later editions (London: Hogarth, 1986; and New York: Grove Press, 1986) included the introduction, written more than a decade earlier.

12. According to Rodman (2003, footnote 17, p. 417), Clare worked hard to control information about Donald that might appear in a future biography. She was particularly jealous of her husband's first wife, Alice, with whom he had exchanged letters after the divorce. Clare found the correspondence in a locked drawer after Donald's death, and she burned it. (Rodman attributes this information to Judith Issroff.) Khan's accounts support this idea. He wrote that Clare insisted that he remove a reference to Alice in his "Homage to Winnicott": "[I have to] delete reference to the first Mrs. Alice W. because the second, Clare, has written a letter soliciting me to delete that mention" (WB, April 9, 1973). Clare also insisted that he eliminate "little remarks that indicate the true character of DWW as a person" in a planned (but never published) introduction to a new edition of Winnicott's *Collected Papers* (WB, February 9, 1974).

13. WB, June 27, 1973.

14. F. R. Rodman, personal communication, January 2002.

15. Phillips 1988. In the acknowledgments, Phillips thanks Khan "from whom I learnt versions of psychoanalysis that were inspiring and intelligible."

16. Khan 1972f.

17. WB, May 25, 1972.

18. Khan 1972i.

19. Personal communication from Bernard Barnett.

20. WB, May 8, 1975.

21. "I have learnt and accepted my aloneness. No woman is going to share my intellectual odyssey" (WB, January 26, 1972).

22. I searched for Roz in many different ways, but was never able to find her.

23. Deirdre Redgrave, like her sister Vanessa, had radical political leanings. As early as September 28, 1970, Khan noted in his Work Book that through Deirdre he had met an impressive black revolutionary, Darcus Owusu. Owusu, according to Khan, was plotting a Communist revolution in the Caribbean, and "he had the conviction and talent to act on his passion."

24. MK/VS, April 19, 1972.

25. In a WB entry on March 17, 1972, Khan notes that several of his close friends were involved with Hakim Jamal. Jamal was an American Black Panther living in London, who was sponsored and "introduced around" by Vanessa

Redgrave. He was a man of extreme charisma and handsome looks, who called himself God. Jamal eventually moved to Trinidad with the ex-wife of "The Eyes," an upper-class woman from London, and she was murdered there—she was hacked to death and possibly buried alive as a consequence of trying to uncover the political corruption of a local Black Panther. Jamal then moved to Boston, where he was murdered by another Black Panther. Jamal may have been a friend of Darcus Owusu (see Footnote 23, above). Jamal's story is told in gripping detail by a former lover, Diana Athill, in a book entitled *Make Believe* (South Royalton, Vermont: Steerforth Press, 1993). Another account is in a chapter of a book by V. S. Naipaul entitled *The Return of Eva Peron* (New York: Knopf, 1980).

26. Interview with "The Eyes," May 2001.

27. MK/VS, April 19, 1972.

28. MK/VS, May 17, 1972.

29. WB, August 8, 1972.

30. WB, November 9, 1972.

31. MK/VS, February 8, 1973.

32. Khan 1975b. Although earlier drafts of this paper had been cowritten with Eva, Khan did not acknowledge her contributions.

33. Khan 1973a.

34. Khan 1973d.

35. WB, February 20, 1973.

36. On this visit, Khan had dinner with the Stollers and the Greensons at the home of the Walter Annenberg heir Lita Hazen, Greenson's analysand (WB, April 26, 1973).

37. MK/VS, April 22, 1973. Khan added: "The only missing element is that neither [Bob nor Sybil] plays backgammon or Canasta."

38. WB, May 1, 1973.

39. Janet still lives in the two-room studio she rented when she returned to Paris thirty years ago. Her quotes come from the meeting we had there in November 1997.

40. WB, April 6, 1973.

41. Postcard, MK to Janet, October 2, 1973.

42. WB, July 30, 1973.

43. Janet told me that Khan wrote her postcards instead of letters because, in her words, "I don't understand letters."

44. WB, March 21, 1973.

45. MK/VS, July 9, 1973.

46. WB, July 30,1973.

47. WB, August 10, 1973.

48. WB, August 9, 1973.

49. WB, September 14, 1973.

50. WB, September 17, 1973.

51. WB, October 7, 1973.

52. WB, October 7, 1973.

53. WB, November 20, 1973.

54. WB, January 15, 1974.

55. WB, October 16, 1973.

56. WB, January 2, 1974.

57. WB, January 27, 1974.

58. WB, June 1, 1972.

59. MK/VS, February 5, 1974. The divorce was not official until May 24.

60. MK/VS, February 5, 1974.

61. The new houseboy was Angelo Gonzalves. Julie Crowther replaced Caroline Hall as secretary.

62. WB, May 9, 1974.

63. Khan 1974a.

64. Khan et al. 1974b.

65. Khan 1975a.

66. WB, May 1, 1974. The discussants were Eric Brenman (a Kleinian), Paula Heimann (a former Kleinian), and Eric Rayner (an Independent).

67. John Charlton provided him with the title, which had originally been *The Finding and Becoming of Self* (WB, April 12, 1973).

68. Megan's ex-husband refused to give me her address or phone number and I was never able to find her.

69. MK/RS, July 4, 1974.

70. MK/VS, July 13, 1974.

71. WB, July 21, 1974.

72. MK/VS, July 27, 1974.

73. WB, July 30, 1974.

74. MK/VS, September 7, 1974. While watching television at the Stollers' beach home in Malibu, Khan had seen Richard Nixon resign from the presidency of the United States. As usual, his interest in politics was limited to psychological considerations: "Nixon is so utterly innocent in his own eyes, and it

is this innocence that makes him evil as a person" (WB, August 8, 1974). "Strange how much loathing in everyone this man Nixon has engendered. As if he could live only in a climate of being hated—that satisfied his hatred of others" (WB, August 28, 1974).

75. WB, October 27, 1974.

76. RS/VS, December 10, 1974.

77. WB, June 2, 1974.

ENDNOTES TO CHAPTER 27

1. WB, January 5, 1975.

2. WB, February 15, 1975.

3. MK/VS, February 25, 1975.

4. WB, February 28, 1975.

5. WB, March 7, 1975.

6. RS/MK, February 5, 1975.

7. WB, March 22, 1975.

8. WB, March 23, 1975.

9. WB, March 27, 1975.

10. The discussants were Anna Freud, Paula Heimann, Malcolm Pines, Lionel Kreeger, and Joseph Sandler.

11. In the earlier meeting in the mid-1960s, Lacan had given a standing-room-only talk at the Institute Français, and Khan interrupted him at one point by going onstage and explaining a difficult concept in his own words (Boynton 2002).

12. Khan commented on the Green lecture: "André's talk was erudite, but arid. Beautifully delivered" (WB, February 10, 1975). The lecture has now been published in Green's book *On Private Madness* (Madison, Connecticut: International Universities Press, 1993, pp. 17–29).

13. RS/MK, March 20, 1975.

14. WB, March 24, 1975, 5:30 a.m.

15. WB, March 29, 1975 8:30 a.m. The reference to "white" nights presumably refers to having the lights on as he reads and writes into the early morning hours.

16. WB, April 22, 1975.

17. WB, May 10, 1975.

18. MK/VS, June 3, 1975.

19. Marie Singer (deceased) was a black American psychotherapist, trained by Anna Freud, who had established an innovative clinic outside of London. She was proudly the granddaughter of a slave and she taught psychology at Eton, to England's elite children (information is from Bob Hinshelwood).

20. WB, June 8, 1975.

21. WB, May 26, 1975.

22. WB, June 13, 1975.

23. CAPS was started in the United States, and then a European branch was established in 1973. Membership was by invitation only and was limited to training analysts and deans of an IPA institute. The purpose of the group was to provide a space for in-depth presentations of clinical material.

24. WB, June 20, 1975.

25. WB, July 4, 1975, 2 a.m.

26. WB, July 14, 1975.

27. Khan1962a.

28. Khan 1972e. Robert Stoller commented on this paper in a letter to Khan, "[This] is the most important paper on dreams since Freud's work. You have opened up the meaning of the dream and, with a brilliant awareness, have given the dream a new dimension in clinical work" (November 13, 1972).

29. Khan 1975c.

30. Khan 1962a, p. 35.

31. Since the dream space, like transitional space, is a "capacity," it cannot be directly observed, but its presence is revealed by a report of a "good dream."

32. Khan 1962a, p. 38.

33. Khan 1972e, p. 314.

34. Two earlier writings, from 1962 and 1972, anticipated the ideas of the 1976 paper: "It is easy to drug oneself into an opaque inert state of sleep. But dynamic sleep is different. It is my experience that all my papers & personal conflicts have been intrinsically worked through in sleep. The waking articulate consciousness only organises and structuralises this substratum of thinking & affectivity" (MK/ZD, August 31, 1962). "One must respect a patient's need not to tell his dream. A patient said today he had a night of rich and healing dreams and on waking had felt better for having dreamt, but couldn't recall any of them to report. My comment was that for him it was not necessary to know his dreams at the present stage of his analysis. It was quite sufficient to experience dreaming them" (WB, June 7, 1972).

35. Khan 1975c, p. 50.

36. WB, March 13, 1975.

37. WB, February 26, 1970.

38. WB, February 23, 1975. Two of Khan's unpublished thoughts about dreams are worthy of further investigation. First: "Recently, I have watched a distinct rhythm in myself. I wake up naturally from within around 8:00 am, and then, if I push myself under into sleep and am woken up later, the 'alive' tone of the first awakening has changed into a dull and negative mood. There is the need in one to nurture and respect the 'wake wish' in oneself" (WB, March 17, 1970). Khan is suggesting that an inner self tells some other self when to wake up, and the two selves work best when the second one listens to the first. The experience rings true for many people. Second: "Hallucinogenic drugs (LSD, etc.) make a person dream while awake, and often this is intolerable to the person. Why does a 'dream' have this difference of affect in sleep and in wakefulness?" (WB, March 19, 1970).

39. WB, July 22, 1975.

40. WB, July 25, 1975.

41. The co-discussants were Michael Fordham and Erik Erikson, with Malcolm Pines moderating.

42. WB, July 25, 1975.

43. WB, July 20, 1975.

44. WB, July 25, 1975.

45. WB, July 28, 1975.

46. WB, August 5, 1975.

47. WB, September 1, 1975.

48. WB, September 12, 1975.

49. The note is quoted in WB, September 16, 1975.

50. He had made sure that there were ample built-in bookshelves for his precious books, possessions that were like people to him: "The only continuity of my life is that with books! those perpetual companions that do not intrude!" (WB, July 6, 1975). "The true nourishment of my mind accrues from living with my books and not just reading them" (WB, May 18, 1975).

51. WB, November 8, 1975.

52. WB, October 12, 1975.

53. WB, September 15, 1975.

54. November 11, 1975.

55. WB, December 13, 1975.

56. WB, November 11, 1975.
57. WB, December 6, 1975.
58. WB, December 23, 1975.
59. WB, December 25, 1975.
60. WB, December 28, 1975.

ENDNOTES TO CHAPTER 28

1. WB, May 27, 1974, Khan's italics.
2. Part of the problem was that heavy drinking was common in Khan's intellectual and upper-class social world. People tended to think that legal and illegal drugs were a much greater danger.
3. MK/SB, June 15, 1963.
4. MK/SB, March 29, 1965.
5. MK/SB, October 3–5, 1965.
6. WB, April 25, 1970.
7. MK/VS, August 26, 1973.
8. Johnson 1999. The general understanding today is that alcoholism results from some combination of genetics, psychopathology, and environmental stress, but experts continue to disagree about the relative significance of those factors.
9. Rayner, foreword to Cooper (1993, p. xvi).
10. Winnicott wrote almost nothing about the problem of addiction, although there is a brief reference (Winnicott 1953) to addiction in general as a problem of the transitional space. In clinical writings, Winnicott mentions alcohol abuse only once, in notes about a case who may well be Khan, where Winnicott interprets that the man is drinking in an attempt to prove that he can have control over the emergence of his symptoms of anxiety and depersonalization (see C. Winnicott et al. 1989, pp. 187–188, Winnicott 1963b). There is no suggestion that the problem of alcohol abuse might require focused attention in the analysis or elsewhere. The extent to which Winnicott failed to grasp Khan's developing problem is suggested in a story told by Khan. He recalls being offered alcohol by Winnicott when they were working together on a Sunday evening in the late 1960s. Winnicott offered him whisky, which Khan helped himself to "generously." A little later, Winnicott suggested, "Pour yourself another" and Khan did so (Khan 1986c, p. 33).

11. WB, September 24, 1975. Like Winnicott, Khan (1972d) published only one clinical case where there is reference to a patient with a drinking problem. Khan claims that he helped this patient quickly with his longtime problem: "I had weaned him from the bottle all too easily." In his article "On Lying Fallow," Khan (1977b) refers to alcoholism as "a failure of the fallow mood" where a person copes with internal anxiety by turning to "exotic" experiences such as drunkenness.

12. It may be of personal significance that, in 1973, Khan recorded a quote from the philosopher Unamuno in his Work Book: "There are moments when to be silent is to be an accomplice" (WB, January 20).

13. See Director 2002, Gabbard 2002, Gerald 2002, Khantzian 1995, Mann 2002.

14. WB, June 8, 1976.

15. Jamison 1993. Bipolar illness is characterized by extreme mood swings and erratic behavior. If alcoholism is involved, there is increased severity of the symptoms.

16. WB, May 24, 1975. Consider also: "Somewhere I have always known and dreaded since adolescence that if I surrendered to my mind it would take over the whole of my life space" (WB, March 18, 1975, 6 a.m.). "Lord! At what speed I work and get things done once I start going. In a strange way I dread my efficiency. It could consume me!" (WB, May 13, 1976).

17. WB, May 25, 1975. Khan's Work Books and correspondences reveal that he was often awake and reading or working as late as 4:00 or even 5:00 a.m.

18. Khan had other symptomatology that suggests bipolar illness. He drank most heavily when he was manic, in contrast to non-bipolar alcoholics, who drink most when they are depressed: "Alcohol has always been my fueling of the counterphobic manic states" (WB, December 6, 1975). (A tendency to drink when depressed came late in his life, in the 1980s, when he had been alcoholic for a long time and was constantly drinking.) His calm periods seemed to come out of nowhere (i.e., without psychological cause) and they coincided with abstinence from alcohol: "I have a distinct inner sense of quietude today, as if I have come through a silent crisis the past many months. A crisis which compelled me to drink heavily. I have no clue about the nature of this crisis" (WB, July 20, 1976). In the calm periods, he missed the excitement of his mania. And he tended to feel "different," as is common in people with bipolar disorders: "Psychic pain: the pain of being separated, the pain of being alone, the pain of being different" (WB, September 1, 1976).

19. For at least twenty years before he died, Khan met all the *DSM-IV* di-

agnostic criteria for the diagnosis of bipolar II disorder (recurrent major depressive episodes with hypomanic episodes): distinct periods of elevated mood, inflated self-esteem or grandiosity, decreased need for sleep, talkativeness, flight of ideas, increase in goal-directed activity, and impulsive behavior.

20. Today there are many choices of medication in addition to lithium for bipolar disorders, e.g., Tegratol, Depakote, Neurontin, Lamictal, and Topamax.

21. Personal communication from Barrie Cooper, November 2000.

ENDNOTES TO CHAPTER 29

1. Khan knew that it was dangerous to modify technique without getting at least peer supervision. Writing to the California analyst Melvin Mandel regarding an especially difficult patient, he said: "It is my experience that with this sort of patient there is always the danger that one gets too over involved from an inherent need for complicity in the patient's illness. If one has a colleague or two to regularly discuss it with, then at least the counter-transference remains properly dosed and shared" (May 2, 1973).

2. MK/RS, July 12, 1972. Critics of therapists who deviate from accepted boundaries tend to think of them as morally corrupt; it is perhaps more frightening to think of them as people who are unaware of the harm they are potentially doing.

3. Some facts about Alexa's life are modified to protect her identity.

4. This is the same treatment as that given to Svetlana Beriosova.

5. Caroline had graduated from high school in Canada, and she needed to pass the A level exams to qualify to go to a university.

6. A "crammer's school" is a small private school where tutors flood the student with knowledge in preparation for exams.

7. It is possible, although troubling, that Khan really believed that he was engaging in an initiation ritual that would help Caroline to become a sexual woman. See this entry in Khan's Work Book from the time when he was treating Caroline. He had just read a review of Dr. Martin Shepard's *The Love Treatment: Sexual Intimacy Between Patients and Psychotherapists* (Wyden Paperback Library) in the *New York Review of Books* (August 31, 1972, pp. 7–8): "Yes, this whole issue . . . needs careful discussion. But we have neither the moral charity nor conceptual tools as yet to creatively explore this predicament of psychotherapeutics" (WB, August 27, 1972).

8. Caroline added: "The little dog Kalu started to often be there in the living room, even though he had never been in the sessions before. Masud painted an abstract painting of Kalu in the park—it was so abstract a painting that you wouldn't have known it was a dog if he hadn't told you."

9. Caroline learned about Khan's alcoholism when I sent her a copy of one of my articles (Hopkins 1998).

10. The person on the phone may have been Beriosova herself.

ENDNOTES TO CHAPTER 30

1. WB, March 29, 1976.

2. WB, January 15, 1976.

3. WB, February 7, 1976.

4. WB, March 19, 1976. Robert Stoller refused to believe in Khan's False Self pathology: "It simply is not true that you are without identity. It—you—lies there going about its own business, having the good sense to ignore both the outside world and your own mad dancing around its central, solid quiet realness" (RS/MK, February 6, 1976).

5. February 28, 1976.

6. The information about Khan's references to supposed illnesses of others comes from J.-B. Pontalis (interview, November 1997).

7. See A. Green, *The Work of the Negative*, London: Free Associations Books, 1993. On the NRP board, Khan and Green were usually allied in decision making, although they liked to debate issues. An anonymous female friend from that era told me: "André and Masud were extremely intimate and close in their sparring. I've never seen two men so close who weren't lovers."

8. WB, March 19, 1976.

9. Khan viewed Pontalis' title as an improvement over the English title: "Perhaps Pontalis, in changing the title of my book, *Privacy of the Self* to *Le Soi Cache* had found me out, quite unconsciously. True! Je me cache! ['I hide myself!']" (WB, February 15, 1980).

10. Khan wrote of Green's introduction: "Its generosity, acumen and insightfulness have left me gasping. What a synthesising mind this man has. No one could do a better review. It has deepened my understanding of my own writing for me. A work of true friendship and creative thought" (WB, May 3, 1975).

11. MK/RS, May 17, 1976.

12. WB, June 15, 1976.

13. WB, June 13, 1976.

14. WB, June 19, 1976.

15. RS/VS, July 1, 1976.

16. WB, August 4, 1976.

17. WB, August 24, 1976. One night the electricity failed and he decided to sleep outside. Still awake at 3 a.m., with his clothes damp from the dew, he went inside and read by the light of a torch. By 4 a.m., the torch had burned out, so he used a kerosene oil lamp: "This is the same lamp with which I studied during all those years 1937–1942 when reading became a strange passion with me. It is the same ambience: little air, soft dry perspiration and the mellow light and heat of the lamp. Yes, the Masud Khan of London found his true beginnings in this light and heat" (WB, August 25, 1976).

18. WB, August 23, 1976.

19. WB, August 24, 1976.

20. WB, August 28, 1976.

21. WB, August 16, 1976.

22. It was a traditional wedding, which included a climactic ritual in which the bride and bridegroom saw each other for the first time in a mirror.

23. Khan had also given this twenty-four-volume set to Sahabzada Yaqub Khan.

24. WB, August 26, 1976.

25. WB, August 31, 1976.

26. WB, September 4, 1976.

27. WB, September 10, 1976.

28. WB, September 4, 1976.

29. Margarita remembers being extremely sensitive to the opinions of her peers and grateful to people who were thoughtful. She told me that once, after a supervision class, a colleague approached her at the elevator and expressed a thought undoubtedly shared by many others: "My friend said: 'Margarita, do you realize that we are envious of you, because you are living out our fantasies? We all would like to live with our analyst.' When she put this into words, without judging, it helped me."

30. WB, September 16, 1976.

31. Twenty-five years later, Margarita told me: "When I think about it now, I regret that neither Masud nor Limentani were influenced enough by the Kleinians. A Kleinian would have seen this whole thing as an experience where

my inner objects were coming alive and being acted out. It was an infantile attempt to get inside the other, and Masud should have known not to take it at face value. He was believing that we were both really in love; I was living in the cloud of transference and it felt like reality. We both needed interpretations, and we needed help to keep the experience in the analysis; nobody gave that to us."

ENDNOTES TO CHAPTER 31

 1. WB, October 14, 1976.

 2. WB, October 11, 1976.

 3. WB, October 17, 1976.

 4. WB, October 17, 1976.

 5. WB, October 18, 1976.

 6. The information on dipsomania is a personal communication from David Mann, M.D.

 7. WB, October 19, 1976.

 8. WB, October 19, 1976.

 9. WB, October 20, 1976. Despite these words, Khan and Margarita were never formally engaged.

 10. WB, October 20, 1976.

 11. WB, October 22, 1976.

 12. Margarita told me how she handled Svetlana, who was in a panic: "Svetlana called while Masud was in the hospital and I took the call. She thought I must be the houseboy's wife, so she spoke to me as if I were a servant, and I just went along with that and tried to reassure her. She phoned every night after that, and I would give her a report on how 'Mr. Khan' was doing. We became very close over the telephone. After Masud went home, he told her who I was, and she appreciated what I had done for her."

 13. Lung cancer is a particularly deadly cancer. In 2005, the reported five-year survival rate for lung cancer is only 15 percent. (J. Brody, "What an Extra Eye on Cancer Can Do For You." *New York Times*, Science Times, August 16, 2005, p. F7.)

 14. WB, October 29, 1976.

 15. It is typical of Khan that he would not have wanted female nurses to help him with physical things. His friends remember that he did not even allow

females to hold his coat in checkrooms of restaurants. This was a remnant of his early life in a very different culture.

16. WB, November 12, 1976.

17. RS/MK, October 26, 1976.

18. This attitude is in contrast to Muslim acceptance of God's will. It is reminiscent of his response in the game reported by Julie Andrews, where the circle of 1960s friends told what they would do if there was about to be an end to the world. Khan had said that he would scream at God in outrage (see Chapter 7).

19. WB, November 12, 1976.

20. WB, December 13, 1976.

21. WB, December 31, 1976.

22. RS/MK, January 7, 1977.

23. WB, December 31, 1976. After the cancer, Khan's use of the third person to refer to himself became a regular part of his writing: losing the "I," he was relating to himself as "he." In psychological terminology, it might be said that his sense of self as subject was disconnected from his sense of self as object (see Ogden 1986).

ENDNOTE TO PART VIII OPENING PAGE

1. WB, January 29, 1980. See also Khan's recording of the words of Fyodor Dostoevsky in 1864: "[I am feeling] anxiety, bitterness, the most senseless rushing about, and, in addition, loneliness—and yet I can't help feeling that I am about to begin to live. Funny, isn't it? A cat's vitality." Khan's comment about the quote was: "At fifty-five plus, I feel exactly the same" (WB, March 9, 1980).

ENDNOTES TO CHAPTER 32

1. WB, December 31, 1976.

2. In Anne-Marie Sandler's memory, it was after her husband, Joseph, had a consultation with William Gillespie "as an elderly wise analyst" that, with Gillespie's urging, a meeting was called to discuss the husband's charge.

3. Letter, A. Limentani to B. Cooper, December 6, 1976 (RSP).

4. The information about the three recommendations comes from Hanna Segal.

5. Letter, B. Cooper to A. Limentani, December 13, 1976.

6. This account comes from various interviews with Barrie Cooper. Cooper notes that he and Limentani had gone to medical school together and that they had a long history of disagreements about the use of psychoanalytic insight in medicine and teaching.

7. WB, December 11, 1976.

8. WB, January 3, 1977.

9. Letter, A. Limentani to B. Cooper, January, 1977—exact date illegible (RSP).

10. Margarita changed analysts because the woman she was seeing was a close friend of Khan and Margarita felt the analyst was overly sympathetic to him. Her new analyst was Tom Haley, an Independent who was uninvolved with the major people involved in the Khan situation. She saw him for three years: "Haley gave me a quiet space where I could talk about myself, and that was a blessing." She told me that a member (unnamed) of the Education Committee was the person who told her she had to leave training: "[He] said that he understood why I had changed analysts, and thought it was a good decision. But I still had to leave. I was expelled for the 'crime' of wanting a neutral analytic space for myself."

11. WB, January 2, 1977.

12. Letter, MK to N. Coltart, January 24, 1977. Khan's statement that he was born a "royal feudal duke" is a fabrication. The author thanks Elizabeth Young-Bruehl for sharing this letter.

13. Kirsner (2000) has written about the reciprocal impact of the reputation and power of the training analyst on his/her students' professional development. Winnicott and Khan are examples of this, with the successes and failures of each being relevant to the other, and Khan's "heirs" would also be carrying his legacy.

14. An (anonymous) British analyst told me: "There were four problems with Masud's affairs: (1) They were too frequent. (2) They were too arrogant. (3) They were a deliberate flaunting of his uniqueness and his power to ignore the rules of the society. (4) He was 'black' and rich, and he was having sex with white women." It is noteworthy that it was Margarita's husband who had made the initial complaint. This is in contrast to most misconduct charges, where it is the patient who complains. Not one of the analysands seduced by Khan ever made a formal complaint. A comment by an (anonymous) London analyst helps to make sense of this. She had a young woman in treatment who had had a sexual

relationship with Khan while in analysis with him (someone not interviewed for this biography). The patient refused to make an ethics complaint, saying she could not do that because Khan had helped her so much in other ways. Charles Rycroft told me something similar: "After Masud was demoted from training analyst, I saw two ladies who had sexual involvement with him while seeing him in analysis, and they both thought he had been marvelous. One said: 'I had no idea anyone could understand me the way Masud did.' The other said, 'It was at least 50% my responsibility and I'm grateful to Masud for what he did for me.'"

15. WB, January 5, 1977.

16. MK/VS, December 12, 1968.

17. WB, February 18, 1977.

18. Khan knew well Miss Freud's personal limitations. We see from a description Khan gave of her in a 1971 letter what a poor choice she was to be his analyst: "How well balanced Miss Freud is & what a price she had to pay for this stance. The girl who used to write poetry could not be more prosaic a human being today. She resigned from her temperament & sensibility to serve her father's cause with a militant normalcy and a sanity of outlook that avoids every experience that is paradoxical & perplexing. She was a 'good' girl and she has aged into a 'good' old woman; she has missed youth & the anguish of being human. Hence she is rather boring. . . . What a deadly price an individual pays for normalcy like hers" (MK/VS, February 10, 1971).

19. VS/RS, March 24, 1977.

20. WB, February 17, 1977.

21. WB, March 15, 1977.

22. WB, January 1, 1977.

23. WB, March 7, 1977.

24. WB, March 26, 1977.

25. VS/RS, June 21, 1977.

26. WB, October 2, 1977.

27. WB, June 25, 1977.

28. WB, July 28, 1977.

29. MK/VS, August 17, 1977.

30. WB, September 21, 1977.

31. Letter, B. Cooper to S. and R. Stoller, September 27, 1977.

32. WB, October 20, 1977.

33. MK/VS, November 9, 1977.

34. WB, January 31, 1978.

35. VS/RS, March 27, 1978.

36. Information about Khan's attacks on Winnicott comes from an e-mail to the author from Patrick Casement, February 27, 2001, and from B. Kahr (1996).

37. On this visit, Khan gave his half-brother Anwar an estate in Chakwal that he had inherited from his father—or possibly just his share of that estate. He may have continued to own yet another property. In 1976, by Khan's report, a distant uncle, the Mir of Chattar, had left him a landed estate in a part of Pakistan that bordered on Iran and Afghanistan. The two had only met twice, at a ninetieth birthday party for Fazaldad and then at Fazaldad's funeral. This uncle had three sons who all died in the 1971 war with East Pakistan. The estate included "vast sheep grazing land" that Khan may never have seen (MK/VS, August 7, 1981).

38. WB, August 29, 1978.

39. WB, August 29, 1978.

40. WB, August 31, 1978.

41. Letter, B. Cooper to R. Stoller, September 20, 1978 (RSP).

42. VS/RS, October 14, 1978.

43. Letter, B. Cooper to R. Stoller, October 5, 1978 (RSP).

44. WB, October 8, 1978.

45. WB, November 23, 1978.

46. VS/RS, October 14, 1978.

ENDNOTES TO CHAPTER 33

1. MK/VS, February 5, 1979.

2. I interviewed Yasmine on two occasions, but she chose not to read the material from Khan's Work Books describing their relationship. It is likely that, had she read the excerpts reported in this chapter, she would have disagreed with some of what Khan writes. Some of the identifying details about her have been modified for purposes of confidentiality.

3. WB, January 13, 1979.

4. John Charlton told me: "I didn't know [Yasmine] very well. Masud kept her for later in the evening" (interview, 1998).

5. WB, December 28, 1978.

6. RS/VS, January 25, 1979. Khan himself gave "treatment" to several

people in his private life. One such person was the French photographer Henri
Cartier-Bresson (d. 2004), whom Khan watched over for more than a decade as
Cartier-Bresson's life went through much turmoil. This story is at least partially
recorded in Cartier-Bresson's private correspondence. Another friend who was
privately "analyzed" by Khan was a well-known public figure. One night after
talking to this man at Hans Crescent from 5 p.m. until 2 a.m., Khan "put him to
bed" in the spare room and commented: "I wonder what makes me take on these
thankless exhausting therapeutic–total care–analytic marathons. It is not that I
consider myself wiser or abler than other colleagues. I really do not. I am different but not necessarily better. It is more the hangover from my feudal upbringing plus ineradicable infections from Winnicott's sensibility" (MK/ZD,
April 10, 1965). The problem with providing therapeutic care for a friend, Khan
said, was that it was impossible for the friendship to stay mutual. From the
"analyst's" perspective, he said, "The whole experience has to be gone through
impersonally: at one remove and with a cold intense sympathy without involvement" (Ibid.).

7. The Stollers' anniversary party started with drinks and an hour of live
chamber music by Mozart and Dvorak, followed by dinner. Khan was well-
behaved because the Stollers insisted on that. Robert wrote to Victor Smirnoff,
"Both Sybil and I [told Masud] that we do not like—cannot stand, will not be
with him—if he persists in his manipulative, dishonest, hateful treatment of
others. The amusing anecdotes are fun and permissible, but when his behavior
either touches us directly or almost directly—as when he is talking about people
and circumstances we know—then we invariably interrupted him, expressed our
disageement and disapproval and repeated, in one way or another, our warn-
ings that we had had enough of that. He was benign and accepting in our dealing with him that way" (RS/VS, January 25, 1979).

8. Thinking about this stormy relationship with Yasmine while sitting at
the beach house in Malibu, Khan wrote about how different he was from the
Stollers: "Little wonder that the Stollers are so healthy and wholesome. There
they are out on the beach: parents, children, grandchild, friends and dogs, whilst
I sit inside and write. Is this phobia?! No, it is a very private sort of discipline in
me. I do not squander myself except on women" (WB, December 31, 1978).

9. WB, December 30, 1978.

10. WB, January 1, 1979.

11. WB, January 3, 1979.

12. WB, January 4, 1979.

13. WB, January 5, 1979. The Stollers had invited Ralph Greenson and his wife to dinner that night but the plans had to be canceled due to the rain. Ralph was already ill, recovering from a stroke, and he died later in the year.

14. WB, January 6, 1979.

15. WB, January 8, 1979. Stoller's emphasis on the importance of controlling behavior, as evidenced in last excerpt, was likely not something that Khan would have heard from Winnicott. Winnicott believed that healthier behavior was the result of insight and thus did not have to be consciously forced.

16. WB, January 9, 1979.

17. WB, January 11, 1979.

18. RS/VS, January 25, 1979.

19. WB, June 19, 1979.

20. WB, January 11, 1979.

21. WB, January 13, 1979.

22. WB, January 13, 1979.

23. RS/VS, January 25, 1979.

24. RS/VS, October 17, 1978.

25. RS/MK, March 7, 1980.

26. WB, January 22, 1979.

27. WB, January 14, 1979.

28. The head of the Publications Committee in 1979 was Tom Haley, the man who had been Margarita's third analyst. Haley was also editor of the IJPA.

29. The NRP article was titled "Infancy and Aloneness." It was reprinted in *Hidden Selves* with the title "Infancy, Aloneness and Madness" (MK3). For the first time, Khan criticized Winnicott in print. He said that Winnicott relied too much on genetic interpretations (i.e., his interpretations took into account the person's early history) and underestimated the importance of a person's False Self madness.

30. Khan 1979b.

31. In 1968, Khan had written to Smirnoff: "I have caused enough distress and harassment to my friends and colleagues by the aberrant antics of my character & temperament. Anna Freud has been very staunchly, though at one remove, behind me, & I don't want to upset her. So I keep postponing writing an evaluative long introduction on the theme of perversions to a collection of my already printed case-studies & articles" (February 3).

32. WB, June 7, 1979.

33. Khan wrote about the sexual relationship: "I am an insatiable sensualist. Lord! I made love for seven hours non-stop, one way or another, with Yasmine last night. Strangely I feel no hindrances of prudence with her" (WB, January 14, 1979).

34. WB, January 22, 1979.

35. WB, June 14, 1979.

36. WB, June 12, 1979.

37. Khan wrote: "I do not see what choice one has with a patient like [Yasmine]. One either steps aside and lets them perish silently and invisibly—or one commits oneself totally, and then one becomes part of the illness. Where one goes from there, and what one does, I do not know" (WB, February 6, 1979).

38. Personal communication from André Green.

39. Green translated a quote for me from his introduction to *Le Soi Cache*. He said that, without knowing it, he had been describing his relationship with Khan when he wrote these paragraphs: "It is frequent that the best friends of analysts are other analysts. This is not just because they are sharing the profession. It hands over the friendship that our practice forbids us to have with our patients. . . . These friendships can be strong and they lead to 'divorces' more dramatic than the divorces of marriage. It is because friendship has become unnatural, what it should never have been."

40. WB, May 30, 1979.

41. WB, May 31, 1979.

42. WB, June 14, 1979.

43. WB, June 15, 1979. Khan wrote that in Woolf's writing and in some of Svetlana's dancing—especially in her performance in *Giselle*—personal madness had been harnessed into extraordinary acts of creativity. "The very first time I saw Svetlana in 'Giselle,' at the end of the first act when she feels jilted and goes mad, I experienced an awed chill, and I knew this was not merely acting, but one day she will BE that. And so it happened" (WB, February 3, 1980).

44. WB, June 14, 1979.

45. WB, June 12, 1979.

46. WB, June 18, 1979. The reader may be surprised to hear what Khan thought True Self living might be like: "Last night I told [Yasmine] that only she and her daughters are keeping me in London. Otherwise, now I would give away all [my possessions], buy myself a one-way ticket to my estate in Lyallpur and leave with my pens, shaver and one Braque lithograph. [Y.] asked me what

I would do there. I said, first take the lethal risk of doing nothing until I feel from within what I want to **do**. [Then] buy a defunct debris-discarded motor-engine of a pre-war Ford lorry, employ five ironmongers, and with their instruction, slowly confabulate a concrete object in metal. Not read at all, and write only from memory" (WB, June 28, 1979). This fantasy sounds like an externalization of the battle to formulate a solid self. The immensity of the task is exemplified by Khan's thought that he would have to employ five ironmongers to help with the task.

47. WB, June 26, 1979.

48. WB, June 20, 1979.

ENDNOTES TO CHAPTER 34

1. MK/ZD, May 15, 1967.

2. *The Idiot* (1868) is one of Dostoevsky's great novels, along with *Brothers Karamazov* (1880), *Crime and Punishment* (1866), and *Notes from the Underground* (1864). There are four main characters: "The Idiot" Prince Myshkin, Parfion Rogozhin, Nastasia Filippovna, and Aglaia Epanchin. Myshkin is an innocent but wise epileptic who is a Christ figure; he returns to Russia from a stay in an asylum in an unnamed foreign country and is accepted at the highest levels of society, even though he never quite fits in. Rogozhin is Myshkin's foil, a man of passion and cruelty. The female characters have similarly opposite characteristics. Nastasia Filippovna, is a passionate and cruel woman who is in love with death, while Aglaia is younger, a gay and sexually naive woman with a loving and proper family. Myshkin falls in love with Nastasia, but she constantly wavers between him and Rogozhin. When Myshkin understands that Nastasia suffers from insanity, his love changes to pity and profound devotion. He falls in love with Aglaia but stays commited to Nastasia. Rogozhin comes to the church as Myshkin and Nastasia are about to be married, and Nastasia willingly runs away with him. Myshkin searches throughout Moscow for the pair and eventually finds Nastasia dead in Rogozhin's home, Rogozhin having stabbed her in the heart. Rogozhin is convicted of the murder and imprisoned, and Myshkin regresses back into his idiocy, becoming a totally mute man who cannot relate to anyone (cf. Khan's childhood symptom of mutism after trauma). Eventually he returns to the foreign asylum.

3. WB, June 19, 1979.

4. MK/VS, April 20, 1975. Khan said elsewhere that the beauty and fatedness of Nastasia Filippovna had haunted him since his first reading of *The Idiot* (WB, March 22, 1975).

5. MK/ZD, August 3, 1965.

6. Letter, MK to Babette Soria, August 5, 1965. (This letter is in the private possession of Babette Soria.)

7. MK/VS, September 30, 1968.

8. WB, August 11, 1973.

9. WB, June 18, 1979. See also: "In all the passionate vehemence, frenzy and pain of Myshkin's tortured soul there resided at the core a simplicity of love, a generosity of solicitude and a tenderness. . . . Yes, he has all the qualities of Dostoevsky's goodness of soul" (WB, February 4, 1980).

10. WB, June 21, 1979.

11. WB, June 19, 1979.

12. WB, June 20, 1979.

13. WB, February 17, 1980. Many of the descriptions of the events of the summer of 1979 come from Work Book entries in 1980.

14. WB, June 21, 1979.

15. WB, June 21, 1979.

16. Robert Stoller had written to Smirnoff about his surprise that Khan was driving again: "Sybil and I were downright astonished that you say Masud is driving his car. That is beyond imagination; in the fifteen years we have known him, we have never seen him drive, and I must admit that the word 'fortunately' comes instantly to mind" (June 14, 1979).

17. WB, June 22, 1979. Five days later, Khan was visited by a policeman responding to a report from the woman that he had damaged her car. He gave a statement and later paid a fine.

18. WB, June 22, 1979.

19. WB, July 11, 1979.

20. WB, June 20, 1979.

21. WB, June 25, 1979.

22. MK/WG, April 27, 1965.

23. MK/ZD, November 9, 1965. See also: "It is the common sense of others that awes me, because I am so lacking in it. My life has always been dramatic and on the grand scale, hence I have missed the ease of ordinariness" (WB, May 8, 1976).

24. WB, January 22, 1976. See also Chapter 7, p. 59.

25. WB, July 11, 1979.

26. See Ogden, 1994.

27. Khan wrote a self-description that could just as well describe Myshkin: "To women, whether patients or in life, I have been a 'shaman': I sense with an uncanny perception a certain madness, pain and incapacity in them, behind all their ruses and expertise to manipulate others, and I volunteer to absorb their sickness into myself, rinse and cure it in myself, and deliver it back as creative capacity to them in the end" (WB, July 12, 1979). Usually Khan saw Myshkin as himself, but sometimes he cast others in Myshkin's role, e.g., Winnicott: "I used to tell DWW that he was just like Dostoevsky's 'idiot' Prince Myshkin: abjectly passive to others and inwardly all-knowing, never losing face in any situation, concerned and caring but utterly un-involved" (MK/VS, July 31, 1980).

28. Robert Stoller was out of touch with Khan in the summer of 1979, but he eventually got a sense of what was happening. In November, when Khan was actually doing better, Stoller wrote to Smirnoff, "Masud's propensity for story telling has increased and he is losing his capacity to differentiate tall tales from reality" (RS/VS, November 2, 1979).

29. WB, October 8, 1979.

30. "If I fail to write significantly about Dostoevsky, I would consider my efforts to actualise my sensibility truly lacking. But I am not ready for it yet" (MK/VS, February 5, 1974).

31. WB, January 26, 1980.

32. WB, March 13, 1980.

33. Bollas (1995) has written about how the victims of serial killers tend to be people who have feelings of helplessness that leave them dependent on a presumed rescuer for help, thus making them more vulnerable to a killer.

34. WB, January 25, 1980. The article was published in NRP, Volume 21, 1980. It is one of Khan's shorter articles in NRP and not one of his best. We see the germ of an important contribution to Dostoevsky scholarship that is poorly developed.

35. Augusto Colmenares, a Khan analysand, told me that in the 1970s, Khan gave him a reprint of the 1955 Penguin copy (introduction by David Magerschack) of *The Idiot* as a reading assignment. Colmenares read this book twice and now, looking back, he speculates about the "more than casual connection" between Khan and Fyodor Dostoevsky: "As for Fyodor [who was epileptic], I would venture the opinion that his main struggle was with psychosis. Yet, to his fortune, he had a built-in mechanism of periodic electroshocks—his

epileptic fits—that arrested the onset of more severe symptoms. . . . For Masud, it wouldn't be farfetched to venture that through psychopathic acting out of his psychosis [in summer 1979], he managed to delay the fall in his own tragic bathos" (letter to the author, February 2002).

36. WB, February 3, 1980.

ENDNOTES TO CHAPTER 35

1. The quote is from *The Idiot*; Dostoevsky is writing about the passion of the fictional character General Epanchin for a younger woman.

2. "[Fleur] has arrived for tea!" (MK/VS, November 6, 1968). "Had a pleasant dinner with [Fleur and her mother]" (MK/VS, November 28, 1968). "Svetlana and I have spent a most unusual weekend of great & delightful happiness with three youngsters [Fleur and her brother and a friend]. Having so many youngsters of an age that I could have bred myself leaves me nostalgic and asking why have I evaded this actualisation in my life" (MK/VS, February 10, 1969). "[Fleur] came to dinner" (MK/VS, March 7, 1969).

3. The account of the relationship between Fleur and Khan comes from Volumes 36–39 of the Work Books, the final volumes, and from interviews with anonymous people. Fleur was adamant about not wanting to talk with me in any depth and she requested that I not talk with her brother or her friends—a request that I honored.

4. WB, January 1, 1980.
5. WB, January 16, 1980.
6. WB, January 20, 1980.
7. MK/VS, January 24, 1980.
8. WB, February 4, 1980.
9. WB, February 4, 1980.
10. WB, March 13, 1980.
11. WB, March 13, 1980.
12. WB, February 4, 1980.
13. WB, February 15, 1980.
14. WB, February 16, 1980.
15. WB, February 11, 1980.
16. WB, February 20, 1980.
17. WB, February 21, 1980.

18. WB, February 20, 1980. The similarity of the triangle of Khan, Fleur, and Yasmine to a triangle in *The Idiot* (Myshkin–Nastasia–Aglaia) suggests that Khan's Dostoevsky delusion had not totally disappeared. He wrote that he felt love based in pity for Yasmine vs. love based in passion for Fleur—the exact split that Myshkin experienced with his two women (WB, January 24, 1980). And he was again overly concrete in equating the fictional situation to real life. Referring to the fictional Nastasia's ultimate choice to be with Rogozhin, who she knew would murder her, and applying the thesis from his own recent paper on Dostoevsky, he wrote: "Yasmine is really psychotic, like Nastasia Filippovna, and is seeking someone— circumstance or person—to kill her" (WB, February 10, 1980).

19. WB, February 17, 1980.

20. WB, February 17, 1980. On this visit, Khan showed X the draft of his Introduction (1981g) to Pontalis's book *Entre le Rêve et la Douleur*. X became tearful, saying that "he had almost given up hope about me writing again because of my alcoholism."

21. WB, February 18, 1980.

22. WB, February 27, 1980.

23. WB, February 22, 1980.

24. WB, February 23, 1980.

25. WB, February 22, 1980.

26. WB, February 24, 1980.

27. WB, February 25, 1980.

28. WB, February 27, 1980.

29. WB, February 27, 1980.

30. WB, February 25, 1980.

31. WB, February 26, 1980.

32. WB, February 29, 1980.

33. WB, February 29, 1980.

34. WB, March 2, 1980.

35. MK/VS, March 3, 1980.

36. WB, March 3, 1980.

37. WB, March 5, 1980.

38. WB, March 6, 1980.

39. WB, March 6, 1980.

40. WB, March 6, 1980.

41. WB, March 6, 1980.

42. WB, March 9, 1980.

43. March 10, 1980 (Khan's italics).

44. The paper pleased him immensely, but it was never published.

45. WB, March 13, 1980.

46. MK/VS, May 19, 1980.

47. VS/RS, September 2, 1980.

48. MK/VS, August 29, 1980.

49. VS/RS, October 26, 1980.

50. VS/RS, December 6, 1980.

ENDNOTES TO CHAPTER 36

1. Khan 1982m.

2. WB, February 16, 1980.

3. In England, a patent agent, in contrast to barristers and solicitors, needs to have a scientific or engineering degree. Gustav's degree was in physics.

4. Gustav's talent for gardening was evident in an unusual garden in the backyard of the house where the ex-wife still lives. In order to deal with excessive shade, he had built a simple but beautiful two-story wood structure that holds a large sunny garden on the second story. Underneath the structure is an exquisite shade garden.

5. Gustav's ex-wife showed me two books given by Khan to her and Gustav. One book was *Hidden Selves*, inscribed: "For [Gustav] who knows the hiddennesses of the Self. With affection and gratitude. Masud. December 10, 1983." The other was Michael Balint's *The Basic Fault*, inscribed: "For Gustav and [his then-wife] to glance through. Much love, Masud, 1984 Jan."

6. The book was published by Penguin in 1982 and by Basic Books in 1984.

7. The book was published by Paddington in 1978.

8. WB, October 11, 1979.

9. Author's note: Luise's reference to the letter opener shaped like a knife was startling to me for a very personal reason. The deceased analyst Marie Coleman Nelson was one of my analytic supervisors and a significant mentor. She knew Masud Khan slightly, having had him as an overnight guest in her Long Island home once when he was lecturing in New York. She told me that, on that visit, Khan stole a knife-shaped letter opener from her desk.

1. Letter, MK to André Green, recorded in WB, March 23, 1971.

1. RS/MK, March 7, 1984.

2. Khan's style of play was both idiosyncratic and Eastern in its style. He had been exposed in childhood to a tradition of oral storytelling and one of his father's favorite quotes came from the Persian poet Sadi: "Well intentioned falsehood is better than mischief-exciting truth" (WB, May 5, 1975). (Khan adapted this idea in his aphorism, "When in a couple someone wants to be cruel, they tell the truth," WB, May 10, 1976.)

3. Personal communication from Jonathan Benson. Cheating was a form of play for Khan, and when he cheated at games, he made no attempt to hide what he was doing. Wladimir Granoff, who considered himself a fellow Oriental because his roots were Russian, told me: "Masud's cheating at card games is totally consistent with Oriental style." People who played games with Khan in the early years remember enjoying his gleeful pursuit of a win.

4. The princes in colonial India were mostly Hindu and Sikh men who, unlike Fazaldad, had held title to their land over many generations. However, some members of Khan's family did intermarry with local royalty; for example, the granddaughter of one of his half-brothers was married to the son of the Nawab of Bahawalpur, who was one of the great princes of India (see Chapter 30). Khan's Pakistani friends were not offended by his use of the term "Prince," according to Sahabzada Yaqub Khan: "Masud pretended to be a prince. I know what the aristocracy is, and he did not have a noble background. The beauty of it was that he knew that he was telling this lie to people who knew that what he was saying was untrue. He was living in a world that was not real, and he knew it and he knew that we knew it."

5. WB, April 15, 1980.

6. Personal communication from André Green.

7. RS/MK, August 19, 1981. Khan also wrote to Victor Smirnoff describing the royal wedding and adding that he had attended "with the title and garb of Prince of Chattar"—Chattar being an estate he had apparently inherited in the 1970s (MK/VS, August 7, 1981; also see footnote 37 in Chapter 32). Khan

and Svetlana had in fact attended a Royal wedding in the early 1960s—the marriage of Princess Margaret and Anthony Armstrong-Jones (later the Earl of Snowdon)—where, because of Svetlana's status and talent, they were asked to be among the first dancers on the floor.

8. Khan also told other friends that he had a daughter, but there is no evidence to confirm this and no rumor about who she might be.

9. RS/VS, January 15, 1981.

10. MK/SS, March 6, 1984.

11. Personal communication from Marie Claude Fusco.

12. Personal communication from John Charlton.

13. Personal communication from Serge Lafaurie. Another part of Khan's story, to which I had no access, involves his Pakistani friends in the 1980s: "He kept his Pakistani friends in a separate compartment of his life. Sometimes an entire entourage of family and friends would descend on the flat" (anonymous friend, 1998, referring to the years 1986–1988).

14. The information about Tahir's death is from Khan (1985a, pp. 131–132). Khalida Khan told me that Tahir was temporarily buried in at Brookwood Cemetery in Surrey, England. Eventually, she said, his body will be returned to Pakistan to be buried on his father's right-hand side, the place reserved for an oldest son according to Rajput custom. See Chapter 38 for an alternative account suggesting that Masud may already be buried in his brother's rightful place.

15. MK/VS, February 18, 1984.

16. WB, March 2, 1980.

17. Barrie Cooper told me that there was a single criterion that distinguished the men who stayed friends with Khan: "It had to do with whether you could relate as a kind of slave to an emperor."

18. Letter, André Green to MK, October 10, 1981.

19. Khan's letter to Green is quoted in a letter he wrote to V. Smirnoff on October 15, 1981.

20. MK/RS, January 12, 1981.

21. Several of these articles have never been published in English. See Gallimard catalogue for NRP, 1970–1994.

22. RS/MK, October 21, 1981.

23. RS/MK, October 21, 1981. Khan stopped making public presentations after a disastrous talk in January 1981. He had read his paper "From Masochism to Psychic Pain" at the Royal College of Psychiatrists (Irish division), and afterward boasted unconvincingly to Robert Stoller: "I was so drunk I can't

remember a damn thing, but I was told I was brilliant" (MK/RS, January 30, 1981).

24. RS/MK, October 27, 1981. A few months later, Khan laid out plans for a trust to be called "The Masud Khan Foundation." There were four trustees: Robert Stoller, Paul Kimber, Harry Karnac, and Gustav (Gustav is a pseudonym for a patent attorney who was Khan's analysand—see Chapter 36) (letter, P. Kimber to R. Stoller, April 15, 1982, RSP).

25. MK/SS, March 1983.

26. RS/MK, October 3, 1983. Stoller ended this letter with the sentence: "I only hope that with this publication, your insides will free you from your prison."

27. The 1985 review in the IJPA was by John Kelly.

28. See this letter to the editor, *London Review of Books*, from Salley Vickers, a British psychotherapist who was commenting on Wynne Godley's article about Khan: "[I] had an encounter with Masud Khan when, on a trustworthy recommendation, [I went to him for supervision] towards the end of his life. . . . His behavior at the first meeting was, to say the least, eccentric; having some idea of what was appropriate in an analyst, I took flight. However, my reasons for wanting to work with Khan were based on his undeniably brilliant writing on psychoanalytic matters and I still recommend these to trainee psychotherapists today" (March 20, 2001).

29. Grosskurth 1999, pp. 163–64.

30. Khan wrote of Bibi Shehnaz to Robert Stoller: "I have been busy trying to habilitate my niece in Flat 7. She grew up in my feudal habitat with some 48 rooms and 37 servants—so coming to stay in a mere 14 rooms and almost non-staff has been quite a task. She is gradually [adjusting to] the Masudic style of living in London, which is quite different from the way the Prince [referring to himself] lives in Pakistan" (March 1, 1983).

31. MK/RS, November 29, 1984.

32. VS/RS, October 26, 1986.

33. "I signed a paper before I went absent saying she is my next of kin" (MK/VS, December 15, 1985).

34. MK/VS, December 15, 1985.

35. MK4. *The Long Wait* originally was to have the title *Aloneness, Passions and Solitudes*. At the same time as Khan planned this book, he also wrote a "Tentative Prospectus" for two other books: *Apostasy, Persons and Certitudes*, a collection of essays on ten psychoanalysts (Melanie Klein, Edward Glover, Anna Freud,

Heinz Hartmann, W. R. D. Fairbairn, D. W. Winnicott, Erik Erikson, Jacques Lacan, John Bowlby, and Wilfred Bion) and *From Sigmund to Freud*, a biography of Freud that would focus on his correspondences—and he prepared an outline for a 200-page book titled *Oedipus the King: Oedipus and After*. The technicalities of these proposals were to be handled by his longtime agent in London, Patricia White. Only *The Long Wait* would come to fruition.

36. MK/SS, November, 1986.

37. Undated letter, MK/SS, 1987. The words suggest that one of Khan's kidneys had been removed when he developed problems that may have been kidney cancer in 1982.

38. MK/VS, November 19, 1986.

ENDNOTES TO CHAPTER 38

1. WB, July 24, 1980.

2. RS/VS, May 22, 1989.

3. Jill Duncan, the librarian for the BPAS in 1987, told me: "Masud could hardly talk in his final years. I told the telephone receptionist, 'If someone calls and you think they are a "breather," put them through to me.' Because it was usually Masud, calling on some business, but the receptionist would think he was a prank caller" (interview, 2000).

4. Khan 1987c. An anonymous therapist told me that the article was published despite its poor quality "out of respect for Khan's prior contributions to psychoanalysis."

5. See McCarthy (2003), Goldman (2001), and Guarton (1999) for perspectives on Khan's willingness to be offensive and outrageousness.

6. Letter, R. Stoller to J. Charlton, September 28, 1989.

7. MK/VS, September 15, 1986.

8. MK 1987b, p. 189.

9. MK 1988d, pp. 92–93.

10. Other Khan analysands whose stories have been reported here tell of Khan attacking them in a similar manner, sometimes with no harm or even with positive results (Peter Elder and Eugene Lerner) and sometimes, apparently, with harm (Wynne Godley). Two American psychoanalysts, Harold Searles and Marie Coleman Nelson (private communication with each, 1996), expressed to me their opinion that critics of Khan's anti-Semitic intervention were making

conclusions based on a limited reading of the case, and that Khan's intervention was justifiable because it was effective.

11. MK4, p. 90.

12. MK4, p. 91.

13. This is a case report that the Chicago analyst John called "subtly pornographic" (letter to the author, August 31, 1998).

14. See footnote 8 of Chapter 37 for another reference to a daughter.

15. RS/VS, September 28, 1988.

16. "The book was a 'kamikaze pilot' job as you say, but I'm quite sure that
[Masud] had no real idea what he was doing to himself" (VS/RS, October 6, 1988).

17. RS/VS, January 16, 1990.

18. Letter, J. Charlton to R. Stoller, October 6, 1988. Charlton told me that
he had assumed that Khan knew his subject matter: "Masud and I were not kindred spirits and it was always a bit of a struggle, dealing with him. But I admired
him, as we all did." But Harry Karnac suggests that there may have been a darker
side to what happened. Chatto & Windus owned Hogarth, which had been publishing the IPL series in collaboration with the BPAS Publications Committee
for many years. The new chair of the Publications Committee was Clifford Yorke.
Under Yorke's tenure, but not at his instigation, the institute changed publishers,
leaving Hogarth for Routledge. Elizabeth Bott Spillius and David Tuckett became
editors of a totally new series, the New International Library of Psychoanalysis.
Was Charlton, in publishing Khan's book through Chatto & Windus, taking revenge on the BPAS for their disloyalty? He admitted to me that he was bitter
about the change: "We felt that the institute had behaved badly when they shifted
horses to a new series. It was all to do with politics."

19. Malcolm, April 9, 1989, p. 25.

20. Here are a few examples of provocative and prejudiced remarks made
by Khan: [Writing from Old Beach Hotel, Monte Carlo, describing Norwegian
tourists] "There is something very unappealing about these Nordic races: they
are bleached and feel as if they have been boiled before being born. Blond, tall-
ish, hairless, and their voices unpassionate and nasal. There is also a chilled feeling about them. And they are always bundled into groups, rarely alone or
separated" (MK/ZD, August 13, 1962). [Writing again from Old Beach Hotel,
Monte Carlo] "Talk of lusting! There is an American queer here: rich and in
his late thirties. You should have seen the rate of salivation in his mouth. Literally like our Kalu [his and Svetlana's toy poodle] when he is watching someone
eat & is smacking his lips. Only Kalu has more dignity" (MK/ZD, August 25,

1962). "Americans are such nice & stupid people. So pleasant to be with, and so unnourishing in the after-image" (MK/VS, September 9, 1969). "My colleagues at the Institute suffocate me with body-distaste by their physical closeness. It is a purely aesthetic reaction of such acrid intensity in me when amongst them. In our Society, psychoanalysis serves to monopolise Unculture in its membership. The members are so ungracious, discourteous and flabby in their manners. It is very painful to live amongst them" (MK/VS, November 14, 1969).

21. Julius 1995, p. 1.

22. Khan had little interest in large-scale social or cultural issues. In thousands of pages of Work Book entries and correspondence, there are only a few comments about such topics and these either express a lack of concern or give a psychoanalytic interpretation of the matter. One example is from September 1965, when India and Pakistan were at war, and Indians were occupying Lahore, just a short distance from the Khan estate. Khan wrote to Dominic that he was more concerned with his patients than he was about Pakistan: "I have reached a point in my own spiritual vision where the fate of even one person is more important than the mass-destiny of a multitude. Today we are at a point of crisis in the development of human ethos where unless the individual is established, the absolute measure of the destiny of the species, we will be lost forever" (September 9, 1965). A few years later, he commented to Zoë Dominic about war in the Middle East in which Egypt had suffered enormous losses in an attack by Israel: "After an orgiastic worry about the Middle East flareup, I have now put it aside. If one can live one's own life well, that is enough discipline & contribution to world peace" (June 7, 1967).

23. Mark Paterson, reported by Cooper 1993, p. 33.

24. Personal communication from Jonathan Benson.

25. Cooper 1993, p. 33.

26. Khan claimed that *he* was an object of discrimination for being non-Jewish: "All of us [at the BPAS] who are non-Judaic are the 'others'! Of course, the moment one says this, one is branded an anti-Semite" (MK/WG, July 29, 1964).

27. Referring to the years prior to the influx of Jewish emigrant analysts, King and Steiner (1991) write: "[A]t that period only two members of the British Society, Barbara Low and David Eder, were Jewish, and the rest came from Scottish, English, or Welsh Christian backgrounds, with a strong bias towards agnosticism and humanism" (p. 5). After World War II, Christians were in the minority, and several sources suggest that there was significant resentment of the newcomers. The intensity of feeling is reflected in a letter written by James

Strachey, a Christian: "Why should these wretched fascists and (bloody foreign-ers) communists invade our peaceful compromising island?" (letter, J. Strachey to E. Glover, April 23, 1940; quoted in King and Steiner 1991, p. 33). The Brit-ish analyst Nina Coltart suggested that one of the reasons why the BPAS did not split after the Controversial Discussions in the 1940s is because the resi-dent British analysts would not have wanted to appear to be anti-Semitic by separating from the Kleinians: "[L]ooking back . . . I think there was a tremen-dous need and longing for peaceable solutions, especially as a lot of the immi-grant analysts were Jewish refugees. . . . As most of the Kleinian analysts were Jewish, I'm sure we didn't want to have any feeling of appearing that we'd booted out the Jewish analysts or got the better of them." (See interview of Coltart in Molino 1997, p. 172.)

28. Rycroft is quoted in Rudnytsky 2000, p. 72.

29. Interview, C. Winnicott with M. Neve 1983, p. 186; quoted in M. Page, unpublished doctoral dissertation, 2002, p. 31.

30. A story told by Khan to Zoë Dominic is an example of anti-Semitism that may have been both playful and offensive: "Redgraves [Michael Redgrave and his wife, Rachel Kempson] took us all out to dinner and your friend Sud was in a hilariously witty mood at the dinner table, amusing everyone a great deal, himself most! Ingrid Bergman asked me what I had lectured on in America and I replied: 'The normalcy of perversions.' She asked, 'And what did they conclude from it?' I replied: 'That I was an anti-Semite'" (MK/ZD, September 27, 1965). A reference to "King Lear" in the final book shows Khan identifying with what he views as Lear's defiant attitude: "Even in madness, Lear seeks bal-ance. . . . His heart cannot break. His frame does. Life is lost, but not the will. Lear does not submit . . ." (MK, 1987b, p. 189).

31. It is perhaps not surprising that Khan attacked Jews for possessing traits that he himself was often accused of having: exclusiveness, a sense of superiority, and a tendency to pursue self-serving interests.

32. Robert Stoller complained: "Masud, when you are removed, it is hard to keep up an intense inner contact with you; for you are out of reach, unimag-inable, too deeply silent" (RS/MK, September 28, 1988).

33. See minutes of informal joint meeting of the BPAS, June 19, 2001.

34. Cooper, 1993, p. 30.

35. VS/RS, December 22, 1989.

36. RS/MK, September 1988 (unspecified date).

37. MK/RS, November 11, 1988.

38. Khan 1988d, p. 97.

39. In "The Long Wait," one of the chapters of his final book of the same title, Khan (1987b) describes the end of Sigmund Freud's life—another good ending, in his opinion: "Freud died a man in grace. [His] end is his greatest virtue. He died a loved father by his exceptional daughter. Destiny had claimed Freud to itself. Thus!" (pp. 196–197).

40. MK/ZD, March 28, 1965.

41. Letter, R. Stoller to Paul Moor, June 28, 1989.

42. Letter to the author, April 20, 2001.

43. Smirnoff 1989, pp. 358–359.

44. The obituary of Khan in the IJPA states that his date of death was June 9, 1989. However, according to Jill Duncan, a retired librarian for the British Society, and Pearl King, who is an historian as well as an analyst, the actual date of death was June 7 (letter to the author from P. King, July 18, 2000).

ENDNOTES TO CHAPTER 39

1. Interview of Werner Muensterberger, July 1999. Also see Boulanger 2004.

2. Smirnoff is quoted in Cooper 1993, p. 37.

3. Most of Fazaldad's ancestors and many of his other children are buried in a different ancestral graveyard in Chakwal.

4. The lack of a memorial service would have upset Khan. Years earlier, in 1967, he was troubled when James Strachey, prior to death, requested that there be no memorial service for him. John Sutherland told Khan that he, Winnicott, and Fanny Wride (a British analyst) had gone in official capacity to Strachey's cremation, even though a notice in the *London Times* had said it was to be private. They were the only people there when Strachey's coffin arrived in the hearse and the body went "straight away" into the fire chamber. Khan referred to Strachey's request as "private mysticism and ghoulish intellectual anti-traditionalism" and he commented that important people should be officially recognized to help the living to mourn (MK/VS, May 4, 1967). The lack of a service for Khan parallels the ending of *The Idiot*'s Prince Myshkin: Myshkin leaves Russia without saying good-bye to anyone.

5. Bollas' obituary of Khan was published on June 26, 1989. Khan had actually written his own obituary, which was never used: "Have just finished

dictating my Obituary at the request of *The Manchester Guardian*, the *Financial Times*, and the *Daily Telegraph*. It is rather uncanny to write one's own obituary in one's own lifetime, but they said they have failed to find anyone suitable to write it—and they need it for their files. I have put all the emphasis on my ancestral inheritance and its end with me, and only tangentially talked of my analytic career" (WB, February 6, 1979). This boastful and inaccurate document can be found in the Robert Stoller Archives and in Willoughby 2005, pp. 246–247.

6. The information had been confirmed for Bollas by Baljeet Mehra, a Pakistani analyst who worked in London. Bollas wrote Robert Stoller about Mehta's communication to him, and Stoller wrote back that he still did not believe it. See correspondence of Stoller and Bollas from June and July, 1989 (RSP).

7. Limentani 1992.

8. Letter, Shaharyar Khan to B. Cooper, July 16, 1989 (RSP).

9. André Green commented, "There is no one single thing that describes Masud—not even that he was Pakistani" (personal communication).

10. NRP, Volume 40, Autumn 1989.

11. *Free Associations*, Volume 21, 1991.

12. VS/RS, December 22, 1989.

13. RS/VS, January 16, 1990.

14. Letter, R. Stoller to anonymous friend, July 7, 1989.

15. July 13, 2003, p. 44.

16. Bollas 1989.

17. RS/VS, January 16, 1990.

18. Letter to the author from André Green, December 12, 1997.

19. MK/VS, August 7, 1981.

20. As Andreas Giannakoulas said in a letter to me, "[Masud's] energies were such that he could neither destroy nor create in small dimensions. The excess in him of every creative or destructive force was notorious" (October 13, 1998).

21. I thank Roger Willoughby for providing me with a copy of Khan's final will.

22. Melanie Stanway Purnell, Khan's former secretary, looked at his signature on a copy of the will that I sent her. She agreed that it did not look like his writing, but she would not make a formal guess that it was fraudulent.

23. There was also a claim by a man in Pakistan that he was Masud's (illegitimate) biological son. This man tried to get the estates for himself, but he was unsuccessful.

24. According to Khalida Khan, one inheritance was a house in Jalalabad that was taken from Ahmed after several years and inherited instead by two of Khan's half-brothers, Akbar and Yusef. Yusef later bought out Akbar's shares, and the estate will be inherited by Yusef's daughter, a married woman with several children. (Yusef had two sons, but both are now deceased.) The current laws allow a female to inherit property.

25. Letter, R. Stoller to P. Kimber, July 11, 1989.

26. Limentani told Stoller that among the papers that were kept was a collection of small diaries with daily entries that were separate from the Work Books. He said he was worried about the eventual release of the content of these diaries: "Unhappily, his account of certain events is quite accurate" (letter, A. Limentani to R. Stoller, February 9, 1990).

27. Letter, R. Stoller to P. Kimber, December 1, 1989.

28. Letter to the editor from Donald Campbell. *London Review of Books*, 23 (6), March 22, 2001.

29. A.-M. Sandler 2004.

30. The meeting was held at 8:15 p.m. at Byron Mews Lecture Theatre, 112A–114 Shirland Road, London W9 2EQ.

31. Sadie Gillespie, who could not be present, sent a commentary that included the comment: "Let us not forget that Masud was one of us. And, not only that, we failed him." And she openly discussed her reluctance to report on other ethical violations that she had witnessed firsthand. For example, she had particular information about Donald Winnicott (her friend) and Margaret Little (her analyst) that she would not reveal out of loyalty to them. Her admission that loyalty gets in the way of profesional reporting was an honest statement about something that most analysts and therapists feel.

32. A.-M. Sandler 2004.

33. Glen Gabbard has noted the particular difficulty for analytic institutes and societies in investigating and acting on violations when training analysts are involved (Gabbard 1995, Gabbard and Peltz 2001; also see Greenberg 1999). But people outside of the BPAS had some very strong feelings about the shared responsibility of Khan's peers for what happened. Harry Karnac, after reading early drafts of this biography, told me:

> The more I read of your work, the more I fume at the blind or blinkered incompetence of the society. How on earth could president after president, committee after committee, against all the evidence accruing of Masud's lack of ethical

behavior, allow him to remain in the society? He continued ruining patients, trainees, and, indeed, the very reputation of the society and of psychoanalysis itself. It really will not suffice to point the finger of guilt at DWW and ignore the rest of them.

And Caroline, the analyst who was sexually seduced by Khan (see Chapter 29), said in our interview:

> The people I'm really angry at now are the people in the BPAS. In 1976, they stopped Khan from seeing their students, but they did nothing to save his ordinary analysands. And I think they acted badly again in 1989, when they expelled him. They found a safe way to get rid of him by acting as if the problem was that he was an anti-Semite. That wasn't the problem—the problem was that he was a psychoanalyst who wasn't doing psychoanalysis, and that had been so for many years.

34. Rayner, Foreword to Cooper 1993, p. xvi.

35. WB, June 12, 1979.

36. MK4, p. ix.

37. MK/VS, August 30, 1970.

38. Khan's personal experience of having multiple noninteracting selves illustrates contemporary analytic writing on the self (e.g., Bollas 1995, Mitchell 1991, Pizer 2001). The latest thinking is that it is the *illusion* of a unitary self, not the actual existence of a unitary self, that allows the person to feel relatively sane. In this way of thinking, it would be inappropriate to question whether or not Khan's Eastern self was really true, since the only important factor is whether or not he had the felt experience of being a True Self at a given moment of time.

39. Eigen 2004.

40. Schmidgall (1994) describes the progression of the tragic life of Oscar Wilde through stages that also fit Khan's life story: The Tragic Flaw (cf. Khan's deformed ear), Differentness, Forebodings, Grand Gestures, a Fall from a Great Height, and, finally, a Long Arch of Suspense Ending in Disaster. For Oscar Wilde, as for Khan, "It was of course, no small advantage that so many large and small supporting roles in the dramatis personae were marvelously acted" (p. 259).

41. Wilde is quoted in Schmidgall 1994, p. 257.

42. The battle of Ayucacho was the final battle between the Peruvians and the Spaniards in the early 1800s, when the Spaniards were defeated and had to leave Peru. I thank Harry Karnac for researching this information.

43. Letter, Augusto Colmenares to Saul Peña, July 24, 2000; translated from the Spanish by Cindy Havens and reprinted with the permission of Augusto Colmenares.

ENDNOTES TO POSTSCRIPT

1. My personal memory is that the subject of the painting was a stage set in disarray, but Tony told me that it is more accurately described as "a weird New York architectural fantasy showing both interior and exterior simultaneously" (personal communication, July 10, 2002). Walton disagreed with Svetlana's summary of the circumstances surrounding the work. He says that he painted it while accompanying Julie Andrews to New York as her fiancé, following the success of the Broadway musical *My Fair Lady*—a tour on which Andrews and Rex Harrison, her co-star, were the constant centers of attention. Tony remembers being a fascinated observer: "I actually enjoyed this period enormously and felt it was an almost ideal way to experience the culture shock that is involved on first becoming a New Yorker. My memory of the painting—which was done in gouache and ink and perhaps a little scotch!—is that it was a sort of fever dream collage of New York environments based on that experience" (letter to the author, May 30, 2002).

2. Gravesite number 4192.

BIBLIOGRAPHY

THE WORKS OF M. MASUD R. KHAN

Compiled by Harry Karnac

PUBLISHED BOOKS

MK1 *The Privacy of the Self: Papers on Psychoanalytic Theory and Technique.* London: Hogarth Press; New York: International Universities Press, 1974. Reprinted in the Maresfield Library Karnac Books, 1996. French edition: *Le Soi Caché.* Paris: Gallimard, 1976.

MK2 *Alienation in Perversions.* London: Hogarth Press, 1979; New York: International Universities Press, 1980. Reprinted in the Maresfield Library Karnac Books, 1989. French edition: *Figures de las Perversion.* Paris: Gallimard, 1981.

MK3 *Hidden Selves: Between Theory and Practice in Psychoanalysis.* London: Hogarth Press; New York: International Universities Press, 1983. Reprinted in the Maresfield Library Karnac Books, London, 1989. French edition: *Passion, Solitude et Folie.* Paris: Gallimard, 1985.

MK4 *When Spring Comes: Awakenings in Clinical Psychoanalysis.* London: Chatto & Windus, 1988. Published in the United States as *The Long Wait.* New York: Summit Books, 1989.

ARTICLES

1950 *Myths of Middle India,* by Verrier Elwin (review). *International Journal of Psychoanalysis* 31:214–215.

1953a *Schizophrenic Art: Its Meaning in Psychotherapy,* by Margaret Naumberg (review). *International Journal of Psychoanalysis* 34:164.

1953b *Psychoanalytic Studies of the Personality,* by W. R. D. Fairbairn (review with D. W. Winnicott). *International Journal of Psychoanalysis* 34:329–333.

1953c *On Not Being Able to Paint,* by Marion Milner (review). *International Journal of Psychoanalysis* 34:333–336.

1954a *The Revival of Interest in the Dream*, by Robert Fliess (review). *British Jour-nal of Medical Psychology* 27:266.

1954b *The Gates of the Dream*, by Geza Roheim (review). *British Journal of Medical Psychology* 27:266–267.

1955a *The Analysis of an Obsessional*, by R. W. Pickford (review). *International Journal of Psychoanalysis* 36:414.

1955b *Symbolic Wounds: Puberty Rites and the Envious Male*, by Bruno Bettelheim (review). *International Journal of Psychoanalysis* 36:416.

1960a Regression and integration in the analytical setting: a clinical essay on the transference and counter-transference aspects of these phenomena. MK1: 136–167. *International Journal of Psychoanalysis* 41:130–146.

1960b Clinical Aspects of the Schizoid Personality: Affects and Technique. *International Journal of Psychoanalysis* 41:430–436. MK1: 13–26.

1961a *Readings in Psychoanalytic Psychology*, ed. Morton Levitt (review). *International Journal of Psychoanalysis* 42:292.

1961b *Identity as Anxiety: Survival of the Person in Mass Society*, ed. Maurice Stern et al. (review). *International Journal of Psychoanalysis* 42:292.

1962a Dream psychology and the evolution of the psychoanalytic situation. MK1: 27–41; *International Journal of Psychoanalysis* 43:21–31. Also in *Dream Discourse Today*, ed. S. Flanders. London: Routledge, 1993, 80–94.

1962b *Letters of Sigmund Freud 1873–1939*, ed. Ernst L. Freud (review). *International Journal of Psychoanalysis* 43:83–86.

1962c Theory of the parent-infant relationship—contribution to discussion. *International Journal of Psychoanalysis* 43:253–254.

1962d The role of polymorph-perverse body experiences and object relations in ego integration. *British Journal of Medical Psychology* 35:245–261. MK2: 31–35.

1963a The concept of cumulative trauma. *Psychoanalytic Study of the Child* 18:286–306. MK1: 42–58.

1963b Ego ideal, excitement and the threat of annihilation. *Journal of Hillside Hospital* 13:3–4.

1963c Silence as communication. *Bulletin of the Menninger Clinic* 27(6). MK1: 168–180. Also in *The Analytic Situation*, ed. H. Ruitenbeek. Chicago: Aldine, 1973.

1964a Ego distortion, cumulative trauma and the role of reconstruction in the analytic situation. *International Journal of Psychoanalysis* 45:272–279. MK1: 59–68.

1964b Intimacy, complicity and mutuality in perversions. MK2: 18–30; and as "The Function of Intimacy, Complicity and Mutuality in Perversions" in *Sexual Behavior and the Law*, ed. R. Slovenko. Springfield, IL: Charles C Thomas, 1965.

1964c Role of infantile sexuality and early object relations in female homosexuality (the). MK2: 56–119. Also in *The Pathology and Treatment of Sexual Deviation*, ed. I. Rosen, 345–402. Oxford: International Universities Press.

1965a Fetish as negation of the self: clinical notes on foreskin fetishism in a male homosexual. *International Journal of Psychoanalysis* 46:64–80. MK2: 139–176. And as *Le Fétichisme Comme Négation de Soi. Nouvelle Revue de Psychoanalyse* 2:77–112.

1966a Comment on "The Role of the Super-Ego in Certain Forms of Acting-out" (Dr. Naiman's paper). *International Journal of Psychoanalysis* 47:293–294.

1966b Role of phobic and counterphobic mechanisms and separation anxiety in schizoid character formation. MK1: 69–81. *International Journal of Psychoanalysis* 47:306–313.

1967 *Écrits* by Jacques Lacan (French edition) (review). *International Journal of Psychoanalysis* 48:611.

1968a Reparation to the self as an idolised internal object: a contribution to the theory of perversion formation. *Dynamische Psychiatrie* 1:92–98. MK2: 11–17. And as *Entre L'idole et L'idéale. Nouvelle Revue de Psychoanalyse* 13:259–264.

1968b The widening scope of trauma: review of *Psychic Trauma* by Sidney Furst. *Psychiatry and Social Science Review* 2.

1968c Introduction (with J. Sutherland). In *Imagination and Reality*, by C. Rycroft. London: Hogarth, i–iv.

1969a On Symbiotic omnipotence. *Psychoanalytic Forum* 135–158. MK1: 82–92.

1969b On the clinical provision of frustrations, recognitions and failures in the psychoanalytic situation: An essay on Dr. Michael Balint's "Researches on the Theory of Psychoanalytic Technique." *International Journal of Psychoanalysis* 50:237–248. And as *Frustrer, Reconnaître et Faire Défaut Dans la Situation Analytique. Nouvelle Revue de Psychoanalyse* 17:115–138.

1969c Role of the collated internal object in perversion formation. *International Journal of Psychoanalysis* 50:555–565. MK2: 120–138.

1969d Vicissitudes of being, knowing and experiencing in the therapeutic situation. MK1:203–218. *British Journal of Medical Psychology* 42:383–395.

1970a Montaigne, Rousseau and Freud. MK1: 99–111. Originally published as

"The Catalytic Role of Crucial Friendship in the Epistemology of Self-Experience in Montaigne, Rousseau and Freud." *Dynamische Psychiatrie* 3:168–178.

1970b Towards an epistemology of the process of cure. *British Journal of Medical Psychology* 43:64–77. MK1: 93–98.

1970c On Freud's provision of the therapeutic frame. MK1: 129–135. Also in *Psychoanalytic Study of Society*, vol. 5. New York: International Universities Press, 1972. And as *Le Cadre Thérapeutique de Freud. Nouvelle Revue de Psychoanalyse* 1:99–104.

1971a To hear with eyes: clinical notes on body as subject and object. MK1: 234–250. Also in *Adolescent Psychiatry* 3:115–131. New York: Basic Books, 1974. And as *L'oeil Entend. Nouvelle Revue de Psychoanalyse* 3:53–69.

1971b Infantile neurosis as a false self organisation. *The Psychoanalytic Quarterly* 40:245–263. MK1: 219–233.

1971c The role of illusion in the analytic space and process. MK1: 251–269. Also in *The Annual of Psychoanalysis*, vol. 1:45–62. New York: Quadrangle, 1973. And as *Toucher Pour Voir. Nouvelle Revue de Psychoanalyse* 4:25–42.

1971d Beyond conflictual dynamics: a tribute to Heinz Hartmann. *Dynamische Psychiatrie* 4:3–8.

1971e Obituary: Donald W. Winnicott. *International Journal of Psychoanalysis* 52:225–226.

1971f Obituary: Donald W. Winnicott. *British Journal of Medical Psychology* 44:387–388.

1971g Bibliographical Note. In *Therapeutic Consultations in Child Psychiatry*, by D. W. Winnicott. London: Hogarth, 397–398.

1971h Foreword. *The Scope of Child Analysis*, V. Smirnoff. London: Routledge, 1–5.

1972a The becoming of a psychoanalyst. MK1: 112–128. And as "Apprenticeship, instruction and communication in psychoanalytical pedagogy." *Dynamische Psychiatrie* 5:1–21.

1972b Dread of surrender to resourceless dependence in the analytic situation. MK1: 270–279. *International Journal of Psychoanalysis* 53:225–230.

1972c Exorcism of the intrusive ego-alien factors in the analytic situation and process, pp. 383–404. MK1: 280–293. Also in *Tactics and Techniques in Psychoanalytic Theory*, ed. Giovacchini. London: Hogarth, 1974.

1972d The finding and becoming of self. *International Journal of Psycho-Analytic Psychotherapy* 1:97–111. *Dynamische Psychiatrie* 10:333–345. MK1: 294–305.

1972e The use and abuse of dream in psychic experience. *Scientific Bulletin of the British Psycho-Analytic Society* 65:18. MK1: 306–315.

1972f Pornography and the politics of rage and subversion. *Times Literary Supplement*, April 2, pp. 350–351. MK2: 219–226. Also in *The Case Against Pornography*, ed. D. Holbrook, pp. 129–143. London: Stacey, 1972.

1972g On D. W. Winnicott. *International Journal of Child Psychotherapy* 1:13–18.

1972h A kind of intimacy: an introduction to Winnicott's *Therapeutic Consultations in Child Psychiatry*. *Scientific Bulletin of the British Psycho-Analytic Society* 60:15–38. Revised version also as Introduction to D. W. Winnicott (1975), *Through Paediatrics to Psycho-Analysis*, Second Edition. New York: Basic Books, xii–l.

1972i Cannibalistic tenderness in non-genital sensuality. *Contemporary Psychoanalysis* 9:294–302. MK2: 177–184. And as *La Tendresse Cannibalique dans la Sensualité Non-génitale*. *Nouvelle Revue de Psychoanalyse* 6:159–167.

1973a Ego orgasm in bi-sexual love. *International Review of Psycho-Analysis* 1:143–150. MK2: 185–196. And as *Orgasme du Moi et Amour Bisexual*. *Nouvelle Revue de Psychoanalyse* 7:315–325.

1973b Obituary: Mrs. Alix Strachey 1892–1973. *International Journal of Psychoanalysis* 54:370.

1973c The role of will and power in perversions. MK2: 197–209. And as *L'alliance Perverse*. *Nouvelle Revue de Psychoanalyse* 8:195–206.

1973d Preface. *The Language of Psychoanalysis*, by J. Laplanche and J. B. Pontalis. London: Hogarth.

1974a Secret as potential space. *Scientific Bulletin of the British Psycho-Analytic Society*. 73:19–34. MK3: 97–107. Also in *Between Reality and Fantasy*, ed. Grolnick et al. pp. 259–270. New York: Jason S. Aronson, 1978. And as *L'espace du Secret*. *Nouvelle Revue de Psychoanalyse* 9:45–46.

1974b [With Madeleine Davis and John Davis] The beginnings and fruition of the self—an essay on D. W. Winnicott. In *Scientific Foundations of Paediatrics*, 2nd ed. London: Heinemann, 1981, pp. 274–289.

1974c The hermeneutic triangle. *Scientific Bulletin of the British Psycho-Analytic Society* 74:33–34.

1974d Grudge and the hysteric. *International Journal of Psycho-Analytic Psychotherapy* 4:349–357. MK3: 51–58. And as *La Rancune de L'hystérique. Nouvelle Revue de Psychoanalyse* 10:151–158.

1974e Editorial note. *Moses and Monotheism*, by S. Freud. London: Hogarth.

1975a Freud and the crises of responsibility in modern psychotherapeutics.

International Review of Psycho-Analysis 2:25–41. And as Freud and the Crises of Psychotherapeutic Responsibility, MK3: 11–41.

1975b Suicide in the condition of consciousness: an essay on Albert Camus' *The Outsider and the Fall*, in *The Black Rainbow*, ed. P. Abbs, pp. 63–91. London: Heinemann, 1975, and as *De La Nullité au Suicide. Nouvelle Revue de Psycho-analyse* 11:155–180.

1975c Beyond the dreaming experience, MK3: 42–50. And as "The changing use of dreams in psychoanalytic practice: in search of the dreaming experience." *International Journal of Psychoanalysis* 57:325–330. And as *De L'Expérience du Rêve la Réalité Psychique. Nouvelle Revue de Psychoanalyse* 12:89–100.

1975d Introduction. In D. W. Winnicott, *Through Paediatrics to Psycho-Analysis, 2nd Edition*. New York: Basic Books, 1975, xi–xxxxix. (Khan's introduction is not included in the 1958 publication of this book.)

1976 From secretiveness to shared living. MK3: 88–96. In *The Human Dimension in Psychoanalytic Practice*, ed. K. A. Frank, pp. 115–123. New York: Grune & Stratton. And as *Tric-trac. D'un Secret L'autre. Nouvelle Revue de Psychoanalyse* 14:231–240.

1977a From masochism to psychic pain. *Dynamische Psychiatrie* 11:165–173. And in *Contemporary Psychoanalysis* 17:413–421. MK2: 210–218. And as *Ne Pas se Souvenir de Soi-Même. Nouvelle Revue de Psychoanalyse* 15:59–68.

1977b On lying fallow: as aspect of leisure. *International Journal of Psycho-Analytic Psychotherapy* 6:397–402. MK3: 183–188.

1978a Introduction. *Dream Analysis: A Practical Handbook for Psychoanalysis*, by E. F. Sharpe. London: Hogarth.

1978b *Entre les Mots et la Mort. Nouvelle Revue de Psychoanalyse* 16:179–182.

1979a Infancy, aloneness and madness. *International Journal of Psycho-Analytic Psychotherapy* 8:271–272. MK3: 181–182. And as *Enfance, Solitude et Folie. Nouvelle Revue de Psychoanalyse* 19:177–178.

1979b *Sigmund Freud: His Life in Pictures and Words*, ed. E. Freud et al. (review). *International Journal of Psychoanalysis* 60:533–535.

1979c Fetish as negation of the self: clinical notes on foreskin fetishism in a male homosexual, part II. MRK 2: 168–176.

1980a *The Psychoanalytic Study of the Child*, vol. 33, ed. E. J. Solnit et al. (review). *International Review of Psycho-Analysis* 7:117.

1980b Murder, frenzy and madness in the logistics of humiliations: notes on

Dostoevsky and *The Idiot*. In *The Yearbook of Psychoanalysis and Psychotherapy*, vol.1, ed. R. Langs. Emerson, NJ: New Concept, 1985. And as *Meurtre, Frénésie et Folie. Nouvelle Revue de Psychoanalyse* 21:225–233.

1980c *D'autres parmi nous. Nouvelle Revue de Psychoanalyse* 20:169–171.

1981a None can speak his/her folly. MK3: 59–87. And as "Speech, the psycho-analytic method, and madness: a case history." *International Journal of Psycho-Analytic Psychotherapy* 9:447–473. And as *Personne ne Peut Dire sa Folie. Nouvelle Revue de Psychoanalyse* 23:83–116.

1981b *Freud, Biologist of the Mind: Beyond the Psychoanalytic Legend*, by F. J. Sulloway (review). *International Review of Psycho-Analysis* 8:125.

1981c *Havelock Ellis, A Biography*, by P. Grosskurth (review). *International Review of Psycho-Analysis* 8:358–360.

1981d The evil hand. MK3: 139–180. And as "The evil contest: from cumula-tive trauma to ego mastery." In *Evil, Self and Culture*, ed. M. C. Nelson and M. Eigen, 124–161. New York: Human Sciences, 1984. And as *La Main Mauvaise. Nouvelle Revue de Psychoanalyse* 24:5–51.

1981e *Countertransference*, ed. L. Epstein and A. H. Feiner (review). *International Journal of Psychoanalysis* 62:128.

1981f *Countertransference and Related Subjects*, by H. F. Searles (review). *International Journal of Psychoanalysis* 62:128–129.

1981g Introduction. *Frontiers in Psychoanalysis: Between the Dream and Psychic Pain*, by J. B. Pontalis. London: Hogarth.

1982a The empty-headed. MK3: 108–138. And as *Du Vide Plein la Tête. Nouvelle Revue de Psychoanalyse* 25:161–197.

1982b *Personal Construct Psychology: Recent Advances in Theory and Practice*, by H. Bonarius et al. (review). *International Review of Psycho-Analysis* 9:107–108.

1982c *Europe's Inner Demons: An Inquiry Inspired by the Great Witch Hunt*, by N. Cohn (review). *International Review of Psycho-Analysis* 9:242–243.

1982d *The Existentialist Critique of Freud: The Crisis of Anatomy*, by G. N. Izen-burg (review). *International Review of Psycho-Analysis* 9:245–246.

1982e *Freud and His Self Analysis* and *Freud and His Patients*, eds. M. Kanzer and J. Glenn (review). *International Review of Psycho-Analysis* 9:246–247.

1982f *Science Against Nature: The Emergence of Human Societies*, by S. Moscovici (review). *International Review of Psycho-Analysis* 9:247–248.

1982g *The Narcissistic Pursuit of Perfection*, by Arnold Rothstein (review). *International Review of Psycho-Analysis* 9:248–249.

1982h *Words Upon Words: The Anagrams of Ferdinand de Saussure*, by J. Staro-binski (review). *International Review of Psycho-Analysis* 9:249–250.

1982i *Dying and Creating: A Search for Meaning*, by Rosemary Gordon (review). *International Journal of Psychoanalysis* 63:91.

1982j *The Dilemma of Human Identity*, by H. Lichtenstein (review). *International Journal of Psychoanalysis* 63:91–92.

1982k *Returning to Freud: Clinical Psychoanalysis in the School of Lacan*, ed. S. Schneiderman (review). *International Journal of Psychoanalysis* 63:95–98.

1982l *The Psychoanalytic Study of the Child*, vols. 34 and 35, ed. A. Solnit (review). *International Journal of Psychoanalysis* 63:98–100.

1982m Preface. MK3.

1983 *Freud and Jung: Conflicts of Interpretation*, by R. S. Steele (review). *International Review of Psycho-Analysis* 10:248.

1984a Prisons. MK4: 1–25. Also as "Fate-neurosis, false self and destiny." *Winnicott Studies* 1:15–25. And as "Prisons." *Nouvelle Revue de Psychoanalyse* 30:77–105.

1984b Negotiating the impossible. In *Listening and Interpreting: The Challenge of the Work of Robert Langs*, ed. H. Rainey, pp. 185–194. New York: Jason Aronson.

1985a Outrage, compliance and authenticity. MK4: 117–138. *Contemporary Psychoanalysis* 22:629–650. And as *L'outrage. Nouvelle Revue de Psychoanalyse* 31:111–128.

1985b True and false esthetics: review of *Creativity and Perversion*, by J. Chasseguet-Smirgel. *Free Associations* 2:61–63.

1986a Thoughts. MK4: 139–174. And as *Pensées. Nouvelle Revue de Psychoanalyse* 33:114–176.

1986b Introduction. *Holding and Interpretation: Fragment of an Analysis*, by D. W. Winnicott. London: Hogarth.

1986c When spring comes. MK 4:26–51.

1987a Foreword. *Winnicott and Paradox: From Birth to Creation*, by A. Clancier and J. Kalmanovitch. London: Tavistock.

1987b *The Long Wait. Psychotherapies* 3 and in *Normal Magazine*, 1987. MK4: 176–197.

1987c Looking at cameos from an experienced analyst's consultation work. *Bulletin of the British Association of Psychotherapists* 18:49–52.

1988a Genius is energy. Review of *The Suppressed Madness of Sane Men: 44 Years of Exploring Psychoanalysis*, by M. Milner. *Winnicott Studies* 3:55–56.

1988b When spring comes. MK4: 26–51.

1988c Empty chairs, vast spaces. MK4: 52–86.

1988d A dismaying homosexual. MK4: 87–116.

Aguayo, J. (2001). Reassessing the clinical affinity between Melanie Klein and D. W. Winnicott—1935–1951: Klein's unpublished "Notes on Baby" in historical context. Paper presented at the 42nd International Psychoanalytical Congress, Nice, France, July 23.

Aron, L. (1996). *A Meeting of Minds: Mutuality in Psychoanalysis*. Hillsdale, NJ: Analytic Press.

——— (2000). Self-reflexivity and the therapeutic action of psychoanalysis. *Psychoanalytic Psychology* 17(4):667–689.

Auerbach, J. S., and Blatt, S. J. (1996). Self representation in severe psychopathology: self-awareness. *Psychoanalytic Psychology* 13:297–342.

Balint, M. (1968). *The Basic Fault*. London: Tavistock.

Beebe, B. (1997). Mother-infant communication: the origins of self and object representations and implications for adult treatment. Second annual Irving Schulman memorial lecture, Institute for Graduate Clinical Psychology of Widener University, September.

Bion, W. R. (1985). *All My Sins Remembered*. London: Karnac.

Black, M. (2003). Enactment: analytic musings on energy, language, and personal growth. *Psychoanalytic Dialogues* 13(5):633–655.

Blatt, S. (1974). Levels of object representation in anaclitic and introjective depression. *Psychoanalytic Study of the Child* 24:107–157. New York: International Universities Press.

Bloom, H. (1996). *Omens of Millennium: The Gnosis of Angels, Dreams and Resurrection*. New York: Putnam.

——— (1998). *Shakespeare: The Invention of the Human*. New York: Putnam.

Bollas, C. (1989). The destiny drive. In C. Bollas, *Forces of Destiny: Psychoanalysis and Human Idiom*, pp. 23–50. London: Free Association.

——— (1995). The structure of evil. In C. Bollas, *Cracking Up: The Work of Unconscious Experience*, pp. 180–220. New York: Hill and Wang.

Boulanger, G. (2004). Lot's wife, Cary Grant, and the American dream: psychoanalysis with immigrants. *Contemporary Psychoanalysis* 40(3):353–372.

Boynton, R. (2002). The return of the repressed: the strange case of Masud Khan. *Boston Review* 27(6):23–29.

Clancier, A., and Kalmanovitch, J. (1987). *Winnicott and Paradox: From Birth to Creation*. London: Tavistock.

Cooper, J. (1993). *Speak of Me As I Am: The Life and Work of Masud Khan*. London: Karnac.

Daniel, P. (2001). Masud Khan and Winnicott. *Bulletin Psycho-Analytical Society* 37:30–33.

Dimen, M. (2001). Perversion is us? Eight notes. *Psychoanalytic Dialogues* 11(6): 825–860.

Director, L. (2002). The value of relational psychoanalysis in the treatment of chronic drug and alcohol use. *Psychoanalytic Dialogues* 12(4):551–580.

Dolnick, E. (1998). *Madness on the Couch*. New York: Simon & Schuster.

Eigen, M. (2004). *The Sensitive Self*. Middetown, CT: Wesleyan University Press.

Fairbairn, W. R. D. (1952). *Psychoanalytic Studies of the Personality: An Object Relations Theory of the Personality*. London: Tavistock.

Fonagy, P., Gergely, G., Jurist, E., and Target, M. (2002). *Affect Regulation, Mentalization, and the Development of the Self*. New York: Other Press.

Frankel, J. (1998). The play's the thing: how the essential processes of therapy are seen most clearly in child therapy. *Psychoanalytic Dialogues* 8(1):149–182.

Franks, A.H. (1958). *Svetlana Beriosova*. London: Burke.

Gabbard, G. (1995). When the patient is a therapist: special challenges in the psychoanalysis of mental health professionals. *Psychoanalytic Review* 82(5): 709–725.

——— (2002). Addiction as mind-body bridge: commentary on paper by Lisa Director. *Psychoanalytic Dialogues* 12(4):581–584.

Gabbard, G., and Peltz, M. (2001). Speaking the unspeakable: institutional reactions to boundary violations by training analysts. COPE study. *Journal of the American Psychoanalytic Asociation* 49:659–673.

Gelber, C. (1998). Erotic Ore: A Study of the Work of Psychoanalyst Robert J. Stoller. Unpublished doctoral dissertation.

Gerald, M. (2002). Follow the bird—a story of survival in the treatment of addictions: commentary on paper by Lisa Director. *Psychoanalytic Dialogues* 12(4):585–592.

Gerhardt, J., and Sweetman, S. (2001). The intersubjective turn in psychoanalysis. *Psychoanalytic Dialogues* 11(1):43–92.

Giovacchini, P., ed. (1972). *Tactics and Techniques in Psychoanalytic Therapy*. London: Hogarth.

Godley, W. (2001a). Saving Masud Khan. *London Review of Books*, February 23, pp. 3–7.

——— (2001b). My lost hours on the couch. *London Times*, February 23, pp. 2–5.

——— (2004). Commentary. *International Journal of Psychoanalysis* 85:42–43.

Goldman, D. (2001). The outrageous prince: The uncure of Masud Khan. In *Hungers and Compulsions: The Psychodynamic Treatment of Eating Disorders and Addictions*, ed. J. Petrucelli and C. Stuart, pp. 359–374. Northvale, NJ: Jason Aronson.

Gorer, G. (1949). *The People of Great Russia*. London: Cresset.

Green, A. (1997). The intuition of the negative in *Playing and Reality*. *International Journal of Psychoanalysis* 78:1071–1082.

Greenberg, J. (1999). Analytic authority and analytic restraint. *Contemporary Psychoanalysis* 35:25–41.

Grosskurth, P. (1986). *Melanie Klein: Her World and Her Work*. New York: Knopf.

——— (1999). *Elusive Subject*. Toronto: Macfarlane, Walter & Ross.

Guarton, G. (1999). Transgression and reconciliation: a psychoanalytic reading of Masud Khan's last book. *Contemporary Psychoanalysis* 35:301–310.

Hazell, J. (1996). *H. J. S. Guntrip, A Psychoanalytical Biography*. London: Free Association.

Heimann, P. (1950). On counter-transference. *International Journal of Psychoanalysis* 31:81–84.

Hopkins, L. (1998). D. W. Winnicott's analysis of Masud Khan: a preliminary study of failures of object usage. *Contemporary Psychoanalysis* 34(1):5–47.

——— (2000). Masud Khan's application of Winnicott's "play" techniques to analytic consultation and treatment of adults. *Contemporary Psychoanalysis* 36(4):639–663.

——— (2004). How Masud Khan fell into psychoanalysis. *American Imago* 61(4): 483–494.

Hornstein, G. (2000). *To Redeem One Person Is to Redeem the World: The Life of Frieda Fromm-Reichmann*. New York: Free Press.

Jamison, K. (1993). *Touched with Fire: Manic Depressive Illness and the Artistic Temperament*. New York: Free Press (Simon and Schuster).

Johnson, B. (1999). Three Perspectives on Addiction. *Journal of the American Psychoanalytic Association* 47:75–96.

Julius, A. (1995). *T. S. Eliot, Anti-Semitism and Literary Form*. Cambridge, England: Cambridge University Press.

Kahr, B. (1996). *D. W. Winnicott: A Biographical Portrait*. London: Karnac.

—— (2002). Masud Khan's analysis with Donald Winnicott: on the hazards of befriending a patient. Unpublished manuscript.

Kanter, J., ed. (2004). *Face to Face with Children: The Life and Work of Clare Winnicott*. London: Karnac.

Kelly, J. (1985). Review of *Hidden Selves. Between Theory and Practice in Psychoanalysis. International Journal of Psychoanalysis* 66:118–121.

Khantzian, E. (1995). Self-regulation vulnerabilities in substance abusers: treatment implications. In *The Psychology and Treatment of Addictive Behavior*, ed. S. Dowling, pp. 17–42. Madison, CT: International Universities Press.

King, P., ed. (2003). *No Ordinary Psychoanalyst: The Exceptional Contributions of John Rickman*. London: Karnac.

King, P., and Steiner, R., eds. (1991). *The Freud–Klein Controversies, 1941–1945*. London: Tavistock/Routledge.

Kirsner, D. (2000). *Unfree Associations: Inside Psychoanalytic Institutes*. London: Process Press.

Kohon, G. (1986). Notes on the history of the psychoanalytic movement in Great Britain. In *The British School of Psychoanalysis: The Independent Tradition*, ed. G. Kohon, pp. 24–50. New Haven: Yale University Press.

Lichtenberg, J. (1989). *Psychoanalysis and Motivation*. Hillsdale, NJ: Analytic Press.

Likierman, M. (2001). *Melanie Klein: Her Work in Context*. London: Continuum.

Limentani, A. (1992). Obituary: M. Masud R. Khan (1924–1989). *International Journal of Psychoanalysis* 73:155–159.

Little, M. (1985). Winnicott working in areas where psychotic anxieties predominate: a personal record. *Free Associations* 3:9–42.

—— (1990). *Psychotic Anxieties and Containment: A Personal Record of an Analysis with Winnicott*. Northvale, NJ: Jason Aronson.

Lomas, P. (2001). Review of "Saving Masud Khan" by Wynne Godley. In *Outwrite: The Journal of the Cambridge Society for Psychotherapy* 3:42–44.

Malcolm, J. (1989). The psychoanalyst plays polo. Review of *The Long Wait (When Spring Comes)*, by Masud Khan, 1968. *New York Times Book Review*, April 9, p. 25.

Mann, D. (2002). A pragmatic convergence in the programs of psychoanalysis and Alcoholics Anonymous. *Journal for the Psychoanalysis of Culture & Society* 7(2):233–240.

Masson, J. (1984). *The Assault on Truth: Freud's Suppression of the Seduction Theory*. Harmondsworth: Penguin.

McCarthy, J. (2003). Disillusionment and devaluation in Winnicott's analysis of Masud Khan. *American Journal of Psychoanalysis* 63(1):81–92.

Merkin, D. (2003). The literary Freud. *The New York Times Magazine*, July 13, pp. 40–44.

Milner, M. (1969). *The Hands of the Living God*. London: Hogarth.

Mitchell, S. (1991). Contemporary perspectives on self: toward an integration. *Psychoanalytic Dialogues* 1:121–147.

——— (1993). *Hope and Dread in Psychoanalysis*. New York: Basic Books.

Molino, A. (1997). *Freely Associated*. London: Free Association.

Ogden, T. (1986). *The Matrix of the Mind: Object Relations and the Psychoanalytic Dialogue*. Northvale, NJ: Jason Aronson.

——— (1994). *Subjects of Analysis*. Northvale, NJ: Jason Aronson.

——— (2001). Reading Winnicott. *Psychoanalytic Quarterly* 70:299–323.

Pearson, J., ed. (2004). *Analyst of the Imagination: The Life and Work of Charles Rycroft*. London: Karnac.

Phillips, A. (1988). *Winnicott*. Cambridge, MA: Harvard University Press.

Pizer, S. (2000). The capacity to tolerate paradox: bridging multiplicity within the self. In J. Christopher Muran (ed.), *Self Relations in the Psychotherapy Process*, ed. J. C. Moran, pp. 110–120. Washington, DC: American Psychological Association.

Pontalis, J. B. (1989). In memoriam Masud Khan, 1924–1989. *Nouvelle Revue de Psychanalyse* 40:335–359.

Richards, V. (1996). Introduction. In *The Person Who Is Me: Contemporary Perspectives on the True and False Self*, ed. V. Richards and G. Wilce, pp. i–iv. London: Karnac Books.

Roazen, P. (1969). *Brother Animal: The Story of Freud and Tausk*. New York: Knopf.

——— (1975). *Freud and His Followers*. New York: Knopf.

——— (2000). Geoffrey Gorer, gentleman scholar. Unpublished paper.

Rodman, F. R., ed. (1987). *The Spontaneous Gesture: Selected Letters of D. W. Winnicott*. Cambridge, MA: Perseus.

——— (2003). *Winnicott: Life and Work*. Cambridge, MA: Perseus.

Roudinesco, E. (1990). *Jacques Lacan and Co.: A History of Psychoanalysis in France, 1925–1985*. Chicago: University of Chicago Press.

——— (1997). *Jacques Lacan*. New York: Columbia University Press.

Rudnytsky, P. (1991). *The Psychoanalytic Vocation*. New Haven, CT: Yale University Press.

——— (2000). *Psychoanalytic Conversations: Interviews with Clinicians, Commentators and Critics*. Hillsdale, NJ: Analytic Press.

Rycroft, C. (1996). In conversation with Jeremy Holmes. *Psychiatric Bulletin* 20:726–732.

Said, E. (2003). *Freud and the Non-European*. London: Verso.

Sandler, A.-M. (2004). Institutional responses to boundary violations: the case of Masud Khan. *International Journal of Psychoanalysis* 85:27–42.

Scharff, J. S. (1992). *Projective and Introjective Identification and the Use of the Therapist's Self*. Northvale, NJ: Jason Aronson.

——— (1994). *The Autonomous Self: The Work of John D. Sutherland*. Northvale, NJ: Jason Aronson.

Schmidgall, G. (1994). *The Stranger Wilde: Interpreting Oscar*. New York: Dutton.

Schoenberger, N. (2001). *Dangerous Muse: The Life of Lady Caroline Blackwood*. New York: Doubleday.

Searles, H. (1982–83). The analyst as manager of the patient's daily life: transference and countertransference dimensions of this relationship. *International Journal of Psychoanalytic Psychotherapy* 9:475–486.

Segal, H. (1979). *Klein*. London: Fontana.

Slochower, J. (1996). *Holding and Psychoanalysis: A Relational Perspective*. Hillsdale, NJ: Analytic Press.

Smirnoff, V. (1989). In Memoriam Masud Khan, 1924–1989. *Nouvelle Revue de Psychanalyse* 40:335–359.

Solway, D. (1998). *Nureyev: His Life*. New York: William Morrow.

Sorenson, R. L. (2000). Psychoanalytic institutes as religious denominations. *Psychoanalytic Dialogues* 10(6):847–874.

Stewart, H. (1991). *Psychic Experience and Problems of Technique (New Library of Psychoanalysis, No. 13)*. London: Tavistock.

Strachey, J. (1934). The nature of the therapeutic action of psychoanalysis. *International Journal of Psychoanalysis* 15:127–159.

Strozier, C. (2001). *Heinz Kohut: The Making of a Psychoanalyst*. New York: Farrar, Straus and Giroux.

Sugarman, A. (1995). Psychoanalysis: treatment of conflict or deficit? *Psychoanalytic Psychology* 12:55–70.

Summers, F. (1999). *Transcending the Self: An Object Relations Model of Psychoanalytic Therapy*. Hillsdale, NJ: Analytic Press.

Sutherland, J. (1989). *Fairbairn's Journey into the Interior*. London: Free Association Books.

Thompson, M. G. (1998). Manifestations of transference: love, friendship, rapport. *Contemporary Psychoanalysis* 34(4):543–562.

Turkle, S. (1979). *Psychoanalytic Politics: Jacques Lacan and Freud's French Revolution*. London: Burnett.

van Dijken, S. (1998). *John Bowlby: His Early Life*. London: Free Association Books.

Willoughby, R. (2005). *Masud Khan: The Myth and the Reality*. London: Free Association.

Winnicott, C., Shepherd, R., Davis, R. & M., eds. (1989). *Psychoanalytic Explorations*. Cambridge, MA: Harvard University Press.

Winnicott, D. W. (1941). The observation of infants in a set situation. In D. W. Winnicott, *Collected Papers: Through Paediatrics to Psycho-Analysis*. London: Tavistock, 1958.

——— (1945). Primitive emotional development. In *Through Paediatrics to Psychoanalysis*, pp. 145–156. New York: Basic Books, 1958.

——— (1947). Hate in the countertransference. In D. W. Winnicott, *Collected Papers: Through Paediatrics to Psycho-Analysis*, pp. 194–203. London: Tavistock, 1958.

——— (1952). Psychoses and child care. In *Through Paediatrics to Psychoanalysis*, pp. 219–228. New York: Basic Books, 1958.

——— (1953). Transitional objects and transitional phenomena. In D. W. Winnicott, *Playing and Reality*. London: Tavistock Publications, 1971, pp. 1–25.

——— (1954). Play in the analytic situation. In *Psychoanalytic Explorations: D. W. Winnicott*, ed. C. Winnicott, R. Shepherd, and M. Davis, pp. 28–29. Cambridge, Massachusetts: Harvard University Press, 1989.

——— (1958). The capacity to be alone. In D. W. Winnicott, *The Maturational Processes and the Facilitating Environment*. London: Hogarth, 1965.

——— (1960). Ego distortion in terms of True and False Self. In *The Maturational Processes and the Facilitating Environment*, pp. 140–152. Madison, CT: International Universities Press, 1965.

——— (1963a). Communicating and not communicating leading to a study of certain opposites. In *The Maturational Processes and the Facilitating Environment*, pp. 179–192. Madison, CT: International Universities Press, 1965.

——— (1963b). Notes for the split-off male and female elements to be found in men and women. In *Psychoanalytic Explorations*, ed. C. Winnicott, R. Shepherd, and M. Davis, pp. 186–188. Cambridge, MA: Harvard University Press, 1989.

—— (1964). *The Child, the Family and the Outside World*. Harmondsworth, England: Penguin.

—— (1966). The split-off male and female elements to be found in men and in women. In D. W. Winnicott, *Playing and Reality*. London: Tavistock, 1971, 72–85.

—— (1967a). The concept of clinical regression compared with that of defence organisation. In *Psychoanalytic Explorations*, ed. C. Winnicott, R. Shepherd, and M. Davis, pp. 193–199. Cambridge, MA: Harvard University Press, 1989.

—— (1967b). D. W. W. on D. W. W. In *Psychoanalytic Explorations*, ed. C. Winnicott, R. Shepherd, and M. Davis. Cambridge, MA: Harvard University Press (1989), 569–582.

—— (1968). The use of an object and relating through identifications. In D. W. Winnicott, *Playing and Reality*, pp. 86–94. London: Tavistock, 1971.

—— (1971a). *Playing and Reality*. London: Tavistock.

—— (1971b). *Therapeutic Consultations in Child Psychiatry*. London: Hogarth.

—— (1972). Holding and interpretation: fragment of an analysis. In *Tactics and Techniques in Psychoanalytic Therapy*, ed. P. L. Giovacchini. London: Hogarth, pp. 1–202.

—— (1988). *Human Nature*. London: Free Association; New York: Schocken.

Winnicott, D. W., and Khan, M. M. R. (1953). Book review of *Psychoanalytic Studies of the Personality*, by W. R. D. Fairbairn (1952). *International Journal of Psychoanalysis* 34:329–333.

Young-Bruehl, E. (1988). *Anna Freud: A Biography*. New York: Summit.

INDEX

Beriosova, Svetlana (*continued*)
  Khan, Masud estrangement, 170–174, 175, 185–187, 188–189, 190–191
  Khan, Masud marriage, 38, 41, 58–68, 77, 90, 150, 152, 159, 160, 165, 197, 198, 364
  meeting with, 391–393
  Winnicott, Donald Woods, 189–190
Berlin, Germany, 183–184
Besobrasova, Marika, 65
Bhutto, Zulfikar Ali, 356
Bion, Francesca, 33
Bion, Wilfred, 30, 33
Bipolar disorder, 261–262
Birdwood, Field Marshall Lord, 12–13, 17
Bisexuality, 133
Bloom, Harold, 129–130
Bollas, Christopher, 210, 357, 378–379, 381, 384–385
Bonaparte, Marie, 337
Bonnard, Pierre, 45
Bonnet, Philippe, 238, 239
Bowlby, John, 21–23, 25
Boynton, Robert, 196
Braque, Georges, 45, 59, 313, 379, 382, 383
Brenman, Eric, 370–371
British Psycho-Analytical Society (BPAS), 239, 244, 263, 279
  Amsterdam conference, 159, 160
  founding of, 30
  Godley affair, 199
  International Journal of Psycho-Analysis (IJPA), 161–162, 386

Khan investigation, 298–301, 325, 370–372, 386
  Khan's death, 379, 384, 385–386
  Khan's ejection from, xxiii, 381
  Limentani, 284
  membership in, 70
  politics within, 21–22, 26–27
  racism, 368
  training program, xxii, 42, 51, 135
Brooks, Peter, 230
The Brothers Karamazov (Dostoevsky), xxiii, 217, 261, 304, 314, 321–322, 326
Burlingham, Dorothy, 337
Burton, Richard, 62, 65

Calder, Alexander, 45
Campbell, Don, 385–386
Camus, Albert, 171, 187, 204, 216, 238–239, 269
Cardwell, John, 179
Cartier-Bresson, Henri, 63, 331, 334
Cartier-Bresson, Martine, 331, 334
Cassou, Isabelle, 45
Cassou, Jean, 45, 313
Catroux, Diomede, 186
Center for Advanced Psychoanalytic Studies (CAPS), 250, 254–255
Chagall, Marc, 77, 189
Charlton, John, 136, 316, 364, 365–367
Child analysis, Khan, Masud, 47–48
Christopher, Sybil, 62
Churchill, Winston, 314
Clavé, Antonio, 45
Clinical work. *See* Analysand interviews